A Companion to Eighteenth-Century Britain

A COMPANION TO EIGHTEENTH-CENTURY BRITAIN

Edited by

H. T. Dickinson

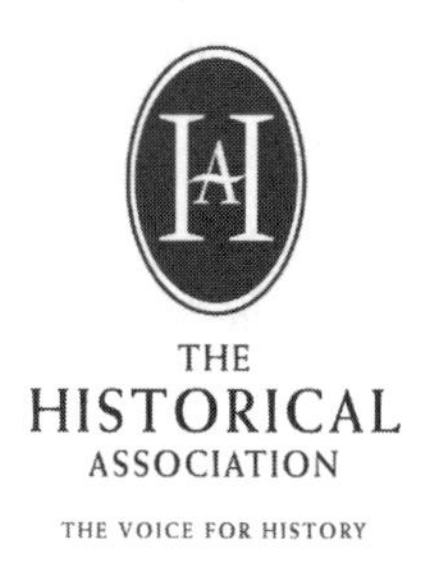

BLACKWELL PUBLISHING
350 Main Street, Malden, MA 02148-5020, USA
9600 Garsington Road, Oxford OX4 2DQ, UK
550 Swanston Street, Carlton, Victoria 3053, Australia

First published 2002
First published in paperback 2006 by Blackwell Publishing Ltd

1 2006

Library of Congress Cataloging-in-Publication Data

A companion to eighteenth-century Britain / edited by H. T. Dickinson.
p. cm. – (Blackwell companions to British history)
Includes bibliographical references (p.) and index.
ISBN 0-631-21837-8
1. Great Britain – History – 18th century – Handbooks, manuals, etc. 2. Great Britain – Civilization – 18th century – Handbooks, manuals, etc. I. Dickinson, H. T. II. Series.

DA480 .C58 2002
941.07 – dc21

2002022769

ISBN-13: 978-0-631-21837-1
ISBN-13: 978-1-4051-4963-1 (paperback)
ISBN-10: 1-4051-4963-9 (paperback)

A catalogue record for this title is available from the British Library.

Set in 10 on 12 pt Galliard
by SNP Best-set Typesetter Ltd, Hong Kong
Printed and bound in the United Kingdom
by TJ International Ltd, Padstow, Cornwall

The publisher's policy is to use permanent paper from mills that operate a sustainable forestry policy, and which has been manufactured from pulp processed using acid-free and elementary chlorine-free practices. Furthermore, the publisher ensures that the text paper and cover board used have met acceptable environmental accreditation standards.

For further information on
Blackwell Publishing, visit our website:
www.blackwellpublishing.com

BLACKWELL COMPANIONS TO BRITISH HISTORY

Published in association with The Historical Association

This series provides sophisticated and authoritative overviews of the scholarship that has shaped our current understanding of British History. Each volume comprises up to forty concise essays written by individual scholars within their area of specialization. The aim of each contribution is to synthesize the current state of scholarship from a variety of historical perspectives and to provide a statement on where the field is heading. The essays are written in a clear, provocative and lively manner, designed for an international audience of scholars, students and general readers.

The *Blackwell Companions to British History* is a cornerstone of Blackwell's overarching Companions to History series, covering European, American and World History.

Published

A Companion to Roman Britain
Edited by Malcolm Todd

A Companion to Britain in the Later Middle Ages
Edited by S. H. Rigby

A Companion to Tudor Britain
Edited by Robert Tittler and Norman Jones

A Companion to Stuart Britain
Edited by Barry Coward

A Companion to Eighteenth-Century Britain
Edited by H. T. Dickinson

A Companion to Nineteenth-Century Britain
Edited by Chris Williams

A Companion to Early Twentieth-Century Britain
Edited by Chris Wrigley

A Companion to Contemporary Britain
Edited by Paul Addison and Harriet Jones

In preparation

A Companion to the Early Middle Ages: Britain and Ireland
Edited by Pauline Stafford

The Historical Association is the voice for history. Since 1906 it has been bringing together people who share an interest in, and love for, the past. It aims to further the study of teaching of history at all levels. Membership is open to everyone: teacher and student, amateur and professional. Membership offers a range of journals, activities and other benefits. Full details are available from The Historical Association, 59a Kennington Park Road, London SE11 4JH, enquiry@history.org.uk, www.history.org.uk.

Other Blackwell History Companions include:

BLACKWELL COMPANIONS TO BRITISH HISTORY

Published

A Companion to Western Historical Thought
Edited by Lloyd Kramer and Sarah Maza

A Companion to Gender History
Edited by Teresa A. Meade and Merry E. Weisner-Hanks

BLACKWELL COMPANIONS TO EUROPEAN HISTORY

Published

A Companion to Europe 1900–1945
Edited by Gordon Martel

A Companion to Nineteenth-Century Europe
Edited by Stefan Berger

A Companion to the Worlds of the Renaissance
Edited by Guido Ruggiero

A Companion to the Reformation World
Edited by R. Po-chia Hsia

BLACKWELL COMPANIONS TO AMERICAN HISTORY

Published:

A Companion to the American Revolution
Edited by Jack P. Greene and J. R. Pole

A Companion to 19th-Century America
Edited by William L. Barney

A Companion to the American South
Edited by John B. Boles

A Companion to American Indian History
Edited by Philip J. Deloria and Neal Salisbury

A Companion to American Women's History
Edited by Nancy A. Hewitt

A Companion to Post-1945 America
Edited by Jean-Christophe Agnew and Roy Rosenzweig

A Companion to the Vietnam War
Edited by Marilyn B. Young and Robert Buzzanco

A Companion to Colonial America
Edited by Daniel Vickers

A Companion to 20th-Century America
Edited by Stephen J. Whitfield

A Companion to the American West
Edited by William Deverell

A Companion to American Foreign Relations
Edited by Robert D. Schulzinger

A Companion to the Civil War and Reconstruction
Edited by Lacy K. Ford

A Companion to American Technology
Edited by Carroll Pursell

A Companion to African-American History
Edited by Alton Hornsby

A Companion to American Immigration
Edited by Reed Ueda

BLACKWELL COMPANIONS TO WORLD HISTORY

Published

A Companion to the History of the Middle East
Edited by Youssef M. Choueiri

Contents

List of Maps

Contributors

Peter Borsay was educated at Lancaster University and is at present Professor of History at the University of Wales, Lampeter. His publications include *The English Urban Renaissance: Culture and Society in the Provincial Town, 1660–1770* and *The Image of Georgian Bath 1700–2000: Towns, Heritage and History*.

Stewart J. Brown took his Ph.D. at the University of Chicago. He is Professor of Ecclesiastical History and Dean of the Faculty of Divinity at the University of Edinburgh. His publications include *Thomas Chalmers and the Godly Commonwealth in Scotland* and *The National Churches of England, Ireland and Scotland, 1801–1846*.

Bob Bushaway gained his first degree and his doctorate from the University of Southampton. He is currently Director of Research Support and Business Development of the University of Birmingham and an associate member of the History department there. He is the author of *By Rite: Custom, Ceremony and Community in England 1700–1880* and of essays in books and journals.

Stanley D. M. Carpenter has higher degrees from the University of St Andrews and Florida State University, Tallahassee. He is now an Associate Professor at the United States Naval War College, Newport, Rhode Island. He has contributed articles to various encyclopaedias and historical dictionaries.

Sean J. Connolly was educated at University College, Dublin and the University of Ulster. He is currently Professor of Irish History at the Queen's University, Belfast. His publications include *Religion, Law and Power: The Making of Protestant Ireland 1660–1760*, *Priests and People in Pre-Famine Ireland 1780–1845* and, as general editor, *The Oxford Companion to Irish History*.

H. T. Dickinson has degrees from Durham, Newcastle and Edinburgh universities and has been Richard Lodge Professor of British History at Edinburgh since 1980. His publications include *Liberty and Property: Political Ideology in Eighteenth-Century Britain* and *The Politics of the People in Eighteenth-Century Britain*.

G. M. Ditchfield was educated at Cambridge University and is now Reader in Eighteenth-Century History at the University of Kent at Canterbury. He is the author of *The Evangelical Revival* and co-editor of *British Parliamentary Lists 1660–1800*.

J. Alan Downie was educated at the University of Newcastle-upon-Tyne. He is currently Senior Pro-Warden (Academic) and Professor of English at Goldsmith's College, University of London. His publications include *Robert Harley and the Press:*

Propaganda and Public Opinion in the Age of Swift and Defoe and *Jonathan Swift: Political Writer*.

David Eastwood was educated at Oxford University and taught there before becoming Professor of History at the University of Wales, Swansea. He is at present Vice-Chancellor of the University of East Anglia. His publications include *Rural England: Tradition and Transformation in English Local Government, 1780–1840* and *Government and Community in the English Provinces 1700–1870*.

Pamela Edwards gained her Ph.D. at the University of London and teaches at Richmond University in London. She is currently a visiting fellow in the History department at Yale University. She has published learned articles in the *History of Political Thought* and *Enlightenment and Dissent*, and is revising her book on the political thought of Samuel Taylor Coleridge.

Jeremy Gregory was educated at Oxford University. He is currently a Senior Lecturer in the Department of Religions and Theology at the University of Manchester. His publications include *Restoration, Reformation and Reform, 1660–1828: Archbishops of Canterbury and their Diocese* and, as co-author, *The Longman Companion to Eighteenth-Century Britain, 1688–1820*.

Richard Harding graduated from Leicester University and took his Ph.D. at Birkbeck College, University of London. He is currently Professor of Organizational History at the University of Westminster. His publications include *Amphibious Warfare in the Eighteenth Century* and *Seapower and Naval Warfare 1650–1830*.

Bob Harris was educated at Durham and Oxford universities. He is currently Senior Lecturer in History at the University of Dundee. His publications include *A Patriot Press: National Politics and the London Press in the 1740s* and *Politics and the Nation: Britain in the Mid-Eighteenth Century*.

Colin Haydon was educated at Oxford University and is now Reader in History at King Alfred's College, Winchester. His publications include *Anti-Catholicism in Eighteenth-Century England, c.1714–80* and (edited with John Walsh and Stephen Taylor) *The Church of England, c.1689–c.1833*.

Eckhart Hellmuth gained his doctorate and his habilitation at the University of Trier. He is currently Professor of Modern History at the Ludwig-Maximilians University in Munich. His publications include *Naturrechtsphilosophie und bürokratischer Werthorizont* and (as editor) *The Transformation of Political Culture in England and Germany in the Late Eighteenth Century*.

Maura A. Henry studied for a time at the University of Sussex and graduated from Smith College in Massachusetts. Having gained her doctorate at Harvard University she has held a number of posts there, including Lecturer in History and Women's Studies and Assistant Director of Women's Studies.

Brian Hill gained his doctorate at Cambridge University and taught for many years at the University of East Anglia, where he retired as Reader in History. His publications include *The Growth of Parliamentary Parties 1689–1742* and *British Parliamentary Parties 1742–1832*.

Geraint H. Jenkins was educated at the University of Wales, Swansea. Formerly Professor of Welsh History at the University of Wales, Aberystwyth, he is now Director of the Centre for Advanced Welsh and Celtic Studies. His publications include *The Foundation of Modern Wales 1642–1780* and *Literature, Religion and Society in Wales 1660–1730*. He is also general editor of *A Social History of the Welsh Language*.

Colin Kidd studied at Cambridge, Harvard and Oxford universities and is now Reader in History at the University of Glasgow. His publications include *Subverting Scotland's Past* and *British Identities before Nationalism*.

Stephen M. Lee is a graduate of Edinburgh University and gained his doctorate at Manchester University. He now teaches at Torquay Boys' Grammar School. He has published articles on aspects of the career of George Canning and is working on a study of Canning and liberal Toryism.

Bruce P. Lenman is a graduate of Aberdeen and has two graduate degrees from Cambridge University. He is currently a Professor of Modern History at the University of St Andrews. His many publications include *England's Colonial Wars 1550–1688* and *Britain's Colonial Wars 1688–1783.*

Emma Vincent Macleod was educated at Edinburgh University and is now a Lecturer in History at the University of Stirling. She is the author of *A War of Ideas: British Attitudes to the Wars against Revolutionary France, 1792–1802.*

Paddy McNally was educated at Queen's University, Belfast and is currently Senior Lecturer in History at University College, Worcester. His publications include *Parties, Patriots and Undertakers: Parliamentary Politics in Early Hanoverian Ireland.*

Gordon Mingay was educated at Nottingham University. He is now retired, but his last appointment was as Professor of Agrarian History at the University of Kent. Among his many publications are two large-scale edited works: *The Victorian Countryside* (2 vols) and *The Agrarian History of England and Wales*, vol. 6: *1750–1850.*

Alexander Murdoch was educated at George Washington University and the University of Edinburgh and is now Senior Lecturer in Scottish History at the latter university. His publications include *'The People Above': Politics and Administration in Mid-Eighteenth-Century Scotland* and *British History 1660–1832: National Identity and Local Culture.*

Patrick Karl O'Brien was educated and taught at the University of Oxford before becoming Director of the Institute of Historical Research in the University of London. He is currently Centennial Professor of Economic History at the London School of Economics. His many publications include *Revolution in Egypt's Economic System: From Private Enterprise to Socialism, 1952–1965* and (with Cagler Keyder) *Economic Growth in Britain and France, 1780–1914: Two Paths to the Twentieth Century.*

John Oldfield was educated at Cambridge University and is at present Senior Lecturer in History at the University of Southampton. His publications include *Popular Politics and British Anti-Slavery: The Mobilisation of Public Opinion against the Slave Trade, 1787–1807* and *Civilization and Black Progress: Selected Writings of Alexander Crummell on the South.*

Martyn J. Powell gained his first degree and his doctorate at the University of Wales, Aberystwyth, where he is at present a Lecturer in History. He has published several articles on British and Irish politics in the later eighteenth century and is completing a study on *Britain and Ireland in the Eighteenth-Century Crisis of Empire.*

John D. Ramsbottom was awarded his Ph.D. by Yale University and is currently an Adjunct Lecturer at the University of Illinois, Urbana-Champaign. He has published articles in learned journals on the Restoration Church of England.

Nicholas Rogers was educated at Oxford and Toronto universities. He is at present a Professor of History at York University, Toronto. His publications include *Whigs and Cities: Popular Politics in the Age of Walpole and Pitt* and *Crowds, Culture and Politics in Georgian Britain.*

John Rule was educated at Cambridge and Warwick universities and is currently a Professor of Modern History at the University of Southampton. His publications include *Albion's People: English Society 1714–1815* and *The Vital Century: England's Developing Economy.*

H. M. Scott was educated at the University of Edinburgh and the London School of Economics. He is currently Professor of International History at the University of St Andrews. His many publications include *British Foreign Policy in the Age of the American Revolution* and *The Emergence of the Eastern Powers.*

James A. Sharpe gained his doctorate at Oxford University. He is currently a Professor of History at the University of York. His publications include *Crime in Early*

Modern England 1550–1750 and *Instruments of Darkness: Witchcraft in England 1550–1750.*

W. A. Speck was educated at Oxford University. He was a Professor of History at Hull and Leeds universities. He is now an emeritus Professor of History of the University of Leeds and at present a visiting professor at the University of Northumbria (Carlisle campus). Among his many publications are *Tory and Whig: The Struggle in the Constituencies 1701–1715* and *Stability and Strife: England 1714–1760.*

Daniel Szechi graduated from Sheffield University and gained his doctorate at Oxford University. He is at present Professor of History at Auburn University, Alabama. His publications include *The Jacobites: Britain and Europe, 1688–1788* and *George Lockhart of Carnwath, 1689–1727: A Study in Jacobitism.*

Richard G. Wilson gained his doctorate at Leeds University and is now Professor of Economic and Social History at the University of East Anglia. His publications include (with T. R. Gourvish) *The British Brewing Industry, 1830–1980* and (with Alan Mackley) *Creating Paradise: The Building of the English Country House, 1660–1880.*

Introduction

H. T. Dickinson

Fifty years ago historians studying eighteenth-century Britain would probably have agreed on what were its most important features. These historians stressed the aristocratic nature and characteristics of Britain, with a long-established landed elite dominating politics and society. They would have emphasized widespread support for a limited monarchy and have highlighted the prestige of a parliament dominated by the landed elite, but they would also have stressed that government and parliament did little to interfere with the lives of most British subjects. They would have acknowledged the importance of agriculture, but would have recognized the growing wealth of the country based on commercial and industrial improvements. They would have praised Britain as an enlightened, modernizing society, becoming increasingly urbanized, secularized and tolerant. They would have celebrated the military, naval and imperial successes which Britain gained in her long rivalry with France, with but a passing nod to the failure in the War of American Independence. Aristocracy, stability, improvement and growing prosperity would have been regarded as the principal features of eighteenth-century Britain.

Today, historians of eighteenth-century Britain are much more sharply divided over what they regard as its central features. There are those who see Britain as very like the *anciens régimes* of continental Europe, dominated by monarchy, religion and the aristocratic elite. There are those who see Britain as significant because of those political, financial, economic, social and cultural changes which were making her the most dynamic and modern society in Europe, indeed in the world. There are those historians who stress stability and cohesion in eighteenth-century Britain, and those who emphasize almost constant instability and the continual tension between the traditional forces of order and the abiding threat to these forces at home and abroad. There are those historians who still stress the significance of the major political and economic developments in eighteenth-century Britain, and those who believe that the most interesting features of Britain are its intellectual, social and cultural developments. Religion has been restored to a central position in British life in the eighteenth century and there is now much interest in intellectual discourse, in the role of gender and of women, and in crime and disorder. Whatever their particular research interests, all historians now agree that eighteenth-century Britain was a vibrant, multi-faceted and multi-layered society that cannot be understood without making an effort to examine the old and the new, the traditional and the dynamic, the changes and the continuities.

This Companion, produced jointly by a range of experts drawn from several countries, endeavours to explain to the student and the intelligent lay reader what were the most important developments in eighteenth-century Britain that have made her such a fascinating subject for serious historical inquiry. It is not an encyclopaedia, so it does not seek to present a comprehensive coverage, in short compass, of all aspects of eighteenth-century Britain. Instead, it covers in greater detail a wide range of important topics which will provide the reader with a sound understanding of many of the most important features of eighteenth-century Britain as they are now being investigated and understood by leading historians in these fields.

The essays in this Companion on politics and the constitution deliberately seek to do justice to the old and the new. They show how much remained unchanged during the long eighteenth century from 1688 to 1815: the importance of the monarch and the strength of crown influence; the domination of parliament by the aristocratic, landed elite; the importance of patronage and influence over election results; the survival of ancient institutions of local government; and the predominance of rather conservative political views among the propertied elite. On the other hand, these essays also show: that the sovereignty of crown-in-parliament became increasingly assured; that, for the first time in its history, parliament met every year after 1689; how political parties rose, declined and began to rise again; and how both central and local government were not entirely dominated by a narrow landed elite, but could be influenced by large numbers of people. Moreover, while Britons enjoyed the rule of law and greater liberties than before, and while Britain became the most efficient fiscal-military state in Europe and developed a particularly effective finance and taxation system, the political system and the ruling elite were seriously challenged at different stages during the century by Jacobite and American rebels, by French revolutionaries, and by domestic radicals.

In economic and social spheres the essays here acknowledge that Britain was primarily a rural country and an agrarian economy, and a hierarchical and patriarchal society, in which a narrow landed elite exercised very considerable power and the majority of the population paid due deference to their economic and social superiors. The peerage remained an exclusive elite which retained wealth, status and power across the whole eighteenth century and well into the nineteenth. The landed gentry also retained and expanded their influence, though they were more open to infiltration by newcomers who gained wealth by other means than the ownership of land. The essays here make it clear that land was not the sole source of wealth, status and power. Over the century parts of Britain at least were gradually being transformed into a modern, urban, commercial and then industrial society. Although many historians now eschew such terms as the 'industrial revolution' and the 'agricultural revolution', because technological change and economic growth and output were simply not that rapid in the eighteenth century to justify these terms, there is no denying that the British economy was advancing on many fronts in a manner and at a rate that made Britain a far more prosperous country and a more advanced economy by the end of the century than she had been at the beginning. These cumulative developments ultimately had a significant effect on British society, creating in particular a more powerful urban middle class, in terms of wealth, status and even power, at least at the local level if not yet at the political centre. It was not only middle-class males, however, who were affected by economic and social changes; both the poor and women of all classes began to escape from those economic fetters and social chains that had previously bound them and still bound a higher proportion of the subjects of other European states.

Contributors to this Companion clearly recognize the fruits of recent scholarship that have stressed the powerful influence of religion in general on eighteenth-century Britain and the significant spiritual, moral and political role of the Church of England in particular. They appreciate that Britain was not so secularized as historians once claimed and that the Church of England was not so politicized as once was thought. On the other hand, they also demonstrate that Britain was more pluralistic and tolerant in religion than most European states. Protestant Dissenters remained a force to be reckoned with throughout the eighteenth century, and Methodists became a rising force in the late eighteenth century. Scotland retained her own distinctive established church after the Union of 1707, but it too faced competition from other sects and churches. In Ireland Protestant Dissent was a major influence in Ulster and in the other provinces the majority of the population remained Catholic. The Catholic question and sectarian divisions bedevilled internal relations on that island and undoubtedly soured relations with Great Britain.

There is now widespread interest in cultural history. There are essays in this Companion that show how eighteenth-century Britain became both highly admired by educated people across Europe and increasingly divided at home between its elite, bourgeois and popular cultures. The landed elite developed an impressively cohesive culture that enabled it to maintain its dominant political and social position. The middling orders in society sometimes sought to ape that culture, but in urban areas an enlightened culture arose which was both distinct from and also intersected with the elite culture of the landed classes. The people at large, in both urban and rural Britain, retained a wide range of cultural practices and traditions, which were distinct from those of their social superiors and which sometimes brought them into conflict with the governing elite. Eighteenth-century Britain developed a popular press which educated, influenced and informed a higher proportion of the population than ever before – and far more of the non-elite than in any other European state. Such a free and active press allowed a wide range of political ideas to be more intensely debated in Britain than in any European state prior to the French Revolution of 1789. Britain's free press and capacity for open political debate were much admired by enlightened opinion in Europe. Her literature and drama were also deeply admired in Europe as Britain escaped to some extent from the cultural hegemony of France. Satiric verse, comedy dramas, and especially the periodic essay and the novel had a profound impact both throughout the British Isles and far beyond their shores. The study of crime and punishment has also become a growth area in British historical studies since the 1970s. This research has demonstrated that the eighteenth-century criminal justice system was neither as brutal nor as chaotic as earlier generations of historians had claimed. It also shows how Britain became one of the first countries to experience the growth of urban and commercial crime, and sought to develop new methods of policing urban areas and punishing those guilty of such crimes.

Abroad, the essays here explain how Britain became a major European power for the first time for centuries and how she felt compelled to wage another 'Hundred Years' War' against France. They also explain the strengths, particular qualities and specific weaknesses of the army and navy, which were so essential to the growth of British power and her remarkable imperial expansion. In the eighteenth century Britain could reasonably claim to be the most liberal country in Europe, and certainly many Britons were enormously proud of their 'liberties', and yet Britain also came to dominate the Atlantic slave trade and to govern large numbers of non-European subjects across the world. These achievements brought resentment and even resistance, as well as political and economic benefits. Without clear government planning or a decided imperial strategy, Britain acquired a large empire across the Atlantic, stretching from Hudson Bay to Trinidad. In the later eighteenth century British ministers drifted into a political crisis with British subjects on the mainland of North America and failed to avoid a disastrous war which resulted in Britain losing these valuable American colonies. This apparent calamity did not, however, have quite the devastating effect on British prestige and power that many contemporaries feared. This was, in part, because Britain remained by far the greatest commercial partner of the new United States and, in part, because Britain began to acquire another, very different, empire in India. Britain's successes and endeavours in wars in Europe and across the world are shown to owe much to her economic power, her financial strength, her rather old-fashioned but vastly augmented army, and her more professional and effective navy. While her successes may have been built on an army, navy and financial system that were not radically different from what they had been at the end of the seventeenth century, they did dramatically alter Britain's position relative to the other major European powers. Britain in 1815 was a formidable power, a far stronger and much more important state than she had been in 1688.

Finally, the essays here take up a recent subject of much historical enquiry: to what extent was there a unified and coherent British state as distinct from a collection of different countries within the British Isles that were increasingly brought under the political sway of England? The contributors to this section of the Companion all seek to show what was distinctive about Scotland, Wales and Ireland, how far different communities flourished across the British Isles, and to what extent they were fully incorporated with England into a greater and more integrated 'British' state. They demonstrate that many different societies and distinct communities continued to flourish across the British Isles throughout the eighteenth century, despite efforts from Westminster in particular to achieve greater political integration. While major strides were made towards the political integration of the various parts of Great Britain, some of those most distant from London were not fully 'Anglicized' (or even English-speaking) by the end of the century. Throughout the century Ireland remained a particular problem and it exploded in rebellion in 1798. The Act of Union in 1800, and the creation of the United Kingdom from 1 January 1801, was an effort to solve this problem and to make all inhabitants of the British Isles into 'Britons', but it ultimately foundered on the rocks of religious, social and economic divisions.

Maps

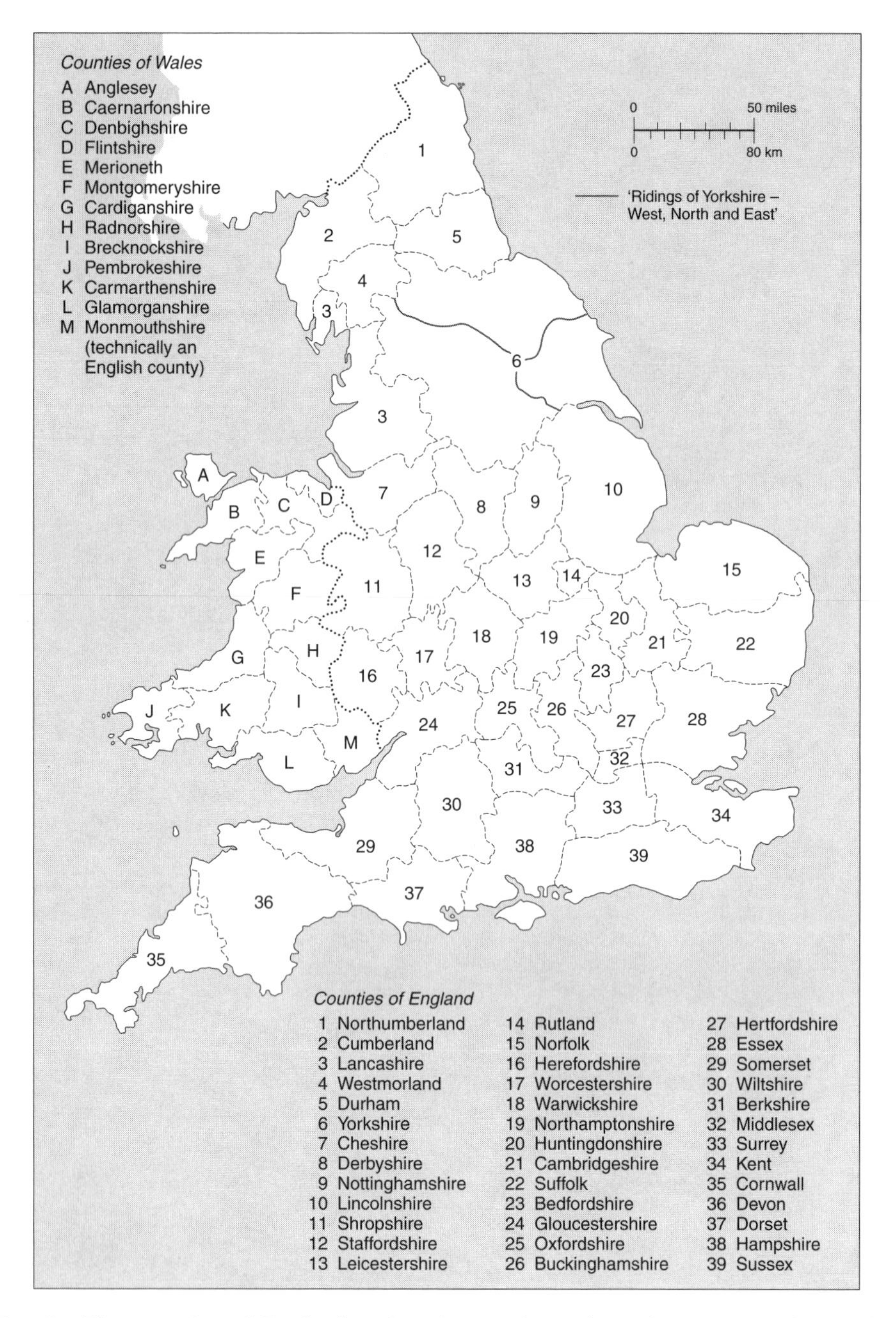

Map 1 The counties of England and Wales in the eighteenth century (adapted from Geoffrey Holmes and Daniel Szechi, *The Age of Oligarchy*, London, 1993).

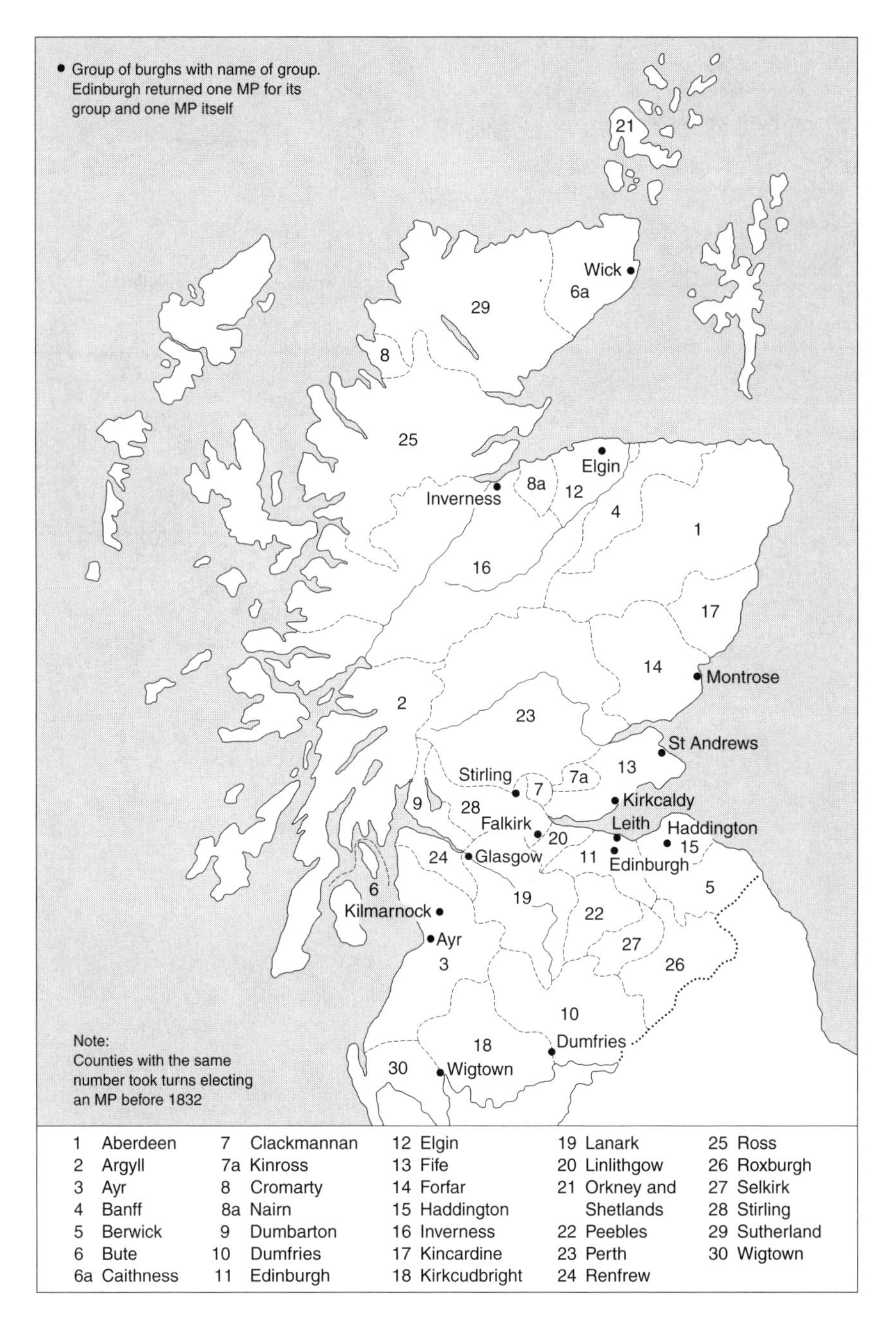

Map 2 Parliamentary constituencies in Scotland, 1707–1832 (adapted from W. A. Speck, *The Birth of Britain*, Oxford, 1994).

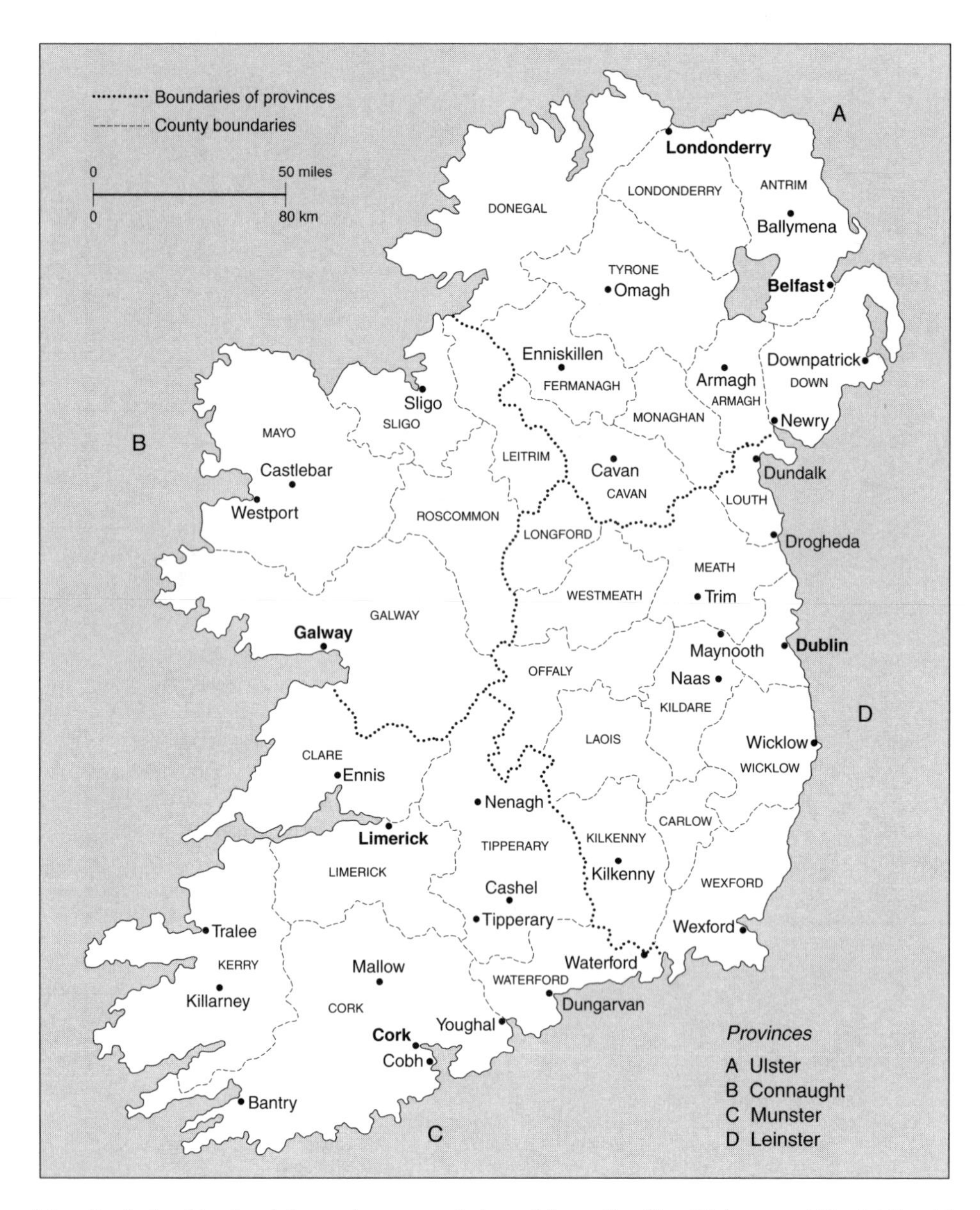

Map 3 Ireland in the eighteenth century (adapted from Geoffrey Holmes and Daniel Szechi, *The Age of Oligarchy*, London, 1993).

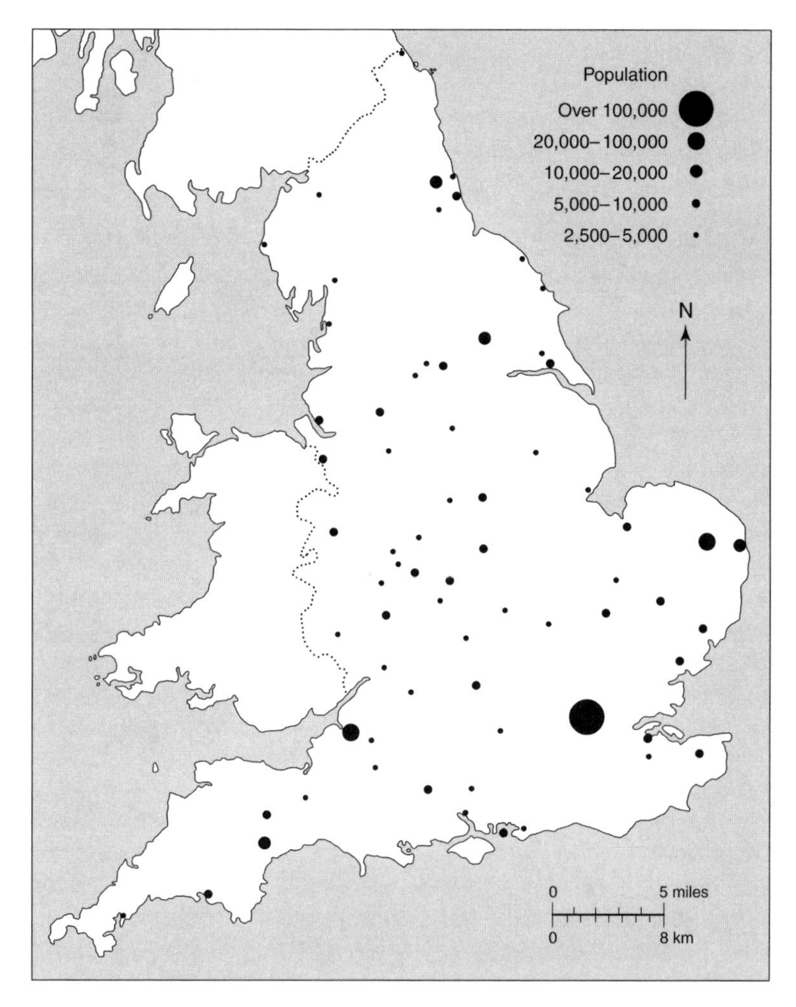

Map 4 Towns with 2,500+ inhabitants in 1700 (adapted from P. J. Corfield, *The Impact of English Towns 1700–1800*, Oxford, 1982).

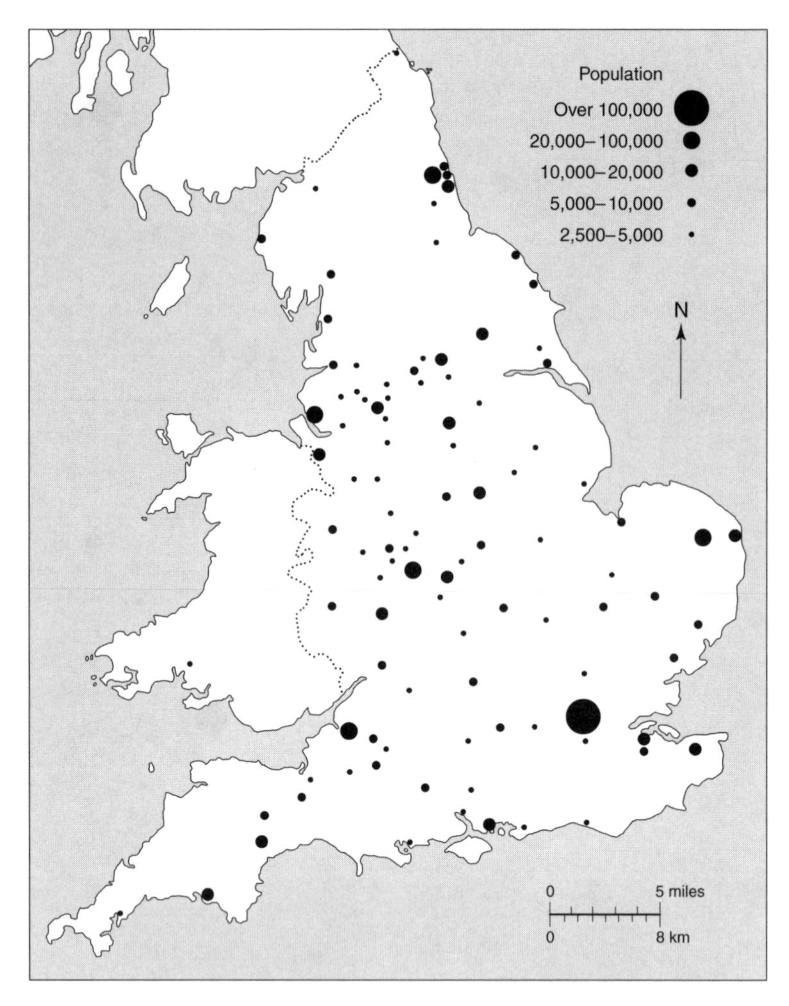

Map 5 Towns with 2,500+ inhabitants in 1750 (adapted from P. J. Corfield, *The Impact of English Towns 1700–1800*, Oxford, 1982).

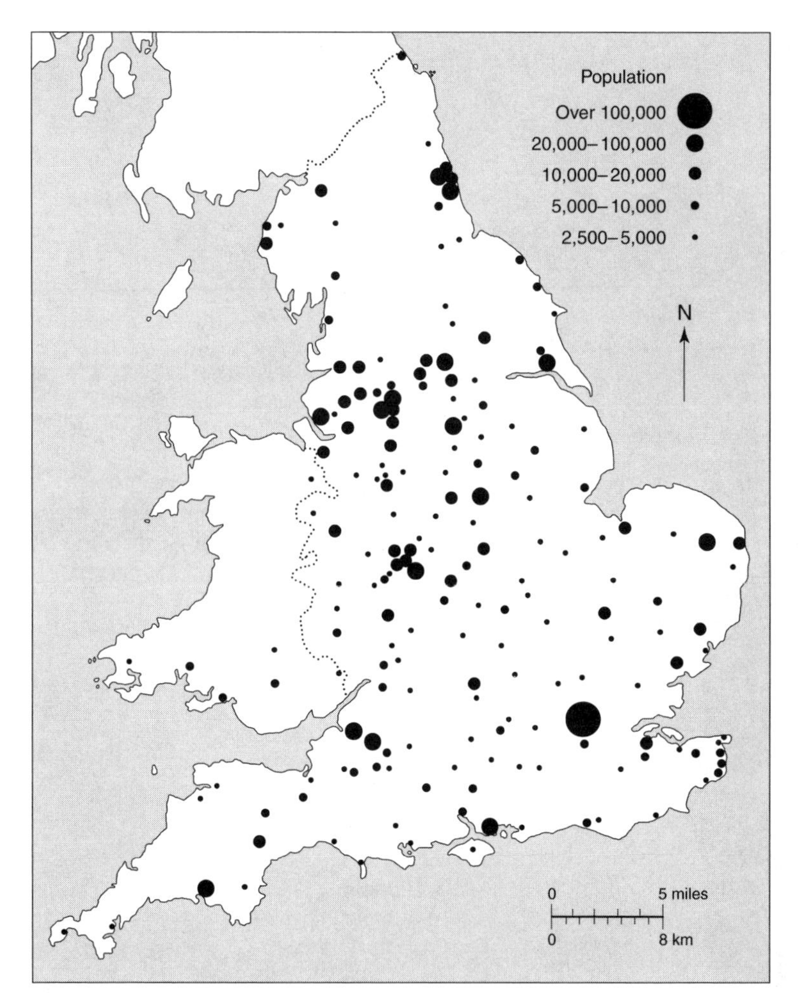

Map 6 Towns with 2,500+ inhabitants in 1801 (adapted from P. J. Corfield, *The Impact of English Towns 1700–1800*, Oxford, 1982).

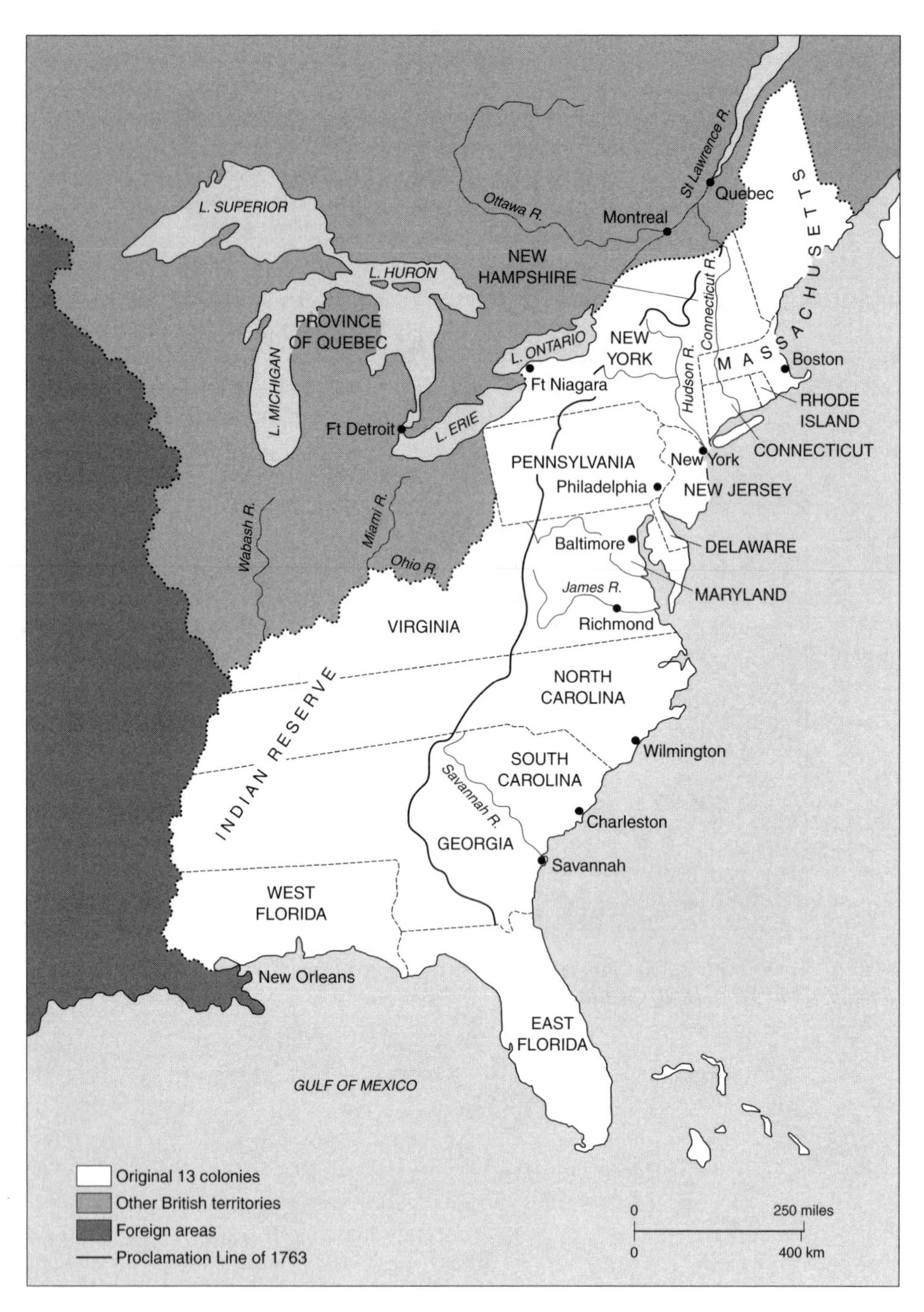

Map 7 British North America *c.*1763 (adapted from H. T. Dickinson, ed., *Britain and the American Revolution*, London, 1998).

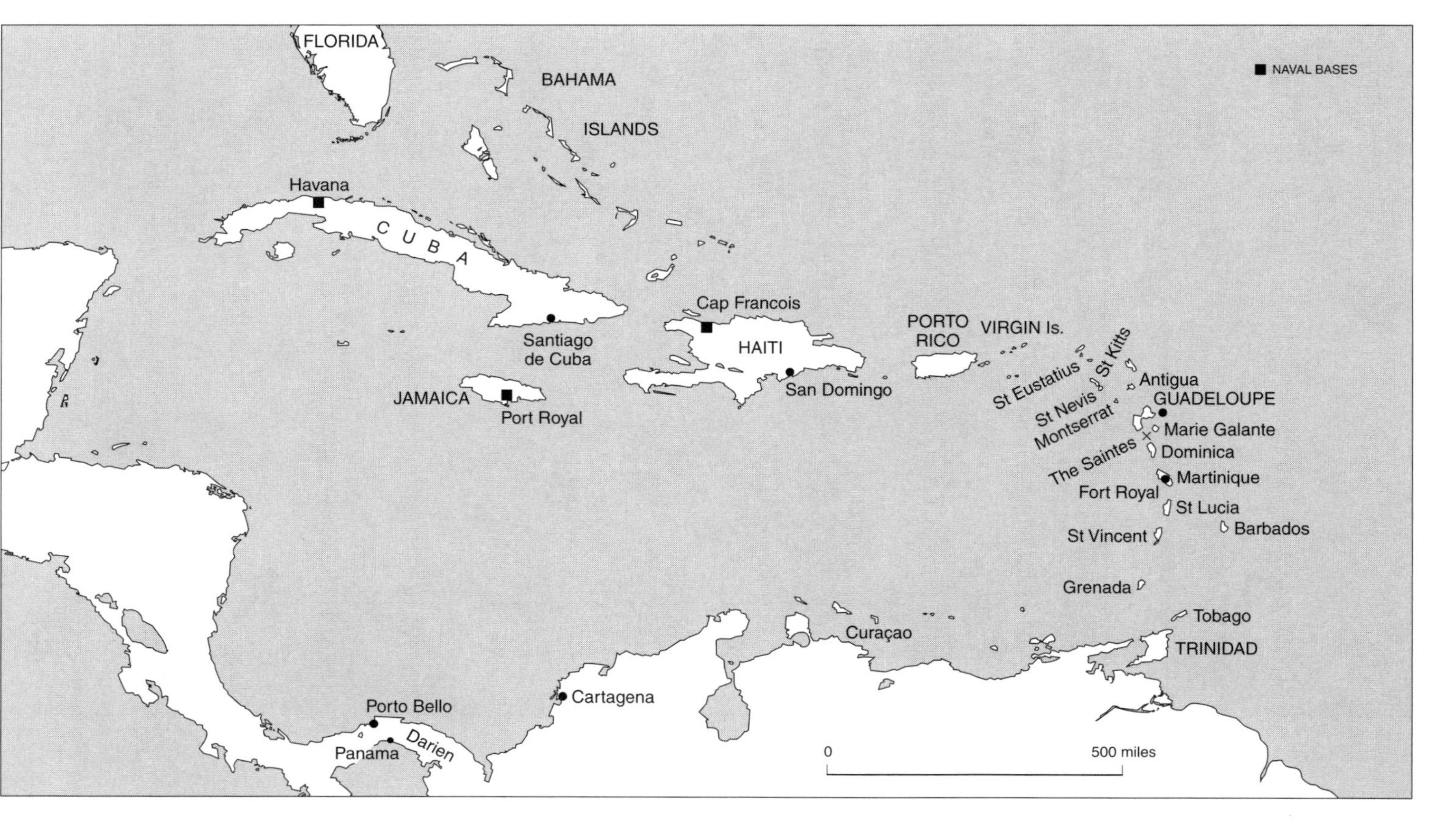

Map 8 The Caribbean in the eighteenth century (adapted from Derek Jarrett, *Britain 1688–1815*, London, 1965).

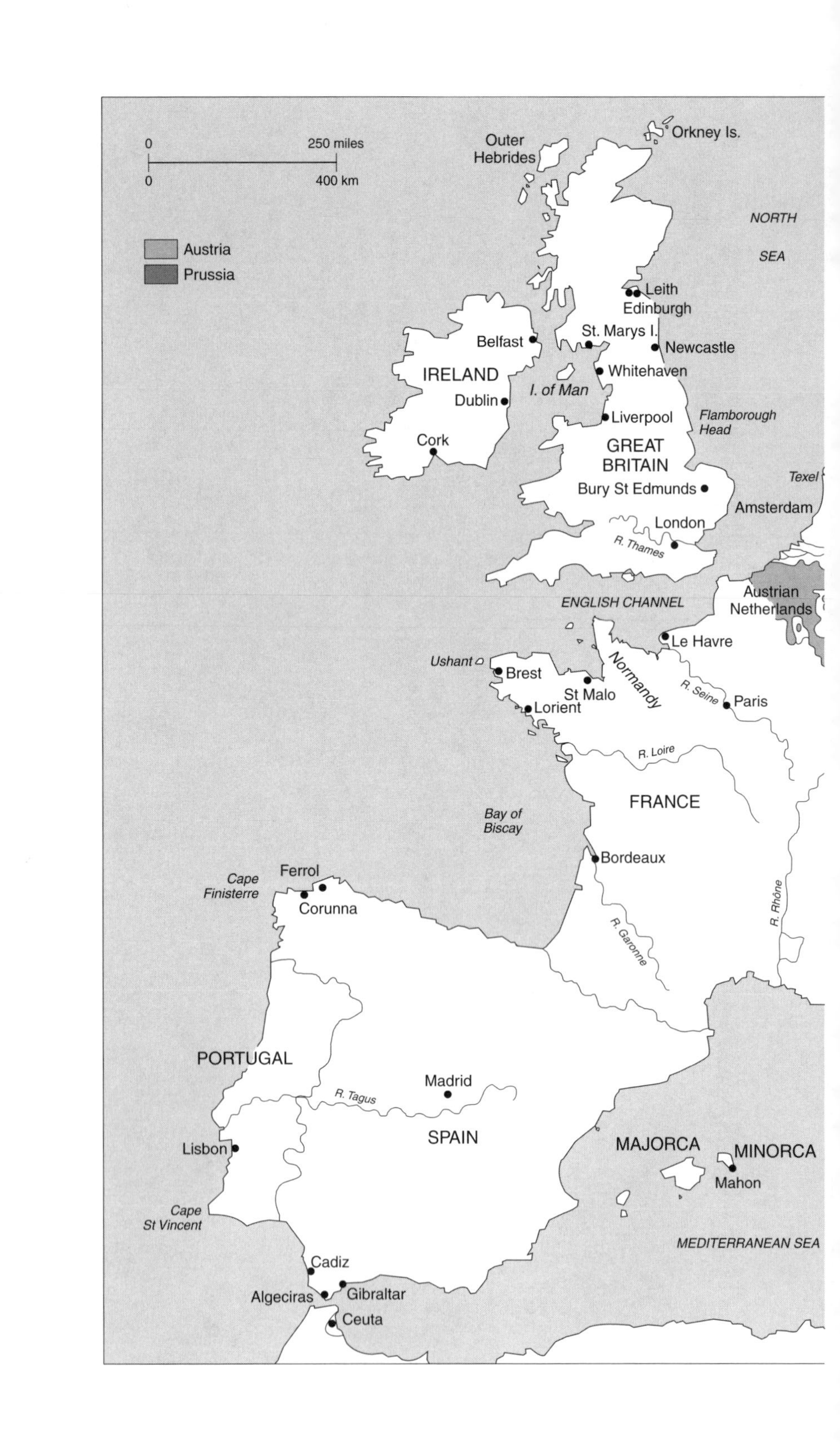

0
250 miles
0
400 km
Austria
Prussia
Outer Hebrides
Orkney Is.
NORTH SEA
Leith
Edinburgh
St. Marys I.
Newcastle
Belfast
IRELAND
Whitehaven
I. of Man
Dublin
Liverpool
Flamborough Head
Cork
GREAT BRITAIN
Texel
Bury St Edmunds
Amsterdam
London
R. Thames
Austrian Netherlands
ENGLISH CHANNEL
Le Havre
Ushant
Brest
Normandy
St Malo
R. Seine
Paris
Lorient
R. Loire
FRANCE
Bay of Biscay
Bordeaux
Ferrol
Cape Finisterre
Corunna
R. Rhône
R. Garonne
PORTUGAL
Madrid
R. Tagus
SPAIN
Lisbon
MAJORCA
MINORCA
Mahon
Cape St Vincent
MEDITERRANEAN SEA
Cadiz
Algeciras
Gibraltar
Ceuta

Map 9 Europe *c.*1775 (adapted from H. T. Dickinson, ed., *Britain and the American Revolution*, London, 1998).

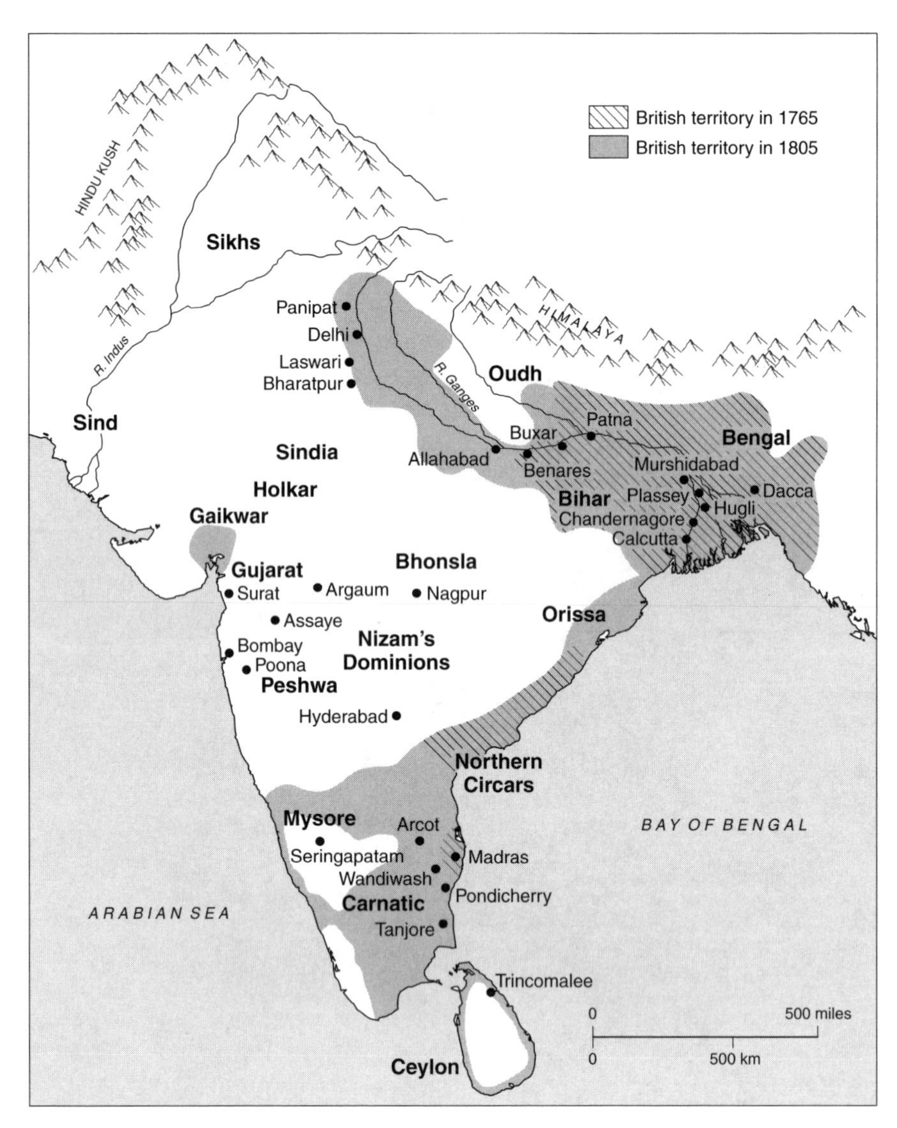

Map 10 Expansion of British power in India (adapted from P. J. Marshall, ed., *The Oxford History of the British Empire*, vol. 2: *The Eighteenth Century*, Oxford, 1998, p. 509).

Part I

Politics and the Constitution

Chapter One

The British Constitution

H. T. Dickinson

The age of the democratic revolution in the late eighteenth century saw the beginnings of modern written constitutions, most notably the American Constitution of 1787 and a succession of constitutions in revolutionary France in the 1790s. The essential feature of the British constitution is not simply that it predates any of these modern constitutions, but that it is *unwritten*. Although some fundamental features of the British constitution were written down in legislative documents – for example, the Bill of Rights, the Act of Settlement, and the Act of Union between England and Scotland – the English (later the British) constitution has evolved over centuries in various ways which were never written down. It is therefore largely a *prescriptive* and an organic constitution.

The evolution of the British constitution was due to prolonged and successive disputes between the monarch and the greater nobility, between crown and parliament, and between parliament and people. These disputes sometimes led to armed conflict and political revolution, but, much more often, they have produced minor shifts in the balance of power and in constitutional arrangements between the various institutions and political agents in the state. Some of these changes were barely detected even by those who helped to make them. It is difficult to trace the shifting balance between crown and parliament that occurred almost imperceptibly throughout the whole eighteenth century or to state with precision what the constitution was at any particular date in that century.

There was very considerable debate in the eighteenth century about both precisely what the constitution was and what it ought to be. These debates existed, in part, because the constitution was unwritten, evolutionary and shifting, but also because there were many and profound disputes between competing groups over how to interpret or amend that constitution. While modern historians may legitimately attempt to define the nature and features of the British constitution in the eighteenth century, they have to acknowledge the near impossibility of performing this task because the constitution never stood still even in periods of relative political stability, because so many contemporary political actors offered very different interpretations of the constitution and because the prevailing theory of the constitution and the actual practice of the constitution were never in exact alignment.

If we wish today to explain the main features of the British constitution, then we need first to look at the contemporary debates on four aspects of that constitution: its origins, its structure, the location of sovereignty and the liberties of the subject. We then need to look at how the political system operated within these constitutional restraints: looking at the role of the monarch and his ministers, at the management of parliament and at church–state relations.

The Ideological Debate on the Constitution

The origins of the constitution

During the eighteenth century three different notions of the origins of the constitution were in contention – divine right, the original contract and the ancient constitution – but only the last of these secured overwhelming support. The upholders of divine right had largely prevailed before the Glorious Revolution of 1688 and Jacobites adhered to this doctrine well into the eighteenth century. The divine right theory had maintained that legitimate authority came only from God and that God favoured absolute monarchy. Kings ruled by the direct command of God and God had established a clear and inviolable rule, namely, indefeasible hereditary succession, to prevent a dangerous hiatus between the death of one ruler and his replacement by the legitimate heir. Subjects could not lawfully oppose the commands of their rulers and could not legitimately decide for themselves who would rule them. They could never possess the right to take up arms against the crown even to protect their lives, liberties and property. The willingness of men of property to put themselves at the mercy of an absolute king can be explained only by their horror of 'mob' rule and their fear of social revolution. They feared the tyranny of the unrestrained multitude more than the power of an absolute king. Some (though not all) Jacobites supported such views in the early eighteenth century, but, by the mid-eighteenth century, fear of a Catholic ruler, and growing confidence in their ability to operate the system of limited monarchy established by the Glorious Revolution, persuaded most men to abandon support for the theory of divine right.

John Locke, in his celebrated *Two Treatises of Government* (1690), had argued that divine right was a slavish doctrine and that the only legitimate form of government was one established by consent and framed in order to secure for all men their natural rights to life, liberty and property. Governors could rightfully exercise power only so long as they preserved the natural rights of the governed. Should they grossly infringe these rights, the governed had the right to resist this abuse of power by force of arms, to dissolve the government, and to erect another which would better preserve the natural rights of subjects. Locke's views were too liberal for most of his contemporaries and only a few radical Whigs endorsed his views in the first half of the eighteenth century. In the later eighteenth century, however, a number of radicals not only revived the notion of the original contract, but were much more explicit than Locke had been over the question of which men gave their express consent to the creation of civil government and how they would ensure that government defended the natural rights of all men. The most famous and influential of these radicals,

Thomas Paine in his *Rights of Man* (1791–2), insisted that all adult males were involved in agreeing to the contracts which established civil society and civil government. He went on to argue that the only way to secure the natural rights of all men was to create a written constitution in which all men had the right to vote for the legislature which would make the laws and control the magistrates who enforced them. Despite the appeal of Paine's ideas to some radicals, support for his desire for a democratic republic was never widespread in Britain, even among advanced reformers.

Much the most widespread and prevalent notion of the origins of the constitution claimed that Britain possessed an ancient constitution which could be traced back many centuries. Many English commentators claimed that English law was customary and immemorial, the monarch's authority had always been limited, the constitution was based on a mixed form of government, the supreme authority in the kingdom was the legislature of King, Lords and Commons, and subjects had the right to resist tyranny. Building upon these foundations, they asserted that the political institutions of the country and the liberties of Englishmen were of ancient vintage. It was firmly believed that this ancient constitution could be traced back to the Anglo-Saxon era before the Norman Conquest of 1066. This concept of the ancient constitution was used by the opponents of royal absolutism. They argued that subjects could throw off the 'Norman yoke' and assert their rights against monarchs who attempted to subvert their liberties. The Glorious Revolution of 1688–9 provided historical evidence of the readiness of the people to justify their legitimate constitutional rights, by force if necessary.

Although a minority of radical Whigs justified the Glorious Revolution by appeals to the contract theory and by claims that the people had forcibly deposed James II because of his abuse of the constitution, the governing elite who successfully carried through the Revolution Settlement (both Whigs and Tories) insisted that they had not done anything so radical. They had sought to restore the ancient constitution by making only a slight alteration in the succession to the crown (in order to remove a Catholic monarch who could not be trusted to uphold the ancient constitution) and by restating the traditional privileges of parliament and the ancient liberties of the subject by such measures as the Bill of Rights and the Triennial Act. They had not claimed that power originated with the consent of the people or that ultimate sovereignty rested in the hands of the people. The Hanoverian succession in 1714, and the defeat of the Jacobite rebellions, both ensured that this view of the constitution would last throughout the eighteenth century. The ruling elite had no desire to see the people appeal to the contract theory or to the right of resistance in order to challenge their own right to govern. They played down the importance of Revolution principles as any sure guide to future political action. They feared that any undue emphasis on the people's right of resistance would undermine the stability of the political and social order which they had established.

When, in the later eighteenth century, radicals began either to claim that the Revolution Settlement had not gone far enough in restoring the liberties of the subject, or that it had justified the people's right to remove a government which infringed their liberties, conservative voices were raised in defence of the older Whig claim that the Glorious Revolution deserved to be celebrated because it had carried through the limited changes needed to restore the ancient constitution. Edmund Burke maintained that the constitution was prescriptive and had developed gradually over many centuries without conscious human contrivance or systematic design. It was the product of history and experience, not the deliberate result of human reason or will. Its authority rested not on any original contract or known first principles, but on the evidence that it had existed time out of mind and had made thousands of adjustments to the needs created by altered circumstances and the changing habits of the people. Burke entirely rejected the radical claim that British subjects had the right to cashier their governors for misconduct and to frame a new constitution for themselves. The Glorious Revolution had been conservative in its intentions and limited in the changes it had made. In essence, it was not so much a revolution made as one prevented.

Burke's case was put so effectively that some radicals abandoned the traditional historic appeal to the ancient constitution. Faced with the powerful claim that history could not be effectively used to demonstrate the traditional liberties of the subject, they appealed instead to reason and morality to justify the rights of the subject. Thomas Paine, in particular, argued that it was not sufficient to look back to the Glorious Revolution or to any earlier historic age. To understand the rights of man it was necessary to go much further back to the state man was in when he was first made by his creator. In Paine's view, it was time to escape from the dead hand of history and the tyranny of the past. Despite his fame and political influence, however, he did not persuade most British radicals to abandon an appeal to the historic rights of the subject under the ancient constitution.

Mixed government and the balanced constitution

Almost all commentators in the eighteenth century described the constitution as a limited or parliamentary monarchy whose main features and greatest virtues were that it was a mixed government and balanced constitution. There was much support for the claim that the structure of the British constitution was the best that could be attained in order to establish authority and preserve liberty on the basis of the rule of law. The constitution was regarded as being a mixture of monarchy, aristocracy and democracy, because the supreme legislature was composed of the crown, the House of Lords and the House of Commons. This mixed form of government achieved the greatest number of advantages and the fewest evils of any political system. Three pure forms of government were recognized: namely, monarchy, aristocracy and democracy. Unfortunately, while each form had its merits, it was also undermined by a serious threat to liberty or authority. Monarchy avoided disputes over who had the legitimate right to exercise authority and it allowed a single ruler to act decisively in an emergency; but it placed the life, liberty and property of the subject at the mercy of one man who might act as an arbitrary tyrant. Aristocracy provided an able elite capable of leading and of offering an inspiring example to the nation, but it could too easily degenerate into a narrow oligarchy of warring, self-interested factions. Democracy offered the greatest liberty to the ordinary subject, but it was often too slow to act and was so inherently unstable that it invariably soon collapsed into anarchy or mob rule. Almost all democracies either ended in bloodshed or were transformed into military dictatorships. On the other hand, a mixed form of government, which incorporated elements of monarchy, aristocracy and democracy, could secure the benefits of each in their pure form while avoiding their disadvantages.

Although mixed government was the best system that human wisdom had ever discovered, it was susceptible to corruption and dissolution if the three component elements did not coexist in harmony. Each element had a natural tendency to pull in its own separate direction and so it was only by carefully balancing them that they could remain harnessed together. Fortunately, the British constitution had secured all the benefits of mixed government because a constitutional balance had then been achieved between the three institutions of crown, Lords and Commons. Each of these institutions possessed its own peculiar privileges and distinct functions. As chief magistrate the king was above the law, was the fount of honour and public office, was the unchallenged head of the executive, and retained various prerogative rights, including the power to summon, prorogue and dissolve parliament. The aristocracy enjoyed the highest honours in the state, sat in the upper house of parliament as of right, and formed the highest court of justice in the land. The members of the House of Commons were the representatives of the people and, as such, defended the liberties of the subject, put forward the grievances of the people and initiated all taxes (and so controlled the supply of money entering the public purse). Besides these individual functions, all three institutions of crown, Lords and Commons combined to form the sovereign legislature. No bill could become law and no money could be raised without being approved by all three institutions in the same session of parliament. There was no strict separation of powers, even though the king appointed all executive posts, the House of Lords was the supreme court of law and the House of Commons voted the public revenue. The executive and the judiciary also interacted with the legislature: the king appointed the judges, who sat in the House of Lords, where they offered legal advice (though they could not vote), they held office during their good behaviour and could be dismissed only by a vote of both houses of parliament. Thus, the British constitution was a complicated system of checks and balances. It preserved the privileges of crown, aristocracy and people, while seeking to secure a harmonious relationship between all three. It was this delicate balance and this constitutional equilibrium that ensured that those twin goals of mixed government were achieved: namely, liberty and authority.

It was not only the governing elite and their loyalist allies who praised mixed government and the balanced constitution. Most reformers, and a majority of those who supported the radical cause, were all convinced that the theoretical structure of the British constitution was without equal in the world. In practice, however, they saw that a monarch who misused his power could still threaten to overturn the delicate balance of the constitution.

The sovereignty of parliament

In the eighteenth century most men were convinced that their property, their privileges and their liberties could be secured only if there existed a single supreme authority from whose decisions there could be no appeal. Political commentators insisted therefore that there must be a supreme, irresistible, absolute and uncontrolled authority in every state if order was to be maintained and anarchy avoided. Throughout the eighteenth century a clear majority of the political nation believed that the combined legislature of crown, Lords and Commons embodied this sovereign authority. Parliament could act as it saw fit and its actions could not be undone by any power on earth except a subsequent parliament. In his immensely influential *Commentaries on the Laws of England* (1765–9), William Blackstone insisted that the British legislature was sovereign and absolute and could change the constitution itself. Blackstone's views were echoed many times in both houses of parliament. None the less, despite such repeated claims, it is misleading to believe that the doctrine of parliamentary sovereignty gained universal approval or that it was unchallenged throughout the eighteenth century. There were criticisms of the sovereignty of parliament from both conservatives and radicals. There were conservative supporters of royal sovereignty not only while there was a Jacobite claimant to the throne, but long afterwards. Indeed, in the late eighteenth century there was a resurgence of support for the authority of the king. Several high church clergymen claimed that the king's authority was still superior to that of parliament. The government of the Younger Pitt even had to condemn the constitutional claims made for George III by John Reeves, one of the government's most fervent supporters, in his ultra-conservative tract, *Thoughts on English Government* (1795).

For most of the eighteenth century many Whig and radical opponents of royal power were also concerned about the concept of an absolutely sovereign legislature. The genuine pride taken in the constitution and in the liberties of Englishmen, and the traditional hostility to arbitrary, absolute power, made many men doubt the wisdom of giving parliament completely unfettered authority. These doubts were expressed in a variety of arguments. One argument maintained that the law of God, derived either explicitly from the Bible or indirectly from the law of nature, was superior to that of any human agency. They stressed that no human power could command what was against the law of nature. The most common line of attack, however, was to appeal to the fundamental laws of the constitution. Sometimes it was claimed that specific constitutional decisions taken in the past were inviolable and could not be altered or repealed by subsequent acts of parliament. The examples most frequently cited were Magna Carta, the Bill of Rights, the Triennial Act and the Act of Union with Scotland. More frequent still were complaints by opposition elements that ministers were introducing legislation which was contrary to the spirit of the constitution. Government policies towards the American colonies in the 1760s and 1770s were frequently condemned in Britain as well as in the colonies for being unconstitutional. The American crisis forced some Whigs to revert to Locke's position: in normal matters of government the legislature was sovereign, but it could not gravely infringe man's natural and inalienable right to his life, liberty and property. The fundamental principles of the constitution were ultimately superior to the authority of parliament. The authority of parliament was bound by the principles of the constitution.

The more advanced radicals located sovereign authority in the people. They insisted that the ultimate authority in the state resided in the collective will of the people, but they did not devise an effective means of establishing the sovereignty of the people. Some radicals did insist that members of parliament (MPs) were not independent representatives, who could vote on motions in parliament as they saw fit, but were delegates who could be instructed how to vote on major issues by the electors who returned them to parliament. A few radicals considered setting up a national convention which would allow the people to resume their sovereign rights and enable them to decide the best means of securing their constitutional liberties. Thomas Paine was convinced that the natural rights of man could be safeguarded only if a written constitution clearly restricted the authority of both the legislature and the executive. In his opinion, it was essential that such a written constitution should be the act of the whole people. It should establish not only the general principles within which government or legislature could operate, but should lay down detailed restrictions on the exercise of power. No part of the constitution could then be infringed either by government or parliament without breaching the trust of the people, dissolving civil government and returning the people to the state of nature.

While the critics of the doctrine of parliamentary sovereignty did not succeed in having it rejected, they almost certainly convinced even its strongest supporters that it was a *legal fiction*. Its value and utility lay in preserving order while allowing for prompt action. These benefits, however, would have been jeopardized by any rash attempts to trample on the rights and liberties of the people. The assertion of the doctrine in the face of American resistance had resulted in the disastrous loss of the American colonies. Thereafter, even the staunchest advocates of a sovereign parliament were fully conscious of the general commitment to the notion of government by consent and the widespread support for the liberties of the subject. Edmund Burke stressed the dangerous consequences that might ensue if the legislature lost sight of the need to carry public opinion along with it.

The liberties of the subject

In the eighteenth century many commentators praised the advantages which British subjects enjoyed as free men living under a free constitution. Although a narrow propertied elite clearly dominated government and parliament, those who admired the existing constitution confidently asserted that the British people possessed as much liberty as was consistent with the preservation of social order. On the other hand, there were also many radical commentators who criticized the actual working of the constitution and they often did so on the grounds that it was failing to safeguard the liberties of the people. There was a profound and prolonged debate between those who were confident that the British people did in reality possess considerable liberty and those who believed that they were being denied their liberty by a corrupt and reactionary governing elite. These differences rested, in part, upon conflicting assessments of what government and parliament were in fact doing to and for the subject, and, in part, on different perceptions of those legitimate rights and liberties which the people as a whole ought to possess. Defenders of the status quo believed that government and parliament were doing as much as possible to preserve the liberties of the subject, whereas critics complained that the governing elite were denying the people their historic, natural and legitimate rights. These opposed views were underpinned by different notions of what rights and liberties British subjects ought and could reasonably expect to possess. No commentator, no matter how conservative, was prepared to assert that the people were without any rights. On the other hand, there was a great deal of discussion and much heated debate over the precise nature and extent of the liberties which British subjects could legitimately demand as their historic or natural rights.

It was accepted by all that every subject had the right to enjoy freedom from oppression and that each individual was free to do some things without interference from government or legislature. There was a moral limit to the power of government or parliament to interfere with the activities of subjects. It was also agreed that this sphere of free action could not be unlimited, because this would mean that no government or parliament could possess any legitimate or effective authority over its subjects. Even at their most limited, it was always claimed that the people's civil liberties ensured the right of subjects to live under the rule of law and to have an equal opportunity of justice. Arbitrary authority was restrained by positive law, ancient custom and common law, or natural law to the extent that no subject could be imprisoned without trial; all men were subject to the same laws administered by the same law courts; no torture could be used to secure a confession; and no accused person could be convicted of a serious offence except after a trial by jury.

Equal justice for all was not seen as the full extent of every subject's claim to civil liberty. There was also almost universal agreement that all subjects had an inalienable right to their property. Locke's views on this particular issue were widely accepted. Even the radicals of the late eighteenth century were prepared to defend both private property and its unequal distribution. Some quite explicitly denied that they desired to invade the rights of private property.

The right to freedom of conscience was another important civil liberty which was conceded by many commentators. From Locke onwards several writers defended the right to freedom of worship, though many denied that Protestant Dissenters, Catholics and atheists could claim the same political rights as Anglican Protestants under an essentially Anglican Protestant constitution. Freedom of worship was given to Protestant Dissenters as early as the Toleration Act of 1689, but the survival of the Test and Corporation Acts ensured that they were still legally denied the right to take office under the crown or to serve in local government. The position of Roman Catholics was much worse. Under the constitution they were probably third-class citizens. Freedom of worship and various political rights and civil liberties were legally denied to Roman Catholics by a series of harsh penal laws passed by parliament in the late seventeenth and early eighteenth centuries. It is true that these were rarely implemented to their full extent, but, none the less, anti-Catholicism was a widespread prejudice in British society and indeed a defining characteristic of that society and its constitution. Anti-Catholicism was so virulent that when parliament sought to relieve Catholics of some of the penal laws in 1778, this minor concession provoked the Gordon Riots of 1780, the worst outbreak of public disorder in the eighteenth century.

The demand for religious toleration generally advanced hand-in-hand with the campaign for a free press and for the free expression of political views. Pre-publication censorship lapsed in 1695 and throughout the eighteenth century there was a very flourishing press in which parliamentary debates were reported, profound political issues could be debated, and frequent and harsh criticisms of the government were advanced. The principle of a free press was rarely challenged. In times of very severe political crisis, of course, the government was able to persuade parliament to impose temporary restrictions on the press, but, more frequently, the government sought to restrict the circulation of the opposition press by imposing stamp duties which would increase the price of newspapers or by subsidizing the press, directly and indirectly, so that it would produce material favourable to the viewpoint of the governing elite. It was always recognized that subjects had the right to bring their grievances and complaints before king and parliament by means of private and public petitioning. In the last resort, moreover, it was generally acknowledged that subjects possessed the natural right to use force to preserve their liberty.

The danger of relying on the right of resistance, however, was that it could be asserted only in a dire emergency when it might already be too late to preserve the people's civil liberties. It made sense, therefore, to ensure that parliament, and, in particular, the House of Commons, was in a position to resist the abuse of power by the executive and was strong enough to defend the liberties of the subject. It was generally agreed that this could be done only if the House of Commons represented the people and their interests. Conservative commentators believed that the House of Commons did effectively represent the people and their interests. It was claimed that parliament represented all the powerful interests in the country since many of the greatest landowners, churchmen, lawyers, financiers, merchants, admirals, generals and businessmen sat in parliament, and MPs were elected from all areas of the country, and by rural communities and urban communities of all sizes and types. Once they were elected, MPs represented all their constituents, not just those who had voted for them. Indeed, they were the representatives of the British people as a whole. Moreover, the fact that large towns, such as Birmingham, Manchester or Sheffield, were not directly represented in parliament did not mean that their interests were neglected by a House of Commons in which there were many MPs representing similar towns. The voters too were men of property who were sufficiently educated and independent to be trusted with the important task of choosing the nation's representatives. The franchise was rightly restricted to men of property, who could be trusted to exercise it wisely. They firmly rejected the radical claim that the vote should be given to the impoverished mob or rabble, who would be easily misled by corrupt men of wealth or by charismatic demagogues. The stability of the constitution depended on the representation of property because only men of independent means could be certain to possess the qualities to exercise a free choice among the candidates standing for election to the House of Commons.

In contrast to those conservative voices who sought to defend the existing electoral system, there were reformers and radicals who insisted that the present restricted franchise returned parliaments which looked only after the interests of men of substantial property and which frequently failed to defend the liberties of most of the people. Whether they looked back to the historic rights of Englishmen under the ancient constitution or they appealed to the universal and inalienable natural rights of men, these radicals insisted that the constitution could not be safeguarded nor the rights of the people secured, unless the franchise was greatly extended. Some wanted to give the vote to all male householders because they would have some property to defend. Some suggested extending the franchise to all men who paid certain taxes and so contributed to the upkeep of the state, while the most radical commentators pressed for a universal adult male suffrage (though only a very tiny minority ever advocated votes for women).

The Working of the Constitution

Although there was constant and sometimes intense ideological debate about the nature of the British constitution in the eighteenth century, the majority of the political elite during most of the period agreed on the major features of that constitution. They generally maintained that Britain possessed an ancient, prescriptive constitution; that liberty and stability were secured by Britain's mixed government and balanced constitution; that the sovereign authority in the state was the combined legislature of crown, Lords and Commons; and that all British subjects possessed the right to justice in the rule of law, and freedom of conscience and expression, but that only a minority deserved the franchise. In order to understand how this system worked in practice, however, it is necessary to look at those political customs and practices which were nowhere embodied in formal acts of parliament. It is necessary in particular to look at the authority of the monarch and royal ministers, the management of parliament, and the relations between church and state.

Crown and executive

In the earlier eighteenth century there were serious disputes and armed conflict about whether the Hanoverians or the Stuarts should sit on the throne, but at no stage was there marked hostility to monarchy as such and there was generally considerable support for those prerogatives of the crown that had survived the Glorious Revolution of 1688–9. After the Glorious Revolution the crown lost some, but not all, of its prerogative powers. The monarch had to be a Protestant (and after 1701 had to be an Anglican Protestant) and had to appoint only Anglicans to offices in the state. The monarch ceased to be able to pass or seriously amend laws without consent of parliament and, because of the constant need for parliamentary taxation, the monarch had to summon annual sessions of parliament in order to finance government policies, particularly costly wars. Queen Anne was the last monarch to veto parliamentary legislation (in the first decade of the century) and, thereafter, the monarch had to accept bills passed by parliament.

Despite these reductions in the prerogative powers of the crown, the monarch still possessed considerable political influence. The monarch was the supreme head of the Church of England. The monarch could still summon or prorogue parliament when it was most convenient to do so. The monarch always remained at the pinnacle of an aristocratic social hierarchy and leading politicians always sought access to the royal court in order to secure royal favour. Court posts conferred honour, distinction, influence and material rewards, but it was the monarch's right to appoint to the leading positions in the government that made it vital for politicians to gain access to the monarch in the royal closet. In the last resort, all government measures required the monarch's approval if they were to have any chance of passing through parliament. The leading government ministers were not in office because a majority in parliament, still less a majority of the electorate, had put them there. Ministers were first appointed by the monarch and only then did they seek majority support in parliament. Ministers could be dismissed at any time by the monarch, even while they seemed to retain majority support in parliament.

The privy council ceased to act as a governing body in the eighteenth century, though it retained some honorific duties and ceremonial roles. The government was dominated by about fifteen politicians who held the highest posts in the state. These men sought to agree government policy in regular meetings of the cabinet or cabinet council, though increasingly the most important decisions were taken in advance by a less formal inner cabinet of about half a dozen ministers (usually including the head of the Treasury, the two secretaries of state, the lord chancellor and the lord president of the council). The monarch ceased to attend the cabinet council in person very early in the eighteenth century. The decisions taken by the inner or efficient cabinet had to be conveyed to the monarch in the royal closet and royal support had to be secured before measures were presented to parliament. The cabinet's view usually prevailed, but it was not the final arbiter of government policy. The monarch always had to be persuaded and the monarch might have very decided views, especially on foreign policy and about other government appointments. Almost all administrations had a leading minister, who, from the earlier eighteenth century, came to be known as the prime minister. He was almost always the head of the Treasury. The prime minister, however, did not have as much authority as modern holders of this title. He did not appoint the rest of the cabinet – the monarch did. Although he might labour hard to bring in his friends and to exclude his rivals, this could be done only by gaining the ear of the monarch, usually through informal meetings in the royal closet. There was no doctrine of cabinet solidarity. Ministers might quite often disagree with one another and compete for the monarch's support for their particular point of view. When the prime minister resigned or was dismissed, it was not necessary for the rest of the cabinet to leave office with him.

The prime minister and his ministerial colleagues had three major political tasks to perform in order to retain royal favour and support: to maintain domestic peace, to avoid unsuccessful wars abroad, and to find the financial resources through loans and taxes to achieve these objectives. These tasks could be performed only with the support of both houses of parliament. As we shall see, this task was greatly eased by the extent of crown patronage. Indeed, it was crown patronage rather than the royal prerogative that allowed the monarch to establish and maintain the executive's powerful influence in parliament.

The management of parliament

There was no separation of powers in the British constitution. The leading members of the government (and even some officeholders whom we might today regard as civil servants) sat in parliament in order to promote the passage of government business through the legislature. The House of Lords did not directly oppose money-raising bills in the eighteenth century and hence its constitutional role was less significant than that of the House of Commons, which did certainly control the purse strings of the state. The Lords however did contain many of the most important men in the country, in terms of wealth and status, and the clear majority of all cabinets were members of the upper chamber. Their debates and their decisions, especially on foreign affairs, religious issues and legal questions, therefore did carry weight. Administrations however rarely had much trouble in persuading a majority in the Lords to support their policies. There were fewer than 200 men qualified to sit in the Lords until the 1780s (another sixty or so were created in the last two decades of the eighteenth century). Some peers never attended because they were Catholics, too old and infirm, or too poor to afford the expense of another house in London. The highest recorded vote in the eighteenth century was when 176 peers voted on the repeal of the Stamp Act in 1766. Normally the attendance rarely reached 120 members, and much lower attendances were quite common. Even the right of peers to vote by proxy did not greatly increase the number of occasions when very high votes were recorded. This being the case, it is not surprising that the government found it relatively easy to dominate the Lords. Most of the leading members of the government and most important courtiers sat in the Lords. So did twenty-six bishops, sixteen elected Scottish representative peers, the most senior army and navy officers, the judges (who could speak but not vote), and several holders of royal pensions. The number of peers holding positions of profit or trust under the crown increased from about fifty earlier in the eighteenth century to around 100 by the later decades. Most lords lieutenant of the counties sat in the Lords and these men recommended the appointment of justices of the peace (JPs) and militia officers. Not surprisingly, therefore, most peers were usually attached to the government of the day and helped it to frustrate most opposition campaigns.

The government found it much more difficult to manage the House of Commons, though even in this chamber ministers suffered relatively few defeats in the eighteenth century. The House of Commons was a larger chamber: 513 MPs prior to the union with Scotland in 1707 and a further forty-five MPs thereafter. The Act of Union with Ireland in 1800 added another 100 MPs. Most MPs were men of considerable wealth and status (a large majority were landed gentlemen, and all were supposed by law to possess substantial real estate), and they cherished at least the impression of being independent of the crown and certainly resented being regarded as servile creatures of the government. Some MPs, however, hardly ever attended debates and 400 was a very high attendance figure in any great crisis. The political loyalties of a significant number of MPs were influenced by crown and aristocratic patronage. Many crown appointments, titles and honours – in the state's bureaucracy (especially in the Treasury) and in the church, the armed forces and the legal profession – were granted to MPs or their relatives and clients. A number of parliamentary seats, including some treasury boroughs, admiralty boroughs, the Cinque Ports and some boroughs in the duchy of Cornwall, returned MPs in the crown interest. By such means crown patronage could strongly influence though not entirely control the votes of about 100 MPs in the earlier eighteenth century and perhaps 200 in the later eighteenth century. This bloc of pro-government MPs was usually known as the Court and Treasury party, though the loyalty of its members could never be absolutely guaranteed when the government faced a severe crisis. Aristocratic influence over MPs was also substantial. Many of these peers were supporters of the government, though, of course, some supported the opposition. About fifty Irish peers or sons of English peers sat in the House of Commons early in the eighteenth century. By the 1740s this number had increased to about 100 and fifty years later it had increased to about 120 MPs.

Peers also influenced the results in a significant number of parliamentary constituencies. They carried considerable interest in about 100 seats in the earlier eighteenth century and double that by late in the century.

Despite the growing influence over MPs exercised by the crown and the members of the House of Lords, the House of Commons could never be managed by patronage alone. Any successful administration had to have other means to influence the votes of the independent backbenchers. The leading ministers gathered able men of business around them to win over opinion-formers on the backbenches. Parliamentary debates were vital in persuading the uncommitted backbencher and hence effective ministerial teams of fine orators and expert debaters had to be deployed. MPs could also be influenced before a session started by efforts to explain government policy through the despatch of circular letters to the constituencies or through ministerial addresses to large numbers of backbenchers in private meetings. Ministers had also to be excellent man-managers, prepared to invite MPs to private meetings or able to lobby or buttonhole MPs in the chamber, and thus win them over to the government side by persuasion. Robert Walpole and Lord North possessed such skills personally. William Pitt the Younger was too cold and aloof to perform such tasks, but the work was done for him by able lieutenants such as Henry Dundas and Henry Addington. Effective administrations also manipulated parliamentary procedures to government advantage. They sought the election of a Speaker of the House, who would be at least sympathetic to the government side, if not usually servile. They worked even harder to ensure that the chairmen of parliamentary committees (especially the committee of supply and the committee of ways and means, which handled financial matters) were government supporters. Debates could be held at times which many backbench MPs found inconvenient: very early or very late in the session, or very late in the day. In a difficult situation popular opposition proposals might be allowed to pass an unmanageable House of Commons, but were defeated in a more compliant House of Lords. In a real emergency even a powerful administration might retreat rather than pursue a policy that was alienating too many MPs. Thus, Walpole abandoned his excise scheme in 1733, Henry Pelham repealed the Jewish Naturalization Act after a few months in 1753, and William Pitt abandoned his Irish trade proposals in 1785. What needs to be recognized, however, is that all successful administrations stayed in office for long periods because their policies were acceptable to the majority of the House of Commons (and also to public opinion outside parliament). Able ministers made shrewd assessments of how to maintain order and stability at home, how to please the most powerful interests in the state, how to raise the necessary loans and taxes to fund government policies, and how to keep the peace abroad or, if necessary, fight successful wars against the nation's enemies. Failure on one or more of these fronts was responsible for bringing down most administrations during the eighteenth century.

Church and state

The Church of England was the most important institution in the state in the later seventeenth century and it was intimately bound up with government, landownership and the social hierarchy. It was impossible to ignore the influence of the church or its authority in all facets of the life of all subjects. At this time the clergy accepted their role as servants of a personal monarchy and as advocates of an authoritarian state. They preached obedience to the powerful in the state and stressed the authority of the king in particular. They regarded disobedience as a sin and exercised a comprehensive control over the morals and religious duties of the laity. The Church of England claimed the loyalty of all subjects in England and Wales and wished to maintain strict religious conformity so that all subjects would be compelled to attend services in its churches regularly.

The Glorious Revolution began a process that saw significant changes in the relationship between church and state. The Church of England undoubtedly lost some of its special privileges. It found it increasingly difficult to support divine right monarchy and to preach its ideological support for the doctrines of passive obedience and non-resistance. The Toleration Act of 1689 formally allowed Protestant Dissenters to worship freely outside the Church of England and gradually Roman Catholics were allowed similar rights in practice. The Act of Union with Scotland in 1707 brought a largely Presbyterian country into the state and recognized the existence of a different state church in the northern kingdom, the Presbyterian Church of Scotland. It was therefore legally possible for many British subjects to choose to attend the services of other denominations than those of the Church of England. All hopes of religious uniformity in the state vanished. The governing institution in the church – Convocation, with its two houses of bishops and representatives of the lower clergy – expressed the dissatisfaction of many clergy in the earlier eighteenth century, but, when the disputes reached fever pitch over the Bangorian controversy in 1717, the government ended its meetings. Apart from a brief meeting in 1741, when no business was actually conducted, Convocation ceased to meet until 1855. The crown, advised by leading ministers, regularly appointed bishops who could be expected to work closely with the government on political matters. The church was regarded by many Whig politicians as an arm of an Erastian state. Furthermore, even the ecclesiastical courts steadily lost authority over the morals of the laity in the early eighteenth century. The lapsing of the Licensing Act in 1695 also meant the end of the powers of religious censorship previously exercised by the church. Unorthodox religious views and anti-clerical arguments flourished in the eighteenth-century press.

Throughout the eighteenth century most conservative clergy of the Church of England wished to return to a situation in which church and state worked together to support an authoritarian regime. Almost all of the clergy wished at least to maintain the remaining privileges of the Church of England. The leading politicians recognized the political value of the church and so an alliance of church and state was maintained, though it was never an alliance of equals but an uneasy agreement which often found some of the clergy dissatisfied with the church's subordinate role. The Church of England remained the state church and from 1701 the monarch was required to conform to the state church not just to exercise supreme authority over it. The Test and Corporation Acts of the later seventeenth century, which laid down that only those who conformed to the Church of England could hold office under the crown or serve in town corporations, remained on the statute books until 1828. Repeated attempts to repeal them failed, though regular indemnity acts after 1727 did enable Protestant Dissenters to evade the restrictions of the Corporation Act.

The twenty-six bishops in the Lords were expected to place their votes and their voices at the disposal of the government and generally did so unless they thought the remaining privileges of the Church of England were in danger. Bishops often wrote pro-government pamphlets, canvassed for pro-government candidates in elections, and delivered pro-government sermons on key dates in the calendar, such as the monarch's birthday, the anniversary of Charles I's execution on 30 January, the anniversary of Charles II's restoration on 29 May, and the anniversary of William III's landing at Torbay on 4 November 1688. The crown and the aristocracy could also exercise considerable authority over thousands of ordinary parish clergy because so many clergymen obtained their livings through lay patronage. The church as a whole still possessed considerable wealth and property and it continued to play a major role in providing education, distributing charity and disseminating news and views. Clerical propaganda played a major role in promoting the notion of a Protestant constitution and of a Protestant people constantly at war with militant Catholicism and French absolutism. In periods of crisis the clergy regularly played an important role in promoting Fast Days and in propagating a conservative ideology in defence of the status quo. Both the ruling elite's right to govern and the duty of subjects to obey were constantly sanctioned by the clergy. The clergy also frequently campaigned against vice and immorality and served the state as well as the church by promoting such moral virtues as humility, sobriety, frugality and industry. Moreover, the church's parish structure remained the basic unit of local government in rural and urban areas and did much to administer the system of poor relief in particular. For a large proportion of the population the Church of England's ceremonies and rituals marked their major rites of passage through life. It offered a focus to their daily lives and a consolation in death.

FURTHER READING

Browning, Reed: *Political and Constitutional Ideas of the Court Whigs* (Baton Rouge, LA, 1982).

Cannon, John: *Aristocratic Century: The Peerage of Eighteenth-Century England* (Cambridge, 1984).

Clark, J. C. D.: *English Society 1688–1832: Ideology, Social Structure and Political Practice during the Ancien Régime* (1985; rev. edn, Cambridge, 2000).

Dickinson, H. T.: *Walpole and the Whig Supremacy* (London, 1973).

Dickinson, H. T.: 'The eighteenth-century debate on the sovereignty of parliament', *Transactions of the Royal Historical Society*, 5th series, 26 (1976), pp. 198–210.

Dickinson, H. T.: *Liberty and Property: Political Ideology in Eighteenth-Century Britain* (London, 1977).

Gibson, William: *The Church of England 1688–1832: Unity and Accord* (London, 2001).

Goldsworthy, Jeffrey: *The Sovereignty of Parliament: History and Philosophy* (Oxford, 1999).

Gunn, J. A. W.: *Beyond Liberty and Property: The Process of Self-Recognition in Eighteenth-Century Political Thought* (Kingston and Montreal, 1987).

Kenyon, John P.: *Revolution Principles: The Politics of Party 1689–1720* (Cambridge, 1977).

Namier, Lewis and Brooke, John (eds): *The House of Commons 1754–1790* (3 vols, London, 1964).

Pocock, J. G. A.: *Virtue, Commerce and History: Essays in Political Thought and History Chiefly in the Eighteenth Century* (Cambridge, 1985).
Robbins, Caroline: *The Eighteenth-Century Commonwealthman* (Cambridge, MA, 1959).
Sack, J. J.: *From Jacobite to Conservative: Reaction and Orthodoxy in Britain, c.1760–1832* (Cambridge, 1993).
Thomas, P. D. G.: *The House of Commons in the Eighteenth Century* (Oxford, 1971).

Chapter Two

The British State

Eckhart Hellmuth

(Translated by Angela Davies)

Historians and historical sociologists have always found the British state both fascinating and irritating. At the beginning of the twentieth century, when Otto Hintze developed his pioneering but still influential theory of state formation, an analysis of conditions in the early modern British state was one of the central planks of his argument. For Hintze, the political and administrative profile of the British state at that time was characterized by 'parliamentarism and self-government', and he contrasted it with the continental variant. This he described as 'military absolutism with a bureaucratic administration', which for him was exemplified by the Prussian state in the eighteenth century. Hintze accounted for the fact that the political and administrative profiles in the two cases were so different by pointing to their respective geopolitical frameworks. In concrete terms, this means that their geographical location forced the continental powers to build up powerful armies. And, in order to finance and maintain such armies, an efficient bureaucracy acting in the spirit of the absolutist state was a prerequisite. Britain, by contrast, as an island state, did not need to maintain large land forces. Consequently, it could dispense with a substantial state apparatus.

Hintze is not the only scholar to have seen Britain as a comparatively stateless nation. A number of authors who have established a link between the state-building process and economic development have argued along similar lines. Among others, Charles Tilly and Brian Downing have suggested that the extraction of resources was simpler in a highly commercialized society like eighteenth-century Britain than in the still predominantly agrarian societies of continental Europe. As a result, it is argued, Britain, in contrast to Prussia, the Habsburg Empire and France, for example, could make do with a slim state apparatus.

War and Taxation

This view of the British state in the eighteenth century, which has left deep traces in the literature, has since been subjected to a thoroughgoing revision. The crucial step in this direction was taken by John Brewer in his book, *The Sinews of Power*, published in 1989, which built on the earlier work of Daniel Baugh, Patrick O'Brien and Geoffrey Holmes. In Brewer's account, the British state of the eighteenth century emerges as a powerful and efficient machine. A fiscal and military apparatus, peerless in Europe, appears in his work. It is not without irony that Brewer operates with an explanatory model that resembles Hintze's in that he establishes a causal connection between war, finance and bureaucracy.

Indeed, in Brewer's account the key to understanding the processes which formed the British state apparatus of the eighteenth century lies in this causal connection. Britain was almost continuously involved in military conflicts for long periods during the long eighteenth century (1688–1815): the Nine Years' War (1689–97), the War of the Spanish Succession (1702–13), the War of the Quadruple Alliance (1718–20), the War of Jenkins's Ear (1739–43), the War of the Austrian Succession (1740–8), the Seven Years' War (1756–63), the War of American Independence (1775–83), the War with Revolutionary France (1793–1802) and the Napoleonic Wars (1803–15). This means that out of about 140 years, Britain was at war for almost seventy. Among the states of continental Europe, only France, Britain's biggest rival, could compare in this respect. Britain's participation in this game of Monopoly of Power, as played by the European states of the eighteenth century, was accompanied by the development of a formidable military apparatus. With the exception of the War of the Austrian Succession, each military conflict in which Britain was involved witnessed an increase in the size of its fighting forces, in both the army and the navy. Whereas parliament had granted money for a good 100,000 men in the army and the navy during the Nine Years' War, by the time of the War of American Independence this figure had risen to almost 200,000. The largest fighting force that Britain mobilized during the long eighteenth century was undoubtedly that which fought in the Napoleonic Wars. At the end of this conflict, about 500,000 men were under arms in the army and the navy.

The shape of the British military apparatus differed substantially from that of its rivals on the continent of Europe. In cases of military conflict, considerable numbers of foreign troops were hired to supplement the regular units of the standing army and large subsidies were paid to foreign powers. In addition, when it was a matter of defending home territory the militia, which was revived on a new basis in the 1750s, could be mobilized. What was different about the military efforts of the British state in the eighteenth century, however, was the significance attached to the navy. The fleet afloat was the largest concentrated population outside London (40,000). To invest in the navy was an obvious step, given Britain's geopolitical situation. Moreover, Britain's role as a global player, whose strategic interests stretched from Calcutta to Boston, and from Jamaica to Newfoundland, demanded that it show the flag on the seas of the world. At the same time, it was extremely expensive to maintain a fleet which, at times of war, could include up to 300 ships of the line (in the Seven Years' War). The infrastructure alone that was required to build, equip and maintain the fleet (dry docks, stores, roperies, building yards, and so on) consumed huge amounts of money. It has been estimated that the per capita cost of a wartime sailor was double that of a soldier in the army.

The military in Britain was not a creature of the monarchical will, as was the case, as a rule, on the continent, but was subject to strict parliamentary controls. Yet even so, spending on military purposes accounted for the vast majority of the state's expenditure. Between 1688 and 1815 more than 80 per cent of the public money spent by the British state went on the army, the navy, subsidies for foreign troops and the repayment of debts incurred as a result of previous wars. Thus, Britain spent a similar proportion of its income on military purposes as did the eighteenth-century Prussian state, which historians frequently see as epitomizing a militarized polity. Moreover, on a per capita basis, Britain spent more on warfare than any other European state in this period. Naturally, the level of spending on the military varied depending on whether the country was at peace or at war, but even in peacetime it was rare for more than one-fifth of state expenditure to be used for civilian purposes. By far the most expensive war that Britain waged during the long eighteenth century was that with Revolutionary and Napoleonic France. It has been estimated that this military conflict, lasting more than twenty years, cost around £1,039 million in current prices and that the total expenditure corresponded to something like six times the value of prewar national income.

With every new military conflict in which Britain was involved, the national debt rose. At the end of the Nine Years' War this had been just under £17 million; by the end of the War of American Independence it had risen to more than £220 million. The war with Revolutionary and Napoleonic France resulted in another explosive increase in the national debt, from £290 million in 1788–92 to £862 million in 1815. Or, to express it in a different way, while at the end of the seventeenth century the national debt amounted to less than 5 per cent of gross national product, at the beginning of the nineteenth century it accounted for more than 10 per cent.

The fact that the British state did not collapse under the weight of this debt was connected, among other things, with the fact that it was able to borrow constantly increasing amounts of money at low rates of interest. The average rate of interest on government loans fell from 8 to 9 per cent to below 5 per cent between the wars against Louis XIV and the wars against Napoleon. Yet government loans were an attractive investment for many contemporaries because the British state was much more creditworthy than its counterparts on the continent. The difference in political conditions was the key to this. Their autocratic character and opaque fiscal policies meant that monarchical regimes on the continent represented a high credit risk and, consequently, their creditors charged high rates of interest. In Britain, the situation was different. Here parliament, which urged financial prudence and transparency, guaranteed the national debt. It earmarked specific taxes for the payment of specific stock issues, so that anyone who invested in government stock had the guarantee of a safe return.

The negative aspect of this was that Britain became one of the most heavily taxed nations in Europe. The British state extracted more in taxes from its subjects than did absolutist France, and from the late seventeenth century the curve of tax revenue was a steeply rising one. Between the Glorious Revolution and the end of the Napoleonic Wars the aggregate net tax revenue grew tenfold. During the same period the total revenue per capita rose by a factor of 4.5. The main burden was carried by England and Wales, while Scotland made only a modest contribution and Ireland hardly contributed at all. This increase in the tax burden was accompanied by a structural change in the tax system. Direct taxes (notably the land tax), which as late as 1700 had formed the main source of the state's income, were eclipsed by indirect taxes, most notably by excise duties, which were levied on many everyday commodities (for example sugar, coffee, tea, tobacco, salt, beer, hops, malt, candles, soap, wine and spirits). Towards the end of the eighteenth century (1790), indirect taxes accounted for 75 per cent of the total tax revenue, the vast majority of which was generated by the excise. There were a number of reasons why this rigid tax system was, on the whole, accepted, despite occasional protests. There were no tax exemptions for particular privileged groups, as was the case in many continental states. Taxes were to a large extent 'invisible'; they were 'hidden' in the price of everyday commodities that were subject to the excise. Above all, however, the British tax system enjoyed a high degree of legitimacy as its source was the will of parliament, not that of an autocratic ruler.

The efficiency with which the British state taxed its subjects was also the outcome of a gradual reform and development of the fiscal administration. Between 1660 and the early eighteenth century this fiscal administration evolved into an effective instrument for ensuring that the state was continuously supplied with money. A number of boards and departments were either newly established or restructured. The Treasury, as the body controlling both income and expenditure, was at the heart of this new institutional arrangement. And the period saw an increase in the number of centrally appointed, highly professional government officials, who helped to create an administration of considerable calibre. Geoffrey Holmes estimates that, by 1720, there were approximately 12,000 permanent employees in government service. The majority of these functionaries worked in the revenue departments and, of these, most worked in the excise. It is highly likely that British society had a greater proportion of government officials than, for example, Prussian society in the eighteenth century.

This 'new' fiscal administration displayed many features that are generally associated with a modern bureaucracy. Its members were full-time employees, who were expected to display loyalty, honesty and devotion to office. Their income came not from fees, but from regular salaries. Promotion within individual departments followed an established system of graded appointments; the main criteria for promotion were merit and achievement. At the end of such a career there was, as a rule, retirement with a government pension. Standards within the service were safeguarded either by entrance examinations, or by a period of practical training. Departments developed their own systems of record-keeping, defined office procedures and routines, and, not least, developed something like an *esprit de corps*. Thus, we have the paradoxical situation that the allegedly weak British state possessed a fiscal administration which, in terms of professionalism and efficiency, was probably unique in Europe.

The Machinery of the State

To define the state is an extremely difficult task. Historians have proposed different solutions. Otto Hintze suggested that the state was an institution with the power of coercion, whose purpose was to maintain the conditions necessary for internal and external security, and to provide for the common good. John Brewer defined the state as a territorially and jurisdictionally delimited political entity in which public authority is distinguished from (though not unconnected to) private power, and which is overseen by officials whose primary (though not sole) allegiance is to a set of political institutions under a single, sovereign authority. Joanna Innes considered the state as consisting of the whole array of institutions which participate in the spending of public monies, and in the legitimate exercise of coercive power. Such attempts to define the state are by no means superfluous theoretical exercises, for upon them depends to some extent how we 'read' the history of the state.

If we accept Joanna Innes's expansive definition of the state, we naturally look at the traditional machinery of local government, which, with its staff and institutions, is difficult to fit into the Weberian idea of the modern state. This traditional machinery of local government gained in importance during the eighteenth century. It seems that the reconfiguration of central government institutions which accompanied the rise of the fiscal-military state absorbed so much energy that central bodies lost interest in intervening at local level. Although new forms of central–local interaction developed, it is quite clear that as far as domestic politics were concerned, state power was highly decentralized. Thus, it is no coincidence that in Britain there were comparatively few institutions at central level. Essentially, in the eighteenth century these were the Treasury, the Navy Office, the Post Office, the offices of the two or three secretaries of state, and the Board of Trade. The Home Office, as a separate institution, was created only in 1782. The central government of other European states could draw upon a much wider repertoire of institutions. The Prussian state in the late eighteenth century, for instance, had more than a dozen ministries and departments whose main purpose was regulating and improving society. In Britain, this job was to a much larger extent the responsibility of the local authorities. This was true, albeit in different ways, of England, Wales, Scotland and Ireland.

Thus, in England, for example, at the level of counties and towns a whole array of people and institutions existed to supervise public relief, guarantee security and administer justice. The most prestigious office in the counties was that of the lord lieutenant. The lord lieutenant, supported by a number of deputies lieutenant, whose number depended on the size of the county, was, as a rule, a peer who normally enjoyed royal patronage. The lord lieutenant commanded the militia and nominated the justices of the peace (JPs), who were the key figures in governing Britain in the localities. They were drawn mainly from among people of wealth and standing, and in the later eighteenth century a considerable number of clergy joined their ranks. JPs were not professional officials such as were increasingly found in the bureaucracies of the continental states during the eighteenth century because they were not remunerated for their work, and they had no formal qualifications for office. Thus, to some extent, they were amateurs. Yet they covered an astonishingly broad field of activities, ranging from judicial functions to a great variety of administrative responsibilities. JPs were responsible for suppressing uprisings, and they were concerned with poor relief, the food supply, and prices and wages. They were considered the guardians of public morals, tightened licensing laws, inaugurated anti-vagrancy campaigns, and dealt with gaming houses and the suppression of disorderly behaviour. They exercised responsibility over roads and bridges, supervised gaols and houses of correction, and appointed parish officers. Above all, however, JPs were also pillars of the British judicial system. Although they were not entitled to decide in cases of life and death, they did try a variety of non-capital cases. In order to fulfil such a large number of functions, they acted either alone, in groups of two or more (petty sessions), or in quarter sessions. The type of business to be done at each level was precisely regulated. Outside the county structure of local government there were about

200 incorporated towns, in which the mayor, aldermen and common councillors enjoyed powers similar to those of JPs. Because of their urban environment, they were forced to devote themselves to issues that were less important in the countryside, such as sanitation, fire prevention, the prevention of begging and prostitution, the policing of markets, and so on.

The most basic unit of administration in England and Wales was the parish. Totalling 15,000 in number, parishes varied greatly in size. About 90 per cent had fewer than 1,000 inhabitants. The administrative tasks were performed by a number of parish officials, including churchwardens, surveyors of the highways, constables and overseers of the poor. Service in the parish offices was unpaid and compulsory. Most of these parish officials were ordinary householders taking their turn at bearing public responsibilities. Some held office for longer periods of time, so that they built up considerable expertise in their particular field. As the various titles of the parish officials suggest, the parish was charged with a wide range of responsibilities. In order to fulfil these duties, parish authorities were entitled to raise taxes. In the course of the eighteenth century it seems to have become increasingly usual to use salaried officers of various kinds at this level.

The older literature on the genesis of the early modern state treated this system of local administration with derision. This criticism is problematic in several respects. First, the differences between British and continental conditions were probably not as great as some historians have assumed. Most continental European states in the eighteenth century had officeholders who would be difficult to fit into the ideal type of a modern bureaucracy. In addition to the officials appointed by the central government, there were frequently elected and amateur local officials, people who had bought or inherited their office, and clergy who performed semi-official functions. Often, too, the organs of the estates were also involved in the administration of a territory. Second, the much-derided English amateur officials were by no means incompetent officeholders entrenched in their local world. Rather, there is much to suggest that we are dealing here with a qualified administrative elite. Of course, it is easy to find evidence that this system of local government could acquire oligarchic tendencies, that its actors allowed themselves to be led by the prejudices and interests of their own class, and that incompetence and corruption did exist. But, at the same time, there are countless examples which point in the opposite direction. Many JPs were undoubtedly committed to the common good, tried to carry out their official business with fairness, were well informed and displayed considerable creativity in solving problems. But, in this context, something else is important. Local officials were not restricted to their immediate environment; they did not act within a largely autonomous cosmos. Rather, they cooperated frequently and effectively with central government. Thus, throughout the whole of the eighteenth century, the British parliament issued a stream of legislation which concerned local government. Similarly, the central executive directly influenced the world of counties and towns via a large number of directives. This does not, however, alter the fact that local officials in Britain enjoyed an unusually high degree of autonomy.

Against the background of the discussion so far, the question arises of whether a highly decentralized system, such as that found in Britain in the eighteenth century, was superior to other contemporary models. This question is all the more justified as historians who study continental Europe are becoming increasingly aware that the equation of centralization with efficiency is highly problematic. If we look more closely at the politics of the absolutist states on the continent, it emerges that bureaucracies working at local level, which were regularly inundated with edicts, were only to a limited extent able to translate the will of the ruler into reality. All this suggests that systems of government which granted local officials a considerable degree of autonomy and freedom of action frequently worked better than more bureaucratic and centralized systems.

The shortcomings of this system of local government were compensated for by the fact that eighteenth-century British society had an astonishing capacity to carry out projects on a voluntary basis. Voluntary societies became active when the established local authorities were unable, or unwilling, to undertake certain tasks. Thus, at the beginning of the eighteenth century, the Society for the Promotion of Christian Knowledge (SPCK) took up the cause of founding charity schools. Or to take another example, in the later eighteenth century the Association for the Prosecution of Felons worked for a stricter enforcement of the criminal law. Voluntary societies were an attractive option for contemporaries because they made it possible to react in a spontaneous and flexible manner. Moreover, Britons often saw in voluntary forms of effort an adequate instrument to tackle certain problems because they had fundamental reservations about 'strong' government. British political society had a deep aversion to anything associated with the taint of absolutism. To minimize state activity was regarded as progress towards greater civilization: 'The more perfect civilization is, the less occasion it has for government, because the more does it regulate its own affairs, and govern itself.' 'Government is no further necessary than to supply the few cases to which society and civilization are not conveniently competent.' These quotations come from Thomas Paine's *Rights of Man*. Paine was a former revenue officer and government official turned political radical. In many respects Paine was undoubtedly a political outsider, yet in his attitude towards the state he captured the spirit of his times. While British society was prepared to accept a formidable fiscal-military apparatus supervised by parliament, any attempt by central government to implement a systematic domestic policy remained anathema.

This does not mean, however, that central government played only a marginal role in domestic policy. In particular parliament, which passed almost 14,000 acts between 1688 and 1801, was extremely active in this area. Although the majority of 'public acts' concerned the fiscal-military state (raising taxes, waging war, and so on), MPs also used this type of legislation to tackle problems such as poverty, vagrancy and crime, and to intervene in the economy and labour relations. Such interventions were, as a rule, largely piecemeal, yet they left deep traces in the lives of contemporaries. This was even more the case with the more numerous 'private acts' of parliament, on the basis of which, for example, the so-called improvement commissions were established. (These numbered about 1,800 by 1830.) These were local statutory bodies whose objective was to provide solutions to specific problems, mainly improving the infrastructure, on an ad hoc basis. It was thanks to the work of these improvement commissions that during the eighteenth century Britain was covered by an increasingly dense network of turnpikes and canals.

Like most European states of the eighteenth century, Britain was also characterized by a mixture of old and new, of central and local power, of state and non-state initiatives. Yet it appears that Britain managed to reconcile these opposing elements more successfully than other states. Perhaps the best example of this is what Joanna Innes has called the 'mixed economy of welfare'. The main pillar of this was poor relief paid out of the parish rates. Towards the end of the eighteenth century, this system raised the remarkable amount of £4 million per annum for distribution among the poor, orphans, the old and the sick. Although this nationwide relief system was executed at local level, its (general) basis was parliamentary legislation in the form of the Poor Law, whose origins go back to the sixteenth century. 'Legal charity' was supplemented by 'voluntary charity'. Thus, for example, voluntary hospitals, founded in many parts of the country, catered for the needs of the sick poor. There were many other subscription-funded charitable institutions, and their number multiplied over the course of the eighteenth century. And, finally, there was institutionalized self-help in the form of 'box clubs' or 'friendly societies', which provided humbler folk with primitive insurance benefits. The fate of those afflicted by poverty and sickness in eighteenth-century Britain was certainly not an easy one, but it was very likely less harsh than in most other European states at this time.

One can speculate whether the success of this highly pragmatic system of domestic administration was partly responsible for the fact that no broad public debate about the goals and tasks of the state developed in British society. In the central European states, in particular, such a debate took place with great intensity. Although these *ancien régime* states were often unable to realize their political goals, there was a permanent discourse in which servants of the state and other enlightenment intellectuals thought about what fields should be permanently brought into the ambit of the state. This intense process of reflection was expressed in a multi-faceted science of government and administration (*Polizei- und Kameralwissenschaften*) and the theory of natural law, which, as it were, provided the blueprint for the interventionist state of the future. Revealingly, there was nothing comparable in Britain.

Corruption and Reform

For the historian, the eighteenth-century British state is difficult to come to grips with because it had several different aspects. It possessed an efficient fiscal and a powerful military apparatus, which allowed Britain to become the dominant world power. Side-by-side with this there was the traditional system of local administration, which, despite its idiosyncrasies, probably worked better than the systems in place in most other European states. But it should not be overlooked that the British state still had an archaic side, for the new administration which the fiscal-military state generated did not replace existing institutions but was added on to them. These older departments in particular, which had not been modernized, attracted increasing criticism and were seen by contemporaries as embodying 'old corruption'. Old corruption involved practices which, at least in the advanced continental bureaucracies, had largely been eliminated by the second half of the eighteenth century. Government offices degenerated into sinecures in various different forms. There were well-paid offices which were not associated with any duties; in other cases, officeholders drew emoluments from an office, but the actual work was done by others who were fobbed off with a fraction of the income from the office. Reversions (the right of succession to an office or place of emolument after the death or retirement of a holder) allowed ministers and high government officials to provide kinsmen with office. Whether they were qualified for the job counted for little. There were other practices that were condemned by contemporary critics: pensions, government contracts and church preferment were showered on those who proved themselves to be loyal supporters of the government of the day.

Such corrupt practices made some critical contemporaries see the British state as a degenerate and parasitic monster which consumed vast sums of tax revenues and had become a vehicle of personal enrichment. Criticisms of this sort had already been voiced during the first half of the eighteenth century, in the context of the 'Country' opposition of the 1730s, for example. But the extra-parliamentary reform movement of the 1760s and 1770s gave this criticism a new quality. Thanks to John Wilkes and to Christopher Wyvill's Association Movement, the idea that the British state was parasitical, wasted taxes and shamelessly enriched a small elite entered the British collective consciousness in an unprecedented way. The disastrous outcome of the American War of Independence only strengthened this tendency. Military failures, a growing state debt and the resulting rise in taxes revived 'Country' criticisms of the corrupt British state. In the early 1780s the Association Movement and metropolitan radicals demanded the end of practices which, in their eyes, were corrupt. The call for parliamentary reform was not least the result of a failure to achieve economical reform, which, it was hoped, would put an end to, in contemporary jargon, 'extravagance'.

Criticism voiced inside and outside parliament in the early 1780s was not without effect. It led to a number of reform measures and steps. From 1780, for example, the Rockingham Whigs made serious attempts to make the machinery of state more efficient and, at the same time, to reduce the cost of running it. The Establishment Act of 1782 abolished 130 'inefficient offices', and for a number of offices casual emoluments were replaced by salaries. Moreover, on Lord North's initiative, the Commission for Examining the Public Accounts was established in 1780. Convinced that government should be as cheap as possible, and disturbed at the dramatically rising costs generated by the central bureaucracy during the American War, the commissioners made a number of radical and comprehensive reform proposals. If they had been realized, they would have wiped out the system of old corruption. But this did not happen. Pitt, who had come to power in 1784, accepted only a limited number of the commissioners' suggestions. No more than three of their numerous proposals were put into practice, and one of these was the proposal to appoint another commission to look into fee-taking in all the public departments. But this commission suffered a similar fate to that of the Commission for Examining the Public Accounts. It stopped work in 1789, after examining only ten of the twenty-four offices originally identified for inspection. The practical effect of its work was minimal. This lack of commitment to reforming the administrative sector is all the more surprising because Pitt, by contrast, pursued the restructuring of the national budget with great vigour. All attempts to restrain the Leviathan failed. On the contrary, the war effort during the war with Revolutionary and Napoleonic France dampened all attempts at reform. The failure to make systematic administrative improvements led to increased criticism of the old corruption – by William Cobbett in particular. The view was widespread that the price the taxpayer had to pay to support the British war machine was simply too high, and that many profiteers – contractors, sinecurists, speculative investors, and so on – were thriving in the shadows of this apparatus, at everybody's cost. Consequently, calls were made for the minimalist state. And, indeed, during the first half of the nineteenth century Britain embarked on the path that led to the minimalist mid-Victorian state, leaving the fiscal-military state of the eighteenth century behind. The end of the Napoleonic Wars marked the beginning of the dismantling or modernization of the British state apparatus, which up to that time had concentrated on one main task: maintaining its formidable war machine. To identify the minimalist state as the objective of reform, and to implement it, was all the easier as in the eighteenth century the British state at central level had taken on responsibility for a much narrower range of tasks than its continental counterparts. The characteristic features of this minimalist state, as they developed in the first half of the nineteenth century, included cheap government, low expenditures compared to other European states, good government, the general acceptance of rational standards of administrative efficiency, and a reluctance to interfere with property rights and market relations.

Thus, Britain embarked upon a path which clearly deviated from that taken by other European states. Many of them – for example, the German states of the early nineteenth century – increasingly intervened in areas of domestic policy, such as education, the economy and social issues, and consequently, their state apparatuses expanded. This difference can be seen from a perspective which Thomas Ertman has introduced into the analysis of the history of the European states, albeit within a different timeframe. Ertman regards the category of *timing* as crucially important in the investigation of the state, arguing that the different patterns of state development in Europe are attributable to the time at which the respective administrative and fiscal systems were developed. There were 'pioneers' and 'latecomers' among the state-builders. The latter had the advantage that they were able to learn from the mistakes made by the former, and could adopt the most recent technologies of government. From this perspective, the question arises as to whether the British state, whose history during the eighteenth century was, despite all its shortcomings, a success story, should be counted among the 'pioneers' who subsequently fell behind the 'latecomers' in the nineteenth century. To put it another way: was the minimalist state which was formed in Britain in reaction to the only semi-modernized Leviathan of the eighteenth century capable of doing what was required of it in the increasingly complex world of the nineteenth century?

FURTHER READING

Baugh, Daniel: *British Naval Administration in the Age of Walpole* (Princeton, NJ, 1965).

Brewer, John: *The Sinews of Power: War, Money and the English State 1688–1783* (London, 1989).

Brewer, John and Hellmuth, Eckhart (eds): *Rethinking Leviathan: The Eighteenth-Century State in Britain and Germany* (Oxford, 1999).

Downing, Brian: *The Military Revolution and Political Change: Origins of Democracy and Autocracy in Early Modern Europe* (Princeton, NJ, 1992).

Eastwood, David: *Government and Community in the English Provinces 1700–1800* (Basingstoke, 1997).

Ertman, Thomas: *The Birth of the Leviathan: Building States and Regimes in Medieval and Early Modern Europe* (Cambridge, 1997).

Harling, Philip: *The Waning of 'Old Corruption': The Politics of Economical Reform in Britain, 1779–1846* (Oxford, 1996).

Harling, Philip: *The Modern British State: An Historical Introduction* (Oxford, 2001).

Harling, Philip and Mandler, Peter: 'From "fiscal-military" state to laissez-faire state, 1760–1850', *Journal of British Studies*, 32 (1993), pp. 44–70.

Hintze, Otto: 'Staatsverfassung und Heeresverfassung' and 'Machtpolitik und Regierungsverfassung', in Hintze, *Staat und Verfassung* (Göttingen, 3rd edn, 1970), pp. 52–83 and pp. 424–56.

Holmes, Geoffrey: *Augustan England: Professions, State and Society 1680–1730* (London, 1982).

Innes, Joanna: 'The "mixed economy of welfare" in early modern England: assessments of the options from Hale to Malthus (*c*.1683–1803)', in Martin Daunton (ed.), *Charity, Self-Interest and Welfare in the English Past* (London, 1996).

Mathias, Peter and O'Brien, Patrick: 'Taxation in Britain and France, 1715–1810', *Journal of European Economic History*, 5 (1976), pp. 601–50.

O'Brien, Patrick: 'Public finance in the wars with France 1793–1815', in H. T. Dickinson (ed.), *Britain and the French Revolution 1789–1815* (London, 1989), pp. 165–87.

O'Brien, Patrick: *Power with Profit: The State and the Economy 1688–1815* (London, 1991).

O'Brien, Patrick and Hunt, Philip A.: 'The rise of a fiscal state in England, 1485–1815', *Historical Research*, 66 (1993), pp. 129–76.

Stone, Lawrence (ed.): *An Imperial State at War: Britain from 1689 to 1815* (London, 1994).

Tilly, Charles: 'War making and state making as organized crime', in Peter Evans, Dietrich Rueschemeyer and Theda Skocpol (eds), *Bringing the State Back In* (Cambridge, 1985), pp. 169–91.

CHAPTER THREE

Finance and Taxation

PATRICK KARL O'BRIEN

Military and Naval Expenditure on Strategic Policies

Britain's Glorious Revolution of 1688–9 marked a decisive shift in favour of a more active and altogether more costly involvement in European and imperial power politics. To check the ambitions of France to hegemony in Europe and to extensive colonization overseas, as well as the French bid to secure and maintain competitive advantages in trade and commerce with the Americas, Africa and Asia, turned out to be unavoidably expensive. Between 1689 and 1803 Britain went to war with France and its allies seven times. Over what is referred to as the Second Hundred Years' War intervals of cordiality, even alliance, marked relations between the two states, but while the power of Britain's 'natural and necessary enemy' waxed and waned, it never ceased to threaten the security of the realm or the interests of the home economy until sometime after the famous defeats of Napoleon – first at sea at Trafalgar (1805), and then on land at Waterloo (1815).

For most of the long eighteenth century (1688–1815) Britain was engaged in preparing for or demobilizing from war. The state's defensive or aggressive stance in foreign, strategic, commercial and imperial policy cost a great deal of money which successive governments borrowed in the form of long-term loans or appropriated as taxes. For example, in real terms (i.e., measured in constant prices) the normal (or peacetime) expenditures climbed by a multiplier of three from around £2 million per annum in the mid-1680s to just over £6 million a century later. Wartime expenditures jumped by a factor of five, if we compare annual levels during King William's (or the Nine Years') War fought against Louis XIV (1689–97) with the war that finally defeated Napoleon (1803–15). Looked at and estimated in *relative* terms, the activities of the British state accounted for tiny proportions of national income before the Glorious Revolution and that ratio rose war after war to reach nearly a fifth during those years of intense conflict immediately before final victory at Waterloo.

In long-term historical perspective the eighteenth century certainly marks a transformation in the levels of intervention and activity undertaken by the state in the affairs of the kingdom. Historians writing standard political histories of the period rarely offer interpretations or indicators of the changing significance that British monarchs, ministers, parliaments, politicians and civil servants have exercised in the economic and social life of the realm. Yet fiscal and budgetary data do allow us to appreciate and to mark discontinuities in the role of the state. For example, between the reigns of Henry VII and the outbreak of the civil wars (*c.*1485 to *c.*1642) the total sums collected as taxation for central or royal government remained roughly constant in real terms. There were some perceptible (but non-sustainable) upswings during the reign of Henry VIII. Most (up to 90 per cent) of the king's revenues were allocated to fund military and naval expenditures, and to service loans incurred to pay for wars, although taxes invariably rose in wartime. By and large (on trend) the total amount of revenues collected for the state hardly changed over time. Since the population and national income of the realm almost certainly increased during the reigns of the Tudors and early Stuarts, this suggests that for some 150 years the burdens imposed on English taxpayers for central government probably diminished.

Unlike its rivals in Europe, in fiscal and financial terms the English state displayed almost no capacity for expansion and active participation in great power politics or for more elaborate regulation of the domestic economy and society. That all changed under the Commonwealth and Protectorate (1649–60), when taxes began to rise discernibly above roughly the stationary levels re-established in the reign of Henry VII. Clearly, it took the singular circumstances of civil war and a republican interregnum to enlarge the English state. That extension in fiscal capacity was consolidated and stabilized after the restoration of the monarchy when the legal and administrative basis for a massive and sustained upswing in revenues (taxes, credit and loans) became institutionalized. This subsequently allowed and (possibly actively encouraged) the state, taken over by William III in 1688, to play a role in great power politics, colonization and international commerce that could not have been sustained under the Tudors and Stuarts.

Between 1688 and 1815 Britain's monarchs and their aristocratic supporters raised the fiscal and financial resources required to transform Britain's geopolitical role in the world and to engage in seven major wars fought against France and its allies. When Castlereagh signed the Treaty of Vienna in 1815, the by then United Kingdom of England, Wales, Scotland and Ireland had emerged as the hegemonic naval power, possessed the largest occidental empire since Rome, enjoyed extraordinary shares of the profits from international trade in goods and services, and its economy was approximately half-way through the first industrial revolution.

In early modern Europe states survived if they possessed sufficient and continuous command over the financial means necessary to defend their territories and citizens against external aggression and to meet internal challenges to their authority. To become more powerful in a universe of contending states and to validate their claims to regulate the presumed autonomy of families, corporations and institutions nominally under their jurisdiction, governments required ever-increasing amounts of revenue. Thus, a successful state can be recognized not merely by its continuity but because it mobilized the resources required for effective action in international relations as well as the force needed to meet domestic challenges to its sovereignty. Historians have recognized the obvious relationship between the power of states and the fiscal means at their disposal, but they are also aware that the connections were never that simple. For example, a 10 per cent increment in revenues rarely implied a proportionate increase in the state's capacity for effective action. Generals and admirals notoriously squandered military resources placed at their disposal. Diplomacy usually proved to be cheaper and sometimes more useful than mobilization for war. Expenditure on bribery, favours, religious persuasion and the propagation of an ideology in support of royal and aristocratic rule cost less than the formal apparatus of coercion and intrusion into private domains, traditionally excluded from governmental control. Compliance with the laws and directives issued by central authorities (for all kinds of reasons unconnected with a state's monopoly of coercion) could be secured more cheaply in some regions and among some populations than others. Nevertheless, in the long run, the relationship between fiscal resources and a capacity for sustained and effective action in the domestic and, above all, in the international spheres prevailed. Thus, the meta-question now addressed by this chapter is this: how did a small state (which endeavoured without conspicuous success to enlarge its fiscal and financial capacity for expenditure under the Tudors and Stuarts) manage to borrow enough money and raise the taxes required to defend the realm and to become so geopolitically and economically powerful among a universe of rival European states?

Taxation

Since its capacity to borrow money ('finance') depended fundamentally on the state's capacity to tax in order to meet regular contractual interest and amortization payments on its loans or accumulated debt, the core of any explanation must reside with the state's success in selecting taxes and the effective implementation of tax policies, rather than with debt management as such. The establishment and evolution of an efficient system for credit and raising loans on the London capital market, however, also contributed to funding British participation in the sequence of wars the state engaged in between 1689 to 1815.

The answer cannot be based on references to autonomous developments in the economic sphere. There is no simple correlation between the growth of the economy and the government's fiscal achievement. Over this period British governments may well have ruled over the most rapidly growing of Europe's competing national economies. That favourable evolution certainly carried whole sections of British society over thresholds of income and promoted patterns of expenditure, where purchases by households on goods and services began first to contribute and then (as private expenditures rose and diversified) to augment public income from indirect taxes. The concentration of households and producers in towns and regions not only increased taxable output flowing through organized markets, but also rendered the imposition and collection of taxes easier to administer. Nevertheless, data – which shows that Britain's national product probably rose by a factor of three between 1688 and 1815, while tax receipts at the Exchequer multiplied around fifteen times – severely qualifies any suggestion which purports to explain fiscal success as a product of economic growth. Rising agricultural productivity, industrialization, urbanization and the reorganization of economic activities into larger firms located within denser zones of production helped, but these developments must be represented as 'contributory' factors and not as major forces behind the fiscal achievements of successive governments after 1688. Instead, that remarkable achievement (which eluded Tudor and Stuart monarchs constrained by a narrow and inflexible fiscal base) can only be accounted for as the outcome of a prior history of disengagement by rulers, of a cheaply protected island realm, from European power politics and wars of religion, and their measured detachment from imperialistic and commercial and colonizing ventures in the Americas, Asia and Africa.

Somehow (perhaps more by necessity than foresight) England's Tudor and Stuart dynasties avoided the proliferation of taxes and accumulation of royal debt that afflicted rival Portuguese, Spanish, Dutch and French powers during the sixteenth and seventeenth centuries. Coming late to European power politics and acting as a 'free rider' upon Iberian and Dutch investments in colonization and commerce overseas, the English state possessed (as Tudor and Stuart rulers long realized) untapped potential for taxation that the traumatic experience of civil war and an interlude of restored stability and institutional innovation brought on stream. In all essentials the foundations of the 'fiscal state' occurred before, not after, the Glorious Revolution.

Its construction began during the 1630s when Charles I attempted to revalue his fiscal kingdom for purposes of direct taxation (and thus to provide the monarchy with a more secure basis for royal borrowing). That attempt led to costly civil wars (1642–8) when soldiers enforced the assessment of taxes levied upon the income and wealth of English families and when both parliament and the king imposed a wide range of new excise duties, many levied upon foodstuffs in mass consumption. After the war, indeed for something like four decades before 1688, the tradition of resistance to the state's demand for money intensified and constrained the powers of the Cromwellian Commonwealth and Protectorate, as well as the restored Stuart monarchy, to widen and deepen the base for taxation and hence for loans, secured upon regular inflows of tax revenues.

Nevertheless, the civil wars must be represented as a conjuncture in the realm's fiscal as well as political history. As usual the necessities of war generated unpopular and resistible, as well as sustainable, innovations in the capacities of the state to levy taxes. For example, the attempts made by the king and by parliament to reassess the base, measured in terms of personal incomes or regional wealth, upon which universal and equitable styles of direct taxes might be levied had occasioned insurrection and revitalized a tradition of resistance to such intolerable innovations. Memories and myths surrounding three decades of violence and strife over taxation between the imposition of ship money and the restoration of the monarchy in 1660 conditioned political attitudes to all forms of direct taxation before Pitt introduced an income tax, at a moment of crisis and threat to the security of the realm, in 1799.

Experiments during the civil wars with a wide and innovatory range of excise duties had also been unpopular, but the principle that indirect taxes could be imposed upon goods and services produced within the realm had been conceded by parliament. Furthermore, that innovation had demonstrated that 'duties' levied on such commodities (as beer and liquors, salt, soap, starch, coal and minerals) could produce significant amounts of revenue for the Exchequer in London.

After the Interregnum, when the English state sought to stabilize royal rule over one of the more lightly taxed societies in Europe, fiscal policies were formulated so as to rebuild trust in the constitution and take account of prospects for compliance with demands of revenue. Charles II and his ministers could do little more but engage seriously with the legal and administrative frameworks required to maintain, and if possible gradually increase, the amount of revenue collected in the more acceptable form of indirect taxes, particularly customs duties. After 1660 parliament replaced all but a small range of the more productive excise duties, but provided for new valuations and rates of duty levied upon a wide range of imports. Ministers and their advisers at the Treasury concentrated upon the rules framing the operations of a largely privatized administration for the assessment and collection of indirect taxes levied upon imports as well as a limited range of domestic production.

Revenues from indirect taxes continued (as had been the practice for centuries) to be farmed out to private individuals or syndicates under a variety of complex contractual arrangements, designed to ensure stable flows of income into the Exchequer year after year. Tax farming offered restored Stuart monarchs an alternative to royal bureaucracy, which was seen as open to antagonism and political interference from parliament, a prey to corruption and prone to prefer patrimonial to the king's fiscal and financial interests.

For the king's purposes the devolution of the administration of taxes into the hands of business syndicates also provided (as it did in Europe before the evolution of modern markets for capital) an institutional mechanism for borrowing money. In common with their continental rivals English monarchs expected to borrow on the security of tax revenues that accrued in the first instance to their agents or farmers. For their part, tax farmers stood prepared not only to manage the assessment and collection of taxes but to risk investing their own and (through networks of affluent clients) other people's money in the form of loans to the crown, because repayments, with interest, could be guaranteed and deducted from the fixed annual rents (i.e., taxes) which they contracted to deliver to the Exchequer.

Farming the royal customs worked best when the kingdom's foreign trade remained free from cyclical downswings and unimpeded by warfare at sea. Farming excise taxes levied on domestic production became equally problematic whenever the economy suffered from recessions connected with bad harvests, plagues or business cycles. At such times tax farmers often submitted claims for defalcations on their contracts to deliver fixed annual sums as rents on tax farms which they found to be subject to unpredictable fluctuations in the amounts of taxation collected upon trade and production.

Yet, whenever they failed to offer stable revenues, a major rationale for the franchised assessment and collection of taxes weakened. When tax farmers made inflated demands for their knowledge and services, the case for a public service became stronger. That occurred in 1670 when Charles II and his ministers found themselves in protracted dispute with a powerful syndicate over terms for the renewal of the lease for customs duties. Apparently, the tax farmers rashly offended the king by demanding prior commitments about defalcations allowable in the event of another war with the Dutch. Unwilling to concede that 'monied men' could raise questions about royal policy, ministers cancelled the contract, repaid loans, put into place and depended thereafter upon the state's own customs service for the assessment and collection of duties on imports.

Tax farming survived, however, for another twelve years for excises. Their gross yields had risen steadily throughout the 1660s and 1670s and the tight system of surveillance, provided for under short leases supervised by commissioners for the excise, meant that the royal ministers took every opportunity to squeeze excess profits out of farmers. Step by step the collection of the excise evolved into a single great farm managed by London merchants and financiers – who in effect operated as agents for the Treasury and who also provided loans and credit on the security of forthcoming revenues. Yet, whenever their profits diminished, farmers cut costs and thereby failed to bring the maximum potential volume of production into the net for taxation. They then attempted to 'recoup' by demanding higher rates of interest for the loans they had contracted to extend in anticipation of future flows of excise duties. As the potential gap between net revenues obtainable from a privatized compared to the public management of taxes narrowed, arguments from the Treasury for direct collection became economically compelling. Indeed, that also came to pass at a time when the political distinction, between a 'metropolitan clique' of tax farmers on the one hand and a royal bureaucracy on the other, lost its historical significance even for opponents of royal power.

Meanwhile, decades of surveillance and negotiation with farmers of customs and excise duties had provided the Treasury and the commissioners of customs and excise with opportunities to monitor the practices of private management and to absorb both know-how about, as well as many of the personnel involved in, the assessment and collection of first customs and later excise duties into departments of state. Thereafter, both departments evolved. The excise rapidly and the customs falteringly and imperfectly developed into bodies of government servants, who matured by standards of the day into relatively effective agencies for the collection of indirect taxes.

Thus, by the time William of Orange secured the throne in 1688, the fiscal system had been reconstructed and can be represented as politically primed and administratively poised to support the accumulation of debt required to sustain the armed forces of the crown through the sequence of major wars fought against France and its allies over the next 127 years. Immediately before James II fled to France the Stuart regime appropriated only 3 to 4 per cent of the national income as taxes, spent some £2 million a year on the army and navy, and carried a tiny royal debt of roughly the same amount. Shortly after Britain's final victory over France at Waterloo in 1815, peacetime taxation had risen by a multiplier of fifteen, compared with James II's brief reign, and the state serviced a national debt which then amounted to nearly three times the national income – a ratio remarkable even by the most profligate standards of debt accumulation undertaken by the Habsburg and Bourbon dynasties to achieve their ambitions in Europe and overseas before and after 1648; or even by the Dutch Republic struggling throughout its golden age to gain and preserve its independence between 1568 and 1795.

Politically primed means that after the civil wars, ministers of the crown reluctantly abandoned serious attempts to make taxes on income and wealth more productive, either by revaluing the base upon which they were assessed or by extending the range and numbers of households brought into the government's net for direct taxation. Policies designed to revalue the wealth of counties, cities, towns, villages, hundreds and households (envisaged in the attempt by Charles I to extend ship money across the kingdom and exemplified by regular universalistic and more equitable assessments undertaken under the Commonwealth) had left behind a memory and a heritage of popular and parliamentary antagonism to any system of direct taxation based upon the *accurate* measurement of income and wealth, either of the households and/or the districts liable to pay taxes to kings and their parliaments. Only very traditional forms of direct taxes collected as quotas, assessed on counties and towns, in relative proportions that had hardly changed since the Middle Ages, remained acceptable to taxpayers. These stereotyped quotas, together with control by local elites over the process of assessment and collection, formed the basis for a moderately productive land tax, which persisted in unaltered form from 1694 to 1798. Other (and widely resented) experiments with 'graduated' poll and hearth taxes assessed in wartime under the later Stuarts and by William III in the 1690s disappeared after 1697. No new and potentially controversial direct taxes emerged before William Pitt's income tax came onto the statute book in 1799. Before that innovation appeared, kings and parliaments could prescribe and legislate, but freeborn propertied Englishmen insisted on keeping the state ignorant about their real levels of income and wealth and set terms for cooperation and compliance by retaining control over the administration of land and all other forms of directly assessed taxation.

To circumvent these political constraints and to avoid any threats to political stability ministers and their advisers turned towards the improvement of legal, institutional and administrative frameworks required to collect rising proportions of revenue in the form of customs and excise duties. That development had proceeded some way by the early seventeenth century; received impetus from the civil wars and Interregnum; and came fully on stream over the century after 1713 when something like three-quarters of all tax revenues received by successive British governments took the form of indirect taxes and when most of the *increment* to the state's income from taxation consisted of excises and stamp duties levied upon the domestic production of goods and services.

War Finance and the Accumulation of the National Debt

For most of the period (1688–1815) when Britain was emerging as Europe's hegemonic naval and imperial power, the state did not control a tax system that was reliable or elastic enough to fund abrupt transitions from peacetime to augmented wartime expenditures. The bulk of extra taxation raised in wartime came from raising the rate of taxation levied from 5 per cent to 20 per cent on a stereotyped valuation of real property. Extra taxation was, however, never sufficient to fund the forces of the crown when fully mobilized for warfare and therefore the raising of loans was needed to circumvent that critical problem. Although proportions of the *extra* money raised as taxes in order to engage in armed conflict varied from war to war (it reached 50 per cent in King William's War, 1689–97, and again during the Napoleonic War, 1803–15), the bulk of funds came from long-term or perpetual loans. Although chancellors of the Exchequer (before Pitt the Younger changed the policy) borrowed most of the money needed to support the mobilization of the armed forces, they imposed indirect taxes to meet interest payments on short-term (unfunded) and above all on perpetual (funded) national debt raised for the expenses of seven wars (1689–97, 1702–13, 1739–48, 1756–63, 1775–83, 1793–1802, 1803–15) fought by Britain's armies and navies. Over the long eighteenth century and the final phase of Europe's mercantilist era, the accumulation of Britain's national debt mounted in line with the state's augmented capacities to tax and pay interest on loans from extra revenues derived largely from indirect taxes. From a ratio of 24 per cent during that brief interlude of peace (1698–1702), the share of the total tax receipts allocated to service the national debt mounted, conflict after conflict, to reach some 60 per cent after the Napoleonic War (1803–15). War after war, as the state exploited its growing potential to borrow funds to support a far more aggressive stance in great power politics, Britain moved from the foot to the apex of the European league table for government indebtedness.

Again unsurprisingly (and in line with histories of its European rivals who had participated more actively in geopolitics and colonization over the sixteenth and seventeenth centuries), Britain's fiscal and financial system passed through but (unlike France, Spain and the Dutch Republic) weathered three serious fiscal and financial crises of the state. The first occurred in the wake of the American War of Independence (1775–83), when Pitt the Younger introduced a sinking fund designed and accepted by parliament as a permanent commitment to redeem systematically the national debt, which had accumulated in the perceptions of the political elite to a dangerous sum outstanding and which in their view threatened the fiscal system, the stability of the constitution and the prosperity of the economy. Similar perceptions, also accompanied by widespread despondency, marked the renewed and even more rapid accumulation of public debt during the war against Revolutionary France from 1793 to 1802. To preserve the financial system while providing funds to meet the rising costs of war and to defeat threats to property from Revolutionary France, Pitt persuaded parliament in 1799 to accept his novel strategy of paying for considerably higher proportions of military and naval expenditure from the proceeds of the nation's first real income tax. Sixteen years later, and after the most costly conflict in Britain's history when (and despite the clear success of Pitt's income tax) the nominal value of national debt amounted to more than double the national income, Lord Liverpool's administration began the task of rebuilding trust in the fiscal constitution, basically by rolling back the state.

Conclusions: Fiscal and Financial Success

England (Europe's most successful fiscal state which emulated several features of Dutch fiscal and fundamental policy) began its irresistible rise after the Glorious Revolution. Between 1689 and 1815 allocations of tax revenues to service a national debt (maturing into the largest in Europe and accumulating to preserve the security of the realm and to carry the state and the economy to positions of naval, imperial, commercial and industrial hegemony) emanated in very large proportion from excise and customs duties. In strictly constitutional terms, the selection of these all-important indirect taxes, the rules prescribed for their assessment and collection, and ultimate control over the departments responsible for the implementation of the laws covering all duties levied on commodities and services fell under the sovereignty of parliament. In political practice the provision of supply for the armed forces of the crown (particularly when British armies and navies were at war), and for the administration of laws and the institutional frameworks required to augment the armed forces, required inflows of revenue into London that remained virtually under the control of an aristocratic oligarchy of Hanoverian ministers reporting to their monarchs. With a state so often at war, parliament almost never refused or hardly ever even cut royal demands for money.

For centuries, as an island with a small presence in imperial ventures overseas, Britain came late to serious participation in European power politics and colonization. After the Glorious Revolution its state arrived on that scene unencumbered by debt, with an underexploited fiscal base and with an aristocratic and monarchical regime that maintained a strong degree of autonomy, in the formulation of its commercial, imperial and fiscal policies, by remaining aloof from its dispersed and heterogeneous bodies of taxpayers and creditors, even while it taxed and accumulated debt on an extraordinary scale.

British exceptionalism in this vital domain of fiscal and financial power had something but rather little to do with the Glorious Revolution, parliaments, liberty and democracy, and owed far more to the construction between 1642 and 1684 of an efficient framework for taxation that subsequently allowed, after 1688, for a massive accumulation of debt that carried the realm through seven wars to reach a pinnacle of power the United Kingdom retained throughout a 'golden age' of Victorian and Edwardian liberal capitalism.

In retrospect, most of the advantages enjoyed by the Hanoverian state flowed from geographical endowments; the detachment or weakness of the Tudor and Stuart regimes in geopolitics; and above all from the fiscal sclerosis that afflicted Britain's major competitors on the European mainland between 1689 and 1815. The inexorable onset of sclerosis (that had also clearly afflicted Britain's fiscal and financial system for several decades after Waterloo) led only to an era of laissez-faire governments. Fortunately, and for more than a century, the rollback of the state did not seriously compromise the Victorian regimes' exercise of hegemony – basically because the struggle against Revolutionary and Napoleonic France had exhausted the capacities of Britain's major rivals to challenge its imperial, economic and geopolitical position in the world economy.

FURTHER READING

Bonney, Richard (ed.): *Economic Systems and State Finance* (Oxford, 1995).

Braddick, M. J.: *The Nerves of State: Taxation and the Financing of the English State, 1558–1714* (Manchester, 1996).

Brewer, John: *The Sinews of Power: War, Money and the English State 1688–1783* (London, 1989).

Chandaman, C. D.: *The English Public Revenue 1660–1688* (Oxford, 1975).

Dickson, P. M. G.: *The Financial Revolution in England: A Study in the Development of Public Credit 1688–1756* (London, 1967).

Dietz, Frederick C.: *English Public Finance 1558–1641* (London, 1932).

Hoffman, Philip T. and Norberg, Kathryn (eds): *Fiscal Crises, Liberty and Representative Government* (Stanford, CA, 1994).

Hoon, Elizabeth E.: *The Organization of the English Customs System 1696–1786* (New York, 1938).

O'Brien, P. K.: 'The political economy of British taxation, 1660–1815', *Economic History Review*, 41 (1988), pp. 1–32.

O'Brien, P. K.: 'Public finance in the wars with France 1793–1815', in H. T. Dickinson (ed.), *Britain and the French Revolution 1789–1815* (London, 1989), pp. 165–87.

O'Brien, P. K.: 'Central government and the economy 1688–1815', in Roderick Floud and Donald McCloskey (eds), *The Economic History of Britain since 1700* (3 vols, Cambridge, 1994), vol. 1, pp. 205–41.

O'Brien, P. K. and Hunt, P. A.: 'England 1485–1815', in R. Bonney (ed.), *The Rise of the Fiscal State in Europe 1200–1815* (Oxford, 1999), pp. 53–101.
O'Brien, P. K. and Hunt, P. A.: 'Excises and the rise of a fiscal state in England, 1586–1688', in Mark Ormrod et al. (eds), *Crises, Revolutions and Self-Sustained Growth: Essays in European Fiscal History* (Stanford, CA, 1999).
Roseveare, Henry: *The Treasury: The Evolution of a British Institution* (London, 1969).
Roseveare, Henry: *The Financial Revolution, 1660–1760* (London, 1991).
Stone, Lawrence (ed.): *An Imperial State at War: Britain from 1689 to 1815* (London, 1994).

Chapter Four

Local Government and Local Society

David Eastwood

Misreading the Eighteenth Century

Local society and particularly local government in eighteenth-century Britain has often been misrepresented. This was an age of oligarchy, when the currency of public life was patronage, repaid in the small change of deference. Landed acres, increasingly manicured and stylized, were a grand metaphor for effortless control by a landed elite. Squires and parsons ruled rural areas with a comfortable complacency, whilst variously growing affluence or genteel decline led to an atrophying of urban government. Walpole's 'Venetian oligarchy' held provincial England in its thrall even more completely than it had subordinated parliament.

The nearest the twentieth century came to an official history of Britain was the *Oxford History of England*. For half a century the eighteenth-century episode in this essentially Whiggish national history was captured in Basil Williams's *The Whig Supremacy 1715–1760* (1939), which held its place until a new wave of scholarship broke with the publication of Paul Langford's successor volume, *A Polite and Commercial People*, in 1983. Williams's picture of local government was puzzlingly dismissive. Provincial institutions and the fabric of local life represented 'an historical scrap book'. England was governed by 'various haphazard methods', which could not be 'dignified with the name of a system'. On the ground there was an 'amazing hotch-potch of authorities and conflicting jurisdictions' which, in the main, were overseen by men drawn from a 'half-educated class'. The powers of the parish had been 'whittled away' and the authority, or 'local despotism', of the justice of the peace now held sway over parish and county. Even urban government had fallen prey to the 'immense power' of the justices of the peace. Moreover, and perhaps most culpably, central government had abrogated its influence in the localities. Relations between central and local government were incoherent, and although parliament sometimes amended or enhanced the role of local government, in essence a petty tyranny was being exercised over petty matters. The history of local government could thus be told in terms of the public activities of 'largely irresponsible' justices of the peace. A few 'vestiges' of an older representative culture aside, the provinces enjoyed no public life.

It is odd and revealing that this caricature of the eighteenth century became so deep rooted. Odd because many of the eighteenth century's most distinctive voices told a different story; revealing because this old orthodoxy represented the triumph of very particular political and historiographical traditions. Henry Fielding, that most brilliantly acute of eighteenth-century novelists, found lurking in the vestries of provincial England, 'schemes . . . which would hardly disgrace a conclave. Here are plots and circumventions, parties and factions, equal to those which are to be found in the courts'. One could here pile quotation upon quotation, tincturing the eighteenth century as a period of almost democratic vitality. The young Frenchman, François de la Rochefoucauld, travelling in East Anglia in 1784, found the administration of justice in provincial England deserving of 'the highest commendation'. Justices of the peace were men of 'the highest reputation', parish constables were 'held in high respect' by the people, whilst farmers adjudicated cases as jurors uninfluenced by 'any personal motive' and with 'the closest attention'. England thus achieved a kind of 'democracy' which avoided the 'unpleasant features of democracy such as factions, risings and so on'. But gathering a small harvest of such quotations does not demonstrate a case by mere weight of accumulation. There are counter-examples as richly etched as a Hogarth print. They merely demonstrate that the eighteenth-century self-image was more complex than some historians' caricatures allow.

What is more important is the political use and historiographical abuse of the eighteenth century. This has deep and specific historical roots and has only been dispelled very recently. The roots of this parody of eighteenth-century government and public institutions lie in the eighteenth century itself. From the 1780s a reform movement gathered momentum, and this movement developed a language and a programme which highlighted 'abuses' and advocated a very different way of ordering society and its local institutions. Beginning with the movement for 'economical reform' in the 1780s and intensified by the more democratic radicalism of the 1790s, reformers developed a critique of the politics of influence, connection and traditional authority. Interestingly this movement had roots in provincial England itself, as Christopher Wyvill's Association Movement built on its Yorkshire base to develop a nationwide organization. This radical tradition came to decry 'old corruption'. Much of the critique of old corruption was elaborated around the politics of Westminster, the growth of pensions, and the machinery of William Pitt's highly effective governmental regime. Nevertheless local politics – whether evidenced by the politics of elections, the composition of the commission of the peace, or the intrusion of the church into civil administration through clerical magistrates and clerical chairs of parish vestries – offered a useful second front for reformers. The apparently oligarchic interweaving of local politics and parliamentary corruption was chronicled in remorseless detail in T. H. B. Oldfield's *History of the Boroughs of Great Britain* (2 vols, 1794) and his *Representative History of Great Britain* (6 vols, 1816). Add William Cobbett's heroically sustained invective against old corruption and the Euclidean certainties of utilitarian reformers, and an awesome critique of the historically informed improvisations of eighteenth-century Britain's local administration was born.

What had begun as the oppositional denunciations of Hanoverian radicals became the stock-in-trade of nineteenth-century reformers. Parliamentary committees and royal commissions from the 1830s teemed with colourful accounts of abuse, incompetence and administrative incoherence. These were marshalled in support of reforming initiatives, whether these aimed to transform the poor law, improve the prisons, raise standards of public health or ensure that the streets were properly policed. Once parliament had been reformed in 1832, the logic, or rather the ideological priorities, which had carried the Great Reform Act were applied to a still more radical overhaul of local government. Carrying these reforms through took much of the nineteenth century. The style of reform changed between the 1830s and the 1880s and 1890s, when county government and parish administration were finally reformed. Nevertheless, one recurrent *leitmotiv* remained: a searing indictment of eighteenth-century administration.

The commissions, especially those on poor law (1834), municipal corporations (1842) and public health (1842, 1843–5), provided a rich quarry for later historians. Happily guided by Whig and liberal certainties, late Victorian and early twentieth-century historical orthodoxy found abundant proofs of the eighteenth century's failings in the great nineteenth-century official inquiries, and thus what had begun as a radical critique became a fixed historical orthodoxy. There were dissenting voices, although interestingly these were often non-English voices. The Prussian jurist Rudolph von Gneist in the 1880s celebrated the eighteenth century's decentralizing tendencies. In 1913 Elie Halévy began his survey of the early nineteenth century by discovering, in his retrospect on eighteenth-century local government, 'the administrative socialism of bygone England'. Yet the mainstream flowed down quite different ideological valleys. Between 1906 and 1929 Sidney and Beatrice Webb produced a nine-volume *History of English Local Government*, whose centre of gravity was an extended survey of eighteenth-century irrationalities and a celebration of the nineteenth century's reforming endeavours.

Conservative historians had less reason to castigate the eighteenth century, but for a variety of reasons averted their gaze from its local institutions and provincial political culture. Parliament, economic progress, metropolitan culture, rather than local institutions and the provinces, were at the centre of more celebratory accounts of Hanoverian England. Moreover, when Lewis Namier published his *Structure of Politics at the Accession of George III* in 1929 a long shadow was cast across the history of the eighteenth century. A simultaneously brilliant, acute and partial reading of eighteenth-century politics, Namier's book became, for nearly half a century, the lens through which the eighteenth century was examined. For Namier patronage, clientage and control were the instruments of power and the currency of politics. Despite critics, Namier carried much before him, and his reading of the eighteenth century was made flesh when the *History of Parliament* began its work in the 1950s. Other historians, who had little sympathy with Namierite politics, found Namierite history served them well. E. P. Thompson, who spoke for a generation of radical historians with and after his publication of *The Making of the English Working Class* in 1963, offered a reading of the eighteenth century full of Namierite themes and nuances. Namier might marvel at a politics of clientage and control whilst Thompson might be repelled by a politics of old corruption, but both were recognizably commenting on the same historical landscape.

The transformation in our understanding of the eighteenth century began in the 1970s and gathered pace in the 1980s. This new history of the eighteenth century is too varied and vibrant to be simply characterized. It has at its core a much more subtle and responsive reading of eighteenth-century politics; a much more vibrant reading of eighteenth-century society and social policy; and a fresh understanding of the nature and trajectory of economic change. For our purposes, though, some other themes can be discerned in this new work. The first is an appreciation that what happened in eighteenth-century Britain happened to a significant degree because of rather than in spite of its public institutions. The second is a recognition that we need to take the eighteenth century's self-evaluation seriously, and that, if the eighteenth century thought of itself as anything, it thought of itself as a period of 'improvement'. Moreover, the theatres of improvement were often, one might even argue predominantly, local institutions and local communities. The century teemed with improvement commissions, local acts to turnpike roads or cut canals, and considerable investment in improving the lot of the poor, the treatment of prisoners and the treatment of the sick. Local government and locally based institutions took the lead in much of this. If we understand that the eighteenth century thought of itself as an age of improvement, whilst historians have chosen to accord this accolade to the nineteenth century, we will understand a good deal.

A Complex Inheritance

It is now a historical commonplace to see England as 'a long formed state'. In the eighteenth century many, though not all, came to venerate Britain's venerable political institutions. Conservatives such as William Blackstone wove his *Commentaries on the Laws of England* (1765–9) around an explanation and a celebration of England's long developed legal and judicial system. When the revolutionary storm broke over Europe after 1789 a chorus of conservative voices extolled England's (for they usually spoke of England) ancient institutions as a bulwark against this rising tide of revolutionary upheaval. Thus, Edmund Burke's *Reflections on the Revolution in France* (1790) was at least as much a panegyric to England's historically refined constitution as it was an exploration of the nature of the crisis of the French monarchy. Radicals took a more sceptical view and by the close of the century had elaborated a connected critique of central and local government. Nevertheless, the strength of British institutions and the mobilization of a British nation in the face of the French revolutionary threat meant that the eighteenth century ended with serious structural reform still a generation away.

It is striking that the institutions of English local government were still more antique than those of central government. Parliament is a late medieval innovation, but the shires and hundreds into which England was divided and the sheriffs, justices and county officers who exercised power within these jurisdictions were older than parliament itself. Shires and hundreds were indeed a hardy legacy of the Anglo-Saxon state. Sheriffs too were first appointed in the eleventh century. Justices of the peace, by name at least, were comparatively recent, first so called in 1351, although their role has deeper roots. Indeed the legal structures of assizes and sessions were a legacy of Henry II's systematic reform of the English law. Towns too could trace their incorporations back to the medieval period, with the curious consequence by the eighteenth century that the pattern of municipal government – those places which enjoyed incorporated status – reflected an earlier pattern of power, patronage and prosperity. The new wealth which the eighteenth century witnessed was, in the main, generated by new centres such as Manchester, Birmingham and Sheffield which, in constitutional terms, remained no more than villages.

By contrast to England, Britain was a new state, fashioned in 1707 through a complex interplay of English and Scottish ambitions. One might have expected the coming together of two states, with distinct cultures and distinct institutions, to have created the impetus for a thoroughgoing reform of political institutions. By 1707 it had become clear that a union could be concluded which fused parliamentary institutions, but which left other public institutions, including the church and local government, unaltered and different north and south of the border. Thus, throughout the eighteenth century, Scotland continued not only with a system of local government which differed from that of England, but those differences became further accentuated when and after heritable jurisdictions were abolished in 1747 as part of the response to the 1745 rebellion. The appointment of sheriffs' deputies in 1748 gave the centre a larger role in Scottish local government than it enjoyed or sought south of the border. Scotland possessed justices of the peace before the Act of Union, and the union certainly animated a magisterial system that was much less energetic than its English counterpart. The greater role enjoyed in poor relief by the church, the particular traditions of the Highlands, and the gradual development of a new culture of local administration after 1748 preserved clear differences between the English and Scottish experiences after the union.

Union with Wales had taken place much earlier, with Acts of Union in 1536 and 1543 producing quite different results. Wales was assimilated to England and, with one exception, Welsh local government by the eighteenth century formally mirrored that of England. Indeed, in the parts of Wales which had easy access to England, both the structures and the operation of local government mirrored those of England, although sometimes, as in Pembrokeshire, with the twist of an English-speaking governing elite exercising power over a Welsh-speaking peasantry. In places nearer to the border, such as Glamorgan, the pattern was less distinctive. In remoter regions, Wales was a less-governed country, with some parts of north Wales having no effective poor law and a weak system of parish administration. What Wales did have, until 1830, was its Court of Great Sessions, the one Welsh institution that had survived the ruthless assimilation of Wales following the Acts of Union. The Great Sessions gave Wales a distinctive and cheap system of justice, although by the eighteenth century it was defended more zealously in west Wales than by landowners in the east. Once serious reform of the English courts began in 1826 its demise was assured and no account was taken of its significance as a national, as distinct from a legal, body.

Thus, the newly formed British state worked with the historically accumulated tools of local government. There were some reforming initiatives but no drive for modernization. In this Britain, and British unionism, was distinct. Many other major European states embarked on systematic reforms of their local government system, either to absorb newly acquired territories, or better to assimilate more remote or independent territories, or to improve the administration of their lands. The Prussians for example reformed local government in 1733 and again after 1749. For much of the second half of the century their legal system was being codified, a task which was not finally complete until 1794. The Habsburgs reformed local government three times: after 1749, after 1760, and between 1781 and 1789. French local government was remodelled with almost geometric precision after the Revolution, whilst a host of minor states emulated the reforming endeavours of their larger counterparts. The European enlightenment was preoccupied with questions of governance. If one adds the American Revolution and subsequent constitution making, where relations between centre and locality were at the heart of the debate, what is striking about eighteenth-century Britain is that there was no attempt to reform its complex local government inheritance. The British way was to innovate within and around existing institutions, but not to innovate on them.

It would be wrong to suppose that no developments had occurred in local government since the medieval period. Many of the major municipal incorporations occurred between the fifteenth and seventeenth centuries. The parish, an ancient ecclesiastical unit, became a unit of secular administration in the Elizabethan period, notably through the acts of 1597 and 1601 which established the parish as a rating unit and gave it responsibility for the relief of the poor. The crucial relationship between parliament and the localities was renegotiated and redefined in the early modern period, and was not finally settled until the Revolution Settlement of 1689–94. By the eighteenth century, though, the period of structural or constitutional alteration was at an end. Although they disagreed as to its political meanings, most of the politically active agreed that the Revolution Settlement was something to work with rather than against.

If we reflect on this, a central paradox emerges. The eighteenth century is a period of little formal innovation in the structures of political life, and yet it is a period that often presents itself in innovatory terms. Improvement and innovation were at the heart of Hanoverian Britain's self-perception. In retrospect the eighteenth century was a period of profound economic change and considerable social development. The coexistence of an essentially conservative constitutional perspective and a dynamic society seems puzzling. The puzzle is resolved if we appreciate that the formal constitution of Britain's political institutions does not describe, or circumscribe, the vitality of its public life. As we will see, innovation took place both within and around these public institutions, notably the institutions of local government. Moreover, the political culture that animated local government, an active local elite assuming a public role, remained and indeed was renewed in the eighteenth century. Finally, in important ways the reforming spirit which often found itself at odds with parliament over parliamentary reform by the late eighteenth century found scope and expression in a flowering of local government and local improvement. In remarkable ways the new wine of reform found its way into the old wineskins of England's local political institutions.

Local Government at Work: Participation and Improvement

People animated local government in eighteenth-century Britain. Where officers lacked energy, institutions ossified and power was haphazardly, even arbitrarily, exercised; when officers had energy and imagination antique institutions acquired new vitality, even new vision. The abuses of eighteenth-century local government were abundantly chronicled in nineteenth-century official enquiries and Whiggish histories in the twentieth century. The personal administration of justice as of political power could be, indeed was, idiosyncratic, but idiosyncrasy erred on the side of indulgence as well as arbitrary excess. Moreover, and this is critical, eighteenth-century Britain was not an intensely governed country. Government expenditure was modest, and taxation and public borrowing were dominated by what historians have lately come to call the 'fiscal-military state'. War, imperial defence and the civil establishment absorbed the majority of public spending. In 1748–50, for example, expenditure by parishes and counties in England and Wales, averaging £730,000, amounted to a shade under 6.8 per cent of total public spending. Similarly, the rate of criminal indictments and criminal convictions was low. The Oxfordshire quarter sessions in the 1780s averaged only around ten committals a year for theft, and though the rate was higher in counties with larger urban populations such as Surrey, indictments for crime were very low by modern standards. These patterns would begin to change in the last quarter of the century, but it is important to understand both the rationale for the Hanoverian system and the political culture of those who made the system work.

The people in Hanoverian Britain were fond of what they took to be their liberties. Idiomatically, English liberties invoked a sense of an ancient inheritance and a contrast with the officialdom that was widely taken to hold the peoples of Europe in thrall to despotic government. The French, Habsburg and Prussian states had their officials, often centrally appointed, sometimes uniformed, and certainly formally accountable to the centre. England, by contrast, had voluntary officers, elected officials, ad hoc commissions. Attempts to introduce a regular police, like attempts to number the people, were defeated in defence of a prized liberty and scepticism about intensive government. Those who wanted to reform or enhance key resources of state power, notably policing, had to work within existing provision or elaborate a quasi-voluntary provision alongside it. John and Henry Fielding, the great London police reformers, offer a cameo of ideology, tradition and reform in the mid-century. Henry Fielding inveighed against 'wild notions of liberty' which explained the 'present lethargic state' of public authorities, whilst still opposing 'pernicious' schemes of European-style police reform. The Fieldings used the authority of their office as magistrates at the Bow Street police office to institute small-scale police reforms from the 1750s. The Bow Street runners achieved a reputation beyond their tiny numbers, and a horse-patrol foundered for lack of funding. Nevertheless this modelled a way forward for many localities, who improved local services through voluntary endeavour, establishing paid watches and mutual-insurance associations to defray the costs of prosecutions. The quest to uphold liberty and enhance efficacy led to numerous experiments and over the course of the next century to a remodelling of the relationship between state and the citizen.

The smallest and most pervasive unit of local government was the parish vestry. Most vestries still met in churches, proclaiming the institution's ecclesiastical origins and reminding villagers that God and Caesar had been married by the English state. The vestry came of age as a secular body when it was given rating power by the acts of 1597 and 1601. This was critical to the development of local government in Britain, giving local authorities power of primary taxation and responsibility for providing for the poor. Until acts of 1818 and 1819 there were few regulatory orders for the vestry. Minutes did not have to be kept, and memory rather than the written record was the currency of business. All ratepayers were entitled to attend and vote in vestries, the most extensive electorate in Britain. In some larger cities, notably London, vestry meetings could be large and boisterous, with larger ratepayers claiming they were outvoted by the smaller ratepayers whose voting rights were disproportionate to their modest fiscal contributions. In rural parishes it was easier to moderate the political authority of the smaller ratepayers by de-rating them. Power here resided with officials. The key officers were the two overseers of the poor, elected annually, and the two churchwardens, one usually elected and one nominated by the incumbent. Parishes also had responsibility for local roads, and elected a surveyor of the highways. Parishes could use rate income for highway repairs, and could oblige parishioners to work on highway maintenance. Parish constables were formally appointed each year, an appointment ratified by magistrates, but many served year-on-year, receiving fees for services performed, and thus quasi-professional.

To the majority of people the only institution of the state they encountered was the vestry. There was an intense pattern of migration in the eighteenth century, driven by economic imperatives and the itinerant labouring gangs at harvest, but this was mostly local migration. In every village there was the vestry, the constable and the overseers. These local elites embodied public authority, and the primary distinction throughout the country was between those who held local office, and might also serve on juries, and those who did not. Richard Gough's famous account of the Shropshire village of Myddle in 1701 is ordered around who occupied which pew in the parish church – a visible political geography. Those who ran the parishes, paid the rates, defined entitlement to poor relief, employed most local labour and filled the benches of juries were, in an authentic and pervasive sense, a governing class. By the end of the eighteenth century perhaps as many as 400,000 people, including some women ratepayers, could attend parish vestries and constituted the pool from which parish officers were elected, a different and bigger electorate than that for parliamentary elections.

If the parish vestry rested on a rather idiosyncratic kind of representative principle, the government of the counties was improvised around the politics of patronage and a highly personal notion of power and status. Here land and power were firmly fused. An act of 1732 fixed the property qualification for being named on the commission of the peace at £100. In most counties the numbers named on the commission of the peace exceeded 200, and amounted to a roll call of the county elite, and the number formally named on the commissions of the peace rose from around 3,000 in 1714 to over 7,000 by 1761. The majority of those named, though, regarded this as a status rather than a responsibility. A much smaller number were active magistrates, in many counties perhaps no more than thirty. Amongst these active magistrates were an increasing number of clerical magistrates. During the intense party political upheavals associated with the 1689–1714 period, commissions of the peace were constantly being remodelled as part of the collateral of party conflicts in parliament and the country. This kind of turbulence disturbed the routine work of local administration. After 1714 justices of the peace found the space and stability to develop county government.

Justices of the peace operated in two theatres: the petty sessions and the quarter sessions. Petty sessions represented the fusion of personal and judicial power at its most intense. Justices dispensed justice from their parlours, held summary sessions in inns and other public places, and decided, often without reference even to a clerk, the outcomes of cases. Summary justice was in their gift, as were its punishments in terms of fines, corporal punishments and, increasingly as the century progressed, imprisonment. More serious offences, from major thefts through offences against the person, to conspiracies and organized crimes, were committed to the higher courts of quarter sessions and assizes. Much judicial business was, however, done in petty sessions. Active magistrates might be clerics such as Reverend Edmund Tew in County Durham, landowners such as William Hunt in Wiltshire, or political notables such as Samuel Whitbread in Bedfordshire, all of whose justicing notebooks have survived. They would generally hold formal sessions either fortnightly or monthly, and would transact other business as and when matters pressed. The more assiduous, too, would use their powers to exercise a significant degree of oversight over parish officers.

The magistrates' achievement was to weld their judicial, licensing and administrative powers into something that operated as a system. The key here was the quarter sessions, which focused, regularized and ritualized magistrates' authority. The quarter sessions were the quarterly meeting of magistrates, along with juries, constituted as a higher court. As the eighteenth century progressed, these quarterly meetings, which generally lasted three days, came to act as the occasion when the county assembled as a social and political entity. Balls, parties, public sermons and court rituals animated especially the first day of the quarter sessions. Those arraigned before the court were treated to rituals of power which ranged from high constables of the hundreds presenting white gloves as 'emblems of purity' betokening no indicted crime in their jurisdictions, through to court officers and court customs which proclaimed the magistracy of the law and the majesty of the magistrates who embodied it.

As so often in British state formation, the quarter sessions were an institution whose role had evolved and mutated. The court had its officers, the most important of which was the clerk of the peace. An ancient office, invariably held by a lawyer, it was rewarded by a system of fees. Many clerks, certainly by the later part of the century, were in effect full-time county officials. Acton Chaplain, clerk of the peace in Buckinghamshire, for example, also held the offices of county treasurer and deputy lieutenant clerk to the lord lieutenant between 1787 and 1813. Elsewhere, the county treasurership was held separately, often by a banker. A county surveyor was appointed with nominal responsibility for county bridges, and when men such as Thomas Telford held the office genuine expertise was available. County sheriffs, who were 'pricked' but in practice served in an honorific rotation, formally had responsibility for the county's gaols. Magistrates themselves had the power to hear appeals from paupers and ratepayers aggrieved at receiving too little or paying too much for poor relief. When one adds to this powers to monitor and regulate migration, responsibility for licensing lunatic asylums and, through the responsibilities of the lords lieutenant, command in the militia, the range of county responsibilities was enormous, and comprehended the elements that make up what later came to be called 'social policy'.

The particular achievement of the eighteenth century was to weld this into a system. The quarter sessions as they came to function were the magistrates' system. Three key developments, which took place in different localities at different points in the century, helped to drive and consolidate this system. The first was the emergence of a regular chairman of the quarter sessions, who became the leading magistrate and often took the lead in developing or coordinating policy. Kent had a regular chairman of the quarter sessions from the late eighteenth century, Gloucestershire not until a century later. Oxfordshire appointed a permanent chairman from the 1770s, and in the person of Sir Christopher Willoughby had, from 1778, a leading penal reformer and perhaps the most important innovator in poor law policy in the late eighteenth century. These chairmen were aided by increasingly professional clerks of the peace, and by an inner cabinet of active magistrates who met sometimes fortnightly and often monthly in adjured meetings of the quarter sessions. By the late eighteenth century this system of quarter sessions and magistrates' power would drive through an experiment in social policy of unprecedented ambition.

The world of eighteenth-century towns was very different. If we define towns as settlements of over 2,500 then in 1700 around 19 per cent of the population lived in towns; by 1800 this had risen to a little over 30 per cent. Behind these figures lay an important story. In 1700 Britain was a comparatively urbanized country, by 1800 perhaps another 1.7 million people were living in towns. Moreover, and more importantly, many of these were new towns or newly expanding towns. The great towns and cities of Britain, places such as Bristol and Liverpool, were being joined by new towns built on new wealth. Yet places such as Manchester, Birmingham, Sheffield and Bradford were, for administrative purposes, mere villages. The incorporated towns remained those that had been historically incorporated. Corporations, too, varied hugely in their role, status and activity. Some corporations, such as those of Banbury and Buckingham, did little more than make the borough's parliamentary returns. Other corporations in places as varied as Bath, Bristol, Congleton, Leicester, Nottingham and Oxford were active and dynamic. Nevertheless the politics of the corporation could be an intensely introspective politics. Rebuilt town halls provided new facilities; they also proclaimed the dignity of the commission. Towns too were places that created new patterns of local government to accommodate growing religious and cultural plurality. In places such as Bury St Edmunds the politics of the corporation was Anglican whereas the local vestries and improvement commissions were dominated by Dissenters, and in more diverse centres such as Bristol a still greater diversity developed within the city's political culture. The world of the corporation was too circumscribed, and the number of corporations too historically limited for corporations to be able to comprehend the diversity and vibrancy of eighteenth-century urban life.

The eighteenth century witnessed something like an urban renaissance. Theatres, public rooms, reading rooms, societies, inns and coffee houses flourished. Leisure, public spaces and social life were commercialized. Building and rebuilding became an insistent rhythm of urban life. The culture of improvement was visible in, and sustained through, urban life. The improving culture was facilitated by perhaps the most striking feature of eighteenth-century urban administration – the rise of the improvement commission. Local acts of parliament established commissions to promote paving, lighting, cleansing, water supply, highways, watching and policing. These commissions gave a new dimension to urban life. They had tax-levying and charging powers; they were armed by significant statutory powers; and they embraced Dissenters as well as Anglicans. In eighteenth-century Bath perhaps £3 million was spent on civic improvement and local development. More than any other development, the establishment of improvement commissions extended and diversified the governing elite of eighteenth-century Britain. Between 1760 and 1799 some 427 new improvement commissions were established. Again nineteenth-century reformers would caricature and condemn these commissions, and certainly the problems of early nineteenth-century urbanization outran their fiscal and political capacity. But in their eighteenth-century context, animated by a civically focused culture of improvement, they were often remarkably well adapted, and were the means through which the eighteenth century achieved municipal reform without a Municipal Corporations Act.

The Eighteenth-Century Achievement

Perhaps the least well understood achievement of eighteenth-century local government lies in the remarkable experiments in social policy that occurred in the later part of the century. Although these experiments were as widely ramified as they were ambitious, they consisted predominantly in a transformation of penal policy and the elaboration of the poor law into integrated welfare provision. As we will see, the nineteenth century appropriated the former and rejected the latter, but both reveal a great deal about the capacity and ideology of Hanoverian local government.

The European enlightenment was profoundly committed to rethinking the notion of punishment and deterrence. The most pervasive outcome of new penal thinking was the penitentiary or prison. Prisons were not new, and had long been places of confinement for those awaiting trial and redemption from debt. They were not, however, places of punishment, still less sites for the reformation of the criminal. Enlightenment thinking opened the way to remaking the prison. Punishment of the body, long characteristic of the western tradition, was increasingly rejected as brutalizing and irrational. Equally irrational was the prospect of brutal punishment as a deterrent to crime. Enlightenment thinking, with its emphasis on associationalist psychology, held out a new prospect of reforming the criminal. If men and women were made bad (or socially inadequate) by circumstances and association, they could be reformed and redeemed by placing them in a controlled environment which substituted rational and benign influences for the vicious and degrading circumstances which had degraded criminals. The prison would both rationally punish and literally remake the criminal.

Interestingly it was in local government more than in parliament that the new enlightenment penology found its resonance. John Howard, pricked as high sheriff of Bedfordshire in 1771, took his responsibilities of visiting and inspecting Bedfordshire prisons assiduously, and was scandalized by the conditions he found. He later embarked on a national programme of visits, a one-man inquiry, which was published in 1777 as *The State of Prisons in England and Wales.* The response would be rebuilding prisons and reforming prison regimes. Again local acts were used, although parliament passed enabling acts in 1779 and 1785. The leading figures in this penal transformation worked from and through local bases. Sir George Onesephorus Paul was high sheriff of Gloucestershire in 1780 and began a process that would make Gloucestershire a model county with new prisons and an integrated penal policy. Paul, a major Gloucestershire landowner, was also an active supporter of Christopher Wyvill's reforming Association Movement, which numbered parliamentary reform among its objectives. Sir Christopher Willoughby, chairman of the Oxfordshire quarter sessions, advised government on prisons policy as well as rebuilding the Oxfordshire county gaol and equipping it with a new regulatory regime in which criminals deemed incapable of reformation were transported and those who responded to the stick of punishment and the carrots of education and religion would remain in the new model prison. In Salford the rebuilt prison was known locally as the New Bayley, after its projector, the chairman of the quarter sessions, Thomas Butterworth Bayley.

All these men were networked. Paul's library shows him to be well read in enlightenment penal theory, and within the thirty-five years between 1780 and 1815 most English county gaols were either rebuilt or substantially remodelled. The effects of these developments were profound. New model county prisons led to the closure of many local prisons. The management of prisons became more considered. The balance between labour, hard labour, education and religion was more carefully calibrated. Prisoners were increasingly carefully segregated, and with greater segregation and more stringent classification came higher building and rebuilding costs. Regular monitoring and magistrates' committees to inspect county gaols became the norm, and prisons and penal policy loomed ever larger in county business.

More profoundly still, the economy of deterrence was being remodelled by this penal revolution. The 'bloody code', which saw the number of capital statutes rise to over 200 by the end of the eighteenth century, was a curious exercise in liberty through terror. The fear of the gallows was expected both to deter and to obviate the need for a vigorous and intrusive police force. Detection might be unlikely but the penalties so astringent that the would-be criminal focused more on the dread of the gallows than on the unlikelihood of apprehension. The logic of punishment in prison, and reform of the criminal through prison, was that this balance between fearsome punishment and haphazard detection should be adjusted. With punishment in prison would come better police. The nineteenth century would draw the conclusions but the foundations had been laid in the eighteenth century. Committals to trial increased by 575 per cent between 1805 and 1840. By 1823 parliament was beginning to regulate prisons, by 1835 it instituted a prison inspectorate, and in 1877 it nationalized all prisons. Within a century the penal experiment of eighteenth-century county government had been appropriated by the Home Office.

The fate of the experiment in poverty and welfare was rather different. As in most periods, attitudes towards the poor in the eighteenth century oscillated between compassion and condemnation. The history of workhouse experiments captures something of this, with more stringent attitudes underlying the Workhouse Act of 1723, yet workhouses also formed a centrepiece of Thomas Gilbert's more humanitarian 1782 act. Interestingly, for much of the mid-century, workhouses where they existed were used by the poor as a resource, without carrying a searing social stigma. Townspeople, for example, entered the Oxford workhouse in much the same way as they might avail themselves of local charities, charitable schools and almshouses. Poverty, or at any rate acute poverty, was cyclical, more often than not occasioned by life-cycles, illness or personal tragedy. In its acute form, for many in the mid-century poverty might be a passing phase rather than a perpetual circumstance. Charitable institutions, like the poor law, were well adapted to ameliorating poverty. The poor law, too, in urban and rural areas, could provide regular support to widows, single-parent families and the aged and chronically sick, without placing a crippling burden on ratepayers. Overseers determined entitlements, vestries gathered rates and modest transfer payments were made to the poor. It would be wrong to idealize this system, and public charity always had its critics, but it did give England and much of Wales a public strategy for assuaging poverty which was largely absent from Europe until Joseph II's reforms in Austria in the 1780s and the revolutionary reconstruction of France in the 1790s. Scotland, with a different legacy from its reformation, continued with the kirk rather than the state as the organizing forum for public charity.

Long-run demographic trends pushing up rural populations, changing patterns of employment in agriculture, enclosure and the decline of customary rights and entitlement, and the dislocations wrought by the American and French revolutionary wars created something like a new poverty by the close of the eighteenth century. Underlying this was what became structural underemployment and a low-wage economy in agriculture, with knock-on consequences for the rest of the rural economy. The dimensions of this poverty were mapped in works such as David Davies's *The Case of the Labourers in Husbandry* (1795) and Frederick Eden's *The State of the Poor* (1797). At the same time the Board of Agriculture, established in 1793, began a series of surveys of all counties and gathered detailed data of wages and prices in 1794. By 1795, with the war still further inflating bread prices, much of rural England was threatened with famine. Like many famines the core of the problem appeared to be a relative income collapse on the part of the poor. The response to this is well known: the development of the 'Speenhamland system', so called after the Pelican Inn at Speen where Berkshire magistrates met in May 1795 to ratify the payment of poor relief in aid of wages. Revealingly, nineteenth-century poor law reformers came to call this the 'magistrates' system', which was accurate enough, but its real origins are deeply revealing of the sophistication which the magistrates' system of local government had now developed.

The real architect of the Speenhamland system was Sir Christopher Willoughby, and the key decision was taken at the Oxfordshire quarter sessions early in January 1795. Willoughby also persuaded Buckinghamshire magistrates to take an identical decision later in January. Willoughby, well networked within local government and an adviser on penal policy, was also a member of the Board of Agriculture established by parliament in 1793. He had been involved in surveying wages and prices in 1794. In short, he had a statistical basis and an analytical context against which to understand the likely impact of massive food price rises in late 1794 and early 1795. The key was not just the depth of poverty, it was also the inadequacy of incomes of those in work. What Oxfordshire magistrates agreed in January 1795 were minimum family incomes, adjusted for the number of children. Magistrates would use their powers to ensure that parishes provided these minimum incomes and all parishes would be circulated with the magistrates' table of allowances, which were also published. The poor now knew to what they were minimally entitled. What Berkshire magistrates did was refine the system by introducing a formal sliding scale based on the price of a standard loaf of bread. However these reforms are characterized, they have the fundamental characteristics of a welfare state: minimum family incomes determined by the state, low wages supplemented from tax income, and modest transfer payments made to the very poor. Improvised in time of war, it was a remarkable achievement.

Like all welfare systems, this invention of the magistrates soon attracted its critics. Thomas Malthus in his *Essay on the Principle of Population* (1798) castigated it as counterproductive, as a humanitarian delusion which actually intensified the poverty it sought to relieve. A generation later, in 1834, the system was torn down amidst an indictment of the unelected magistrates who had constructed it. The system created in 1795 became institutionalized in ways which its projectors had perhaps not envisaged. By the end of the Napoleonic Wars it had become massively expensive, with poor relief expenditure exceeding £8 million in 1818. In trying to meet the challenges of an essentially rural poverty, magistrates overextended the Hanoverian system of local government. Without being representative of or accountable to the ratepayers, they made demands which ratepayers came to regard as excessive. They made the poor into a transparent public charge. For this, and more, magistrates came to be reviled. In fact, the language in which they cast their decision, which was measured and paternalistic, reflected the values which had come to animate county government in the later eighteenth century. It was the language of ambition rather than complacency.

In penal policy and poor law reform county government found a reforming energy that matched the improving enthusiasms of urban Britain. Of course the overall record of eighteenth-century local government is patchy, and like all systems of administration which rely heavily on individuals, it reflected the particularity and partiality of individual visions. To more systematic and bureaucratic cultures it looked hopelessly, indeed wilfully, unsystematic. Critics were wrong to suggest that it was wholly unrepresentative – vestries and some urban bodies were formally and often actually representative – but patronage, particularly within the magistracy, was at least equally characteristic. What eighteenth-century local government does demonstrate, however, is that local self-government retained its resonance for the governing elites of the provinces. Moreover, and most important, public life in eighteenth-century Britain was far more broadly based and far more pluralistic than the century's Whig and radical critics ever suggested.

FURTHER READING

Beattie, J. M.: *Crime and the Courts in England 1660–1800* (Oxford, 1986).

Borsay, Peter: *The English Urban Renaissance: Culture and Society in the Provincial Town 1660–1770* (Oxford, 1989).

Corfield, Penelope J.: *The Impact of English Towns 1700–1800* (Oxford, 1982).

Eastwood, David: *Government and Community in the English Provinces 1700–1870* (Basingstoke, 1997).

Hay, Douglas, Linebaugh, Peter and Thompson, E. P.: *Albion's Fatal Tree: Crime and Society in Eighteenth-Century England* (London, 1975).

Hey, David (ed.): *The History of Myddle: Richard Gough* (Harmondsworth, 1981).

Ignatieff, Michael: *A Just Measure of Pain: The Penitentiary in the Industrial Revolution 1750–1850* (London, 1978).

Innes, Joanna: 'Parliament and the shaping of eighteenth-century social policy', *Transactions of the Royal Historical Society*, 5th series, 40 (1990), pp. 63–92.

Jenkins, Philip: *The Making of a Ruling Class: The Glamorgan Gentry 1640–1790* (Cambridge, 1983).

Langford, Paul: *Public Life and the Propertied Englishman 1689–1798* (Oxford, 1991).

Neuman, Mark: *The Speenhamland County: Poverty and the Poor Laws in Berkshire 1782–1834* (London, 1982).

Rogers, Nicholas: *Whigs and Cities: Popular Politics in the Age of Walpole and Pitt* (Oxford, 1989).

Webb, Sidney and Webb, Beatrice: *History of English Local Government* (9 vols, London, 1906–29).

Whetstone, Ann E.: *Scottish County Government in the Eighteenth and Nineteenth Centuries* (Edinburgh, 1981).

CHAPTER FIVE

Parliament, Parties and Elections (1688–1760)

BRIAN HILL

During the century and a half before 1688 parliament grew in importance: most similar institutions in Europe disappeared under the impact of absolutist monarchy. Co-opted by Henry VIII to legitimize his seizure of supreme authority in the English church, parliament acquired a major stake in the political establishment. Succeeding reigns saw parliamentarians challenge the crown's authority in national finance, the law and even government. In the civil wars of the 1640s, however, the Long Parliament's resort to force proved dangerous, for the army turned against the parliament itself. After 1660 a restored monarchy recovered some of its powers by prolonging the life of the compliant Cavalier Parliament for nearly two decades. When this body became too turbulent Charles II and James II used their prerogative power to dissolve both it and the four succeeding short-lived parliaments, and also claimed the right to suspend or dispense with existing legislation. A growing cult of divine right monarchy, demanding passive obedience and non-resistance from subjects, appeared to threaten earlier parliamentary gains, and the political nation removed James in the Revolution of 1688 with minimum use of force.

The Post-Revolution Political System

In the aftermath of the Revolution most peers and members of parliament (MPs) were agreed that a further enhancement of their power was needed, and they passed the Bill of Rights to limit the powers of monarchy, the Triennial Act to regulate the life of parliament, and the Treason Act to prevent monarchs from using treason law against political opponents. Above all, MPs ensured that parliament would have regular and prolonged meetings, providing a permanent forum to counter monarchy's continuous presence. This objective was achieved by a variety of means, especially the voting of financial supplies to government for only one year at a time. The sanction process was aided by the need of post-Revolution monarchs to raise money for expensive wars against France. Determined and sustained use of the power of the purse, to prevent rulers from ever again intimidating or dispensing with parliament, transformed the political scene, assisting a long-term process of reducing the power of the crown.

Of all changes after 1688 none was more visible than parliament's continual presence, compared with the long periods of non-parliamentary rule experienced under the Stuarts and earlier, such as the 'eleven-year tyranny' of the 1630s and two intervals of nearly three years each in the 1680s. Moreover, from 1689 onwards the business of both houses took up many months of every year, in contrast to the often truncated parliamentary proceedings of a few weeks, or even a few days, before 1688. Beyond permanence and frequency of meeting, MPs were not prepared to go. The electoral system remained largely unchanged and there was no general desire to revive experiments of the Interregnum in the 1650s such as a wider franchise, equal distribution of borough seats by number of voters, or the abolition of the House of Lords. Such measures would have smacked of republicanism, social equality and equal distribution of property, ideas which post-Revolution society was not prepared to air openly, though these ideas lingered on among common men and intellectuals until the time was ripe for a new outburst from the later 1760s, in the era of 'Wilkes and Liberty'.

The new prestige which parliament enjoyed even outside Britain in the eighteenth century, as a result of successfully establishing its regular presence on the political scene, had some important results for the nature of government. Under the Stuart monarchs financial supplies offered by the Commons had rarely erred on the side of generosity. The various expedients by which these monarchs had tried to supplement their income, such as secret subsidies from a foreign power, prerogative taxes of dubious legitimacy, and the sale of irreplaceable assets, had resulted in a marked and national lack of confidence in Stuart kingship. But four or five years of parliamentary financial control after the Revolution of 1688–9 brought remarkable changes. With parliament willing and able to allot taxation for funding interest payments on government loans, the resources of an increasingly prosperous financial community were opened dramatically, allowing William III to fight a major war on a scale never available to his predecessors. Britain's military successes under Marlborough in the next reign were the direct result of a new confidence in government, signalled by such major steps as the Million Loan of 1693, the foundation of the Bank of England in 1694 to channel City wealth into the Treasury, and the gradual emergence of a funded national debt.

By the late seventeenth century the parliament of England and Wales had a lower house of 513 members, a number enhanced by forty-five new members in the union with Scotland's parliament in 1707, bringing the total for the Commons of Great Britain to 558. Nearly all English constituencies returned two members, a practice not phased out until the nineteenth century. Two-member constituencies allowed some flexibility, since electors could use their second votes to allow minority parties or groups to acquire the second seat. Rival parties sometimes agreed informally to put forward only one candidate each, avoiding the expense of a contested election. The national electorate was large enough to express public opinion fairly accurately, especially in the larger-franchise constituencies, even though representation deteriorated somewhat as population increased, while a new 'last determinations' law in 1729 hampered the increase of voters by custom. There was no secret ballot and electors identified in poll books were open to various pressures, especially in the smaller boroughs.

Contemporaries recognized two types of constituency: counties and boroughs. The forty counties of England, which returned eighty members, had a uniform franchise, the forty-shilling freehold, and each enjoyed electorates of several thousands. Large urban boroughs too could have thousands of voters. But the great majority of borough seats had electorates of only a few hundred, in some cases even fewer. It was the small electorates in particular which stood open to patron pressure, bribery and corruption, and made up the legendary 'pocket' boroughs. The widely varying franchises prevailing in the boroughs, based on ownership of property, payment of local rates, freedoms, or membership of corporations, aided dubious electoral practices. English counties and the large-franchise boroughs, having too many voters to be in any patron's pocket, enjoyed much prestige as true indicators of public opinion, and their representatives in parliament were regarded as the elite of MPs. General interest in politics was not confined to voters. Wider participation in political discussion was ensured by the newspaper press, which grew rapidly after parliament's inadvertent abandonment of censorship in 1695. By 1760 there were four dailies, five or six thrice-weeklies and four weeklies serving London and the southeast, and dozens of other weeklies elsewhere. Knowledge of current political issues spread far more widely than in pre-Revolution days, adding to electoral pressure on MPs from informed public opinion. The right of petition to parliament was widely used, sometimes concerted between areas, and was not confined to voters.

Under the Triennial Act of 1694 parliament had to be re-elected at least once every three years. The intention of its devisers was not only to ensure the continuity of parliament but also to lessen the opportunity for ministers in the Commons to build up a subservient 'Court party' of officeholders without the electorate having an early opportunity to reject them. In practice general elections came so often, on average every two years between 1695 and 1715, that the constituencies remained in constant turmoil, and ministerial management of the Commons often became impossible. The Septennial Act of 1716 increased the permitted time between elections to a maximum of seven years, and parliament often subsequently went the full period. If the earlier measure helped to ensure the legislature's permanence, the later one retained this but calmed political life and allowed a new growth of patronage in both Westminster and its constituencies.

Membership of the House of Commons consisted overwhelmingly of landed gentry, though there were increasing numbers of lawyers, financiers and businessmen. The latter elements used their wealth to buy into substantial landownership, as required by an act of parliament of 1711. There were no working-class MPs, though patrons could sometimes evade this landed qualification act and could bring into the Commons able men who did not themselves possess the necessary landed property. Many candidates for election paid large sums for their seats, though the outcome of such expenses was far from guaranteed in any but the most docile of constituencies. MPs were unpaid as such and many had an adequate private income to sustain the expenses of being an MP, but some sought remuneration from government offices, many of which are now held by permanent civil servants. Major 'placemen', who held government office, were usually expected to vote for the government of the day. Other perquisites such as honours, local offices, tax collectorships and magistracies were welcome to all MPs, for either themselves or their supporters; but such lesser benefits did not carry so much obligation to the government, if any.

The House of Lords was of similar social composition to the lower chamber, but peers were on the whole richer. The hereditary principle dominated, with a minority of bishops and senior law officers as non-hereditary members. The absence of any responsibility to an electorate made the Lords particularly prone to pressure from crown or ministers, and the upper house was usually compliant to government's wishes. Peers could sometimes apply restraint to the Commons but usually tried to avoid confrontation with the elected chamber, especially over money matters, for by 1689 the convention that the Lords could not reject money bills was already observed. Where taxation was concerned, the peers preferred not to offend public opinion, which they accepted was better represented by the Commons.

The complex systems of elections which had grown up over centuries differed in detail almost from borough to borough, giving rise to many anomalies. With local practices prevailing it was often difficult for returning officers to know exactly who was entitled to vote. Such dilemmas gave rise, at the opening of parliament after every general election, to the hearing of disputes between those who had been returned as certified winners and those who claimed to have been defeated by illicit means. The decisions taken on disputed elections actually swung the balance against Robert Walpole's long ministry in December–January, 1741–2, or could enhance an existing majority, as when, after the 1715 election, a Whig majority voted to replace thirty-one duly returned Tories by Whig claimants but to reject the claims of all forty-six Tory petitioners. Not until Grenville's Act of 1771 was a fairer system of determining election disputes devised, and a uniform borough franchise was not introduced until the first Reform Bill in 1832.

Without the increased importance of parliament after the Revolution the development of a new type of political party could not have taken place. In the Cavalier Parliament, Court and Country parties had existed, but these differed in important respects from later parties, for they possessed little idea of competing to exchange the roles of office and opposition. The Court party, looking to the monarch as its leader and wishing to serve the government, could not by its nature go into opposition. The Country party, a diverse set of MPs who voted on issues as they saw fit and who were generally critical of the expenses and practices of government, could not enter government *as a party*. Soon after the Revolution, however, the new Tory and Whig parties underwent several major interchanges between government and opposition, and parliament witnessed regular conflicts between these two parties. With the Whig ascendancy from 1714 to 1760 ministerial changes became less frequent and were confined to Whigs.

The Whig and Tory parties differed from their modern successors in some important respects: they had no national organization linking constituencies with the parliamentary party, and any constituency organizations bore only embryonic resemblance to those of today. In parliament mechanisms to make supporters available for important divisions were effective but primitive by modern standards, especially in lacking the sanction of reporting dereliction of duty to any local party organization. A party in office could use the junior Treasury ministers to exert some discipline on its supporters in the Commons, while opposition leaders could ensure attendance at divisions only through voluntary party managers.

The names Tory and Whig originally arose as terms of abuse: meaning, respectively, Catholic Irish outcasts and Presbyterian Scottish outcasts from pre-Revolution

Anglican society. The two terms were first used at Westminster during the Exclusion crisis of 1679–82, when the taunt of Tory was applied to the crown's supporters and that of Whig to its opponents. Three successive parliaments were dissolved by Charles II when the Commons brought in bills to exclude his brother James, a Catholic, from the succession. After Tories joined Whigs reluctantly and briefly in order to protect the Church of England and remove the Catholic James II in 1688, their differences were renewed by fresh issues which divided the nation between 1689 and about 1720. Thereafter, the residue of such issues kept party differences alive in a situation of continuous Whig dominance until 1760, when new circumstances dictated a collapse of both parties and a slow emergence of successors which was not completed until early in the nineteenth century.

Whig–Tory Rivalry, 1688–1714

As soon as the immediate Catholic threat was removed in 1688 there came to the fore the deeply contentious rivalry of Anglican Episcopalians and Protestant Dissenters, hardened by two generations of persecution and counter-persecution (though this had been temporarily suppressed in the common cause against James II). The Toleration Act of 1689, by which Anglicans recognized the Dissenters' right to worship in their own way, did not extend to the removal of the civil disabilities under which the Dissenters had been placed by the Test and Corporation Acts of the Cavalier Parliament, including exclusion from all government and local offices. The practice of some Dissenters of occasionally taking Anglican communion in order to obtain office under the crown or to join a borough corporation angered Anglicans, just as Anglican insistence on making a test of the sacrament infuriated Dissenters.

To religious differences were added grievances concerning the Dissenters' control of dozens of boroughs where the corporation or freemen constituted the electorate. Purges of corporations to control national elections took place under Charles II and James II. The burning resentments of the local oligarchies thus dispossessed came before parliament as early as 1689, and control of the borough seats continued to be sharply contested between Dissenters, who voted for Whig candidates, and their opponents who favoured Tories. Bishop Burnet noted in 1708 that the party differences existed not only in parliamentary elections but even in the yearly elections of mayors and corporations, and that in every corner of the nation the two parties stood, as it were, listed against one another.

In parliament wartime expenditure on an unprecedented scale after 1689 proved increasingly politically divisive, with Tories favouring relatively cheap naval and only limited land operations, while the Whigs favoured more expensive military intervention in Europe against France's armies. To pay for extended and expensive war the Whigs were prepared to support the financial revolution which saw the creation of the Bank of England, the national debt and a new system of public credit. The Whigs supported the financial interests of the City of London, who stood to gain from lending to the government at high wartime rates of interest, while the Tories sympathized more with the country landowners, who paid the land tax that helped to meet the interest rates on the large war loans raised by the government and sanctioned by parliament.

The two related questions of defence of the established Church of England and the safeguarding of the Protestant succession were never far from the fore. The Tories' main commitment remained always the safety of the Church of England, whether against Roman Catholics or Protestant Dissenters, a defining principle of their party because the Whigs, though mainly Anglican (as MPs were required to be), were more tolerant of Protestant Dissenters and favoured them as reliable election supporters. But the Whigs' main aim from the Exclusion crisis onwards was rejection of the Catholic Stuarts. Although the majority of Tories demonstrated in 1688, 1715 and 1745 that they too were basically loyal to the Protestant succession, enough 'Jacobite' supporters of the exiled House of Stuart remained within their ranks to cast doubt on the whole party's commitment to the Hanoverian succession. This helped to ensure that only the Whig party could claim undivided loyalty to the Protestant cause.

In the early 1690s the committed Tories and Whigs in the Commons were still a minority of its members. At first most MPs stood aloof from the party men, regarding them as extremists. This opinion had much truth. Both groups had to undergo decisively changed patterns of thought to adapt themselves to the post-Revolution world. The Whigs at first still possessed the mentality of opposition. In the Exclusion era they had shown a marked antipathy to monarchy, often favouring a republican model of government. King William, however, was needed to preserve the Protestant religion, and the Whigs had to work with him in parliament by dropping their former fanaticism. This they duly did, aided by the rise of more circumspect leaders known as the 'Junto' (John Somers, Charles Montagu, Thomas Wharton and Edward Russell). These four assumed control of William's ministry in 1694–5, when Montagu established government credit by founding the Bank of England. With their accession to power the Whigs' older republicanism and radicalism declined, to be replaced by a pursuit of power and support for the new post-Revolution monarchy.

The Tories immediately after the Revolution also presented a spectacle of ideological disarray, and were forced to adjust their traditional ideas. Formerly the party of the Court, they had joined in the removal of James II rather than allow him to threaten the position of the Church of England, of which he was legally the head. But though they had resisted James despite their preference for the theories of passive obedience and non-resistance, they still initially hesitated to form a concerted political opposition to William and Mary, even though these monarchs had plainly been called into their position by parliament rather than by divine right. The Tories' reluctance began to change, however, when Mary, on whose share of the throne they had insisted, died in 1694. The Tories moved cautiously into opposition, led by the earls of Nottingham and Rochester, assisted by a small band of 'Old Whigs' discontented with the political ambitions of the Junto. Tory opposition became overt when a temporary peace with France in 1697 encouraged calls for government economy and the disbandment of much of William's army.

For three years Tories and Old Whigs called themselves the New Country party, combining the image of respectable Country patriotism with the reality of the Tories' first furious party opposition. By 1700 a tense situation in which the ministry could not carry even routine business in the Commons came to an end with the replacement of the Junto by Rochester and the Tories. By this time these had so far abandoned their traditional stance of subservience to monarchy that, Rochester bluntly told the king, princes must not only hear good advice, but must take it. Although infuriated, William had to stand by while the Tories placed further extensive limitations on the powers of monarchy in the Act of Settlement of 1701 that decided the line of succession (after William's death and that of his half-sister, Anne). The succession of the deeply Anglican Anne to the throne in 1702 benefited the Tories.

By Queen Anne's reign (1702–14) MPs are seen, from surviving division lists, to be voting solidly with one party or the other, with only about one eighth of them ever cross-voting; smaller groupings within or outside the major parties were no more significant than in most modern periods of predominantly two-party strife. Even the House of Lords displayed greater than usual party affinities. From the outset of Anne's reign Tory ministers carried out a sweeping purge of opponents from office at all levels, following Somers's example under William and Mary. Mounting Tory xenophobia was directed against the Dutch and other foreign Calvinists who played a vital role in the City of London. The Tories also found it increasingly difficult to support the raising of the huge loans and the voting of the high taxes needed to support the efforts of Lord Treasurer Godolphin and the duke of Marlborough to defeat France in the War of the Spanish Succession (1702–13). Outside parliament what has been called a 'Divided Society' echoed and reinforced the marked political differences between the two major parties at Westminster.

Early in Anne's reign the most serious party difference concerned the Dissenters' control of scores of borough seats by obtaining places through occasional conformity to the tests imposed in the Cavalier Parliament's Corporation Act. The Tories' indignation at this practice and their hunger for more parliamentary seats, together with their fear of a Puritan political revival, produced three attempts in Anne's first three years to introduce severe financial penalties for occasional conformists, threatening to alarm the City of London and end loans from its mainly Dissenting community. Finally, the high churchmen's 'tack' of an occasional conformity penal bill onto a tax bill in the Commons (to avoid rejection in the Lords) was averted only by a combination of Lord Treasurer Godolphin's placemen, moderate Tories and the Whig party, but at the cost of making political concessions to the Junto. These, serving in a special commission, were allowed to steer through a parliamentary union between England and Scotland. The union strengthened the provisions for the Protestant House of Hanover to succeed Anne in both kingdoms; but the further advantage for the Junto lay in the forty-five new MPs from Scotland, the native land of Whiggery, who entered the newly united House of Commons in 1707 and helped to swing the balance in favour of the Whigs. The Junto were able to force the queen to give them office – against her inclination – a year later.

The last six years of Queen Anne's reign saw an appearance of partisan fanaticism greater than anything seen since the Exclusion crisis. War weariness, especially among land taxpayers, was widespread. The Whigs, however, with the approval of the elector of Hanover, set out to prolong the war with France for the advantage of the elector's Austrian suzerain, the Holy Roman Emperor, and also so that France, the principal sponsor nation of King James's son 'James III', would remain Britain's enemy if Anne died soon. The methods used by the Whig ministers went far beyond national interest: the Dutch allies were bribed to put aside reasonable French peace proposals, and negotiations with France were sabotaged by excessive British demands.

The Junto's worst action, in the eyes of most English opinion, was to impeach the high church clergyman, Henry Sacheverell, for preaching a sermon 'In Peril among False Brethren', indicting Godolphin's ministry and appearing to favour the succession of the House of Stuart. Sacheverell was the most vociferous spokesman for the surviving Jacobite sentiment and political theory held especially strongly in the lower clergy's house in the Convocation of Canterbury, the church's premier institution. But the use of impeachment, parliament's principal instrument of political retribution, against a clergyman aroused clamorous resentment not only from high Tories but also from moderate public opinion, rallying to the clarion call of 'the Church in Danger'. The queen replaced Godolphin and the Junto in 1710 by Rochester and her confidant Robert Harley, who called an election which gave a landslide victory to the Tories, despite Harley's own efforts from the Treasury to restrain the high churchmen. Moderation was swept aside in a Tory frenzy of desire for peace and fear for the safety of the Church of England.

The great achievement of the Tory ministry of 1710–14 was the eventual bringing of the War of the Spanish Succession to a successful end by the Treaty of Utrecht in 1713. At home, however, the ministry was wracked with serious political problems. Whig extremism provoked equal extremism, with the high Tories being led from within the new ministry by Henry St John (later Viscount Bolingbroke). An act of parliament was at last passed in 1711, setting heavy penalties for occasional conformity, and an even more draconian measure, the Schism Act, was intended in 1714 to destroy Protestant Dissent itself by strangling its educational system. The Tories were largely united in support of these measures, but they were badly divided on how to cope with the succession to the childless Queen Anne. Any expectation on the part of concealed Jacobites to restore the Stuarts peacefully was destroyed in 1713–14 when a substantial minority of 'Hanoverian' Tories voted on key occasions alongside the Whigs for fear that the Protestant succession was in danger. It was clear that the Stuart claimant to the throne could only be imposed by force and that an armed invasion by the Stuart Pretender, James Edward, would not find strong enough Tory support in parliament. The feared possibility of civil war on Anne's death was avoided because *parliamentary* strife proved sufficient, rather than armed conflict, and the moderate Tories moved once more to the political centre in a brief alliance with Whigs against the high Tories in order to secure the Protestant succession of the Hanoverian George I in 1714.

'The Rage of Party', as the historian J. H. Plumb called these events, was never to be as great again in the eighteenth century. But Plumb's belief that a growth of political and social stability in the era of Robert Walpole rectified the instability of the period before 1714 needs some modification, for the principal growth of stability began with the Revolution Settlement itself. The highly contentious period from 1689 to 1714 provides the first example of representative political institutions taking the strain of volatile events without breaking. Early in 1714 both sides were reported to have been drilling for a resort to arms. That Queen Anne's death was followed by the peaceful accession of George of Hanover is a testimony to the basic soundness of institutions devised during the first quarter of a century after the Glorious Revolution.

The Whig Supremacy

The Hanoverian era presents a spectacle of parliamentary tranquillity compared to that of William III and Anne. A ratio of voters to population estimated for 1722 at one to four adult males deteriorated somewhat as population increased; and the period saw the institutionalization, with some modification, of many changes made since the Revolution. Parliament continued to sit regularly for many months of each year, though general elections became less frequent after 1716. The concept of a permanent national funded debt became better accepted despite the ill-advised South Sea scheme of the early 1720s that attempted to reduce it precipitately. The nature of parties underwent some further modification as a result of decades of Whig dominance, but as government was always run exclusively by Whigs, while the Tory party remained permanently the focus of opposition, the new situation did not amount to a revival of the pre-Revolution Court and Country pattern. Some Whigs now joined in opposition from time to time, the better to force their way into office, but the Tories were stubborn in their refusal to enter any ministry except as a party, and they have been shown to have a remarkably consistent pattern of opposition voting and of political independence from dissident Whigs.

The decline of the Tory party after 1714 was due to systematic suppression by a combination of royal preference, Whig patronage and the electorate's revulsion against the excesses of Anne's last ministry. The first step was the displacement of virtually all Tories from office or place, perquisite or favour. The purge was even more thorough than the Tory one in 1702. An election in 1715 returned 341 Whigs to 217 Tories, almost reversing the result of 1710 and reflecting a major swing of floating voters, who moved from fear on behalf of the Church of England in 1710 to alarm at the Stuart threat to the Protestant succession by 1715. In 1717 Convocation was suspended, effectively removing the high churchmen's main propaganda platform. Finally, the ministry extended its control of parliament by the Septennial Act, reducing the frequency of general elections and giving longer tenure to the existing Whig majority.

Whig dominance of government and parliament helped to consolidate the party's control of the smaller borough constituencies for some decades. That the Tory party survived in parliament as an effective, if reduced, party was due to factors beyond the powers of Whig managers to control, particularly the large electorates in some boroughs and in the English counties. In 1715 these counties returned forty-nine Tories to thirty-one Whigs, strongly against the trend in the smaller boroughs of under 1,000 voters that elected 234 Whigs to 124 Tories. The overall Whig victory reflected an imbalance in the size of constituency electorates, for the overall number of votes for each of the parties across the nation was about equal. Substantial Tory majorities in the large-franchise constituencies were cast for a few score candidates, while relatively small electorates in the numerous small boroughs returned hundreds of Whigs. The smaller boroughs did not again return a majority of 'Tories' until the rise of a new party system at the end of the eighteenth century and beginning of the nineteenth.

The rise of Robert Walpole followed the first split among the Whigs in 1717. Despite the obvious overtones of a struggle for control of patronage among a party now too large to satisfy all its claimants, the issues which divided the two main groups were substantial and important. Lord Stanhope at first prevailed, but his ministry's use of British resources to further the interests of George I's German possessions gave cause for objections by Lord Townshend and his brother-in-law, Robert Walpole. In domestic policies Stanhope represented an idealist element closer to the original Whigs of the Exclusion era, while Walpole appeared more pragmatic. All Whigs agreed to repeal the Occasional Conformity and Schism Acts, but Stanhope wished also to remove the Test and Corporation Acts of Charles II's reign and allow Protestant Dissenters to take a wide range of offices. The Townshend–Walpole group's preference was for retaining the tests, since Dissenters would vote for Whig candidates anyway, and there was every reason to mollify the Anglican church which included most English people and which the Whigs needed to win over from the Tory cause. A large body of Walpole Whigs helped the Tories to reject Stanhope's scheme, together with his proposal to strengthen the House of Lords by means of the Peerage Bill, moving politics closer to the centre against the Whig party extremity.

Walpole's primacy (1721–42) rested on a control of parliament arising from a powerful combination of party principles and patronage. In the House of Lords ministerial pressure on the bishops, obtained by judicious career advancement from poor to rich bishoprics, accounted for up to twenty-six votes, twenty-five of which saved Walpole from a defeat on one major occasion in 1733. Government management, aided by Scotland's staunch Whiggery, ensured that only one Tory was returned for the northern kingdom in the 1722 election, and none in 1727. Most Scottish MPs were co-opted into the ranks of the Court and Treasury party (those placemen who could usually be counted upon to vote on the government's side). But a putative eighteenth-century maximum of 200 placemen by 1760 never dominated the Commons of 558 members, and the ministry relied for survival on the large number of Whigs who, regardless of patronage, supported Walpole's formula of combining support for the House of Hanover with low taxation and restraint on the expensive overseas policies of the Hanoverian monarchs.

In the light of such powerful ministerial control it is hardly surprising that the main tactic of opposition was to maintain that Walpole's following was but a corrupt revival of the Court party of old, and that true patriotism lay with Country members, whether Tory or Whig. So far as some issues were concerned there was some truth in this. Peace with France had removed sharp issues of war strategy and expense. But other major party issues still remained: Walpole's domination of the Episcopal hierarchy did little to detach the lower Anglican clergy and laity from the Tories, and there remained too the overarching question of whether a successful Jacobite restoration could yet be staged, an event which some Tories secretly wished for but almost no Whig could contemplate. The rival fears of the Church in Danger and the Hanoverian monarchy in jeopardy continued to keep the rank-and-file members of the two parties far apart. The taint of Jacobitism by association was a powerful bogey to prevent too many disaffected Whigs from joining for very long with any genuinely Tory opposition, while what has recently been called the 'Jacobite fringe' of the Tory party was in reality too ineffective to endanger the House of Hanover.

Walpole's tenure of the Treasury saw the beginning of the role of a 'prime' minister, one who could carry much of the authority formerly attached to the crown itself. He largely dispensed with the new, larger cabinet, which had been formalized in Anne's reign, and relied instead on a small inner cabinet, stretching the powers of a minister up to, some said beyond, their possible limit. With the backing of most Whigs, the Townshend–Walpole group was able to manoeuvre George I's preferred minister Lord Carteret, a convert from Toryism, out of harm's way, while Walpole's acceptability to the Commons ensured that when George II came to the throne in 1727 his favourite, Spencer Compton, fared likewise. Thereafter, complaints that Walpole was so ambitious that he was usurping the power of the king grew more clamorous. Since Walpole's authority came from parliament (and not just from royal favour), he was also dependent on that parliamentary support. He always showed himself aware that if he lost his majority he would lose power, as he eventually did in 1742.

The reign of George II saw the emergence of a social trend which was to continue down to 1760 and beyond. Acts of parliament for enclosure of land and for punishing crimes against property increased. No general protest from the lowest classes was easily possible, and rumblings of discontent were confined to riots or voting for government opponents, even for suspected Jacobites. The high point of ministerial conciliation of landed society was Walpole's reduction of the land tax to one shilling in the pound (the wartime level being four shillings) and increases of other indirect taxes. A new salt duty which fell mainly on the poor met widespread resistance. But it was the proposal to subject wine and tobacco to excise duties which aroused the greatest public hysteria in 1733 and also strong parliamentary resistance in a year before a general election. The ministry was forced to withdraw the intended duties after its majority fell briefly to sixteen in the Commons.

After this display that parliament could closely reflect national opinion, a residue of the agitation was seen in 1734 with a Tory electoral gain of seventeen seats. Even more ominous for Walpole was the appearance of a large number of Whigs committed to the opposition. Further Whig defections, together with an unsuccessful war on which Walpole reluctantly embarked in 1739 (after considerable public pressure), reduced his immediate majority to about twenty in the general election of 1741, and Walpole fell from office early in 1742 after losing a series of disputed elections, brought down by a transient combination of Tories and opposition Whigs.

Henry Pelham's ministry from the mid-1740s to the mid-1750s did more to cement post-Revolution developments than did Walpole's. He made better use of the cabinet and set up a consolidated fund to combine miscellaneous items of the national debt at a lower rate of interest. Pelham and his elder brother the duke of Newcastle ensured that the Tories gained little. Pelham inherited the support of the 'Old Corps of Whigs' in parliament, both independent Whigs and Court and Treasury men, and Walpole's longstanding reluctance to place Tories in office was shared by the new ministers, who settled mainly for shuttling various cliques of Whigs in and out of office.

Pelham's greater willingness to conciliate rival Whigs by a share of office pro tem strengthened him in a revival of ministerial clashes with the king, which were prompted by George II's policies in the War of the Austrian Succession. Within four years of Walpole's fall the Pelhams forced George II to abandon ministers he favoured, especially the reinstated Carteret, and they organized cabinet and other ministers, some forty-five in all, in a mass resignation to secure a set of concessions that included the appointment to office of William Pitt, whom the monarch detested.

The Pelhams followed their coup by an early election in 1747, resulting in victory against ill-prepared Tories and Whig opposition groups and bettering Walpole's election result of 1734.

The revival of Whig disregard of royalty in issues of national importance upset more than the king. His eldest son, Prince Frederick, determined that when he came to the throne he would not be humiliated like his father. A way lay open for him to secure parliamentary support in the failure of all but a few English Tories to support the Young Pretender Charles Edward's rebellion of 1745, suggesting that traditional Tory loyalty to monarchy might, except in the case of a dwindling body of Jacobites, be diverted to service of the House of Hanover. Within two years of this event Prince Frederick came to an understanding with the Tories that in return for their cooperation he would, when he came to the throne, abolish 'all distinctions of party', remove their exclusion from office and give them a share of local appointments and commissions in an effective militia. The Tories and Frederick's Whig followers provided the only opposition to Pelham in the Commons until the prince's early death in 1751. In these few years he had succeeded in beginning the new direction in politics which his elder son Prince George was to follow.

The Walpole–Pelham system began to fall apart when Newcastle took control of the Treasury on his brother's death in 1754. A general election in that year gave the Old Corps of Whigs their usual victory, with a low Tory party return of 106 MPs and only some forty-two Whigs currently in opposition. But Newcastle was soon forced to share power with William Pitt after serious setbacks in a major new war with France (which started in America in 1754 and spread to Europe in 1756). The Tories in parliament sealed a new alliance with the young Prince George and ceased opposition for the first time since 1714, following the lead of the prince's court, though old party disputes continued in many areas and walks of life in the late 1750s.

Conclusion

The period from 1688 to 1760 saw a new map of political life come into being. Parliament functioned continually, rivalling monarchy's own permanence and making possible novel governmental structures. Deficit finance based on loans funded yearly by parliamentary taxes provided the means for post-Revolution governments to fight Britain's expensive wars of the eighteenth century, which raised her to the rank of a first class power. The new Whig and Tory parties of the 1690s, relieved of immutable Court and Country roles, competed for office within a permanent parliamentary framework, and though party animosities sometimes ran to extremes they did not slide over into physical force, apart from the occasions when a parliamentary minority supported the Jacobite rebellions of 1715 and 1745. The Tories' worst nightmare was a revival of militant Puritanism under a new Oliver Cromwell, but post-Revolution Dissenters were no Puritans and had little remaining political ambition except to share the political rights open to others. The Whigs' fear of a new restoration of the Catholic Stuarts had more reality, but few Tories could countenance the return of the Stuart Pretender unless he abandoned Roman Catholicism, which he always refused to do. Party dialogue gradually marginalized extreme views and strengthened the centre, with moderates combining in the crises of 1688–9, 1704, 1714 and 1719.

The electoral system in the constituencies did not change markedly in the early eighteenth century, though patron management became more systematic. Pressure for electoral reform had to await the 1760s and beyond. The later radical mythology of an all-powerful system of rotten boroughs needs, however, to be treated with caution, for even in closed constituencies public opinion, if aroused, could override the bastions of patronage. Strong public interest could greatly affect general elections, as in 1710, 1715 and 1734. The Triennial Act, in reaction against the Stuarts' habit of either keeping a favourable parliament too long or doing without one altogether for long periods, kept politics overheated for two decades after 1694, whereas the Septennial Act of 1716 arguably placed too much power in the hands of government by lessening the frequency of elections.

The pace of changes after 1688 was too rapid for all of these developments to be immediately absorbed into political life. But most changes were considered and temperate, more so than those of the Interregnum of the 1650s, and they certainly proved longlasting. The weaknesses and misunderstanding of the national debt came to light in the South Sea crisis of the early 1720s, and had to be rectified. Thereafter, Britain's credit system was always a major advantage in her expensive wars against France. General elections became less frequent after 1715, but they remained regular and far from subject to a return of royal whims. Because of the 'proscription' of Tories under George I and George II the parties lost momentum, but both survived despite the forecasts of critics. George III planned the end of Whig dominance, and the original parties were dissolved in the 1760s amid rapidly changing ministries. From this process a reformed and leaner Whig party emerged in opposition by the 1780s, facing a new party of government under William Pitt the Younger, which became the basis, by the early nineteenth century, of a revived Tory party. None of the major political developments of the post-Revolution era – annual sessions of parliament, political parties, the national debt and deficit finance, the Protestant succession, the post of prime minister and the role of the cabinet – was lost, for they were inextricably tied together.

FURTHER READING

Black, Jeremy: *Robert Walpole and the Nature of Politics in Early Eighteenth-Century Britain* (London, 1990).

Clark, J. C. D.: *The Dynamics of Change: The Crisis of the 1750s and the English Party Systems* (Cambridge, 1982).

Colley, Linda: *In Defiance of Oligarchy: The Tory Party 1714–1760* (Cambridge, 1982).

Dickinson, H. T.: *Walpole and the Whig Supremacy* (London, 1973).

Dickinson, H. T.: *Liberty and Property: Political Ideology in Eighteenth-Century Britain* (London, 1977).

Dickinson, H. T.: *The Politics of the People in Eighteenth-Century Britain* (Basingstoke, 1995).

Hill, B. W.: *The Growth of Parliamentary Parties, 1689–1742* (London, 1976).

Hill, Brian W.: *The Early Parties and Politics in Britain, 1688–1832* (London, 1996).

Holmes, G. S. (ed.): *Britain after the Glorious Revolution 1689–1714* (London, 1967).

Holmes, Geoffrey: *British Politics in the Age of Anne* (London, 1967).

Kenyon, John P.: *Revolution Principles: The Politics of Party 1689–1720* (Cambridge, 1977).

Monod, Paul K.: *Jacobitism and the English People 1688–1788* (Cambridge, 1989).

O'Gorman, Frank: *Voters, Patrons, and Parties: The Unreformed Electoral System of Hanoverian England 1734–1832* (Oxford, 1989).

Owen, John B.: *The Rise of the Pelhams* (London, 1957).

Plumb, J. H.: *The Growth of Political Stability in England, 1675–1725* (London, 1967).

Rogers, Nicholas: *Whigs and Cities: Popular Politics in the Age of Walpole and Pitt* (Oxford, 1989).

Sedgwick, Romney (ed.): *The History of Parliament: The House of Commons, 1715–1754* (2 vols, London, 1970).

Speck, W. A.: *Tory and Whig: The Struggle in the Constituencies 1701–1715* (London, 1970).

CHAPTER SIX

Parliament, Parties and Elections (1760–1815)

STEPHEN M. LEE

In the world of late eighteenth-century politics, parliament was not simply the arena in which the ruling elites negotiated compromises for the running of the country in their own interests, but it was also the focus of attention for much wider sections of the population, both the franchised and the unenfranchised alike. In terms of the constitutional theory of the eighteenth century, sovereignty lay with the crown-in-parliament in which each of the three components of the balanced constitution, King, Lords and Commons, exercised a restraining influence on the others. The monarchy retained considerable powers in this period, powers which were at the centre of the political debate, but increasingly, as the eighteenth century progressed, the balance of power between the two houses of parliament swung in favour of the House of Commons, continuing a process that had begun in 1688. This is not to say that the House of Lords was powerless. Not a few peers were great borough patrons and controlled the votes of many MPs in the Commons. Peers such as the duke of Norfolk, who had interests in eight constituencies, or Earl Fitzwilliam, who had interests in six, could exercise a considerable influence over events in the Commons. The potential for the exercise of such influence actually increased during the first long ministry of William Pitt the Younger (1783–1801) as a consequence of his ennoblement of a number of prominent borough patrons, such as James Lowther, who in 1790 controlled seven seats in four boroughs and was also able to return both county members for Westmorland and one for Cumberland. Moreover, the Lords were not averse to using their status as a revising chamber to exercise a veto over legislation to which they objected. Indeed, the Lords could on occasion be the key factor in bringing down a ministry, sometimes with the connivance of George III, as was the case with the fall of the Fox–North coalition in 1783 or of Pitt's first ministry in 1801. Nevertheless, it remains the case that the Commons was increasingly the more influential house of parliament and has as a consequence been the primary focus of attention for parliamentary historians.

Turning then to the lower house, typically MPs came from Anglican aristocratic or gentry backgrounds and were commonly educated at the public schools and at Oxford or Cambridge. Many, at times up to 20 per cent or more, were the heirs to peerages marking time until they succeeded their fathers, or they were the younger sons of nobles who would make their political careers in the Commons (such MPs often sat for seats controlled by their fathers or elder brothers and were the primary channel for the exercise of noble influence in the lower house). None the less, the number of MPs who came from outside the charmed circle of landed society did grow in the late eighteenth century. At the general election of 1761 only around 15 per cent of the 558 MPs came from 'non-elite' backgrounds, but this had risen to around 26 per cent (excluding MPs from Ireland) by the general election of 1812. Despite this slight weakening of the hold of the aristocracy and gentry over the House of Commons, however, in this period parliament remained a stronghold of the landed orders, although it should be remembered that many peers and country gentlemen had industrial and commercial interests which gave them a knowledge of affairs outside the confines of the agricultural economy that formed the basis of their wealth and position in society.

The Electoral System

In legislative terms the electoral system by which these MPs gained their seats in the Commons remained relatively unchanged in the period 1760–1815. None the less, the campaign for 'economical reform' in the late eighteenth century did reduce the scope for ministries to influence the composition of the Commons and the number of placemen declined markedly over this period. Crewe's Act and Clerke's Act, both passed in 1782, respectively disenfranchised revenue officers and barred government contractors from having a seat in parliament; although their impact is difficult to quantify, they probably did work as intended and helped to diminish the influence of the executive over the composition and conduct of the legislature. The impact of Crewe's Act, for example, was felt in those ports which previously had a large proportion of revenue officials among their electorates and who, employed as they were by the crown, may have been inclined to return the crown's nominees. Curwen's Act of 1809, which forbade the buying and selling of parliamentary seats, also had an impact on the executive, as Lord Liverpool admitted in 1812, by lessening its ability to return ministerial candidates. The most far-reaching changes to the system of parliamentary representation came, however, as a result of the Act of Union with Ireland in 1800, which added 100 MPs to the Commons, bringing the total to 658, and increased in so doing the number of open constituencies.

Beyond these pieces of legislation, the electoral system also underwent a number of important changes in its practice. One reason for this was the growth of the British population, particularly in places that were unrepresented in parliament (such as Leeds, Manchester, Sheffield and Birmingham), which meant that the proportion of voters to the general population became steadily smaller. In the early part of this period the electorate was about 4 per cent of the total population (or less than a fifth of the adult male population). This figure would continue to decline towards 3 per cent on the eve of the Reform Act of 1832 (or less than a sixth of the adult male population). Furthermore, the number of contested constituencies in general elections declined in a period when elections were arguably more frequent. Thus, while the first six general elections of the period (1761, 1768, 1774, 1780, 1784 and 1790) saw an average of sixty-nine contests in the 245 English constituencies, the last five

(1796, 1802, 1806, 1807, 1812) saw an average of only sixty-four (in any one election the highest number of constituencies contested was eighty-one or 33 per cent in 1774, a figure not exceeded until 1818). This decline in the number of contested elections was due partly to the increased frequency of general elections, but also to the rising cost of returning a candidate to the Commons. In 1807 Earl Fitzwilliam spent around £100,000 in Yorkshire alone in order to return his son as MP for the county. It should be emphasized, however, that the absence of a contested election is not evidence for the absence of political conflict in a particular constituency. Many constituencies, both counties and boroughs, saw a great deal of overt political activity, such as canvassing, fundraising and the formation of election committees, even though the contest did not proceed to a formal poll, usually because one or more of the candidates pulled out rather than risk the expense of a contested election when they divined that they did not have the requisite support to win the poll. It is in the recognition of facts such as these that recent research, most notably by John Phillips and Frank O'Gorman, has come to emphasize the dynamic and participatory aspects of the unreformed electoral system and to reject the Whiggish caricature of the operation of the electoral system that predominated in earlier historiography.

This Whiggish idea that the unreformed electoral system consisted either of electors entirely in thrall to their social betters, who decided how they should dispose of their votes, or of voters venally disposing of their franchise to the highest bidder, in constituencies totally unrepresentative of the population of Britain, will not stand up to modern analysis. Rotten and pocket boroughs and electoral corruption certainly existed, but to elevate these features of the system into its defining characteristics is illegitimate, as it would also be illegitimate to use the experience of large open boroughs like Westminster or counties such as Middlesex to provide typical accounts of unreformed elections. Even in constituencies where deferential relationships predominated and in which voters felt obliged to vote for the candidate preferred by their landlord or employer, it was usually the case that a voter would customarily be required only to commit one of his two votes in such a fashion. Moreover, a vote for a patron or a patron's candidate can be seen as a deferential response to the paternalistic role of the patron in the constituency, as expressed through, say, charitable works (such as establishing hospitals or schools) or simply through the economic benefits bestowed by the patron's patronage of local craftsmen. Any borough patron who became complacent about his voters and who was perceived by them to be neglecting their interests could soon find himself rudely awoken by an electoral rebellion. In 1806 in Malton, for example, Earl Fitzwilliam lost control of the constituency as a result of the perception among voters that he did not treat it well during the famine of 1799–1800. The electoral system in the eighteenth century was, thus, a facet of the operation of the wider social system and was one of the ways in which that system reproduced itself. Elections were one aspect of the relationships of paternalism and deference which went some way to ameliorating social conditions in an economically unequal and socially hierarchical society.

Given that electoral behaviour was part of a wider matrix of social behaviour, that voting was in many ways as much a social act as a political one, it is unsurprising that the issues which dominated elections throughout this period were local in nature, often centred around control of the constituency. Commonly, the chief issue in many contested elections was the battle between a local electoral oligarchy, be it a single family or a body such as the local corporation, and 'independents' who wished to break the stranglehold over the constituency. Taking the 1802 general election as an example, one finds independents succeeding in freeing up at least one seat and in some cases two in nine constituencies: Berwick, Beverley, Boston, Chippenham, Grantham, Grimsby, Morpeth, Queenborough and Warwick. None the less, as the period progresses one can detect the intrusion of national issues into the electoral arena, partly as a result of the growth of the press and the emergence of new political techniques such as mass petitioning. (It should be noted in passing that the practice of mass petitioning in support of campaigns such as those in favour of the abolition of slavery, the relaxation of laws discriminating against Dissenters or Catholics, and parliamentary reform, or the equally numerous loyalist petitions during the American crisis or during the 1790s following the impact of the French Revolution on Britain, served to reinforce the centrality of parliament to political life in Britain.) In certain general elections national issues were more prominent than in others. The constitutional crisis of 1783–4, which began with the dismissal of the Fox–North coalition and the installation of the ministry of William Pitt the Younger by George III in December 1783, played a significant role in the election of April 1784. In 1807, as a response again to the dismissal of a ministry by George III, this time the Ministry of All the Talents over a measure of Catholic relief, the cry of 'No Popery' was raised by supporters of the Portland ministry in perhaps as many as nine of the eleven county contests and fifteen of the fifty-eight borough contests. This general election was the closest thing to a single-issue election in this period, but even then the question of Catholic relief had a discernible impact in only 35 per cent of the contested constituencies.

A further feature of general elections in this period was that they were always won by the incumbent ministry. Ministries were defeated in parliament or were dismissed by the king; they did not lose office as a result of general elections and general elections were only called early in order to strengthen the ministry concerned. Thus, following the election of 1761, which was required both under the terms of the Septennial Act of 1716 (the previous one having occurred in 1754) and by the fact of the death of George II and the accession of his grandson George III, elections took place as required every six or seven years until the 1784 election, which took place after only four years of the 1780 parliament. The 1784 election was called by Pitt and George III in order to resolve the constitutional impasse of the parliamentary situation in the early months of 1784. The use of government influence and a widespread tendency for many borough patrons to support the king's minister, whoever he was, unless there were pressing reasons to do otherwise, resulted in a victory for Pitt. Similarly, the elections of 1806, 1807 and 1812, all of which were called early in conventional terms, were intended by, respectively, the newly formed Talents, Portland and Liverpool governments as measures to strengthen a ministry already in office.

The Re-emergence of Party

Once parliaments were elected, this raised for contemporaries and for subsequent historians the issue of how the MPs were to organize themselves once they arrived in Westminster. Indeed, one of the most contentious issues for modern historians of eighteenth-century politics is the question of the role that party played in the politics of the time. The old Whiggish accounts tended to assume simplistically that a two-party system existed in England continuously from the emergence of the labels Whig and Tory during the Exclusion crisis of 1679–81. The massive impact of the work of Lewis Namier and his seminal study, *The Structure of Politics at the Accession of George III* (1929), saw the emergence of a consensus which rejected both the Whig interpretation generally and, more specifically, any meaningful role for the concept of party as a useful analytical tool for historians. The Namierite consensus also denied the usefulness of politicians' expressed political principles as a means to understanding their behaviour, regarding all such expressions as post facto rationalizations of baser desires for power, profit and place that were better explained by a focus on the kinship and patronage structures in which politicians operated. It is only in recent decades that the importance of the role played by parties and political principles has been reinscribed by historians into the historiography of Hanoverian Britain. Thus, while it is true to say that the majority of backbench MPs for most of the period 1760 to 1815 can be regarded as, in the description used at the time, 'independent country gentlemen' who would normally give their support to the ministry of the day, it is also the case that during this period more and more of the important, active politicians can be ascribed a meaningful party label and that this period saw the emergence of both the early nineteenth-century Whig and Tory parties. Moreover, these were parties which defined themselves in ideological terms.

The most fundamental and continuous ideological divide in British politics in the late eighteenth and early nineteenth centuries was over the proper scope of royal prerogative, an issue that lay at the heart of both Whig and Tory ideology. It was through the prism of changing attitudes to the royal prerogative that most, perhaps all, the major political issues of the day were viewed, at least in part. The dominance of this issue was established early on, in the struggles of the 1760s. For George III and his supporters, his behaviour in that decade was simply an attempt to reassert the legitimate rights of the crown in the political process; to his opponents his behaviour was that of a potential tyrant which it was the duty of the aristocracy of the country, as embodied in the Whig party, to resist, as their forebears had resisted the despotic tendencies of Charles II and James II in the seventeenth century. In contradistinction to this were those politicians, like Chatham, North, Shelburne and the Younger Pitt, who, whatever their individual differences of emphasis, ultimately regarded it as their duty to protect the crown from the dominance of party politicians who were unconstitutionally intent upon limiting the powers of the crown in their own factional interests. Later, in the early nineteenth century, the Tory party would organize in part on the basis of a common desire among its members to defend the royal prerogative.

George III may not have been the despot-in-waiting of the old Whig myths, but he certainly wished to free himself from what he regarded as the overmighty influence that Whigs such as the duke of Newcastle had exercised over his grandfather. George III's decision to end the proscription of Tories at court, his explicit desire to install anti-party ministries, and his attempts to exclude the Pelhamite or Newcastle Whigs from office, as manifested in such episodes as the Massacre of the Pelhamite Innocents of 1762, when many supporters of Newcastle were ousted from their positions in government, transformed the position of the Whigs during the 1760s. The

Whig party under the first two Georges had operated in essence as a party of government. In the changed political environment of the 1760s the Newcastle Whigs had to adjust both organizationally and ideologically to opposition. This period saw the emergence of the marquess of Rockingham as the most significant Whig leader, replacing the fading Newcastle, who never fully adjusted to the role of an opposition politician. Rockingham, on the other hand, partly influenced by his role as a major landowner in Yorkshire, introduced noticeable oppositional, 'country' elements to the ideological make-up of the Whig party, which had previously been dominated by 'court' elements that emphasized ideas of service to the crown. The impact of the Edgcumbe affair of late 1766, in which Rockingham was only partly successful in his attempt to induce his supporters in the ministry of William Pitt the Elder, earl of Chatham, to resign over the dismissal of the Rockinghamite Lord Edgcumbe by Chatham, further emphasized the oppositional nature of the Rockingham Whigs by splitting off the ministerial or Chathamite wing of the party. This reduced the size of the party but it did give it greater ideological coherence.

Rockinghamite ideology was ultimately based on a particular interpretation of the events of the 1760s, an interpretation which provided a lasting legacy for good or ill to later generations of Whigs. For the Rockinghams, George III's behaviour towards the Whigs who had served his forebears so loyally was evidence of his absolutist tendencies. Moreover, his promotion of non-party ministries and the elevation of his former tutor, the earl of Bute, to positions of political importance, and ultimately to the head of a ministry, was taken by the Rockinghams as a betrayal of the sound constitutional practice of Whig party government. Even after the retirement of Bute from active politics the Rockinghams suspected that he and others (notably Lord Mansfield and Charles Jenkinson) were exercising 'secret influence' over the king and destabilizing each successive ministry, including their own of 1765–6. Opposition to this system of unconstitutional 'secret influence' became the defining ideological tenet of the Rockingham Whig party and its successor, the Foxite Whig party. Moreover, the only defence, it was argued, against 'secret influence' was party government. This paranoid style of politics was later elevated to the level of political ideology in Edmund Burke's classic defence of Rockinghamite party principles, *Thoughts on the Cause of the Present Discontents* (1770), and it remained a central feature of Whig politics throughout this period. Indeed, the tendency to interpret everything in terms of 'secret influence' was exacerbated by later events. Lord North's long government fell in 1782 and he was succeeded by a ministry led by Rockingham and the Chathamite earl of Shelburne. This inaugurated a period of political and ultimately constitutional crisis which only reinforced the Whig suspicions about the misuse of royal prerogative and 'secret influence'.

Rockingham's untimely death in July 1782 meant the government fell into the sole hands of Shelburne, who was brought down in 1783 by what many saw as an unprincipled alliance of the followers of Lord North and the Whigs led by the duke of Portland and Charles James Fox. This led to a short-lived ministry nominally under the premiership of Portland but dominated by the two secretaries of state, North and Fox, and universally known as the Fox–North coalition. This ministry fell when the king urged his supporters in the Lords to vote down the government's East India Bill. George III then dismissed the ministry and installed William Pitt the Younger as first lord of the Treasury in December 1783. Despite repeated defeats for Pitt's ministry in the Commons in early 1784, however, George III persisted with his chosen minister and the general election of 1784 confirmed Pitt's hold on the reins of government. All this simply reinforced the Whig belief in the malign effects of 'secret influence' and the use of the royal prerogative. The Whigs believed that the Fox–North coalition had been brought down unconstitutionally by the actions of George III and that the ministry of Pitt had been similarly unconstitutional in its origins. The Whigs were thus confirmed in their belief that they were the guardians of the constitution; the party of aristocrats standing between the monarchy and the people, with the task of preventing the worst excesses of either, monarchical tyranny or democratic mob rule, from predominating; and the sole possessors of political virtue, excluded from power only by unconstitutional means. In the circular arguments that often predominated in Whig politics at the time, their very exclusion from office was seen as proof of their political virtue.

Such sentiments sustained the Whig party for the remainder of this period, but the ideological obsession with the royal prerogative and 'secret influence' was not without its limitations, as the Regency crisis of 1788–9 showed. Given the obvious hostility of George III to the Whig party, especially after 1783, the Whigs under the leadership of Fox had aligned themselves with the reversionary interest of the Prince of Wales. When George III fell ill in late 1788, Fox's argument, for an immediate and untrammelled regency for the prince on the grounds of hereditary right, sat very uneasily with the Whigs' previous rhetoric about the dangers inherent in the unlimited exercise of the royal prerogative, especially since Pitt's regency proposals had the Whiggish principles of parliamentary limitation of the monarchy at their heart. George III's recovery was a disaster for the opposition Whigs. Furthermore, the obsession with the royal prerogative often prevented the Whigs from adapting successfully to changing circumstances. The insistence of the Foxite wing of the Whig party that the French Revolution of 1789 was an indication that the French were undergoing their own equivalent of 1688, an analysis which they stuck to despite increasingly obvious evidence to the contrary, is an illustration of how the Foxites became trapped within an ideological prison in which any and all events, no matter how unprecedented, could be interpreted in terms of their relationship to the Whigs' aim of limiting the rights of the monarchy. The realization that this was no longer legitimate under the changed conditions brought about by events in France was a major factor in driving a wedge between the conservative Portland Whigs and their Foxite colleagues. In the end the Portland Whigs went over to Pitt in 1794 when their fears about the impact on Britain of the ideas of the French Revolution and the war against France overcame their distaste for the unconstitutional way, as they saw it, Pitt had been installed in office. The Foxite wing of the Whigs remained in opposition and stuck to its ideological guns. Later events surrounding the dismissal by the king of the Ministry of All the Talents (1806–7), in which the Whigs were the largest part of the coalition of which it was formed, yet again only reinforced the tendency of the Foxite Whigs to interpret everything in terms of royal power. Overall, the Whig party in this period, by cleaving to its obsessions about 'secret influence', gained a degree of ideological coherence at the price of near permanent exclusion from power. Even when their old patron George, Prince of Wales finally came to power as regent in 1811–12, he preferred to stick with his father's ministers (now referred to as 'Tories') rather than bring in Whig ministers committed to the reduction of crown influence and seduced into defeatist attitudes towards the war against Napoleon by their objections to the growth of the executive branch of government that such a war necessitated.

It is clear, therefore, that the Whig party, first the Rockinghamite and then the Foxite, emerged as a party predominantly of opposition, only briefly holding office during these years (1765–6, 1783 and 1806–7). Crucially, the very ideology of late eighteenth-century Whiggery was an ideology of opposition. Unable to rely upon the machinery of government to supply the infrastructure of party, the Whig party led the way in organizational developments in this period, particularly during the 1780s. It developed election funds, formed political clubs (particularly significant was the Whig Club), and began to use the press, especially what was in effect the party organ, the *Morning Chronicle*, to promote its political interests.

It was developments such as these that allowed the Whig party to survive and recover from the repeated setbacks it experienced in the late eighteenth century. The Edgcumbe affair helped reduce the size of the Rockingham Whigs in the Commons from 111 to fifty-four MPs. This figure rose during the following years, reaching seventy-seven after the election of 1780 before falling back again in the aftermath of the crisis of 1782–4 to fifty-nine after the election of 1784. The party rallied during the late 1780s, reaching a peak of 146 in 1792 just prior to the secession of the 'Third party' and of the Portland Whigs. These losses reduced the Foxite rump of the Whig party to under seventy in the later 1790s. Again the party rebuilt itself, having around 150 members in the Commons by 1815.

If one turns to the emergence of a Tory party, by the early nineteenth century the process of party formation is not as clear as it is in the case of the Whig party and the issue is more contentious, with many historians arguing that no such Tory party emerged at all. This, however, would be to go too far. The old, early Hanoverian Tory party, tainted by Jacobitism and proscribed by the first two Georges, had a continuous existence right up until the late 1750s and early 1760s, when a combination of factors, such as the collapse of Jacobitism as a potential threat to the Hanoverian state in the decade after 1745, the political crises of the mid-1750s and the removal by George III of the proscription of Tories at court, brought an end to a discernible Tory party. The new Tory party which had emerged by 1815 had no organizational connections with the early Hanoverian party, but it did share some of the ideological obsessions of the early Tories, seeing itself, for example, as the defender of the established church. In the mirror image of the process undergone by the Whig party, however, which moved from a party of government to one of opposition, the Tory party that emerged in the early years of the nineteenth century was essentially a party of government predicated on loyalty to the existing constitution, whereas the Tory party under George I and George II was one of opposition, sometimes going to the extent of opposing the very basis of the Hanoverian succession.

Toryism in its late eighteenth- and early nineteenth-century form can be said to have emerged first as an ideology, and then as a party. In ideological terms, this form of Toryism can first be seen to stir in the domestic loyalist response to the American crisis. This was in turn greatly reinforced by the reaction in Britain to events in France after 1789 and the impact of 'French' ideas in Britain, a reaction compounded by the impact of the subsequent wars against the French revolution and against Napoleon. Defence of the monarchy and the church against the republican and atheistical principles of the French Revolution was added to an already antipathetic attitude amongst most Tories towards radicals, Dissenters and Catholics. In popular terms this found its most militant manifestations in 'Church and King' mobs and in John Reeves's Association for the Preservation of Liberty and Property against Republicans and Levellers. In more elevated political terms, the role of Burke's *Reflections on the Revolution in France* (1790) in the genesis of this new Toryism is crucial but should not be overestimated. Burke's opposition to political reform and his defence of the established constitution certainly spoke to many natural Tories, but his liberal attitudes towards Catholicism and imperial issues made him an unsuitable role model for many in the future Tory party. The true role model for the early nineteenth-century Tory party was Pitt the Younger, or rather the mythical view of Pitt that emerged in the years after his death. This was despite the fact that Pitt had favoured parliamentary reform in his earlier career and had left office in 1801 due to George III's opposition to a measure of Catholic relief intended to accompany the Act of Union with Ireland. Fortunately for Tory mythmakers, Pitt did not leave the sort of documentary record behind him that Burke bequeathed to posterity, and this made it easier for them to turn Pitt into a proto-Tory root-and-branch defender of the established constitution in politics and religion, and to establish the cult of this mythical Pitt as one of the key ideological pillars of early nineteenth-century Toryism. The rapid rise of Pitt Clubs as rallying points for Tories in the country was solid evidence of the success of this mythopoeic endeavour.

Toryism became, thus, an amalgam of attitudes centred around the defence of the established aristocratic, landed, Anglican order against both internal opponents (radicals, Catholics and Dissenters) and external enemies (chiefly the French). A central element in this was a defence of the royal prerogative, which inevitably placed this emergent Toryism on the opposite side of the political divide to the Whig critics of 'secret influence'. Many of the politicians whose ministries were to be one of the means of fostering such attitudes, such as North and Pitt the Younger, would have rejected the label 'Tory'. Pitt, for example, always considered himself an 'independent Whig' and self-consciously adopted the non-party principles of his father, Chatham, and of Shelburne as the organizational basis of his long first ministry (1783–1801). Indeed, so inhibiting was Pitt's influence that it was only in the years after his death in 1806 that a Tory *party* can be said to have emerged. Upon Pitt's death, his followers, the Pittites, found themselves excluded from the coalition that was the basis of the Ministry of All the Talents. Excluded thereby from access to the machinery of government, the Pittites found themselves, as the Whigs had done before, in the position of having to develop organizational solutions of their own to compensate for this exclusion. Once back in office in 1807, the party character of the ministry was enhanced by the events surrounding the 'No Popery' election of 1807, an election that began to see the widespread return of the term 'Tory' to the lexicon of British politics. The process of party formation was further facilitated after 1810–11 by George III's removal from the political scene by illness and his replacement as regent by his less able and less active son. This helped to complete the shift from king's party to Tory party that had begun in 1801 with the rift between George III and Pitt. Significantly, this was a process that went on in both the Commons and the Lords, with the first decade of the nineteenth century witnessing the beginnings of the transformation of the party of the crown in the House of Lords into adherents of the Tory party. The year 1812 and the establishment of the Liverpool ministry, which reunited most of the factions into which the Pittites had split in 1801, can be usefully regarded as the effective point of consolidation of a Tory party of government. Estimates of the size of the Tory party are more difficult and less meaningful than those which can be arrived at for the Whig party. This is largely because it is difficult to distinguish Tories from the broader group of Court and Treasury members who naturally supported the government of the day and independent country gentlemen who habitually supported the ministry and contributed substantially to government majorities. For what it is worth, one can identify certain groups that emerged in the aftermath of the break-up of the Pittite coalition in 1801 and would go on to form the core of the Tory party as it emerged in the next decade. Pitt had about sixty personal followers in the Commons, Addington between thirty and forty, Canning around fifteen, with other figures such as Castlereagh and Wellesley leading even smaller groups. From 1812 or so, however, it becomes more legitimate to see the government majority itself as constituting the Tory party (and the opposition minority constituting the Whig party for that matter) as the number of nominally independent MPs declined and most MPs henceforth can be given a party label of one sort or the other.

When one turns away from the world of political parties at the national level, at Westminster, and begins to consider parties in the country at large, in the constituencies, one must recognize that there was an essential discontinuity between party at the national and local levels. When the parties emerged at the centre and then began to attempt to extend their influence at the constituency level, they immediately encountered a pre-existing world of local parties, which had survived continuously throughout the Hanoverian period and which were conditioned by the sort of political issues hinted at earlier, often relating to political control of the constituency itself. Consequently, to be successful, parties at the centre had to work indirectly through local networks of influence. In party terms, therefore, the relationship between parties at the centre and parties in the localities was a dialectical one, with the parties at Westminster forced to accommodate themselves to local political culture while at the same time being able to imbue that culture with wider national elements. A classic example of this came in Liverpool in 1812 when George Canning, out of office but a key figure in the development of early nineteenth-century Toryism, took on two Whig candidates of national standing, Henry Brougham and Thomas Creevey, in an election that inseparably mixed local and national issues in the context of a vibrant local political culture. All three candidates were shocked by the level of popular party-political participation that an election in Liverpool involved and were exhausted by the numerous speeches they had to make and political clubs they had to visit. Moreover, the interaction between local shipping interests and national policy regarding the Orders in Council of 1807 and the war with America neatly illustrated the way local and national issues intertwined. It would not be until well after the period under consideration here, and partly as an unintended consequence of the registration clauses of the Great Reform Act of 1832, that national parties would come anywhere close to imposing their identities on local parties and local political culture.

The emergence in the period 1760–1815 of recognizable Whig and Tory parties at the national level should not delude us into believing that the emergence of a two-party system was either a smooth or inevitable process. The history of the two-party system in this period is one of discontinuity and false starts as much as it is of gradual evolution. If one looks at the political history of the late eighteenth and early nineteenth centuries, one finds an alternation between periods of often short party-political turmoil separated by longer periods of relative stability of party arrangements. Thus, beginning with the 1760s one finds a decade of factional chaos as the leading politicians readjusted themselves to cope with the new conditions brought about by the accession of George III. One key indicator of this is the fast turnover of ministries as both king and politicians jockeyed for position. Between 1760 and 1770 there were five ministries: those of Newcastle (up to 1762); Bute (1762–3); Grenville (1763–5); Rockingham (1765–6); Chatham (1766–8); and Grafton (1768–70). From 1770 to 1782 one sees, by contrast, a period of government by a single ministry, that of Lord North. In turn, this was followed by another brief period of constitutional crisis and party realignment in the years 1782–4 (although it could be argued that the period of instability should be extended back as far as 1779 to include the last years of North's premiership). The Rockingham ministry (1782), the Shelburne ministry (1782–3) and the Fox–North coalition (1783) saw widespread political realignment and gave a great stimulus to party formation on the Whig side of the political divide in particular. Again, in turn, this was followed by a lengthy period of ostensibly non-party government during Pitt's first ministry (1783–1801), which was followed by another decade of political and factional crisis, analogous to the 1760s and accompanied by a similar rate of turnover of ministries as politicians adjusted themselves first to the collapse of the Pittite coalition, and then to the death of Pitt himself: Addington (1801–4); Pitt again (1804–6); the Ministry of All the Talents (1806–7); Portland (1807–9); and Perceval (1809–12). Only with the establishment of the Liverpool government in 1812 was a period of ministerial stability re-established under a Tory party of government. It is essential to realize, however, that ministries are not synonymous with party systems. If one looks behind the changing roll call of ministries one finds that the crucial assumptions and structures of the political landscape of late eighteenth- and early nineteenth-century politics fall into roughly two phases or party systems, with the crucial change coming in the years after 1801. Prior to 1801 the general pattern was one of non-party or even anti-party governments, especially those of North and Pitt, being confronted by party oppositions, respectively the Rockingham and Foxite Whig parties. After 1801 one sees a move towards the acceptance of the principle of organizing as a party among the followers of Pitt, and from around 1812 onwards one can see in operation a two-party system in which a party of government, the Tories, confronts a party of opposition, the Whigs.

The period 1760 to 1815 was, then, an important one for the history of parliament and of party politics in Britain. It saw the emergence of two parties at the national level that began also to take the first tentative steps towards imposing themselves on the parties and political culture of the localities. Moreover, it was a period which saw the emergence of a two-party system in parliament, albeit a system in which one party, the Tories, was permanently in power until the Reform crisis of 1830, and the other, the Whigs, found themselves consigned to continuous opposition.

FURTHER READING

Christie, Ian R.: *British 'Non-Élite' MPs 1715–1820* (Oxford, 1995).

Clark, J. C. D.: 'A general theory of party, opposition and government, 1688–1832', *Historical Journal*, 23 (1980), pp. 295–325.

Dickinson, H. T.: *Liberty and Property: Political Ideology in Eighteenth-Century Britain* (London, 1977).

Foord, A. S.: *His Majesty's Opposition 1714–1830* (Oxford, 1964).

Large, David: 'The decline of "the Party of the Crown" and the rise of parties in the House of Lords, 1783–1837', *English Historical Review*, 78 (1963), pp. 669–95.

Namier, Lewis: *The Structure of Politics at the Accession of George III* (2nd edn, London, 1957).

Namier, Lewis and Brooke, John (eds): *The House of Commons 1754–1790* (3 vols, London, 1964).

O'Gorman, Frank: *The Whig Party and the French Revolution* (Basingstoke, 1967).

O'Gorman, Frank: *The Emergence of the British Two-Party System 1760–1832* (London, 1982).

O'Gorman, Frank: *Voters, Patrons, and Parties: The Unreformed Electoral System of Hanoverian England 1734–1832* (Oxford, 1989).

Pares, Richard: *King George III and the Politicians* (Oxford, 1953).

Phillips, John A.: *Electoral Behavior in Unreformed England: Plumpers, Splitters and Straights* (Princeton, NJ, 1982).

Sack, James J.: 'The memory of Burke and the memory of Pitt: English conservatism confronts its past, 1806–1829', *Historical Journal*, 30 (1987), pp. 623–40.

Thorne, R. G. (ed.): *The House of Commons 1790–1820* (5 vols, London, 1986).

Chapter Seven

The Jacobite Movement

Daniel Szechi

'Jacobites' is the name given to the supporters of the exiled (main) branch of the Stuart dynasty after the Revolution of 1688. The origins of the term are straightforward: it derives from the Latin translation of James II and VII's name: *Jacobus*. The origins, development, dynamics and repercussions of the Jacobite moment in the history of the British Isles are, however, much less clear-cut.

The Jacobite Risings

The military history of the movement is well known and may be briefly summarized. In the aftermath of the Revolution of 1688–9 two areas in the British Isles ultimately remained loyal to James: Ireland (except parts of Ulster) and the central core of the Highlands of Scotland. In Ireland James personally took command in 1689, but was unable to secure control of the whole island because of Ulster Protestant resistance, notably at Enniskillen and Londonderry. William III built up a counter-force of his own in northeastern Ireland in 1689–90 and advanced south to defeat James and his Franco-Jacobite army at the battle of the Boyne on 1 July 1690. James then fled Ireland, leaving the remainder of the war to his generals. In 1691 Williamite forces won a second battle against the Jacobites at Aughrim on 12 July, then besieged Limerick, which finally surrendered on 3 October 1691, effectively terminating the war in the British Isles. The Highland war in Scotland was seen by both sides as a sideshow to the war in Ireland, but was none the less a very damaging affair. The rising begun by Viscount Dundee in May 1689 was primarily a war of raid and counter-raid, though there were a few small battles. In the first of these – the stunning Jacobite victory at Killiecrankie on 17 July 1689 – the Jacobites lost their best commander, Dundee, in the closing minutes. This led to a Jacobite reverse at Dunkeld on 21 August. The war then diminished into a series of raids by Jacobite clans on their Williamite neighbours and Lowland areas close by the Highlands until spring 1690, when a substantial Jacobite force heading for the Lowlands was routed at the Haughs of Cromdale on 1 May. The Jacobites then reverted to raiding and harassing government forces and their supporters. When the Jacobite army in Ireland surrendered, all hope of reinforcement evaporated and the clans accordingly negotiated a surrender of their own. The onset of peace in Scotland was, however, marred by the massacre of the Macdonalds of Glencoe on 13 February 1692 by government forces after their chieftain had already submitted, an atrocity which was to have repercussions in the Highlands for generations to come.

The next major Jacobite rising took place in northern Scotland and northern England in 1715–16. The rebellion officially began on 6 September 1715 at Braemar, where the self-proclaimed leader of the Jacobite movement in Scotland, the earl of Mar, formally declared himself at war with the government at Westminster by raising the standard of James 'VIII' (James II's only surviving son, James Francis Edward Stuart, the 'Old Pretender'). He then collected a formidable army at Perth and lesser forces in other parts of the Highlands and in the northeastern and southern Lowlands, in which at one time or another as many as 20,000 Scotsmen may have appeared in arms. This makes the '15 the biggest, and potentially the most dangerous, of all the Jacobite rebellions. Fortunately for the British government, it was also one of the most incompetently conducted. Mar was a career politician trying to mend his fortunes and had little idea how to use his army. Consequently, it sat at Perth, apart from a couple of brief forays southward (one of which culminated in a drawn battle against government forces at Sheriffmuir on 13 November), until the end of January 1716, when, despite having been joined by his putative monarch, Mar felt compelled to retreat north in the face of a strong government advance out of Stirling. Mar and the Old Pretender fled Scotland on 4 February 1716 and the Jacobite army disintegrated shortly afterwards. The rising in northern England was a much smaller affair that would never have got off the ground if it had not been reinforced by Jacobite rebels from the southern Lowlands led by Viscount Kenmuir and a force of Highlanders under Brigadier William Mackintosh of Borlum sent by Mar. Like the Scottish army, it suffered from very poor leadership and was consequently browbeaten into surrendering after an otherwise successful resistance at the battle of Preston (12–13 November 1715).

The last significant Jacobite rising occurred in 1745. Charles Edward Stuart (the Old Pretender's oldest son) landed in Eriskay on 23 July and by 19 August had persuaded sufficient clan chieftains to follow him to make a viable rebellion. The Jacobites then evaded government forces sent to attack them, seized Edinburgh by a *coup de main* and destroyed the only substantial government army in Scotland at Prestonpans on 21 September. Charles Edward soon thereafter persuaded his Scottish officers to march into England, promising the English Jacobites would join them in large numbers. The Jacobite army crossed the border on 8 November and reached Derby on 5 December, having decisively outmarched and outmanoeuvred its opponents. There, however, the Scots demanded it return to Scotland. Few English Jacobites had in fact joined them, and Charles Edward's officers feared isolation and defeat in a hostile country. By dint of more deft manoeuvring the Jacobite army returned to Scotland virtually unscathed on 20 December. There it regrouped and on 17 January 1746 handed the government forces another defeat at Falkirk. The sheer weight of government reinforcements was, however, beginning to tell and Charles Edward was forced to order a retreat further north, towards Inverness, on 1 February. The Jacobite army was finally brought to bay at Culloden moor near Inverness on 16 April, and there comprehensively defeated. A rally at Ruthven between

17 and 20 April was aborted by Charles Edward's decision to fly the country, which effectively terminated the '45. Despite the decisive nature of its victory, however, the government forces followed up their triumph by savagely harrying the Highlands for several months, leaving a legacy of bitterness that has endured to the present day.

These moments in British history from 1688 to 1760 are only the best-known highlights of the Jacobite movement. There was in addition a brief insurrection in the Highlands in 1719, and abortive attempts by France to invade the British Isles in conjunction with planned Jacobite uprisings in 1692, 1696, 1708, 1744, 1745 and 1759, and by Spain in 1719. As well, quite apart from all these rebellions and invasion plans, Jacobite plots and conspiracies against the existing order were discovered in 1689–90, 1704, 1716–17, 1720–2, 1725–7, 1730–2 and 1750–2. Moreover, these were only the occasions when the authorities had to take dramatic action against the Jacobites, in terms of arrests, formal investigations and executions. Hence, to this already long list of Jacobite events we need to add serious conspiracies that fizzled out before drastic intervention was called for in 1709–10, 1713–14 and 1758–9.

The total is quite instructive. In the course of seventy-two years the Jacobites were responsible for three major rebellions, one minor rebellion, seven planned foreign invasions (two of which actually saw foreign troops land in mainland Britain), and between seven and ten major conspiracies against the state. On average there was a serious Jacobite-related 'event' in the British Isles every one to two years between 1689 and 1722, and every three to four years between 1740 and 1760. Even leaving aside the literally hundreds of other occasions during this period when plebeian English, Scots and Irish rioters against the existing order voiced Jacobite sentiments (for whatever reasons), this is an impressive record.

When we add to this picture of a British polity episodically plagued by Jacobite unrest, statistical estimates of how many people were actually, physically involved in the two major Jacobite uprisings in Scotland, the results are equally illuminating. In both 1715–16 and 1745–6 the Jacobites never controlled more than half of Scotland. None the less, when we take into account the turnover of recruits, i.e., men who joined up, served for a time, and then went home, we arrive at an approximate figure of 20,000 Scots in arms in 1715 and 13,500 in 1745–6. Given that adult males of military age comprised about 25 per cent of a total population of about 1 million in 1715 and 1.2 million in 1745, this means that in the region of 8 per cent of adult Scotsmen served in the Jacobite army in 1715–16 and around 4.5 per cent in 1745–6. By way of comparison, if such figures were duplicated in a Scottish uprising in 2002 the rebels would be fielding 250,000 and 140,000 men, respectively. By any standards, both had sufficient support to pose a major threat to the Whig regime.

Moreover, the frequency of Jacobite events and the degree of support they mobilized on at least two occasions directly challenge old (but persistent) historiographic orthodoxies regarding the stability of the British polity. Even leaving aside the question of how much support the Stuart cause enjoyed in Catholic Ireland, it is clear that no other European *ancien régime* power, except perhaps Poland, faced anything like such a persistent, dynastic/ideological challenge from dissident elements in its own population.

So what prevented the Jacobites from overthrowing their opponents? The underlying strength of the Whig regime, enjoying as it did complete command of the formidable resources of the British fiscal-military state, an unimpeachable commitment to maintaining Protestantism in the British Isles and (by mid-century) the prosperity with which the Hanoverian dynasty and the Whig regime were generally associated, certainly had something to do with it. None the less, the internal dynamics of the Jacobite movement had a central role to play in the final outcome of the struggle, and thus it is to the nature of Jacobitism in the three kingdoms that we must next turn.

Ideology and Objectives

The Jacobites were agreed on only one thing – that the restoration of the exiled James II (1633–1701) and, subsequently, his son, James Francis Edward Stuart (1688–1766), and grandson, Charles Edward Stuart ('Bonnie Prince Charlie', 1720–88), was the best way to achieve their other objectives, whether confessional, political or economic. They did not agree on how best to achieve a restoration or what kind of polity a restored dynasty should reign over.

The chronic internal disagreements that always plagued the Jacobite movement stemmed from the Jacobites' own personal, confessional and national rivalries. Jacobitism enjoyed different levels of support and was centred on different elements in each of the three kingdoms, and, in addition, had a strong base overseas in a pan-European emigrant community. Each element in each kingdom pulled it in a different direction.

England and Wales

In England and Wales Jacobite support derived from three main sources: Nonjurors, Tories and Catholics. The Nonjurors were devout Anglicans who refused to accept the Revolution of 1688–9. In 1689 the Williamite regime imposed an oath of allegiance to William III and Mary II on the clergy of the Church of England. Five bishops, led by the archbishop of Canterbury, William Sancroft, and over 400 lower clergy refused to take the new oath (i.e., became non-jurant; hence Nonjurors) while James II, to whom they had sworn an oath of allegiance at his coronation in 1685, still lived, and were in consequence stripped of their benefices. A small number of primarily elite laity followed them in their exodus from the Church of England. Both lay and clerical Nonjurors were convinced Jacobites, in that they wanted the restoration of the exiled Stuarts and the intolerant high church Anglican regime of the early to mid-1680s, but this did not mean that they were all equally active in supporting the exiled dynasty. A strong quietist tendency soon took hold among the Nonjurors, and many were content simply to withdraw from public affairs and devote themselves to leading pious and exemplary lives. And though a few rejoined the Church of England after James II's death, most remained aloof, adhering to their own schismatic true Church of England. It was this illegal church's congregations who were the bedrock of activist Nonjuring Jacobitism from the 1700s onwards, for in each generation (1689–1760) the Nonjuring church gave rise to a cohort of pious, zealous recruits for every Jacobite conspiracy and uprising that came their way. They were never very numerous (perhaps 1 per cent of all gentry families), but they made up for their paucity of numbers in their dedication to the Jacobite cause.

The English and Welsh Tories played a major, if unenthusiastic, role in the overthrow of James II. It is, therefore, at first glance surprising to find some of them adhering to the exiled Stuarts, particularly in the 1710s and 1740s. The drift back towards allegiance to the dynasty on the part of some English and Welsh Tories owed something to inchoate sentimentalism concerning the Stuarts, in that every Tory gentleman had, or believed he had, an ancestor who fought for Charles I, but more to the peculiar political circumstances of the 1710s and 1740s. There were always a few Tories who were crypto-Jacobites, but in the early 1710s a large number became apprehensive about the likely fate of the Church of England if, as seemed increasingly likely, the Hanoverian dynasty (which was poised to succeed to the throne when Queen Anne, the last surviving Protestant Stuart, died) favoured the Whigs over the Tories. Since support for the Church of England against its Dissenting and Catholic foes was the essence of Toryism, and the Whigs were generally viewed as the friends and allies of Dissent, most Tories were very unhappy at this prospect. Nevertheless, most of them restricted their opposition to the Whig regime established after the Hanoverian succession to public criticism and parliamentary action. A small minority of Tories, however, began to dabble in Jacobite conspiracy with a view to restoring the Tory hegemony of Queen Anne's last years, while their plebeian counterparts rioted and attacked Dissenting churches. Going by the concrete results, in terms of Tory recruits to Jacobite armies and money smuggled overseas to fund the Jacobite cause, most of this was sound and fury signifying nothing. Foreign powers in conflict with the British state, such as France, Sweden and Spain, were, though, episodically impressed with the potential support a strong, nationwide political party like the Tories could deliver in the event of an invasion of the British Isles, if, as the Jacobite government-in-exile persistently claimed, they were wholeheartedly committed to the Jacobite cause. And in the 1740s, when the Tories were angry at having been used by their opposition Whig allies to lever Sir Robert Walpole out of office, only to be unceremoniously dumped as soon as their Whig friends were offered a share in government, some leading Tories asked the French to launch an invasion of England to restore the Stuarts. The invasion was prevented in early 1744 by bad weather, Royal Navy intervention and a resurgence of Tory faintheartedness, but it well demonstrates the power of the Tory chimera to draw Britain's international rivals into direct action in favour of the Stuarts. It does not, however, redound to the credit of those Tories who had claimed they were willing to rise for 'the king over the water' (a notorious Jacobite toast). The sincerity of their pledges is further cast in doubt by their supineness during the '45, when Charles Edward Stuart persuaded his Scots Jacobite army to march as far as Derby by promising them English Tory support, and was then forced to turn back because they had delivered so little. In fairness, it should be noted that the English and Welsh Tories who participated in these conspiracies always flatly stated that they would not turn out unless a large foreign army was landed in England in support of a rising. It is equally the case that this, too, was symptomatic of their irresolution and half-heartedness.

Taken as a whole, the English and Welsh Catholic community was by contrast resolutely loyal to the exiled Stuarts. Though some of the old Catholic families had initially tried to restrain James II's zeal for pro-Catholic reforms, instead favouring a more cautious approach that they hoped would not alienate his Tory political allies, most were eventually caught up in his confident enthusiasm. This was transformed into real hope by the birth of the Prince of Wales on 10 June 1688, which seemed to portend a self-perpetuating pro-Catholic regime. The Catholic community was correspondingly badly exposed when James's government collapsed in the face of William of Orange's invasion. Priests were openly celebrating Mass in publicly licensed chapels and Catholic officers and gentlemen were prominent at all levels of the army and administration. The consequences in the short term were dire: the Catholic church was badly disrupted, as mobs attacked its chapels and magistrates went on priest-hunts all across England and Wales, and Catholics generally were unceremoniously thrown out of office, arrested, fined and otherwise harassed by partisans of the new order. Even after the excitement of 1688–9 had died down, the Williamite regime kept a close watch on the Catholic community for the rest of the 1690s, and arrested and interrogated large numbers of elite Catholics whenever it feared a Jacobite conspiracy was afoot. Despite the disruption and difficulties all this exposed them to (perhaps in part because of them), the English and Welsh Catholics stubbornly sustained their ties to the exiled court at St Germain in the hope that a Stuart restoration would at least secure them religious toleration and might be the precursor to the reconversion of England and Wales to Catholicism. They also held most of the offices at the Jacobite court and were a key component in every Jacobite plot and invasion plan from 1689 to 1715. Where they were strongest, in Lancashire and the northwest, they may even have formed a small underground army, ready to march at short notice to join any uprising or invasion. And in 1715 a hugely disproportionate number of Catholics did turn out to join the Anglo-Scottish Jacobite army that briefly advanced into England as far as Preston. Even so, the total number of English Catholics involved was very low (no more than a few hundred), which starkly highlights the fundamental problem with Catholic support for the Jacobite cause in England and Wales: there were simply too few of them to make a substantial difference. The Catholic community in England and Wales constituted no more than 2 per cent of the population, and though there were pockets in the northwest where the proportion of Catholics may have been as high as 20 per cent, even there they could be no more than an adjunct to a general uprising. For all their loyalty and zeal they could not go it alone. This problem was underscored in the aftermath of the '15, when the Whig regime systematically hit the English Catholic community as a whole with punitive taxation and determinedly sought to expropriate the property of those who had been involved in the rebellion. The Catholic community had accumulated a good deal of experience in ways of evading and blunting such measures since the sixteenth century and it was able, eventually, to do so again after 1715, but it never recovered its former significance in Jacobite affairs. Thereafter, although English and Welsh Catholics remained prominent at the exiled court, and remained quietly loyal to the Stuart dynasty until the late eighteenth century, they played no further role as a community in Jacobite plans and conspiracies. In 1745 a handful of English and Welsh Catholics joined Charles Edward on his march to Derby, but the great majority, even in the northwest, stayed quietly at home and sat out the storm.

England was the economic and demographic powerhouse of the developing British state. As such, it was the prime target for a foreign invasion and/or a Jacobite uprising, for by winning control of England the Jacobites, like William III, would be in a position to overawe and dominate the other kingdoms. Yet it was in England that the Jacobites were weakest. Only the tiny Nonjuror and Catholic communities can be said to have been truly committed to the Stuart cause (and, it should be noted, for fundamentally opposed reasons in terms of their non-dynastic objectives). The Tories periodically seemed to offer a broader, stronger base of support, but in a crisis they always proved a broken reed. Hence, if the Stuarts were ever to be restored, the Jacobites had to find a powerful alternative source of support.

Scotland

Hence the significance of Scotland for the Jacobite cause. Given that control of England was the key to control of the British Isles, the obvious next best thing to a strong party in England and Wales was one in Scotland. Because Scotland and England had a land frontier, a Jacobite takeover of Scotland would potentially secure an excellent springboard for an invasion of England. The Jacobites were, then, fortunate that political and military events in Scotland after 1688 ensured that Scotland became a real source of strength for the exiled Stuarts.

Though the Scottish political nation was bitterly divided in 1689, it was far from inevitable that this would fall out to the advantage of James II and his heirs. One of the abiding legacies of the great civil war of the mid-seventeenth century in Scotland was the division of the country into two hostile religious camps. On one side stood the kirk by law established. This was the state church created by the new religious settlement enacted after 1660. It was a strongly Protestant institution, but one presided over by bishops after the fashion of the Church of England (though without the medieval holdovers that characterized Anglicanism) and one which placed a heavy emphasis on the subjects' obligation to be loyal and obedient to the earthly powers ordained by God, and in particular the reigning Stuart dynasty. Separated from the kirk by an insurmountable barrier of ecclesiology were the various strains of Covenanters. These were the surviving remnants of the Presbyterian regime in church and state who controlled Scotland from 1638 to 1650. They refused to accept the reinstitution of episcopacy after 1660, resisted the imposition of ministers loyal to the Restoration settlement of the kirk and withdrew (led in many cases by their former Presbyterian pastors) from their parish churches to worship in field conventicles. There they continued to uphold the righteousness of the Solemn League and Covenant and the church settlement of the mid-1640s, and when the government attempted to suppress them by force they resisted in arms. Covenanting was at its strongest in the southern Lowlands, while the Episcopal kirk was strongest in the northeastern Lowlands and Highlands. Either church could have served the Williamite regime well. The Episcopalian kirk was entrenched in parishes throughout Scotland and prided itself on its loyalty to the powers that be. The Covenanters were zealous Protestants who were delighted by William's victory over the popish King James. What swayed the balance between them was the Episcopalian bishops' decision to withhold their support from the Williamite regime. Civil war soon followed, in the form of Viscount Dundee's rebellion and the subsequent Highland war of 1689–91, and consequently William III had little choice but to take the former Covenanters as his allies. The price of their support was a wholesale purge of the kirk, as the ex-Covenanters expelled their rivals, re-established Presbyterianism and abolished episcopacy. In effect, the establishment and the alienated minority of the pre-1688 era exchanged places. Henceforth, the Presbyterian heirs of the Covenanters controlled the kirk and their former Episcopalian enemies were forced into schism and resistance outside it.

Since the Episcopalians amounted to 25–30 per cent of the population well into the eighteenth century, they posed a serious threat to the stability of the new order in Scotland. Yet they were not quickly, or ever entirely, committed to the Jacobite cause. Forays by the Jacobite Highland army into the heartland of Scottish Episcopalianism, the northeastern Lowlands, during 1689 initially drew only limited support from the Episcopalian community. Only as the new controllers of the kirk began to intrude into the localities, prosecuting Episcopal ministers who refused to leave their charges and imposing Presbyterians in their stead (regardless of local landowners' rights and opinions), did the tide of Episcopalian opinion turn decisively in favour of the exiled Stuarts. The Highland war was winding down before this could have any significant impact on its outcome, but the war in turn created new grievances that strengthened Jacobitism's appeal within Scotland, even outwith the Episcopalian community. Most notoriously, the massacre of the Macdonalds of Glencoe in February 1692 shocked and disgusted a broad spectrum of Scots after news of it began to circulate some months later, and contributed to their gathering alienation from the Williamite regime. The hidden engine driving this process was, however, the enforced dependence of the Revolutioners (as they were known) in government in Edinburgh on their English counterparts. The government of Scotland was effectively bankrupted by the costs of waging the Highland war and was only able to fight it to a conclusion because of English subsidies and English troops, all supplied with ill-grace by the government at Westminster, which considered Scotland a tiresome distraction. Their government's visible dependence on the fickle favour of English politicians rankled with many Scots (not just the Jacobites), and this resentment came to a head over the Darien affair of 1696–9. This was an attempt by the Royal Company of Scotland Trading to Africa and the Indies to plant a Scots colony on the isthmus of Darien (now in modern Panama). The venture was ill-judged and almost doomed to failure, as Scotland did not possess the resources successfully to plant a colony in such a fever-infested part of the world in the teeth of Spanish opposition without substantial English support. Since Spain was England's ally and the English parliament had no intention of backing an interloping Scottish venture begun in defiance of English disapproval, such support was not forthcoming. None the less, it seized the imagination of the Scots as a nation, and close to 25 per cent of Scotland's liquid assets were invested in the venture. The nation was consequently appalled and angry when it proved a dismal failure, and politicians and people soon fastened the blame on Scotland's government and the English connection.

Just as the Darien affair was drawing to a close, however, a succession crisis loomed. William III had no children, and hence, according to the terms of the Revolution Settlement, when he died his sister-in-law Princess Anne of Denmark, James II's last surviving Protestant child, was set to inherit the throne. Unfortunately, her last surviving child died in 1700, and as she was too infirm for there to be any realistic hope of her producing another heir, it became apparent that the Stuart dynasty's non-exiled branch was about to die out. The nearest Protestant heirs to the throne were the Guelph Electors of Hanover, and these were confirmed as Anne's heirs by the English Act of Settlement in 1701. Many in the Scots parliament, however, saw this dynastic crisis as a golden opportunity either to end the union of crowns between Scotland and England that had existed since 1603, or to extract some serious trade concessions from the English in return for accepting a continued dynastic union. Both elements therefore collaborated to block passage of a similar act of succession through the Scots parliament, precipitating a major confrontation between the English parliament, which was determined to make Scotland accept the Hanoverian succession, and the Scots political nation. The eventual outcome was the union of England and Scotland in 1707, in which Scotland got its trade concessions, but at the price of its independence. This bargain was a bitter pill even for those Scots who basically supported it for religious or economic reasons (the union also guaranteed the continued Presbyterianism of the kirk), but it incensed a great many more who did not accept the deal. Shrewd political management, a good deal of horse-trading and some straightforward bribery none the less secured the passage of the Act of Union through the Scottish parliament despite the vocal disapproval of most of the Scottish political nation. And the group best placed to capitalize on their discontent were the Jacobites, who first promised to repeal the union almost immediately after it was passed. Thereafter the Stuart cause in Scotland became inextricably identified with the cause of Scottish independence. This was the mainstay of the Jacobites' appeal there clear to the end of the Jacobite era, and even reached beyond the Episcopalian community that was the bedrock of their support to attract a small minority of Presbyterians, who valued an independent Scotland more than they valued the guaranteed ascendancy of the Presbyterian kirk under the terms of the union.

Jacobite support in Scotland was thus much more substantial than in England. By the early eighteenth century the exiled Stuarts could count on relatively solid support from the alienated Episcopalian community, which also included many Highland clans. In addition, though few Presbyterians identified with the national cause so strongly as to go openly against their church's strictures on the subject (which increasingly identified the well-being of the kirk with the continuation of the union), a significant minority remained hostile to the union which the Jacobites were pledged to overturn. For at least a generation after 1707 this minority periodically seemed to offer hope of a pan-Scottish alliance to restore the Stuarts and end the union, which gave the Jacobites hope of a grand patriotic alliance and a national uprising – which in turn enhanced the attractiveness of Scotland as the site for a Jacobite insurrection.

Ireland

If Scotland was a source of strength for the exiled dynasty, prima facie Ireland should have been ten times more valuable. It had an alienated *majority* rather than an alienated minority, powerful cultural and economic grievances focused on the English connection and strong overseas connections that should have boosted its chances of securing foreign help. Yet Ireland was the dog that did not bark after 1691.

Part of the reason for Ireland's apparent quiescence lay in its recent history and its experiences in the Revolution of 1688. The populations of all three kingdoms undoubtedly underwent prolonged suffering and trauma in the course of the great civil war of the mid-seventeenth century. England is estimated to have suffered 190,000 casualties due to fighting, disease and the other incidentals of early modern conflicts, amounting in total to something in the region of 3.7 per cent of the population (by way of comparison, Britain suffered a total population loss of 2.61 per cent as a result of World War I – a war that undoubtedly scarred the national psyche for the rest of the twentieth century). Scotland suffered more than England, losing an estimated 6 per cent of its total population. Ireland, however, outstripped them both: modern estimates of its population loss between 1641 and 1660 are in the region of a staggering 40 per cent. Ireland was, consequently, just beginning to recover twenty-five years later when James II succeeded to the throne, and the mass of the population was doubtless chary of repeating its experience of civil war. Nevertheless, we should not underrate either the resilience of the Irish, nor the appeal James's religion held for the 75 per cent of the Irish population who were Catholic. The new king was, correspondingly, initially very popular in Ireland, and he in turn favoured the Irish more than any of his predecessors in that its Catholic population featured prominently in his plans to build up a solid Catholic presence in government and the military throughout the British Isles that would outlive him and secure the religious toleration he wanted to leave as his legacy. Hence, when William of Orange invaded England, Ireland was the only one of the three kingdoms which stayed resolutely loyal. William's successful usurpation, however, stimulated a general uprising by the Protestants of Ulster in the spring of 1689 and the ensuing civil war lasted from then until the autumn of 1691.

Ireland was not alone in suffering a civil war between 1689 and 1691 (Scotland did too), but, as with the great civil war, there can be no doubt that Ireland suffered more than its sister kingdoms. The Jacobites put up a determined resistance to the Williamites, which had the usual consequences in terms of towns besieged, bombarded and plundered, farms burned and population displaced. Fortunately, the war was relatively brief and was not characterized by massive human slaughter on the scale of the mid-seventeenth century, which in turn opened the way to a surprisingly quick recovery. Indeed, by the mid-1690s the Irish economy was expanding so rapidly that English merchants were complaining about Irish competition.

From the Jacobite point of view, far more serious than the human and material damage inflicted by the fighting were the terms on which the war ended. For the Articles of Limerick profoundly affected the nature of Jacobite support in Ireland. By the articles some 15,000–16,000 Jacobite troops were given the choice of peacefully returning home, transferring to the service of William III or withdrawing to France to carry on the war. Over 14,000 chose to leave for France, and it was this corps of Irish exiles who were to form the basis of the Irish brigade in the French army for the next three generations.

In principle, the creation of a Catholic Irish army overseas was a positive gain for the Stuart cause. Once James was gone, the Old Pretender and his son Charles Edward were soon adopted as icons of hope by their erstwhile (Catholic) Irish subjects, and featured as yearned-for rescuers, indeed the living embodiment of Catholic Ireland's coming salvation, in Gaelic *Aisling* poetry and peasant folklore for nearly a century. They would, the poets promised, redeem Ireland and fulfil long-held plebeian Catholic dreams of overturning the land settlement that underpinned the Protestant Ascendancy. And consequently, over the next seventy years, tens of thousands of young Irishmen responded to the lure of adventure, idealism and opportunity represented by the Irish brigades to slip away to France (and later to Spain too), and join their compatriots in arms in the belief that some day they would return to Ireland in triumph. They thereby escaped the discrimination and poverty that was their lot in Ireland and entered a prosperous exiled community that prided itself on its loyalty to the Stuarts. The problem was that the Stuarts never controlled the Irish brigades. They were a valued, elite corps of the French, and subsequently Spanish, armies and were cherished and rewarded as such. And, inevitably, the officers and men of the brigade responded warmly to such treatment, so that as the years went on, and plans to use the Irish brigade as the spearhead of a French invasion of the British Isles came and went, it became in effect a bridge for the naturalization and absorption of Jacobite Irishmen into French and Spanish society rather than a Stuart army in waiting. In addition, by bleeding off the boldest and most militant young men in the Catholic population, the very existence of the brigades fostered quiescence in Ireland. If their poetry and the oaths they took to their secret societies are anything to go by, Catholic peasants still dreamed of a Stuart restoration clear to the end of the eighteenth century, but many of their best and brightest young men and the sons of the remnants of the Catholic elite who might have led them in rebellion in Ireland were overseas fighting and dying for France and Spain.

Rather than being a dog that did not bark then, Ireland was one that was too enervated to make much noise. Despite their experiences in the mid-seventeenth century, the Catholic Irish fought hard for the Stuart cause in the 1690s, which they saw as the vehicle for the re-establishment of a Catholic ascendancy in Ireland and the assertion of Irish sovereignty against English domination (which objectives, it should be noted, directly conflicted with the aims and agendas of their Protestant Scots and English fellow-Jacobites), and during the Jacobite war of 1689–91 their economy and society suffered accordingly. It is not, therefore, altogether surprising that a more cautious spirit prevailed for a generation or so thereafter. This in turn was insensibly reinforced by the steady siphoning off of many of the more restless spirits within the Irish Catholic community by the Irish brigades in the service of France and Spain. And, while it was all too apparent to later generations that these units were not necessarily phenomena that were in the best interests of the Catholic Irish, it was much less clear-cut at the time. In a sense, many of the young Irishmen who undertook the hazardous journey overseas to join the Irish brigades were actually rebelling against the existing order in Ireland, and clear up to 1759 the promise they would surely one day return as part of a French invasion force headed by the Stuarts was a major draw for new recruits.

The exiles

The final community towards which the Stuarts could look for support was not located in the British Isles, but in continental Europe. Accustomed as we are to looking westward, across the Atlantic to America and the Caribbean, when we think of migration out of the British Isles in the late seventeenth and eighteenth centuries, it is easy to overlook the substantial migration of British peoples to the rest of Europe. It began to tail off, and the outflow of migrants to refocus on the American colonies, from about the 1720s, but a significant British diaspora survived on the continent until the second half of the eighteenth century, and it was an abiding source of support for the exiled Stuarts.

Each of the three nations had its zones of preferred settlement. The Jacobite English and Welsh overseas community was the smallest, which is not surprising as it stemmed disproportionately from the elite among the tiny Catholic minority. It was thus a community that was primarily church-centred, and hence revolved around the long-established continental bastions of the English Counter-Reformation, such as the Jesuit college at Douai and the English College in Rome. The only other Jacobite Englishmen and Welshmen permanently resident in Europe were a scattering of, primarily Catholic, English and Welsh officers serving in foreign armies. Though the community's size was briefly boosted by the flight abroad of some English and Welsh Jacobites in 1689 and 1716, it always remained small and weak compared to the others. Hence, the English and Welsh community on the continent was the least helpful from the point of view of the exiled dynasty.

The Scottish Jacobite continental community was significantly larger than its Anglo-Welsh counterpart. It, too, contained a network of Counter-Reformation institutions, including colleges in Paris and Rome, but its main source of recruits was primarily Protestant Scottish refugees fleeing government retribution in the aftermath of the '15 and '45. Merchants and professionals (mainly physicians) as well as military officers were involved in this migration (though many of the poorer elite exiles did not turn up their noses at the thought of going into business), and they seem to have moved into existing Scottish expatriate commercial communities and hence adapted better to their host societies than their more elite counterparts. This meant that significant elements of the Scottish Jacobite community on the continent were evanescent, in that they were rapidly integrating with their surrounding societies, but by the same token it tended to mean that they were soon well connected in ways that proved very useful to the Jacobite movement. Hence the ability of Scottish merchants in Gothenburg to facilitate projects like the raising of troops in Sweden for service in the '45 and the negotiation of loans in Paris by the Jacobite court using the good offices of Scottish bankers long resident in the city. The Scottish exile community was always, however, a diminishing asset because the merchants and professionals were in the process of assimilating and the elite refugees for the most part returned home as soon as it was safe to do so. To maintain a viable expatriate community there needed to be a constant flow of new immigrants, and as the eighteenth century wore on more and more Scots emigrants sought new lives in America rather than in traditional destinations in Europe.

The Irish Jacobite diaspora was much more limited in geographic scope than its Scottish counterpart, being virtually confined to Catholic Europe and France and Spain in particular. Like the Anglo-Welsh community, it too had well-established Counter-Reformation institutions at its core, but in the Irish case the sheer size of the immigrant community meant that the church did not dominate its activity or its connections with the societies in which it was domiciled. The expatriate Irish community, both mercantile and military, consistently supported the exiled Stuarts whenever they had the opportunity, and given the Irish military exiles' status as elite corps in the French and Spanish armies and the major role played in the expansion of French overseas commerce by Irish merchants like Antoine Walsh, they were well placed to persuade the governments of their host nations to listen to overtures from the Jacobite government-in-exile. It is no coincidence that Charles Edward Stuart sailed for Scotland in 1745 on a ship owned by Walsh accompanied by 700 men of the Regiment de Clare and that the very last Jacobite invasion attempt, in 1759, was originally set in motion by the extremely well-connected Thomas Arthur Tolendal, comte de Lally, and commander of the Irish brigade in France.

Each of the exile communities favoured its own nation's agenda in the event of a Jacobite restoration, and this led to clashes on an individual and national basis at the Jacobite court. But in practical terms such squabbling mattered little. All three elements of the Jacobite diaspora were willing to do what they could to get the Stuarts home. Despite their mutual jealousies they recognized that until a Stuart was back on the throne they could never achieve the rest of their respective agendas. And without the support, and especially the local connections, freely provided by the immigrant communities of the three nations, the Stuart cause would have been crippled, and must soon have languished and died. Moreover, of the three diasporas there can be no doubt that the most important and consistently supportive was the Irish.

Conflicting agendas

It will be readily apparent by this point that – beyond the restoration of the dynasty – the aims and objectives of the various strands of Jacobitism were highly divergent. In England and Wales after 1714 the Tories' and Nonjurors' aims were purely revanchist, i.e., getting the Whigs out and putting the Tories back in – permanently. They certainly did not envisage any change in the status quo regarding England's imperial domination of the rest of the British Isles. The only difference between them was how extreme the new restoration settlement should be. By contrast, the English and Welsh Catholics' only real ambition was to secure a sympathetic monarch who would protect them from Protestant zealots. In Scotland almost all Jacobites were committed Scottish patriots-cum-nationalists and saw a Stuart restoration as the way to end the union with England. Beyond that, the Episcopalians (i.e., the great majority of Scottish Jacobites) aimed at the restoration of Episcopalianism in the kirk and some degree of revenge upon their Presbyterian foes. In Ireland the Jacobites (who were almost all Catholics) aimed at the restoration of the Catholic church as the state church, the return of land confiscated from Catholics over the course of the seventeenth century and the breaking (or at least the severe attenuation) of English control over the Irish parliament.

It is clear that these secondary ambitions were not compatible. The English and Welsh Tories had no intention of relinquishing English control over Ireland, or, after 1707, over Scotland. Neither they nor the Scots wanted to see a Catholic state in Ireland; both were suspicious of Catholicism and wanted to grant the Catholics nothing beyond the most minimal, grace-and-favour, religious toleration. In addition, the Tories were contemptuous of the Scots, whom they regarded as importunate beggars, and the Scottish Jacobites were the heirs to the fine old Scottish tradition of anglophobia. And all these prejudices, suspicions and jealousies – and their associated personality clashes – were the meat and drink of politics at the exiled court from 1689 to the 1760s.

Great Power Politics

Yet, as we have seen, the Stuart cause remained vital and dangerous for over seventy years. What sustained it so long, despite its internal contradictions as a movement within the British Isles, was the ability of the Old Pretender and his son to keep the dynasty's adherents in the three kingdoms focused on the most immediate issues: restoring the dynasty, and their supporters' fundamental acceptance of that basic starting point. Beginning very reluctantly with James himself in 1693, the exiled monarchs steadily compromised everything the regnant James II had stood for in terms of the role of the monarchy in church and state in order to satisfy their adherents and keep them cooperative. This in turn enabled the Jacobite court to present an agreeable image of itself to every potential foreign backer. When negotiating with Spain, for example, the exiled dynasty played up its Catholic credentials and secretly promised to work towards the re-establishment of Catholicism in all three kingdoms. By contrast, when it negotiated with Sweden the dynasty blandly pointed up its ironclad, public commitment to maintaining the Protestant settlement throughout the British Isles, thus assuaging any qualms the Vasas might have had about reinstalling a Catholic dynasty in a Protestant kingdom. The net effect was to give the exiled Stuarts a financial and political lifeline, for this ability to make themselves acceptable to the major powers of Europe, whatever those great powers' own agendas might be, secured a trickle of support just sufficient to keep the movement alive until the 1750s.

It was, of course, also greatly to the advantage of the other great powers of Europe to have a viable Jacobite movement (in the sense of one able to foment a rebellion in some part of the British Isles) ready to hand. Several of the major dynasties of Europe, among whom the French and Spanish Bourbons were the most important, genuinely sympathized with the plight of the exiled Stuarts, but *realpolitik* dictated that they could not always openly favour their cause. Hence, the peace of Ryswick in 1697, the peace of Utrecht in 1713 and the peace of Aix-la-Chapelle in 1748 – the treaties that ended all three major wars of the Jacobite era – all contained clauses requiring the Bourbons to abandon the Stuarts and expel them and their adherents from their territories. And France, Spain and the other great powers of Europe duly observed the letter of such commitments, but not the spirit – unless it served their interests. Thus, despite their treaty obligations, both France and Spain quietly subsidized the Stuart court (and hence the Jacobite movement) for most of the century after 1688. In time of war, or even just tension with Britain, they could then either openly or semi-covertly encourage the Jacobites with money and arms and/or the promise of an invasion force. This in turn would nicely distract the British government and force them to keep troops, ships and resources at home that otherwise would have been deployed against the Bourbons in continental Europe, the West Indies or North America. In the event of a serious Jacobite uprising, there was, too, the delicious possibility (so they believed) of a Jacobite victory, or at the very least a catastrophic civil war that would knock Britain out of whichever war was currently under way. Even being seen to be semi-covertly encouraging the Jacobites could be useful in terms of international relations, as it encouraged British governments to make diplomatic concessions in the hope of avoiding serious trouble. Because Britain was also one of the most aggressive *ancien régime* powers, the Jacobites (the like of whom existed nowhere else in Europe) were especially useful for Britain's rivals and so the other great powers kept the Stuart cause going for as long as they could.

Successive defeats, periodic bouts of government harassment, gathering despair and disgust at the boorish, drunken paranoia of Charles Edward Stuart after the '45 progressively eroded Jacobite support in mainland Britain. By the mid-1750s all the Stuarts' major adherents there had ceased communication with the exiled dynasty. Only Ireland (and in particular the Irish diaspora) remained loyal. And the Jacobite movement effectively died there in 1759, when the last French attempt to invade Britain in the name of the Stuarts had to be abandoned after the Royal Navy defeated its French counterpart at the battle of Quiberon Bay. Thereafter all that was left of the movement was the ageing, dwindling group of exiles attached to the Stuart court at Rome and a scattered handful of diehards in the British Isles.

The Legacy of Jacobitism

The repercussions of the Jacobite phenomenon were as complex as its roots in the three kingdoms. In England and Wales Jacobitism became associated in the popular imagination with boneheaded reaction, despite the fact that in its final phase there Jacobitism had embodied an agenda that was quite radical (including statutory freedom of the press, annual, reformed parliaments and the disbandment of the standing army). In Scotland the defeat of the Jacobites was the death knell of Episcopalianism, which shrank to a tiny minority church, and also served to damn anything resembling nationalism for well over a century. The sentimental Jacobitism popularized by Sir Walter Scott might superficially appear to have made it more respectable, but the implicit burden of his stories was that the Jacobites were noble, foolish children. Only in Ireland did Jacobitism leave a cherished legacy. Catholic peasant secret societies such as the Whiteboys and Defenders retained references to the Stuarts in their oaths and rituals. And like the Irish brigades they now form part of the mythistory of modern Ireland, symbolizing the constancy of Irish resistance to English rule. From a nationalist perspective, Jacobitism came to be seen as an early vehicle for Irish national aspirations; nationalism *avant la lettre*.

In terms of British history in this period, there can be little doubt that the Jacobite phenomenon implicitly questions a number of existing orthodoxies. The persistence and violence of Jacobite resistance reinforces the argument that eighteenth-century Britain may not have been as stable a polity as is commonly believed. The nationalist edge to Scottish and Irish Jacobitism challenges the assumption that modern nationalism was a product of the French Revolution or the nineteenth century. The fundamentally religious nature of Jacobitism in all three kingdoms implies that the age of confessional war did not end with the great civil war in the British Isles. Jacobitism is thus a dog in the manger for the orthodox view of the eighteenth century, and as such continues to be a fruitful producer of the scholarly discords through which history advances as a discipline.

FURTHER READING

Baynes, John: *The Jacobite Rising of 1715* (London, 1970).

Bennett, G. V.: *The Tory Crisis in Church and State, 1688–1730: The Career of Francis Atterbury, Bishop of Rochester* (Oxford, 1975).

Cruickshanks, Eveline (ed.): *Ideology and Conspiracy: Aspects of Jacobitism, 1689–1759* (Edinburgh, 1982).

Cruickshanks, Eveline and Black, Jeremy (eds): *The Jacobite Challenge* (Edinburgh, 1988).
Fritz, Paul S.: *The English Ministers and Jacobitism Between the Rebellions of 1715 and 1745* (Toronto, 1975).
Hopkins, Paul: *Glencoe and the End of the Highland War* (rev. edn, Edinburgh, 1998).
Lenman, Bruce: *The Jacobite Risings in Britain 1689–1746* (London, 1980).
McLynn, Frank J.: *France and the Jacobite Rising of 1745* (Edinburgh, 1981).
McLynn, Frank J.: *Charles Edward Stuart: A Tragedy in Many Acts* (London, 1988).
Miller, John: *James II: A Study in Kingship* (Hove, 1978).
Monod, Paul K.: *Jacobitism and the English People 1688–1788* (Cambridge, 1989).
Pittock, Murray G. H.: *The Myth of the Jacobite Clans* (Edinburgh, 1997).
Szechi, Daniel: *Jacobitism and Tory Politics, 1710–14* (Edinburgh, 1984).
Szechi, Daniel: *The Jacobites: Britain and Europe 1688–1788* (Manchester, 1994).

Chapter Eight

Popular Politics and Radical Ideas

H. T. Dickinson

Eighteenth-century Britain was a monarchical state, with an aristocratic legislature and an established state church, but it was still widely regarded as one of the freest societies in the world. The ruling aristocratic elite dominated the royal court, the cabinet, both houses of parliament and the law courts, and expected the state church to teach the common people to obey those in positions of authority. The elite were convinced that they had the right to govern their social inferiors and they believed that democracy was inherently unstable and would inevitably degenerate into anarchy. This did not mean, however, that this elite believed that they could act in an arbitrary, oppressive or tyrannical fashion. They were expected to maintain public order, to deliver justice to all, and to uphold the rule of law and the lives, liberty and property of all British subjects. Whilst they believed that only a propertied minority should play an active role in the government of the British state, they did concede that all men possessed certain civil liberties and were free men living in a free state.

The political life of eighteenth-century Britain was dominated by the aristocratic elite, but it was not controlled by them in every respect. Many men outside the ranks of the elite played an active role in parliamentary elections or engaged in political campaigns to influence the decisions taken by the elite who sat in parliament. In the numerous and growing towns of Britain the commercial and professional middle classes created their own distinctive political culture, in which the press and voluntary societies played a major role, and they learned to dominate urban politics. Even poor British subjects learned how to restrict the power of the ruling elite, and even sometimes to influence their decisions, by combining together in crowd demonstrations and popular disturbances. Without an adequate civil police force, and reluctant to deploy a large army at home in policing duties, the ruling elite were often compelled to adopt a conciliatory stance rather than resort to repressive tactics in order to respond to the numerous direct challenges they faced to their authority from their social inferiors. For their part, the middle classes and even the poor became increasingly politicized during the eighteenth century and, by the later eighteenth century, they began to campaign for political reforms which would make the ruling elite more responsible to the people at large. Many of them began to cast off the ideological fetters made for them by clerical and conservative propagandists and they engaged in a prolonged and profound debate on the rights of men in general, and the liberties of British subjects in particular. In the earlier eighteenth century British subjects critical of the governing elite tended to adopt the ideology and programme of the parliamentary opposition and mainly sought to purify the existing constitution of its abuses. By the later eighteenth century radicals and reformers had begun to appear outside parliament and began to enlist widespread support for policies which would make parliament accountable to an extended electorate. By the end of the eighteenth century even those ordinary British subjects, who still admired the existing constitution and who opposed radical reform, were prepared to act independently of the ruling elite in defence of a political system which they freely chose to support.

The People and Parliamentary Elections

The right to vote in parliamentary elections was restricted to adult males who possessed certain property qualifications. In the counties the franchise was possessed by freeholders who owned land valued for taxation purposes at forty shillings (two pounds) per annum. In the boroughs the franchise varied, ranging from members of the town council, through all freemen possessing certain properties and privileges, to all householders paying certain local rates and taxes. In the earlier eighteenth century the total electorate in England and Wales was about 300,000 men, about 23 per cent of the adult male population. By the late eighteenth century the total had increased to about 400,000 voters, but this was now only about 17 per cent of adult males. The total and percentage were much lower in Scotland, where there were only about 3,000 voters. The larger English counties had thousands of voters. In a handful of English boroughs 40 per cent or more of the adult males possessed the vote, and in a significant number of boroughs the proportion was about 25 per cent. The majority of voters across the whole country were men drawn from the middling ranks of society, though about 15 per cent of voters were drawn from the poorer sections of society. In nearly all English constituencies the voters possessed two votes. Even in the smallest of these constituencies the local aristocratic patron could usually only command one of these votes. The electors usually cherished their votes and desired to exercise some control over how they were cast. In the smaller constituencies they expected to be asked for their vote and to be rewarded in some manner for disposing of it as the local elite requested. In the larger constituencies they often prided themselves on their political independence and they might rebel against powerful patrons who sought to dictate how they should use their votes.

The propertied elite certainly made determined efforts to dominate parliamentary elections and in the many small constituencies they could usually ensure that their candidates were elected, often without an actual contest at the polls. Only in the minority of large county and borough constituencies, with voters running into the thousands, did really serious contests, involving the views of the voters, take place. Parliamentary elections were very expensive to contest and MPs required substantial property qualifications to sit in parliament, and hence only rich men sat in parliament. But these facts do not mean that the voters could ever be taken entirely for granted. All candidates competing in the larger constituencies and even patrons seeking to manage the smaller constituencies had to court and woo the voters. Voters were canvassed and courted, treated and flattered, even when no poll was expected. In the larger constituencies the candidates had to spend a great deal of time, energy and money in order to canvass the electors and get the voters to the polls. While the direct bribing of voters was extremely rare, candidates and their patrons were expected to place their economic resources, social status and political influence at the service of the voters. They were expected to spend money in their constituencies to the benefit of the voters, to contribute generously to the erection of public buildings and the creation of local amenities, and to distribute charity when times were hard. Whenever possible they were also expected to help their constituents to secure minor government posts and contracts, leases of land and property, and access to local schools and hospitals. They refrained from treating the voters as servile dependants, but sought instead to earn their gratitude by the skilful use of their patronage. Wise patrons and candidates tried to influence voters with great tact and careful preparations. They accepted that electoral deference had to be earned, and could not be commanded. Any MP who neglected his constituents after the election might find it difficult to retain his seat at the next election.

Electoral activity was never confined solely to those constituencies that went to the polls or even to those qualified to cast a vote. Even small constituencies and safe seats were carefully nursed and regularly canvassed. When a poll was required the voters could expect benefits and favours in return for the political service that they were expected to perform. They were transported to the polls free of charge and reimbursed for the expense of taking time off to travel and to cast their votes. Contested elections in the larger constituencies could extend over several days. This increased the political excitement and, since voting was in public and was openly expressed, these elections could draw in excited spectators who were not even qualified to vote. Such elections became a public spectacle and even an emotionally charged theatrical event. Music, effigies, gun salutes, firework displays, bonfires and bell-ringing – as well as a great deal of eating and drinking – could enliven proceedings and entertain the whole community. As a form of street theatre parliamentary elections drew many voters and many non-voters into the accompanying crowds, audiences, processions and celebrations. On occasion these festivities could get out of hand and degenerate into electoral riots when the social order was temporarily inverted.

Contested elections were more numerous in the earlier and later decades of the eighteenth century. In most contested elections the voters were primarily concerned with local issues and they expected their MPs to represent their local interests in parliament whenever necessary. National interests and issues impinged on parliamentary elections only when the political elite themselves were sharply divided along ideological, religious or party lines or when the nation faced a major crisis at home or abroad. When such issues split the elite, the votes of the electorate were worth more to rival candidates and the voters could gain more for putting them at the disposal of these candidates. Political tensions also allowed the voters in the larger constituencies even greater independence from the governing elite seeking their votes. They expected more from their MPs and were more willing to attempt to instruct their MP on how to vote in parliament. By the late eighteenth century voters in some thirty to forty constituencies were ready to put up and vote for independent or even radical candidates.

Pressure-Group Politics

Although the great majority of the British people were excluded from direct representation in the decision-making institutions of the state, they did learn to bring pressure to bear upon government and parliament and to defend their own vested interests by organized press, petitioning and lobbying campaigns. A high proportion of the bills passed by parliament were private or local bills which were not drawn up by the government, but were proposed by backbench MPs as a result of pressure applied by their constituents. Many of these bills were drafted by local vested interests outside the governing elite and were discussed in the local community and promoted in the local press before being promoted in parliament by local MPs. Parliament therefore did not just advance and support measures to safeguard the interests of the aristocratic landed elite who dominated the composition of both houses, but passed legislation to promote the interests of a wide range of people who had no direct influence on the government.

The great financial corporations, such as the Bank of England, the East India Company and the South Sea Company, could bring considerable influence to bear upon government and parliament and secured government action or legislative measures to promote their interests. So could less powerful trading companies such as the Russia Company, the Levant Company and the Hudson Bay Company, as well as the wealthy merchants and planters involved in the prosperous West Indian trade. At times, groups of independent merchants and manufacturers based in different towns, but engaged in the same line of business, combined through press, petitioning and lobbying campaigns to influence the decisions of government or parliament. The wine and tobacco merchants, for example, combined in effective opposition to Robert Walpole's excise bill of 1733, while the cider interest forced the repeal of the excise tax on cider in 1763, and the merchants and manufacturers trading with the American colonies helped to secure the repeal of the Stamp Act in 1766. By the late eighteenth century industrial lobbying had become standard practice among the manufacturing interests in the industrializing areas of the country. The cotton masters of Manchester, for example, were able to persuade William Pitt to abandon his cotton tax in 1785 and to amend his proposed trade concessions to Ireland.

Much weaker economic interests could also influence government and parliament. The smaller tradesmen of Newcastle-upon-Tyne could persuade parliament to pass an act in 1774 which protected their interests in the common land of the Town Moor. Even ordinary working men could sometimes persuade parliament to protect their interests. While parliament often passed legislation limiting the activities of combinations or trade unions of workers, it did on occasion listen to the grievances of specific groups of workers. In 1721, for example, violent protests, combined with more sophisticated lobbying and over ninety petitions from all parts of the country, persuaded parliament to forbid the importation of foreign calicoes that was causing considerable unemployment among English weavers.

Organized pressure groups were established not just to serve material interests, but to promote particular religious and moral causes. The Church of England had enough political influence to be in a position to defend most of its privileges throughout the eighteenth century, and it had enough support among the population at large to enlist opposition to many efforts to promote the interests of religious minorities.

Efforts to repeal the Test and Corporation Acts, which restricted the political rights of Protestant Dissenters, were defeated by political influence within parliament and popular pressure from without. The Jewish Naturalization Act of 1753 was swiftly repealed later that same year following virulent anti-Semitic propaganda in the press, formal protests from grand juries and municipal corporations, widespread public petitions and constituency instructions to MPs. Resentment against minor concessions to Roman Catholics in 1778 led to the founding of the popular Protestant Association, massive petitions for repeal, and the alarming Gordon Riots in London in June 1780 when the capital was virtually out of control for several days. And yet, some minor concessions were gained by religious minorities as a result of their own efforts to organize effective petitioning and lobbying campaigns. The Quakers secured the right to affirm rather than to swear oaths and the Protestant Dissenters secured regular annual Indemnity Acts, from 1727 onwards, that allowed them to evade the political restrictions imposed by the Test and Corporation Acts. Men of religious conviction in different denominations also sometimes combined together to achieve moral reforms. They created such voluntary organizations as the Society for the Reformation of Manners and the London Abolition Society. From 1787 onwards the latter organized the greatest extra-parliamentary campaign of the whole eighteenth century, in opposition to the Atlantic slave trade. In 1792, for example, there was a massive press campaign in favour of abolition and over 500 petitions, many signed by thousands of ordinary people, rained down upon parliament. The conservative opposition to abolition in parliament prevented repeal until 1807, but the moral argument in favour of repeal had been won among the people at large many years before this piece of legislation was passed.

Popular Disturbances

The most common and the most effective forms of plebeian politics in eighteenth-century Britain were the peaceful crowd demonstrations and the popular riots. Crowd activity, both peaceful and violent, was a major form of group expression by the common people. It brought together onto the streets significant groups of ordinary people, whose numbers, proximity and direct action allowed them to combine effectively in order to worry and even influence their social superiors. The common people engaged in a wide range of collective behaviour, much of it stressing social order and integration, on festive, ceremonial and celebratory occasions and in recreational, patriotic and popular assemblies. Peaceful crowds might gather to celebrate coronations, military and naval victories, parliamentary elections and civic ceremonies, and local festivals. They might also provide audiences at political rallies or spectators at executions and sporting events. In periods of tension, however, crowds could gather in a more aggressive and hostile mood in order to engage in social protests and political demonstrations. Riots were widespread, frequent, even endemic. Sometimes they did involve a degree of near mindless violence, but much more often they were rational and legitimate protests against a variety of grievances and they were clear manifestations of the economic grievances, social attitudes and political will of the common people.

There were literally thousands of riots and popular disturbances in the eighteenth century. They occurred across the length and breadth of the country, but much more often in urban areas than in rural areas because these towns had concentrations of poor workers experiencing similar grievances. Some protests involved only a few dozen people hurling abuse, but many involved larger numbers using intimidatory tactics and a degree of physical violence, and a few involved thousands of rioters in near insurrectionary violence. Nearly all riots were provoked by specific grievances which alienated the local community. These grievances were of many kinds, but most fell into a few general categories. The most common form of popular protest was the food riot, when crowds protested not just at the shortage and high price of food, but attacked those who were making an excessive profit out of their distress. There were also many riots which developed out of industrial protests, before the organized strike became the more effective response of workers complaining about low wages or poor conditions. There were also numerous popular protests against new taxes, land enclosures, toll roads and forced recruitment into the army, navy or militia. Popular riots – sometimes incited or at least condoned by their social superiors – were also aimed at despised religious minorities, such as Roman Catholics, Jews, Methodists and Protestant Dissenters. In all such disturbances it is possible to see the rioters defending traditional rights and customary practices against innovations which they saw as changing their world for the worse.

A few riots (such as the Sacheverell Riots of 1710 and the Gordon Riots of 1780) descended into near social anarchy when order was restored only with the greatest difficulty. Most riots, however, were much more restrained affairs when the crowd acted in a fairly disciplined fashion in order to gain specific objectives by attacking clearly defined targets. Most crowds were not lawless mobs, but were fairly cohesive groups united by a common sense of grievance and a desire to achieve a limited objective. Most participants were not young delinquents, criminals, vagrants or misfits, but were employed young workers and sober family men driven to violence by a failure by the authorities to defend their customary rights and traditional practices. Most riots did not descend into indiscriminate violence or heavy loss of life. The crowd generally attacked the property of those they wished to frighten, rather than their persons, and they usually resorted to violence only after more peaceful means had failed. Very few people were killed by the many thousands of rioters who resorted to direct action in the eighteenth century. When fatalities did occur, the vast majority were caused by the forces of order deployed to suppress the riots.

The ruling elite had no effective civilian police force at their disposal and they were usually reluctant to use the regular army or the militia (which was established in the later eighteenth century) to maintain order. The suppression of riots by military force was generally a last resort. Whenever possible, the ruling elite and the local magistrates tried to restore order by offering some concessions to the rioters. When riots were suppressed by force, the authorities punished as few of the rioters as was consistent with the restoration of good order and due subordination. Since riots were endemic and the forces of law and order were of limited effect, the ruling elite preferred conciliation rather than forcible repression.

Politics in the Urban Community

It was in the towns, and especially in the larger towns, that popular politics in all its manifestations flourished most vigorously and most persistently. Eighteenth-century

Britain saw not only a doubling of its total population, but a significant growth in the number of people living in towns. The percentage of people living in towns of over 5,000 inhabitants rose from 13 to 25 per cent over the century. By 1801 London had a population of nearly 1 million people, fourteen other towns had a population of over 20,000 inhabitants, and another thirty-three towns had between 10,000 and 20,000 inhabitants. Political leadership in these towns was provided by the burgeoning middle classes, who sometimes made up 30 to 40 per cent of the inhabitants. Towns were more open societies than the rural areas and in them men could use their wealth acquired in commerce, manufacturing and the professions to buy status and to challenge the domination of political life by those of superior birth. Urban communities were the centres of economic growth, social mobility, religious tensions and popular disturbances. Literacy rates were always higher in urban areas and towns were the centres of a thriving print culture that educated and informed the middle classes in particular. Most towns witnessed the growth of voluntary clubs and societies that provided their members with instruction, fellowship and mutual support. These clubs encouraged a growing willingness to participate in public life. They refused the patronage of the aristocratic elite and demonstrated the independence of their members. By the later 1760s many of these clubs, particularly those promoting instruction and debating, had begun to advance a political reform programme.

In over two-thirds of the boroughs the town councils or corporations were dominated by the wealthier inhabitants, who served for life and who filled any vacancy by co-opting new members. In the more 'open' boroughs, which included London itself, the freemen could elect the members of the corporation. No matter how the town was governed and the corporation was chosen – and some growing towns such as Westminster, Birmingham and Manchester did not even have a town council – the governing elite usually faced a challenge to their authority from the broad body of inhabitants whenever they sought to abuse their local powers. The City of London, with the largest and most sophisticated urban community in the country, was regularly the scene of political disputes involving many thousands of its inhabitants. Most other large towns frequently saw the decisions of the town corporation challenged by the local middle classes in particular. Similar disputes might greet the decisions taken by parish vestries which collected the poor rate and surveyed the local highways. Town corporations and parish vestries often had to defer to these challenges and to seek consensus rather than confrontation. If towns and parishes were to be governed effectively and harmoniously, the local elite sitting in these or similar governing bodies had to secure a broad measure of agreement from among the large number of middle-class inhabitants in these urban locations. In addition to these older institutions, the later eighteenth century saw the creations of hundreds of new statutory authorities set up to deal with the town-planning problems faced by these urban communities. Arising out of local demands, and set up only after local discussions and consultations, these authorities were established by local acts of parliament which defined their function, jurisdiction, organization and composition. These statutory authorities covered a wide range of activities and duties. They included bodies to establish or properly maintain harbours, docks, bridges, canals, markets and burial grounds. Even more important were the statutory authorities to establish workhouses and turnpike trusts, and the improvement commissions that were set up to deal with the lighting, paving, cleaning and policing of the streets. These various statutory bodies and commissions were often managed by small property owners and they occasionally involved large numbers of ordinary rate-paying householders. More men of modest property had some role in managing the affairs of their towns as the eighteenth century progressed.

The ruling elites in urban communities might often try to act as cosy oligarchies that could protect their own interests and ignore those of the majority of their fellow inhabitants, but they could not always achieve these objectives. Many corporations and even parishes were riven by political disputes and these conflicts often involved a significant proportion of the local inhabitants. There were frequent disputes about parliamentary elections, the choice of local officials, the creation of new freemen, access to local charities and amenities, and the raising of local rates and taxes. As numerous new statutory authorities and improvement commissions were established, these disputes multiplied. Improved amenities cost money and, since not all local inhabitants believed that they benefited from such improvements, they were reluctant to fund them. Local disputes could be both intense and prolonged when it was widely believed that those in positions of authority were abusing their powers, encroaching on the rights of their fellow citizens, and were lining their own pockets at the public's expense. Too flagrant an abuse of power and too ostentatious a monopoly of privilege provoked hostility and attracted widespread condemnation. There was an increasing recognition that the only way to make urban governments accountable to a wider public was to allow a higher proportion of townsmen a legitimate political role in their local communities. By the later eighteenth century there were many demands to open up town government to a wider municipal electorate. From 1784 the Convention of Royal Burghs in Scotland began a prolonged campaign to achieve such municipal reform, and similar demands were made in a large number of English boroughs, including Birmingham, Bristol, Liverpool, Manchester and Southampton. There were bitter attacks on local oligarchies and increased demands for the creation of urban institutions that commanded greater public support and were more accountable to a wider municipal electorate. Although municipal reform was delayed until the 1830s, urban oligarchies in late eighteenth-century Britain nearly always faced local political opposition when they tried to increase or to abuse their authority.

Radical Ideas

In seeking to understand the political role that ordinary British subjects played in the eighteenth century, we need to recognize that many commentators of the period argued that Britons were free men living in a free society. No commentator, no matter how conservative, was prepared to argue that the common people were without any rights or liberties at all or that they had to submit to the whims of an arbitrary tyrant. There was general agreement that all Britons possessed a range of civil liberties and that the powers of government were limited by positive laws and customary rights. All commentators accepted that British subjects had the right to live under the rule of law and ought to have the opportunity of equal justice in the nation's courts of law. Arbitrary power was restrained by positive law, ancient customs or natural law to the extent that no subject could be imprisoned without trial; all men were subject to the same laws administered by the same law courts; no torture could be used to secure a confession; and no accused person could be convicted of a serious offence except after a trial by jury. There was also almost universal agreement that all subjects had an inalienable right to their property, no matter how little they possessed. No government could legitimately seize or even tax any man's property except by due process of law in parliament or in the courts of law. The right of freedom of conscience was another important civil liberty that was widely conceded. The intellectual justification of religious toleration made great strides during the eighteenth century so that no man could be forced to accept particular religious opinions or to attend a particular form of worship. The state ceased to look into men's souls and the right of freedom of conscience was broadly accepted. While full political rights (for example, the right to hold office in the state) might be denied to some religious minorities (including Protestant Dissenters, Roman Catholics and Jews), the state did not impose its religious beliefs on its subjects. The free expression of political views, provided they were not libellous, seditious, treasonable or subversive, was also granted to all subjects. The right to address the monarch or to petition parliament was never infringed and the policy of pre-publication censorship of the press by the state or the church was abandoned in the 1690s. The press might be taxed, but these levies never prevented the steady growth of a free political press throughout the eighteenth century. The existence of a free press was widely recognized as one of the most valuable civil liberties possessed by the British people. In the last resort, it was also widely accepted that the British people could forcibly resist arbitrary tyranny, although it was confidently asserted that this right would never need to be used so long as parliament met regularly and Britain's excellent constitution remained in being.

While it was generally acknowledged that all Britons possessed a number of vital civil liberties, there was much less agreement about which subjects deserved to possess the parliamentary franchise or the right to exercise a positive role in the decision-making processes of the state. Conservative commentators were content to restrict the franchise, the right to sit in parliament and the right to hold political office at local and national level to those who possessed particular property qualifications. When they referred to 'free men', they invariably meant those who owned sufficient property to be economically independent. Radical suggestions that the supreme authority in the state rested with the people at large rather than with the wealthy, propertied elite ran up against the widely accepted counter-argument that sovereign authority lay with the combined legislature of King, Lords and Commons. The ruling elite and men of conservative disposition were therefore content to see political power limited to a narrow propertied oligarchy. Men of more radical opinions began to demand that most men, perhaps even all men, should possess the right to vote for their representatives in parliament and to hold the government to public account. The logical conclusion of this radical claim was the demand for a democratic republic, though only a handful of extreme radicals in the 1790s went this far.

In seeking to justify the extension of political liberty to a broad range of British subjects, radical commentators used a number of arguments and appealed to quite different intellectual traditions. One popular line of argument put great stress on the appeal to history, experience and prescription. It was maintained that England (later extended to the whole of Britain) possessed an ancient constitution which had long guaranteed the historic rights and liberties of the subject. Some radicals claimed that these rights had been very extensive in the distant Anglo-Saxon past, had been undermined by the Norman Conquest of 1066, but were in the process of being slowly recovered thereafter by sustained popular pressure for the restoration of lost political rights. A very different defence of liberty rested on the claim that God had endowed all men with inalienable natural rights. These natural rights to 'life, liberty and property' had to be converted into civil liberties which could be properly protected only if all men were able to exercise a positive political role in the state by electing their representatives and holding them to account for their public actions.

Some critics of parliamentary sovereignty insisted that the legislature had no legitimate power to command what was contrary to the historic rights of the subject, the inalienable rights of man, the law of nature, or such fundamental laws of the constitution as the Bill of Rights, the Triennial Act or the Act of Union with Scotland. For much of the eighteenth century critics of existing political practices, inside and outside parliament, condemned the growth of crown patronage and expressed the fear that this patronage was being exploited to undermine the independence of parliament and to subvert the liberties of the subject. It was widely believed that once a majority of MPs had been seduced by government office and crown favour, then arbitrary power would be as firmly established as if parliament and voters no longer existed. To counter this threat, it was argued that MPs and voters must resist the temptations offered by honours, office and rewards from the crown, and reforms must be passed which would scale back the extent of political patronage at the disposal of the crown and government ministers. By the late eighteenth century a number of radicals were arguing that reforms of this kind did not go far enough to safeguard the liberties of the subject. They insisted that parliament must be subordinated to the sovereign will of the people and political reforms needed to be enacted that would make government and parliament accountable to the people at large. This led to proposals for free, fair and frequent elections which would make parliament more responsive to the electorate. Some reformers were content to argue for the abolition of small parliamentary constituencies, the transfer of these seats to the counties and to unrepresented towns such as Birmingham, Manchester and Sheffield, and more frequent general elections. The more radical reformers went beyond this and advocated a major extension of the franchise, at least to all male householders, though some radicals such as John Cartwright and Thomas Paine favoured universal manhood suffrage. These radicals also favoured the abolition of property qualifications for MPs and even advocated the payment of MPs. By 1780 a really radical programme of parliamentary reform was being advocated, though it was supported by only a minority of reformers, who themselves were almost certainly outnumbered by conservative opinion.

The democratic leanings of nearly all reformers and radicals stopped short of advocating the positive political rights of women. Adult females were regarded as mere appendages of men and as dependants of their male relatives. Only a handful of radicals ever even broached the issue of extending the vote to women. Most radicals were also content to limit their political demands to a reform of the process by which the people elected their representatives to the House of Commons. They had no wish to abolish monarchy, aristocracy or the hereditary right to rule. Furthermore, only a few radicals were prepared to go beyond a demand for extensive political reforms. They thought that a more democratic House of Commons would automatically implement changes that would reduce the tax burden on the people and eliminate many of the social and economic grievances of the poor. Most radicals explicitly denied that they had any wish to challenge the social hierarchy or the very unequal distribution of wealth and property in eighteenth-century Britain. A handful of the extreme radicals did maintain that political equality was impossible in a society where gross economic inequality was allowed to persist. Thomas Paine, for example, wanted to slash the costs of government, to tax extensive landed estates very heavily and to use the proceeds to fund a variety of social welfare payments to the poor, including old age pensions and child and maternity allowances. Thomas Spence went even further and advocated the abolition of private property altogether. He advocated the creation of parish corporations that would own all the land and natural resources within their boundaries. Each parish would then rent these annually to the highest bidders and use the proceeds to create a range of social amenities, including schools and housing, and to make equal quarterly payments to all inhabitants, men, women and children alike. His extreme proposals won few adherents.

Radical Campaigns

Popular movements dedicated to the radical reform of the British constitution did not exist in the earlier eighteenth century and did not develop until the era of the American and French Revolutions. In the period before the 1760s most critics of the existing constitution and opponents of prevailing political practices concentrated their attacks on the growth of an aristocratic and propertied oligarchy, on the extension of crown patronage which threatened to give the crown and government ministers too much influence over peers, MPs and voters, and on the increase in political corruption at all levels of the political process. While the prerogative powers of the crown had been successfully curtailed after the Glorious Revolution of 1688–9, a new, more insidious danger to the independence of parliament and the liberties of the subject had emerged in the form of crown patronage, which appeared sufficient to corrupt both parliament and people. This patronage system had been created by the growth of the national debt and the system of public credit, by the raising of large armies and navies, by the growth of a government bureaucracy needed to manage the national debt, supply the armed forces, and raise the revenue to fund them all. Crown patronage enabled the king and his favourite ministers to persuade peers and MPs to sell their political integrity and their political independence in return for offices, promotions, titles, honours and material profit. Widespread and persistent criticism was launched at the whole system of public credit, the growth of the armed forces, the expansion of the bureaucracy, the wide array of new taxes imposed on the people, and the number of peers and MPs rewarded by the crown in return for their votes in parliament. Efforts to introduce legislation to curb crown patronage failed and, because they did so, some critics urged instead a measure of parliamentary reform. They advocated the abolition of small parliamentary constituencies, the transfer of these seats to the counties and larger boroughs, more frequent general elections, and the election of more independent and patriotic MPs. They did not urge an extension of the franchise.

These critics of political corruption did not seek to enlist the support of the lower middle classes, still less the support of the poor. They concentrated their attention on winning the support of backbench MPs and the existing voters. They hoped to persuade these men to safeguard the independence of parliament and to preserve the liberties of the subject by exploiting the growing power of the press. A growing number of the wide range of political prints (newspapers, periodicals, pamphlets, books and graphic prints) were devoted to political subjects and issues. The intense propaganda campaigns waged in the press enabled the parliamentary opposition to the ruling oligarchy to articulate their political programme and to bring politics out of the restricted arenas of court and parliament. The press played an increasingly important role in advising its readers about the decisions taken by government and parliament, and it helped the voters to organize effective petitioning, propaganda and lobbying campaigns in opposition to the governing elite. A growing number of newspapers became critical of the government and the growth of oligarchy was most resisted in the larger county and borough constituencies. It was from these constituencies that most effective petitioning and lobbying campaigns were launched to influence the behaviour of backbench MPs and even to instruct them on how to vote in parliament on crucial issues. The City of London, where there was always considerable opposition to the national government, frequently led these nationwide petitioning and instruction campaigns. Campaigns such as this helped to defeat Robert Walpole's excise scheme in 1733 and forced the repeal of the Jewish Naturalization Act in 1753, and seriously weakened Walpole's administration in 1739–42 and helped bring down the duke of Newcastle's administration in 1756. These were important, but limited, achievements, because they failed to prevent the growth of oligarchy.

By the later eighteenth century many decades of political, social and economic change had combined to create a growing body of opinion critical of the power and policies of the aristocratic elite. Commercial expansion, urban growth, the beginnings of industrialization and a growing population had produced, and was continuing to increase, a middle class whose advancing wealth and improving education inspired demands for greater social status and increased political influence. The middle classes had begun to establish their own voluntary organizations, to inform themselves about public affairs, and to develop advanced notions about their political rights and liberties. They became increasingly critical and independent of the landed elite and transformed some of their clubs and societies into vehicles for coordinating campaigns to challenge the political influence of their social superiors and to increase their own representation in parliament. The flourishing and expanding press of the later eighteenth century played a major role in educating a wide public on the important political issues of the day and enabled those demanding reform to spread their ideas across the whole country. A succession of major crises facing the nation helped to convince a large body of public opinion that parliamentary reform was essential if these crises were to be tackled effectively. The alarm raised by the political decisions taken by the young George III after his accession in 1760, the dramatic irruption of the demagogic John Wilkes onto the popular political stage in the 1760s, the prolonged and ultimately disastrous dispute with the American colonies, and the profound ideological challenge and costly wars created by the dramatic French Revolution, all generated severe political pressures which encouraged large numbers of ordinary Britons to support demands for political change. These political crises had a cumulative effect in that they deepened the sense of unease about the existing constitution and widened the circle of those who supported the cause of political reform.

While no historian now believes that George III waged a determined campaign to increase his prerogative powers at the expense of the rights of parliament or the liberties of the subject, a considerable body of opinion in the 1760s did come to fear that the king was threatening to disturb the balance of the constitution and was leading a conspiracy against liberty in his efforts to secure an administration that satisfied him. Public fears were deliberately exacerbated by disgruntled politicians and particularly by the unscrupulous John Wilkes. Major press campaigns persuaded many outside parliament that a constitutional crisis had been created by the political ambitions of George III. Wilkes was even more successful in convincing many people that he was a political victim of politicians who were acting unconstitutionally in attempting to silence his efforts to criticize the government and in seeking to debar him from a seat in parliament, even though he was repeatedly elected to the House of Commons by the voters of Middlesex in 1768–9. This allowed Wilkes to pose the major political question of whether the membership of the House of Commons was to be manipulated by a narrow aristocratic elite or was to represent the interests of the electorate as a whole. Even more fundamental questions were raised by the American crisis which developed over a period of more than twenty years from the early 1760s. The ill-judged policies of successive British administrations to tax the American colonists and to impose the authority of parliament on the colonies provoked intense and widespread resentment in America. Unresolved, the political crisis led to a disastrous war which saw the American colonies gain their independence by force of arms. This shocked the nation and undermined support for the existing constitution. The dramatic and astonishing events in France, for a quarter of a century after the outbreak of revolution in 1789, had an even greater impact on political events in Britain. The French Revolution inspired more profound ideological debates and raised a greater challenge to the existing British constitution than the events in America had done. The political impact on Britain was dramatic and it galvanized many thousands of Britons into discussing the rights of man and the need to reform the British constitution. An enormously costly war between Britain and France, and years of economic distress, helped to recruit mass support for those radicals demanding political change in the 1790s.

The reformers of the later eighteenth century appealed to the historic rights of Englishmen and increasingly to the natural rights of all men. They supported a wide range of reforms, including attacks on crown patronage, demands for greater religious equality, the abolition of the slave trade and, especially, the reform of parliament. The various campaigns for reform had some gentry support, but were largely led by urban middle-class radicals, especially in London and the larger towns. This leadership developed a whole range of intellectual justifications for reform and they exploited the press to impressive effect. They established dozens of political clubs and societies, from the Society of the Supporters of the Bill of Rights in 1769 to the Yorkshire Association in 1779, the Society for Constitutional Information in 1780, and the London Corresponding Society in 1792. Although there was never a fully integrated radical movement at any stage in the later eighteenth century, great efforts were made to coordinate the activities of a broad spectrum of clubs, societies and associations. These societies debated political questions, spread reform propaganda, mounted nationwide petitioning campaigns, and organized innumerable dinners, processions and public meetings. These activities educated the people about their political rights and enlisted them in a number of campaigns for various reforms, especially for parliamentary reform. Although mainly led by educated men from the middle classes, they increasingly rallied many thousands of men from lower down the social scale, especially in London and the larger towns. What the radicals never established was a united movement, an agreed leadership, a coherent platform or a unified strategy. They were always split between moderates and genuine radicals, and, apart from a heavy reliance on the written word and constitutional petitioning, they had no effective strategy to achieve their political objectives. Popular riots and industrial strikes might serve the specific grievances of sectional interests, but they were never used for political purposes. Although a small revolutionary movement emerged in the later 1790s (and was soon destroyed), there was very little desire for change through political revolution on the French model.

Radical demands were firmly opposed by the powerful ruling elite. The government never lost its nerve and was adept at using counter-propaganda, repressive legislation and the legal process as well as the occasional deployment of armed force to suppress the more dangerous radicals. Many radical leaders were arrested, harassed, silenced or driven into exile. The elite made use of the deference habitually displayed by large numbers of ordinary Britons, especially in rural areas, and promoted loyalism and opposition to radicalism across the country. Large numbers of ordinary Britons were ready to follow the political lead of their social superiors and to enlist in a loyalist campaign to preserve the existing constitution and safeguard the prevailing social order against domestic radicals, colonial rebels and French revolutionaries. Popular loyalists used the press, joined political clubs and societies, attended crowd demonstrations and petitioned crown and parliament as effectively as did the popular radicals, but in order to preserve not to undermine the status quo. It is impossible to understand the intensity and the volatility of political divisions in the 1790s without appreciating how many ordinary Britons enlisted in both the radical campaign for reform and the loyalist efforts to oppose radical change. It is very likely, however, that more ordinary Britons were loyalists rather than radicals by the end of the eighteenth century.

FURTHER READING

Barker, Hannah: *Newspapers, Politics and Public Opinion in Late Eighteenth-Century England* (Oxford, 1998).

Bonwick, Colin: *English Radicals and the American Revolution* (Chapel Hill, NC, 1977).

Christie, Ian R.: *Wilkes, Wyvill and Reform: The Parliamentary Reform Movement in British Politics, 1760–1785* (London, 1962).

Christie, Ian R.: *Stress and Stability in Late Eighteenth-Century Britain: The British Avoidance of Revolution* (Oxford, 1984).

Clark, Peter: *British Clubs and Societies 1580–1800: The Origins of an Associational World* (Oxford, 2000).

Dickinson, H. T.: *British Radicalism and the French Revolution 1789–1815* (Oxford, 1985).

Dickinson, H. T. (ed.): *Britain and the French Revolution 1789–1815* (Basingstoke, 1989).

Dickinson, H. T.: *The Politics of the People in Eighteenth-Century Britain* (Basingstoke, 1995).
Goodwin, Albert: *The Friends of Liberty: The English Democratic Movement in the Age of the French Revolution* (London, 1979).
O'Gorman, Frank: *Voters, Patrons, and Parties: The Unreformed Electorate of Hanoverian England 1734–1832* (Oxford, 1989).
Rogers, Nicholas: *Whigs and Cities: Popular Politics in the Age of Walpole and Pitt* (Oxford, 1989).
Rogers, Nicholas: *Crowds, Culture and Politics in Georgian Britain* (Oxford, 1998).
Thompson, E. P.: 'The moral economy of the English crowd in the eighteenth century', *Past and Present*, 50 (1971), pp. 76–136.
Stevenson, John: *Popular Disturbances in England 1700–1870* (London, 1979).
Wilson, Kathleen: *The Sense of the People: Politics, Culture and Imperialism in England, 1715–1785* (Cambridge, 1995).

Chapter Nine

The Crisis of the French Revolution

Emma Vincent Macleod

The revolution in France which began in 1789 provoked a crisis in Britain of constitutional, political, social, religious and strategic dimensions. By mid-eighteenth-century standards the British state was relatively liberal and open; indeed, it was often favourably compared with that of absolutist France by British and continental commentators alike. Britain was ruled, not by an absolute monarch, but by a mixed government and balanced constitution of King, Lords and Commons. Ordinary people enjoyed civil liberties which included the rule of law (equality before the law for all subjects), freedom from torture and arbitrary imprisonment, the right to trial by jury, the right to petition the crown and parliament, and freedom of expression, of worship and of the press. It was nevertheless an oligarchical and aristocratic system that was weighted heavily in favour of the monarchy, the landed (male) elite and the Church of England at the expense of the less well-off, women and non-Anglicans, who were excluded from the formal political process and from constitutional rights and power. During the early years of the French Revolution, French politicians sought to define citizenship more inclusively, recognizing the rights of subjects irrespective of their birth or religion and, later, regardless of their wealth or race. This chapter explores why the French Revolution had the capacity to provoke a crisis in Britain. It then investigates how serious this crisis really was.

Why did the French Revolution Generate a Crisis in Britain?

The French Revolution was able to threaten British stability because it offered an example of a successful revolution in church and state and because it posed a substantial military threat. It is important to recognize, however, that the British crisis was not generated solely by the French Revolution. It was also dependent on the fact that the existing order in Britain was in a position to be challenged in all of these dimensions by the time the revolution erupted in France. Because the eighteenth-century British state was one of the most liberal regimes in the world, its subjects had great freedom to question publicly the actions of the current government or even the nature of the political, social and religious order. By the time of the outbreak of the French Revolution this had become an increasingly common practice.

Criticism was encouraged by the propagation of enlightenment principles. These stressed the value of the individual's use of reason at the expense of the acceptance of revelation, authority and tradition. Enlightenment writers such as John Locke and Voltaire had challenged people's habitual submission to the authority of the established forms of government and religion, and by the later eighteenth century their ideas had been diffused to a wide circle of intellectuals and political thinkers in Britain. A related, but separate, phenomenon was the emergence and growth of a political reform movement in Britain since the 1760s. Commercial growth, population increase and urbanization had expanded the wealth, confidence and power of the urban middling orders, some of whom began to demand more political influence at a national level. The metropolitan press and, in its footsteps, the provincial press flourished on relatively high urban literacy rates and the emergence of such issues as the Wilkesite protests and the American Revolution. Societies and pressure groups, such as the Society of the Supporters of the Bill of Rights (formed in 1769), the Yorkshire Association (1779) and the Society for Constitutional Information (1780), began to meet to debate political questions and to organize petitions in favour of political reform. By the 1780s a regular opposition grouping was also forming inside parliament, around the leadership first of the marquess of Rockingham and then of the duke of Portland and Charles James Fox. This opposition did not yet operate as a modern political party, its adherents were often motivated by self-interest and opportunism, and it was not as radical as the extra-parliamentary reformers; but it was more organized than before, and it increasingly acted as a self-conscious political connection and as the parliamentary partner of reformers outdoors.

As well as providing a major issue for the developing British radical movement to debate, and a focus for popular discontent in Britain, the American Revolution had prefigured the impact of the French Revolution on Britain in several other ways. The French Revolution was physically nearer to Britain, and it was a more fundamental upheaval; but because the American colonists had revolted against British rule they had shaken British complacency with particular force. Thomas Paine's pamphlet *Common Sense* (1776), the securing of American independence and the later American debate over the constitution of the new state raised debates in Britain over fundamental political issues.

The liberalism of the prevailing regime, the influence of enlightenment ideas, the previous emergence and growth of a radical movement 'out-of-doors', the expansion of the press and the impact of the American Revolution therefore combined to make Britain vulnerable to political and constitutional challenge before the French Revolution broke out. The increasing population of Britain, and the growing tendency of the British population to live in towns, constituted a social threat to the dominance of the traditional elite. The rate of population increase accelerated in the last third of the eighteenth century, and the proportion of the population living in towns also rose markedly. While Edinburgh and London had been the only cities of more than 50,000 inhabitants in 1750, there were eight such cities by 1801. The more heavily populated an area, the more difficult it was for the gentry and traditional local ruling authorities to control its population. This created a political challenge, for elections were more likely to be contested and MPs were more liable to be presented with instructions from voters in vigorous urban constituencies; but it was the social challenge presented by large numbers of the lower orders living in such dense settlements that most disturbed the elite. When the French Revolution broke out, its social menace to the British elite was amplified because they were already contending with a swiftly changing social structure.

The ability of the French Revolution to endanger the existing order in Britain therefore rested on British vulnerability to such a challenge at the end of the eighteenth century. It was also produced by the nature of the revolution itself, both as an instance of a successful revolution, and as an expansionist threat. The first reason why the French Revolution was in itself a threat to British stability was that it provided a practical demonstration of replacing the existing order in church and state with a more egalitarian system – an example that proved attractive to a significant number of British subjects. French ideas of republicanism, popular sovereignty and religious toleration encouraged British reformers to question the benefits of the present constitutional, political, social and religious system in Britain.

Most British commentators on the early months of the French Revolution, whether conservative or reformist, approved of the events taking place in France. 'We saw a great people reclaiming the inheritance of men, and boldly aspiring to be free', Thomas Hardy, professor of ecclesiastical history at the University of Edinburgh, explained later (*The Patriot* [Edinburgh, 1793], p. 4). Some thought that the French were following the British example, set a hundred years earlier in the Glorious Revolution, of establishing a constitutional monarchy, a measure of political liberty and a degree of religious toleration. Some were simply content that Britain's traditional rival and enemy was likely to be preoccupied with domestic matters for some time to come following such an upheaval. Others, however, hailed the further progression of the French Revolution, past the point at which British constitutional change had stopped at the end of the seventeenth century, towards more fundamental alterations.

On 4 November 1789 the economist and Unitarian clergyman, Richard Price, preached a secular sermon, entitled *A Discourse on the Love of Our Country*, to the Revolution Society, which had met to celebrate the anniversary of the Glorious Revolution. Price applauded the revolution in France as a worthy successor to the Glorious Revolution and the more recent American Revolution, in its establishment of popular sovereignty – that is, the right of the people 'to chuse our own governors; to cashier them for misconduct; and to frame a government for ourselves' (pp. 28–9). The Revolution Society agreed to send a congratulatory address to the National Assembly in Paris. A year later, the eminent political thinker and MP, Edmund Burke, attacked Price's sermon in his book *Reflections on the Revolution in France*. Burke argued that the French Revolution was a much more subversive and extensive overturning of political and social structures than the Glorious Revolution had been. It was, he claimed, a fundamental assault on the established institutions (the monarchy, the aristocracy and the church) which upheld law, order, property, religion and morality – it was an evil revolt against the very foundations of European civilization. It should be condemned rather than admired or imitated. As well as many publications in support of his views, Burke's work attracted at least a hundred replies, the most famous of which was Thomas Paine's *Rights of Man*, published in two parts, in March 1791 and February 1792. Writing at a later stage of the revolution than

Price, Paine went further in arguing for the application of revolutionary principles to British politics and society. He, like Price, was greatly influenced by the American Revolution as well as by events in France, and he argued against hereditary monarchy and aristocracy as corrupt, irrational and ineffective. He claimed that all men had a natural right to an active political voice, and that such a system of government would establish a much fairer society, with support for the poor, the sick and the old.

Paine's work also drew many replies and, together with the increasing violence of events in France, this pamphlet debate now divided British opinions on the French Revolution, so that the earlier consensus of complacent approval broke down. Many people were inspired by Price, Paine and the French example. In 1790 many Dissenters campaigned (unsuccessfully) for parliament to repeal the Test and Corporation Acts which barred them from holding public office unless they received communion under the rites of the Church of England at least once a year. On 14 July 1790 political dinners were held in London, Liverpool, Edinburgh, Yarmouth and elsewhere to commemorate the first anniversary of the fall of the Bastille in Paris, and further addresses of congratulation were sent to the revolutionaries in France. In 1791 more Bastille dinners were held, and radical societies and clubs were established in such places as Manchester, Birmingham, Norwich, Sheffield, Derby, Dublin and Belfast to debate Paine's views and the events of the French Revolution. These were dominated by middle-class professionals and manufacturers, but they were increasingly concerned to promote awareness of political rights among working men. The moderately reformist Association of the Friends of the People was formed in London in April 1792 by opposition Whig MPs and other members of the social elite. Many other, more radical, societies were formed in 1792, with a higher proportion of artisans and tradesmen in their membership. The London Corresponding Society (LCS) was established in January, and in June the Society of the Friends of the People was formed in Lowland Scotland, where previously there had been very little popular interest in politics. In December 1792, May 1793 and October 1793 the Scottish radicals held national conventions – a term clearly borrowed from the French National Convention. More daringly still, they were joined by English and Irish delegates for a 'British Convention' in Edinburgh in November–December 1793. Radical newspapers were also established, such as the *Manchester Herald*, the *Sheffield Register* and the *Edinburgh Gazetteer*, and many tracts and pamphlets were published and circulated widely in favour of a radical reform of parliament.

British radicals were not wholly united in exactly what reforms they sought. It is true that most agreed in demanding the six points of parliamentary reform: universal manhood suffrage, annual parliaments, equal constituencies, the secret ballot, the abolition of property qualifications for MPs, and payment of MPs. Most radicals, moreover, were eager to obtain parliamentary reform not only for its political benefits but also because they agreed with Paine that it would result in social and economic benefits for the poor, because taxes would be lowered through the elimination of government corruption. Only a few, however, emphasized that they wanted ordinary working men to participate in actually governing the country. A few radicals were overtly republican, but most attacked the monarchy and the House of Lords only implicitly. Very few advocated political rights for women, although Thomas Spence and George Phillips did so. Mary Wollstonecraft questioned women's exclusion from citizenship, but she did not call explicitly for the vote. Other writers, such as Mary Hays and Thomas Holcroft, used their novels to imply that the position of women in British society ought to be improved.

Although many people were impressed by the example of the French Revolution and the interpretation of its principles for the British context by Paine and others, many others were increasingly unhappy with these developments by 1792 and were inclined to agree with much of Burke's analysis. They believed that the British system of a parliamentary monarchy and the rule of law, combined with a property-based social order, was what guaranteed British liberties and commercial prosperity. Inequality was both natural and divinely ordained, and hereditary power was necessary to ensure stability and order. The radical movement, inspired by the French example, seemed to threaten not only the established institutions of government, but also the social hierarchy, justice and security of property.

Church and King clubs emerged in 1790 to oppose the campaign to repeal the Test and Corporation Acts, and they often resorted to violence to intimidate Dissenters and reformers. A Church and King mob destroyed the house, library and laboratory of the well-known Unitarian radical politician and scientist, Joseph Priestley, in Birmingham in July 1791, after the local Bastille Day celebrations. In May 1792 a royal proclamation was issued against the publication and distribution of seditious literature, aimed particularly against Paine's *Rights of Man*. In response, many people demonstrated their loyalty to the existing constitution and social order in public addresses, letters, pamphlets and newspaper articles. The Association for the Protection of Liberty and Property against Levellers and Republicans was founded in London in November 1792, with the approval of William Pitt's government. Hundreds, possibly thousands, of local Loyal Associations were swiftly established all over Britain.

This sharp polarization of British political opinion over the French Revolution and the debate on the British constitution did not incorporate everyone, even of those who were politically conscious and literate. There was a small but significant number of liberal politicians who admired the early stages of the French Revolution and who wanted moderate parliamentary reform in Britain, but who disapproved of the violence and extremism perpetrated in France (especially after the abolition of the monarchy in August 1792) and who did not support universal manhood suffrage or social change at home. Some of these turned to loyalism as the crisis deepened, believing it to be safer or more legitimate than continuing liberalism in the current climate. More than half of the pre-1792 opposition group in parliament moved to the government benches by the summer of 1794, under the leadership of the duke of Portland. Others stood firm, however. Those MPs who remained in opposition under Charles James Fox, together with a significant number of people outside parliament, had a difficult middle path to steer, while each side put pressure on them to declare for its principles. They were often accused by loyalists of supporting radical goals, and it is true that they sometimes made common cause with the radicals, such as in their opposition to the war against France (1793–1815), or when they were particularly horrified by repressive government legislation, such as the Two Acts of December 1795, which they saw as dangerously anti-libertarian. They did not, however, support the full radical programme and they often disappointed the radicals by their lukewarm assistance.

The French Revolution, therefore, provoked a crisis in Britain by providing an example of constitutional, political, social and religious upheaval which inspired some in Britain and appalled others. The French effort to export their revolution by force of arms greatly aggravated the threat it posed to Britain. Austria and Prussia declared war on France in April and June 1792, respectively, but the French Republic then proceeded to demonstrate aggressive tendencies of its own. It unilaterally declared the River Scheldt (which opened to the sea on Dutch territory) free for international navigation on 16 November 1792, contrary to longstanding international agreement. On 19 November 1792 it offered to assist all peoples who wished to overthrow their monarchs; and on 15 December 1792 it declared its intention to requisition occupied countries in order to sustain its military and proselytizing activities. Since French troops had overrun the Austrian Netherlands (Belgium) in November and appeared to be poised to invade the Dutch Republic, it was impossible for the British government to regard the French Revolution any longer as irrelevant to British strategic interests. The Dutch Republic was a British ally. Moreover, French control of the Low Countries would allow the French navy to menace a wider stretch of the British coastline. On 1 February the French Republic declared war on both Great Britain and the Dutch Republic. The British conflict against France lasted until 1815, except for a truce between March 1802 and May 1803, and it involved Britain in a war of unprecedented scale. Britain sustained 315,000 casualties and spent £1,500 million in loans and taxes during the war. No other state sustained war against France for so many years as did Britain.

When war broke out, patriotism persuaded some liberals and reformers to support the government. Many others, however, opposed the war as unjust, unnecessary and a heavy burden on the British people. The 'Friends of Peace' were a network of liberal, often Dissenting, men spread throughout the country, but based mainly in London and the northwest of England. They were often supported by the Foxite or opposition Whigs in parliament, but it was they who provided the leadership of the British anti-war protest throughout the wars against France. They organized sizeable petitions for peace and used the liberal press to great effect, while many Dissenting churchmen used official fast-days to preach against the continuance of the war rather than to pray for its success. The radicals were also hostile to the conflict, because they supported the French Revolution, even in its conflict against Britain, and because, they argued, it was a waste of blood and money. The anti-war activities of the radicals centred on trying to inflame and exploit popular discontent in an attempt to put pressure on the government to introduce measures of reform.

While the French Revolution posed a very serious strategic danger to Britain in the long war of 1793–1815, this was not a new threat. The Revolutionary and Napoleonic Wars were the seventh major conflict between Britain and France since 1689, yet Britain's professional army in 1793 was small, disorganized, badly equipped and poorly staffed, and Britain's coastal defences were minimal. Furthermore, Ireland had already begun to give cause for concern before 1789. There, too, a reform movement had developed from the 1760s and had been inspired by the American Revolution, which had appeared to constitute a parallel case to the Irish situation. Recognizing that Ireland, like the American colonies, was subject to the Westminster parliament despite possessing its own legislature, Irish 'patriots' had exploited the exigencies of the war to press successfully for commercial and constitutional concessions from Westminster. Ireland, therefore, was not only a potential 'back door' to Britain for an invading French force, it was a back door which might be opened wide by welcoming Irishmen interested in achieving further concessions and perhaps even independence from Britain.

How Severe was the Crisis?

Historians differ over the extent to which the existing British order was really threatened during the 1790s and early 1800s. Some have argued that the British establishment faced the possibility of revolution during these years. Certainly the government and the ruling elite had undoubted cause for alarm because of the scale of the political, social and military threats to stability which arose during these years. These may be summarized under the headings of mass protest, organized extra-parliamentary politics, insurrectionary activities and state insecurity.

During the period 1789–1815 there were many crowd protests and demonstrations – probably well over 1,000 in England and Wales alone. Most of them concerned either the price and supply of food or military issues (recruitment to the army, the navy or the militia, or mutinies within the forces), but there were also many arising from political grievances and industrial disputes. The cost of living, forced up by population increase and repeatedly poor harvests, rose by 30 per cent between 1790 and 1795, its rate of increase doubling after the outbreak of war in 1793. Wages also rose, but not sufficiently to match price rises, and underemployment and rising wartime taxation aggravated the difficulties. The most frequent and widespread rioting occurred in 1795–6, 1799–1801 and 1811–13. Riots, however, were a common form of local protest in the eighteenth century, and local elites were used to dealing with them by a combination of concession and repression. What made the crowd disturbances of the 1790s and the early nineteenth century particularly worrying to the authorities, apart from their frequency, were indications that some rioters were beginning to hold national government and its policies (such as the war) responsible for their economic hardship. Previously, local figures and local circumstances had usually been blamed. The radicals therefore appeared to be achieving some success in their attempts to mobilize crowds and politicize mass discontent. Demands for relief became conflated with demands for reform by some rioting crowds and bill-posters.

As well as attempting to exploit unprompted expressions of local discontent, the radicals also arranged their own mass demonstrations, in which they mixed political and economic protests together. In 1795 the LCS held several 'monster meetings' to demand political reform and to protest against the war, economic hardship, the government's proposals to pass acts outlawing 'seditious meetings' and 'treasonable practices', and the Pitt administration in general. Tens of thousands of people attended the meetings held in St George's Fields on 29 June, in the fields near Copenhagen House on 26 October and 12 November, and in Marylebone Fields on 7 December 1795. Ten thousand people were reported to have attended an open-air meeting on the moors outside Sheffield to protest against the war on 10 August 1795. The Friends of Peace organized sizeable petitions for peace in 1795, 1797, 1801, 1807–8, 1811–12 and 1813. The Edinburgh petitions of 1795 and 1797 contained around 8,000 and 11,000 signatures, respectively, and the petition sent from

Yorkshire in 1801 carried some 30,000 signatures. One of the most alarming features of the radical movement to the authorities was its largely middle-class leadership and its skilful exploitation of middle-class networks. Educated, middle-class, professional men were less easily dismissed as ignorant or intent on destroying property rights than working men, and they were able to provide finance and organizational skills. Systematic, planned defiance of government policy was much more frightening to the elite than familiar, pragmatic, spontaneous rioting. Societies such as the Sheffield Constitutional Society and the LCS were highly organized. They operated a system of divisions and branches, at first from practical convenience to members and later in order to avoid the restrictions of the Seditious Meetings Act of 1795.

More disturbing still, however, was the fear that some radicals were actively planning insurrection. Government ministers recalled parliament early and summoned the local militia in London in December 1792 because they were convinced that a rising was being planned there. More than thirty leading radicals were arrested between April and July 1794, of whom eighteen were indicted on a charge of high treason. Ministers believed that their demands for parliamentary reform were merely a cover for a more sinister and revolutionary scheme. They suspected that the radicals were planning another national convention with which to replace parliament, and that the radical societies were arming in preparation for forcing a change of constitution. Apart from Robert Watt's farcical 'Pike Plot' to seize Edinburgh Castle, exposed in May 1794 (and for which he was executed), there was little conclusive evidence for these beliefs before 1795; but it is more likely that the government was right to be suspicious in the later 1790s.

The Society of United Irishmen, directly inspired by the French Revolution, had been established in Belfast and Dublin in 1791 as a non-sectarian reform society. After considerable disagreement over their precise political aims, in 1794 the United Irishmen declared their support for universal manhood suffrage. The unwillingness of the Irish administration to concede any reforms eventually caused the United Irishmen to operate clandestinely and to seek French military assistance, incited by a militant, republican minority led by Arthur O'Connor and Lord Edward Fitzgerald. A substantial French force sent to invade Ireland in December 1796 was only turned back by stormy weather, and it would only have found a small British force in Ireland had it managed to land. When rebellion finally broke out in Ireland in May 1798, however, the reverse was true. Only a small French force was sent over to help, and it arrived too late. The insurrection was also defeated by the divisions and disorganization within the United Irishmen, by their failure to harness properly what was also a popular Catholic rising, and by the government's arrest and suppression of the United Irish leadership before the rebellion erupted.

The significance of the United Irishmen was not restricted to Ireland, however. As early as December 1792 the Dublin society had sent a fraternal address to the national convention of Scottish radicals meeting in Edinburgh, although the convention had voted not to answer it, finding it too dangerously radical. Two Irish delegates (Simon Butler and Archibald Hamilton Rowan), however, along with three English representatives (Charles Sinclair, Maurice Margarot and Joseph Gerrald) attended the British convention in Edinburgh in November–December 1793. By 1795 the United Irishmen were working to achieve a union of insurrectionary forces in Ireland, France and Britain. Agents established secret, oath-bound societies of United Englishmen, United Scotsmen and United Britons, greatly helped by Irish immigrants already living in Britain (including many who fled to the mainland both before and after the Irish Rising of 1798). A minority of the native British radical movement, including several prominent LCS members, supported their subversive and militant activities. The United Societies were most successful in recruiting support in London, the northwest of England and central Scotland, and they seem to have attracted people into membership from lower down the social scale than the radical societies had previously managed. It is impossible to discover how many people in Britain were really committed to a policy of violent revolution, but there is certainly evidence of arming, military drilling and hope of French military assistance in both Scotland and England to give substance to the government's fear that the country was harbouring fifth columnists who posed a serious danger to its security. Colonel Edward Despard was executed in 1803 for planning an armed insurrection in London in 1802. The 'Black Lamp' disturbances in west Yorkshire in 1801–2 may have included an element of political conspiracy; and it also seems likely that, while the violent Luddite machine-breaking disturbances of 1811–12 in Nottinghamshire probably only represented industrial grievances, those in south Lancashire and west Yorkshire reflected political aspirations as well.

Also extremely disturbing to the authorities was evidence that radical literature was being circulated among the armed forces in an attempt to incite them to mutiny. The most alarming instance of this was the mutiny of the Channel fleet stationed at Spithead and the Nore in April and May 1797. The protest at Spithead seems to have been almost wholly motivated by poor pay and working conditions, and the dissidents there were quite swiftly placated; but the mutineers at the Nore demanded greater concessions, were better organized, and were less easily subdued. It was widely believed that radicals had been involved in instigating the resistance, and although the sailors at Spithead emphasized their loyalty, there is some evidence of United Irish activity within the fleet and of contact between sailors and United Irishmen and LCS members on shore.

Nevertheless, the potential threat to the British state and its existing political and social order was always greater than the actual crisis, because France was never able to defeat Britain by armed force or even to land a significant invasion force, and because the radicals were never able to mobilize a sufficient proportion of the British population against the establishment and the existing system. Britain's ability to keep France at bay for twenty-two years, and eventually to triumph over it, can be attributed to several factors. Although Britain's financial system was severely strained, it proved far more efficient at raising taxes and loans than any system adopted in France. Britain's growing national economic prosperity and its rate of population increase, despite the war and the hardship it caused to individuals and to sectors of the population, supplied the men and money needed to sustain such a long war. French trade and industry were damaged badly by the revolution during the 1790s, by Napoleon's Continental System after 1806, and by the effects of war on land and at sea. British trade fluctuated throughout the conflict, but on the whole its level of prosperity was sustained. The British navy, expanded and reformed during the war, ensured that France was never able to mount a serious invasion attempt (except that driven away from Ireland by bad weather in 1796) and that British colonial possessions, which were responsible for so much of the country's wealth, were not only defended adequately but were significantly increased during the course of the conflict. France ultimately had to be overcome on land, however. Britain was involved in various alliances during the war, but this was mostly a frustrating experience since the other participating European nations tended to have different aims from Britain and were prone to withdraw from the conflict, leaving Britain isolated in the struggle against France. Although the British army began the war in poor condition, various reforms, together with the experience of continuous warfare in the Iberian peninsula under Wellington for over five years, eventually turned out troops that even their demanding general thought were probably the best in the world. A revived European alliance involving all the great continental powers was nevertheless necessary to defeat Napoleon conclusively between 1813 and 1815.

The British government's ability to defeat the radicals at home can similarly be explained by a combination of weaknesses on the part of the radicals and actions taken by the government and by their loyalist supporters. The radicals were never able to mobilize enough of the British population to topple the existing order. Despite the evidence of widespread food shortages and disease at certain times during the war years, of deep resentment against military and naval recruiting, of extensive discontentment caused by high taxation, and of great sympathy in some places (such as Norwich, Sheffield and Paisley) for the radical agenda, it remains the case that the radicals could not rally the majority of Britons to continuous, active support of their cause. The scale of discontent and agitation, while deeply alarming to the authorities at times, never presented a truly serious challenge, far less an irresistible one, to the old political and social order. The vast majority of riots were not revolutionary or even politically radical in intent, although radical groups may have tried to exploit them for their own ends; and local elites often managed to undermine the politicization of economic hardship by means of increased poor relief and charity.

The failure of radicalism in this period was partly due to the various measures the government took to suppress it. These measures were intended to deter potential radical supporters, although in the opinion of radicals and liberals they created the real constitutional threat. The government passed a series of repressive pieces of legislation, including the Traitorous Correspondence Act (1793), which banned all forms of trading with revolutionary France and, unusually, required anyone going to France to carry a passport; the Two Acts against Treasonable and Seditious Practices and Seditious Meetings (1795), which respectively clarified and extended existing law on treason and sedition, and required magistrates to be informed in advance of meetings of more than fifty people; an Act condemning Seduction from Duty and Allegiance of members of the armed forces (1797); an Act against Administering Unlawful Oaths (1797); and the Combination Acts (1799–1800) which made men who organized industrial activity liable to summary trial before a magistrate. In 1799, moreover, the United Societies, the LCS and all oath-bound societies were banned. A number of leading radicals were imprisoned for lengthy periods, sometimes without trial, when habeas corpus was suspended between 1794 and 1795 and between 1798 and 1801. Close surveillance was kept over radical activities, with the small secret service collecting details from magistrates, customs officials and the post office all over the country. Spies, informers and *agents provocateurs* were used; and prominent radicals were tried for sedition in Scotland in 1793–4 and for treason in England in

1794. Pitt even considered supporting legislation that would have given magistrates the power to withhold licences to preach.

The Pitt administration was largely successful in suppressing radical meetings, publications and societies. At first glance, this is not surprising, given the weight of legislation it enacted. It should be remembered, however, that ministers did not have access to unlimited force with which to compel obedience from the British population. They could and did use regular troops and militia men to suppress disturbances, but both forces were finite. Britain had only a small professional army, and regular troops were usually needed in Ireland or abroad. In any case, military force was used sparingly against British subjects because overuse was traditionally regarded as a form of tyranny. Even the new repressive legislation was very seldom used. No radical was ever actually prosecuted under the Treasonable and Seditious Practices Act (1795), and only two men were executed for treason in the whole of the 1790s. The government could not by itself remove the radical threat. It had to rely on the support of part of the community and the acquiescence of the rest. It is not, therefore, enough to argue, as some historians have done, that the radicals presented a real danger to the stability of the British state which was only met by the severe repression of government measures. Ministers had to depend upon popular assistance.

The government's anti-radical campaign was heavily reinforced by local loyalists. They published a vast quantity of conservative propaganda, written to suit various classes of readers and often distributed freely or at a greatly subsidized rate, and they far surpassed their radical counterparts in terms of volume, sales, variety, and social and geographic spread. Some loyalist writers were paid by the Treasury, but most wrote independently. Most churchmen supported the government and the existing order, and many sermons were preached and published to reinforce the loyalist message. Loyalists also harassed local radicals into silence or even support for conservative addresses and petitions by withdrawing custom from them, refusing them licences to trade, or prosecuting them for sedition. Militant conservatism also found very popular expression in Volunteering. From the start of the war, gentlemen living on the south coast of England began to form themselves into mounted patrols to defend their property against any French attack. In March 1794 ministers permitted the establishment of official Volunteer companies for defence both against French invasion and domestic radicalism. These were at first composed almost wholly of the comfortably off, who could afford to buy their own uniforms and equipment, but mass enlistment was encouraged in 1798, when fears of French invasion heightened. By 1805 Britain had a Volunteer force of some 450,000 men – the largest organization in the country. Although Volunteer units were not always entirely reliable, and although individuals might enlist for a great variety of reasons, Volunteering served nevertheless as a powerful weapon of visible propaganda which was clearly identified with the defence of the British constitution.

By contrast, the potential strength of the radical movement was never fully realized in this period. It never gathered either middle-class or lower-order support *en masse* more than temporarily or occasionally, attracting few rural labourers or domestic servants. It was disadvantaged by internal divisions over its programme and strategies. Particularly during its revolutionary phases, it naturally suffered from a lack of coordination because it was forced to operate underground. Even during these periods, there was no resort to revolutionary violence despite much insistence in radical literature on the right to resist, and despite evidence of obscure groups arming and drilling which never seemed to progress further than providing an outlet for the discontent of their members. Although a few revolutionary conspirators planned violent action, most radicals relied instead on constitutional strategies such as petitioning and demonstrating peacefully, neither of which posed any danger to the state. Evidence supplied to the government of insurrectionary intentions and plans by informers and spies, who had infiltrated radical meetings and networks, was often wildly exaggerated. At the treason trials of 1794, the government went to almost incredible lengths to prove the existence of a treasonable conspiracy, even changing the legal interpretation of the statute on treason, and yet it was unsuccessful in its attempt to convict the defendants. The administration frequently grasped at straws such as the unlikely Pop-Gun Plot of 1794, or the trial of the millenarian prophet Richard Brothers in 1795, in its attempt to convince the nation that the internal threat from radicalism was real, so that they could deal harshly with the radical societies. This may prove that the government believed that the menace was real; it does not prove that the danger was in fact genuine.

Most seriously, there was no successful invasion by the French that might have galvanized native revolutionary forces. Even if the French had invaded successfully, it is open to question how the radicals would have responded. Some claimed to be waiting in readiness to join an invading force; but others, especially by 1798, were dubious about French good faith and suspected that the invaders might be more interested in extending an increasingly despotic military empire than in fraternally promoting republicanism. It is unlikely that more than a small minority of radicals would have supported a French invasion of Britain, although their rhetoric often suggested otherwise. Indeed, while the French Revolution was the catalyst for the crisis of the 1790s in Britain, it was also responsible for weakening the chances of success of the radical movement. The increasing violence and extremism of the internal government of France, and then its blatant military expansion abroad, lost it a great deal of sympathy among radicals and reformers in Britain, and lent support to the arguments of Burke and other conservatives who had denounced the French Revolution and opposed any similar meddling with the British constitution. Moreover, once hostilities were declared between Britain and France, the radical movement itself lost support because, while they had traditionally assumed the character of 'true' patriots, they gained an anti-patriotic image because of their continuing enthusiasm for the French Revolution at a time when France was at war with Britain.

The opposition Whigs in parliament and their supporters out-of-doors clung to the middle ground in the debate. They did not succumb to government and loyalist alarmism, but maintained a position of opposition to the war and to the government's repressive policies, and they lent the radical movement a certain amount of support, representing individual radicals in the sedition and treason trials, befriending many radical leaders and working with them on issues of shared concern, such as the peace petitions and the opposition to the Two Acts. The aid that they gave the radical movement by defending the right to freedom of speech and of the press, or simply by taking an oppositionist stance in parliament and in the press, however, should not be confused with support for such radical principles as universal manhood suffrage. They may not have yielded to conservative alarmism, but nor did they succumb to radical blandishments. The liberal opposition in parliament and in the country may have made it less easy for the government to repress the radicals, but it did not endanger the British state.

The view that Britain was on the point of revolution in the 1790s or early 1800s does not sufficiently acknowledge the fact that there was widespread acquiescence in the existing system. In some people outright support for the prevailing order was created by conviction, by francophobia, perhaps, by fear of French invasion, or by agreement with the conservative view of the benefits of the existing British state and constitution. In others a practical, if not an ideological, conformity stemmed from intimidation by the loyalist community; in others still, from lack of political awareness or from simple apathy. If the magnitude of the crisis threatening the British political and social order in the years following the French Revolution has not always been recognized by some historians, those who wish to redress this balance should not forget the strength of ideological and practical loyalty which enabled the old order to survive the crisis almost unscathed until well into the nineteenth century.

FURTHER READING

Christie, Ian R.: *Stress and Stability in Late Eighteenth-Century Britain: The British Avoidance of Revolution* (Oxford, 1984).

Cookson, J. E.: *The Friends of Peace: Anti-War Liberalism in England, 1793–1815* (Cambridge, 1982).

Cookson, J. E.: *The British Armed Nation 1793–1815* (Oxford, 1997).

Curtin, Nancy J.: *The United Irishmen: Popular Politics in Ulster and Dublin 1791–1798* (Oxford, 1994).

Dickinson, H. T.: *British Radicalism and the French Revolution 1789–1815* (Oxford, 1985).

Dickinson, H. T. (ed.): *Britain and the French Revolution 1789–1815* (Basingstoke, 1989).

Dickinson, H. T.: *The Politics of the People in Eighteenth-Century Britain* (Basingstoke, 1995).

Elliott, Marianne: *Partners in Revolution: The United Irishmen and France* (New Haven, CT, 1982).

Emsley, Clive: *British Society and the French Wars 1793–1815* (Basingstoke, 1979).

McFarland, E. W.: *Ireland and Scotland in the Age of Revolution* (Edinburgh, 1994).

Macleod, Emma Vincent: *A War of Ideas? British Attitudes to the Wars against Revolutionary France, 1792–1802* (Aldershot, 1998).

Meikle, H. W.: *Scotland and the French Revolution* (Glasgow, 1912).

Morris, Marilyn: *The British Monarchy and the French Revolution* (New Haven, CT, 1998).

O'Gorman, Frank: *The Whig Party and the French Revolution* (Basingstoke, 1967).

Philp, Mark: *The French Revolution and British Popular Politics* (Cambridge, 1991).

Spence, Peter: *The Birth of Romantic Radicalism: War, Popular Politics and English Radical Reformism 1800–1815* (Aldershot, 1996).

Thompson, E. P.: *The Making of the English Working Class* (1963; 2nd edn, London, 1968).

Wells, Roger: *Insurrection: The British Experience 1795–1803* (Gloucester, 1983).

Part II

The Economy and Society

Chapter Ten

Manufacturing and Commerce

John Rule

By the standards of the time at the beginning of the eighteenth century, Britain already had a successful and developing economy. The agricultural predominance characteristic of traditional economies was already shrinking, and it was to continue to do so through the century with increasing momentum in the final decades. Recent reassessment and augmentation of the employment data in the much-used surveys of Gregory King (1688) and Joseph Massie (1759) have tended to the view that Britain in 1700 had even larger commercial and manufacturing sectors than used to be thought. By 1688, 27.7 per cent of the population was engaged in industry, building and commerce, and by 1759, 36.8 per cent. Such proportions were significantly in excess of the European average, which for industry was 12.6 per cent in 1700 compared with Britain's 18.5 per cent. In 1800 the respective figures were 18.6 per cent and 29.5 per cent. By the time of the first census in 1801, the 11.2 per cent of the population employed in trade, when added to this latter statistic, produces a figure of over 40 per cent, ahead now of the 35.9 per cent employed in agriculture. Although technological change was still slow, it is reasonable to suppose that more value per head was produced in manufacturing and commerce than in traditional agriculture and, accordingly, that the value of the output of the former began to exceed that of the latter from at least the beginning of the eighteenth century. Statistics like these, derived as they are from male employment data, may well understate the overall importance of industry, for, relatively speaking, more women than men were disemployed by the agrarian changes of the century, and young women especially were available for industrial employment, particularly, but far from exclusively, in the still persistently domestic textile manufactures.

Writing *A Tour through the Whole Island of Great Britain*, around 1700, Daniel Defoe portrayed an England of active manufacturing regions: in Devon, where for 20 miles around Exeter the trade of serges was carried on; in Norfolk, where for as many miles about the city of Norwich the stuff-weaving trade was carried on; in Essex, where for nearly 40 miles in every direction the bay-making trade was carried on; in Wiltshire, where from Warminster to Malmesbury, inclusive of all the great towns of Bradford, Trowbridge, Westbury, Tedbury, Frome and Devizes, the manufacture of fine Spanish and medlay clothing and drugget-making were carried on; in Gloucester and Worcester, where the white-clothing trade for the Turkey merchants was carried on; in the counties of Warwick and Stafford, all around the town of Birmingham, where the hardware manufacture and cutlery trade was carried on; in Yorkshire and Lancashire, round and about the great manufacturing towns of Manchester, Sheffield, Leeds and Halifax, where the well-known manufactures of cottonware, ironware, Yorkshire cloths, kersies, etc. were carried on.

It is hardly a complete list. It mentions none of the great artisan manufactures of London, nothing of the mining of coal, tin, lead or copper. It is perhaps half a century too soon for the rapid rise of the potteries of the Staffordshire towns. It is confined to England: not so serious an omission then, but following the Union of 1707, Scotland too was to make significant manufacturing progress. It is notable too for the fact that it does not confine manufacturing activities to the named towns alone, but includes the districts that surrounded them. Certainly a feature of the eighteenth-century development of the English economy, which was clearly linked to the growth of industry and commerce, was increasing urbanization. In 1700 it has been estimated that 13.4 per cent of the population lived in towns of 10,000 or more inhabitants. By 1800, 24 per cent did so, and this compared with just 10 per cent for north and west Europe minus England. But even in Lancashire, the 'cradle' of the factory system, manufacturing growth produced a thickening of the population over the countryside as much as it did in distinct urban areas. Manufacturing then had both urban and rural forms, often within the same industry. Typically, urban artisans made the better-quality goods. Superior cutlery was made in Sheffield to that produced in the surrounding settlements. Wolverhampton and Willenhall made locks, while the Black Country's villagers, women as well as men, made chains and nails. Coventry's silk ribbons were higher-priced than those woven in rural Warwickshire. There are many other examples, but it would be incorrect to suppose that in Britain rural manufacturing was generally a matter of crude production deriving from the seasonal and gender-spared labour of farming households. Rural manufacturers were an industrial labour force often well established in the countryside. Many may have kept up small-scale farming, but in textiles, in mining and in metal-making, it had become for most households a subsidiary activity.

Many historians now avoid using the term 'industrial revolution', with its connotations of rapid transformation to the modern factory system; others will allow it as having value for the nineteenth but not the eighteenth century. It has even been suggested that it better describes the period from the 1880s rather than the 1780s (Price 1999: 17–22). If, however, references to a 'great discontinuity' in the closing decades of the eighteenth century have been largely abandoned, it is still possible to view them as years in which significant developments in technological and organizational terms took place, which inaugurated two centuries of breaking and rebreaking of tradition. This does not imply that manufacturing developments earlier in the century were insignificant, for the later acceleration towards the modern manufacturing system was preceded by a long period of steady growth and by the expansion and modification of traditional methods of production.

Modern assessments certainly point towards a less sharply broken growth profile even than that offered by Deane and Cole in their pioneering work of 1962. Particularly influential in this regard has been the work of Crafts. It is axiomatic that the rise of a modern industrial economy depends on an increase in the rate of capital formation, and gross domestic investment did increase steadily through the eighteenth century from 4 per cent of gross national product in 1700 through 7 per cent in 1780 to 7.9 per cent by 1801. It did not, however, exceed the 10 per cent level, which has been associated with industrial 'takeoff', until the 1820s.

Textiles

By the mid-eighteenth century textiles nationally employed more than 100,000 families and the spectacular rise of cotton manufacture was only just beginning (woollen cloth still outproduced cotton into the early nineteenth century). In 1700 woollen and worsted cloths accounted for 70 per cent of English domestic exports and still accounted for 50 per cent at mid-century. The major areas of production by then, with the Devonshire serges already falling away, were East Anglia, around Norwich, for lighter worsteds; the western counties embracing parts of Wiltshire, Gloucestershire and Somerset for the traditional heavy woollen cloths; and the West Riding of Yorkshire, rapidly rising to predominance and producing both cheaper woollen cloths and worsteds. Merchant capitalism continued to organize production in the west country, putting to work thousands of cottage-based handloom weavers, who, in turn, depended on an even larger number of spinners. West Riding woollen cloth production depended on the extended households of small working clothiers. It was here that the factory system was to develop in the early nineteenth century, but the 15 per cent weighting in total manufacturing which woollen and worsted cloth contributed in 1770 derived at this time from well-established methods of production.

At the beginning of the eighteenth century much linen was being imported, but, aided by protective duties, home production made impressive strides. English output quadrupled between 1720 and 1775, but the greater share of output continued to come from Ireland and Scotland, which together had 700,000 spindles by the mid-nineteenth century compared with 265,000 in England and Wales. It was perhaps Scotland's greatest manufacturing triumph. Based in the five counties of Forfarshire, Perthshire, Fife, Lanarkshire and Renfrewshire, the value of linen produced rose from £103,000 in 1728 to £1,116,000 in 1799. Silk was less important but still outweighed cotton in its contribution to total manufacturing in 1770. Its progress can be measured from the increasing volume of raw silk imported. Around 1700 this amounted in value to £500,000, which had doubled by the 1770s and reached £1.25 million by 1815. The greatest concentration of silk cloth weavers was in the Spitalfields district of London, where their notorious readiness to take riotously to the streets was a matter of consternation to the city's authorities. Coventry and its neighbourhood dominated the manufacture of ribbons. The process of 'throwing', that is, the production of silk yarn, underwent a precocious mechanization. Thomas Lombe's water-powered mill at Derby was in production by 1720, and, followed by others in Macclesfield, Stockport and other towns in north Cheshire and south Lancashire, it can be considered a true pioneer of factory production.

In south Lancashire, however, it was cotton which in the last quarter of the century was to signal the coming transformation of British manufacturing. Like silk, its progress can be measured from the imports of its raw material. British consumption of raw cotton was 1.2 million pounds in 1760 and rose through 6.5 million pounds by 1780 to 51.6 million in 1800; an amazing rate of growth in a generation. By 1815 its weighting in British manufacturing was 8 per cent out of a total textile weighting of 27 per cent. It still lagged behind wool at 11 per cent, but it outweighed silk and linen combined. In terms of technological advance cotton production headed wool. Cotton yarn was being spun in water-powered mills following Richard Arkwright's water-powered mill at Cromford in 1771, and steam power was coming into use for coarse yarns from the mid-1780s and, with the adoption of the spinning mule, for the finer varieties by the 1790s. By 1811 there were over 4 million steam mule spindles spread over more than fifty mills in the Manchester district alone. The age of the factory was truly beginning. None the less, although Edmund Cartwright patented a power loom as early as 1785, mechanized weaving only became established in the second quarter of the nineteenth century. In the meantime the number of handloom weavers turning the factory yarn into cloth increased from 75,000 in 1795 to 225,000 in 1811, by which year factory employees, women and children predominant over adult males, exceeded 100,000. Outside of Lancashire and Cheshire cotton manufacture became located in Scotland. Its main centre was Glasgow and the smaller settlements such as Paisley. In this district by 1809 some forty-one cotton-spinning mills employed 932 men, 2,449 women and 17,792 children.

Textile yarn, wool, silk and cotton, was not just manufactured into cloth. The manufacture of hosiery through framework knitting was the dominant industrial employment of the east midlands, with Nottingham and Leicester its main centres. Producing stockings on knitting frames had already driven more traditional methods to the margins by the beginning of the century. By 1740 around 5,000 frames were at work and, by the time the Luddite disturbances of 1811–12 convulsed the district, there were six times as many, giving employment to 50,000 persons. Glovemaking employed similar numbers by then at and around its main centres of Yeovil, Worcester and Hereford. The leather industry generally in the 1770s was second only to wool in the value it added to manufacturing output. Like garment manufacture generally, production came from legions of handworkers: tailors, shoemakers and others. These could be found in most towns, but were most numerous by far in London, where they tended to form one of the poorest sections of artisan manufacture.

Coal

Coal output increased fivefold over the century, even though steam power was only exceptionally used before the nineteenth century (by 1830 the 1800 output level had doubled again). The contributions of the British coalfields varied. Most significant was the great coalfield of northeast England, whose output rose over the century from 1,290,000 to 5,395,000 tons. In terms of its share of total output, this was actually a fall from 43 to 30 per cent. Scottish output rose from 450,000 to 2,000,000 tons, although its share fell from 15 to 13.3 per cent. Besides the northeast only the west midlands headed Scotland in 1800 with an output of 2,550,000 tons: a share of 17 per cent. With approximately 60 per cent of output coming from these three areas, the bulk of the remainder in 1800 was coming in order of output from south Wales, Lancashire, Yorkshire and the east midlands. Smaller amounts were produced in Cumberland, the southwest and north Wales. Figures of this magnitude indicate the importance of the prodigious availability of coal to the eighteenth-century economy. Of course much of it was burned in domestic hearths: urban Britain, given its climate, could hardly have expanded at the rate it did otherwise. London had been consuming coals brought by the collier vessels sailing from the Tyne since the sixteenth century. There was, however, an increasingly varied use of coal for manufacturing purposes, even before the first steam-powered cotton mills appeared, following James Watt's critical breakthroughs in the closing decades of the century. Even before the end of the seventeenth century coal was being used to heat, boil, brew, smelt and malt, and its uses were rapidly expanding. Petitioners in 1738, who complained of its high price, included glassmakers, brewers, distillers, sugar bakers, soap boilers, smiths, dyers, brickmakers, lime burners, founders and calico printers. Industries said to be threatened by a miners' strike in Bristol in 1792 included glass houses, copper refineries, lead works and distilleries. None of these involved using steam power, which only began to make its appearance from the 1780s. Whitbread's London brewery, for example, purchased its first Boulton and Watt engine in 1786 in order to grind malt, although it had long been using coal to heat its vats. The delayed and sporadic spread of coke smelting in ironmaking contrasts with earlier use in non-ferrous metal smelting. By the 1750s the combined value of copper, tin and lead approached £1 million. Output continued to increase. In 1788 the value of copper alone exceeded that of pig iron. Particularly as the core ingredient of brass, it was vital to Birmingham's metal trades, which by the middle decades of the eighteenth century employed around 20,000 workers, whose labour was being made significantly more productive through the use of the lathe, stamp and press. Iron was of course forged with coal to be made usable by village blacksmiths, through Black Country nailmakers to Sheffield's skilled metalworkers. The diversifying uses of coal in eighteenth-century manufacturing provided Britain with an invaluable leadership in coal technologies: the beginnings of the energy breakthrough which has been seen as the essence of the industrial revolution. Even before Watt's translation of reciprocal into rotary motion, steam engines were playing a crucial role in draining mines, for which purpose sixty Newcomen engines were in use from Cornwall to Newcastle by 1733, and 300 by 1780. As Watt's engines were added, the number of steam engines working at British mines was around 1,200 by the end of the century.

Iron

Abraham Darby's 1709 discovery of coke smelting notoriously diffused only slowly, although later historians have largely ceased to blame this on industrial secrecy, indicating instead problems with the pig iron produced and the little cost advantage to smelters. From 1750, however, coke smelting rapidly overtook the use of charcoal with iron output doubling by 1780. The locating of iron manufacture on the coalfields was completed over the second half of the century. In 1806 England produced 149,000 tons of iron, Wales 72,000 tons and Scotland 23,000 tons. This was almost treble the 1780 British output of 62,000 tons. Critical to this huge expansion were Henry Cort's two transforming inventions patented in 1784: the puddling furnace and the rolling mill. Usable bar iron could now be produced in huge quantities that were removed from dependence on reforging with charcoal and water-powered hammers. Heavy regional concentration followed with over 90 per cent of English and Welsh output coming in 1806 from south Wales and the three counties of Yorkshire, Shropshire and Staffordshire. From the 1780s the iron industry had taken on a locational pattern and a scale of operation that were to persist until the second half of the nineteenth century. The availability of mass-produced workable iron transformed the size of the iron hardware industry. Exceptional works like Boulton and Watt's famous Soho works in Birmingham produced steam engines, munitions and other large items, but in 1800 most of the iron output of Shropshire and Staffordshire was being made up in the region's foundries and forges into utensils, tools, locks, nails, and so on, for the most part by vast numbers of small producers. The great steel manufacture of edged tools and cutlery in and around Sheffield similarly continued to be made by skilled artisans in small forges attached to their cottages.

Other Manufactures

Of other manufactures, both glass- and paper-making experienced significant growth. The former, like metals, had become increasingly dependent on coal. The combined output of bottle and white glass doubled over the second half of the century to reach 19,400 tons by 1800. Although the opening of the famous Ravenshead works at St Helens in 1773 was a significant event in the history of plate glass manufacture, glass-making most noticeably established itself around Dudley and Stourbridge in the west midlands and in the northeast around Newcastle. Coal was essential for firing the reverbatory furnaces. Paper-making was not coal dependent, but water was essential in its processes and the mills had to be situated on riversides. Output increased steadily over the first half of the century, but then more dramatically to produce by 1815 a sevenfold increase over the level of 1714. This increase was closely linked to the growth of printing and together they accounted for around 2 per cent of total manufacturing output by the later date.

Pottery was another success story of eighteenth-century consumer goods production. By mid-century London, Worcester, Derby and Liverpool were among those with porcelain works, but the real growth was to come from the common wares of Staffordshire. As late as 1730 that county's potters were still using local clays and selling in their own area, but by 1760 the Weaver Navigation was transporting six times as much pottery as twenty years previously. The leading entrepreneur, Josiah Wedgwood, was sending most of his wares to London and beyond. He was perhaps exceptional, but he nevertheless represents a rapidly growing manufactory. The 'Potteries' – the five towns around Burslem – developed into one of Britain's most distinctive manufacturing districts, Burslem alone having 150 potteries by 1762.

Shipbuilding

Shipbuilding was unusual among industries because it was in part a state enterprise. The Royal Dockyards individually were the largest industrial sites operating in the British economy. Even the newest, Plymouth, employed over 1,000 men by mid-century. At the time of the American War in 1776 the total establishment at the six yards was around 10,000 men. At the height of the Napoleonic War in 1813, the greatest of them, Portsmouth, employed 3,582 men. The Royal Navy's demand for ships naturally depended on the needs of war; hence, after a few years of peace, this number had fallen to 1,610 men by 1822. The dockyards were amalgams of skilled labour. At Portsmouth in 1803 there were 900 shipwrights, 140 sawyers, 200 rope-makers, 100 carpenters and 140 caulkers, supported by 350 general labourers.

Much naval shipbuilding was contracted out to private yards, mostly to those on the Thames, but, by the time of the American War, orders were increasingly being placed in the northeast. Merchant shipping even at times of war vastly exceeded naval shipbuilding in both numbers and tonnage. In 1810 the merchant fleet of 12,198 vessels was sixteen times bigger than the Royal Navy. By the end of the eighteenth century London, still, and the northeast, more recently, dominated the building of vessels of 200 tons and above. In 1790–1, 150 of these were built: twenty-five on the Thames and eighty-eight in the northeast. In terms of share of total tonnage the former contributed almost 16 per cent and the latter 40 per cent, with the south coast contributing 15 per cent, the northwest 14 per cent, and the remaining tonnage being shared between East Anglia and the Bristol Channel. Not all British registered ships were built in England. Although the Clyde had no shipbuilding firms before 1800, playing no part in the age of the wooden ship, in the middle decades of the century up until the American War a significant contribution came from the North American colonies: one in three ships by 1776.

The Organization of Manufacturing

It would be surprising if, given its wide product range and its not inconsiderable geographical reach, British manufacturing had not exhibited diverse forms of organization. What is clear, however, is that the characteristic forms of industrial capitalism existing by the middle decades of the nineteenth century were still uncommon at the end of the eighteenth century. Large concentrations of capital and labour, in factory, engineering or ironworks or in deep mining, although they existed, and indeed increased after the 1770s, did not generally predominate with regard to output or employment. What is also clear is that merchant capital, derived from the profits of commerce to a significant degree, underwrote both the production and the purveying of manufactured goods. In textiles, by 1800, if a few mills in wool and worsted production and several employed on silk are added to the 900 cotton-spinning mills by then operating, a total of 1,000 textile mills is a reasonable estimate. But few of them were large and all of them employed women and children in larger numbers than men. To a much greater extent textiles were produced from a combination of merchant capital and cottage labour, traditionally known as the 'putting-out system'. Under this system large employers certainly existed, but they did not typically manage labour on particular sites of production. They put out materials to and collected finished work from an army of dependent outworkers, such as handloom weavers or framework knitters. Many putting-out merchants were very substantial indeed. To count as 'substantial' in the west country woollen manufacture a clothier needed to put out to at least thirty to forty households. According to Defoe at the beginning of the century some of Gloucestershire's 'gentlemen clothiers' were worth from £10,000 to £40,000. In East Anglia, too, it was merchant capital, not independent manufacturing, which controlled the making of cloth. Of the major districts, only in the West Riding did the independent, small working clothier with an extended household predominate. In the late eighteenth century there were still more than 3,000 independent clothiers in the region. These clothiers purchased their wool from the staplers and, assisted by family, apprentices and perhaps one or two hired journeymen, took it through all the stages of manufacture to the undressed cloth. There was a low capital threshold and, in marked contrast to the situation in the west country, a small social gap between master and journeymen since the latter could aspire to the status of the former. The system's survival had depended on a favourable credit relationship with the merchants who took up the cloth and on the combining of manufacturing with the running of a small farm.

Such men hardly survived elsewhere. Even in the West Riding the newer worsted section of the cloth manufacture was largely organized under the putting-out system. In neighbouring Lancashire, cotton, in the several decades when it flourished in a pre-factory form, followed the same pattern. In 1736 one merchant claimed that he and his brother put out to more than 600 looms – and it then needed around four female wheel-spinners to keep each loom supplied with yarn. In 1758 another capitalist claimed to employ 500 persons, while by 1812, in the era of factory-spun yarn, several spoke of employing more than 1,000 outworkers. These controlling manufacturing capitalists had for the most part emerged from a merchant background. By the time weaving followed spinning into the factory in the 1830s, the population of outworking handloom weavers peaked at around 250,000, and some employers were distributing warps to weavers over distances of up to 30 miles. In the east midlands stocking manufacture, hosiers filled the role of the clothiers. One hosier in 1813 claimed to put out to more than 300 framework knitters, while by the end of the following decade several kept more than 1,000 frames at work.

Textiles were not alone in presenting the proto-industrial system under which merchant capital organized cottage labour to produce for often distant markets. The system was also prevalent in the final stages of iron and other metal manufacturing. At the bottom of the ladder more than 12,000 workers, women as well as men, were employed at their cottage anvils to turn the iron rod put out by iron merchants into nails. One from the Black Country claimed to put out to more than 1,000 homes. No other branch of the iron trade was as populous, but other iron goods were similarly produced from put-out bar or sheet iron. Brass wares were similarly manufactured; in 1767 one merchant claimed to put out this metal to be worked by more than 2,000 persons. Such workers – along with the weavers and knitters – can indeed be considered as a labour-selling outworking proletariat, but the boundaries were not always clear. In cutlery manufacture, for example, cheaper cutlery was made in the same way from put-out steel, but the finer wares on which Sheffield's reputation rested allowed a greater degree of independence. Very little capital was needed to set up the characteristic small forges and 'little masters' survived well into the nineteenth century. Even if in theory working on their own raw materials, and selling the product of their labour, rather than labour power itself, they were usually dependent on merchant suppliers through credit and commonly sold their product to the same merchant, so that what might be described as a 'price' was in reality more like a piece rate. Similar arrangements existed through Birmingham's matrix of small workshops. True putting-out arrangements dominated in the manufacture of simple objects like buttons, but even where merchant capital did not put out, it typically controlled the trade through the prices at which it bought in the products. Cutting prices was not to the recipient so very different from cutting wages, even if it did permit the continuance in some sense of the independent producer.

The greatest centre of artisanal production was London. Workers in the larger trades such as tailoring, shoemaking or even, by the end of the century, watchmaking were numbered in thousands. In many trades, especially in some of the more skilled and specialized, elements of the guild-style of mobility from apprentice through journeyman to independent master remained. But, increasingly, London's manufacturing trades depended on a class of permanent wage-dependent journeymen. These often existed alongside small struggling masters, the price of whose independence was poverty. In tailoring, for example, it was the West End tailors who insisted on working for time wages on their merchant-employers' premises, while the lower-quality work of the East End was done at home for precarious piece rates. A similar division between 'honourable' and 'dishonourable' sections existed in shoemaking and in hat manufacturing. Watchmaking, on the other hand, was largely organized in its Clerkenwell location as an urban putting-out trade. The division of labour was extreme and the 'watchmaker', who put his name on perhaps several thousand completed watches, might have employed as many as 300 workmen in the manufacture of the separate components. In some trades journeymen, such as compositors in the expanding printing trades and some building craftsmen, were paid premium wages, while at the other end of the scale common labourers working in paint works and lead works received little for working in life-destroying conditions.

Heavy Industry and Mining

By the middle years of the century, in iron founding, artisan ownership had passed away. It needed around fifteen men to operate the smallest of works with a single furnace and forge. In the charcoal era, even when single-owned, the smelting and forging were often carried out at geographically separate sites. After mid-century large complex units began to appear where both coal and iron existed. Arthur Young in the 1770s estimated that several hundred were employed at Crawley's near Newcastle, 1,000 were employed at Coalbrookedale and 500 at Rotherham, although he usually included colliers as well as ironworkers. In Shropshire ironworks tended to be larger, but a typical size elsewhere was 200 to 300 persons. Technological advance, especially from the 1780s, made for increasing size and concentration with the increasing use of water-powered slitting and tilting machinery. Large ironworks were created by the bringing together of processes where water power was available.

The reciprocal action of steam engines was widely adapted to the draining of mines decades before Watt enabled the translation of steam power into rotary form. As a consequence the eighteenth century saw the birth and significant spread of deep underground mining for coal and metals, although shallower, small-scale mining persisted alongside it through the century, especially in older mining areas such as the Forest of Dean. In its more advanced areas, however, mining underwent a significant degree of capitalization. By 1800, for example, several copper mines in Cornwall were already individually employing a thousand workers, when women and children engaged in surface tasks are included. Coal-mining enterprises too were becoming larger. By the early nineteenth century the average labour force on the northeast coalfield was 300, 200 of whom worked underground. The links between coal mining and landowning were close, with landed families, like the Fitzwilliams of Yorkshire or the Lowthers in Cumberland, emerging as a distinct class of 'coal-owners'. At the end of the seventeenth century a visitor to Cornwall wrote of tin mines as typically employing around twenty men and boys, but things changed dramatically when around 1740 copper displaced tin in importance, with significant expansion in the 1780s enabled by improvements in steam pumping. By the end of that decade, behind the several mines employing a thousand workers, were dozens whose labour force was measured in hundreds. As a whole Cornish mining for copper and tin occupied more than 10,000 men, women and children by 1800. Lead mining employed a smaller total, but here too some enterprises present examples of significant capitalism, particularly in the northern Pennines, where the Quaker-owned London Lead Company was the dominant enterprise. It seems reasonable to suppose that metal mining in Britain employed at least 13,000 workers and coal mining at least 60,000 by the end of the eighteenth century.

It has commonly been suggested that a distinguishing trend of an industrializing economy, in addition to an increase in investment in manufacturing and mining, is a shift from circulating to fixed capital: that is, from capital tied up in raw materials, part-processed goods and those awaiting marketing, towards buildings, plant or, in the case of mining, shaft sinking. Estimates suggest that the ratio of fixed to circulating capital in Britain moved from less than 1 : 1 in 1760 to 3 : 1 by 1860. It would seem, however, that most of this shift did not become marked before 1800, nor dramatic before 1830. This reflects the gradual and piecemeal takeoff of the factory system, once the unrepresentative nature of the cotton industry is recognized. Even in the cotton industry trends can be exaggerated. The typical share of fixed capital in large enterprises around the end of the eighteenth century was under a fifth of total investment. In wool even the precocious example of Benjamin Gott's enterprise at Leeds in 1801 reveals a circulating capital almost two and a half times as large as that committed to fixed capital. Coal mining exhibits a similar pattern of growth over the eighteenth century, but at rates less dramatic than those of the early nineteenth century. The annual rate of capital formation certainly increased from £83,000 in 1760 to £211,000 in 1790, but by 1810 an annual investment of £776,000 has been estimated.

Even if demands for fixed capital formation generally were, by later standards, less than dramatic, growing enterprises still had to find increasingly larger amounts of operating capital of all kinds. The role of merchant capital, especially involved in the expansion of the putting-out system, has already been mentioned, but there are important examples of merchants going further and becoming factory builders, especially in cotton. Yet it has also been shown that at the great woollen centre of Leeds surprisingly few of the merchants followed the example of Benjamin Gott in employing their profits directly in the factory system, while in the manufacture of hardware Matthew Boulton, famous for his association with James Watt, was also exceptional in his creation of the giant Soho factory in Birmingham. Direct investment is not, however, the whole story. What merchants did often provide was credit both for the purchase of raw materials and for the take-up of finished goods. This was an enabling role of immense importance to the growth of eighteenth-century manufacturing.

Mining, for coal or metal, had special capital needs. The sinking of shafts and the installation of pumping engines presented a formidable 'hump' of investment before any profits were returned. We have already noted the role of landowners as 'coal-owners' and increasingly, as the iron industry developed over the century, ironmasters became considerable investors in coal mines. The flow of capital from iron dynasty names like Cort, Darby, Wilkinson and Crawley became very important after 1780, most clearly indicated by such integrated concerns as Coalbrookedale in Shropshire or Ambrose Crawley's giant works in Durham. Non-ferrous metal mining, based in hard-rock areas, was not only expensive to initiate and develop, but was much more speculative as a venture, with the risk of not finding significant ores always present. In the tin and copper mines of Cornwall the risk was spread through the use of the 'costbook system'. Under this a group of 'adventurers' formed a company and subscribed capital relative to their agreed share, with profits being distributed at intervals, but with proportionate calls being made on them when investment was needed. This system brought into the mining industry capital not only from landowners, but from merchants, bankers, professionals, and indeed from anyone seeking a speculative investment. A similar system operated in the lead mines of Derbyshire. Mining as a whole was unusual in its capital needs and in the ways in which they were met. Major organizational problems had to be grappled with at a time when most of the rest of industry was still in the handicraft stage.

Meeting Markets

The rise of manufacturing came in response to enlarging markets. Not all commerce is concerned with the supply and exchange of visible goods, but that is what the eighteenth century would mostly have understood by it. Of course not all traded visible goods arise from manufacturing. The increasing commercialization of agriculture was as evident a feature of the age. Overseas colonial trade brought profits from re-exported products such as tea, sugar, coffee and tobacco. It also brought the gains from the trade in black slaves. Foreign trade tends to attract more attention than domestic trade, although the total volume of the latter is much the larger. At the beginning of the century domestic exports accounted for around 7 to 8 per cent of national output; by 1750 this had risen to 10 to 12 per cent and by 1800 to around 17 per cent. Exports accounted for perhaps a fifth of the increase in the output of the economy as a whole. After mid-century, however, they were predominantly made up of manufactured goods. It was in respect of particular manufactures like cotton and iron that they mattered most. These industries were making spectacular productivity gains and were driving the increase in the share of manufactured goods exported from a fifth in 1700 to a third by 1800. Possibly, over the century as a whole, exports may have accounted for 40 per cent of the increase in manufacturing output. In 1700 trade with Europe dominated both imports and exports, but by 1800 less than a third of imports came from the continent and it accounted for less than a fifth of exports. Trade with North America and the West Indies, on the other hand, increased more than six times between 1700 and 1815. The North American colonies were especially important as a market enabled by the high per capita incomes of its rapidly growing white population to consume not just textiles, but iron and other metalwares, and pottery. In short, of Britain's overseas markets,

North America was the most like an extension of its home market in the range and depth of its consumption.

In contrast, Africa took little apart from increasing trade goods after 1780 that were exported to secure the black slaves in the numbers required by the expanding plantation economies of the Americas. It is hard to evaluate just what direct contribution this evil traffic made to British trade as a whole. Three ports – Bristol, Liverpool and London – participated in measurable degrees, with the role of the last declining significantly relative to the other two. Between 1772 and 1775 the average of 161 ships active in the trade from the three ports was double the number active in the 1730s and 1750s. Over the third quarter of the eighteenth century slavers made up from a quarter to a third of the merchant fleet. Abolition of the trade came in 1807. Neither was the Orient an avid consumer of British goods. It was notoriously a source of expensive imports. These included the tea brought in via the East India Company's monopoly that grew from £500,000 in value in 1700 to almost £2 million by 1780.

Overall, while it would be misleading to describe British manufacturing success over the century as 'export led', the role of overseas trade was to add both dynamism and extra growth. The role of the North American market both before and after the American Revolution was especially important. It was estimated in 1808 that of 50,000 persons, not including 20,000 nailmakers, engaged in hardware production in Birmingham and its region, as many produced for American consumption as did for the home market, while the former was also said to provide employment for 6,000 Sheffield cutlery workers. Cotton goods sold more widely. Exports were small before 1770, but by 1815 four yards of cotton cloth were being exported for every three sold at home. Cotton had accounted for 84 per cent of the increase in manufactured exports between 1784–6 and 1794–6. Its rise, as it displaced and then offset the traditional role of wool textiles, was to spearhead technological and organizational changes which, through their unprecedented lowering of production costs and the transformation of achievable output levels, demonstrated the possibility of making as well as meeting markets.

If export growth stimulated manufacturing growth, it was the home market which sustained it. Its eighteenth-century enlargement was critical. Population growth was fundamental, but also important was a steady, although not spectacular, downward spread of consumption. Indeed, some historians insist on a 'consumer revolution'. Population growth became rapid only after 1750, so the real problem is to explain how an expansion of the home market began even before then, and why it was not reversed by demographic expansion. What seems to have taken place was a widening and deepening demand for goods previously hardly purchased by those below society's upper ranks. Even in better-paid working-class households, goods which have been described as 'decencies' began to appear, making the difference between tolerable living and mere subsistence: soap, some new 'groceries' such as tea and sugar, a few items of pewter, brass or earthenware, basic metal wares and, by the end of the century, some cotton goods. Several explanations for the growth in the consumption of manufactured goods have been offered. In the first half of the century slow population growth placed no strain on grain supplies, thus bringing down food prices, which must have had some effect on the household income available for the purchase of non-food items. Later demographic research has supported the idea that in the period before about 1760 the consumption/production ratio was favourable, with the number of dependent children historically low. A rising rate of population growth after 1760 diminished these advantages, but there was no general erosion of living standards. For increasing numbers of people entering the market was not in any case a matter of choice, since self-sufficiency, payment in kind and living-in service were declining, especially in the southern counties. Generally, wage dependency was on the increase in manufacturing and in agriculture. Much, however, can be more positively explained by the growth of purchasing power among the middle ranks of society; from farmers, professionals and merchants to tradesmen, shopkeepers and the upper ranks of the skilled artisans. Even by the beginning of the century such people formed a bigger fraction of the population in Britain than they did elsewhere. Demand increased both from the increase in their numbers and from the rising prosperity of many in this group. But what share of the population did they represent? It has been suggested that economic growth and changing structures drew perhaps 3 million households above the line at which some degree of spending on other than necessaries became possible. In some cases increased purchasing power came from increasing employment opportunities for women and children. Wedgwood pottery, Black Country kettles, Sheffield cutlery and the whole range of Birmingham's small metal wares were certainly exported, but it was in British households that they first came to hold the middle ground between upper-class luxury and the penury of the labouring classes. The supply-side evidence tells a simple story. Goods were manufactured to an increasing volume and range, beyond the extent that even successful exporting can explain. To the 'commercial revolution' associated with the latter, at least some concept of a 'consumer revolution' must be added. Most people were not part of it, but to sustain the developing manufacturing economy of eighteenth-century Britain, it is only necessary that between a quarter and a half of a growing population were included.

FURTHER READING

Berg, Maxine: *The Age of Manufactures, 1700–1820: Industry, Innovation and Work in Britain* (2nd edn, London, 1994).

Clarkson, L. A.: *Proto-industrialization: The First Phase of Industrialization?* (London, 1985).

Court, W. C. B.: *The Rise of the Midland Industries, 1600–1838* (Oxford, 1953).

Crafts, N. F. R.: *British Economic Growth during the Industrial Revolution* (Oxford, 1985).

Daunton, Martin: *Progress and Poverty: An Economic and Social History of Britain 1700–1850* (Oxford, 1995).

Davis, Ralph: *The Industrial Revolution and British Overseas Trade* (Leicester, 1979).

Deane, Phyllis and Cole, W. A.: *British Economic Growth, 1688–1955* (Cambridge, 1962).

Flinn, M. W.: *The History of the British Coal Industry*, vol. 2: *1700–1830: The Industrial Revolution* (Oxford, 1984).

Harris, J. R.: *The British Iron Industry, 1700–1850* (London, 1988).

Hoppit, Julian: *Risk and Failure in English Business 1700–1800* (Cambridge, 1987).

Hudson, Pat: *The Industrial Revolution* (London, 1992).

McKendrick, Neil, Brewer, John and Plumb, J. H.: *The Birth of a Consumer Society: The Commercialization of Eighteenth-Century England* (London, 1982).

Price, Richard: *British Society 1680–1880: Dynamism, Containment and Change* (Cambridge, 1999).
Rule, John: *The Experience of Labour in Eighteenth-Century Industry* (London, 1981).
Rule, John: *The Vital Century: England's Developing Economy, 1714–1815* (London, 1992).
Schwarz, L. D.: *London in the Age of Industrialization: Entrepreneurs, Labour Force and Living Conditions, 1700–1850* (Cambridge, 1992).
Wrigley, E. A.: *Continuity, Chance and Change: The Character of the Industrial Revolution in England* (Cambridge, 1988).

CHAPTER ELEVEN

Agriculture and Rural Life

GORDON MINGAY

The Importance of Agriculture

Agriculture was by far the largest occupation of England in the eighteenth century. In 1700 it is estimated to have occupied directly 45 per cent of a population of 5 million, i.e., some 2.25 million people. A century later this number had grown, though the proportion was considerably less: some 36 per cent were then employed of a much larger population, something over 3 million out of more than 8.5 million people. While continuing to shrink as a proportion of the total, the numbers in farming continued to rise until the 1850s, when it was still the largest occupational group.

The remarkable achievement of agricultural progress in the eighteenth century was to feed, with a smaller proportion of the total, a non-agricultural population that expanded from an estimated 3.75 million to about 5.5 million, and this at a time when imports, though growing, accounted for only a small proportion of total food supply. In addition to food, of course, agriculture was producing increased quantities of important raw materials used in both country crafts and urban industries, such as timber, wool, hides and tallow (for candles) as well as dyestuffs and medicinal plants.

Apart from landowners and their families, whose incomes came mainly from farm rents and the profits of their estates, and the farmers and their labourers, many country residents depended in large part on the agricultural community for their living. These included the many craftsmen who found part of their market among landowners, farmers and labourers, such as workers in the cloth and clothing industries, building workers such as masons and carpenters, and workers in leather, as well as tradesmen, maltsters, brewers and distillers, corn and cattle dealers and drovers, millers, butchers and innkeepers. The rural professional class, made up of clergymen, attorneys, doctors, surveyors and estate stewards, also looked to the land for custom. It is interesting to examine the occupations of small country towns and remark how many of the inhabitants were employed in these various callings. The little Yorkshire town of Wetherby, for instance, with a population of only 912 in 1776, had twelve farmers and gardeners, employing four apprentices living in and fifty-one labourers. But in addition, there were eight professional men, including an attorney, three apothecaries and surgeons, an excise officer, two schoolmasters and a curate. As many as fourteen provision dealers supplied the neighbourhood, together with a linen-draper, an ironmonger, a whitesmith and gunsmith, and seventy-one craftsmen, who included six blacksmiths, five wheelwrights, three saddlers, two coopers, a tanner, a skinner, a glover, besom-maker and a farrier. There were, furthermore, a postmaster, a brewer, a miller and fifteen innkeepers, employing thirty-seven servants living in. This varied range of occupations reveals that agriculture provided the foundation of many people's lives, and it illustrates the significance of the agricultural community as a market for townsmen's products.

Of course, in more remote districts farming occupations loomed larger, accounting in small townships for perhaps as many as a third of all the households. On the other hand, in the larger country towns farmers were relatively scarce – only three in the Aylesbury of 1798, for example, out of 549 persons whose occupations were listed, and five in Buckingham out of 217 for the same date. In both places, however, like Wetherby there were many whose occupations were closely associated with the land. 'Labourers' made up over 30 per cent of Aylesbury's occupations, with numbers of these, no doubt, engaged in producing, processing and transporting the produce of the land.

In the countryside at large the size and character of the agricultural community varied considerably with the nature of the farming. Pastoral farming – rearing, fattening and dairying – was more common in the moister western half of the country, with the uplands given over to the rearing of cattle and grazing of sheep, and the midlands and west country to fattening and dairying. Arable farming was found, however, in favoured areas such as the Vale of Glamorgan and Salisbury Plain, and was widespread over the midland counties where in many districts the ancient open-field system still prevailed. The growing of grain crops was a main feature of the drier eastern half of the country, though even here large enclaves were given over to pasture, and an individual county, such as Kent or Lincolnshire, showed numerous variations and specialities, influenced by soils, local climate and availability of markets. Pastoral farming employed fewer people than the equivalent acreage of arable, about half as many according to the contemporary view, though in fact much of the farming everywhere was mixed in character, with arable and livestock as essential elements of an enterprise. Local specialization might include, for instance, the growing of barley for malting, hops for brewing, the rearing of horses, cheese-making, mustard or canary-seed, crops for dyestuffs such as weld and woad, and others used as both dyes and in medicine.

Pastoral farming generally gave rise to smaller communities than did arable with its large demand for hands to plough, sow and harvest. Partly because of availability of labour, crafts were more likely to be found in pastoral areas, although their location was influenced also by markets and the supply of raw materials. Heavily wooded areas fostered charcoal-burning, ironmaking and the fashioning of fencing, posts and gates. Such areas, too, lacking the presence of magistrates, were frequently the resort of robbers, footpads and coiners.

In general, however, the agricultural structure was made up of three main elements, landowners, farmers and farmworkers, each with different functions and very different incomes. By the later eighteenth century independent landowning farmers were in a minority, though their numbers varied from one district to another. The bulk of the land, perhaps 80 or 90 per cent of it, was in the hands of great landowners and gentry. Many of them, it is true, kept a home farm for the convenience of having a supply of fresh food ready to hand for their large households, but generally they did not go in for farming for an income. They preferred to leave this risky and troublesome business to tenant farmers, who, while often possessing some land of their own, rented additional acreage from landlords. This enabled them to employ their resources more profitably: contemporaries believed that farmers earned as profit a third of the value of their output, another third going to meet the costs of farming, and the other to the landlord in rent. Landowners, however, rarely received in rent more than about 3 per cent of the value of their land after allowing for outgoings, a factor which made farmers more willing to rent land than to own it.

Small farmers were engaged in various kinds of mixed and more specialized farming, and there were also large numbers of smallholders and 'husbandmen' who made a living, part-time or full-time, by dairying on common or rented land, by growing vegetables and fruit, or raising poultry. They were certainly more independent than the labourers, who generally had no land except perhaps access to a common, and who relied mainly on their wages.

The labourers fell into two main groups: those, mainly young and unmarried, who were farm servants, living in with the farmer and hired and paid by the year; and those who lived out in cottages and were paid by the day or at piecework rates for particular tasks. The latter, the day-labourers, were clearly less secure and had to give up their cottage when changing master; although in practice they often worked for years for the same farmer, when it was a common practice for farm servants to move on each year. Sometimes farm servants who saved their wages were able in time to set up as small farmers, the farmer helping them to begin by running their sheep with his own flock. Farm servants were more commonly found in northern and western areas where pastoral farming was the rule, day-labourers were scarce, and a regular workforce was required to look after the livestock. There were also numbers of semi-independent workers who made a living by carting coal, wood and building materials, and by 'higgling' or dealing in small quantities of poultry, eggs and vegetables, or by offering some special skill such as a knowledge of draining, hedging, well-digging or mole-catching.

Most farmers had no leases and, formally, little security. In practice, however, for reasons of securing votes and gaining popularity, landlords generally kept their rents low and revised them only at long intervals, and they were concerned to help their better tenants through difficult years. The last thing a landlord wanted was to have to take a farm 'in hand', for the losses arising from having to provide himself the stock and supervision of a farm could be heavy. In the village community the farmers shared with prominent tradesmen the unpaid duties of local administration, in the work of churchwarden, overseer, parish constable and surveyor of the highways. These posts were unpopular since they attracted a great deal of criticism as well as taking up time, and sometimes a farmer would approach his landlord to use his influence to have him excused from serving. Consequently, the parish work was often ill-done, if done at all: the church roof might leak for lack of repairs, the poor relief might be inadequate or inconsistent, vagrants and petty criminals might roam unchecked, and the roads become mired, flooded and sometimes impassable.

These parish functions were overseen by the county justices of the peace, mostly landowners but including in their number representatives of the church and trade. The numbers of justices rose considerably in the course of the century, but the actual work of petty and quarter sessions was usually carried out by a small active minority. Again the duties were unpaid, and the four shillings allowed a day was very far from meeting a conscientious justice's outgoings. The active justice, indeed, undertook an onerous round of attending sessions and other meetings, visiting prisons and houses of correction, supervising the work of overseers and inspecting roads and bridges, as well as issuing a variety of licences and certificates. The work occupied several days a week, and the frequent journeying round the neighbourhood in all weathers was not the least of the burdens.

It was from the more important landowning families that the lord lieutenant and high sheriff of the county were selected, and the parliamentary representation of a county could continue in the hands of a very few families over long periods, with elections often infrequent. When, however, there were elections to be fought, landowners promised to a candidate the votes of those of their tenants who possessed the franchise and canvassed them accordingly (though usually they could command only one of their tenants' two votes). Furthermore, they bought up property in villages and country towns in order to control more votes. When in command of a sufficiently valuable influence they gained favour with the county's great landowners, who thus were able to combine the separate strands of electoral control to form powerful groups in parliament.

The Prosperity of Farming

It would be a mistake to assume that those engaged in agriculture enjoyed a quiet, unchanging existence. A major new influence in their lives began to be felt about the middle of the century with a more rapid rate of population growth after a long period of near stagnation. A long-term effect of this growth in numbers and consequent expansion of the market was to raise the prices of agricultural products. There was at first some slack in the capacity of farming to respond to the new stimulus, but in the course of a decade or two, and despite an increase in the area under cultivation and the adoption in some areas of improved techniques, prices showed an upward tendency. Those of wheat and other grains began to rise gradually from about 1760, and there was a very marked upswing in prices as a result of the bad harvests of the 1790s.

In the decades before 1760 the price of wheat fluctuated around an average of 31–32 shillings per quarter (eight bushels), while barley and malt ran at some 18 shillings. (Prices varied considerably across the country as local markets were affected by differences in harvests and transport conditions, but the general trends were similar.) In the forty years after 1750 the average price moved up appreciably to over 40 shillings for wheat (reaching in some years over 50 shillings), and for barley to some 21 shillings. The deficient harvests of the 1790s forced prices up to an average of about 53 shillings for wheat and some 31 shillings for barley. The years 1794–6, which saw the allowance or 'Speenhamland system' of poor relief become widespread, were particularly bad, with wheat at over 68 shillings and barley over 34 shillings.

The prices of livestock products fluctuated less, changing little except in occasional years before 1765, through there then appeared a general upward trend, and again prices were especially high in the years after 1793. These years, of course, saw the onset of the prolonged wars with France, when rising numbers of consumers combined with difficulties in importing food, and most especially with remarkable runs of extremely bad seasons, to raise grain prices to unheard-of levels, indeed in some years to near famine conditions.

In the course of the century, therefore, farmers were exposed to two main movements in prices. Before about 1760, generally low prices together with a more or less stagnant market created an unfavourable climate for farming, although the difficulties did encourage some experimentation with new techniques and, especially, trials of new or unfamiliar crops. Thus, the use in arable rotations of root crops like turnips and grasses such as clover and sainfoin spread on suitable soils, particularly in East Anglia, while enterprising men tried the possibilities of, for instance, rapeseed, hops, woad, madder and vines. In livestock there was experimentation also, with breeders making efforts to improve existing breeds of cattle and sheep, although the great age of livestock improvement began after mid-century.

The 1730s and 1740s, with the exception of the very bad year of 1740, were particularly marked by low grain prices, especially in the midlands. Landowners were obliged to intervene to keep their tenants on the farms by accepting unusually high arrears of rent and by giving assistance with payment of taxes and other outlays normally considered the tenant's responsibility, such as purchases of seed and repairs. Even so, tenants threw up farms and numbers absconded, leaving accumulated arrears unpaid. Landlords had to write off bad debts and tried to encourage their remaining tenants to carry on by offering rent reductions and improvements to buildings. The agricultural depression in some grain areas appears to have resulted from the bountiful harvests of the time coupled with only a small increase in demand except for the growing market among the swelling population of London.

The economic climate began to change after 1750 when the general increase in consumers' numbers tended to outstrip agricultural production and harvests were less plentiful. At the same time transport improvements gave better access to ports and growing towns. Even so, exports of grain continued, though on a diminishing scale, until the 1790s. Further experimentation with livestock and advanced cropping systems were encouraged by more profitable markets, and landlords continued, as earlier, to improve the efficiency of their farms by expanding the holdings of the better tenants at the expense of the incompetent. The most remarkable feature of the second half of the century, however, was the reorganization of a substantial proportion of the farmland by means of enclosure.

During the first sixty years of the century landlords' farm rents were generally low and suffered downward pressure in the 1730s and 1740s. Subsequently, however, following the rise in prices, rents began to rise. Throughout the century there was a marked difference between the rent paid for land in open fields, generally some 6–8 shillings a year per acre, and that already enclosed, 10–15 shillings. Rich pasture yielded even higher rents. Landlords kept their woodlands in hand, to be cut and replanted at regular intervals and the wood sold to dealers. Timber was an important source of revenue on many estates and if minerals were present landlords themselves exploited the mines or leased them out to entrepreneurs. Quite often there were also ironworks and other enterprises, including brick-kilns, lime-kilns and even textile works. Those landlords who took an interest in farming techniques used the home farm for experiments and brought their tenants round to see for themselves the effects of new rotations, more quickly fattened livestock and more efficient implements.

The rise in rents in the later decades of the century was not due solely to higher prices, though many landlords took advantage of the more prosperous times to revise rentals which in some cases had been unchanged for as long as a century. Where owners made permanent improvements, such as rebuilding a farmhouse, providing a new barn or cowshed, and installing more effective drainage of wet soils and flood protection, the rents would be raised to obtain a reasonable return on the expenditure. The largest rent increases, however, followed on the enclosure of open fields and commons when not only were common rights abolished and the farms made more compact, but former waste land worth cultivating was incorporated in the farms. The post-enclosure rents varied with location and the nature of the soils, but in some cases might show a doubling or trebling of the former value.

Rising rents enabled landowners to live on a more luxurious scale and helped to pay for extensions to the house, enlarged and newly landscaped parks, and such extravagances as private menageries, costly follies and newly built ruins. Entertaining, sport and political activity also benefited from the new affluence, and dowries and legacies reached dizzier heights. From surplus income some owners financed an entrepreneurial role beyond the bounds of the estate, putting money into turnpikes and canals, river navigations and harbour improvements. The transport enterprises were usually local ones which gave better access to distant markets for tenants' produce and the owner's mines. And, though to a lesser extent, the landlords' example was followed by the wealthier farmers. It has been calculated that one-third of all the investment made in eighteenth-century canals came from landowners. Much of this investment affected nascent industrial areas. Of course, not all owners enjoyed the same opportunities or showed the same enterprise, and some of them opposed river navigations and turnpikes where the effects were likely to damage the local markets enjoyed by their tenants. But generally the need for better transport conditions was widely recognized, as may be seen also in the newly constructed parish roads that accompanied many enclosures. Landowners' enthusiasm was encouraged by the social and business connections they had with local merchants and industrialists, sometimes tempting them to invest in overseas trading and shipping ventures.

Landowners' industrial and transport investments, and to a lesser extent those of farmers too, were locally very significant. They were particularly important in the exploitation of coal, the essential material for the new iron industry as well as the new source of power, the steam engine. The advance of areas such as the Black Country, the West Riding, Lancashire and Newcastle hinged on coal, and it formed the main cargo of most northern canals, rivers and ports. The willingness of landowners to invest, if often on a very limited scale, was a major factor in fostering the new economy of coal, iron and textiles that was to dominate the next century. In seeking private profit the landed interest advanced the industrial age.

Agricultural Improvement

It used to be believed that an 'agricultural revolution', the counterpart of a parallel 'industrial revolution', occurred in the decades after 1760. A large body of research published over the past fifty years has produced, however, a quite different picture of agricultural progress. In the first place the introduction of new crops has been taken back into the sixteenth century. There was a large time-gap, however, between the first introduction and the widespread use of novel crops on a field scale, which often did not occur before the middle of the eighteenth century. Second, the role of the famous innovators – Jethro Tull, 'Turnip' Townshend, Robert Bakewell and Coke of Holkham, for instance – has been reassessed and their achievements placed in a wider context of long-term improvement. Third, the importance of parliamentary enclosure, once seen as an essential prerequisite of technical advance, has been revised as its geographical limitations have been re-emphasized and its consequences for farming seen in more realistic terms. Lastly, valuable attempts have been made in recent years to calculate the size of the increases in output and productivity achieved, producing more sober figures than used to be put forward.

The new crops, such as clovers, sainfoin, lucerne and turnips, were employed to help solve the age-old problem of restoring fertility to the soil after the inroads made by grain production. Adoption of these crops, it is now known, restored nitrogen to the soil and also provided additional fodder for carrying larger numbers of livestock, whose manure was the traditional means, together with bare fallowing or resting of the land, of putting the soil back into good heart. The crops made it possible to reduce or dispense with fallowing (which, however, remained the practice for restoring fertility and reduction of weeds in areas where the new crops were not adopted), as well as enabling more stock to be carried on a given acreage. Novel rotations which included clovers, grasses and turnips were first introduced in central Norfolk and high Suffolk, where the light soils were well suited to them and the feeding and manure of the sheep were basic elements in the farming system. Investigation has revealed that the proportion of farms in Norfolk and Suffolk growing turnips rose from about 20 per cent in the 1680s to 50 per cent in the 1720s, but turnips did not become an essential part of crop rotations until the middle decades of the eighteenth century. The growth in cultivation of clovers was less remarkable, found on about 10 per cent of farms by the 1690s and on 20 per cent by 1740. The main diffusion of turnip husbandry came after 1750, and towards the end of the century the hardier Swedish turnip or 'Swede' was preferred in order to avoid losses caused by frost and disease to which turnips were liable.

The celebrated 'Norfolk system' was a four-course cycle of wheat, turnips, barley and clover. The growing of legumes has now been traced back to medieval times, but again widespread use developed only in the eighteenth century. In practice a wide variety of rotations came to be used in Norfolk, and the cultivation of turnips, in particular, depended very much on soils and other local conditions, though it was already common in suitable areas early in the century. The spread of new rotations after 1750 was limited by the problems of dealing with acidic soils and removal of restrictions on freedom of cropping. In the midlands 'ley farming' was practised, in which the plough was 'taken round the farm', with an individual field cropped continuously for a period of years and then restored to fertility by a grass ley, also lasting some years, followed by a new cycle of crops.

The prolonged period of the diffusion of new crops indicates that the importance of such a figure as Townshend has been exaggerated, though it is true that turnips were widely cultivated on his Raynham estate by the first decade of the century. Thomas Coke comes much later in the story, and indeed the growing of turnips and clovers, the use of long leases to encourage investment by tenants, the drilling of seeds and the use of oil-cake for feeding cattle were already well established on his estate when Coke was but a boy, and, in fact, can be traced back to the previous century. Coke was instrumental, however, in improving local breeds of stock, and his sheep-shearings or private shows became an important event in the farming calendar, when numerous visiting experts were entertained and the opportunity taken to praise the work of his leading tenants.

The advance of improved livestock, similarly, has a long if somewhat obscure history before Robert Bakewell became famous in the 1770s. He was certainly the best known of the breeders who attempted to create superior stock by crossing existing animals – cattle, sheep, horses and pigs. Bakewell, however, was only one of such men and, in fact, was only partly successful; his New Leicester sheep fattened more quickly but had serious disadvantages, while his longhorn cattle enjoyed even less success. The more lasting work of stock improvement came from later breeders such as George Culley and the Collings brothers, and John Ellman, the originator of the improved Southdown sheep.

The development of farm machinery and implements was subject to many obstacles. Early seed drills, such as that of Tull, had been preceded by the designs of seventeenth-century writers. Tull, however, may have been the first to make and use a working machine, though the drill spread only slowly and was not widely used before late in the century. But another device, Tull's horse-hoe, was valuable for better cultivation and keeping down weeds among drilled, as opposed to broadcast, seeds, but was wasteful of land. A multitude of different designs of ploughs existed, though in East Anglia the wheeled plough drawn by only two horses was an important innovation for light soils, replacing the heavy, cumbersome implements that required large teams of horses or oxen. Signs of advance came with the greater use of the Rotherham plough, a model based on Dutch designs, and in 1785 Robert Ransome of Ipswich obtained a patent for making shares of cast iron. About the same time there also appeared the threshing machine, which was adapted to hand power, horses or a steam engine. This was an important device which obviated the slow, dusty work of threshing corn by hand, and came into wide use during the labour shortages of the Napoleonic Wars. There were also improved designs of carts and other farm equipment, but the major difficulty with all these innovations was that of finding blacksmiths, millwrights and wheelwrights who could produce them from unfamiliar designs. Only with the advent of Robert Ransome and the threshing machine was there glimpsed the beginnings of an agricultural machinery industry.

The nature of soils – undrained heavy clays were not suited to the new husbandry – and variations in local climate held up progress, and in addition there was the profound conservatism of many farmers and farmworkers. Arthur Young, the best-known agricultural writer of the later part of the century, was fond of drawing the contrast between the forward-looking enterprise of large farmers and the blind backwardness of many small men. Small farmers, it is true, often lacked the means of innovating, something that they regarded as the folly of those who could afford to lose money. Their conservatism, however, was rooted in an intimate knowledge of the land and its limitations, as well as in ignorance.

The farmworkers were apt to be intensely suspicious of new ways of doing things, and their obstinacy was accompanied by careless handling of valuable stock and new implements. It is not surprising, then, that farming standards varied greatly from district to district and there was much backwardness. The diffusion of new ideas by means of private shows, correspondence between leading farmers and their tours of well-known advanced farms was slow and largely confined to a coterie of landowners and prominent farmers. The point is well illustrated by the small circulation, a mere few hundred, of Young's periodical, the *Annals of Agriculture*, intended as a forum for new ideas, which began publication in 1784.

A major feature of eighteenth-century improvement was the reorganization of a large part of the farmland by enclosure of open fields, commons and waste lands. This was a process already in train in previous centuries, but in the eighteenth century enclosure by private act of parliament was added to existing procedures. There were then three main forms of enclosure: the piecemeal fencing in of small acreages, a gradual process which over the years nibbled away at the fields; larger-scale enclosure by agreement among the owners; and compulsory enclosure by the authority of private acts.

It is not known how much land was affected by the first two forms, but in some areas that enclosed by agreement was considerable. Parliamentary enclosure, which became the favoured procedure after about 1750, is estimated to have affected some 24 per cent of the total area of England and Wales, though geographically it was very unevenly spread. Most of the open fields enclosed by private act were in the midlands, where in four counties they still occupied as much as 50 per cent of the area, while in another ten counties in or adjacent to the midlands some 30 to 40 per cent of the land was affected. It follows that parliamentary enclosure was experienced much less in the more peripheral regions where, indeed, surviving open fields were unusual. Enclosure of waste lands, however, occurred mainly in northern England and Wales since such land was generally scarce in the midlands.

The object of enclosure was to abolish the remaining open fields (which in some parishes were small in area) and terminate the common rights governing the use of the land. The commons were brought into the farmlands, together with any waste lands that were worth cultivating or could be exploited for minerals. The result was the creation of a new pattern of fields and closes divided by hedges or walls, with the occupiers having sole access to the land and free to cultivate it as they wished. The new flexibility of land use might mean that old worn-out arable was converted to pasture, or old pasture was ploughed up, or the adoption of some form of ley husbandry where the arable and pasture were alternated. For a variety of reasons, however, the farmers often continued with their familiar two or three crops and a fallow, as had been the general rule in the open fields. Nevertheless, the advantages of sole access still made them willing to pay a higher rent for enclosed land than they had paid when it was in open fields and subject to common rights. Landowners, who met the costs of the enclosure, recovered their expenditure from higher rents and also obtained control of former commons and wastes for mining or building purposes. Frequently, opportunity was also taken to build new parish roads and to end long-running disputes by commuting the tithes.

The long-term effects on farm output were certainly beneficial, if difficult to estimate, although the rise in post-enclosure rents gives some rough indication of the advantages to the farmers and the possibilities of achieving higher profits. The extent of the more frequently debated social effects is also uncertain. A number of salient points emerge, however. First, the money costs of enclosing did not fall on the community but only on those who owned the land enclosed, although farmers had to move their farming to another part of the parish. Second, although it has been argued that some small owners had difficulty in meeting their share of the costs and may have been forced to sell up, there are reasons for thinking that the extent of this problem may be exaggerated. Third, with the disappearance of the commons the cottagers usually lost access to land for keeping a cow and obtaining fuel, and this resulted in poverty and migration. Again, however, the dimensions of the issue are unclear for it is known that many cottagers had no right to the common or, if they did, failed to exercise it. Cottagers who possessed rights often rented them out to dairymen or horse-keepers, and it was these who lost their independence when the common was enclosed. Those who could prove a right were compensated, though the compensation was often insufficient to provide a reasonable substitute for the amenities lost. Last, the unenclosed common was in fact often worth very little: overgrazed, ill-drained and covered with furze and bracken.

In summary, there were undoubtedly some small occupiers and cottagers who were deprived of part or all of their livelihood by enclosure, though their numbers are uncertain. Offsetting this in some degree was the compensation that enclosure often meant more intensive agriculture and higher output, which needed more labour for production, processing and transporting. It is a relevant consideration that the worst of the rural poverty of the late eighteenth century and early nineteenth century was to be found in southern and western counties where there was only limited enclosure, and it is significant that these were also areas lacking the industrial growth which in the heavily enclosed midlands offered increasing employment opportunities.

The increase in total farm output over the eighteenth century owed much to a considerable expansion of the cultivated acreage through the taking in of commons and waste lands, as well as to a rise in productivity as land and labour became used more efficiently. The estimates of total output differ according to the method of calculation, but the figures suggest an increase of something between 59 per cent and a perhaps improbable 91 per cent, with the larger part of the increase coming in the second half of the century. Land productivity, the increase in output per acre, rose between 15 and 38 per cent, while the productivity of labour rose by between 41 and 70 per cent, with the improvement spread evenly over the two halves of the century. The rise in the yields of cereal in Norfolk and Suffolk, the home of the most improved farming, was 35 per cent. These figures have to be set against an increase in the area under cultivation of 38 per cent.

The lack of adequate statistical sources for the period makes these estimates the best we are likely to obtain. Taking them at their face value it appears that, allowing for the expansion in the area cultivated, the increase in output per acre was of the order of some 20–50 per cent. (It has to be borne in mind that the rise in the farm area involved the cultivation of soils inferior to those already in use.) Given the slow diffusion of innovations and their limitations, the increases in output and productivity were quite remarkable. They hardly amount, however, to an 'agricultural revolution' comparable with the massive increases in output that have characterized the period since the Second World War, but they had great significance in the context of the eighteenth century.

The increase in output in the second half of the century is estimated at between 29 and 64 per cent, and if the truth lies somewhere between these two extremes, it suggests that agriculture was reasonably successful in meeting the concurrent rise in population, which was about 50 per cent. The fact that prices rose substantially towards the end of the half-century emphasizes the importance of harvest conditions and suggests also that supply was then tending to lag behind demand, especially in cereals. By the middle 1790s the effects of poor seasons put pressure on living standards and resulted in widespread resort to the poor law.

Agricultural advances in both the increase in the area cultivated and in improved farming practices achieved, therefore, considerably higher total output, though this was evidently not sufficient to meet the needs of a rapidly expanding population, the more particularly when harvests were poor. Nevertheless, this was a considerable achievement, even if it was merely the natural response of businesslike landowners and farmers to the profits to be made from more rewarding prices. The rise in labour productivity certainly has economic significance for, in effect, agriculture was feeding a larger non-agricultural population with a smaller share of the labour force, leaving more hands to be used elsewhere in the growing trade and industry of the time.

Rural Society

The rural communities of the eighteenth century were made up of diverse strands: the landowners, farmers, farmworkers, tradesmen, country craftsmen and a number of professional men. And not to be forgotten were the rural poor, the very young and old, but many of them of employable age, if incapacitated or temporarily ill, together with orphans, deserted wives with young children, servants who had lost their place, vagrants, beggars and petty criminals.

Landowners' estates varied greatly in size and revenues. For the great majority most of their income came from farm rents and the profits of timber and other estate resources. Many, however, enjoyed substantial incomes arising from mortgages, urban property, holdings in canals and turnpikes, and investments in the funds such as Bank of England or South Sea Company stock. A smaller number might also have an income from government office or sinecures in the church, while some had ventured on industrial or trading projects, and not a few lived on the returns from naval prize money or a fortune gathered in India or the West Indies. The range of incomes was very wide, from the princely £10,000–£50,000 of the great landowners, down through the £2,000–£10,000 of the ranks of the gentry and the few hundreds which supported the relatively modest but still comfortable lifestyle of country squires, the wealthier parsons and well-endowed widows. The great owners needed a minimum of some £10,000 a year to live in the style expected of them, i.e., to support a large family mansion with its grounds and amenities, and to afford to make the annual visit to London for the winter season. Each of these absorbed £5,000 a year or more, and the outlays could be much higher when the mansion and park were on a grand scale, with perhaps secondary mansions to be maintained in other parts of the country.

In summer there were always many visitors, people who called on social errands or on matters of estate or political business, while numbers of relations made protracted stays. Servants were necessarily numerous, and though the majority cost little beyond their keep, as much as £50 or £100 a year was paid for a competent butler or a French cook. Outdoors there were carriages, racehorses and riding horses to be maintained, perhaps boats and boatmen, and even as a curiosity a resident hermit. Gamekeepers were needed to deter poachers, and a professional huntsman and kennel hands where hounds were kept. The rising popularity of hunting and shooting meant low rents for the tenants and other compensation for the depredations of sport.

In winter family and servants were transported expensively to London. The season involved a costly social round of assemblies, tea parties and balls, and opportunity was taken to attend parliament, consult with one's doctors and lawyers, and make visits to dressmakers and tailors. This was the time also for ordering articles difficult to obtain in the country, a new coach, stocks of wine, new wigs, the latest books and a portrait painted by a fashionable artist. Not least, it was the great opportunity for disposing of an unmarried daughter or two, and cementing valuable family alliances into the bargain. Some of the wealthiest owners kept a large house in the capital especially for the season, but those with more restricted incomes rented a house or merely some rooms. Even modest country gentry attempted a London visit at least once in their lives, and it could be done quite cheaply by staying in an inn.

There were other calls on landed wealth. Owners always had an eye out for properties coming on the market that would round off the park or strengthen their hold on a parish and might in time lead to an enclosure or increase the family's political influence. Those owners who dabbled in politics expected to have to meet large bills at election time for the conveying, entertaining and influencing of electors, and in the longer term the maintaining of an influence meant charging low rents to keep the voters complaisant. Improvements to the house, perhaps the construction of an entirely new house, and the extension and landscaping of parks ran away with many thousands.

Among the more burdensome and inescapable outgoings, however, were the expenses of family. The owner's bride received in return for her dowry a proportionately large jointure, an income to keep her in independent style in widowhood. A wealthy bride could insist, too, on 'pin-money' or a private income as part of the marriage contract, as well perhaps as a house in London. The younger sons of the marriage were not usually costly for, unlike the heir, they received a cheaper education and subsequently only the means of setting them up in the church, the law, the army or even in trade.

Daughters, however, were another matter. To be married off to a suitor of suitable status required a dowry or portion, and in the eighteenth century marriage among the wealthy became so commercial that the size of the dowry was a bride's chief attraction, and go-betweens might be employed to find an attractive dowry or a groom of high status. The two families' lawyers met to thrash out the marriage settlement, and while the expected level of dowry varied with status the daughter of a great owner would be likely to offer some £10,000, and much larger dowries were not uncommon. Numerous daughters and large portions to be paid – usually in the form of land – led to the decline of some families and, of course, the aggrandizement of others. For the sake of the dowry financially embarrassed owners were willing to accept the daughter of a wealthy merchant or industrialist despite the social slur this would cast. As in the later eighteenth century incomes rose with rising rents, there was also a tendency for dowries to rise and, in consequence, families found themselves in difficulty when large dowries had to be paid. Sometimes only part of the sum was paid immediately, with the balance treated as a long-term debt on which interest was paid.

Lastly, when he succeeded the heir might find that he was heavily encumbered by debts arising from earlier extravagance, in which unpaid portions ranked high. If indebtedness reached crisis point trustees were appointed to administer the estate, and they were often able to save the situation by enforcing a regime of strict economy and by selling land to pay off those debts carrying the highest rates of interest. One difficulty was that a large part of the estate might be settled, i.e., its revenues were reserved for meeting certain family payments and the lands could not be sold and might be mortgaged only up to certain sums. Sometimes the situation was so grave that a private act of parliament had to be sought in order to break the settlement and allow the lands to be sold. The urgent need for revenue was a factor in raising rents and might bring on an enclosure to exploit waste land that was known to have coal or could be sold for urban development.

Similar problems could face lesser landed families, if on a smaller scale. Minor gentry and country gentlemen necessarily lived modestly and avoided the excesses of the great owners. Lower down the social scale marriage and its financial implications were less of a commercial matter, even if the status of a bride or groom was something to be taken into account. Gentry estates were often small and compact enough to be supervised personally instead of by a steward or professional land agent, and close personal knowledge of the farms and their tenants made for more efficient and economical management. The gentry, however, were as important in their own small districts as were the great landowners in their wider sphere. Some regions, like the home counties and south Wales, were dominated by gentry estates and their owners had control of the parliamentary seats as well as county administration.

Nevertheless, there were numerous ties that bound landowners great and small into a degree of unity. They might be as divided by political conviction as by wealth, but their education, outlook and even lifestyle possessed common characteristics and there was, of course, a general concern with issues affecting landed property as well as enthusiasm for country sports. There were, naturally, many exceptions. Some owners, large and small, interested themselves in the complexities of agricultural improvement, though many did not; some were businesslike and assiduous in their estate dealings, others careless and indifferent; and not a few were scholars who rarely emerged from their libraries. Superior education and leisure as well as wealth imposed responsibilities; for seeing that the affairs of the district were properly managed, that vagrants and wrongdoers were brought to justice and help given to those who needed a letter or reference written, or to accept money to be held in trust (on which interest was paid) against the time when perhaps an apprenticeship was to be bought. The squire would provide a feast when there was a birth or anniversary in his family or news of a victory at sea. Owners also expended small sums in charity, largely confined to old tenants or servants fallen on hard times, and larger sums were bequeathed to the church or an almshouse. The lady of the house managed the estate when her husband was away but still found time to provide simple remedies for the sick and cook food for honest wayfarers who called at the kitchen door. Some squires even paid an annual fee to a doctor to treat the sick of the parish or paid an inoculator to safeguard the parish against smallpox.

Wealthier farmers lived in much the same way as the lesser squires, though more closely involved, of course, in the details of farming. Some of them were in a big way of business, renting a number of farms in adjacent parishes and managing them through bailiffs until their sons were old enough to take them over. These were the men who corresponded with innovating farmers and made tours to see others' improvements for themselves. Very probably much of the advance of agricultural improvement was due to their efforts rather than those of dilettante landlords. By the later eighteenth century they lived in some style with their own carriages and servants, their sons educated for a profession as an alternative to farming, and their daughters sent to acquire the social graces at boarding schools. They were sufficiently well thought of to ride with the landlord's hunt, if not considered suitable for a shooting party, a ball or elevation to the justices' bench.

The small farmers were generally held in some contempt. They lacked education, lived little better than did the farmworkers and were in a weak bargaining position *vis-à-vis* their landlord, although it was uncommon for a small tenant to be turned off who farmed reasonably well, paid his rent and in his private life was not a disgrace to the estate. Indeed, small farms were often passed down through one family for generations, from father to son, to a widow, even a daughter, while large tenants usually moved on at the expiry of a lease. The small man was expected to be backward and lacking in enterprise, though often he could more easily ride out a difficult period than could the more extended large farmer. One factor in survival was his dependence on family rather than hired labour, and he was also able to obtain loans from neighbours who had cash to spare; another was the landlord's willingness to allow the rent to run into arrears because he wanted to keep his farms occupied and his local popularity intact. Furthermore, the small farmer often had relations farming nearby from whom he could borrow implements, horses and seed as well as money. He was certainly looked down upon by contemporary experts, such as William Marshall and Arthur Young. Many were believed to be given to immoderate consumption of drink.

If small farmers employed few hands except at harvest time, the great arable farmers employed a score or more of men in addition to women and boys. The condition of the farmworker varied with his employer and his wages varied from district to district, and even from farm to farm, while the more highly prized men like bailiffs, shepherds and men in charge of valuable stock earned something above the average. About 1770 a female farm servant was paid in addition to her board and lodging between £3 and £5 a year when a young maid would have £7 or £9, and an experienced head servant £8–£12. Farm servants were in the habit of changing masters every year and this meant that within a limited area they could gain a wide experience. Hours for both servants and day-labourers were long: from before light until dark in winter, and from six to six in summer, with even longer hours in the better-paid busy seasons. But though they worked a long day, the pace of work was often slow with numerous breaks for refreshment.

Wages of both farm servants and day-labourers tended to rise in the later eighteenth century. About 1770, before this improvement, day-labourers were generally paid about a shilling a day in winter, 1s 6d at haytime and 2s–2s 6d at harvest. Women received six or eight pence a day in winter, eight or nine pence at haytime and one shilling at harvest. Children as young as seven or eight were able to earn in a week a shilling or so. Altogether the weekly income of a labourer who was regularly employed, with help from his wife, might average some 10–12 shillings a week, but work was not always continuous and hands were often laid off in bad weather, though some farmers would find them odd jobs to do in the barn. The cottage, frequently very rudimentary, might be a simple two-room erection of mud and stud or wattle and daub, though new and more substantial brick cottages became more common in the course of the century. Sometimes the labourers were quartered in an old farmhouse or barn that had been divided up for the purpose. Cottages might be provided free but were often rented at some 20–40 shillings a year, representing a considerable drain on income. Farm servants, for their part, slept in the garrets of the farmhouse or in an outhouse and ate in the kitchen or perhaps with the farmer's family.

The farmers sometimes sold their surplus produce to their workpeople, grain or flour, meat and milk, though the low prices charged might be offset by poor quality, the produce being such that the farmer could not sell at market. A regular daily allowance of ale, or in the west country cider, was customary, and in some instances was so large as to constitute an important element of diet and an inducement to stay on the farm. In consequence, many farmers brewed their own ale. Often a load or two of fuel was dropped at the cottage door by the farmer, though outside coal-mining areas it might consist only of peat or furze. Coal fuel was a great advantage for providing a warmer home and more hot food. Lastly, in a village that still retained its common, the labourer might have the right to gather additional fuel and use the pasture to keep a cow and fatten a pig at home, while in season there were berries and medicinal herbs to be collected. Often it was the wife and children who looked after the cow and pig, and came home burdened with laboriously collected fallen wood and twigs. The cow was valuable for its milk and the pig was often sold when fat in order to meet heavy occasional expenses such as those for winter clothing, a child's apprenticeship or a funeral.

The seasons greatly influenced farmworkers' lives. Winter was a period of hardship when wages were at their lowest, and they came home in clothes sodden from working in the rain to a damp and draughty cottage with only a smoky peat fire and water to be fetched from a well or a pond. The husband's illness meant a reduced income and there was always the possibility of his suffering an accident. Accidents, in fact, were surprisingly frequent, partly through the handling of sharp tools and working in half-light. Illness, an accident or early death of the husband might well mean resort to parish relief. But in coal areas farmworkers were better off because the higher industrial wages tended to raise the floor of farm earnings.

Haytime and harvest not only meant relatively well-paid work but also plentiful food and drink. A supply of both strong and small beer might be accompanied by a variety of pies, pasties, cheese, milk, beef, bacon, pickled pork, beans and pease. The allowance of beer was a quart a day, and the hands might eat five times in the course of a day which lasted until eight o'clock. The country women might enjoy a comfortable existence, engaged only in cooking and cleaning and leaving all the work in the fields and caring for livestock to the men. But this might not be typical of all districts.

There had always been poverty and distress in the villages but mainly affecting a few individuals too young or too old to work. Their plight was often relieved by a small weekly payment from the parish or the provision of a rent-free cottage. Large villages and country towns built workhouses for the homeless, and in East Anglia there were some unsuccessful attempts to make the able-bodied pay for their keep by setting them to work and selling the produce. The parish, too, often paid for the care and education of pauper children, provided treatment for the sick and injured, and licensed adults to beg for alms. The supplementing of the earnings of people in work by weekly doles of money was already in use in some parishes on a regulated basis when in 1795 the Berkshire justices issued the famous Speenhamland scale, relating the parish payment to the price of bread and the size of the family. Considerable sums were also given in private charity: landowners and some farmers often looked after their own employees, and in the dear years of the middle 1790s subscribed to funds used to buy bread, grains or flour for resale at subsidized prices.

Considerable difficulties stand in the way of calculating average income since the amount of time paid at piecework rates varied, the earnings of the wife were very uncertain, and the value of access to a common, if available, differed greatly from place to place. There is also the considerable possibility of illness or accident, and hence it is easy to understand the need to seek poor relief, even when men were fully employed, as the century drew to a close with sharply rising food prices.

A few tradesmen and craftsmen were present in many villages, but they tended to congregate in the larger settlements and country towns. The more successful of them lived comfortably above the level of workpeople and even that of small farmers, employing apprentices, journeymen and a domestic servant or two. The trades of butcher, baker and innkeeper were well represented, while craftsmen proliferated in the building industry and there were numerous blacksmiths, wheelwrights and millwrights, as well as a variety of other occupations. Many combined a little farming, dealing or carrying with their main calling. Their services were in demand from landowners – many great houses were built and kept in repair by local craftsmen – from farmers and the few professional families, in addition to their fellow tradesmen and craftsmen. In some areas many country inhabitants were engaged in other occupations, in branches of the textile and clothing industries, in mining or quarrying or in the iron industry, and there were also numerous persons concerned with horses, as breeders, carriers or jobbers who hired out their animals.

The agricultural community could not have functioned without a very wide range of skills and services, and rural trades, crafts and domestic industries offered outlets for employment of the children of small farmers and farmworkers so that the pressure of large families on low incomes was relieved. The better-off families offered a major outlet for young girls to train as domestic servants, and the sight of a girl of thirteen, armed with her box, leaving her cottage home for the establishment of a superior family was commonplace. Furthermore, as the country's population grew, so too did the demand for the work of those country people offering their services and skills.

There was much migration. While many small farmers and their workpeople were firmly rooted in the countryside, there were many who had moved to find work and homes. Most of the movement was short-distance, within a radius of 20 or 30 miles, and for many their goal was merely a nearby country town whose varied occupations and sprinkling of well-to-do families promised a chance of betterment. Movement was hampered in some degree by the settlement laws, which were designed to establish and limit local responsibility for relieving the poor, but their restrictions affected mainly those already on relief and particularly those with large families. In practice, areas with growing needs for additional labour were able to draw freely on districts of plentiful labour.

The eighteenth century saw much change in the countryside, varying prosperity and greater affluence contrasted with deeper poverty. 'Merrie England' was not entirely a myth and could be said to exist in aristocratic sport and entertainments, the heavy eating and drinking of many people, and the simple feasts provided by the better off for village people. But many families lived hard, comfortless lives always on the edge of poverty, and desperation drove some to poaching and theft, while years of unusually high grain prices saw riots and attacks on millers and corn dealers. In the techniques of farming there was in some areas remarkable progress, to the benefit of the food supply. Nevertheless, the gap between rich and poor, always huge, widened further, and it was a less stable, less homogeneous rural society that met the intensifying strains of the more rapid industrial growth and eventual decline.

FURTHER READING

Armstrong, Alan: *Farmworkers: A Social and Economic History, 1770–1980* (London, 1988).

Beckett, J. V.: *The Aristocracy in England 1660–1914* (Oxford, 1986).

Chambers, J. D. and Mingay, G. E.: *The Agricultural Revolution 1750–1880* (London, 1966).

Hammond, J. L. and Hammond, B.: *The Village Labourer* (new edn, London, 1978).

Howell, David W.: *The Rural Poor in Eighteenth-Century Wales* (Cardiff, 2000).

Martins, Susanna Wade and Williamson, Tom: *Farming and the Landscape in East Anglia, c.1700–1870* (Exeter, 1999).

Mingay, G. E.: *English Landed Society in the Eighteenth Century* (London, 1963).

Mingay, G. E.: *The Gentry* (London, 1976).

Mingay, G. E. (ed.): *The Agrarian History of England and Wales*, vol. 6: *1750–1850* (Cambridge, 1989).

Mingay, G. E.: *Parliamentary Enclosure in England: An Introduction to its Causes, Incidence and Improvements 1750–1850* (London, 1997).

Overton, Mark: *Agricultural Revolution in England: The Transformation of the Agrarian Economy 1500–1850* (Cambridge, 1996).

Thirsk, Joan (ed.): *The Agrarian History of England and Wales*, vol. 5: *1640–1750* (Cambridge, 1985).

Turner, Michael: *English Parliamentary Enclosure: Its Historical Geography and Economic History* (Folkestone, 1980).

Chapter Twelve

The Landed Elite

Richard G. Wilson

The basic task of the historian of landownership in eighteenth-century Britain is to explain how, in an economy increasingly driven by industrial and commercial forces, the landed classes retained their traditional influence. Indeed, it is maintained they did so past the great Reform Act of 1832 to the last quarter of the nineteenth century. The question can be put another way. Did their political authority, their social and cultural embrace of Britain's industrial and financial leaders, create a brake on Britain's early economic supremacy? Was the world's first industrial nation forced to carry the weight of a traditional seigneurial class? Historians attempting to answer these big questions have concentrated upon those factors underpinning the economic buoyancy of the aristocracy, especially the growth in size of the landed estate, and the relative openness of the landowners' ranks to newcomers.

The best starting point for this discussion is an identification of the landed classes. So far as their number is concerned there are two fixed points: the famous calculations of England's wealth and social structure made in 1688 by the herald and pioneer statistician Gregory King, and the remarkable series of parliamentary papers known as the 'New Domesday', published between 1872 and 1876, which recorded the owners and gross annual values of estates of one or more acres of land in the United Kingdom. King identified a roughly tripartite division: 160 peers (with average incomes of £2,800) and twenty-six bishops (£1,300); 800 baronets (£800), 600 knights (£650) and 3,000 esquires (£450); and lastly, 12,000 gentlemen (£280). A mere 1.2 per cent of the population, they enjoyed around 15 per cent of the nation's total income according to King's calculations. The figures derived from the 'New Domesday' pinpoint the large landowners' position more precisely: some 4,217 persons owning more than 1,000 acres (usually designated as the minimum size necessary to allow owners gentry status from the rental income of their land) owned 55 per cent of the land surface of England and Wales; around 11,000 owners held two-thirds of the United Kingdom's total land area in the late 1870s. Both calculations underline the dominant position of the landed aristocracy and gentry in terms of their wealth and their key role in rural society. Although twentieth-century historians have disputed the fine print of King's figures, especially in terms of incomes (the estimates are too low) and the number, wealth and status of the 12,000 gentlemen, his figure of 4,586 landowners, ranging from great duke to parish squire, roughly equates with the population of around 5,000 country houses and with the total of 4,217 owners in the mid-1870s. It is not asserted from this evidence that the size of estates remained constant over about two centuries, but that their number roughly seems to have done so. The number of large landowners is therefore small, the size of their holdings impressive, their incomes and influence immense.

The Landed Aristocracy

In any debate about the dominance, exclusiveness and closed nature of the Georgian landowning classes it is necessary to isolate the peerage. Their significance was far greater than their numbers at first sight suggest. Gregory King was accurate enough with his estimate of 160 English peers in 1688. A century later (the first two Georges especially balking at its extension), there were still only 200 in 1780. Thereafter numbers rose quite sharply, to 267 in 1800 and 400 in the 1860s. Of course, creations were more prolific than these figures suggest, for peerages (as even the most cursory perusal of the thirteen volumes of the *Complete Peerage* reveals) frequently became extinct, especially between 1660 and 1750, years of acute demographic crises which spared neither those of high birth nor full stomach. Taking into account that the population of England and Wales quadrupled between 1700 and the 1860s, creations did not keep pace with this increase. The English peerage, unlike its continental counterparts, remained small until the late Victorian period.

What set this tiny group apart from its hereditary titles – barons, viscounts, earls, marquesses and dukes? In fact, the English peerage had few legal privileges beyond summonses (not automatic for either Scottish or Irish peers) to the House of Lords. It was not heavily taxed, but this was true of all landowners after 1720 when the exactions of the land tax, introduced to fund the long wars against France in the 1690s and 1700s, eased and the government instead resorted increasingly to loans served by revenues raised principally from indirect customs and excise duties spread across the whole population. Of course, the small size of the peerage itself guaranteed exclusiveness. There were only 1,003 persons who held peerages across the course of the eighteenth century.

Moreover, recruitment was self-perpetuating since new members were drawn almost entirely from within the peerage class itself. A few generals, admirals and very successful lawyers were ennobled, but their family and social connections were almost invariably with the peerage and large landowners. Otherwise, a regular route of advance to the English peerage was laid down which effectively restricted it to the wealthiest landowners: ownership of a large country estate sufficient to sustain a peer's dignity; a prestigious seat in parliament; an Irish peerage; and, finally, to guarantee a seat in the House of Lords, an English one. But it was often slow progress, requiring frequent personal application to the king and his ministers. Sir John Rous, a Suffolk baronet, leading landowner and MP for Suffolk from 1780 to 1796, always hankered after a peerage, but believed in 1785 he did not have an income to support it. Two good marriages later he applied for one in 1790 and in 1794. But he was only successful at the 1796 dissolution of parliament, and had to wait a further twenty-five years, with persistent jogging of the prime minister's memory, before he was raised to the earldom of Stradbroke. Similarly, Edward Lascelles stressed to Pitt in 1796 (when he applied for his childless uncle's recent barony to be remaindered in his favour), that he was of very ancient family in Yorkshire, an old MP and heir in entail to Lord Harewood's landed estate, which was one of the largest in England, as likewise heir presumptive to almost the largest monied property. In other words, a peerage should recognize an identifiable weight of landed property and political clout.

Not only did the peerage remain exclusive, it retained its political power across the century. True, its collective influence in the House of Lords *vis-à-vis* that of the House of Commons gently waned from the early eighteenth century. As John Cannon put it succinctly, 'there was hardly any major role for the House of Lords to play. They were firemen in a town without any fires and consequently, they could allow their hoses to rot'. But the peerage's hold on the Commons, both through the return of MPs by direct constituency control and more directly through family members occupying a large number of seats, was firm. In the parliament of 1784, 107 sons of peers (and the figure was rather lower than usual) sat in the Commons. And there were as many more with close ties of marriage and connection. It was, however, in their grip on the country's executive that the peerage's power is most readily illustrated. No fewer than 60 per cent of the peerage held office of one kind or another. The 1743 cabinet of sixteen members included six dukes and the archbishop of Canterbury. Only as late as 1859, when Britain's industrial supremacy was already at its height, was the balance of the cabinet tilted in favour of non-peerage members.

The peerage also had enormous influence at county level. Since its numbers were tiny, those regularly residing in any county could usually be counted on one hand. Demonstrating this pattern as late as 1865, the map illustrating Sandford and Townsend's *Great Governing Families* included 178 peers and only thirty-four other large landowners in thirty-nine English counties. In Norfolk, for example, England's foremost agricultural county, never more than half a dozen peers ruled the roost, although several more held secondary estates there. They provided automatic social leadership in the counties, headed up rival political factions, topped every charitable list. Invariably, they filled the office of lord lieutenant, and since lords lieutenant nominated all justices of the peace, the de facto rulers of the countryside, the appointment remained an important one. More generally, enormous deference was paid to peers. In the early eighteenth century, when they arrived at their country seats from London, members of the peerage received the local gentry and members from the neighbouring corporation, exactly like a minor German prince, to endorse their political and social leadership in the county. When the newly created Earl Fitzwalter went down to his Essex estate in the summer of 1730, he spent £10 4s at the Saracen's Inn in Chelmsford upon his neighbours who came to see him, including the local minister and 130–140 of the principal inhabitants of the town.

The peerage's prominence at every level of the nation's life was, of course, ultimately based on their wealth. It has been estimated that the average income of the peerage in 1690 was £5,000 to £6,000 (twice King's reckoning); a century later it was £10,000. Except during the French wars (1793–1815), this gain was not seriously eroded by inflation. But averages conceal as much as they reveal. Struggling to keep pace even with his untitled landowning neighbours, the net income of the second duke of Manchester in the 1740s was no more than £3,000. Already some in his rank boasted means at least ten times as large. By the 1790s the really great *grands seigneurs*, such as the dukes of Bedford, Bridgewater and Devonshire and the Egremonts, Shelburnes and Rockinghams, had incomes approaching £40,000 or even £50,000, and were richer than many of the small independent rulers of the continent. Certainly, the houses they built, Petworth, Chatsworth, Wentworth, Woodhouse, Woburn and so on, were palaces.

The Wealth of the Peerage

How had these big increases in peerage incomes come about? The evidence to answer this question is not in short supply. The literature on the landed estate is voluminous. The most recent survey of landownership, alive with examples, runs close to 800 pages. For each of the few thousand sizeable estates, scattered randomly across the diverse regions of England, experience a different evaluation; each revealed a different demographic profile of ownership. Yet, whilst historians disagree about the impact, timing and weighting of various factors, all are of the opinion that the growth of the large estate and the increasing wealth of their owners was abundantly evident after 1660.

Three principal causes appear to have worked together to produce the right conditions: the use of the strict settlement or entail allowing estates to be passed from one generation to another largely intact (somewhere between half and two-thirds of land owned by large landowners was so settled); the negotiation of advantageous marriage settlements between landed families and sometimes with the richest bourgeoisie; and the increased reliance upon mortgages to fund territorial expansion, family settlements and estate debt generally. Manipulation of these three features was at the core of all dynastic landed ambition. Classically, they led to the evolution of the great ten-, twenty- and thirty-thousand-acre estates that were such a marked feature of British life in the eighteenth and nineteenth centuries. The finances of the second earl of Nottingham (1647–1729), balancing the dowries of his two wives, his earnings as secretary of state (1689–93, 1702–4), sales of outlying property and of his house at Kensington to William III in order to buy a great estate and build a vast house at Burley-on-the-Hill (together costing some £80,000) and to provide portions of £52,000 for his thirteen surviving children, show exactly how the system worked. In the process borrowing could not be avoided, but the fact that he owed a mere £22,000 on his death in 1729, a modest sum by peerage standards, underlines his way-above-average competence in financial matters.

Of course there were wider influences without which the strategies and devices of settlements and mortgages could not so easily have operated. After 1688 the great upheavals of the seventeenth century, which had so thoroughly destabilized the land market and so troubled landowners, subsided. At home, political stability and domestic peace, with few major internal disturbances, returned. The Revolution Settlement, enshrining the power of property, was immensely favourable to agricultural and political development and to colonial expansion alike. Interest rates after the 1690s were low; agricultural prices and incomes rose appreciably after 1750. Rents reflected these increases and also the enormous benefits to landlords of enclosure in its last great parliamentary phase running from around 1750 to 1820. Certainly, landowners shared fully in this general prosperity of agriculture.

The majority of large landowners, as the economic benefits of agricultural improvement were brought home to them by a rapidly growing literature on the subject, increasingly invested in their estates, improving their tenanted farms, providing leadership in agrarian progress, planting trees for prosperity and future gain. There were also landowners, again driven by economic motives, who had the opportunity to exploit, because of the location of their estates, either urban expansion or mineral resources. Peers like Earl Grosvenor (later duke of Westminster), Earl Fitzwilliam and the duke of Bedford were at the top of the tree of peerage incomes, not only because they were amongst the largest landowners, but also because they were the fortunate beneficiaries of either prime London building leases or mineral rights and exploitation. Moreover, many landowners involved themselves, though not necessarily taking the lead, in developing river navigations, turnpike roads and, after 1760, canals. And all landowners, even if they made but a small contribution in these productive areas of investment, condoned the developments in agriculture, industry and transport that slowly transformed Britain, in the two centuries after 1660, into the first industrial nation. In this way the traditional landed classes did not act as a brake on an economic progress that was the envy of their continental neighbours.

The records of negotiations and transactions surrounding settlements and borrowing, purchases, rentals, leases and sales of land filled the muniment rooms and estate offices of every country house. But there were landowners, usually the largest, whose incomes were made up from other sources besides land, urban leases and mineral profits. Some, with breathtaking examples such as the first duke of Chandos, Sir Robert Walpole and the Fox family, did well from political place and office, especially during periods when Britain was at war. Cannons and Houghton, two of the greatest country houses of the early eighteenth century, were monuments to government place. Many a peerage family's finances were reinforced, if less spectacularly than those of Chandos and Walpole, from the profits of office. Revelations in the clamorous prelude to reform after 1815 discussed scores of sinecures, realizing thousands of pounds annually for those influential members of the peerage who struggled most successfully to acquire them. It can be argued that the first earl of Leicester, who took over thirty years to build Holkham Hall, the finest Palladian house in Britain (he spent a massive £92,000 on the house and its landscape), did so in large measure from the proceeds of two government sinecures. These were the right to collect dues on shipping passing Dungeness lighthouse and the office of postmaster-general. Together they produced a net £3,600 a year, a large sum for a peer whose building and landscaping activities were on such a scale that they led him to live in perpetual debt.

Expenditure and Cultural Pursuits

In a brief examination of the expenditure and cultural pursuits of the peerage generalization is again difficult – in this case because, even with a restricted group like the peerage, members of it were, unlike men engaged in the professions, or merchants, financiers and industrialists, freer to follow their own inclinations. Good, impartial, thoroughly professional advice from agents, attorneys and bankers was nothing like as sound as that provided by accountants and financial advisers in the twenty-first century. Although minorities were far better managed than they had been by the controversial Court of Wards before the civil wars, and the trust had become an established and venerated, peculiarly British institution, family members and friends who acted as trustees were no more far-sighted than the general run of landowners. For all these reasons, landowners still possessed considerable latitude in determining the fate of their estates through their approach to debt and expenditure.

Yet if this independence is reflected in the different histories of families, estates and houses, the peerage and largest landowners nevertheless shared a common culture. This was grounded in their education. Increasingly, there was a preference for a public school education (chiefly at Eton and Westminster) in the classics, often followed by matriculation at Oxford and Cambridge, before undertaking the great pinnacle of elite education in the eighteenth century, the Grand Tour – a sojourn of many months and often years, principally in Italy. Sir Brinsley Ford recorded around 6,000 'tourists', the great majority of whom were drawn from the landed classes, in his *Dictionary of British and Irish Travellers in Italy, 1701–1800.* There must have been many more whose visits went undocumented. Then, on their return from abroad, according to their means and inclinations they could indulge themselves in the common pursuits of their class, hunting, horseracing and gambling, and on inheritance, building, collecting, landscaping and improving their estates. In all these various activities they were guided by the fashions of their peer group, usually picked up in long visits to London, often of seven or eight months in the year, and a growing literature on every aspect of these interests.

To fund dynastic ambitions, control of political institutions, extravagant lifestyles, great building, landscaping and collecting schemes or estate improvements, the majority of landowners appear to have resorted to borrowing on the strength of low interest rates and rising incomes. Strict settlements were no bar, indeed they fuelled it. Life tenants were able to incur surprising levels of debt. Indeed, many landowners shared the same culture of debt and insecurity that pervaded the financial, commercial and industrial worlds in this period. The scale of landowners' debts depended, of course, upon resources and prospects. Lesser landowners, usually more cautious, borrowed a few thousand pounds. But the peerage, again varying in their needs and prudence, could and did borrow profusely. Wealthy they may have been, but this did not necessarily guarantee a high liquidity rating for many of them. Debt was therefore a way of life and one which became a more pronounced feature for all landowners in the course of the eighteenth century as they built, bought more land and made more extensive family settlements. Spending way beyond income across long periods was the usual course. The problems at Houghton, the Palladian show house of the 1740s, after Sir Robert Walpole's death in 1745, were twofold: his grandson was incompetent; but the prime minister and his heir, the second earl of Orford, who died in 1751, had already accumulated debts of over £100,000, largely from building, collecting and prodigal lifestyles. Without the fruits of political office and place, these were difficult to sustain on a landed income of only £8,000 a year. The estate and house were reported to be in poor condition in the 1770s. The fate of Sir Robert's picture collection, the most celebrated and expensive of its day, sold at a bargain-basement price of around £40,000 in 1779 to Catherine the Great of Russia, was sealed, in spite of all Horace Walpole's protestations, from the moment of his father's death.

The duke of Newcastle sustained a long and famous political career, properties in eleven counties, five large houses and seventy servants, with the grandest of ceremonial lifestyles, by servicing an ever-escalating debt. In the early 1720s he enjoyed a net annual landed income of around £17,500 and earned another £5,000 from his secretaryship of state. At the outset of his career he improved his houses but laid out little on his estates, for spending, not investing, was the key to the duke's make-up. By 1748 his debts had reached a dizzy £286,000. Inevitably, land sales and limited retrenchment followed. Unlike the duke of Newcastle, the third duke of Richmond inherited a considerable surplus in 1756. He was also personally frugal, checking his account books to the penny, but over forty years later he was £95,000 in debt through making land purchases to extend a modest estate and to extend a modest house, neither initially matching ducal status. Although many landowners were heavily in debt, they almost all stopped short of the danger point. But only just. The second Earl Verney when he succeeded to Claydon in 1753 had an income of £10,000 a year; a decade earlier he had married a London mercantile heiress with a colossal dowry of £40,000. Throwing himself into building, politics and pleasure with Hogarthian abandon, he was forced to flee to France to escape his creditors and to sell the contents of the incredibly extravagant house he had built, which boasted the finest suite of rococo rooms in England. In the early 1790s his heir wasted no time in demolishing two-thirds of it. Lenders – bankers in London who specialized in landed debt, financiers and those members of the commercial rich who dealt in mortgages and annuities – certainly gave landowners a large degree of latitude when negotiating mortgages and bonds. By the early nineteenth century conventional practice was based on a formula, taking into account net rental income, which allowed lending up to half the value of the property mortgaged.

Massive, increasing wealth, a predilection for borrowing and extravagant, emulative lifestyles are always powerful forces likely to produce excesses amongst the tiny minority of those who share them. Ample leisure, diverse interests and copious incomes, principally based upon the seeming bedrock and permanence of land, certainly allowed the peerage in the eighteenth century to follow routes to excess which enlivened the letters and journals of their contemporaries and have fascinated or appalled historians ever since.

The Landed Gentry

The 4,400 landowners King identified in the 1690s and the 3,817 non-peerage landowners whom John Bateman in 1883 reckoned owned estates of more than a thousand acres in England and Wales (there were a further 6,500 in Scotland and Ireland, generally a good deal less rich) were a much more varied group than the peerage. In 1883 some 175 possessed estates of 10,000 acres plus, which placed them at least on a par with the average peer with whom they almost always had close connections of blood and marriage; just over 1,000 gentry owned estates of between 3,000 and 10,000 acres and 2,529 lesser gentry occupied between 1,000 and 3,000 acres. In the eighteenth century the picture was probably not very different. Each county displayed a heterogeneity of gentry population. A handful rubbed shoulders with the peerage in terms of wealth; at the other end of the spectrum there were those who struggled on the margins of landed gentility, even when agricultural prices and rents began to improve from the 1750s after a century of generally low farm incomes. To keep a household, stable and garden sufficient for the dignity of a justice of the peace and for membership of county society, to marry off daughters and to educate and place younger sons advantageously, and to improve farms, was quite difficult on the minimum £800–£1,200 generated by the smallest estates. Unless there were sizeable earnings from other sources there was no surplus, especially when rents, arrears and agricultural prices plummeted to new depths in the second quarter of the century. Davy Durrant of Scottow in Norfolk provides an instructive example. Although the Durrants obtained a baronetcy in 1784 and owned 2,935 acres a century later, they were average Norfolk squires, even if their incomes were well in excess of King's 1695 guidelines for the lesser gentry. Durrant's day-book reveals his expenses and outgoings from 1738 to 1755. In those eighteen years his expenditure averaged £980. He lived comfortably, enjoying the sufficiency of polite society – regular journeys to Norwich and Great Yarmouth, a calendar of assemblies and clubs, and the frequent purchase of books and plate. He was a justice of the peace and the bearers at his family's funerals clearly show him to be a member of county society; his household included a footman, coachman, gardener, cook and three or four maids. But he could do no more than repair his house and modestly update it. A major rebuild, achieved neither stylishly nor extensively, had to wait until the 1780s. Durrant's pleasant, circumscribed county world was a far cry from that of the great peerage families in Norfolk, the Townshends, Walpoles and Cokes.

Lesser titles, hereditary baronetcies rather than knighthoods, seem to have created further distinctions amongst landowners. Initially, at least in 1611 when the order of baronets was founded, grants as of right were awarded to those who met the strictly defined criteria of landed wealth and birth. But creations were soon much exceeded by the first three Stuart kings so that the order, originally restricted to 200 members, had swollen to close on a thousand by the early 1680s. The one detailed study of the baronetage, for Yorkshire, reveals an unexpected picture. Of the ninety-three creations between 1611 and 1800, no fewer than seventy-two (77.4 per cent) dated from before 1672. A mere five originated between 1697 and 1775. Nevertheless, at least in Yorkshire, the order of baronets was characterized by a wide-ranging and growing diversity. Because creations were chiefly of the Stuart period, large numbers did not survive the demographic crisis which straddled the turn of the seventeenth century. Although the wealth of the Yorkshire baronets varied significantly, the way forward for those who prospered and survived (a dozen were advanced to peerages) was through prestigious marriages, the choice of responsible trustees during minorities, small families, businesslike management, consolidation of the core estate and, above all, the capacity to make realistic wills and settlements.

The general mechanism of the gentry's aggrandizement in the eighteenth century, whatever the size of their estate, was exactly the same as that we have seen enriching the peerage: the enforcement of strict settlement to assist the descent of estates more or less intact in a period of demographic uncertainty; the negotiation of mortgages to allow the extension and consolidation of estates and to aid bigger family settlements; and the bargaining of marriage settlements to achieve dynastic ambitions and to refuel family resources. Those at the base of the gentry pyramid, although they appear to have operated all these devices, clearly did so less extensively. Yet those families whose estates and enterprises allowed them to benefit from urban land sales and the granting of building leases, from mineral royalties, or from parliamentary enclosure and exceptional agricultural improvements, fared well, especially after the 1780s when the pace of urbanization, industrialization and agrarian development quickened. Only in the province of government office and place, which in any case gradually became less lucrative after the 1780s, did the gentry do less well than the peerage, who assumed virtually exclusive rights to shake the tree of state and court patronage.

Country Houses

This range of peerage and gentry wealth and pretension is now best encapsulated in a survey of country houses. There are, however, problems in peeling back the layers of our perceptions to the core of their original social and cultural purposes. Now we think, after decades of their demolition and subdivision to institutional use, of even the smaller houses as being formidable undertakings beyond the reach of the largest lottery prize. In the eighteenth century they were simply the residences of the nation's ruling, landed elite, instantly recognized symbols of power and status. A survey of the whole stock of country houses provides a straight fit between the wealth and heterogeneity of the landowning classes in the eighteenth century and the hierarchy of houses they built or remodelled.

The largest houses of the grandest peers cost tens of thousands of pounds, took years to build and employed scores of local labourers and skilled craftsmen drawn from London and nearby urban centres. It was these houses which were on the route of every genteel tourist in Georgian Britain, whose numbers much increased as turnpike roads and the sprung carriage made journeys easier. Access to the largest houses was not difficult. Norfolk, with the two largest architecturally exciting houses of the 1740s and 1750s – Holkham and Houghton – was a magnet for tourists wanting to keep abreast of the latest building styles in the mid-eighteenth century. Yet these gentlemen excursionists never visited more than half a dozen houses in the county, with one exception all the seats of peers.

A quick survey of five Yorkshire houses underlines the sharp distinctions between houses and the marked gradations of landed society. It is a pattern of the latter's material culture which, to a greater or lesser degree, fits across Britain. Castle Howard cost the third earl of Carlisle £78,000 between 1699 and his death in 1738, an enormous amount split almost equally between the Vanbrugh house and his massive landscaping schemes – the great obelisk from which miles of avenues radiated, 7 miles of stout park wall, castellated gates and mock bastions, walks through a 100-acre wood, a pyramid, a parterre and terrace with obelisks, urns and statues in profusion, two temples and, the crowning glory, Nicholas Hawksmoor's mausoleum, itself costing more than the vast majority of country houses. This was building and landscaping on the grandest scale. Horace Walpole, the most acerbic of country house visitors, was bowled over with the results forty years later. Lord Carlisle built Castle Howard, since his political career was brief, principally from an estate income increased through efficient administration. In the West Riding, Harewood House symbolized the wealth and growing political significance of the Lascelles family. Henry Lascelles, immensely rich from victualling, custom collections and plantation owning in the West Indies, bought the Harewood estate in 1739 (it quadrupled in size over the next 140 years). His son, Edwin, built one of the showiest houses in England in the 1760s and 1770s. He spent over £40,000 on the house. Almost £7,000 was paid to Thomas Chippendale, some of whose men worked throughout most of the 1770s furnishing and fitting it out to perfection. A similar sum was expended on the park laid out by Capability Brown's plans, including submerging the old house in a lake which was the centrepiece of Brown's design.

Coming down the scale of Yorkshire house from Castle Howard and Harewood, Sledmere House (1787–92) in the Yorkshire wolds represents the ambitions of those greater gentry who enjoyed the fruits of mounting agricultural prosperity after 1750. Its builder, Sir Christopher Sykes, second baronet, was a sharp businessman – banker, land speculator and great encloser – who had made a superb marriage. He spent, well within his means, a meticulously recorded £18,143 on building Sledmere, largely replacing a house itself no more than thirty years old. But the great majority of landowners in Britain had to proceed with building and landscaping schemes on far more restricted budgets than those of Edwin Lascelles or Sir Christopher Sykes.

Many lesser landowners (as indeed did some of the largest) simply remodelled the houses they inherited so that they conformed to the changing pattern of social life and in the process created lighter and more spacious rooms. High on the list of improvements were a bigger eating room, which on occasion could double for dancing, a library (an essential feature introduced into almost every Georgian country house), and better suites of bedrooms and dressing rooms. Turning a house around and remodelling the interior were not in themselves cheap or necessarily satisfactory solutions, and it could be an almost constant preoccupation. Some landowners, therefore, when their circumstances were right, often on marriage or inheritance, built new houses, a good stable block and set of brick kitchen garden walls, and created a park (the status demarcation of a decent eighteenth-century country house) of at least a few score acres. Many of these houses were built for a few thousand pounds. In Yorkshire, a couple of them indicate the range. Thorp Arch Hall was built to the designs of John Carr of York between 1749 and 1756 for William Gossip, a newcomer to the county's gentry, who had bought the 1,074-acre estate for £8,725 in the early 1740s. The house, a plain five-bay villa, four rooms to a floor, flanked by two attached three-bay wings, was well finished by skilled craftsmen whom Carr engaged in York. The house was built for around £3,480, a sum close to that for Ormesby Hall, another five-bay, two-and-a-half-storeyed ashlar-faced North Yorkshire gentry house, probably designed by the amateur architect Colonel Moyser around 1750 for the Pennyman family.

When books of country house design printed in English began to proliferate after the 1720s, some architects attached costs to their plans. Since they were targeted at the major sector of the market, the lesser landowners, they seldom ran to more than a few thousand pounds. These were probably seldom realized in practice, since most projects ran way over budget; yet evidence, like that of Thorp Arch and Ormesby, indicates that houses were built for the lesser gentry in the £3,000 to £5,000 range in the mid-eighteenth century, a cost band which seems to have at least doubled by the end of the Napoleonic Wars in 1815.

An Open Elite?

It is these smaller houses which fit the contemporary dissection of eighteenth-century society revealed by the social tables of King, Massie and Colquhoun. There does not appear to be a yawning gap between those of the smaller gentry and those of urban grandees. Just as landed incomes at the lower end fused with those of the richer merchants, industrialists and members of the more lucrative professions, so did their houses. Landed society remained aristocratically cohesive way beyond 1800, but it was not a permanently closed world of impenetrably large owners. Architecturally and culturally in Yorkshire there is an obvious descent from Castle Howard, through the houses of the greater gentry such as Sledmere, to those of the smaller landowners at Thorp Arch and Ormesby. These smaller houses suggest that the county's ruling elite was neither closed nor fossilized. It was possible for newcomers to afford houses and estates like these. Then the ascent could begin. There was an 'openness' that existed at the lower levels of landed society, with obvious close links of material culture between them and the trading and professional elites. Socially, this phenomenon was extremely important in the early stages of Britain's industrialization, for by and large its landed classes condoned the momentous changes that took place.

But how genuinely 'open' was landed society? Were newcomers very numerous in the general population of landowners? These questions have greatly exercised historians evaluating in recent years the nature of English society until the late nineteenth century. From evidence ranging from 1540 to 1880 and taken from three counties of varying distances from London – Hertfordshire, Northamptonshire and Northumberland – it has been argued that the number of people selling property was always relatively small and that the newcomers from trade or business were equally small in number and were socially unimportant. More generally, the Stones maintained English landed society remained a closed elite until the end of the nineteenth century. Rubenstein in his studies of the very rich added an extended coda to this argument. He concluded that those bankers, brewers and industrialists who became millionaires and half-millionaires in increasing numbers, as Britain's prosperity reached new heights after 1815, tended not to buy land in quantities which would have given them a place in Bateman's collection of landowners owning at least 2,000 acres. Thus, wealthy newcomers from finance, trade and industry made little impact in the world of established large landowners and a competing bourgeois elite was created and flourished. Rubenstein's findings, like those of the Stones, have been hotly contested. Do they, in any case, fit the eighteenth century?

Two points in the discussion about newcomers require further clarification – the turnover of land to allow them entry to landed society, and the origins of the newcomers themselves. There does seem to have been a considerable and regular turnover of land. Estates of assorted sizes came onto the land market as families faced serious debt or demographic crisis (which most of them at some stage did). As family fortunes fluctuated, some estates grew as successful owners consolidated them by frequent purchases. Sir John Griffin Griffin spent £54,384 on scores of transactions, large and small, to round out his north Essex estate at Audley End in the late eighteenth century. The estates of other families declined as their owners sold at least outlying portions of their properties, sometimes scattered across several counties, to meet contingencies. Few estates remained static across the generations. Supply and demand factors also shifted over time, varying significantly as distances from London increased. The amounts of land sold are impossible to calculate precisely. Disraeli in 1846 believed that not less than a third of the land in Buckinghamshire had changed hands in the previous twenty years. In Cambridgeshire, Daniel and Samuel Lysons noted as early as 1806 that out of 235 families recorded as living in the county in 1433, only one was now resident and even its descendant had moved house. Estimates have been made of the infiltration of newcomers to the gentry of Essex, Oxfordshire and Shropshire in the eighteenth and nineteenth centuries. There were clear variations between each, but in none was there stability. In Essex a quarter of large landowners had nineteenth-century origins, with almost a half making their appearance in the eighteenth century; in Oxfordshire the nineteenth-century figure was similar, but fewer, around a third, had originated between 1700 and 1800. In the more remote county of Shropshire, where ancient gentry families were more predominant, one-sixth were of nineteenth-century origin, a quarter in the previous century. The figures for Shropshire are not inconsistent with those for the 'aristocratic' counties of Northamptonshire and Northumberland. In Lincolnshire, a buoyant land market after the 1730s was sustained by London merchants, those from Leeds, Hull and the midlands, besides men of wealth from the towns of Lincolnshire itself. On all counts, however, significant numbers of newcomers infiltrated landed society after the Restoration. Generally they did not break into the ranks of the largest landowners, whose estates tended to change hands less frequently. Men like Henry Lascelles were unusual. More often, newcomers bought small or moderate-sized estates. If a dynasty was established (and the estates of newcomers appear to have had the most rapid turnover of all estates), their descendants built them up on the pattern common amongst successful landed families.

Who were the newcomers? Some of course had connections through family or marriage with the old gentry, especially if their fortunes derived from great achievements in the armed services or law, two regular sources of new wealth at least before the second quarter of the nineteenth century. Nabobs, too, whose riches were derived from the East Indies or those whose fortunes came from lucrative sugar plantations in the Caribbean, could again establish themselves readily in county society via a seat in the House of Commons and a good marriage. There were also merchants and financiers in London, prominent in the organization of government borrowing and city affairs, who made large fortunes across the century especially during times of war, who were often returned as MPs, and who bought estates usually in the home counties. And there were genuinely new men. Take Peter Birt, West Yorkshire colliery proprietor and farmer of the Aire and Calder navigation's lucrative tolls. He lived almost on top of his coal mines, but these pits enabled him to raise Wenvoe Castle in Glamorganshire. He bought the south Wales estate in 1775 and immediately commissioned two top architects to rebuild it during the most trying recession of the eighteenth century. John Byng visited Wenvoe in 1787; he liked neither the house nor its owner: his new-built house and all his sterling improvements exhibited bad taste and bourgeoisity. Byng was most glad to get away from the owner and his vulgarities.

The type, not all as assertive of his wealth as Mr Birt, seems to have been numerous amongst the very richest men in industrial and commercial life for, down at least to the agricultural depression of 1880, most new men of great fortune bought estates.

Besides its social attractions, land produced stable incomes (at least in comparison with trade), allowed the easy raising of loans upon its security, and provided the necessary property qualifications that were essential for justices of the peace and MPs. Of course, the vast majority of merchants and industrialists did not have the means to buy even a small estate and build. This is unsurprising. At most, when times were prosperous, they enjoyed a suburban villa such as those surrounding London which so delighted Daniel Defoe in the 1720s, or one of those gaudy scarlet houses springing up like mushrooms in the neighbourhood of large manufacturing towns. Nevertheless, each major industry and each major port, town or city (besides London, itself the most powerful engine of new wealth) enabled a handful of the most successful men across the eighteenth century to make fortunes large enough to enable them to buy estates in neighbouring counties. The process of gentrification and aggrandizement could then begin. Often the breakthrough in the establishment of a landed dynasty came with the second generation. The father provided the means and took the initiative; the son acquired polish, enjoyed the permanency a landed income guaranteed, immersed himself in the ways of the landed gentry, and usually ran down the family's business interests. William Milner, so wealthy he was known as 'Alderman Million', lived next to his cloth-packing shops and warehouses beside the grimy River Aire in central Leeds for over thirty years after he had bought the Nun Appleton estate in 1709. He rebuilt the great tumbledown mansion of the Fairfaxes, who had fallen on hard times, in the next three years. But it was left to his Eton-educated son, given the estate and created a baronet in 1717 on marrying the daughter of the archbishop of York, and returned as MP for York five years later, to enjoy a landed lifestyle. Thereafter, the latter's most obvious connection with Leeds was to be buried in the parish church with his forebears.

So long as newcomers lived by the unwritten rules of the old landed gentry, enjoyed hunting, shooting and, before the 1770s, cockfighting, were not extreme in politics or religion, so long as they were hospitable, appeared at the local assemblies and race meetings, treated their tenants generously and fairly, educated their children like those of other landowners, and generally showed the good manners of polite society, they were soon accepted in the county. Membership of the bench, appointment as high sheriff, a commission in the militia, Volunteers or Yeomanry, were more or less automatic for the owners of a good landed estate. Initially, newcomers from trade and industry were never going to meet the social criteria of the closed circle of peerage families, but an expensive education, good marriage, membership of parliament and a deep pocket could work wonders in the second and third generations. At the level of county society acceptance does not therefore appear to have been difficult if its ground rules were sensibly followed. The path of advancement was well signposted from the sixteenth century onwards. A country estate and a fine house were the most obvious way, in a highly wealth-conscious society, by which the most affluent could demonstrate their great riches and success to the world.

This relative openness of British landed society in the eighteenth century was important. True, the peerage provided an almost impermeable gratin at the top, but at the lower levels there was a clear acceptance into its ranks of newcomers who knew the worlds of finance, commerce and industry and who, because of their businesslike approach, made in turn good agricultural improvers. On the other hand, the traditional landowning hierarchy in Britain seems to have been responsive to the economic advantages of urban development, mineral exploitation and transport developments besides estate improvement. Clearly, all parties enjoyed the political power, cultural and leisure resources and economic benefits which the ownership of land conferred. The pursuit of these goals does not appear to have stopped the forward-looking majority of landowners participating in, indeed encouraging, these changes which an expanding home and foreign trade and industrial and agricultural development required.

FURTHER READING

Bateman, John: *The Great Landowners of Great Britain and Ireland* (London, 1883; reprinted Leicester, 1971).

Beckett, J. V.: *The Aristocracy in England 1660–1914* (Oxford, 1986).

Cannon, John: *Aristocratic Century: The Peerage of Eighteenth-Century England* (Cambridge, 1984).

English, Barbara: *The Great Landowners of East Yorkshire 1530–1910* (Hemel Hempstead, 1990).

Girouard, Mark: *Life in the English Country House* (London, 1978).

Habbakuk, John: *Marriage, Debt and the Estates System: English Landownership 1650–1950* (Oxford, 1994).

Kelch, Ray A.: *Newcastle, A Duke without Money: Thomas Pelham-Holles, 1693–1768* (London, 1974).

Mingay, G. E.: *English Landed Society in the Eighteenth Century* (London, 1963).

Parker, R. A. C.: *Coke of Norfolk: A Financial and Agricultural Study, 1707–1842* (Oxford, 1975).

Roebuck, Peter: *Yorkshire Baronets, 1640–1760: Families, Estates and Fortunes* (Oxford, 1980).

Rubenstein, W. D.: *Elites and the Wealthy in Modern British Industry: Essays in Social and Economic History* (Brighton, 1987).

Stone, Lawrence and Stone, Jeanne C. Fawtier: *An Open Elite? England 1540–1880* (Oxford, 1984).

Thompson, F. M. L.: *Gentrification and the Enterprise Culture: Britain 1780–1980* (Oxford, 2001).

Williamson, Tom: *Polite Landscapes: Gardens and Society in Eighteenth-Century England* (Stroud, 1995).

Wilson, Richard and Mackley, Alan: *Creating Paradise: The Building of the English Country House, 1660–1880* (London, 2000).

Chapter Thirteen

The Middling Orders

Nicholas Rogers

The notion of the middling orders is something of an oxymoron. The conventional idea of a society of orders presumed a formal hierarchy of estates and degrees, and by extension a myriad interdependencies, headed by men of distinction, conferred by noble birth or royal appointment and patronage. It saw society as a series of vertical linkages, delineating obligations and reciprocities between superiors and their subordinates. The notion of 'middling', however, presumed a horizontally stratified society. It denoted an interposition between high and low, rich and poor, between those of inherited wealth on the one hand, and those who had to work for wages on the other. Yet, in the eighteenth century, middling orders was acceptable usage, for this was a transitional age, broadly speaking, between a society of status hierarchies and that of class.

The language of the 'middle', whether middling orders, middle ranks or the middling sort, came into general usage during the seventeenth century. Such language was rarely used before 1630, but thereafter it was used to denote people who occupied the middle ground in the hierarchies of wealth, status and power, and aspired to some social and economic independence. By the early eighteenth century definitions of society as tripartite, with identifiable strata of rich, middling and poor people, became quite commonplace. Sometimes authors would even attempt to attribute particular characteristics to such strata. Thus, the *Free-thinker* in 1718 commented that 'the Middling People of England are generally Good-natured and Stout-hearted'. Those troubled by the decline of political independence at the hands of a more expansionist wartime state, where contracts and minor offices were mobilized to secure political allegiance, would sometimes trumpet the virtues of the middling sort as the natural repository of political virtue and disinterested conduct. On 9 June 1753, for example, the *Protester* argued that 'the middle rank of the people' was the most 'solid resource' in times of political crisis. Those preoccupied with the burdens of taxation upon particular sectors of society often earmarked the middling sort as a special interest group. In the debate over assessed taxes at the end of the century, for example, politicians agonized over how Pitt's wartime taxes would affect the fortunes and response of the 'middle class', the 'middling class', the 'middling orders' or the 'middling walks of life'.

As these terms suggest, the language of orders and class was interchangeable in the eighteenth century. Class was synonymous with 'category'. It lacked the sociological connotations of collective consciousness or identity with which it became associated in the nineteenth century. Moreover, since the language of the middle was often used discursively or as a rhetorical device or strategy, it is not easy to determine the sociological contours of those who comprised the middling sort. Some historians would charge that such a task is foolhardy, in any case, since in their eyes language is constitutive of reality rather than a prism through which social realities can be seen. But by and large historians have offered some reflections as to who the middling sort were in the eyes of themselves and contemporaries.

Status and Security

In the seventeenth century the middling orders referred principally to the independent small producers in agriculture and industry. With the development of agrarian capitalism and more commercial forms of farming, many of these smallholders declined in status, so that by the eighteenth century the middling sort in the countryside connoted the larger tenant farmer and employer of agricultural labour and the merchant-middleman who controlled the distribution (and only indirectly the production) of Britain's diverse products. In rough terms, these capitalists of the countryside numbered about 225,000 in 1688, rising to 320,000 by 1800, when the population of England and Wales was about 8.5 million. They were joined by a diverse group of tradesmen and professionals whose presence illustrated the increasingly complex nature of Britain's market society and the growth of the state. This group numbered perhaps 170,000 in 1700 and about 475,000 in 1801, a threefold increase in a century where the total population did not even double. In fact, as the eighteenth century progressed, the term middling sort increasingly privileged urban over rural occupations. It came to mean merchants, tradesmen, substantial shopkeepers and master manufacturers, as well as the emergent professions of medicine, teaching, the law, and the civil and armed forces. Within the elite regiments of the army, and in the more genteel sections of the professions, the links with the landed gentry and even aristocracy were close, principally because the convention of male primogeniture forced younger sons to seek their fortunes elsewhere. Even among London apothecaries, links to gentlemanly, if not landed, society could be intimate. Yet among those more active in international trade and commerce, the links with gentry society became fewer over time. Among the cream of London businessmen, for example, that is, among the directors of the larger monied companies such as the Bank of England and the East India Company, the proportion that hailed from the landed gentry ran at 13 per cent for the first half of the eighteenth century, roughly half of what it might have been a half-century earlier. Here at least, the businessmen formed an increasingly indigenous elite, with 40 per cent having fathers in London business before them. The same appears to be true of other urban elites as well. While prone to adopting a genteel lifestyle, they were increasingly self-selecting in their membership.

It is difficult to determine just how large the middling orders were in Georgian Britain. So much depends upon where one chooses to draw the lines demarcating the middling from those above and below them. Based on the contemporary and quite impressionistic calculations of Joseph Massie and Malachy Postlethwayt, the middling sort might constitute 20 per cent of the population if an annual income of £50 is the agreed criterion; 40 per cent if the level of income is dropped to £40 per annum. Many historians would balk at a middling class comprising 40 per cent of the population, and certainly in London an income of £40 per annum would not qualify. It might be that 40 per cent of the population aspired to middling status in the eighteenth century, for spending, social aspirations and the marshalling of wealth were as important as getting it. Even so, it is doubtful that the middling sort increased dramatically in the course of the eighteenth century, at least relative to the total population.

In practice the middling sort of the eighteenth century might not have prided themselves on their independence from the landed gentry to the same extent as they had done earlier. This was because some of them were linked, as attorneys and stewards, very intimately to the gentry, and because, as the patrons and officeholders with provincial towns, they shared in an urban renaissance that was gentry directed. Even so, all members of the middling sort would have placed a premium on sound economic management, perseverance, utility and plain speaking. Only the richest would have sent their sons to elite public schools, whose value-systems were rarely conducive to a profitable and virtuous business career. Dissenting academies, or schools in Geneva and Amsterdam, were preferred by the highest echelons of the middling orders, grammar schools for the rest. Many attended school for a few years before being apprenticed into a trade or business. The practical orientation of this training did not necessarily mean that the middling sort deferred automatically to those above them. By the middle decades of the century there was a growing criticism of seemingly aristocratic traits, especially the fondness for luxury, French taste, gallantry and the lack of application among gentlemen in general. These traits were thought to be undermining the moral and military fibre of the country at a time when the expansion of empire and trade were important national goals. Within this context, the middling sort saw themselves as men of substance whose palpable economic and political contribution to society – as employers, consumers, officeholders and property owners – entitled them to recognition and respect; or so they, their wives and widows would have anticipated.

The search for security was an unending quest for the middling sort and something that certainly informed many aspects of their behaviour. Because businessmen faced the prospect of prison for debt and bankruptcy, it was important, in an age where limited liability was unknown, to shore up one's credit. Many of Daniel Defoe's comments on the urban tradesmen betray a keen awareness of living within one's means, staying solvent, establishing good credit. Although Defoe recognized and accepted many of the important developments associated with the financial revolution – the rise of public credit, the speculation in stock, the capacious market in debentures and bonds – he was also concerned that tradesmen should not be absorbed with the reckless gambling in stocks and shares that accompanied the growth of financial instruments. Similarly, he was troubled that the emulation of the landed gentry or quality would ruin tradesmen. The high consumption of the middling sort, the general improvement in their material life, continued to raise anxieties about businesses being wrecked by the folly of fashion and luxury.

The concern for safe investments and eliminating business risk guided middling conduct in a number of ways. It was critical to build up a satisfactory network of friends and associates in order to offset a liquidity crisis and potential loss of credit. In previous centuries urban guilds insulated merchants and traders from business crises, and while their formal economic function as the regulators of production and labour declined in the eighteenth century, their informal function as mobilizers of credit remained important. Such associations, and other public forums, whether urban councils, chapels, vestries, turnpike trusts, school, library, hospital or workhouse boards, were also important sites for the diversification of assets and partnership building. Mid-eighteenth-century common councilmen in London, for example, dabbled very extensively in urban property and public stocks, building up small fortunes from the experience and knowledge that they gleaned from their associations with other businessmen. Over the course of the eighteenth century this civic identity gave way to more plural forms of sociability. After 1760 there was a rapid increase in voluntary association: in urban clubs and in masonic lodges, particularly in the unincorporated towns; and there also seems to have been an upsurge in newspaper readership from the mid-century onwards as war and government increasingly determined the conditions of trade and credit.

Voluntary associations were all the more necessary because bankruptcy was commonplace, especially after 1760, when the rate of bankruptcies more than matched economic growth. In fact, the crises after 1770 revealed quite clearly the increasing dependence on confidence, and on bills of exchange and accommodation notes, as well as the growing integration of the different realms of private finance. Before country banks emerged to offer loans, businessmen were very reliant upon friends and kin. Indeed, such informal networks very likely enhanced one's credibility with country banks as well.

In these circumstances it is hardly surprising that marriage alliances were often shaped by business imperatives, especially by the inadequacies of the early modern marketplace. In mid-eighteenth-century London the marriages of big businessmen seem to have been modestly kin-based, where religious persuasion and ethnicities were important factors, as they were among Huguenots and the Dutch. Otherwise London marriages seem to have been noticeably endogamous at the occupational level, despite the Hogarthian fiction that the London *nouveaux riches* aspired to ancient titles. Nearly 40 per cent of London's big bourgeoisie in the mid-century decades married within the circles of commerce, a figure that may be even higher given the larger number of unknowns (36 per cent).

What is particularly instructive about bourgeois marriages in this era is the age at which aspiring businessmen married. Although some 40 per cent of all London aldermen married in their twenties, a further 40 per cent married at thirty-five years or more. City directors also tended to marry relatively late: nearly 35 per cent in their early thirties and over a quarter at aged thirty-five or older. This is in marked contrast to the peerage and the landed gentry, most of whom, if they were inheriting sons at least, tended to marry in their early twenties. Smaller businessmen in the metropolis tended to marry in their twenties, although a quarter married at thirty years or more. The timing of these nuptials suggest that London businessmen married when they had or were about to secure partnerships and spread their economic wings. The richer the trader, the greater the age gap between him and his wife; as much as ten years for the richest, perhaps two to three for the average trader. The portions such men received, as much as £10,000 for the largest merchants, provided them with crucial injections of capital as well as important business contacts. Even amongst smaller fry, there was a good chance that a newlywed could double his capital upon marriage.

Marriage in middling circles seems to have been a mix of affection and interest, with the accent likely on the latter. Daughters may have been given the right to refuse partners, but the circles within which they could choose were limited. Daughters and nieces were sometimes cut off from their inheritances when they defied their parents' or uncle's wishes. On the other hand, London's businessmen do not seem to have necessarily sacrificed their daughters' futures to the imperatives of patrilineal descent. Where wealthy businessmen died without sons, and in the middle decades of the eighteenth century over half of them did so, estates were normally divided among the daughters. They were not given smaller legacies so that some surviving kinsmen might inherit the lion's share. In part, this distribution was made easier by the fact that relatively few businessmen left large landed estates. A lot of their money was in stocks and shares. Similarly, while businessmen did sometimes tamper with their wives' separate estate when their commercial affairs were hard pressed, they do not seem to have tried to control their wives from the grave, by revoking their legacies if they remarried. They simply strove to ensure that their children's legacies were protected in that eventuality. This quest did not prevent them from allowing their wives to play an important role as the executrix of the will or as a joint executor. This was particularly the case where there were children who were minors, and where the mother would be expected to offer guidance about marriage and careers. All in all, the testamentary practice of London's biggest businessmen suggests that they were less interested in male primogeniture and patrilineal descent than the landed aristocracy and more willing to accommodate the interests of wives and daughters in the quest for social ambition and financial security. Whether this holds true for other middling groups remains to be seen. While widows played an important role in the administration of their late husbands' estates in the earlier decades of the century, they may have become less active over time, reflecting perhaps the growing trend towards separate spheres for men and women.

For most women of the middling sort, of course, the possibilities of concentrating upon domestic duties and perhaps being a trophy wife were extremely limited in the eighteenth century. This was so even though 40 per cent of all married women mentioned in the interrogatories of the church courts in early eighteenth-century London declared no income other than their husbands'. It was so because women's informal participation in their husbands' trades, especially in retail, was notoriously underreported. But those middling married women who did report a trade separate from their husbands' almost invariably worked in the garment or retail industry. Such women were expected to run their own concerns and place their husbands' trading interest ahead of their own. Indeed, husbands were entitled to the profits of such enterprises even though they did not shoulder the risk. This made it difficult for any wife to aspire to a modicum of economic independence. Such businesses were normally subordinated to the wider ambitions of the family. The prospects for single or widowed women in trade were not much better, because the range of opportunities remained small. Often it resided in sweated trades like millinery, or in general provisioning or pawnbroking. Such predicaments enhanced the attractiveness of financial security through marriage for most middling women. It explains why, in advice books, novels and diaries, the marriage match became such an obsession and anxiety.

Influence and Interest

One of the major issues surrounding the middling sort in the eighteenth century concerns their relative weight in society. There was a time when it was believed that the middling sort were culturally dependent upon their superiors, aping their fashions, aspiring to country house wealth and status. Historians invoked Bernard Mandeville and theories of social emulation to explain why British consumption soared in the eighteenth century under fashionable aristocratic pacemakers, and why noble grovelling became a practised art. This deference extended to the political sphere as well. A close examination of the personnel of the House of Commons revealed that middling membership remained small and hardly increased throughout the century. Only a small cohort of merchants and lawyers consistently achieved parliamentary status, comprising at best 15 per cent of the House; and some of these men were entangled in the patronage of the greater landlords. Men of new wealth, such as manufacturers, seldom graced the corridors of parliament.

Both of these views have undergone some revision in recent decades. It has been shown that the contribution of the middling sort was critical to economic consumption and that the middling sort could aspire to fashionable taste on their own terms. Money rather than privilege became the chief currency of culture, so that anyone who could translate their wealth into a modicum of gentility was eligible to enter polite society. In fact, the compulsion to ape the aristocracy became less compelling to a public unimpressed by upper-class dissipation, fashionable frippery and its 'effeminate' effects in the mid-century decades of bellicose mercantilism. The quest for green-acres among the richest of businessmen became less appealing by the mid-century decades, as public funds became a stable investment and country villas more convenient locales for the socially amphibious men of commerce. By the end of the century, in fact, there were middling modes of taste that were gaining considerable popularity in the provinces. One revolved around the cult of Thomas Bewick of Newcastle, an engraver and writer whose homespun genius was thought to touch the sublime more successfully than more polished artists.

In the political realm it was indisputable that the landed aristocracy dominated the political machinery of the state, but political power could never be reduced to a matter of personnel; that is, to the influence exercised by powerholders and their clients. To begin with, the middling sort of people could influence politics through the power of the lobby. Interest politics of this kind was not peculiar to the eighteenth century, but its dimensions changed quite dramatically as the fiscal requirements of the state and its active promotion of industrial production touched a wider variety of interests, and as parliament's status as a policy-making body grew. Lobbying parliament became an increasingly sophisticated art, advanced through local representatives or professional agents, and sometimes through nationwide petitioning campaigns. Some of these campaigns were very successful. Shopkeepers from a wide range of towns across the country, for example, vigorously petitioned parliament in the 1780s and forced Pitt to amend and ultimately repeal his retail tax.

Such tax revolts were largely reactive. Small men of property could not hope to monitor the activities of parliament or the executive as closely as the Bristol Merchant Venturers, or the West India planters, or the East India Company, all of whom regularly had representatives in parliament looking after their business, even standing committees to draw up legislative agendas. Interest groups of this permanence were sometimes powerful enough to influence policies that disadvantaged the landed interest in the House. Textile manufacturers, for example, regulated the Anglo-Irish trade to their advantage. They were also able to prohibit the export of wool despite repeated complaints from English farmers. Rarely, of course, were broad-based economic interests in opposition to one another in a sustained and dramatic manner during the eighteenth century. The one exception was the battle between the landed and financial interest in the early decades, fuelled by a Tory antipathy to Dissent. During the 1780s, for example, when textile manufacturers argued that the prohibition on foreign or Irish wool would increase rural unemployment and impose higher poor rates on landowners, the interdependence of trade and land was emphasized. The same was true in the debates over the corn bounty and the sugar acts.

In fact, the clash of large-scale interests was not as formidable in the eighteenth century as it was to become in the nineteenth, when the battles over cash and corn threatened to pitch an entrepreneurial middle class against an overly protected landed elite. What characterized the century was the pragmatic pursuit of interests by myriad pressure groups, both landed and mercantile. Middling support was important to the turnpikes and canals that grew apace in the middle decades of the century, as it was to a variety of statutory bodies delegated with the tasks of urban improvement and policing. This gave rise to an essentially conservative, pluralistic propertied order in which substantial sections of the middling class joined the gentry as the co-sponsors of improvement.

Yet lobbying and local activism could breed its discontents. Merchants and industrialists were sometimes frustrated by the time and expense of lobbying MPs unfamiliar or indifferent to their projects. Even where trades had direct representation, MPs could be tetchy about the demands imposed upon them. Merchants and manufacturers did not always find the structures of landed power to their taste and their experience of local government occasionally amplified their unease. In Southampton middling ratepayers and councillors chafed at the attempt to increase taxes to turn the town into an aristocratic spa. Middling participation on statutory bodies for urban improvements was not necessarily conducive to class harmony, either. It could generate criticisms of corporate privilege and by extension 'aristocratic' habits of rule. This was because the commissioners for some trusts were both salaried and elected by ratepayers, rules that encouraged greater public accountability and scrutiny. Such rules and expectations led middling radicals to call for a more open participatory style of politics in the 1770s, bringing the national reform agenda in line with the practice of local association.

Most middling men lacked the resources and contacts to be big players in the politics of interest. Their only hope of influencing national politics was through the vote. Yet the electoral structure of the eighteenth century was based on a hotchpotch of electoral privileges and freedoms that frequently constrained rather than enhanced middling voices. Over the century, proportionately fewer and fewer men had the franchise, fewer than 15 per cent by 1800. And fewer constituencies actually went to the polls. Among the English counties, for example, where middling freeholders had an opportunity to exercise their choice, contested elections declined from 46 per cent in the opening decade of the century to 16 per cent by the end. Among the larger industrial counties, where merchants and manufacturers frequently had a freehold, the decline was as dire. Only in the larger cities and towns did the proportion of electoral contests consistently run at over 50 per cent. Where middling voters were able to exercise a choice in relatively large numbers, they were not always deferential. In contested county elections, for example, middling freeholders showed no tendency to follow the lead of the local squire. Indeed, in some situations, voter truculence could be quite marked, as it was in the wake of Walpole's excise bill of 1733 and over the legitimacy of the Fox–North coalition some fifty years later.

In the larger urban constituencies the thickening of local economies made patron–client politics more problematic. Although the local gentry or oligarchy was able to control the electorate at its source, by regulating the number of eligible voters, it was often vulnerable to big shifts in middling opinion. In towns like Norwich and Bristol voter participation was high, and rose with civic responsibility. Middling masters and vestrymen were more likely to vote consistently over time than more plebeian voters, for whom the attractions of treating and venality were greater.

Although the middling sort did not speak with one voice in city politics, there were occasions when its influence was crucial. In the 1730s urban merchants and tradesmen revolted against Walpole's fiscal policies and pacific foreign policy, demanding a purification of political life and a more open, accountable politics. During the Seven Years' War (1756–63), when Britain lost Minorca, there were further calls for political reform to eliminate placemen from parliament and to accommodate more mobile sources of wealth. On this occasion, military defeat also led middling spokesmen to criticize the aristocratic nature of military command and to make a great parade of successful generals like James Wolfe, who rose through the ranks by virtue of his talent.

Middling voices also surfaced once more in support of John Wilkes, whose flamboyant career in Middlesex and the City of London threw up a number of political issues with which middling tradesmen and merchants could identify: reform of the debt laws, accountability before the law, judicial process, a reformed magistracy and freedom of the press. The last issue was particularly important, because the press of the 1760s and 1770s was beginning to break free of elite political patronage and control and establish itself as an independent voice. Indeed, Wilkes's middling supporters enhanced the power of the press by safeguarding printers from arbitrary arrest and opening parliamentary debates to public scrutiny. At the same time, Wilkes's middling supporters pioneered new forms of political association and campaigned for more delegatory forms of representation that would give their interests a more direct voice. By helping make Wilkesite politics convivial, accessible and commercial, middling radicals enhanced the 'public sphere', that realm of social life outside government auspices from which a genuine engagement of public issues could be launched. In fact, the Wilkesite movement brought together two middling concerns: the desire to associate against debt and to associate for a more open politics. The men who clubbed together to protect themselves from bankruptcy, whether in masonic lodges or pseudo-masonic fraternities, provided much of the infrastructure of Wilkesite politics. They were among the people who had used political instructions and peti-

tioning to mobilize support on a national basis from 1734 onwards. As a survey of the addresses and instructions reveals, most emanated from the larger towns where middling folk were well placed in positions of authority and leadership. By the end of the century they also included some of the unenfranchised urban constituencies where the manufacturing interest was prominent, places like Birmingham, Halifax and Sheffield.

This did not mean that the middling sort were necessarily radical. Despite the salience of Wilkes's middling supporters on the Bill of Rights Society, some wealthy merchants, professionals and tradesmen rallied to the crown in 1769 and 1775 and rejected radical, even opposition Whig, candidates. In the 1781 Bristol by-election, for example, in which the Tory George Daubeny ran against the radical Whig and American, Henry Cruger, the larger manufacturers divided their votes quite evenly among the two candidates, while professionals and genteel trades voted decisively for the Tory. By the time of the French Revolution, middling voters were rallying to King and Country in greater numbers, and the middling vote in the country was increasingly divided by religion, with the more radical Dissenters adhering to the Foxite Whig and independent candidates.

Yet it would be possible to show that middling notions of respectability and virtue helped set the political agenda from the 1770s onwards. During the first half of the century the private lives of politicians were seldom a matter of public scrutiny. The main source of criticism focused upon their dependence on the state or the market. This quintessentially 'Country' vision continued after 1760, but it was conjoined with a moral critique of high politics that sought to probe the relationship between public and private spheres. The pacemaker in this regard was Vicesimus Knox, the headmaster of Tonbridge School, whose enormously popular essays emphasized the inextricable links between private and public virtue and the need to promote 'decency and regularity', 'temperance and industry' and 'religion and fortitude' in defending liberty. The same line of argument was taken up by Richard Price, who linked Britain's political troubles during the American War to her profligacy and impiety. Such appeals would attract those of an Evangelical stamp who were alarmed at upper-class dissipation and its abrogation of true Christian stewardship. Amid the trauma of the Gordon Riots of 1780, the call for moral virtue acquired the status of a patriotic venture as much as the campaigns for economic and parliamentary reform.

The changing moral climate of late eighteenth-century politics may be illustrated by comparing John Wilkes to the next demotic politician in London, Charles James Fox. Wilkes, a ruthless social adventurer, was admired for his rascality. Although some would excoriate him for publishing the *Essay on Woman* and for frequenting brothels, others would revel in the exploits of the waggish, squinting, leering hero of liberty that William Hogarth so ironically portrayed. Fox, by contrast, was increasingly reviled for his rakish habits. Along with the Prince of Wales, Fox was cast as the degenerate politician unfit to govern the country. By the same token, the moral respectability of the king had begun to restore his popularity among his middling subjects after the loss of America and the Scottish 'invasion' of high politics led by Lord Bute. George emerged as a signifier of domestic probity and obstinate patriotism, a homely and honest contrast to meretricious politicians and as providing a reassuring stability in the midst of national flux and humiliation.

By the mid-1780s the foundations of what later became a middle-class social and political sensibility had been basically laid. Political and social virtue no longer rested on a country house ideal, with its paternalistic responsibilities and conventions of landed stewardship. Rather, it rested on men of character, whose domestic felicity, moral integrity and forthright dealing made them the health and vigour of a state. Such a vision increasingly privileged men of mobile wealth and sought to reconcile the older traditions of patriotism and disinterested service to the state with the realities of a more dynamic society. Such a definition did not exclude landed proprietors, but it challenged narrow definitions of landed hegemony and denied virtue to both aristocratic voluptuaries and to those who lacked the necessary means to respectability and responsibility. On this score, even conservatives such as Thomas Gisborne could agree. In his opinion, the higher classes of society could continue to play a leadership role if they could shake off the luxury and sycophancy that surrounded their station. At the same time, men of commerce could enhance the science of political economy and enlarge the 'liberal prospect of commerce', as well as situating political virtue in the bedrock of the Christian family. While Gisborne thought buying and selling tended to narrow the imagination and coarsen the contractor, he also saw great advantages to the nation in the middle-class pursuit of commerce if pursued with integrity, punctuality, industry, prudence and freedom from extravagance. While a liberal education would be a tonic to business, Gisborne also saw a role for female domestic felicity in his overall plan. In his view God had not endowed women with demanding close and comprehensive reasoning, but with qualities and talents that were particularly suited to the domestic sphere. Modesty, delicacy and a sympathizing sensibility were the quintessential qualities of women, and ones essential to domestic nurture. Here, in embryonic form, was the middle-class fusion of political and private virtue that would come into fruition after the Reform Bill of 1832. It featured a measured acceptance of responsible aristocratic leadership, a necessary infusion of middle-class values to revivify the body politic, and a fully elaborated ideology of separate spheres. With Gisborne, we are at the cusp of middling sensibilities becoming middle class.

FURTHER READING

Barry, Jonathan and Brooks, Christopher (eds): *The Middling Sort of People: Culture, Society and Politics in England, 1550–1800* (Basingstoke, 1994).

Corfield, P. J.: 'Class by name and number in eighteenth-century Britain', *History*, 72 (1987), pp. 38–61.

Davidoff, Leonore and Hall, Catherine: *Family Fortunes: Men and Women of the Middle Class* (London, 1987).

Earle, Peter: *The Making of the English Middle Class: Business, Society and Family Life in London, 1660–1730* (London, 1989).

Hoppit, Julian: *Risk and Failure in English Business 1700–1800* (Cambridge, 1987).

Hunt, Margaret: *The Middling Sort: Commerce, Gender, and the Family in England 1680–1780* (Berkeley, CA, 1996).

Langford, Paul: *A Polite and Commercial People: England 1727–1783* (Oxford, 1989).

McKendrick, Neil, Brewer, John and Plumb, J. H.: *The Birth of a Consumer Society: The Commercialization of Eighteenth-Century England* (London, 1982).

Money, John: *Experience and Identity: Birmingham and the West Midlands 1760–1800* (Montreal, 1977).

Rogers, Nicholas: *Whigs and Cities: Popular Politics in the Age of Walpole and Pitt* (Oxford, 1989).

Smail, John: *The Origins of Middle-Class Culture: Halifax, Yorkshire, 1660–1780* (London, 1994).

Wahrman, Dror: *Imagining the Middle Class: The Political Representation of Class in Britain, c.1780–1840* (Cambridge, 1995).

CHAPTER FOURTEEN

The Labouring Poor

JOHN RULE

According to Defoe in 1709, below the middle ranks who 'live well' came four groups: the 'working trades who labour hard, but feel no want'; the country people, farmers, etc. who 'fare indifferently'; the poor, 'who fare hard'; and the 'miserable who really pinch and suffer want'. Just above the labouring poor he placed those with some skill and the artisans whom he embraced under the general term 'mechanics'. Together these sections of society can be considered in general terms as the labouring poor. For even the presumed superior life of the artisan could in the eighteenth century be a precarious one. In British terms at least, artisans are more usefully considered as a working-class elite than as a section of the middling ranks.

The Nature and Treatment of Poverty

In general terms most eighteenth-century labouring people were poor and many of them unable to survive on their earnings without supplementation from poor relief. Some were wretchedly poor and dependent poverty could be a longlasting condition, or an occasional one experienced in times of particular difficulty or at unfavourable stages in the lifecycle. It has been estimated, for example, that between 1760 and 1802 in Staffordshire, by no means among the poorest counties, in a normal year around 10 per cent of households were unable to purchase sufficient bread over the year even if they spent all their earnings on it. In years of higher food prices this proportion doubled, while in food crisis years such as 1766, 1795–6 or 1800–1, in excess of 40 per cent would be in this situation.

Only a small section of the population was wholly or permanently dependent on poor relief: predominantly those described as the 'impotent' poor such as the old, the widowed, the orphaned and the infirm, whose situation was contrasted with that of the 'able-bodied' poor. At the end of the seventeenth century Gregory King distinguished between those who increased and those who decreased the wealth of England, estimating the latter, who included all those whose annual incomes fell short of subsistence expenditure, to total more than half of the population, although the average degree of deficiency was small. Many lived in a marginal situation and the dependent poor in normal times made up around a quarter of the population. But it was a condition into which from time to time many fell. Lifecycle poverty brought into dependency not only the old, but many households with the infant burdens of early married years. Women were especially vulnerable if unmarried or widowed because few employment opportunities existed that afforded them living wages.

Much has been learned by historians about the levels of relief and the willingness with which it was given. The polemics that drove the great poor law amendment of 1834 presented a bleak and hypercritical view of the 'old poor law'. Elizabethan in origin, it was firmly based on the parish as the unit of rate and relief. Modern historians have assessed it as generally neither ineffective nor ungenerous. At least, that is, until the steeply rising food prices and rapidly increasing population of the last decade or so of the eighteenth century transformed the burden of support. Needs assessed locally were often met effectively. Wherever possible children were expected to work, and for that reason writers like Defoe praised the expansion of manufacturing. Operating in a local context, those who administered the poor law were often more generous than might be suggested by the rhetoric of national pamphleteers who discoursed on the burden of the profligate and the idle. The former knew that situations could change and that in time many who had paid the poor rate could become dependent on relief. The real abuses were to be found in the crowded urban parishes; in the context of rural society the poor law was part of the 'moral economy' of expectation, with adequate relief being viewed as a popular right.

No such right of the able-bodied to relief was presumed in Scotland. There the act of 1579 placed no requirement on the parishes to set a rate. It was assumed that voluntary contributions administered through the kirk would support the impotent poor. Even then there was an expectation that alms from begging would play a role. Parishes could seek permission to levy a rate exceptionally, but only a minority through the eighteenth century did so; legal decisions in 1751 and 1752 effectively allowed the landowners to veto such actions. There were signs that as the eighteenth century advanced, more parishes, especially in the rapidly developing Lowlands, were having to think in terms closer to the English model. In general, however, different demographic pressures and systems of labour hiring, as well as the greater incidence of subsistence farming, allowed the differences between the two poor relief systems to persist, and indeed to allow English hardliners to point to Scotland as an example of how things might be better done.

The willingness of the English poor to complain over the heads of the overseers to justices of the peace does seem to indicate different expectations. General regulation was undertaken by the quarter sessions, but from 1691 individual justices on receipt of complaints could overturn what they considered failure on the part of parish officials to give appropriate relief. Poor relief was not always a question of doles in money or in kind such as clothes or shoes. The poor law required that work and habitation be found for those able-bodied who needed them. Relief for widows was often dependent on their giving up their children at the appropriate age to apprenticeships found for them by the parish.

Sums given were usually small, but until the closing decades of the century brought inflation, so too were the earnings they supplemented. The philanthropist

Jonas Hanway estimated in 1766 that the 'mass of people' lived on £5 a year. And when prices were moderate, a rural family with three or four children could be supported on one shilling to 1s 6d per day. In 1730 it was estimated that a poor man in constant employment could earn from four to five shillings a week. At such levels a poor relief payment of sixpence or one shilling or the payment for items of clothing, shoes or even tools could indeed make a significant difference. But if, as some disgruntled observers saw it, this situation had given rise to dependency and a culture of expectation, it was an expectation which would be met only in the parish where the would-be relief recipient had a 'right of settlement'. According to the law, entitlement came only in the parish of birth unless this was later displaced by serving an apprenticeship or completing a complete year of hiring in another parish, or inhabiting a property there of qualifying value. The harassing of those caught out by need in a parish where they could claim no legal settlement was the darker side of the eighteenth-century poor law associated both with forced removals, notably of pregnant women, and with evasive practices such as short-time hiring for less than a year, or the pulling down of cottages.

The right to be relieved in one's own parish was one reason for popular hostility to workhouses when several parishes combined to build one to hold down the costs of poor relief, a course of action allowed by an act of 1723. Even stronger was the popular view of the workhouse as an institution designed to imprison the poor. Popular opposition certainly restricted the spread of the workhouse system into some areas, East Anglia for example. But only one in nine Oxfordshire parishes had a workhouse in 1777 and nationally it would seem that in 1775 there were 2,000, a large enough number, but there were 17,000 parishes. Even where they existed outdoor relief continued alongside them. In 1802 only a twelfth of relief recipients were workhouse inmates. Increasing national cost after mid-century brought some hardening of attitudes, but it was only in the final decade that spiralling costs brought about a profound crisis in poor relief. At mid-century the annual cost of poor relief was estimated at £689,971. By 1783–5 it was close to £2 million and by 1803 in excess of £4 million. The two great hunger crises of 1795–6 and 1800–1 clearly made a contribution, but there is no consensus view over the role of more structural factors. Recently there has been a tendency to take more seriously the social consequences of the rush of parliamentary enclosures, while wartime inflation and dislocations played an aggravating role. Before the great war with France ended in 1815 expenditure on poor relief in the crisis year of 1812 approached £8 million. Of the expedients adopted to cope with the escalating burden the best known is the Speenhamland system, named after the Berkshire village where it was first implemented in 1795. It was based on a system of family allowances, determined by family size and the price of bread, to supplement the earnings of rural labourers who were increasingly unable to secure a full week's employment from the farmers. It was perceived by its critics as encouraging feckless breeding, improvident early marriage and a greater sense of welfare dependency, but historians have tended to view it more kindly than did the ideologues whose sights were beginning to turn towards the remedies that were eventually realized in the new poor law of 1834, with its hated principle of 'less eligibility' and its despised and resented institution of the union workhouse.

Working Lives

Part of the classic narrative of the industrial revolution is the insistence that it brought about major changes in the ways in which very many people – men, women and children – experienced working lives. To write now of a 'transformation of work' has become less convincing. The emphasis on gradual change, with the persistence, or even growth, alongside highly capitalized industry of alternative technologies with different deployment and organization of labour, is associated with a reminder that work in a factory was still not, even by the mid-nineteenth century, the experience of the larger part of even the non-agrarian workforce. Nevertheless, there are evident trends in the nature of work in the later eighteenth and early nineteenth centuries which do indicate that for many workers, the daily grind was being significantly affected in a number of ways by the changes taking place in the developing economy of the period. Many of these changes were already well developed by the mid-eighteenth century, while others had still some distance to proceed by the middle of the nineteenth. Change, too, was not necessarily experienced in the same way or in the same direction by men, women and children.

By the eighteenth century the British economy was already distinguished by the extent to which the proportion of its agriculturally employed population had declined. By the time of the first census in 1801, little more than a third were still so employed; by 1851 only a fifth. Before 1801 accurate estimation is made difficult by the persistence of dual occupations. Entries such as 'weaver-husbandman' or 'tinner-husbandman' were common in parish registers. Arguably, by 1700 agriculture was already employing only around a half of the employed population. To this degree the period of the industrial revolution did not mark a hugely dramatic shift in movement out of agriculture, but it made it more rapid and presented it in an aggravated form.

Eric Hobsbawm has argued that labour in an industrial society is different from pre-industrial work in four main ways (1968: 66–70). In the first place in an industrial society labour became overwhelmingly the labour of proletarians: that is, of those who had no real source of support other than a wage. This dependency changed the employment relationship. The old language of 'master and servant' described a complex of mutual obligations. The new vocabulary, deriving from the increasingly dominant idea of a 'labour market', moved in a dehumanizing direction through 'hand' or 'operative' to see, in economic terms, the 'worker' as a commodity linked to the employer only by a 'cash nexus', although ideas of a free contract between 'labour' and employer still assumed the subordination of the former to the latter. Second, industrial labour imposed new rhythms of work. Work time for increasing numbers of workers was no longer determined by the task in hand, by the length of daylight, or by the varying dictates of the season. Factory work most clearly symbolized work becoming routinized, regular and monotonous, with a pace dictated by the demanding motion of powered machinery, but what has been described as 'productivist pressure' was also intensifying labour in mines, workshops and, via the sweating-down of piece rates, in sites of domestic production.

Third, Hobsbawm pointed out that with industrialization labour increasingly took place in the large town or city. It was not until 1851 that half of the population were living in towns, but over the eighteenth century the fraction had grown to a third. Whatever happened to wages, there is little doubt that urban living by the early nineteenth century amounted to a deterioration in the quality of life. The jerry-built, overcrowded, slum-ridden towns brought bad air, pollution and the rapid spread of disease – a situation which in its scale was already being prefigured in eighteenth-century London and was beginning to develop in Manchester by the 1790s. The mortality differential between the country and the town had narrowed over the later eighteenth century, but in the early nineteenth it widened again. Urban disamenities are not measured in morbidity and mortality alone. The social relations of the countryside were not immediately transferable. In time the urban working-class culture and community, subsequently to be admired and even romanticized, was formed, but in the beginning the industrial town was seen as the very negation of community. Its labouring population was feared as a class apart, literally so as towns increasingly zoned into class segregation. A class apart was a class needing to be controlled through religion, schooling and, eventually, the new police. Once again it was only in London that such fears significantly manifested themselves in the eighteenth century.

Finally, Hobsbawm argued that pre-industrial experience, tradition, wisdom and morality provided no adequate guide for the kind of behaviour which a capitalist economy required. The new society based on the cash nexus and increasingly committed to the laws of the 'market' completed the dispensing with what Edward Thompson influentially called the 'moral economy' of the eighteenth century. In food riots the crowd had attempted to impose 'just' food prices, while artisans sought to defend 'rights' to employment and to customary wages. It was not easy for such groups to accept that wages should be determined in an open labour market, unsegmented by particular properties in skill, still less that men could be replaced in the interests of costs and productivity by machines. As much as to a 'moral economy', eighteenth-century workers and consumers appealed to a prior political economy, which allowed a regulatory paternalist role for the state. Over the early years of the nineteenth century many were to learn that laissez-faire was becoming the ideology of government as well as of capitalist employers.

In general terms Hobsbawm's four distinctions retain validity. But to take account of recent research and of shifts in approach, each needs closer attention. In the creation of a wage-dependent proletariat the prime process in Britain was not that of peasants entering factories. The peasantry had substantially disappeared and the factory brought only the last act in a lengthy drama. Already by 1776, Adam Smith could accept that the separation of labour and capital was normal. The wage-dependent fraction of the population probably exceeded two-thirds by 1800. In this respect Britain was unusual. The arrival of the factory system had had by then only a slight effect, and, in terms of male employment, the mine and ironworks were at least as important. It could be argued that the growth of a waged proletariat was rather a cause than a consequence of the industrial revolution. It not only supplied a more mobile labour force but a growing one, for the proletariat married younger and had more children. It was also a labour force in which the division of labour and the distribution of critical skills were well developed. The lower orders in Britain also had greater disposable income than elsewhere, and thus offered a wider and deeper market for the simple goods of the early industrial revolution.

Part of the emergence of the proletariat derived from the increasing spread by the beginning of the eighteenth century of manufacturing into the countryside, via the putting-out system operated by merchant capitalists. Their materials were made up in outworking cottages into cloth, hosiery, hardware, cutlery or nails. Historians have described this development as 'proto-industrialization' and observed its appearance and expansion in many parts of western Europe. In Britain it seems to have been especially marked by an earlier and more complete separation from agriculture. Weavers, framework knitters, cutlers and metalworkers quite rapidly became an industrial labour force dwelling in the countryside, rather than a manufacturing peasantry dividing its time seasonally between farming and manufacturing. Although the cottage as a site of production was based on family labour, the typical rural manufacturing worker in Britain neither owned the materials on which he worked, nor disposed of the product of his labour. In short, he was wage dependent.

To these rural workers must be added an urban proletariat that was increasing in size. Over most of Europe the eighteenth century was one of urban stagnation. England and Lowland Scotland were exceptions. Here towns grew in fulfilment of a variety of functions, but important among them was the growth of urban manufacturing. This accounted for the rapid expansion of Birmingham and the metalworking towns of the Black Country; of Sheffield, the great centre of cutlery manufacture; of textile centres for wool such as Leeds, Halifax or Norwich, or for cotton centres like Manchester and its neighbouring towns in south Lancashire; of Stoke as a centre for pottery and of dockyard towns such as Portsmouth, Plymouth and Chatham. London was still the largest centre of urban manufacture with many thousands of tailors, shoemakers, hatters, watchmakers, silk weavers and others. A large proportion of workers were artisans, the possessors of a 'trade', who thought themselves above the common labourer. Nevertheless, by the mid-eighteenth century fewer and fewer of them were independent in the sense of being self-employed, working on their own materials and selling their own product. Most had become permanent journeymen, as waged workers in the trades were called. They may have sold *skilled* labour, and at times of advantage in the labour market at a high price, but they were still wage dependent.

These several tendencies were also to be found in other countries, but the unique occupational structure of eighteenth-century Britain was the outcome of their greater and more rapid development there. In agriculture too the parliamentary enclosures of the late eighteenth and early nineteenth centuries were the last act in the creation of a landless waged labour force, which contrasted sharply with the predominantly peasant-based agriculture found elsewhere. Although peasant agriculture still persisted, especially on the Celtic fringes, the formation of an agricultural proletariat was another distinguishing feature of Britain's pattern of economic development.

The industrial revolution, then, came at the end of extended and varied processes that formed the waged labour force. It was nevertheless responsible for changing the form of a section of the labouring classes into the classic urban industrial working class for which Marx and Engels prophesied the revolutionary role of overthrowing capitalism. Two phases of proletarian class formation were distinguished by Marx. As well as the *expropriation of the product*, whereby the worker ceased to work on his own materials and to market his own product, which we have already discussed, he also identified the *expropriation of nature*. This takes us to Hobsbawm's second point, for it refers to the process of alienation through which the worker loses real control over the labour process (that is, the way in which he works) when he comes under supervision and has to adapt to the dictated rhythms of machine production. There were alternate bouts of intense labour and of idleness, whenever men were in control of their own working lives. That a man could control his own pace when working in his cottage is clear, but the pattern was characteristic too of small workshops, where men paid by the piece came and went. This did not pose too many problems for employers with little investment in fixed capital. Such work rhythms survived into the middle decades of the nineteenth century, epitomized by taking 'Saint Monday' as an unofficial holiday in the small workshops of Birmingham and Sheffield. The weekly rhythm of the outworker was as familiar to potters and weavers as it was to metalworkers. Monday was a holiday, Tuesday a slow day, then a quickening pace until a hectic Friday made up the output needed to make adequate wages. So widespread was the taking of Saint Monday that it has been suggested that it was in fact part of a 'regular' week in work which effectively began on Tuesdays. Justices of the peace as well as employers considered its observance a great irregularity.

The factory system with its expensive running machinery could hardly tolerate such attitudes. Disciplining workers to accept factory time was a major concern of the early factory masters. To this end they developed clocking-in systems and imposed disproportionately large fines for casual attendance and for lateness. For the most part they were successful and the second generation of factory workers had become accustomed to the time-discipline of the factory. By the 1830s the agitation for a shorter working day reveals their acceptance of a rigid division between work and non-work time and a wish to control the length of the former, rather than instinctively reacting to its imposition. It is obvious from its very nature that factory production imposed a new kind of discipline.

Hobsbawm's third point, that with the industrial revolution labour became increasingly urban, becomes especially marked after 1815. The early textile mills, whose machinery was powered by running water, tended to need rural sites, such as that chosen for Richard Arkwright's pioneering cotton mill at Cromford in 1770. It was the problem of recruiting labour to sparsely populated locations that led to the infamous employment of pauper child apprentices. With the advent of steam power, factories could be established in the middle of towns amongst adequate local supplies of 'free' child labour. Even before the factory era workers in many manufactures suffered in health, due to accidents, as in mining, to the deadly effects of breathing dust, as in cutlery grinding, or to muscle strain from repetitive actions, or to cramped and confining working positions, such as tailors (who suffered both from working bent over and cross-legged and from eyestrain), and to poisoning, as in the case of lead-using plumbers, painters and potters, while it was their use of mercury that drove the hatters mad. The cotton mills, too, had their peculiar occupational disease: bysinosis, a lung condition caused by the fine particles of lint which filled the air in low-ceilinged and ill-ventilated workplaces.

Such conditions took their toll, but in general the greater mortality and morbidity found in the industrial working class were increasingly explained by the atrocious living conditions in industrial towns, aggravated by poor diets. The comparative mortality figures, presented in Edwin Chadwick's famous report of 1842, may be flawed by modern standards, but the story they tell is clear enough. A Manchester labourer had a life expectancy of seventeen and one in Leeds of nineteen. At the other extreme, one in small-town Truro had a life expectancy of twenty-eight and in rural Rutlandshire of thirty-eight. That living as much as working conditions were responsible is indicated by the fact that at fifteen for labourers, life expectancy in non-factory Liverpool was even worse than in Manchester.

Contemporaries presented the industrial towns as bleak in more senses than the material conditions of life. Engels was not alone in presenting Manchester and its like as the antithesis of community in the old village with its class reciprocation, face-to-face relationships and mutual assistance and support. In fact, the migrants to the industrial towns carried something of the old ways with them, and in a rather short span of time surviving old ways mingled with new ones deriving from work comradeship, neighbourhood, kinship and association in chapel or trade union to create a distinctive urban working-class culture that later came to be celebrated by sociologists for its cohesion and mutuality.

Hobsbawm suggested a fourth difference: pre-industrial outlook and experience offered no adequate guide for the kind of behaviour that a capitalist economy required. He contrasted the moral economy of the past with the economic rationality of the capitalist present. A *mentalité* of customary rights and traditional expectations was faced increasingly through the eighteenth century with the erosion of the paternalist regulation of the economy associated with the Tudor and Stuart eras, and with changing employers' attitudes. Although it has been argued that there was much that could be described as 'paternalist' in the relations between the mill owners and their workers, the tendency was otherwise. At the end of the eighteenth century the London saddlers were still celebrating in verse the *Memory of Queen Elizabeth*, still 'dear to journeymen' because 'her glorious rules' had checked 'tyrannic masters' and protected 'workmen's rights'. Edward Thompson wrote of the crisis point produced by the imposition of laissez-faire upon and against the will and conscience of the working people, which came in the early nineteenth century. He had especially in mind the Luddite resistance of the east midlands framework knitters and the wool croppers of the West Riding in 1811–13, in which attacks on machinery were paralleled by unsuccessful petitioning campaigns to persuade government to regulate the trade and prevent employers from cutting wage rates through employing unskilled labour in association with machinery. The same decade also saw in 1813 the repeal of the section of the Elizabethan Statute of Artificers, which had allowed magistrates to impose wage rates, and in 1814 of that which restricted trades to those who had been properly apprenticed to them, despite strong resistance to the repeal by skilled workers. A number of trades were recording their frustration as petitions to parliament failed to secure a degree of protection from changing employer practices. The cotton workers did so in 1811 when they failed to secure a minimum wage. Government by the end of the eighteenth century had become largely convinced that interference in the economy by the state was to be avoided. In 1806 a House of Commons committee declined to impose regulation on the employment conditions of journeymen calico (cotton) printers, even though it accepted that many employers were forcing down wages by taking on large numbers of so-called apprentices. Instead, they preferred to stress the salutary effects of leaving the masters and journeymen to settle their affairs between themselves.

Left to themselves, workers generally had little choice but to take whatever the labour market offered in wages and terms of employment. In the early nineteenth century rapid population growth, enhanced by an influx of unskilled Irish, ensured that the balance of power in the labour market usually tilted towards the employers. Skilled workers had more ability to protect their standards, but some, like the handloom weavers, found that their skills were first made less valuable through too rapid an increase in their numbers, and then redundant through the introduction of powered machinery or the alternative deployment of unskilled, often female, labour. From the late seventeenth century, but with a noticeable spread and increase in the eighteenth, many groups of skilled workers had been uniting in organizations which were then usually called 'workers' combinations' to use collective action to protect their living standards, and even, in favourable contexts, to advance them. 'Strike' in its modern sense is at least as old as the 1760s, when it was in common usage by London's well-organized journeymen tailors.

What a later age would come to know as trade unionism clearly predated the industrial revolution, and in Britain its craft origins still characterize it. Adam Smith in 1776 accepted as commonplace that workers combined against their employers for 'defensive' and 'offensive' purposes. Recent work has stressed how often workers used collective action to wrest wage increases from employers, but as often the early trade unions were defensive in their aims, seeking to protect existing standards of living and conditions of work and hire. Their rhetoric often looked back to 'better days'. 'Innovation' was the enemy, whether it involved the use of new machinery or simply new ways of organizing work. Research now suggests that these early trade unions were often successful in securing wage advances and in imposing a degree of constraint on the actions of employers. But the real advantage usually lay with the latter. Success was hardly possible unless the economy was prospering, with labour in demand and employers anxious not to lose output. In trade depressions actions were mostly defensive and likely to fail given the difficulties that they faced. These included that of funding long strikes and a precarious legal situation even before the Combination Acts of 1799 and 1800 generally proscribed workers combining to raise wages or reduce hours. The acts remained in force until 1824. Although their level of enforcement and overall effect is disputed by historians, they undoubtedly hindered the progress of trade unionism in the newer manufacturing districts in the industrial north and midlands, even if they had only limited impact on the well-established organizations of London's artisans. After 1824 trade unions operated in a more favourable though far from comfortable legal situation in which they still faced considerable hostility from employers, the press and the authorities. They were able to take hold among some new groups of skilled workers associated with the industrial revolution, such as engineers and cotton mule spinners, whose position had become more secure while that of displaced skills like handloom weaving and calico printing declined.

To a marked extent the purposes of early trade unions, shared by early nineteenth-century political movements such as Owenism and Chartism, was resistance to the dynamic force they increasingly identified as 'capitalism'. As they articulated their opposition to its encroachment on their traditional ways and expectations, they began to present themselves as 'labour'. They developed a language which reflected this identity, and a consciousness which, although it was restricted and even exclusive in its own time, extended more widely as the nineteenth century progressed and helped to form the ideologies and perspectives of later working-class movements.

Women and Work

From the time of the industrial revolution itself there has been much debate over the impact that it made on women's work. Until recently only a handful of scholarly works were directed at the subject, but this is no longer the case. The list of titles that directly address this topic has lengthened with the advance of women's history. This work has tended to stress that only a minority of women who worked did so in the classic industrial revolution context of the textile factories that began to emerge from the closing decades of the eighteenth century, but it has nevertheless been the situation of these millworkers that has been in the forefront of contemporary discussion and of subsequent historical debate. Factory work was seen as transforming women's work by removing it from the home and from the constraints of the family economy of cottage manufacture. To the extent that women entered the labour market as independent wage earners, this could be viewed as an important step towards economic emancipation.

This sense of transformation has also been highlighted by historians, who have noted a 'tremendous' increase in the availability of work for women outside the home, which was of vital importance in destroying the family wage, bringing improved status and better conditions. This has been seen as the beginning of the most important and most beneficial of all the social revolutions of the last two centuries, the emancipation of women, but others have also stressed that the industrial revolution introduced the idea that men's wages should be sufficient to maintain a wife and family and that women should make their contribution by looking after the home. The emergence of the ideal of the male 'breadwinner', and the related one of separate spheres for men and women, was certainly one of the most potent and significant developments of the period. In fact, it was a development not easily directly attributed to the industrial revolution. It could even be seen as an ideological constraint, working against the free labour which should have provided employers with as much as they needed of the cheapest available labour. Female participation in the waged economy probably declined after the 1820s. This happens to coincide with the highest average family size in British history, when women even more than usual experienced repeated pregnancies and continuous childrearing. For whatever reasons it seems that through several decades of especially rapid industrial growth industrialists made only modest use of female labour. The factory girls were given unusual opportunities, and even for them their 'independent' years were closely linked to the lifecycle commonly ending with marriage. Indeed, the productive activity in the outside waged economy of women seems to have declined after the eighteenth century. Even in textiles it was outside the factory, in the home-based needle trades, that the largest expansion of female employment took place, along with domestic service. It is hard to escape the conclusion that despite the insistence of an earlier generation of historians that the industrial revolution widened women's opportunities, their contribution to the various forms of manufacturing persisting and developing in the eighteenth-century economy was proportionately greater and of more significance. This was not simply a response to the fact that women were cheap: they were generally paid a third to a half of male wages. In some parts of the country they were also increasingly available. In agriculture female participation seems to have experienced an overall decrease in the cereal-producing regions after the mid-eighteenth century. The evidence on seasonal employment suggests that they were moving from working at the harvest to less reliable and less well-paid springtime activities. By the second quarter of the nineteenth century a sexual division of labour had become marked. The scythe, never used by women, had generally replaced the bagging hook and the sickle by 1790 and had done so even earlier in the south. The experience of the pastoral counties was different. Here there was no decline in, and even possibly rising real wages for, female specialization in livestock, dairying and haymaking, but the purpose of most later eighteenth-century enclosures was to increase the amount of arable land. The demand for female labour was linked to organizational and technological changes which enhanced the profits that could be made from employing women. By the end of the century in some manufactures such as calico printing, spinning and button-making, increasing employment of women was linked to new methods of production that did displace men. The total new employment for women outside agriculture, grow as it did, was not sufficient to offset entirely their declining earning opportunities in that sector. Where employment was available even at women's wages, it allowed family earnings to rise more clearly above the level of destitution.

Child Labour

So, too, did the earnings of children where work was available for them, and they formed a significantly higher proportion of the population then than in later western populations. The factory system became notorious for its use of child labour, but of course it did not initiate the expectation that the children of the labouring poor should work wherever possible. In cottage-based industry they were usually employed at home within the family economy, assisting in the many tasks that existed alongside a main activity such as cloth weaving. Defoe at the beginning of the eighteenth century praised the woollen manufacture of the district around Norfolk, where there was not any hand unemployed, if they would work, and children of four or five years of age could everywhere earn their own bread. He made similar observations of the other main textile regions. William Temple, the best-known spokesman for the great west country woollen manufacture, stressed that it was mainly the opportunity for usefully employing the labour of children which lifted the living standards of manufacturing households well above those dependent solely on agricultural employment. Of course, children were employed in agriculture, but in general only fitfully and seasonally when particular tasks such as stone-picking or bird-scaring presented themselves. Many children were employed outside the family home or holding. In some mining districts they worked both above and underground. As apprentices they worked in situations in the trades that could be as harsh as those encountered in early nineteenth-century cotton mills. All this does not make simple sentimentalists of those who insist on the special nature of child employment in the latter. This is especially true of the system under way in the closing years of the eighteenth century of taking unfree pauper apprentices from their home parishes to the newly emerging mills of the midlands and the north. That era was short-lived. Steam power in the early nineteenth century brought the factory into the town and the need for transporting labour to rural water-powered mills ended. But while it was happening it is fairly associated with a particular systematization and brutalization of child labour.

Standards of Living

Overall it is hard to overcome the data deficiencies and identify any clear trends in living standards. Regional variations were marked, with family earnings becoming larger in the midlands and north, where manufacturing employment both influenced the labour market for men and gave greater opportunities to women and children. Generally, over the south, the west and the southeast, real wages declined from the middle decades of the century, as earnings fell behind rising food prices. Although London wages were higher, here too real wages seem to have been in decline across the artisan and building trades, with an especially marked decline over the 1760s, almost as marked as that in the better-known difficult decade of the 1790s. In Scotland, too, the situation in industrializing Lowland areas was markedly different from that in the Highland regions, where, as in north Wales, a near-subsistence peasant economy persisted. Overall demographic expansion did to a degree threaten economic well-being and it seems, although experiences varied between regions and between occupations, that the 'vital revolution', the sustained rise in population that set in by the mid-eighteenth century, while in outcome hardly justifying the extreme pessimism of Malthus cannot be wholly dissociated from the tightening circumstances of many of the eighteenth century's labouring poor.

FURTHER READING

Berg, Maxine: *The Age of Manufactures, 1700–1820: Industry, Innovation and Work in Britain* (London, 1994).
Clarkson, L. A.: *Proto-industrialization: The First Phase of Industrialization?* (London, 1985).
Hay, Douglas and Rogers, Nicholas: *Eighteenth-Century English Society* (Oxford, 1997).
Hill, Bridget: *Women, Work and Sexual Politics in Eighteenth-Century England* (Oxford, 1989).
Hobsbawm, E. J.: *Industry and Empire: The Economic History of Britain since 1750* (London, 1968).
Lees, Lynn Hollen: *The Solidarities of Strangers: The English Poor Law and the People, 1700–1948* (Cambridge, 1998).
Malcolmson, R. W.: *Life and Labour in England, 1700–1780* (London, 1981).
Marshall, Dorothy: *The English Poor in the Eighteenth Century: A Study in Social and Administrative History* (London, 1969).
Mitchison, Rosalind: 'The making of the old Scottish Poor Law', *Past and Present*, 63 (1974), pp. 58–93.
Porter, Roy: *English Society in the Eighteenth Century* (Harmondsworth, 1990).
Randall, Adrian J.: *Before the Luddites: Custom, Community and Machinery in the English Woollen Industry 1776–1809* (Cambridge, 1991).
Rule, John: *The Experience of Labour in Eighteenth-Century Industry* (London, 1981).
Rule, John: *Albion's People: English Society 1714–1815* (London, 1992).
Schwarz, L. D.: *London in the Age of Industrialization: Entrepreneurs, Labour Force and Living Conditions, 1700–1850* (Cambridge, 1992).

Snell, K. D. M.: *Annals of the Labouring Poor: Social Change and Agrarian England, 1600–1900* (Cambridge, 1985).
Thompson, E. P.: *Customs in Common* (London, 1991).
Valenze, Deborah: *The First Industrial Woman* (Oxford, 1995).
Wells, R. A. E.: *Wretched Faces: Famine in Wartime England, 1793–1803* (Gloucester, 1988).

Chapter Fifteen

Urban Life and Culture

Peter Borsay

In the eighteenth century the British Isles became the most dynamic area of urban development in Europe, and – perhaps – in the world. In 1700 the proportion of the population of Britain and continental Europe living in cities of over 10,000 people was roughly similar (at around 9 per cent), but by 1800 it was almost twice as high in Britain (16 per cent) as on the continent (9 per cent). The rapid urbanization of the British Isles in the eighteenth century should be seen as part of a longer-term historical process. During the Renaissance the economic and cultural heartlands of urban Europe had been located in the Mediterranean; by the seventeenth century the centre of gravity was shifting northwards and westwards, manifesting itself in the Golden Age of Amsterdam and the Dutch Republic; in the following century the mantle passed to the islands of Europe's Atlantic archipelago. The effect of urban growth on the life and culture of those who occupied the British Isles, and particularly their towns, was to be immense, but it did not follow some simple universal or progressive pattern; rather, it was a multi-faceted phenomenon, characterized by variety, ambivalence and complexity.

The British Isles was not a homogeneous entity. Sharp environmental differences, allied to very different courses of historical development, ensured that the impact of urbanization varied considerably from country to country and region to region. The proportion of the population living in towns of over 2,500 people may scarcely have shifted at all in eighteenth-century Ireland, remaining at about 12 per cent; in England and Wales it grew from just under 20 to just over 30 per cent; and in Scotland it trebled from around 12 to 36 per cent. This picture itself masks dramatic regional variations. Huge areas of central and west Wales enjoyed only a minimal urban presence; in Scotland urban growth was heavily focused on the narrow belt of land in the western and eastern Lowlands, which included Edinburgh and Glasgow; and in Ireland – whose crude rates of urbanization were depressed by a burgeoning rural population – town life was much stronger to the east in Leinster (and was strengthening in Ulster) than to the west in Connaught, whose relative environmental marginality left little potential for the development of an extensive urban network.

The elements of contrast and diversity in the British urban experience were reinforced by the enormous variation in size and character between different towns. At the very top of the urban hierarchy, and in a class of its own, presided London. Between 1500 and 1700 it increased its population almost tenfold to become, with half a million inhabitants, the largest city in western Europe; by 1800 it had swelled to a million people and, with Peking (Beijing) and Edo (Tokyo), was the largest city in the world. Dublin's eighteenth-century growth was almost as remarkable. In 1700 it had a population of around 50,000 to 60,000; by the 1820s this was approaching a quarter of a million. By 1800 Glasgow and Edinburgh had roughly 80,000 inhabitants each, though Glasgow had grown the fastest during the course of the century, with about 20,000 inhabitants in 1700 compared to Edinburgh's 50,000. Beyond these metropolitan complexes came the provincial towns. Their dynamism should not be underestimated. During the sixteenth and seventeenth centuries London's share of the population of England and Wales rose from 2 to 10 per cent. That this trend did not continue in an upward spiral, that – despite its continued monstrous growth – London's slice of the national demographic cake remained more or less stable across the eighteenth century, reflects the way that urbanization came to permeate the English urban system as a whole. Most striking was the dramatic rise of the industrial towns and ports of the midlands and north, so that by 1750 Birmingham, Liverpool and Manchester (each with around 20,000 people) were already among the top six provincial English towns, having not figured in the top twenty in the 1670s. Urbanization helped fill out the middling to upper tiers of the urban hierarchy, and to close the awesome gap between London and the rest; between 1700 and 1800 the number of towns of over 2,500 people in England and Wales trebled from sixty-six to 188. But this did not alter the fact that throughout the British Isles the vast majority of towns remained very small. In the late seventeenth century 90 per cent of the thousand or so towns in mainland Britain had populations of under 2,500. Many of these places were tiny; for example, half the towns in Sussex in the 1670s had populations of 1,000 or under, and even in 1801 the proportion still stood at a quarter. It might be thought that during the course of the eighteenth century small towns – under the impact of modernization, rationalization and urban 'massification' – would have gone to the wall, but generally this was not the case. In Scotland and Ireland hundreds of small settlements were either newly founded or remodelled, especially from the middle of the century, which possessed, whatever their size, some urban characteristics. A number developed into full-blown towns, such as Inveraray (Strathclyde), laid out in about 1740, and Westport (Co. Mayo), established in about 1780. England's rich endowment of towns, and the maturity of its urban system, meant that there was less scope for the creation of new towns, but the evidence is that its established network of small towns held up remarkably well, sharing in the processes of urban growth and prosperity, until the early nineteenth century. It must be said, however, that there were distinct regional differences, with the small towns of the north and west midlands faring much better than the less economically dynamic southwest and East Anglia.

Given the huge spectrum of urban settlements to be found in the British Isles, from the largest city in the world to arguably the smallest – in 1720 the parish of the cathedral town of St David's, located in the far western extremities of Wales, contained 1,316 people, of whom fewer than 500 actually occupied the urban core –

any attempt to establish a universal urban experience would be an illusive goal. Yet there were certain common features which, at the most basic and pragmatic level, distinguished urban life from that in the countryside. Towns were places to which people came. This reflected the underlying function of almost every town, that of a market centre. However impressive the rates of urbanization witnessed during the eighteenth century, the British Isles in 1800 was still a predominantly rural society, with the need for central places in which to buy and sell its produce. This went not only for agricultural goods, but also – of great importance in a Britain reaching the peak of its proto-industrial phase – the output of rural industry. Thus, the textile towns of the West Riding of Yorkshire were not at this stage so much centres of manufacture as of marketing. Twice a week clothiers would arrive *en masse* from the surrounding hamlets, carrying the textiles woven in their homes, to congregate at the great cloth market in Leeds that stretched along Briggate to the Market House, though from 1711 it was being accommodated in the impressive new White Cloth Hall. A similar rural invasion took place in Shrewsbury every Thursday, where flannel woven in the hamlets across the border was brought 'weekly in very great quantities', so that though, as Daniel Defoe wrote, 'they speak all English in the town . . . on a market day you would think you were in Wales'. The growth of the rural linen industry in eighteenth-century Ulster brought yarn and cloth to the buoyant markets of its towns, the majority of which, even in 1800, still had populations of under 2,500. But the flow of goods was not one-way. Rural industrialization reduced the workforce's capacity to produce its own foodstuffs, so that a trip to market was also essential to stock up the larder, sometimes requiring large-scale agricultural imports from outside the region. The impact of the periodic ebb and flow of industrial and agricultural produce, and of the people that accompanied them, on the sights, smells and general ambience of the town is something that is scarcely imaginable to those used to the sealed and sanitized world of the modern superstore and supermarket. Unprocessed food arrived in wagons and carts, on horseback or simply on the backs of people; often it came live on the hoof, with cattle, pigs, sheep and poultry driven into the town – complete with the odours of their bodies and ordure – to be sold in (and sometimes slaughtered close to) the open street. In the smaller towns transactions would be concentrated in a single multi-purpose marketplace, but in the larger places trading would spill out across the central commercial area, the streets of which can today still retain the names of the products they accommodated.

This necessity for trade created in both the greatest city and the smallest town a sense of human and physical movement, and a mixing of inhabitants and visitors, that would have distinguished all urban communities from their surrounding villages. In ports the toing and froing of peoples and products was accentuated by the regular arrival and departure of ships, which often traded across considerable distances. The burgeoning west coast ports of Glasgow, Greenock, Cork, Bristol and Liverpool, with their commercial links not only to Europe but also across the Atlantic, were international communities, whose life pulsated to the rhythms of Virginia and Barbados as well as – and recent work on Bristol suggests more than – those of their local hinterlands. The central role played by trade in the urban economy highlighted the town's service function. Unlike the position in the countryside, a high proportion of the population would be employed in the tertiary sector. Many of the male workforce were involved simply in moving around goods and people – porters, carriers, carters, dockers, watermen, bargemen, sailors, chairmen and such like. In Newcastle-upon-Tyne there was a tightly knit, fiercely independent group of workers called keelmen, devoted simply to shifting the prodigious quantities of coal mined along the Tyne Valley from the quay to the collier ships moored in the river; and in Bath the chairmen who conveyed the polite visitors around the town formed a similarly specialized, self-conscious and at times truculent occupational category. Alehouses, taverns and inns were the cogs of the transport system – accommodating travellers, and feeding and stabling horses – but they also provided an extraordinarily wide range of other services and, particularly in road and drover towns, would have generated a good number of jobs. Towns were, in addition, geared to meeting the rapidly expanding demand for professional and quasi-professional services in areas such as the law, medicine, finance, education, architecture and music.

The most characteristic institution of the urban tertiary sector was the retail outlet. Surviving inventories and newspaper adverts suggest just what a range of goods shops might stock, and in the larger towns they were able to reach a high degree of specialization and sophistication. Some shops were simply instruments of distribution, but many also doubled as places of production, such as tailors, bakers, confectioners, shoemakers, gunsmiths and clockmakers. Indeed, townspeople were heavily involved in making as well as selling goods. Most of this production, however, was geared towards servicing a local market, was based on working or processing agricultural products (such as in the leather trades and malting), and was of a craft character, located in the home or small workshop. Where towns were engaged in primary industrial output it tended to be at the end of the chain of production. In the textile trades this involved the finishing processes, such as fulling and dyeing. The bulk of spinning and weaving occurred in the countryside, though there were important exceptions to this; for example, stuff weaving took place on an extensive scale in the 'Over the Water' district of Norwich, and silk weaving in London's Spitalfields. Ports also contained significant pockets of industrial activity, not only shipbuilding yards, but also manufacturing plant – such as that for the refining of sugar, tobacco and salt, for metal smelting, and the production of pottery, glass and soap – associated with their ready access to fuel and unprocessed raw materials. During the industrial revolution powerful centrifugal forces emerged, arising in part from the development of steam-powered technology, which concentrated primary industrial production in large-scale, urban-based units such as factories. Signs of this process were already evident by the later eighteenth century – even earlier if one counts John Lombe's large water-powered silk mill constructed at Derby in about 1720 – but this was not typical of the pre-modern experience.

Probably the most important urban occupational categories, and among the most invisible in the records, were housewives and servants, working not only in the domestic household but also, and one suspects often simultaneously, in hostelries, shops and businesses where a cheap and flexible labour supply was required. Women made up the bulk of those involved, and it is the appeal of urban domestic service (in the 1690s around 80 per cent of London's domestic servants were female) which accounts for the markedly low male to female ratios (in 1700 often in the region of eighty to ninety men to every hundred women) to be found in the majority of English towns. Men made a much stronger showing in those centres with a robust industrial base, such as the emerging ironmaking town of Merthyr Tydfil or the dockyard town of Portsea, but urban life as a whole was heavily coloured by the presence of young female migrants, under pressure to leave the countryside, where there was limited permanent agricultural work for women and pay was low. Though it is known that villages were far from static populations, migration was a critical feature of urban life – in the late seventeenth century between a half and two-thirds of residents were incomers – adding to any town's transient character. Without migration the high levels of urbanization achieved in the eighteenth century would have been unobtainable. The smaller and medium-sized centres may have been able to contribute to their own growth, but the larger cities were so unhealthy that they could not even have held their own, let alone fuel the spectacular rates of expansion many achieved. Notoriously, London killed off more than it created, so that its rise to global greatness rested on a steady tide of migrants; between 1650 and 1750 it has been estimated that net immigration stood at around 8,000 a year. Most incomers came from a relatively short distance away, strengthening the contacts between towns and their immediate hinterlands. Though the larger cities were able to recruit over longer distances, London's base narrowed during the course of the eighteenth century as the capital faced stiff competition from the expanding industrial towns and ports of the English midlands and north, and of south Wales. Ironically, migrants contributed to the high urban mortality rates, since they were particularly vulnerable to illness and disease, their bodies unprepared for and unimmunized against the killer diseases, such as smallpox, lurking in the city.

The flow of people in and out of the town contributed a large part to the urban experience. But migration is something which needs to be read through the prism of the social structure. The great bulk of incomers came from the potentially (if not actually) poor, to whom the principal attraction of the town, in comparison to the countryside, was the prospect of better employment opportunities, especially for women, young adults and families, and of higher wages and securer and steadier jobs. It would be misleading to imagine that the eighteenth-century town delivered on all these counts, but its inherent economic buoyancy ensured that it did a better job than its early modern predecessor, where the demand for urban employment often outstripped supply. That said, the majority of migrants were not well off, and they carried their socio-economic baggage with them. Economic growth and the increasing easing of formal employment restrictions, such as those imposed by the craft guilds, offered greater opportunities for personal mobility than in earlier generations, but the town – whatever its image – was not a huge escalator able to advance the careers of all those who entered it. The common migrant, unless going into service, would have joined the generality of less-well-off townspeople – not infrequently they would have lodged temporarily with relatives, or in alehouses – who lived in the town's suburbs or in narrow alleys and enclosed courtyards situated to the rear of main thoroughfares. Poverty was an endemic feature of urban life, and if its sharper edge was being dulled a little by the early modern development of a parochial system of relief, migrants' access to this might have been restricted by their 'outsider' status.

Not all migrants were poor. Significant numbers also came from better-off backgrounds. Some of these would arrive as already established businessmen and women, and would be welcomed into the town because of the economic and social benefits it was believed that they could bring; a newspaper printer, a school teacher or a dancing master might introduce valuable services, a successful trader could generate new employment opportunities. Others would take up apprenticeships in jobs with good career prospects. At the top end of the range, particularly among merchants and the expanding professions, this would involve a hefty apprenticeship fee, severely limiting the social pool from which recruitment occurred. Thus, merchant apprentices arriving in early eighteenth-century Edinburgh and Aberdeen were drawn overwhelmingly from the middle strata of Scottish rural and urban society, and it was not uncommon for the Yorkshire and Lancashire gentry to place their younger sons with the gentlemen merchants of Leeds and Liverpool. The appeal of the Georgian town to better-off migrants reflected the growing size and profile of the urban middling orders and the rising quality of living, for those able to afford it, to be found there. It was the improved sense of urban amenities – fine shops, attractive buildings, cleaner and wider streets, improved piped-water supplies and a widening range of fashionable leisure facilities – that attracted the social elite (and especially women) to visit and reside, temporarily or permanently, in towns. So powerful was this trend that a whole category of residential and resort towns – notably the county towns, spas and seaside resorts – emerged to cater for the demand. The wealthier citizens had traditionally occupied the central or principal commercial areas of the town. This pattern of social zoning remained the norm for much of the eighteenth century. From at least the middle of the century in the provinces, and earlier in London, there are however signs of the middle-class flight to the suburbs that during the nineteenth century was dramatically to change the social geography of towns. This reflected the fact that by the end of the eighteenth century the town, as primary industrial production became increasingly focused upon it, was beginning to lose its appeal to fashionable society. A striking example of changing attitudes to the town among the elite is the case of Warwick. In the replanning after a major fire in 1694, the fifth Lord Brooke, the owner of the castle, sought to integrate his imposing home and the townscape. A century later his successor threw a great perimeter wall around the castle, destroying homes, slicing some streets in half and isolating others, all in the interests of distancing himself from his urban adjunct.

The second earl of Warwick's attempts to seal his great residence from the town was an extreme manifestation of power. It mirrored the way many country house owners at the time were remodelling their rural estates to create hermetically sealed environments free from the presence of the common people and their employments. But it would be wrong to give the impression that the rural elite normally exercised such influence over the town. Some notion of an independent, self-governing community was close to the heart of what it was to be a town. In England, Warwick was unusual, though not unique – Arundel, Petworth and Whitehaven also spring to mind – in accommodating the principal residence of a member of the aristocracy. There were curiously few parallels of the German *Residentzstädten*, used as a power base by a religious or secular potentate. In Ireland the Protestant landowning elite established planned settlements on their estates (and sometimes in proximity to their country houses), but development was achieved through cooperation with rather than domination over their urban tenants. Indeed, landlords had a self-interest in cultivating a strong urban middle class since this would enhance the economic prospects and rental potential of settlements, as well as shifting the costs of development and maintenance on to the shoulders of townspeople. The English rural gentry paid close attention to the pattern of urban politics because around 80 per cent of parliamentary seats were located in boroughs, but their relations with town governors and voters were usually based on reciprocity rather than supremacy, and they were normally careful – as, for example, with the Grosvenors at Chester – not to ride roughshod over the town's independence. It must also be said that, by and large, the gentry were only too happy to leave the nitty-gritty of local governance to authorities within the town. Here a complexity of bodies was involved – not just corporations (present in only a quarter to a third of the towns in England and Wales), but also the more common court leets and vestries, together with a proliferating corpus of official and semi-official organizations, including workhouse boards, improvement commissions, trusts, charities, hospitals and voluntary societies. Urbanization, as it placed growing pressure on the traditional modes of government, tended to expand the range of bodies involved. This multiplicity of institutions points to the inherent plurality of power in the town, providing opportunities for participation in the urban polity for those from the leading citizens to the petty bourgeoisie. The diffusion of power did not stop there. Every household and workshop, every church and chapel, every club and society represented – to some degree – a nexus of power, capable of influencing the lives of those within, and sometimes without. Moreover, there were bodies of 'alternative' authority, such as the crowd or 'mob', present throughout the eighteenth century, capable, at least temporarily, of empowering their membership. The town was thus a locale in which power was a ubiquitous phenomenon, more so than in the countryside; but this should not conceal the fact that it was heavily concentrated in the hands of men, and in particular those occupying the upper echelons of society.

In evaluating the character and significance of eighteenth-century urbanization, qualitative change was as, if not more, important than quantitative change. Towns were undergoing a cultural transformation, which though not measurable in terms of crude statistics, none the less altered profoundly the way urban life was conceived and valued. Towns became – and became seen to be – attractive and fashionable places, and the idea and ideal of the town came to occupy a new prominence in people's minds. One of the most striking manifestations of this process was the remodelling of the town's physical appearance. Vernacular (or locally determined) forms of urban architecture were replaced by a single international style based on the classical tradition. Out went timber-framed structures, with jettied irregular facades and thatched roofs, and in came the brick or ashlar 'box', with a well-proportioned and symmetrical front, employing classical ornamentation and roofed in tile or slate. The quality of street space was boosted by improved paving, cleansing and lighting; novel large-scale architectural forms were introduced like the terrace, the crescent and the square; there was a surge of investment in public buildings (in the broadest sense, from town halls to churches and chapels), and there was a new interest in town planning. Paralleling this enhancement of the urban fabric went a wide-ranging upgrading of the town's cultural facilities. The provision of commercial theatre and music was greatly expanded, as was access to print culture, with the emergence of the London and provincial press, and the growth in bookshops, libraries, coffee houses and book clubs. Fashionable recreational life was transformed with the development of public walks and gardens, the commercialization and urbanization of sports such as horseracing and cricket, and the rise of the assemblies and of a spectacularly rich variety of clubs, societies and associations. During the eighteenth century around 12,000 town-based clubs were established in England, 3,000 in Scotland, and 750 in Wales. These developments impacted on some locations more than others. English towns felt the effects first, reflecting the earlier growth and wealth of their urban and rural clientele. The metropolitan centres were the powerhouses of change, pioneering new cultural forms and movements; the Scottish enlightenment, for example, was forged in the universities and clubs of Edinburgh and Glasgow. In the provinces cultural change was felt first, and most deeply, by the provincial capitals, county towns, spas and seaside resorts, though what is remarkable is the extent to which it permeated, to some degree, the entire urban system. Some surprisingly small places, able to capture a niche in the local market for residential and cultural services, blossomed into centres of polite living and elegant architecture; for example, Ashbourne in Derbyshire, Stamford in Lincolnshire, Ludlow on the Welsh borders, Cowbridge in the Vale of Glamorgan and Armagh in Ulster (a cathedral town, but with fewer than 2,000 people in 1770). Even the most diminutive settlement was capable of being touched. Concealed to the rear of the timber-framed White Lion in Eye in Suffolk – a town with a population of perhaps 1,000 in 1700 and still under 2,000 in 1811 – stands a Georgian brick extension with a gem of an assembly room, complete with minstrels' gallery, while the fine eighteenth-century brick facades of tiny Montgomery's domestic and public buildings (there is a town hall of 1748) show how the cultural renaissance was able to penetrate even the depths of rural mid-Wales.

The physical and social embellishment of the town raised its image and influence. This resulted not just from the visibility and scale of change under way, but also the manner in which the new forms of urban life embodied a spirit of enlightenment that became the dominant culture of the age. It was an ethos that was outward-looking. It celebrated the national and international scene, drawing inspiration from the major metropolitan centres and leading resorts – London, Dublin, Edinburgh, Bath and Brighton – and, beyond these, the continent and the great cities of the classical and Renaissance world. Because of their function as gateways, towns were particularly suited to providing local society with access to external ideas and fashions. But towns were not simply the conduits for an elevating culture, they were also its natural location. Central to the British enlightenment were the notions of politeness and civility, ideas which emphasized man's (and to a lesser extent woman's) special capacities as sociable and rational beings. It was the public character of urban life, and its inherent potential for social and intellectual interaction, that made the town the locale *par excellence* for the enlightened citizen. The new urban culture was modelled specifically to realize this potential. The emphasis – in organizations and institutions such as the assemblies, pleasure gardens, clubs and coffee houses – was upon creating contexts that encouraged a sort of positive human friction, the effects of which, it was felt, would be to polish and refine the inner and outer person. Buildings were constructed to reflect these needs; assembly rooms and public walks were exercises in open planning, which left little space to hide, while the development of the terrace, crescent and square created a form of collective domestic architecture in which the needs of the individual dwelling and householder were subsumed within the larger whole. It is not surprising that these novel types of urban architecture were pioneered, and reached their apogee, in the leading social centres. The spas and seaside resorts, indeed, became the equivalent of a modern cruise liner or holiday camp, in which visitors led, and were required to lead, an intensely corporate lifestyle. This was encouraged by the existence of a set of mores and norms that stigmatized privacy and aloofness, and of a rigid daily cycle of activities requiring the company to be in the same place, doing the same thing, at the same time. This routine was itself part of a shared annual cycle of leisure which herded polite society from one venue to another – from the metropolitan capitals or the county towns for the winter season, to the spas and urban race meetings between spring and autumn.

The cultivation of sociability was in some respects an urban-led campaign, orchestrated by London-based media such as Addison and Steele's *Spectator* (1711–12), or by figures like the legendary Beau Nash, master of ceremonies at Bath and Tunbridge Wells. One key objective was to civilize a backward and boorish rural gentry, whose religious and political prejudices, never mind intellectual deficiencies, had, since the civil war of the mid-seventeenth century, introduced dangerous divisions into the body politic. The idea of the town as an agent of civilization had a long pedigree, and it was a tradition which the enlightenment – with its roots in the urban world of classical Greece and Rome, and its mission to release humankind from its barbaric condition – was in a strong position to exploit. The notion had a particular resonance in the Celtic 'peripheries' of the British Isles, which contained vast tracts of land with low population densities and a relatively weak urban presence, whose peoples, attached as they were to seemingly primitive customs and languages, were an obvious target for attention. It was to cultivate and civilize these areas, and to connect them to the economic and political heartlands of Britain, that many small towns and villages in Ireland and Scotland were founded or 'modernized'. A feature they shared was some element of planning, such as uniform housing, broad and straight thoroughfares, large regular marketplaces and the provision of public buildings. The outcome was often planning at its most minimal, but the forms adopted were clearly drawn from metropolitan models, and their symbolic meaning and function – as beacons of order and agents of progress, amidst a sea of rural backwardness – was obvious enough. During the eighteenth century, particularly the latter part, the civilizing role towns played became closely allied to dynamic notions of 'improvement'. This was something not only to be found in the urban context – rural modernizers were only too keen to invoke its spirit in the design of their gardens and the running of their estates – but towns were especially receptive to it. Improvement commissions, directed at reforming the urban environment, were established in many places – over a hundred had been set up in English towns by 1800 – and most clubs and societies were dedicated, in the words of Edinburgh's Rankenian Society, to 'mutual improvement by liberal conversation and rational enquiry'. It was this commitment to change and betterment, to the point at which it had become a moral category and a duty, which energized those responsible for shaping urban life.

Though in the eighteenth century the dominant ethos and image of the town was that of a centre of enlightenment, in reality this represented only a partial view of urban life and culture. Counterbalancing the tendency to look outwards was one to turn inwards. Towns, especially those with a long history and strong regional ties, often had an acute sense of their own local identity. The eighteenth century witnessed in England an upsurge in the compilation of town histories, which could embrace notions of progress within a narrative that was rooted in a wholly local past. Architecturally, external models might be drawn upon, but these were modified to express local identities and needs. The spectacular Piece Hall at Halifax, opened in 1779, with its vast open atrium enclosed by tiers of arcades, was probably an attempt to reconstruct a Roman forum; but it was firmly adapted to selling the products of the local textile industry – the arcades accommodated over 300 shops and offices – and was in a long line of impressive West Riding cloth halls built in the eighteenth century. Towns might aspire to be sociable places, but there were definite limits to this. Though the spas and resorts promoted a corporate ethos, in practice – given that so many of the visitors were there in pursuit of status, money and spouses (and the three were closely interrelated) – the prevailing atmosphere could be one of intense rivalry and competition. Moreover, as in the late eighteenth century the middling orders began to flood into the watering-places, the aristocracy and gentry either retreated to small and isolated resorts, such as Teignmouth in south Devon and Aberystwyth and Tenby in southwest Wales, or abandoned the notion of public sociability in favour of a more privatized lifestyle based on exclusive social gatherings.

The urban public sphere, and the ideal of sociable behaviour that oiled its operation, were always qualified phenomena. There were widely recognized physical boundaries which demarcated and protected the life of the private individual. The domestic threshold was one such frontier, though with urban dwellings often doubling as alehouses, retail outlets and workshops, and frequently accommodating lodgers, the dividing line within the house between the public and private spheres might be highly fluid. That said, the open nature of street space was itself compromised by occupational, ethnic and social zoning, which created mini-communities in which outsiders would be made to feel uncomfortable. On the face of it civic buildings facilitated and celebrated the public life of the town, yet access to the more prestigious of these, such as the fine town halls being constructed at the time, was often highly restricted, limited to the governing body of the town and their cronies. Religious buildings might be seen as venues to gather together the whole community in public worship, but with the erection of separate denominational chapels (following the Toleration Act of 1689), the rise of the exclusive proprietary chapels, and the use of private pews to segregate those who attended Anglican churches, clerical buildings tended to reinforce rather than mitigate social divisions. Clubs and associations promoted high degrees of sociability between their membership, but they were by their very nature private associations, with internal bonding bought at the price of greater external exclusivity. The same could be argued for polite urban leisure as a whole, where it was clear that the easy social intercourse and 'democratic' behaviour that the spas and resorts encouraged among their visitors was intended to apply only to those who were considered gentlemen. At Bath tradesmen were excluded from the principal assembly rooms, and John Wood, the architect of Queen Square – that prototype of sociable architecture – argued that 'the intention of a square in a city is for people to assemble together; and the spot whereon they meet, ought to be separated from the ground common to men and beasts, and even to mankind in general'.

If, in practice, the sociable character of urban culture was problematic, so also was its civilizing and improving role. Improvement was a concept to which the upper and middling orders as a whole, along with the more skilled and ambitious sections of the lower orders, would have readily subscribed. But what each group meant by improvement could be very different. Whereas for the gentry who visited or lived in towns it was an aesthetic, intellectual and social notion that depended upon heavy conspicuous consumption, the middling orders and petty bourgeoisie placed much greater stress on religion, morality, thrift, sobriety, work and respectability. In the *Rake's Progress* (1735) Hogarth – whose popularity reflected his capacity to articulate the views of bourgeois Londoners – presents a remorseless critique of how metropolitan leisure and luxury could corrupt the social elite, and in *Industry and Idleness* (1747) he charts the very different careers of two apprentices, the one choosing the easy but fatal path to personal and social ruin, the other the difficult but ultimately effective route to self-realization and worldly success. That a culture of improvement, nurtured in the town, could civilize urban and rural dwellers would have been a widely accepted, if not universal, belief among the ruling orders. But it would have been less clear to those who were to be civilized. Enlightenment and improvement were not just cultural but also social and political strategies. For the town to act as a civilizing agent necessarily involved subjugating rural society to urban norms. Because these standards drew heavily upon metropolitan models, and especially upon London – the great dynamo at the heart of the Atlantic archipelago – then the civilizing process was in some measure a cultural tool for bringing the provinces and the peripheries under the control of the centre. In a multi-national polity like the British Isles this process, especially where it involved the plantation of new towns in parts of Ireland and the Scottish Highlands, also took on a colonial dimension.

Those perceived to be in need of civilizing were to be found inside as well as outside the town. A wide range of charities and organizations were established, and campaigns initiated, with a strong middle-class involvement in their running, which were dedicated to curbing and refining what was considered the rude and primitive behaviour of the urban lower orders. Frequent targets were prostitution and improper sexual activities, petty crime, disorderly behaviour, violent animal sports, sabbath breaking and drunkenness. Alongside strategies to suppress these activities went more subtle efforts to reform behaviour through programmes of low-level mass education – as in the hundreds of 'blue-coat' schools established in the early decades of the eighteenth century – and carefully structured charitable interventions, such as the Magdalene hospitals for fallen young women. This reforming ideology undoubtedly had some impact on working people, among sections of whom the idea of self-improvement seemed to offer a means to avoid or escape from the ever-present abyss of poverty. Many urban artisans and petty shopkeepers also saw in the discussion of intellectual issues and current affairs at clubs and debating societies an opportunity for collective social and political education, one consequence of which was an emerging strand of political radicalism. Alongside a popular acceptance of elements of the improvement package also went much indifference and hostility. For there existed a traditional (but not unchanging) alternative culture which embodied many of the features of town life that the reformers sought to undermine. For example, violent recreations such as bear- and bull-baiting, bull-running, cock-fighting and cock-throwing, street football, sword- and dagger-fighting and pugilism – all accompanied by heavy drinking and gambling – were common activities. Street celebrations of festivals in the traditional calendar – such as Shrove Tuesday, May Day and Midsummer's Eve – remained widespread, and the public thoroughfares and marketplaces were not infrequently the location of raucous demonstrations, some of a political or economic character, others – such as the charivari or skimmington – directed at maintaining the sexual norms of the community. This was a culture as viable, vibrant and – in its own terms – 'civilized' as that which sought to reform it.

Though it was capable of embracing all sections in society, it became more and more focused among the common people as urban elites withdrew their participation and support. There could be considerable resistance to attempts by the improvers to undermine longstanding practices – the Stamford bull-running, for example, took fifty years of hard campaigning (1780–1830) and substantial intervention by outsiders to bring to an end – which suggests that for many townspeople customary culture remained central to the self-image and operation of the urban community.

The clash between the two cultures often resulted in a process of 'negotiation', in which the outcome was an amalgam of old and new. This was indicative of the deep but complex impact of urbanization on eighteenth-century Britain. There were major national and regional variations; the metropolises enjoyed sustained growth and dynamic new cities emerged, but this was not in general at the expense of the smaller towns, which remained the bedrock of the urban system; industrialization began to shape the pattern of urban growth, but it did so at this stage without fundamentally altering the town's primary economic role as a centre of craft manufacture and trade; and the middling orders strengthened their presence, but heavy migration tended to reinforce rather than alter the traditional distribution of wealth and power. The profile and status of towns strengthened substantially, as they became the engines of an enlightenment culture – dominant among the elite and middling orders – that was outward-looking, sociable, civilizing and improving; but the manner and extent to which this modified the true character of urban and rural life was qualified by the counteracting forces of localism, privacy and social class, by the politicized and ambivalent nature of improvement, and by the persistence of traditional forms of urban culture.

FURTHER READING

Borsay, Peter: *The English Urban Renaissance: Culture and Society in the Provincial Town 1660–1770* (Oxford, 1989).

Borsay, Peter (ed.): *The Eighteenth-Century Town: A Reader in English Urban History 1688–1820* (London, 1990).

Brewer, John: *The Pleasures of the Imagination: English Culture in the Eighteenth Century* (London, 1997).

Clark, Peter (ed.): *The Transformation of English Provincial Towns* (London, 1984).

Clark, Peter: *British Clubs and Societies 1580–1800: The Origins of an Associational World* (Oxford, 2000).

Clark, Peter (ed.): *The Cambridge Urban History of Britain*, vol. 2: *1540–1840* (Cambridge, 2000).

Corfield, Penelope J.: *The Impact of English Towns 1700–1800* (Oxford, 1982).

Cruickshank, Dan and Burton, Neil: *Life in the Georgian City* (London, 1990).

Devine, T. M. and Jackson, Gordon (eds): *Glasgow*, vol. 1: *Beginnings to 1830* (Manchester, 1995).

Dickson, David (ed.): *The Gorgeous Mask: Dublin 1700–1850* (Dublin, 1987).

Estabrook, Carl B.: *Urbane and Rustic England: Cultural Ties and Social Spheres in the Provinces, 1660–1780* (Manchester, 1998).

Graham, Brian J. and Proudfoot, Lindsay J.: *Urban Improvement in Provincial Ireland 1700–1840* (Group for the Study of Irish Historic Settlement, np, 1994).

Houston, R. A.: *Social Change in the Age of Enlightenment: Edinburgh 1660–1760* (Oxford, 1994).

Sweet, Rosemary: *The English Town 1680–1840: Government, Society and Culture* (London, 1999).

Chapter Sixteen

Women and the Family

John D. Ramsbottom

Perhaps more than most areas of history the study of women and the family is inevitably shaped by present-day judgements. Although few scholars have been generals, diplomats or revolutionaries, all have gathered personal experiences and expectations as members of families. Moreover, from our perspective, the history of the family in eighteenth-century Britain encompasses themes of contemporary academic and political relevance. In the years since Lawrence Stone's pioneering work feminist scholarship has contributed insights about women's dependent status in society that seem to be borne out in the eighteenth century as well. Simultaneously, the rereading of primary sources through the lens of gender has added a new dimension to our picture of everyday realities. Concerns about the position and status of women in modern society naturally affect the meaning that historians attach to developments in the past.

For the early modern period generally scholarly debate has been shaped by the concept of patriarchy, that is, the male-dominated system that prescribed socially acceptable roles for husbands, wives and children. During the eighteenth century the prevailing ideal of civil society required that wives be economically dependent, confined to the home, and committed intellectually and spiritually to their own subordination. At the same time, however, women played crucial roles in the pursuit of two goals that increasingly found expression in family life: the accumulation of property and the quest for advancement in 'respectable' society. Evidence of this apparent contradiction between growing female responsibility and continued subjection emerges at every level of the complex social spectrum of eighteenth-century Britain. How this evidence should be interpreted, however, has proved a controversial question.

The attention now paid by historians to women and the family is justified in part by the demographic facts of the period. The aristocracy had particular reason to be concerned with the twin issues of marriage and childbirth. The average family size among the peerage had fallen throughout the seventeenth century; by the early Hanoverian years the peerage as a class was not reproducing itself, and many family lines became extinct. But in the population as a whole the proportion of people who never married dropped from the 1680s until at least the 1760s. The age at first marriage for women fell steadily and substantially from about twenty-six years to about twenty-three, with most of the decline occurring during the second half of the century. Higher estimates of female celibacy among Scottish women (between 20 and 30 per cent) seem to be based on questionable sources, although their age at marriage was slightly higher than in England. Broadly speaking, by the end of the century, men and women seem to have been more likely to marry and changing economic conditions encouraged them to do so earlier.

The conventional view of women's destiny is clear enough. Early in the century John Evelyn gave his grandson advice on raising daughters to be instructed in useful things and in all modesty so to become a good wife. In 1781 a Scottish judge declared, 'To make a good husband, is but one branch of a man's duty; but it is the chief duty of woman, to make a good wife' (Vickery 1998: 289). Preparation for marriage and motherhood was the overriding goal of women's education and upbringing. The view of women propounded in seventeenth-century literature – that they were irrational and prey to their own unlimited sexual appetite – was gradually replaced with the notion that their natural condition was innocence. Thanks to the influence of biblical concepts as interpreted by Puritan writers, women came to be valued for their potential contribution to the godly household. The emergence of this kind of companionate marriage did not make for equality, but women's moral, intellectual and spiritual virtues were openly acknowledged and fostered. According to feminist scholars, however, this ideology of femininity itself constituted a tool of subordination; now young women were taught to master their own dangerous passions in the interest of the male-headed family.

Patriarchy appears equally powerful in the realm of the law. It is a truism that the common law of England transferred ownership of a woman's personal property to her husband upon marriage; it also put her real property under his control. This was part of the doctrine of coverture, enunciated by William Blackstone, in which the very existence of the woman is suspended or entirely merged and incorporated in that of the husband. Moreover, primogeniture ensured that daughters could inherit the landed estate only if there was no living son. The same preference was observed in Scotland. Nor could the wife dispose of inherited lands without her husband's consent, and he controlled the usufruct of her dowry lands. Prior to the eighteenth century, however, changes in actual practice affected the legal rights of women – whether favourably or otherwise is still the subject of debate. For example, among the landed classes, the development of the 'strict settlement' in the later 1600s meant that daughters could be passed over in favour of a collateral male; these binding arrangements for the next generation were made at the time the parents married. The strict settlement may have assisted the decline of patriarchy, in that younger children were expressly provided for in its terms. But it may also be that this trend reflected a reversal in the fortunes of female heirs and a general growth of anti-female sentiment in eighteenth-century England. In many instances the old common law would have guaranteed daughters a larger estate than they now received. Strict settlement also converted the jointure, a provision for the wife's widowhood, to a charge upon the real estate, which descended to a male; this kind of jointure was naturally worth less than the dower under common law (one-third of the estate itself). Moreover, a legal judgement in 1760 allowed brides who were still minors to sign away their rights to the larger amount. In these ways property became more concentrated in the hands of a patriarchal elite.

Alongside these indications of continuing patriarchy in the eighteenth century, many historians have detected the simultaneous rise of the affectionate nuclear family, and in precisely the same social class. Among the peerage, we are told, marriage was becoming the cornerstone of domesticity. Already by the early 1700s aristocratic couples paid lip-service to an ideal of intimacy in their private correspondence, even in the case of the widow of an Irish peer, who quickly married the writing master by whom she already had several children. By the century's end, upper-class spouses began using familiar forms of address with one another, and the norms of domesticity would soon require that their public behaviour as well would bear witness to the intimacy of married life. In 1784 a visiting Frenchman estimated that three-quarters of marriages in the educated classes were based on affection, a situation that struck him as unfamiliar.

About sexual intimacy within marriage we know little enough. Private correspondence and a few surviving diaries are our only sources, and generalization is hazardous. For many couples, concern about pregnancy must have been in the background. The chief methods of contraception in this period were natural, and refraining from actual intercourse must be numbered among them. Perhaps as a result, in eighteenth-century town society, which offered greater opportunities for extramarital liaisons, infidelity among husbands was common, and wives seem to have accepted, even expected, such behaviour. The ordeal of Margaret Boswell, who was married to James Boswell for twenty years, was surely not unique except in the thoroughness of its documentation. By his own careful account, Boswell insisted on sleeping with his wife regularly, in spite of her illness and his own frequent visits to prostitutes. Of course, we should not assume that all wives treated their husbands' physical demands with dismay or indifference. Ladies' allusions to the comforts of the marital bed are simply less explicit, and they are typically couched in the context of the overall relationship. What makes the eighteenth century different from previous eras is that such tenderness was openly reciprocated by some men, even years after marriage.

Without being too precise about the origins or extent of the affective family – and some scholars would maintain that this ideal was by no means new – one can see how it might have spread. As rising generations of the peerage became used to different standards in their own unions, they might abandon the custom of using a child's marriage to forge a family alliance. The change in attitude was gradual, however; prior to mid-century, parents were still known to beat or confine non-compliant daughters. Nor is it difficult to point to examples of aristocratic girls whose marriages to older men were arranged and who were widowed young. On the other hand, although Hardwicke's Marriage Act (1753) made a father's consent necessary for the marriage of minors in England, it could have represented a rearguard action in defence of an already weakening patriarchy. In any case, it is clear that most of those who eloped to Scotland, where only the exchange of vows was required for a legal union, were not aristocratic couples but rather ordinary folk who wanted a cheap, private marriage.

Daughters were permitted greater freedom in choosing a partner, but genteel parents also did all they could to ensure that their children planted their affections in prudent soil, and tried to prevent them marrying beneath their social class in particular. Moreover, generally speaking, the higher the social class of the bride and groom, the greater the age difference between them. In the aristocracy, where the exchange of property still formed a large part of the marriage settlement, the husband might be ten years older; the gap narrowed among the middle classes. Ultimate approval of the match would depend in part on its suitability from the financial point of view, but, as one sensible scholar has put it, few girls faced a clear-cut choice between love on the one hand and money on the other.

We are afforded only a few glimpses of how women themselves experienced courtship, a period during which they could hope to enjoy the attentions of a suitor while controlling the pace of the evolving relationship. On the one hand, the young woman often had a key role in the negotiations: that of mediating between her parents, particularly the father, and the suitor. On the other, the popular literature of the later eighteenth century embodied romantic notions of passion and sympathy. Lovers were expected to meet not only in public assemblies or in the woman's home, but also clandestinely. Even before mid-century, however, the practice of making exaggerated protestations of ardour was being satirized by observers and ridiculed by some women. Only widows, of course, were in a position to benefit from experience. Following the death of her first husband, chosen for her by her uncle, the aristocrat Mary Granville refused ten offers of marriage, including several from men who were her social peers, before choosing an older clergyman. In the case of a determined suitor who was not quickly accepted, the siege might go on for years. It seems reasonable to think that this prolonged personal contact prior to marriage might make for more affection within it.

Recent research suggests, moreover, that marriage did not invariably remove women's financial independence. Aristocratic husbands usually gave their wives 'pin-money', a sum based on the marriage portion, for expenses such as clothes, personal items and charities. Further developments in the law permitted wives to have separate property within marriage. Already by the seventeenth century prenuptial settlements gave the wife more independent control over property than traditional coverture would have allowed. Farther down the social scale, this separate estate came to include not only real estate but stock in trade, cash and investments. A commercial man might prefer to create a separate estate for his wife after marriage, since property in these settlements was legally insulated from the demands of his creditors, but a separate estate created even without the husband's consent might be legal if he were a wastrel. Thus, middle-class women might retain control over some of the property they brought into a marriage, in particular bequests from female relations. In many cases, though, it was a remarrying widow who took these precautions, thus underlining the relatively weak position of wives.

The evolving concept of motherhood did more to increase women's power over their own lives. Among the upper classes, it has been argued, childbearing was essentially a service performed in the interests of the paternal line. Unlike in the seventeenth century, however, childbirth ceased to be seen in religious terms as the great trial of suffering that females faced on the way to full womanhood. Instead, by the end of the period, women were happy to be delivered, when possible, without knowing it. In the course of gaining more control over this process, eighteenth-century wives appear to have sacrificed the support of traditional midwives to the judgement of the emerging medical establishment, which was dominated by men. Indeed, upper-class women could command the services of male physicians, some of whose advice concerning diet and exercise was actually helpful. In some cases the husband engaged the best available practitioner, but in others the woman exercised a degree of choice that some men saw as an insidious challenge to male authority. When it came to the 'accouchment' itself, contemporary medical knowledge was frequently inadequate, though often the failure was in not intervening soon enough rather than letting nature take its course. Maternal mortality rates ranging from 4 to 7 per cent are lower than one might expect, but no individual mother could be certain of survival.

The period of 'lying-in' that followed delivery has been seen as either a period of protective isolation or a deliberate inversion of normal patriarchy. The ritual implications of this custom, based on the notion that newly delivered mothers were 'unclean', surely declined, but most genteel women by tradition did observe a period of withdrawal lasting up to six weeks, often ending with a service of thanksgiving or churching. They might enjoy the exclusive company of female relatives and friends, who drank caudle, a spiced wine, and exchanged advice or, as husbands saw it, gossip. What was formerly done at society's behest was now done mostly for the comfort of the mother, and she was increasingly able to maintain emotional ties with her own mother and sisters as well as her husband's family. By the early nineteenth century, however, some women themselves found confinement too restrictive and wished to make childbirth an altogether less intrusive event.

Breastfeeding was another area in which the changing attitude towards motherhood affected women's lives. Since the seventeenth century Puritan authors had advocated maternal nursing, and by the late eighteenth century it was widely accepted among the upper classes. The practice occasionally met with disapproval from the husband, who reluctantly observed a taboo on sexual relations during the nursing period, and, after mid-century, it was often the wife who made the decision in favour of breastfeeding. Some relations might wish her to stop in order to resume childbearing. The relatively short birth intervals among the aristocracy indicate that such arguments often prevailed, and of course some wives might not wish to nurse. The contraceptive effect of lactation was widely understood; in fact, there is some evidence that later in life, upper-class wives deliberately took advantage of it in order to avoid further pregnancies. By the same token the proportion of infants dying in their first year declined in aristocratic families, especially after 1750, and this has been attributed to early maternal breastfeeding. It seems likely that the mother's emotional attachment to her child also was aided by this practice.

In the classes just below the aristocracy, an increased interest in family life accompanied the preoccupation with outward 'respectability' that was becoming evident by the 1780s and 1790s. During the Evangelical revival, concern with individual salvation elevated moral probity above the claims of rank through birth. Here historians have located a principal source of the doctrine of 'separate spheres', an ideology that stressed the special fitness of women for carrying out a moral reformation in society. Anglicans and Nonconformists alike stressed women's essential, if subordinate, role; success as a wife was extolled as a high attainment in female excellence and woman's brightest glory. Not all scholars attribute this development to late eighteenth-century religious influence. According to Anthony Fletcher the domestic cult of womanhood based on complementary spheres was well established several decades before the Evangelical revival, and it has also been observed that prescriptive views of woman's role in the family are at least as old as Aristotle. To what degree, then, did the actual experience of women during the eighteenth century reflect an ever-tightening domestic encirclement?

Irrespective of social class, the expectations placed upon mothers certainly competed with both the marital relationship itself and with any sense of personal freedom. Although most genteel mothers employed at least a nursery maid, pregnancy and early childrearing took at least a decade out of their lives. They lacked the time or energy for their accustomed correspondence or social visits. There is even greater reason to suppose that domestic life brought new challenges for women in the middling classes. For one thing, the sheer physical demands of motherhood were felt more keenly. Demographic studies of Scotland suggest that the interval between births was generally a little over two years; on average, married couples in England produced seven children. Because middle-class couples married later, the wearying cycle of pregnancy and delivery was compressed into a short span of time and went on without large numbers of servants to help. Elizabeth Cadbury, mother of the founder of the cocoa factory, had ten children in fourteen years. Finally, the proportion of marriages broken by the death of one spouse was still high enough, especially early in the century, to increase the overall level of remarriage; the result was a significant number of 'blended' families in which women were raising the children of a former wife as well as their own. At any level below that of the gentry, women would also have been directly engaged in the education of young children. By the eighteenth century a mother's tender influence was seen as less likely to spoil a child, and in any case, men were more often absent from the home.

Nor was the emotional toll any less burdensome. If some women had the luxury of nurturing their infants in a new way, as individuals with a promise of survival, the evidence also suggests that the mortality rate for children aged between two and four did not decline significantly during the eighteenth century. The sense of loss if the child died must have been that much more acute. The existing studies of the role of mothers suggest that the sentimental view of childhood was not entirely a Victorian invention, but maternal pride and doting had to be matched by sheer stoicism during bouts of smallpox or other illnesses. In addition, wives were also expected to manage the household, if not to confine themselves to it. The specific nature of housework obviously varied from class to class, but there was never any doubt about whose job it was. For women with few or no servants, of course, cooking and laundering clothes were the principal chores, and these tasks were not as yet significantly eased by technological improvements. The introduction of the cast-iron range combined the functions of a cooking stove with the production of hot water, but fireplaces in general were only as efficient as the chimneys, and cleaning them was a laborious and dirty job.

For her part, the mistress of the middle-class house usually held the view that the best sign of good domestic management was the extent to which it went unnoticed. New standards of cleanliness required almost constant labour, which the lady of the house supervised, armed with the house keys and a memorandum book. Preserving, distilling and curing were still a part of the seasonal routine in the countryside, even if the products were for domestic use rather than sale. The genteel housewife also ordered in groceries on a large scale, prepared medicines and provided clothing for her children, often long after they had left home. Increasingly, social status was determined by ownership of consumer goods, and women made most of the family's purchases, apart from luxury items such as furniture. They might commission their husbands to buy items from town, and they kept track of current fashions.

The other half of household management – or, in wealthier households, almost the whole of it – lay in the supervision of servants. The turnover among domestic help was notoriously high. Early in the century half of the servants employed by the Scottish receiver-general remained less than a year, and more modest households suffered similar rates of attrition. Some mistresses deliberately gave their maids a minimum of training lest they leave for another position. Most upper-class households at the beginning of the century boasted as many menservants as possible, but a stiff tax imposed on male domestics in 1777, and strictly enforced against appeals, seems to have curtailed their popularity. Thus, the mistress's power over hiring and firing probably grew as female servants came to outnumber males. Indeed, there is abundant evidence that wives resented their husbands' interference in household affairs, especially if it tended to undermine their authority among the servants. The ecclesiastical courts recognized such conduct as a form of abuse and as supporting grounds for a separation.

Historians must certainly entertain the idea that this domestic monopoly conferred power on women. 'The Domestic oeconomy of a family is entirely a woman's province', one father advised his daughter in 1774 (Vickery 1998: 127). On the other hand, there was already some resistance to allowing this role to become all-consuming. As early as 1722, Thomas Gisborne complained that recently housekeeping had been 'too much neglected by Ladies of Fashion' who considered it fit only for 'Women of Inferior Rank and Condition, as Farmers' Wives, etc.' (Davidson 1982: 193). At the turn of the century, one Evangelical author felt compelled to affirm the scriptural grounds for considering domestic management 'the indispensable duty of a married woman', regardless of her other interests or abilities. 'No mental endowments furnish an exemption from it; no plea of improving pursuits or literary pleasures can excuse the neglect of it' (ibid.).

Given these constraints, middle-class women could not ordinarily venture far beyond the domestic sphere. But at a slightly lower social level, business itself still remained very much a family affair. Wives were expected to contribute to the family's subsistence wherever possible, and not just in the traditional areas of women's work, textiles, petty retail and victualling. Unlike in England, in Scotland women inherited the right to trade on their own from their fathers who were freemen of the burgh; wives could even pass this freedom on to their own husbands who were not burgesses. Although they did not always work literally side-by-side, a married couple shared the principal tasks of a commercial business, and women often handled bookkeeping, correspondence and stocktaking. The same seems to have been true in London. In legal matters, collecting a debt for example, the wife would act equally for the business, if she was the one involved in the transaction. In short, there is no evidence that these women were cut off from the wider community in a private world of domesticity.

Overall, it may be useful to think less in terms of separate spheres than of overlapping ones. If the woman was free from the necessity of working, she could undertake philanthropic labour as her share in a family partnership. The marriage of William Gray, a Yorkshire solicitor, and his wife Faith was a triumph of accounting and time management, within which she pursued 'scientific' projects such as the founding of a spinning school for the children of the indigent poor. Likewise, among the lower middle classes, one could argue that there was an egalitarian strain to the notion of a family alliance in joint pursuit of financial solvency. Careful marriage was a key ingredient of success: it is no exaggeration to say that a man's relationship to his wife's family could make or break him. Wives served a vital function by finding business partners among their kin and places for the children.

At a deeper level, however, focusing on the precise character of the wife's activities may be mistaking a different job for a distinct identity. Just as the bounds of domesticity were not limited by the physical setting – women could fill acceptable roles even outside the home – so the wife's performance of tasks that would today be identified with personal independence did not necessarily signal such an understanding on her part. In some cases the position of the wife could also be defined as that of 'deputy husband'. In this guise, she temporarily carried out essential duties for the family, but without leaving her own special household functions and certainly without challenging her husband's authority.

The control of property marked the limit of female independence. Custom as well as law dictated that the man, as head of household, would assume the role of guiding the family fortunes, and, as assets accumulated, so the male predominated. In the seventeenth century it had been common for husbands to name their wives as executors of their wills, thereby suggesting that they would at least share in the management of property. By contrast, among the families of middle-class manufacturers in eighteenth-century Birmingham and Sheffield, men appointed their wives only about one-third of the time, less often than they did their male friends. Both wills and trusts were widely used by middle-class women in midland towns to pass on property bequeathed to them by their own families. But their choice of executors seems to reflect an understanding of women's limited power in such matters; for example, only about 20 per cent of the executors named in their wills were themselves female.

Finally, although the emergence of a consumer culture permitted wives to invest in property appropriate to the family's status, their autonomy in such matters is difficult to demonstrate. Inventories from the early eighteenth century suggest that women of the middling classes, both rural and urban, might choose to acquire a range of newly available decorative goods, such as pictures, looking-glasses and table linen. They also appear to have attached their sense of identity to items of furniture and especially clothing, which they often bequeathed to others not as family but as personal possessions. This pattern may have meant that women of the period had desires for these kinds of goods that they could not satisfy as long as they lived in a household headed by (and thus dominated by) a man.

Domestic roles and responsibilities in households that had less status or property at stake are more difficult to illuminate. Over the course of the eighteenth century new patterns of family life undoubtedly took shape among the lower classes, and by the later nineteenth century it was possible for some women to remain at home as full-time housewives without endangering the economic welfare of the family. But in the early industrial age the effects of the overall economic transition were more widespread and on the whole tended to underline women's importance as wage earners.

Widespread mobility of women in search of work played a major role in this transition. Fewer and fewer rural families had land to pass on, and so could not provide a dowry as an incentive to remain in the village and marry. By the end of the century as many as half of the marriageable girls in the Scottish Highlands were involved in seasonal migration to jobs as agricultural servants on Lowland estates, where they generally remained less than a year. The numbers of female immigrants to Edinburgh also increased, as women sought positions in domestic service. While there, even temporarily, they met and married men in the capital.

The extent to which eighteenth-century agriculture saw an alteration in the nature of women's work is the subject of ongoing debate. In some areas the sexual division of labour changed, with women being excluded from an equal share in tasks such as ploughing, reaping and threshing. The introduction of the scythe in place of the lighter sickle meant that women no longer took a principal role in reaping – although evidence from Yorkshire shows that this part of the harvest was done exclusively by women with sickle in hand as late as 1787 – and some 'rational improvements' in agriculture led to new seasonal employments for the wives and children of cottagers. The contention that gender-based change occurred seems best supported in Lowland Scotland, where the pace of agricultural reform quickened in the second half of the eighteenth century. Here the population was older in demographic terms than in England, and skilled male labour was scarce. 'Hinds' were hired only if they could bring a wife to help, and farming was rationalized, with men confined to ploughing and carting with the horses while women were employed in other fieldwork such as weeding and thinning. By contrast, in Essex, sexual differentiation of agricultural labour seems to have been well in place by 1700.

Thus, the economic activities of the sexes were already different though not necessarily unequal in importance. Indeed, the existence of rural domestic industry throughout the British Isles had long since given women the opportunity to contribute to household income. Prior to the arrival of factories, the women of one Yorkshire valley flocked, on sunny days, with their spinning wheels to some favourite pleasant spot to pursue the labours of the day. In northwest Ireland separate households consisting entirely of poor women and children survived by spinning linen yarn. Such by-employment of women made a valuable, often indispensable, contribution to a family's subsistence. In rural Scotland perhaps 80 per cent of adult women were engaged in spinning, which they pursued while men farmed and fished. The steady expansion of flax spinning in most Lowland areas was made possible by the employment of women outside the harvest season; in the Highlands, farming was on such a small scale that women had time and incentive to spin. By the 1790s a typical rural household in southern England might derive as much as half its earnings from the wife's labour.

It is in this context that the emerging factory system made its impact. The development of machine spinning in some regions of England cut the wages of women in cottage industry or put them out of work completely. On the other hand, during the Napoleonic Wars at the end of the century, domestic industries that relied largely on female labour benefited from protection against foreign competition. Lace-making and straw-plaiting, located in the southern and midland counties, were far more remunerative than spinning. Moreover, as it proceeded, the industrial revolution itself actually expanded home-based work. Manufacturing processes were broken down into smaller and simpler tasks, thereby increasing the demand for unskilled labour. Some of the most striking gains in productivity were achieved not through mechanization in factories but by employing more women and children in the domestic setting. Employers were eager to take advantage of cheap female labour wherever possible. But largely because women's work was seen as supplemental – and a husband in Essex could be paid directly for his wife's spinning – female wages were never equal to that of males and in fact fell during the course of the century by as much as one-half. In Scotland the justices set maximum wages for women's farmwork at 60 per cent of men's; in Yorkshire women reapers earned 10d a day, while the men who bound the sheaves got two shillings. Feminist historians would rightly note that the rewards of labour were distributed according to gender; from the standpoint of family formation, however, the important thing was the overall opportunity for work.

This combination of changes was accompanied by a shift in patterns of courtship and marriage that some have called a 'sexual revolution'. Capable of earning adult wages, young people, women as well as men, could begin courtship and to contemplate marriage without the assistance or consent of their parents. The average age at marriage fell, more sharply for women than men, and the incidence of prenuptial pregnancy rose. In arable areas of southern England premarital pregnancy was 'covered up' by marriage, but the overall rate of bastardy also increased, noticeably in the north and west of England, where unwed mothers could find work near home. In Scotland, the rate of premarital pregnancy could be extremely high – comprising one-third of brides in one northeastern parish – although the proportion of infants conceived out of wedlock who were actually born illegitimate is harder to establish. Again, the support of grandparents made it possible for single mothers to work and perhaps eventually to marry.

On the other hand, contemporary comment suggests that many in the lower orders, particularly in urban areas, regarded the middle-class definition of matrimony with indifference. In the 1790s a magistrate in London observed the prodigious numbers among the lower classes who cohabited together without marriage. In Scotland, unlike England, divorce was permitted on grounds of adultery or desertion, and the number of suits for divorce, though minuscule by modern standards, rose sharply at the end of the century. But these involved only persons who bothered to take action in court; in fact, a great many Scottish divorce cases involved spouses who had long since set up house with someone else. In Scotland the breakdown of kirk supervision of morals, especially after 1780, together with the pressures and opportunities of urbanization, ushered in an era of serial monogamy.

Lower-class unions, therefore, were first and foremost practical arrangements. In 1743 a handbook advised female servants that once married they should expect to continue working: 'none but a fool will take a wife whose bread must be earned solely by his labour and who will contribute nothing towards it herself' (Shoemaker 1998: 205). Migration to the cities only reinforced this expectation. Especially in London, with its seasonal employment cycles, families might be maintained entirely by the wife's work during slack periods in the male-dominated artisan trades. Yet for many working-class women, especially in the metropolis, it was difficult to form durable relationships. Single women who had come to London from the countryside frequently became victims of failed courtship, being left alone with an illegitimate child. Such women had spent only a year or two in service before becoming pregnant, and their ability to contribute economically to a stable union had declined. Their partners were no more securely established and were prone to break promises of marriage that, in village society, might have been enforced. According to poor law records, in mid-century Colyton, Devon, about 10 per cent of marriages were affected by desertion. Moreover, the principal reason for desertion seems to have been the lack of regular employment for men and, in such cases, the separation was often temporary. But the rate of desertion was as much as three times higher in metropolitan London than in the countryside and men tended to abandon their wives more often when there were opportunities to enlist in the army or navy.

Thus, research into the lives of lower-class families has revealed a range of motivations largely unknown to their social superiors. As many as half of all women, and therefore most plebeian wives in both England and Scotland, belonged to a category that modern observers would call the working poor. For them, much of life consisted in organizing the various sources of a meagre livelihood. In addition to keeping a small shop or taking in washing or sewing, they might pawn goods or arrange loans on pledges of property in order to see the family through a crisis. Although the husband's employment might be irregular, the loss of a wage-earning partner was nevertheless among the worst disasters that could befall any wife or mother. Poor law examinations indicate that even middle-class women could be reduced to pauperism in short order if deprived of the man's contribution to the household income; in Edinburgh, burgesses' widows frequently petitioned for assistance with burial expenses.

Insecurity, financial as well as emotional, played a role in many if not most instances of maternal 'neglect'. Deliberate infanticide was perceived to be a growing problem – both Scotland and England enacted capital statutes against it during the seventeenth century – but research has shown that the vast majority of those accused were never-married women acting on their own. By contrast, child abandonment in eighteenth-century London was generally an act of desperation by a mother who had already nurtured the child for several months. Foundling children were 'dropped' in public places in the hope that they would be discovered and rescued. Occasionally a note testified directly to the impact of poverty, as in the case of an abandoned wife who was not able to support herself and not having any family or friends. Even so, in Hanoverian London, widows and abandoned wives with dependent children made up fewer than half of those considered for relief, suggesting that they were regarded as able to pay their own way. Poor mothers were often occupied finding employment or apprenticeships for their offspring; if they developed a mercenary attitude towards their children, it is hardly surprising.

In this way marriage, one of the expedients for survival open to poor women, could also lead to poverty. Moreover, there are clear signs that the nuclear family was not expected to take sole responsibility for wives and mothers who had ceased to be able to care for themselves. In London very few widows lived with their sons or daughters. This pattern may be attributable to the existence of state poor laws in England; throughout most of the period, widows on their own were customarily favoured in the distribution of parish relief. By the 1790s, however, parish pensions were no longer being granted disproportionately to female recipients, and increasingly women had the workhouse to look forward to in old age. The roots of the 'feminization of poverty' can be traced to the eighteenth century.

Social class was evidently an important determinant of women's experience. Among the relatively well-to-do, the eighteenth century saw a hopeful broadening in the possibilities of family life, and with this came an expansion in the responsibilities of wife and mother. The duties of the middle-class household were understood to be shared, although the result was not an equal partnership. Farther down the social scale, we are reduced to inference about women's desires and expectations. Clearly their best hope lay in fashioning a union that combined financial stability with mutual respect. Women brought dowries or skills to a marriage in order to create the basic unit of production and so presumably they expected more out of it than being chattels. Common sense alone invites this conclusion, but the sequel is harder to summarize. We must beware of using evidence of dysfunction to infer the norm. Even allowing for this, however, the traditional institution of marriage was showing signs of breakdown under economic and social pressure.

For the majority of women, their future in a family was more a matter of personal choice than before, but it was no more secure for that. In an economic environment that promised to reward risk-taking, many men had difficulty coping with setbacks. In 1699 a Scottish court heard that a husband whose creditors had seized his wife's property to satisfy his existing debts – 'at which she grudged' – had abandoned her. Although she vowed she would be content to beg her bread with him, he declared that he did not love her. Under duress a man's concern for his reputation might revert to the crudest patriarchy. In late eighteenth-century London, it was not unheard of for middle-class husbands of rape victims to use this violation as a pretext to leave their wives.

Tensions within the lower-class family tended to be resolved to the disadvantage of women. Despite their nearly equal ability to contribute to income – or rather because of it – they suffered from gender stereotypes. Husbands could not accept financial dependence on their wives' wages without damaging their accustomed authority. It makes sense to see in this conflict the origins of the Victorian 'male breadwinner' ideology – the belief that the husband must be capable of supporting a family on his earnings alone. Does this imply, as Deborah Valenze has asserted, that the subsequent restriction of women's employment reflects a concerted effort to promote a domestic role that would curtail female activity outside the home? The process was not necessarily so deliberate as this suggests. The code of domesticity and female dependence could gain ground in more spontaneous ways. For example, prosperous plebeians seeking respectability might feel obliged to embrace the middle-class virtue of sexual self-control. But because of the long-established double standard in such matters, a woman's reputation was far more vulnerable to rumour than a man's. Upward social mobility required restricting her sphere of activity, not his.

Domestic discord can readily be detected in eighteenth-century judicial records, and its causes seem to relate in part to these attitudes. Although the law was not on their side, working wives might believe that they were entitled to keep their wages; the resulting quarrels over control of the family budget could lead to violence. A woman like the Edinburgh housewife who had supported the family without any assistance from her drunken and profligate husband might be rewarded with abuse. Wife-beating continued to be legal – even the so-called 'rule of thumb' limiting the size of the rod to be used was not a binding precedent – and the courts tolerated physical correction of wives for disobedience or gossip somehow damaging to the husband's reputation. Although it is clear that excessive beating done in a fit of rage could be seen as 'unreasonable' or 'unmanly', it was not until the Victorian era that legal opinion turned decisively against corporal punishment of wives as utterly inconsistent with modern manners. Ironically, as men's abusive behaviour became less acceptable and its details (especially sexual) more repellent, domestic violence simply disappeared behind the walls of respectability.

Generally speaking, in fact, the degree to which a wife actually enjoyed respect for her judgement rested on her ability to ignore her individual concerns. Domestic harmony, as portrayed by commentators such as Addison and Steele at the beginning of the century and by Evangelicals at the end, depended upon the wife's exclusive devotion to her husband's comfort and welfare. Popular culture dispensed harsh condemnation for the sharp-tongued or scolding wife. Yet her own survival hung on factors beyond her control; she might suddenly be left destitute by her husband's failure, brought on by decisions in which she had little if any voice. To cite one example, in mid-life, Rachel Welby's husband dropped his post as a schoolmaster without consulting her and embarked on Anglican ordination, hardly the high road to prosperity. Soon after taking orders, he died, and she was obliged to turn the schoolhouse into a boarding house in order to support her children. For couples precariously poised in the middle class, a business or personal setback could create a crisis to which the woman had to respond – large families raised under tight financial circumstances extracted a high price from the wife. In the case of Ann Taylor, an Essex housewife, her husband's illness, at a time when she had four children under age eleven to care for, stretched her Evangelical faith to the breaking point.

For many women of all classes, religion still provided the best emotional refuge and defence. In the 1710s Lady Sarah Cowper found an outlet for the anger and frustration of an unsatisfactory marriage in a diary that recorded her struggles against her husband's controlling behaviour in household matters. Rather than rebelling outright, she adapted the counsel of Christian forbearance into a vindication of her own female virtue. Likewise, in their private letters and diaries, middle-class widows might eulogize a lost spouse as 'the best of husbands'. This rather formulaic expression, while compatible with a profound sense of grief, also helped to sustain the relict's duty towards family and kin in her independent role.

In sum, family life was no less complex in eighteenth-century Britain than it is today. In order to fully understand women's experience, it is important to treat the family both as a functional unit in demographic and economic terms and as an ideal type whose members felt and met their obligations in different ways. In this regard it is difficult to overstate the value of reassessing existing categories of original sources and, where possible, exploiting new ones. Documents of every variety, from account books to parish poor records, can potentially shed light on family relationships and societal expectations. Perhaps through them it will be possible to refine our definition of domesticity to take fuller account not only of class and regional differences in family structure, but also the perceptions of the participants. During recent decades the history of the family has developed new scholarly appendages and reached maturity as a discipline. But realizing its full power to illuminate the eighteenth century depends upon outgrowing the preoccupations of the late twentieth.

FURTHER READING

Clark, Anna: *Women's Silence, Men's Violence: Sexual Assault in England, 1770–1845* (London, 1987).

Davidson, Caroline: *A Woman's Work is Never Done: A History of Housework in the British Isles, 1650–1950* (London, 1982).

Fildes, Valerie (ed.): *Women as Mothers in Pre-industrial England* (London, 1990).

Fletcher, Anthony: *Gender, Sex, and Subordination in England, 1500–1800* (New Haven, CT, 1995).

Hall, Catherine and Davidoff, Leonore: *Family Fortunes: Men and Women of the English Middle Class, 1780–1850* (Chicago, 1987).

Hunt, Margaret: *The Middling Sort: Commerce, Gender, and the Family in England 1680–1780* (Berkeley, CA, 1996).

Lewis, Judith: *In the Family Way: Childbearing in the British Aristocracy, 1760–1860* (New Brunswick, NJ, 1986).

Mendleson, Sarah and Crawford, Patricia: *Women in Early Modern England, 1550–1750* (Oxford, 1998).

Rendall, Jane: *Women in an Industrializing Society: England, 1750–1880* (Oxford, 1990).

Sanderson, Elizabeth C.: *Women and Work in Eighteenth-Century Edinburgh* (Basingstoke, 1996).

Sharpe, Pamela: *Adapting to Capitalism: Working Women in the English Economy, 1700–1850* (Basingstoke, 1996).

Sharpe, Pamela (ed.): *Women's Work: The English Experience 1650–1914* (London, 1998).

Shoemaker, Robert B.: *Gender in English Society 1650–1850: The Emergence of Separate Spheres?* (London, 1998).

Spring, Eileen: *Law, Land and Family: Aristocratic Inheritance in England, 1300–1800* (Chapel Hill, NC, 1993).

Stone, Lawrence: *The Family, Sex and Marriage in England, 1500–1800* (London, 1977).

Trumbach, Randolph: *The Rise of the Egalitarian Family: Aristocratic Kinship and Domestic Relations in Eighteenth-Century England* (New York, 1978).

Valenze, Deborah: *The First Industrial Woman* (Oxford, 1995).

Vickery, Amanda: *The Gentleman's Daughter: Women's Lives in Georgian England* (New Haven, CT, 1998).

Part III

Religion

Chapter Seventeen

The Church of England

Jeremy Gregory

The Church of England in the eighteenth century has received criticism from almost every quarter. R. H. Tawney's acerbic condemnation of it as 'a servile appendage to a semi-pagan aristocracy' is echoed in most of the writing about the established church in the years between 1688 and 1800. Tawney's negative judgement pithily summarizes some of the most often-cited charges against the eighteenth-century church and highlights the ways in which it has been accused of giving up its independence and of toadying to those in power. Historians have observed the servile nature of the church in a number of ways. At the level of high politics bishops have been blamed for slavishly following the priorities of government ministers (even sacrificing the church's own interests if necessary), and of being voting fodder for the government in the hopes of securing ever more lucrative preferment. At the local level parish clergy have been criticized for bowing to the requirements of the local elite. Tawney's charge of aristocratic domination also picks up on the fact that, after 1750 at least, members of the aristocracy were increasingly tempted into joining the church as a profession. Moreover, Tawney's linking of the church with the aristocracy also reminds us that the church was a major landowner and part of the property-owning elite, and, so the criticism goes, increasingly out of touch with popular culture and opinion. His use of the word 'semi-pagan' reflects the still often-accepted view that the society within which the church operated, and indeed the church itself, was more influenced by classical than Christian norms and frames of reference. This was, after all, the age of reason, and the cult of rationality which is seen to have characterized the established church is thought to have led to the downgrading of spirituality and faith, supposedly resulting in a backlash against the church in the Evangelical revival of the late eighteenth century and in the Oxford Movement of the nineteenth century.

Similar criticisms to Tawney's were made during the eighteenth century itself when Methodists, Nonconformists and others chastised the church for its lack of zeal and its worldliness, even charging it with corruption. In the nineteenth and twentieth centuries historians frequently restated their judgements, pointing to a litany of abuses which, they claimed, typified the church during this period. These failings are still referred to in many of the general books on the period. The ills most often flagged up for adverse comment include pluralism, which meant that clergy frequently were non-resident in their parishes; the issue of tithes, which led to disputes between clergy and those who were not members of the church, and antagonism from parishioners who resented clergy gaining from improvements in agricultural production; the increasing gentrification of the clergy, which supposedly distanced clergy from the great majority of their parishioners; and a slothful attitude to pastoral work, which left their parishioners bereft of pastoral care. Cathedrals received a particularly bad press as being centres of torpor, if not scandal. In short, the eighteenth-century Church of England has frequently become a byword for lax standards and for pastoral negligence, indicating an institution that had fallen far short of the standards and ideals of the church of the sixteenth and seventeenth centuries or of the nineteenth century. Perhaps even more damningly, historians have viewed the Church of England as an increasing irrelevance to the period. Several studies have treated it as marginal to the life of the nation, giving it only a few paragraphs or pages in their wider surveys. In the age of enlightenment and in a century where secularization has been viewed as a hallmark, the church is seen to be playing an ever more minimal role, cut off from the period's most important and significant developments.

These, however, are not the only ways that the history of the church in this period can be approached. More appreciative comments about the eighteenth-century church can be found, especially from the late nineteenth century, and in particular with the publication of Norman Sykes's *Church and State in England in the Eighteenth Century* in 1934. Sykes pointed out that the church was more efficient as an organization, and its clergy more hardworking as individuals, than had previously been recognized. To a certain extent the criticisms of earlier historians can be shown to be based on the biased opinions of the church's opponents, or the result of anachronistic expectations, judging the eighteenth-century church by late nineteenth-century standards. During the last twenty years or so, however, there has emerged what might be called a revisionist school of historians whose detailed work, particularly on what the church was doing at the local level, has modified and in some cases reversed the more negative opinions of some of their predecessors. Rather than dwelling on the failures and shortcomings of the established church, they have highlighted instead its successes and its strengths, and have argued that in many respects the church was more effective than at any time since the Reformation. Other scholars have argued that, far from being a corrupt and inefficient institution, the church had begun to reform itself long before the administrative reforms of the nineteenth century got under way and had already begun to clamp down on abuses such as non-residence and pluralism. Some historians have even suggested that the Church of England clergy remained more in tune with popular mores than has often been supposed. Yet, as might be expected with historical fashions, revisionism has been followed by a post-revisionism, which is wary of some of the upbeat claims of the revisionists, and is concerned that they are ironing out the real structural and pastoral problems faced by the church. There is, at the moment, a debate between 'optimists' and 'pessimists' about the state of the church in the eighteenth century, and, for the sake of balance, it should be acknowledged that the present writer is by and large of the optimistic revisionist camp.

Several historians have recently shown that the church was much more powerful in the political, cultural and social life of the nation than the conventional image of this as a period of enlightenment and secularization would lead us to suppose. In his *English Society 1688–1832*, J. C. D. Clark argued that the established church was one of the trinity of forces (along with the monarchy and aristocracy) that dominated English society. Other historians have pointed to the ways in which cultural and intellectual life – despite the traditional emphasis on secular enlightenment – was still conditioned and shaped by the church and the clergy. For example, it should not be underestimated how far the church dominated the media in this period. More titles were published under the broad category of religious works than under any other category (the vast majority of these written by Church of England clergy), and the sermon was by far and away the most potent means of spreading ideas, not only about issues of belief and theology, but also about politics, society and the economy. In any case, it is possible to overplay the tension between the enlightenment and religious values. In England, at least, enlightenment and piety often went hand-in-hand, and the church and its clergy can, in various areas of activity, such as education, be seen as leading forces of enlightenment.

But in talking, as historians often do, of 'the eighteenth-century church', we are making some assumptions that need to be examined at the outset. The phrase suggests that there was something peculiar about the church in this period that marked it off from the church in the seventeenth or the nineteenth centuries. While there were certainly some aspects of the church that were distinctive in the century, and these will be emphasized below, it does need to be recognized that the church and its clergy shared concerns and problems which had preoccupied the church in earlier periods, and which would continue long after the century was over. In matters of church administration and organization, for instance, and in the business of providing services and pastoral care, the role of the church was little different from that in earlier or later times. Furthermore, many of the failings and shortcomings which are sometimes seen as being somehow particular to the church in this period – such as pluralism and non-residence – were issues that had plagued the church since the Middle Ages. The phrase 'the eighteenth-century church' also suggests that we can write about the church as though it had a single voice and operated in the same way in all parts of the country. But the church in this period, as in any other, was not monolithic as an institution, and too frequently historians have argued from either a positive or a negative instance to claim that this was true of the church as a whole. If we are talking about the church's pastoral care, for example, we have to realize that there were likely to be huge variations, dependent not only on environment and geographical factors (clearly making the experience of the church in a growing urban and industrial centre such as Newcastle-upon-Tyne very different from that in rural Much Wenlock), but also on the abilities and inclinations of individual clergy. Moreover, the fortunes of the church could change over time. The church in 1688 was not necessarily the same as in 1800. Having said this, there were some overarching considerations about its position which lasted throughout the period and which to some extent justifies an attempt such as this to give an overview of the church in the eighteenth century.

Context

It is not always sufficiently appreciated how far the most important contexts for understanding the preoccupations and position of the church in the eighteenth century were the Reformation of the sixteenth century and the civil wars of the seventeenth century. It was during the Reformation period that the church's close links with the monarchy and parliament were forged, and it was then that the overriding anti-Catholicism of the period was formed. Eighteenth-century clergy were as suspicious as their predecessors of 'popery', and the fear that the Reformation might be undone and that Catholicism would again be restored shaped a surprising amount of eighteenth-century sermonizing, tract writing and pastoral endeavour. It has, indeed, been argued that anti-Catholicism was the major ideological determinant not only of the clergy but of most English men and women in the century after 1688, which is suggestive of the ways in which the eighteenth century was heavily influenced by attitudes assumed during the Reformation. The upheaval caused by the civil war was an equally potent determinant in shaping clerical assumptions in our period. To a large extent the memory of what happened when the world was turned upside down formed the habits of mind and fashioned the behaviour of Church of England clergy from the late seventeenth to the early nineteenth centuries, making them suspicious of groups or movements which it was feared might undermine the position of the church. The memory of the Great Rebellion when the church had been overthrown, the archbishop of Canterbury executed and Anglican clergy harried in their parishes became deeply fixed within Anglican consciousness, and the fear that there might be another civil war often determined the eighteenth-century clergy's responses to events. The eighteenth-century church was very conscious that in the previous century its very existence had been severely under threat and its members had been driven underground.

The position of the church in the eighteenth century was also shaped by several crucial late seventeenth-century events and pieces of legislation. First, the Restoration of 1660 had restored not only the monarchy but also the Church of England as the established church of the nation with special rights and privileges (such as allowing twenty-six of its bishops to sit in the House of Lords), and the Corporation Act of 1661 forbade those who dissented from the church from holding a municipal office. The Act of Uniformity of 1662 proscribed worship outside the auspices of the church and enshrined the Anglican Book of Common Prayer as the standard for liturgy and worship. The church's dominant place within the political and social life of the country was strengthened by the Test Acts of 1673 and 1678, which ensured that to hold political office under the crown or to be an MP it was necessary to be a member of the Church of England.

Second, the Glorious Revolution of 1688 could be seen as establishing the Protestant nature of the monarchy, which cemented the link between the monarchy and the church. In popular mythology, the trial of the seven bishops, led by Archbishop Sancroft, was a clear statement of the church's suspicion of the popish activities of James II and their acquittal helped to establish the lawfulness of opposition to the Stuart regime. That the church had played such a large role in legitimating opposition did, as we shall see, have a divisive impact among the clergy, but in the long run it strengthened the connections between the church and the crown. Indeed, one reason why Roman Catholics were not given full emancipation until the nineteenth century was that George III believed that such a move would go against his coronation oath to maintain the position of the established church.

Third, the Toleration Act of 1689, which was often seen as a concomitant of the Glorious Revolution, maintained the establishment position of the church, while giving limited concessions to Nonconformists. The act, although contested with some clergy wanting it repealed and others wanting it to be extended, nicely summed up the position of the Church of England throughout the eighteenth century as established, yet (at least in comparison with other periods, and with other churches in Europe) broadly tolerant of some at least of its rivals. Although commonly known as the Toleration Act by contemporaries and by later historians, it was, however, originally entitled an 'act for exempting their majesties' Protestant subjects dissenting from the Church of England from the penalties of certain laws', which indicates that it was less tolerant than has sometimes been suggested. Protestant Dissenters could legally worship only in unlocked meeting houses, providing they had been licensed, and their minister subscribed to the Thirty-Nine Articles of the Church of England (a set of doctrinal statements defining the position of the church, originally written in the sixteenth century and appended to the 1662 edition of the Book of Common Prayer), except those concerning baptism and church government. The act clearly proscribed Roman Catholic worship. Nevertheless, the act became important for the self-definition of the church as one which was charitable and enlightened (at least compared with its competitors), and where persecution of Dissent was seen to be a hallmark of popery. And although evidence can be found of mobs stoning and harrying Dissenters, and pulling down their meeting houses, the Anglican clergy at least had to work within a framework where they persuaded rather than persecuted Nonconformists back into the fold. It is this frame of mind which in part explains why clergy were so eager to publish their views in print, as a way of competing with, rather than persecuting, Nonconformists. Clergy do seem to have generally treated Protestant Dissenters with respect. Some clergymen not only had a positive view of Dissenters but also saw both Anglicans and Nonconformists as their parishioners, a lingering suggestion of the view that the Church of England had a responsibility for all the nation. What was of more concern to Anglican clergy was the apparently growing sector of the population who did not attend any form of religious worship (the Toleration Act itself was widely suspected of having encouraged them to attend no place of worship at all), and it was against this group that the church might combine with the Dissenters. This shared pastoral purpose can be witnessed by Anglicans working with Dissenters in the societies for the reformation of manners (in the 1690s and early eighteenth century) and in educational projects such as charity schools.

These late seventeenth-century developments as outlined above effectively shaped the position of the church within the life of the nation for the next 120 years, thereby giving the period some kind of structural coherence (the Test Acts were not repealed until 1828, and Roman Catholics were not given emancipation until 1829). How far the legislative position of the church means that England should be seen as a 'confessional state' in the eighteenth century has recently been a matter of some debate. Clearly, sections of the English population did not conform to the church, even though some Dissenters, through the practice of occasional conformity, made themselves eligible for public office. Nevertheless, the centrality of the church's legal position did have a profound impact on political and social life, ensuring that the state, the English universities, the army and the civil service were Anglican strongholds, and in the localities clergy were often justices of the peace (JPs) and as such were responsible for the administration of local government. Perhaps a more accurate description of the church's position is not as a confessional state so much as an Anglican hegemony. Although its position was contested, the church effectively dominated society and politics, and sought to marginalize those who challenged its role. It needs to be stressed that many churchmen believed that the interests of church and state were in fact inseparable and interdependent, and that enemies of the church were also enemies of the state. A good indication of this attitude can be seen in the church's response to the Jacobite rebellions of 1715 and 1745 when the vast bulk of the clergy and the church's hierarchy supported the Hanoverian regime. Again, at the end of the century, the church was a staunch defender of the government during the French Revolution, believing that threats to the state would also be destructive to the church, and to true religion generally.

From the perspective of the period itself – and certainly from the point of view of those who were outside the church – the political link between church and state gave the church an enviably powerful position, making the state appear subservient to the church. Most clergymen, and most lay politicians, would not have seen the church as an adjunct to the state; rather, the established church was integral to English law and society and there was no distinction between its political and spiritual roles. In any case, the political connection between church and state could work to the advantage of the church. Individual bishops could and did vote against the government of the day, and, over certain issues when the church's interests were felt to be at stake, such as the Quakers' Tithe Bill of 1736, which, it was feared, threatened the church's economic position, bishops acted as a group to defeat the proposal (with fourteen bishops voting against the bill, and eleven abstaining). Other attempts during the 1730s to curb Anglican privileges were largely abortive. And while the late eighteenth century did see a number of acts to relieve the position of those who were outside the church (such as the Dissenters' Relief Act of 1776, and the various measures to soften penalties against Catholics in the 1770s and 1780s), nevertheless the parameters established in the late seventeenth century remained remarkably intact at the end of the eighteenth century.

Church Parties and Politics

It is sometimes suggested that the events of 1688–9 had a profound effect on the Church of England as an institution. In the first place they have been seen as damaging to the personnel of the church. One of the most obvious consequences of the Glorious Revolution for the Church of England was that some of its members refused to take oaths of allegiance and supremacy to William and Mary for fear of breaking their oaths to James II. These included the archbishop of Canterbury, William Sancroft, eight bishops (three of whom died before they were deprived of their posts), about 400 parish clergy and some laymen, as well as virtually all the Scottish Episcopalian clergy and one Irish bishop. Some historians have suggested that these Nonjurors robbed the church of its most conscientious and saintly clergy and, by depriving the church of those most likely to have maintained its ideals and vigour, contributed to the supposed corruption and torpor of the period. In actual fact, relations between the Nonjurors and those who conformed to the church were not as hostile as the printed debates between them would imply (the first archbishop of the new regime, John Tillotson, died in the arms of the Nonjuror Robert Nelson), and in any case it is doubtful whether those who became Nonjurors had differing views on pluralism and non-residence, those areas where the eighteenth-century church has most often been criticized.

Historians have also argued that the events of 1688–9 helped to divide the clergy into two broad camps which lasted throughout the eighteenth century: high church and low church. Broadly speaking, high churchmen upheld the belief in sacraments and ritual, the authority of the church hierarchy, the close relationship between church and state, and were suspicious of Dissenters (with some high churchmen being amongst the most vociferous for the repeal of the Toleration Act). On the other hand, low churchmen gave a relatively low place to the claims of the episcopate and frequently sympathized with Dissenters. Another way in which 1688–9 high and low church clergy have been seen to have split is with reference to their political affiliation, with high churchmen being allied to the Tories and low churchmen to the Whigs.

It is clear that these divisions might come to the fore at times of political and religious controversy. One famous instance was the Sacheverell affair of 1710. The high churchman Henry Sacheverell preached in St Paul's Cathedral on 5 November 1709, taking as his text 'In perils among false brethren', which attacked the Whig government for allegedly putting the Church of England in danger by favouring the Dissenters. Following his outspoken sermon (of which, it has been estimated, over 100,000 copies were sold, and read by perhaps half a million people), Sacheverell was impeached in February 1710 for seditious libel. Riots broke out in London on the night of 1–2 March, and Dissenting meeting houses were burned down. The election of October 1710 resulted in a strong Tory victory on the back of the 'Church in Danger' slogan. As a result of this victory some significant pieces of legislation were passed in favour of the church (the Occasional Conformity Act of 1711, which forbade the Dissenters occasionally conforming to allow them to take up political office, and the Schism Act of 1714, which effectively prohibited Dissenting schools). These acts were later repealed under a Whig government in 1719.

Some historians have also seen the political divisions as operating not only within the clergy, but, at least for the first half of the century, between the predominantly Whig bishops and the overwhelmingly Tory parish clergy. An indication of this is the so-called Convocation controversy of the early eighteenth century. Convocations were assemblies of clergy which met alongside parliament. In 1689 and between 1700 and 1717 disputes arose between the Whiggishly inclined upper house (made up of bishops and senior clergy) and the more Tory lower house (made up of the parish clergy). After 1717 Convocation was suspended, and the church lost its central meeting forum. But by the 1730s, as a number of recent studies have shown, these political divisions within the clergy had softened and in large areas of the country (such as Yorkshire, Kent and Sussex) parish clergy were predominantly voting Whig. To a large extent this was because the various Whig ministries had shown that they were not acting to destroy the church, and that in fact the church was safe in Whig hands. In the late eighteenth century, some of the political divisions of the early century reappeared with the development of more liberal political ideas, and certainly some clergy shared in the radical critique of government. But the French Revolution, and the fear of unrest at home, ensured that the vast bulk of clergy were vociferous supporters of the political establishment.

We should, in any case, be aware that the divisions between high and low churchmen were often the products of propaganda and satire, and did not necessarily reflect reality. Although a number of clergy can be placed into these categories, what is increasingly receiving attention are the ways in which clergy did not fit into these neat labels, and in particular, the identification of Whigs with low churchmanship and Tories with high churchmanship is not a hard and fast rule. Indeed, by the 1730s and 1740s many of the leading Whig clergy can be seen to be high churchmen, suggesting that Whiggery and high churchmanship could go hand-in-hand. A good example of this might be Edmund Gibson, bishop of London, 1723–48. His Whig credentials are clear – he was a firm ally of Sir Robert Walpole's and he effectively dominated ecclesiastical patronage during the 1720s and 1730s – but in many ways he was a high churchman too, with his insistence on maintaining the rights and privileges of the church. And outside periods of political tension, clergy who belonged to either the high or the low church camp could work together, particularly over pastoral matters. And, despite some historians' stress on divisions between the clergy, during the eighteenth century these divisions were, arguably, not as great as splits in the periods before 1688 and after 1800. Rather, there were shared beliefs and priorities, such as the need to preserve the church from the twin threats of popery and Protestant Nonconformity (and this was a recurrent theme of countless sermons and tracts denouncing the evils of both its rivals), which to a remarkable extent helped to bind clergy together. This sense of a shared identity was important in the self-definition of the church and helped to ensure that there was, in the long run, more that bound them together than drove them apart.

Intellectual Developments

As far as the world of ideas is concerned, it is often argued that the church was dominated by reason rather than by faith or spirituality. In large measure, however, the church's stress on reason has been exaggerated or misrepresented. Rather than vaunting reason for its own sake, clergy tended to emphasize not only the reasonableness of Christianity (against atheism and Deism), but the reasonableness of the Church of England against what was understood to be the fanaticism of its rivals. The emphasis on reason was in any case a reaction against the perceived misguided enthusiasm and irrationality which, according to the Church of England, pervaded not only Roman Catholicism but also Dissent. Nevertheless, it would be wrong to suggest that the weight placed on reason indicated a preference for classical rather than Christian authorities. Church of England clergy (predominantly university-educated) saw a congruence between classical and Christian forms of thought (and in that they followed in the tradition of the Christian humanism of the sixteenth and seventeenth centuries). And in some ways clergy can be seen as leading the attack on the unwarranted role of reason in religious matters. For example, the future bishop of Durham Joseph Butler's *The Analogy of Religion* (1736) was widely believed to have vanquished Deism, and the idealist philosophy of George Berkeley, later bishop of Cloyne, as demonstrated in his *Treatise Concerning the Principles of Human Knowledge* (1710) and his *Three Dialogues*, combated the materialism of Locke and Newton.

In the period after 1688 those clergy who stressed the importance of reason in religious matters were often equated with latitudinarianism (a term of abuse used from the late seventeenth century to characterize those clergy who, while conforming to the church, attached relatively little importance to dogmatic truth, ecclesiastical organization and liturgical practice). Influential clergy here included Benjamin Hoadly, the bishop of Bangor, whose sermon of 1717, 'My Church is not of this World', advocated private judgement and sincerity over ecclesiastical authority, provoking the so-called Bangorian controversy which led to the suspension of Convocation. Hoadly has traditionally been seen as representing the worst aspects of the Georgian church, although modern research indicates that he was more conscientious and spiritually concerned than his detractors have thought. Latitudinarians were also often associated with liberal theology and in some cases were suspected of unorthodoxy, especially Arianism and Socinianism (Arians believed that although created by God, Christ had not in fact coexisted with God from eternity; Socinianism was more extreme, in that it denied the pre-existence of Christ and asserted that Jesus was merely a good man). A number of influential Church of England clergy can be placed in this group. For example, Samuel Clarke, the rector of Westminster, wrote *The Scripture-Doctrine of the Trinity* (1712), which appeared distinctly Arian. Clergymen with theologically liberal ideas were particularly favoured by Queen Caroline during the late 1720s and 1730s, and again reached some prominence in the church in the 1760s and 1770s, with Francis Blackburne, the archdeacon of Cleveland, and Richard Watson, the bishop of Llandaff. Blackburne's *The Confessional* (1765) was a stinging attack on the authoritarianism of the church establishment, and he and others attacked the church for making it compulsory for clergy to subscribe to the Thirty-Nine Articles. After the Feathers Tavern petition of 1772, a handful of clergy, headed by Theophilus Lindsey, left the church for Unitarianism.

Yet the importance of latitudinarian ideas, at least in terms of liberal theology, can be exaggerated. At one time it used to be common to use the term latitudinarian as a label to describe the dominant temper of the Georgian church as a whole. But it is clear that the vast majority of clergy – and especially those who received promotion within the church – were soundly orthodox in their views. Even Hoadly, who has been seen as an archetypal latitudinarian, can be seen to have placed increasing emphasis on orthodoxy as his career progressed, and it is significant that those with the most liberal theological views felt that they had to leave rather than stay in the church.

In any case there were challenges to the latitudinarian view from two major quarters: Evangelicalism and renewed high churchmanship. Although Evangelicalism will be considered in more detail in a later chapter, it needs to be stressed how, from the 1740s and quite distinct from Methodism, a not insignificant number of clergy began to revive the 'religion of the heart' and thereby challenged what to them seemed an undue emphasis on the role of reason in religious matters. These included William Grimshaw, Samuel Walker, Thomas Jones, Henry Venn and William Romaine. Certainly, by the 1760s, it is possible to talk of an Evangelical grouping who sought to combat what they perceived to be clerical apathy, while accepting Anglican discipline. They emphasized the importance of moral earnestness and proclaimed salvation by faith. By the end of the eighteenth century the most prominent members of the Anglican Evangelicals were known as the Clapham sect (because they lived in the village of Clapham in south London). Believing in personal salvation through good works, they campaigned on behalf of the abolition of the slave trade and were involved in a number of other humanitarian causes, including Sunday school reform and promoting a high standard of public morality. Significantly, two of the most influential members of the Clapham sect, William Wilberforce and Hannah More, were lay members of the church.

A second attack on the latitudinarian position came from the Hutchinsonian circle of clergy. These were largely Oxford-educated clergy who rose to some prominence within the church after 1760 and who stressed the centrality of the Trinity and the limits of human reason in religious matters. The group took their name from John Hutchinson (1674–1737), whose writings on natural philosophy and theology became the basis of their work. He had argued that a proper reading of the Bible demonstrated that both it and the natural world held sure proofs of the Trinity. The chief target of the Hutchinsonians (who included George Horne, later bishop of Norwich, and William Jones of Nayland) were the Unitarians and the Rational Dissenters, in particular Joseph Priestley and Richard Price, who were responsible for leading the attack on the Anglican liturgy from the 1770s.

One of the significant intellectual developments of the period in which clergy from across the clerical spectrum participated was in the interest in science and the natural world through the study of natural theology. Broadly speaking, natural theology is the belief that human reason can know the attributes and existence of God, and his purposes, from the evidence of the natural world, and was not dependent on information gleaned from the Bible. As a theological method it relies on the image of God's two books, the book of nature and the book of revelation, both of which could lead to Christian truths. The popularity of natural theology in the eighteenth century was crucial in the dissemination of the new science and in encouraging people to look more closely at the natural world. It also fitted in with enlightenment thought, emphasizing as it did the power of human reason to make connections between this world and divine truths.

A concomitant of natural theology was the argument from design. This held that the existence of a purposeful creator responsible for the world could be gleaned from the evidence of order and harmony in the universe. In this scientific and religious activities were seen as inseparable: religious priorities prompted scientific investigation. The most obvious examples of clerical endeavour in this respect were the Boyle lectures, which were established by the will of the leading chemist Robert Boyle (1627–91) for 'proving the Christian religion against notorious infidels'. This type of thinking reached its apogee in William Paley's (the archdeacon of Carlisle) *Natural Theology* (1802). These examples indicate that Anglican clergy were part of the wider intellectual culture of the age.

The Church and the Parishes

The church in the eighteenth century has received most of its criticism for its pastoral record. Whatever other charges have been levelled at it, its failure to minister effectively to its parishioners has been one of the most enduring, and it has been voiced by social historians as well as by historians of religion. But it needs to be remembered that many of the supposed pastoral shortcomings of the Church of

England during the eighteenth century were often the consequences of having an administrative structure that had hardly altered since the Middle Ages. The organization of the church into twenty-seven dioceses and nearly 11,000 parishes in England and Wales and the geographical distribution of parishes and clergy were little changed from the fifteenth century, and this meant that the church was not well equipped to deal with the upsurge in population after the 1740s with the growth of towns such as Manchester and Sheffield.

Nevertheless, it would be wrong to downplay some of the ways in which clergy were able to use their resources to provide at least adequate pastoral care. Although historians used to argue that industrialization and urbanization were twin problems for a church which supposedly did better in a rural context, we can exaggerate the ways in which these two developments were necessarily detrimental to the life of the church. It is, for example, often suggested that the church in the eighteenth century failed to build new churches to meet the growth of the towns, and the impression is often given that apart from the fifty new churches act of 1711, which attempted to build new places of worship in newly populated districts of London (with only ten in fact being built), little was done until the church-building explosion of the nineteenth century. In actual fact, some of the newly smart urban centres such as Bath, Warwick, York and Newcastle-upon-Tyne provided a rich environment for the church: in all these towns, and in many others, churches were either newly built or refurbished, congregations were large and clergy benefited from the pleasures of urbane society. And in parts of Lancashire (the area that witnessed the greatest upsurge in population and where industrialization was furthest developed, placing the greatest strain on its resources) the church, through its use of newly built chapels of ease, was able to accommodate a greater percentage of the population in 1800 than it had in 1740. Even in Manchester, whose population growth in the last thirty years of the century astounded contemporaries, the church was not negligent in providing new places of worship, and eight new churches were built in the city.

The pastoral failings of the church have sometimes been blamed on the bishops, who, it is often asserted, were frequently out of touch with their dioceses, being more involved with the House of Lords than with their diocesan clergy. But the image we have had of bishops who were negligent of their dioceses is in many ways a misleading one. Despite their involvement in politics, it is clear that the church had many conscientious diocesans, who took care to monitor the clergy under their control and to provide pastoral oversight. Of course there were exceptions, and because there was no system for retirement, elderly bishops might lose a grip on their task, but modern research at the diocesan and local level has revealed much more active leadership than previously assumed. For instance, despite the often-held view that archbishops of Canterbury in the eighteenth century were by and large unconcerned with the well-being of the church, several of them were outstanding administrators, such as Thomas Tenison (1695–1715), William Wake (1715–37), Thomas Secker (1758–68) and John Moore (1783–1805), and throughout the eighteenth century a number of diligent bishops can be found. One of the consequences of research into the diocesan archives has been to uncover correspondence between bishops (or their officials) and the parish clergy which indicates that bishops were more in contact with their subordinates than used to be supposed. In particular, much recent research has used the extensive replies written by clergy to the questions asked by the bishops as part of their triennial visitation of their diocese. These not only provide us with remarkable information concerning the church's role in individual parishes (such as its personnel, the number of services offered and who attended, and how often children were catechized), they also provide information concerning the numbers of Catholics and Protestant Dissenters in the parish, and the number of inhabitants. As yet, no one has attempted to collate the evidence from all the dioceses over the century; but some preliminary conclusions can be attempted.

Much of the writing about the parish clergy in the eighteenth century has been based on literary evidence and has focused on the stereotypes of a clergy divided into the extremes of the fox-hunting parson or the woefully poor curate. Recent studies have indicated that most clergy fell well between these extremes. By and large the clergy were a graduate profession (the vast bulk of those who were ordained had been to either Oxford, Cambridge, Trinity College, Dublin or one of the Scottish universities). This matched the church's desire to have a learned ministry and in its propaganda it liked to contrast this fact with the supposedly unlettered status of its Dissenting rivals. It is true that, as the century progressed, an increasing percentage of clergy came from what might be broadly called the gentry ranks, but the wholesale gentrification of the clergy can be exaggerated. A significant number of clergy (perhaps over a quarter) even at the end of our period came from rather more humble origins, and were less likely to have been out of touch with ordinary parishioners than the pessimistic interpretation suggests, and an increasing number had fathers who had also been clergy. Certainly, a large number of parishes, as a consequence of pluralism, were staffed by curates and some of these lived up to the image of the poorly paid lumpen proletariat, but many were at the early stages of their career and would move on to more settled and more lucrative employment. Beneficed clergy (those in permanent employment) were either vicars or rectors: the distinction being that rectors (since they received the tithes on all produce within the parish) were likely to be richer than vicars, who only received 'small' tithes (usually just on the minor products of the parish). The lot of those who were most poorly remunerated was somewhat alleviated during the course of the century through Queen Anne's Bounty (established in 1704), which, through funds diverted from government resources and by raising extra money, was able to make a significant improvement to the less well-endowed parishes.

As far as the pastoral work of the clergy is concerned, it is of course impossible to generalize, depending as it did on the inclinations of individuals (although it is clear that bishops were not content with the most minimal pastoral cover). There are examples, to be sure, of negligent clergy, but by and large the pastoral dedication of the parish clergy is more impressive than the traditionally hostile picture would suggest. The broad results of the visitation surveys indicate that services were regularly given on Sundays (with the pattern of two services being more frequent in the north and west, and one service in the south and east), and that the laity were happy to attend, as long as there was a sermon. The furnishings of many eighteenth-century churches, and especially those that were refurbished or new built in the period, confirmed the ascendant place of the pulpit (and sermon) within the interior of the church. The dominance of the pulpit within the church, and especially the three-decker pulpit (which figured prominently in Hogarth's satirical prints), was much derided by nineteenth-century church reformers who accused their forebears of neglecting the sacrament, but it is indicative of the central role given to the sermon, and of 'the word' more generally within eighteenth-century religious life. The chief pastoral aim of eighteenth-century clergy was to initiate parishioners into the fundamental message of the Reformation and to educate them out of popery and superstition.

The visitation returns indicate that clergy were involved in catechizing children (a form of question and answer designed to inculcate the most essential religious truths), although this was usually only for part of the year, and clergy admitted to their superiors that sometimes parents were reluctant to send their children. Another common complaint made by the clergy was the reluctance parishioners had in taking holy communion, but whether this was because they devalued the sacrament, or whether they felt unworthy to receive it, is not clear. The returns also show a broad difference between rural and urban parishes. In the towns it was much more common to find weekday services being offered and attended, and some of the larger urban centres had communion once a month and occasionally every Sunday. In rural parishes, by contrast, clergy found it hard to take parishioners away from the agricultural routine and in many rural parishes weekday services had long since died out. The visitation returns also demonstrate the wider role of the church and the clergy in the life of the parish. Clergy frequently had the role of supervising the local school, managing charitable funds and organizing poor relief, and as such played a vital role within the parish community.

Two of the most significant and longstanding Anglican pastoral initiatives of the period were the foundation of the voluntary societies: the Society for the Promotion of Christian Knowledge (SPCK) in 1698 and the Society for the Propagation of the Gospel in Foreign Parts (SPG) in 1701. Their founder, Thomas Bray, was a high churchman who nevertheless wanted to support non-partisan initiatives for reforming religious life and for eradicating popery. The SPCK fostered a range of activities, including establishing a corresponding society for pooling and collecting information on the church's work in the localities, encouraging the development of parish libraries and, increasingly, publishing and disseminating religious tracts and pamphlets as a way of spreading religious education. During its first thirty years it also seems to have had a special role in encouraging the establishment of charity schools. The SPG reveals the extent to which the church in the eighteenth century can be considered to be a missionary church; recognizing that its mission was not only to its English parishioners, but also to those in its colonies. Another example of the church's links with religious groups outside the British Isles were the various funds organized by the church for the support of Protestants in Europe who were suffering from persecution by Roman Catholics (and collected through the church briefs).

In all these areas of concern the church showed itself rather adept at raising funds for its activities and was particularly successful in getting money from the laity for its ventures. The SPG and the Corporation for the Sons of the Clergy (which supported the widows and the children of deceased clergy) raised money through annual concerts and services at St Paul's Cathedral. The ways in which the church was able to extract money from the laity points to one of the most important developments within the Church of England in this period, what has been termed the laicization of religion. It is this development, rather than the conventional stress on this being an age of secularization, which is the hallmark of the Anglican history of the period. Most histories of the church concentrate either on the church as an institution, or on the clergy, but it needs to be recognized that a considerable emphasis was placed by clergy on the role of the laity. Rather than being under the thumb of the laity, the church, it could be argued, was rather successful in persuading the laity to support church-led projects. Although as yet there are only a few studies of lay piety for this period, nevertheless, what is emerging is a considerable body of people who not only attended the services provided by the church, but who also wanted to help the church in other ways and to participate in debates about religion more generally. The aristocracy were certainly less 'semi-pagan' than Tawney claimed, and several, such as the duke of Newcastle, the earl of Dartmouth and Lady Betty Hastings, were pious defenders of the church. Not many lay people, of course, were like Samuel Johnson, who wrote sermons, but the general support for the church, not only in the fundraising activities mentioned above, and in the regular payment of tithes, but also in donations to individual parish churches (most of which dated from the medieval period and were increasingly in need of repair), is impressive and certainly challenges the view that the church was increasingly marginal to the life of parishioners. It has also become an axiom of much writing on the church in this period that it had lost its hold over the lower orders. Certainly in this – as perhaps in all periods – signs of disaffection can be shown, particularly towards individual clergy and over particular grievances. But this did not mean that the church as an institution had lost its place in the hearts and minds of ordinary parishioners. The famous Church and King Riots of the 1790s, which amongst other things mobbed the Dissenter and radical political thinker Joseph Priestley's house in Birmingham and destroyed his laboratory, were not very edifying, but they indicate that the church could still inspire popular loyalties.

It is often said that one of the clearest testimonies to the failure of the church in the eighteenth century in the pastoral sphere was the existence of Dissent, and especially of Methodism. If the church was as successful as some of the more optimistic judgements would have us believe, it can reasonably be asked, why did Nonconformity exist and why did Methodism develop? Although other chapters deal with these topics in detail, it is worth stressing here that these factors in themselves are not a necessarily useful guide to the successes or failures of the eighteenth-century church. In the first place, by the 1730s several contemporaries were noticing a decline in 'Old Dissent' as many erstwhile Dissenters had by now conformed to the Church of England, including some, like Thomas Secker, a future archbishop of Canterbury, who had initially contemplated becoming a Nonconformist minister. The reasons for the decline in Old Dissent are varied: some blamed the internal wranglings over doctrine; some pointed to the ways in which the confessional state severely limited opportunities for Nonconformists to have significant political, social and educational positions if they remained outside the church; and others blamed the decline of Old Dissent on the effects of the Toleration Act, which supposedly weakened the backbone of Nonconformity. Whatever the reason, it is clear that the church gained from winning over some former Dissenters and as a consequence the challenge of Dissent weakened. It is also necessary to stress that Methodism should at least in the first instance be seen as a movement from within the Church of England, rather than as a Dissenting movement operating outside it. John Wesley, himself the son of the rector of Epworth, remained an ordained member of the Church of England throughout his life, and although he could be sharply critical of contemporary practice, his energies were devoted to reforming the church from within. Wesley's efforts to keep the movement he founded within the church – by encouraging his followers to attend both church services and the Methodist meeting, and his insistence that Methodist meetings should not clash with the times of church services – may not have been respected, or even put into practice, by all of his followers, but, at least until his death in 1791, Methodism was as much an Anglican as a Dissenting phenomenon.

So, in conclusion, how useful or appropriate is Tawney's verdict on the church in the eighteenth century with which this chapter began? It is a judgement which, at least until the last twenty years, has commanded general assent. On the basis of recent research, however, we can now challenge such a statement and suggest that the church was at best less servile and more spiritually alive than has often been supposed. The Church of England, even at the end of the eighteenth century, was a powerful presence in the life of the nation and, despite the challenges from Dissenting groups and from pressures placed on its resources through population growth, it can be shown to have successfully maintained the strong place it inherited from the seventeenth century. In some areas, such as pastoral ministry and education (and refreshed by the Anglican Evangelicals), it is arguable that the church was more active at the end than at the start of our period. Nevertheless, there were, in the last decade of the century, indications of new pressures on the church's position. During the 1790s, and as part of the widespread reaction to the French Revolution, church authorities became more suspicious of Dissenters, and more jealously guarded the church's position. In that decade, too, the radical critique of the church's privileges became more widespread.

FURTHER READING

Bennett, G. V.: 'Conflict in the church', in G. S. Holmes (ed.), *Britain after the Glorious Revolution, 1689–1714* (London, 1969).

Bennett, G. V.: *The Tory Crisis in Church and State, 1688–1730: The Career of Francis Atterbury, Bishop of Rochester* (Oxford, 1975).

Chamberlain, Jeffrey S.: *Accommodating High Churchmen: The Clergy of Sussex, 1700–1724* (Urbana, IL, 1997).

Clark, J. C. D.: *English Society 1688–1832: Ideology, Social Structure and Political Practice during the Ancien Régime* (1985; rev. edn, Cambridge, 2000).

Gascoigne, John: *Cambridge in the Age of the Enlightenment: Science, Religion and Politics from the Restoration to the French Revolution* (Cambridge, 1989).

Gibson, William: *The Achievement of the Anglican Church 1689–1800: The Confessional State in Eighteenth-Century England* (Lewiston, 1995).

Gibson, William: *Religion and Society in England and Wales 1689–1800* (London, 1998).

Gibson, William: *The Church of England 1688–1832: Unity and Accord* (London, 2001).

Gregory, Jeremy: *Restoration, Reformation and Reform, 1660–1828: Archbishops of Canterbury and their Diocese* (Oxford, 2000).

Hempton, David: 'Religion in British society, 1740–90', in Jeremy Black (ed.), *British Politics and Society from Walpole to Pitt* (Basingstoke, 1990).

Jacob, W. M.: *Lay Piety and Religion in the Early Eighteenth Century* (Cambridge, 1996).

Mather, F. C.: *High Church Prophet: Bishop Samuel Horsley (1733–1806) and the Caroline Tradition in the Later Georgian Church* (Oxford, 1992).

Smith, Mark: *Religion in Industrial Society: Oldham and Saddleworth, 1740–1865* (Oxford, 1994).

Sykes, Norman: *Church and State in England in the Eighteenth Century* (Cambridge, 1934).

Tawney, R. H.: *Religion and the Rise of Capitalism: A Historical Study* (London, 1926).

Virgin, Peter: *The Church in an Age of Negligence* (Cambridge, 1989).

Walsh, John, Haydon, Colin and Taylor, Stephen (eds): *The Church of England, c.1689–c.1833: From Toleration to Tractarianism* (Cambridge, 1993).

Ward, W. R. (ed.): *Parson and Parish in Eighteenth-Century Surrey: Replies to Bishops' Visitations* (Surrey Record Society, 34, 1994).

CHAPTER EIGHTEEN

Religious Minorities in England

COLIN HAYDON

The Legal Framework, Distribution and Numbers

The principal religious minorities of eighteenth-century England were Protestant Dissenters – the 'three denominations', Presbyterians, Independents (i.e., Congregationalists) and Baptists, and also Quakers – and Roman Catholics. The years 1687–9 had seen the formulation of a longlasting framework respecting these groupings. In 1687 James II's Declaration of Indulgence authorized the public worship of both his Catholic co-religionists and Protestant sectaries. Following the Glorious Revolution, the Toleration Act (1689) confirmed the freedom of worship of Protestant Dissenters, provided they were Trinitarians – an important stipulation – and they registered their meeting houses with the local magistracy or episcopal authorities. Yet, concerning civil matters, the Corporation Act (1661) remained in force, debarring from borough corporations those who refused to receive the sacrament according to the Church of England's rites. The Test Acts also remained in force; the first Test Act (1673) required an officeholder, civil or military, to take the Anglican sacrament within three months of assuming his post, and to make a declaration against transubstantiation; and Catholics were additionally disadvantaged by the second Test Act (1678), which excluded them from parliament. James II's fall brought renewed persecution of Catholics. Their worship was proscribed and an Act against Popery of 1700 recast the penal laws. But in the eighteenth century, the statutes – aside from those concerning public life and the act imposing a double land tax – were rarely enforced, and, after 1760, magistrates and the courts discouraged prosecutions, thus favouring much de facto toleration. In 1778 parliament modified the penal code, removing its heaviest penalties and permitting land purchase by Catholics; Catholics were granted freedom of worship in 1791. None the less, parliament did not abolish the sacramental test until 1828 and conceded Catholic emancipation only in 1829. Throughout the eighteenth century in England, Anglican hegemony was clear in law. On paper, at least, the kingdom was a 'confessional state'.

At the start of the eighteenth century, England's Catholic population was most conspicuous in the north, and especially in Lancashire, in the west midlands and in

Table 1

Denomination	*Estimated numbers*	*Percentage of total population*	*Congregations*
Presbyterians	179,350	3.4	637
Independents	59,940	1.1	203
Particular Baptists	40,520	0.8	206
Quakers	39,510	0.8	672
General Baptists	18,800	0.4	122

Sources: Julian Hoppit, *A Land of Liberty? England 1689–1727* (Oxford, 2000), p. 220; Michael R. Watts, *The Dissenters*, vol. 1: *From the Reformation to the French Revolution* (Oxford, 1978), p. 270.

London. Though not exclusively so, Catholicism outside the capital was markedly seigneurial in character: priests acted as chaplains to landed families and ministered to their Catholic tenants. As for the Dissenters, the Evans List (1715) shows concentrations of General Baptists in Buckinghamshire, Kent and Lincolnshire, and of Particular (i.e., predestinarian) Baptists in Bedfordshire and Hertfordshire. Independents were strongest in Bedfordshire, Cambridgeshire, Essex, Hertfordshire and Northamptonshire; Presbyterians in Cheshire, Devon, Dorset, Lancashire, Northumberland and Somerset. The three denominations' ministers were dependent on the financial support of their hearers and some central funds. Quakers had strength in Cumberland and Westmorland, in Bristol, and in London and in counties to its north. A disproportionate number of Dissenters, when compared to the whole population, were town dwellers, employed in, or directing, commerce, trade and manufacturing. Many Dissenters worked in the clothing trades. Quaker ironmasters included Abraham Darby I (1677–1717) and John Hanbury (1664–1734); there were famous Quaker bankers, clockmakers and physicians. Denominational connections, and the Dissenters' qualities of self-discipline and honesty, aided business ventures.

It is difficult to estimate the number of Roman Catholics, but it seems likely that in England and Wales there were some 60,000–70,000 in 1700 and around 100,000 by 1800. Seigneurial Catholicism declined in England, as prominent laymen – including seven peers – conformed to the established church, but the faith expanded in provincial towns, including Bath, Birmingham, Bristol, Liverpool, Manchester, Preston and Worcester. In the early eighteenth century, General and Particular Baptists, Independents, Presbyterians and Quakers constituted less than 7 per cent of England's population. Table 1 shows the different denominations' estimated numbers, their size *vis-à-vis* the whole population and congregations in England in *c.*1715.

Old Dissent's numbers declined in the early eighteenth century. Prosperous Dissenters became Anglicans; enlightenment reason sapped faith; endogamy stunted Baptist, Independent and Quaker growth. Between 1714 and 1731 some fifty ministers joined the established church. In London and Middlesex the three denominations' congregations fell from 112 in 1727 to seventy-two in 1776. At Stratford-upon-Avon there were 300 Presbyterians in 1715; but, by 1782, according to an episcopal survey, there were just a few Methodists and no other Dissenters. Old Dissent revived, however, in the late eighteenth century, and, partly under

Evangelicalism's influence, experienced an increasingly sharp rise in the late eighteenth and early nineteenth centuries. Between 1750 and 1800, Independent members swelled from 15,000 to 35,000, Particular Baptists from 10,000 to 24,000.

Besides these Protestant Dissenters and Catholics, there were some other religious minorities. Following the Revolution of 1688–9, the archbishop of Canterbury, five bishops and some 400 priests refused to swear allegiance to William and Mary. Deprived of their sees or livings, they formed, with their lay supporters, the Nonjuring church. They held their own, illegal, services, though some also attended worship in the parish church. Gradually reabsorbed into the Church of England in the eighteenth century, their regular episcopal line ended with Robert Gordon's death in 1779, though a Nonjuring church survived in Manchester into the nineteenth century. There was also a Jewish community. Oliver Cromwell permitted the Jews' return and thereafter Ashkenazi and Sephardi Jews emigrated from the continent to England. Synagogues were opened in London – the Duke Street synagogue was established in 1690 and that in Bevis Marks in 1701. Eighteenth-century immigration was slow. There were only some 6,000 Jews in England by the 1730s. Outside the capital there were, by 1800, organized Jewish communities in some seaports, growing cities and in the fashionable towns of Bath and Brighton. Though excluded from public life, Jews in London dominated the trade in coral and diamonds; some invested in Bank of England and East India stock, and acted as jobbers. The great Jewish financier Sampson Gideon (1699–1762) advised Walpole and Henry Pelham.

There were, in intellectual circles, Deists – of whom more later. There were few open atheists, denying any deity's existence on reasoned grounds: under the Blasphemy Act (1698), atheists could be prosecuted. Deeply disturbing to Christians, however, were the countless humble 'atheists', whose ignorant, dogged indifference or hostility to organized Christianity is noted in such sources as Anglican consistory court papers, sermons and tracts. Finally, there were some tiny groupings, like the Muggletonians and the French Prophets, originally Protestant refugees from the Cévennes.

Religious Life

Early in George I's reign there were more than a thousand Dissenting ministers in England, and around 1,400 by the mid-1720s. Some – but only a small minority – were graduates of Scottish or Dutch universities. Most ministers were trained in English Dissenting academies, opened in the late seventeenth and eighteenth centuries. Among the most famous of these establishments, in Hanoverian times, were Northampton (under Philip Doddridge) and Warrington (where Joseph Priestley, the great scientist and intellectual, taught). The academies fostered a spirit of enquiry amongst their students and displayed a tolerance of differing opinions. Consequently, some became hothouses of radical theological – and political – ideas. The denominations' views of education varied: the Presbyterians stressed the need for a well-educated ministry, whereas the Independents maintained that the spiritually, if not academically, gifted could preach the gospel. Roman Catholic priests were trained in seminaries abroad – at Douai, Lisbon, Rome, Seville and Valladolid – for their task in England. England was viewed as a *pays de mission* and its Catholic church was ruled by Vicars Apostolic, such as Bonaventure Giffard (1642–1734) and Richard

Challoner (1691–1781), a superb administrator. Until the end of the century, regulars – above all, Jesuits, but also Benedictines, Dominicans and Franciscans – outnumbered the secular clergy. The English seminary priests were assisted by the chaplains of the Catholic embassies in London and by the foreign Jesuits who came to England after their expulsion from France (1764) and Spain (1767), and after the society's suppression in 1773. The French Revolution's persecution of the Catholic church drove many *émigré* priests to England, though most eventually returned home.

Some Dissenting academies also educated those not intended for the ministry: Daniel Defoe, for example, attended the academy at Newington Green. A range of subjects besides classics and theology was favoured; history, mathematics, modern languages and science might form part of the curriculum. Under Queen Anne Tories and high churchmen denounced the academies as nurseries of sedition; and in 1714 the Tories passed a bill prohibiting Nonconformists from teaching – a measure designed to curtail an educated Dissenting ministry and to smash Presbyterianism. The Whigs, however, repealed this Schism Act in 1719, and the academies prospered; the Warrington Academy, in particular, achieved a dazzling reputation in the later eighteenth century. Indeed, some pious Anglicans sent their sons to the academies instead of the universities, with their reputation for debauchery. Teaching by Catholics was illegal until 1778, when the first Relief Act permitted it: before then, on paper, Catholic schoolmasters were liable to perpetual imprisonment. For their general and higher education, sons of the Catholic nobility and gentry were sent (also illegally) abroad: to the colleges at Douai and Dieulouard, and to the Jesuit college at St Omer until 1762, and later at Bruges and then Liège. Girls were sent to convent schools, such as that at Cambrai. In England the famous Sedgley Park school for boys in Staffordshire was opened in 1763; for girls there were convent schools at Hammersmith and York. Priests might provide some Catholic education for country children. The French Revolution brought the closure of the overseas English colleges and their re-establishment in England.

Free enquiry among the Dissenters fostered the growth of Arianism and Socinianism, both anti-Trinitarian doctrines. Arianism represented Christ as a subordinate deity to the Father; Socinianism denied Christ's divinity and pre-existence, and hence rejected the doctrine of the Atonement. The issues exploded when James Peirce, a minister to a Presbyterian congregation in Exeter, came under suspicion of Arianism in 1716 and later stated that he believed the Son and Holy Ghost to be divine persons, but subordinate to the Father. In 1719 London's Dissenting ministers met at Salters' Hall, where the majority of Independents and Particular Baptists, upholding Calvinism, insisted on subscription to Trinitarianism, while a majority of Presbyterians and General Baptists did not – thereby potentially allowing a slide into Unitarianism. Although less divisive, English Catholicism was also beset by tensions during the eighteenth century. Jansenism, and Clement XI's bull *Unigenitus* (1713) condemning it, caused disputes, not least at Douai. In Jacobite times there was a spectrum of opinion as to the degree to which a principled accommodation with the government was possible. In 1719 Earl Stanhope backed a scheme for a measure of toleration; but it ultimately foundered, chiefly because of disagreements about it among the Catholics themselves. There was unedifying friction between the secular and regular clergy. Late in the century the Cisalpines showed a marked suspicion of foreign Catholicism and undue interference from the papal curia. Calls for an elective episcopate elicited counter-blasts from John Milner (1752–1826).

From the Nonconformists' conflicts a distinct 'Rational Dissent' or Unitarianism emerged, eclipsing Arianism and maintaining a belief in God's absolute unity and the humanity of Christ. Although Unitarian worship was proscribed, the law was rarely enforced; and, in 1813, an act was passed 'to relieve persons who impugn the doctrine of the Holy Trinity from certain penalties'. After the Salters' Hall conference, significant numbers of Presbyterian pastors and congregations chose to espouse Unitarianism; and eventually most did. Similarly, concern about Trinitarian doctrine among the General Baptists took many of their ministers and congregations into Unitarianism; though the Particular Baptists, who lacked a central forum in which to debate the issues, were shielded from such divisive tendencies. Independency was little affected by anti-Trinitarian thinking, and, indeed, its numbers were swelled by Presbyterians alienated by the progress of such notions among their ministers. (Priestley's brutal Socinian language, in particular, could horrify: Christ, he declared, 'is as much a creature of God as a loaf of bread'.) In London, a Unitarian chapel was opened in Essex Street in 1774 by Theophilus Lindsey (1723–1808), formerly rector of Catterick, after parliament's rejection of the 1772 Feathers Tavern petition requesting the abolition of subscription to the Thirty-Nine Articles by Anglican clergymen. From 1782 Lindsey was assisted at Essex Street by John Disney (1746–1816), also formerly an Anglican parson; Disney became the chapel's sole minister after Lindsey's retirement in 1793. Attenders at the chapel included many fashionable, important and influential figures, notably the third duke of Grafton and Sir George Savile, MP for Yorkshire. Naturally the appeal of Unitarianism, with its spirit of daring enquiry and its exacting theology, was to gentlemen and intellectuals, not to the populace, unable to grasp the niceties of, and thinking behind, its doctrines.

Catholic priests sought to proselytize. They had some success, notably in the mid-1730s. In 1733 one Catholic cleric wrote of 'the incredible success we have had in bringing proselytes of all ranks to our communion', and another, Monox Hervey, working in London in 1730–4 and 1753–6, converted ninety Protestants. Protestants were dismayed by Catholic proselytizing in the 1730s and 1760s. Itinerant missioners aimed in particular to convert the inferior or middling sort of people. Old Dissent was initially suspicious of the Evangelical revival (though Doddridge felt differently). Introspective Calvinist pastors and congregations disliked Methodism's enthusiasm and facets of the Wesleys', or Whitefield's, theology; since Dissenting worship was legal only in licensed meeting houses, should ministers emulate Methodist preaching in barns and fields? Yet, in time, the Evangelical awakening revitalized the Independents and Particular Baptists. In 1770 the New Connection of General Baptists was created by Orthodox (Trinitarian) General Baptists, uniting the Evangelical Baptists, instituted by David Taylor at Barton-in-Fabis, Leicestershire, with Dan Taylor's Evangelical General Baptist churches; the Old Connection gradually joined the Unitarians. By 1800 the New Connection numbered 3,403 members. From the 1780s the Independents and Baptists used itinerant preachers and formed county associations in order to evangelize effectively. Some former Methodists also swelled Dissenting numbers. Lacking central ties, most of Whitefield's societies, and many of the countess of Huntingdon's, became Independent churches. Some Evangelical converts, disillusioned with the Church of England and angry at John Wesley's refusal to break with it, became Baptists or Independents.

The worship of the three Dissenting denominations was essentially similar. Congregations met for prayers and the exposition of scripture, to hear sermons (usually an hour long), and to celebrate monthly the Lord's Supper. There was increasing congregational singing, first of psalms and, as the century advanced, of hymns. Two Sunday services were held; at home there was family devotion. Fasts were organized for special occasions. As Quakers rejected liturgies and the sacraments, meetings lacked structure; though, increasingly, recognized 'public Friends' led worship. Dissenters' lives were strictly monitored: impure conduct incurred censure and, potentially, excommunication, though the practice of ministers and congregations varied. Breaches of discipline included neglect of worship, drunkenness, sexual lapses, malicious or loutish behaviour and, often, frivolous recreations. Like the Dissenters, Catholics set store by sermons, plainly delivered, though of course the mass was central to their worship. There was emphasis on regular Sunday services, less on the seasons and feasts. Priests heard confession and catechized children; days of abstinence were observed. Pilgrimages continued to St Winifred's shrine at Holywell (Flintshire). Catholics encouraged the nurturing of spirituality through prayer and meditation. But there was stress too on devout living in the world, following the tradition of St François de Sales. Dissenting ministers and Catholic priests alike deplored religious indifference and, eyeing different targets, denounced false doctrine. Both encouraged philanthropy.

When Edward Gibbon, as an undergraduate, was attracted to Catholicism, he had no difficulty in finding a Catholic bookseller in London. Catholic works were published abroad and, increasingly, in England. There were Bibles, editions of the church Fathers, breviaries, missals and small books of devotion. There were controversial works such as Challoner's *The Unerring Authority of the Catholick Church, in Matters of Faith* (1732) and *A Caveat against the Methodists* (1760). There were histories: Charles Dodd's *The Church History of England* (1737–42), Challoner's *Memoirs of Missionary Priests* (1741–2) and Joseph Berington's *The State and Behaviour of English Catholics, from the Reformation to the Year 1780* (1780). But the most enduring works were the devotional – notably Challoner's *Garden of the Soul* (1740) and the many reprints of Gother's works, such as *Instructions for Particular States and Conditions of Life* (1689). Dissenters too published much. Sermons rolled from the press. Most were mundane, a few explosive: when in 1789 the Arian Richard Price (1723–91) welcomed the French Revolution in his *Discourse on the Love of Our Country* (printed in 1790), Edmund Burke was appalled. Polemical works included sermons preached against popery in 1735 at Salters' Hall, and then published. The *Account of the Ministers . . . ejected by the Act of Uniformity* (1702) and *A Continuation of the Account* (1727) by Edmund Calamy III (1671–1732) illuminated the history of seventeenth-century Nonconformity. Guides to Christian living included Doddridge's *The Family Expositor* (1739–56) and *The Rise and Progress of Religion in the Soul* (1745). And there were the hymns of the Congregationalist Isaac Watts (1674–1748), the principal collections being *Hymns and Spiritual Songs* (1707) and *The Psalms of David* (1719). Sixteen editions of Watts's hymns were published during his lifetime.

Places of worship reflected the legal standing, status and theology of the congregations. Before 1689 Dissenters had largely worshipped in private houses, rented rooms or barns. After the Toleration Act's passage, congregations converted cottages into meeting houses or erected purpose-built ones. Most were simple buildings, light, with plain-glass windows and white walls. Pews ran along three sides of the building, and galleries might provide additional seating. Seating was segregated by sex and arranged according to the amount of pew-rent paid; sometimes important families had fine pews. Except in Quaker meeting houses, there was a pulpit, raised to emphasize the centrality of the Word, and before it stood a communion table. Some town meeting houses were impressive and stately, but even humble buildings doubtless inspired pride and affection in those who paid for their erection and maintenance. Until 1791 Catholic chapels were illegal, though increasingly ignored by magistrates. In country districts, services were traditionally held in attics or upper rooms in gentry homes. As the century proceeded they were moved downstairs (the genteel wanted minimal intrusion) or separate chapels were erected. In London worship was conducted in a variety of settings: in garrets, for the Irish poor; in a hired room, as at the Ship Tavern, Holborn; in small mass-houses; in the embassy chapels – most splendidly, in the beautiful Sardinian. In provincial towns there were houses containing a chapel and a priest's home. As Catholic confidence increased in the 1770s chapels became more elaborate; that at Wardour Castle, Wiltshire, was decorated in flamboyant Italian style. The Relief Act of 1791 legalized Catholic places of worship.

Broadsides against Christianity itself were launched by the Deists, believers in a supreme being quite unlike the Judaeo-Christian God. Espousing Newton's conception of a mechanistic universe governed by immutable laws, they saw proof of the deity's existence in nature, but doubted notions of divine intervention in human affairs subsequent to the creation. They were distrustful of revelation. Thus, in his *Christianity not Mysterious* (1696), John Toland (1670–1722) maintained the existence of a benevolent creator but rejected revelation as, for him, reason was the only foundation of all certitude. The Deists also distrusted prophecy. Anthony Collins (1676–1729), for instance, in his *Discourse of the Grounds and Reasons of the Christian Religion* (1724), denied that the Old Testament prophesied the events of the New, preferring an allegorical to a literal reading. Deists scorned belief in particular providences and miracles, suspensions of physical laws. The free-thinking divine Conyers Middleton (1683–1750) denied the evidence for miracles after Apostolic times. (For David Hume, with a reputation for atheism, human testimony was worthless when weighed against the evidence for unvarying natural laws.) Doubtful of revelation, and emphasizing the unreliability of the scriptural texts (as demonstrated by biblical scholars), Deists decried religious dogma, insisting that unprovable doctrines should not be imposed by clerical or state authority.

For Matthew Tindal (1655–1733), author of *Christianity as Old as the Creation* (1730), true religion was simply 'a constant disposition of mind to do all the good we can', thereby answering the creator's purposes. Deists judged religions by utilitarian criteria. They praised religions whose teaching (including the promise of reward or punishment in the afterlife) inculcated moral virtue and promoted social harmony, fostering right conduct towards others, learning, tolerance, civic duty and patriotism. Some eastern religions were lauded for their social utility. So was the paganism of ancient Rome: in this spirit, Edward Gibbon, in *The Decline and Fall of the Roman Empire* (1776–88), wrote that the 'various modes of worship, which prevailed in the Roman world, were all considered by the people, as equally true; by the philosopher, as equally false; and by the magistrate, as equally useful'. By contrast, the Christian churches' failings were manifold in the Deists' eyes. Priests encouraged superstition so as to promote the masses' credulous dependence upon them; by such 'priestcraft', they obtained material wealth and temporal power. Christianity divided men and nations; the intolerance of medieval Catholicism, and later of Protestantism and Counter-Reformation Catholicism, had spawned persecution, civil strife and wars. More generally, clerical obscurantism stifled reason and intellectual enquiry.

Politics

The politics of both the Catholic and Dissenting minorities gave governments cause for concern at different points in the century. Until at least 1746 Catholics were perceived as resolute supporters of the exiled Catholic Stuart dynasty. Catholics formed between two-thirds and three-quarters of the English rebel army in 1715. In the '15 and the '45 rebellions, the penal laws were activated. Following the '15's suppression, the property of Catholic rebels was sequestrated by the government and in 1723, after the Atterbury plot's discovery (in which Catholic involvement was, in fact, minimal), a levy of £100,000 was imposed on the community. Yet by 1745 Catholic Jacobitism was largely sentimental: as Berington noted in his *State and Behaviour of English Catholics*, very few Catholics were engaged in the rebellion. When James Edward Stuart died in 1766, the Vatican recognized George III's title and, by the late 1770s, leading politicians regarded Catholics as very dutiful and loyal subjects. The French Revolution's assault on the Catholic church further linked Catholicism with loyalism.

The Protestant Dissenters maintained their links with the Whig party from the seventeenth into the eighteenth centuries and were naturally unswerving supporters of the Hanoverian succession. In 1715 there were Dissenting ministers in Lancashire who encouraged their congregations to assist the government's troops against the Jacobites; in 1745 John Wiche, Baptist minister at Salisbury, declared that 'as *Christians*, as *Protestants*, as *true Englishmen*', his flock's duty to George II was unquestionable. Later in the century, however, there was Nonconformist agitation – chiefly from the Radical Dissenters – for civil equality in law, the abolition of subscription to Trinitarian doctrine by ministers and schoolmasters, and the ending of the church–state alliance. There was Dissenting support for Wilkes and demands for parliamentary reform. From the 1760s to the 1780s most leading Dissenting ministers were hostile to the government's American policy and the war; Richard Price's *Observations on the Nature of Civil Liberty* (1776) sold 60,000 copies. In the late 1780s and in 1790 Dissenters campaigned for the repeal of the Test and Corporation Acts, and the radically minded welcomed the French Revolution (they were prominent in the Society for Constitutional Information and the London Revolution Society). Conservative observers denounced the Dissenters as potential subversives or revolutionaries. But many Dissenters had little interest in politics and orthodox congregations feared changes that might encourage the growth of anti-Trinitarianism. The French Revolution alarmed most Dissenters, with their leaders and the Dissenting Deputies (formed as a pressure group in 1732) producing loyal addresses to George III.

Among the populace there was much religious bigotry. Anti-Catholic sentiment was grounded on concerns that the papacy might intervene in domestic politics and on doctrinal tenets; on a fear of potentially or actively hostile Catholic kingdoms; and on a horror of 'popish cruelty'. For Hanoverian militants, Catholic Jacobitism was intolerable. In 1745–6, during or after the Young Pretender's rising, Protestant mobs menaced Catholics and attacked mass-houses at Gateshead, Liverpool, Newcastle-upon-Tyne, Ormskirk, Preston, Stokesley (Yorkshire) and Sunderland. In June 1780, following demands for the 1778 Relief Act's repeal by the English Protestant Association, headed by Lord George Gordon, London experienced a week of colossal 'No Popery!' rioting. Gordon's subsequent conversion to Judaism produced much anti-Semitic ribaldry, but that was minor compared to the savage anti-Semitic press campaign which had followed the passing, in 1753, of the Jewish Naturalization Act, permitting parliament to naturalize individual Jews. So great was the outcry that the 'Jew bill' was repealed later in the same year. Protestant Dissenters also sometimes faced popular hostility. In 1710 support for the high church Dr Henry Sacheverell, who had denounced Dissent from the pulpit, unleashed massive anti-Dissenter rioting in the capital and smaller disturbances elsewhere. As ardent Hanoverian supporters Dissenters were the victims of Jacobite mobs: in 1715 over thirty meeting houses were ransacked in Lancashire and the west midlands. During the French Revolution, militant loyalists and 'Church and King' mobs targeted Dissenters as a dangerous fifth column. In July 1791 anti-Dissenter riots erupted in Birmingham: meeting houses were wrecked; Priestley's home and laboratory were destroyed; and the houses of other Dissenters were pillaged. Thereafter, Rational Dissent declined sharply. Other anti-Dissenter riots soon occurred elsewhere.

Local circumstances could mitigate hostility. Early in the century it was noted that at Norbury in Derbyshire the Fitzherberts, Catholic aristocrats, were unassailable, and nothing could be done about their priest's proselytizing. In 1733 there was a threat of renewed anti-Catholic persecution in the north, following some conversions. In 1745 a letter was found near Poole in Dorset, apparently revealing Jacobite scheming by a local Catholic gentleman; but the authorities dismissed it as malicious and improbable. In villages hostile stereotypes seemed inapplicable to neighbours and relations; there was therefore a large measure of practical toleration. The Protestant Dissenters sought political power in the localities and aimed to influence parliamentary elections in some corporation and freeman boroughs. Presbyterians and some Independents (but not Baptists) might evade the Test and Corporation Acts' provisions and qualify for office, or election to corporations, by occasional conformity – i.e., intermittently taking the Anglican sacrament. In 1711 the Tory government outlawed this – though the practice was justifiable as an expression of Dissenting–Anglican fellowship; but, in 1719, the Whigs repealed the Occasional Conformity Act. Thereafter there was a de facto acceptance of officeholding by Dissenters, and their service on corporations: the Act for Quieting and Establishing Corporations (1719) and indemnity acts, passed almost annually from 1727, drew the teeth of the Test and Corporation Acts. In any case, some Dissenters simply risked the hazard of prosecution. Dissenters dominated politics in some towns – notably Coventry, Nottingham and Portsmouth – and had considerable power in others, such as Bristol.

They, with low church Anglicans, formed the bedrock of Whig support in the constituencies. Eighteenth-century Dissenting MPs, or their supporters, were careful to cultivate the low church electorate.

Both the Catholics and Protestant Dissenters – notably the Protestant Dissenting Deputies – lobbied the powerful in support of their interests. Catholics, led by the duke of Norfolk, made weighty intercessions with the considerable men of the House of Commons against a proposal in 1706 to tighten the penal laws. Following the '15 rebellion and the Atterbury plot, prominent Catholics desperately sought to placate the government. The envoys of Catholic states intervened on behalf of the Catholic minority and maintained close ties with its leaders. The 1778 Relief Act was secured by the negotiations of a group of Catholic gentlemen, acting independently of the clergy. The skilful negotiations with the Younger Pitt's government of a second Catholic Committee, chaired by Lord Petre, steered by Charles Butler (1750–1832) and including clerics, produced the granting of official toleration in 1791. Parliament could prove hostile to Dissenters' calls for change: was not toleration, and connivance at officeholding, enough? The Lords in 1736 rejected a bill promoted by the Quakers to alter the method of tithe collection. A petition of 1792 to legalize Unitarianism was rejected by the Commons. Above all, parliament refused to repeal the Test and Corporation Acts in 1736, 1739, 1787, 1789 and 1790. None the less, in 1722 it was made easier for Quakers to affirm rather than swear oaths, as their beliefs required. Although in 1772 and 1773 the Lords rejected relief bills to exempt Dissenting ministers and schoolmasters from subscription to the doctrinal parts of the Thirty-Nine Articles, a bill effecting this was passed in 1779. Dissenters not only lobbied for themselves but also supported liberal causes, notably the abolition of the slave trade. The penal reformer John Howard (1726?–90) was a Dissenter.

Under the Hanoverians politicians' treatment of religious minorities was careful and usually well judged, in step with political realities and educated opinion. Regarding the Catholics, parliament adjusted the penal code following Jacobitism's demise and gave a legal basis to the de facto toleration effected by justices of the peace, juries and judges in the later eighteenth century. Faced with hostility the legislature might retreat, but could stand firm. The Jewish Naturalization Act of 1753 violated the sense of the people and raised discontents, and was repealed accordingly; but in 1780, parliament refused even to modify the first Catholic Relief Act following the Gordon Riots. As for the Dissenters, politicians after 1714 maintained, and extended, their toleration. From 1723 Nonconformists even received the *regium donum*, a crown grant for their ministers. But parliament repeatedly refused to repeal the Test and Corporation Acts, because it saw them as a formal expression of the constitution's essential Anglican character.

Conclusion

E. P. Thompson once disparagingly contrasted the self-preserving retreat of Dissent with the positive energy of Puritanism. Similarly, the Catholic Committees' patient negotiations and the Catholics' armed support for the '15 were clearly different things. Yet the danger posed to the established church proved ultimately to lie less in Catholic Jacobitism or a reborn Dissenting radicalism than in the increase, at first slow, then more rapid, of non-Anglican worshippers from the later eighteenth century. In 1800 this danger was not pronounced in numerical terms, but the rising trend was ominous; and, after John Wesley's death in 1791, the Methodists formally broke with the Church of England and drifted into Dissent. By 1811 Evangelical Dissent was proliferating so markedly that Viscount Sidmouth proposed a bill to check its expansion. It was not enacted; and Nonconformity continued to grow, spawning a number of new sects. Catholicism burgeoned too in the nineteenth century, boosted by converts from Protestantism and by considerable Irish immigration. Badgered by the Whig government in the 1830s, the privileged position of the Church of England was under threat. Providentially or otherwise, the Church of England remained the established church; but its standing was horribly bruised when the religious census of 1851 showed that the Dissenting and Catholic churches commanded the allegiance of nearly half of those attending religious services in England.

FURTHER READING

Bossy, John: *The English Catholic Community, 1570–1850* (London, 1975).
Bradley, James E.: *Religion, Revolution and English Radicalism: Nonconformity in Eighteenth-Century Politics and Society* (Cambridge, 1990).
Clark, J. C. D.: *English Society 1688–1832: Ideology, Social Structure and Political Practice during the Ancien Régime* (1985; rev. edn, Cambridge, 2000).
Duffy, Eamon (ed.): *Challoner and his Church: A Catholic Bishop in Georgian England* (London, 1981).
Haydon, Colin: *Anti-Catholicism in Eighteenth-Century England c.1714–80: A Political and Social Study* (Manchester, 1994).
Israel, Jonathan I.: *European Jewry in the Age of Mercantilism, 1550–1750* (Oxford, 1985).
Mullett, Michael A.: *Catholicism in Britain and Ireland, 1558–1829* (Basingstoke, 1998).
Perry, Thomas W.: *Public Opinion, Propaganda and Politics in Eighteenth-Century England: A Study of the Jew Bill of 1753* (Cambridge, MA, 1962).
Redwood, John: *Reason, Ridicule and Religion: The Age of Enlightenment in England, 1660–1750* (London, 1976).
Rowlands, Marie B. (ed.): *English Catholics of Parish and Town, 1558–1778* (Totton, 1999).
Spufford, Margaret (ed.): *The World of Rural Dissenters, 1520–1725* (Cambridge, 1995).
Watts, Michael R.: *The Dissenters*, vol. 1: *From the Reformation to the French Revolution* (Oxford, 1978).

Chapter Nineteen

Methodism and the Evangelical Revival

G. M. Ditchfield

Evangelicalism, of which Methodism was an important feature, was (and remains) a complex and far from an exclusively British phenomenon. Although it is best understood as a series of spontaneous revivals, notably in Germany, North America and different parts of the British Isles, there were significant common features. Evangelicalism was primarily a Protestant phenomenon, which reaffirmed the fundamental Reformation values of the supremacy of scripture and the right of individual judgement in religious matters. It won relatively little open support in Catholic Europe. The clearest and most accessible definition has been provided by David Bebbington, who identified four central Evangelical characteristics. These characteristics are biblicism; crucicentrism, with the doctrine of the atoning death of Christ as the means of the forgiveness of sins and the reconciliation of God with man; conversionism, with its insistence on the necessity of a new birth, frequently marked by a conversion experience; and activism, which involved a compulsion to share with others the message of the gospel. To this list may be added a deep pessimism as to the corruption of human nature based on a profound belief in original sin; an acceptance of the human facility of reason but not an excessive rationality which might lead to scepticism and unbelief; and a continuous process of self-analysis. John Wesley kept a detailed journal in which he sought to account to God for every moment; Howell Harris, rightly described as the first and most eloquent of the Welsh Methodists, compiled diaries of which no fewer than 284 volumes survive.

Although much attention in British historiography has focused upon the 1730s, when Methodist field-preaching began on a substantial scale, the origins of the revival may be found in a series of separate developments over the previous half-century. W. R. Ward has identified the early stirrings of revival in the crisis that engulfed Protestantism in late seventeenth-century Europe. By the 1690s the success of the Counter-Reformation had reduced the Protestant states of Europe to the north-western fringes of the continent. At the same time, Protestant minorities in Catholic states encountered a greater degree of persecution, of which the best-known example was the expulsion of the Huguenots from France after Louis XIV's revocation of the Edict of Nantes in 1685. Part of the response to this perceived threat was an attempt to reinvigorate the Protestant religion, especially in Martin Luther's home state of Saxony, with an emphasis upon inward experience, a domestic approach to worship and lay participation. Much of this emphasis came from the German Pietists, a group whose priorities included a deeply personal relationship with God sealed by a 'new birth'. Two key figures in the Pietist movement were Philipp Jakob Spener (1635–1705) and August Hermann Francke (1663–1727). The latter became professor of theology at the University of Halle and the philanthropic institutions which he helped to establish there acquired an international reputation. Francke's printing press provided biblical translations in many European languages and stimulated a response among the Protestant minorities in the Habsburg empire and elsewhere. The social inclusiveness of Pietist house meetings, and their lay involvement, anticipated several Methodist practices in the British Isles. One common feature was a quasi-democratic undercurrent which caused alarm in official circles. In the 1690s the Lutheran authorities in Saxony expelled some of the Pietists from their territory. But Pietists found succour in other German Protestant states and by several means their message was propagated within and beyond continental Europe.

The later years of the seventeenth century and the early years of the eighteenth witnessed an immense Protestant diaspora. The displacement of the Huguenots, the flight of refugees from the Palatinate of the Rhine during the War of the Spanish Succession and the expulsion of the Lutheran minority from the diocese of the Catholic archbishop of Salzburg in 1731 all served to intensify the challenge to the Protestant religion and the urgent need for renewal. It is notable that several leading Evangelical clergy within the Church of England came from Huguenot backgrounds; William Romaine and Charles Edward de Coetlogon are among the best-known examples, while the Salzburgers helped to establish settlements in the newly founded British colony in Georgia. Other prominent Methodists, such as Vincent Perronet, vicar of Shoreham, and John Fletcher, Wesley's designated successor, originated from Protestant communities in Switzerland. Above all, perhaps, the Moravian church, with its pre-Reformation origins in central Europe, its status as an ancient Episcopal church and its revival in Saxony under the leadership of Count Zinzendorf (1700–60), played the largest part in bringing the ideas and fervour of the German revival to Britain and its colonies. The willingness to travel and sometimes the necessity of emigration were considerable factors in the geographical extent of Evangelicalism. One of the legacies of this Protestant diaspora was a profound anti-Catholicism, evident in Evangelical writing and preaching, in Britain and elsewhere.

Evangelicalism in effect consisted of a series of independent and spontaneous revivals in diverse and separate locations, brought together by print culture and improved communications by land and sea. In 1734 Jonathan Edwards (1703–58), the Congregational minister at Northampton, Massachusetts, helped to set in motion a series of highly emotional conversions, perhaps prompted by a number of sudden and unforeseen deaths, and his preaching drew widespread attention throughout New England. Although criticized in some quarters for excessive emotionalism, Edwards, too, acquired an international reputation with his publication of *A Faithful Narrative of the Surprising Work of God in the Conversion of many hundred souls in Northampton* (1737). He emphasized the local and specific causes of these events, which owed nothing to developments in continental Europe. In 1740 George

Whitefield (1714–70), attracted by Edwards's success, visited New England and subsequently helped to transform the limited range of Edwards's conversions into a much wider phenomenon in North America which came to be known as the 'Great Awakening'. News of the work of Edwards spread rapidly to Britain. It came to the attention, for instance, of William McCulloch, Presbyterian minister of Cambuslang (Lanarkshire). McCulloch presided over a brief but spectacular revival in 1742 during which he recorded the experiences of his converts. Many of them, like those of the German Pietists, were drawn from the artisan, servant and unskilled classes; a significant number were women. Quite independently of these developments, a revival had begun in Wales. Howell Harris (1714–73) underwent a conversion experience which began on Palm Sunday 1735 at Talgarth and which led him, although he was never in holy orders, to an effective career as an itinerant preacher. Harris's conversion owed much to the Anglican spirituality in which he had been brought up, and the painful awareness of sin with which it was accompanied led him to seek an immediate personal reformation, with intensive prayer and self-denial. In cooperation with Daniel Rowland, the curate of Llangeitho, Harris not only promoted revival in Wales before the open-air preaching of the Wesleys began in England, but helped to give it an Anglican leadership.

Although these revivals were clearly autonomous and owed much to specific local conditions, they became connected through the vital medium of print culture. News of their progress was reported in detail across the Atlantic and between Britain and the European continent. This was a period of significant expansion of the newspaper and periodical press. McCulloch publicized his activities through his *Glasgow Weekly History*, while Whitefield published seven volumes of *Journals*, recording his missionary progresses, between 1738 and 1741. The personal narrative became a staple product of Evangelicalism; both in terms of the recounting of personal experiences and the description of preaching campaigns, it was a crucial means of propaganda. Revivals were attributed by participants to outpourings of the divine grace, for which prayers could be offered; when such prayers appeared to be answered, revivals acquired the character of self-fulfilling prophecies.

The international dimensions of, and explanations for, Evangelicalism cast considerable doubt on the once-fashionable explanation for the revival in England, which stressed the pastoral deficiencies, materialism and spiritual aridity of the Church of England in the Georgian period. A process of cautious revisionism, identifying the conscientious parochial attention and charitable commitment of the bulk of the Anglican clergy, was begun by Norman Sykes in the 1930s and received reinforcement in 2000 from Jeremy Gregory's detailed analysis of the diocese of Canterbury and William Gibson's examination of the church's benign cultural influence. An alleged Anglican inadequacy can hardly be held accountable for developments in Germany or Scotland. A more plausible explanation for the revival is a reaction against a tendency towards a rather dry, intellectualized manner of preaching that was common among the Protestant Dissenting denominations in England, as well as within the established church. Some of that preaching appeared to countenance a heterodox approach to such fundamentals of Christianity as the doctrine of the Trinity. Evangelicalism strongly reaffirmed those fundamentals and was sharply critical of theological tendencies such as Arianism and Socinianism, which questioned the Trinity and even the divinity of Christ. In his book *The Deity of Christ* (1785), Henry

Venn of Huddersfield wrote of Socinianism as 'poison'. There were, however, more positive cultural factors. Prominent among them, as identified in a key essay by John Walsh, was the legacy of spirituality and lay piety bequeathed by the late seventeenth-century Church of England. After its restoration in 1660, and particularly after the legal toleration accorded to Protestant Dissenters in 1689, the church was obliged to compete with other Protestant sects for the allegiance of the population. One of its responses to that challenge was a re-emphasis on voluntary activity, personal moral reform in the private sphere coupled with reformation of manners in the public sphere, personal asceticism and a high devotional standard among the clergy. It found expression in a series of small religious societies for private Bible study and voluntary activity. Many early Evangelicals emerged from high church Anglican backgrounds, where such values were highly regarded. A formative text for such people was the Nonjuror William Law's *Serious Call to a Devout and Holy Life* (1728). Another 'tap-root' of the English revival was the endurance of seventeenth-century Puritan values, notably the sense of a highly personal relationship with God, intense self-analysis and lay participation. The moderate Puritanism represented by Richard Baxter survived in the spirituality of many early eighteenth-century Dissenters, some of whom, notably William Bagshawe (1628–1702), the 'Apostle of the Peak', in Derbyshire, undertook itinerant preaching several decades before the rise of Methodism. In his *Dictionary of the English Language*, first published in 1755, Dr Johnson defined a Methodist as 'one of a new kind of Puritans lately arisen, so called from their profession to live by rules and in constant method'.

The expression 'Methodist' was first applied to the leading members of the 'holy club' which was formed at Oxford University in 1729–30. Some of its members, notably John and Charles Wesley, were Tory in their politics and one, John Clayton of Manchester, had unambiguous Jacobite sympathies. It is not fanciful to regard the early Oxford Methodists as reacting against the political domination of the Church of England by the Whig regime of Sir Robert Walpole. They urged personal reformation rather than political reform, and their priorities involved ministering to the poor, visiting the sick and consoling the imprisoned. They did not yet engage, however, in the field-preaching for which Methodism later became famous. It was not until 1735 that Whitefield experienced a 'new birth' and not until May 1738 that John Wesley felt his heart 'strangely warmed' at the celebrated Moravian meeting at Aldersgate Street in London. Indeed, the Moravian contribution to Wesley's own 'conversion' cannot be overestimated. He had been favourably impressed by Moravians during his unsuccessful mission to Georgia in 1735–7 and it was Moravian influence that led him to transform his rather formal religious observance into a genuine religion of the heart, when, in his own words, 'I felt I did trust in Christ and Christ alone for salvation; and an assurance was given me that He had taken away *my* sins, even *mine*, and saved *me* from the law of sin and death' (Rack 1989: 144). One of Wesley's early associates at Oxford, John Gambold, subsequently joined the Moravians and became the first English-born Moravian bishop.

Methodism emerged in the first place from the Church of England. It enjoyed the support of a significant number of Anglican clergymen, whose conversions were quite independent of the efforts of the Wesleys. They included John Berridge of Everton, William Grimshaw of Haworth and Henry Venn of Huddersfield. Their assistance was vital, since many clergy were suspicious of Methodist preachers and denied them access to their pulpits. As parish clergy, however, they were restricted in their ability to travel. John Wesley, by contrast, as a fellow of Lincoln College, Oxford (an office which he held until his marriage in 1751), was never a parochial clergyman and his boast that the world was his parish became something of a legend. Early in 1739 Whitefield invited him to join his preaching campaign in the Bristol area and he followed Whitefield and Harris in spreading the gospel in open-air meetings. Possibly the unusually harsh weather in 1739–40, the sharp increase in food prices and public anxiety occasioned by the outbreak of war with Spain helped to concentrate attention on matters of the spirit and the path to salvation. Some of the earliest conversions were made among those who had suffered economic hardship. The colliers of Kingswood, which became the site of the famous Methodist school, were among the first Methodists, and Bristol, too, became an early centre of Methodism.

The traditional image of Methodism presents Whitefield as the star preacher and public performer, John Wesley as the vital organizer as well as preacher, and Charles Wesley as poet and hymn writer. Recent research has broadly confirmed this impression. Whitefield travelled extensively in America as well as Britain and died there, exhausted, in 1770. He drew immense crowds to his meetings. On 14–17 June 1755 the *Whitehall Evening Post*, not a friendly commentator, estimated that he 'made an Harangue to 30,000 people' in Moorfields, where he had a chapel. Wesley, although he covered the length and breadth of the British Isles, including Ireland and the Isle of Man, and made forays to continental Europe, never returned to America after his Georgia expedition and was always in a position to keep a tight control over his British followers. Many of those followers were lay men and women, since the bulk of the Anglican clergy were suspicious of his methods. The clergy particularly deplored the 'democratic' implications whereby unlettered lay preachers bypassed the educated church hierarchy in order to bring the offer of salvation directly to the people, and in the process frequently berated the upper orders for neglect of their religious duties. Wesley himself had to deny that he was a Leveller on the one hand or a Jacobite – a particularly serious charge in the 1740s – on the other. Recognizing that his followers needed firm, indeed authoritarian, leadership, by the mid-1740s he had organized them into a hierarchy of local societies, regional circuits and districts. A national conference, which met annually, was composed of lay preachers chosen personally by Wesley and became the main instrument of his domination. In the local societies Methodist adherents were divided into bands and classes for Bible study, self-analysis and possible reproof or even expulsion for backsliding. The rigour of Methodist discipline is one reason why the number of Wesley's followers seems surprisingly low, in comparison with the influence attributed to the movement. In 1767 there were only 25,911 Methodists in the British Isles (22,410 of them in England) and there were only 72,476 at the time of Wesley's death in 1791 (Rack 1989: 237, 437). These figures, however, reflect only formally registered adherents and not the thousands who heard and were influenced by Methodist preaching.

Dr Field's analysis of Methodist membership in the second half of the eighteenth century shows that it was drawn disproportionately from skilled artisans and craftsmen, particularly in textiles, manufacturing and mining. Methodism seems to have appealed particularly to those whose occupations involved risk and danger, such as Cornish tin miners and fishermen. It also drew support from soldiers, either engaged in continental operations or in garrison towns in Britain; in Kent it won numerous adherents among the dockyard shipwrights and carpenters at Sheerness. Although Wesley himself showed extraordinary charity towards the poor, and although many Methodists were close enough to real poverty to feel or to fear its impact, Methodism did not win much support among the destitute. A notable feature of its membership is that more than half of Methodist adherents were female, with a predominance of single women over single men. Methodism offered women a role, notably in domestic visiting but also at times as preachers, which was not available to them elsewhere. Some female preachers, such as Ann Trip in Leeds, acquired considerable reputations. Methodism certainly provided opportunities for a small number of wealthy women, of whom the best known is Selina, countess of Huntingdon (1707–91), to endow Methodist chapels. Methodism tended to flourish where Anglican provision was weakest, such as upland areas where parishes were largest, and where displacements of population, provoked by changing patterns of employment, had occurred.

Methodism, however, attracted at least as much hostility as support. Many of its early meetings were characterized by a conversionist zeal that bordered on fanaticism, with convulsions and apparent disregard for social propriety. The derogatory term 'enthusiasm', defined by Dr Johnson as 'a vain belief of private revelation', was frequently applied to them and in 1749 the bishop of Exeter, George Lavington, published a fiercely anti-Methodist tract entitled *The Enthusiasm of Methodists and Papists compared*. In many communities Methodists were regarded as menacing outsiders and encountered physical violence; at least one of their itinerants was killed by a mob. Their use of ill-educated, sometimes female, preachers seemed to challenge the social order. Moreover, when Methodists attacked the pleasures of the poor, such as gambling and drinking, they could easily be portrayed as killjoys. One of their responses to such stigmatization was to take over and christianize ancient 'pagan' festivals and to introduce an element of spectacle, such as the Moravian 'lovefeast', or even of entertainment. Even more serious, however, were divisions within Evangelicalism itself. In the 1740s Wesley broke with the Moravians over their alleged 'antinomianism', while the Welsh revival was hindered by an equally bitter controversy between Harris and Rowland. Wesley and Whitefield had for many years differed over doctrines of salvation. Wesley took the Arminian position, which held that Christ had died for all humanity and that salvation was open to all who genuinely sought it; Whitefield preached the predestinarian insistence that Christ died only for the elect. Arminians argued that the Calvinist position nullified efforts to gain conversions; Calvinists retorted that salvation depended on God's free grace for the elect, not the free will of corrupt humanity. After Whitefield's death the controversy took on a more bitter form; Wesley and John Fletcher both wrote anti-Calvinist tracts and the *Arminian Magazine*, founded by Wesley in 1778, kept the dispute alive. The countess of Huntingdon sympathized with Whitefield's position; her followers split from Wesley's and in the early 1780s left the Church of England to form a separate Dissenting sect. The Calvinist theology of the Presbyterian Church of Scotland restricted Wesley's converts north of the border to very low numbers.

The major problem for Methodism at the end of the eighteenth century was its relationship with the Church of England. Wesley was insistent that his followers should not secede from the established church, but the need for preachers in England, Scotland and North America led him to ordain a small number of men as Methodist clergy in the 1780s. This was a clear gesture towards separation and after Wesley's death in 1791 there were further moves in that direction. The demand that preachers be allowed to administer the sacraments, and the association of some Methodists with the radical ideas of the 1790s, helped to turn Methodism into a distinctive Dissenting denomination, although this process was far from complete by 1800. A more radical, plebeian group broke away from Wesley's followers in the mid-1790s to form the 'New Connection'; it was strongest in the midlands and northwest of England. Other groups which left the main body during the first decade of the nineteenth century combined to form the more durable 'Primitive Methodists'. Wesley's own political conservatism – seen especially in his support for George III and Lord North at the time of the American rebellion – has tended to obscure the genuine radicalism of other Methodists, such as Samuel Bradburn of Manchester. There is reason to question the validity of the celebrated thesis which ascribes Britain's avoidance of revolution in the 1790s to the socially and politically conservative influence of Evangelicalism. It is doubtful whether Evangelical, and particularly Methodist, numbers were sufficient to exert such an influence. Admittedly, Methodist membership increased at a faster rate than that of the population of Britain as a whole, but it still formed barely 1 per cent of the population in 1801. Even if sympathetic attenders, as well as formal members, are included, a total of no more than 210,000 to 300,000 in 1791 is cautiously suggested by Dr Rack (Rack 1989: 438).

The longer-term impact of Evangelicalism upon British society was immense, however. Methodism became the largest Nonconformist denomination in the nineteenth century. Many Evangelicals, clerical and lay, continued to exercise a theological and broader cultural influence within the Church of England. The older Nonconformist denominations took up Evangelical ideas and methods. From the later eighteenth century Evangelical values began to win acceptance in elite circles. Roger Anstey has demonstrated the Evangelical contribution to the successful movement for the abolition of the British slave trade in 1806–7, while Boyd Hilton has claimed for Evangelicalism a major role in the development of laissez-faire ideology. One of the most powerful Scottish Evangelicals, Thomas Chalmers (1780–1847), was the inspiration for a new social gospel of moral paternalism. Most important, perhaps, was the ability of Evangelicalism to transform the lives of numerous ordinary individuals. Few documents bear the hallmark of the Evangelical obsession with time and personal accountability more firmly than the diary of W. E. Gladstone. If, at times, Evangelicalism combined a morbid obsession with sin and a stultifying sobriety, it also promoted enterprise, application and a spirit of hope.

FURTHER READING

Anstey, Roger T.: *The Atlantic Slave Trade and British Abolition 1760–1810* (London, 1975).

Bebbington, D. W.: *Evangelicalism in Modern Britain: A History from the 1730s to the 1980s* (London, 1989).

Ditchfield, G. M.: *The Evangelical Revival* (London, 1998).

Field, C. D.: 'The social composition of English Methodism to 1830: a membership analysis', *Bulletin of the John Rylands University Library of Manchester*, 76 (1994), pp. 153–69.

Gibson, William: *The Church of England 1688–1832: Unity and Accord* (London, 2001).

Gregory, Jeremy: *Restoration, Reformation and Reform, 1660–1828: Archbishops of Canterbury and their Diocese* (Oxford, 2000).
Hempton, David: *Methodism and Politics in British Society 1750–1850* (London, 1984).
Hilton, Boyd: *The Age of Atonement: The Influence of Evangelicalism on Social and Economic Thought 1785–1865* (Oxford, 1991).
Podmore, Colin: *The Moravian Church in England, 1728–1760* (Oxford, 1998).
Rack, Henry D.: *Reasonable Enthusiast: John Wesley and the Rise of Methodism* (London, 1989).
Sykes, Norman: *Church and State in England in the Eighteenth Century* (Cambridge, 1934).
Tudor, G.: *Howell Harris: From Conversion to Separation 1735–1750* (Cardiff, 2000).
Walsh, J. D.: 'Origins of the Evangelical revival', in G. V. Bennett and J. D. Walsh (eds), *Essays in Modern English Church History: In Memory of Norman Sykes* (London, 1966).
Walsh, J. D.: *John Wesley, 1703–1791: A Bicentennial Tribute* (London, 1994).
Ward, W. R.: *The Protestant Evangelical Awakening* (Cambridge, 1992).
Watts, Michael R.: *The Dissenters*, vol. 1: *From the Reformation to the French Revolution* (Oxford, 1978).

CHAPTER TWENTY

Religion in Scotland

STEWART J. BROWN

Eighteenth-century Scottish religion was infused with the spirit of Presbyterianism. Throughout the century a large majority of the Scottish people adhered to the Presbyterian Church of Scotland, the church by law established. They were taught from childhood the strict Calvinist doctrines of the Westminster Confession of Faith, including the awesome majesty of God and the predestined eternal fate of each soul. Their worship was defined by the Westminster Directory, giving emphasis to preaching, scripture readings and extempore prayer. Their piety was intensely Bible-based. Their national church was governed not by bishops, but by a hierarchy of representative ecclesiastical courts, made up of ministers and elders. Their national identity was shaped by the struggles and the martyrdom of the seventeenth-century Covenanters.

The Presbyterian Church of Scotland differed fundamentally from the Anglican establishment in England and Wales. It was indeed an anomaly that an eighteenth-century state should have two distinct established churches, but it was an anomaly that the British state had been reluctantly forced to accept. When the Reformation had come to Scotland in 1560, the country was an independent kingdom. The Reformation had gained broad popular support in Scotland, and had been pursued *against* the opposition of the crown. Scotland's reformers had looked for their doctrinal and ecclesiastical models not to Canterbury and the English Reformation, but to the Geneva of John Calvin. While initially prepared to accept a version of episcopacy, by the later 1570s the Scottish reformers embraced Presbyterianism. In 1603 Scotland's king, James VI, acceded to the throne of England as James I, and England and Scotland were united under a single crown. James and his son, Charles I, sought to strengthen this union by moving the Scottish church towards convergence with the Episcopal Church of England. Scottish Presbyterians, however, resisted such efforts. Their resistance culminated in a popular rising in Scotland in 1637–8, under the banner of the National Covenant, which by the early 1640s plunged Britain and Ireland into revolution and civil war, and brought the execution of Charles I and the establishment of the Commonwealth in 1649. When the monarchy was restored in 1660, Charles II reinstated episcopacy in the national churches of both Scotland and

England, and revived the effort to move the Scottish church towards convergence with that of England. Again, this was met by violent resistance from the Presbyterian Covenanters. The state, in turn, waged brutal war on the Covenanters. In the 'killing time' of the 1680s, Covenanters worshipped in secret on the hillsides and could be executed on sight. Following the Glorious Revolution of 1688–9, William III sought to end the religious strife by acquiescing in the decision of the Scottish Convention to re-establish Presbyterianism in the Scottish church. It was for William a matter of political expediency. The majority of the Scottish people seemed committed to Presbyterianism, and he had no wish to continue the warfare against the Covenanters. He declined the advice of his high Anglican advisers that he must, for truth's sake, continue the effort to impose bishops on the Scottish church. When, five years after William's death, England and Scotland entered into the legislative union of 1707, securities were added to guarantee the Scottish Presbyterian settlement.

The Structure of the Church of Scotland

The eighteenth-century national Church of Scotland, then, was Presbyterian. This meant that it was governed not by bishops, but by a hierarchy of church courts, rising layer upon layer from the kirk-session at the parish level, to the district presbytery, the provincial synod and, finally, the national General Assembly. Fundamental to Scottish Presbyterianism was the parity of ministers: no individual minister was superior to, or exercised authority over, a fellow minister. At the base of the Presbyterian system was the parish. The whole territory of eighteenth-century Scotland was parcelled into approximately 970 parishes, each with a parish church and minister. A new minister was ordained when appointed to his first parish. He was assisted in his parish ministry by a number of elders – usually between seven and twelve, but often as few as one or two – who were also ordained. These latter were termed 'ruling elders' and were unpaid; the minister was a 'teaching elder' and was paid a stipend. The minister and ruling elders met together regularly as a parish court, or kirk-session, which had responsibility for supervising the moral and spiritual life of the parishioners, and overseeing parish education and poor relief. In rural parishes the kirk-session shared local authority with the parish court of heritors, or principal landowners. In burgh, or town parishes, the kirk-session shared authority with the magistrates and burgh council.

Above the kirk-session was the presbytery, a court that exercised a territorial jurisdiction over several contiguous parishes, usually between eight and eighteen, within a convenient travelling distance of one another. There were some seventy presbyteries in the eighteenth-century church. A presbytery included the minister and one ruling elder from each parish within the presbytery's boundaries, and it usually convened once a month. Presbyteries would hear appeals against kirk-session decisions, examine and license candidates for the ministry, ordain new ministers to parish livings, and supervise the work of ministers within their boundaries. They had the power to depose ministers for heretical teaching, neglect of pastoral responsibilities or immoral conduct. Further, they could recommend motions ('overtures') for church legislation or statements of church policy to the higher church courts. The next higher court above the presbytery was the synod. This was made up of all the members of several contiguous presbyteries, and normally met twice a year, in the spring and in the autumn, for sessions lasting two or three days. There were sixteen synods in the church. Synods heard appeals against presbytery decisions and reviewed actions taken by presbyteries. They could also recommend overtures for church legislation or policy to the next higher court, the General Assembly. The General Assembly, or supreme ecclesiastical court in the Church of Scotland, met in Edinburgh once a year for a week-long session, usually in late May. It consisted of three to five representatives from each presbytery, and a ruling elder from each royal burgh and university, making a total of some 360 members, with about 200 ministers and 160 ruling elders. It met in the presence of a lord high commissioner, a nobleman who represented the monarch, and it was presided over by a moderator, a minister who was elected by the assembly for a term of one year. The General Assembly was the court of final appeal against decisions taken by the lower church courts. It also had the power to approve overtures for new acts of church law (these overtures then had to be approved by a majority of presbyteries before becoming law). At the close of its annual session, the General Assembly appointed a commission, which met for brief sessions in Edinburgh three times during the year to handle ongoing assembly business. While all members of the General Assembly were named to the commission, in practice the difficulty of travel meant that attendance was restricted to members who resided near the capital. This gave the clergy in the neighbourhood of Edinburgh a particularly strong influence over church government, and made such livings desirable to ministers who aspired to roles of national leadership. All church courts, with the exception of kirk-sessions, were conducted in public, open to spectators from all social orders.

The doctrinal standards of the Church of Scotland were defined by the Westminster Confession of Faith. This was a systematic exposition of Reformed doctrine drafted by the Westminster Assembly of Divines in 1645–6, adopted by the Church of Scotland first in 1647 and again in 1690. The Westminster Confession left little room for diversity of belief. It proclaimed a transcendent God who had ordained all things from before the beginning of time by his divine decrees. God's decrees included the predestination of the elect saints to salvation and of reprobate persons to eternal damnation. The Confession insisted in uncompromising language on the total depravity of human nature and on salvation by grace alone. All candidates for the ministry were required to subscribe to the Confession and promise to teach its doctrines. Children were taught its doctrines through the Shorter Catechism. Worship in the church was defined by the Westminster Directory of Public Worship (1645), which provided for a simple service, emphasizing the sermon, extempore prayer and the singing of psalms, without instrumental accompaniment. The church recognized two sacraments, baptism and communion. Baptism was normally conducted in the parish church in the presence of the congregation, though in the course of the eighteenth century baptism in private homes became normal among the middle and upper classes. In most parishes, communion was celebrated once or twice a year, in sacramental occasions of three or four days' duration. These events could attract hundreds of people from neighbouring districts for prayer meetings, catechism, preaching and special worship services. In these communal festivals, or 'holy fairs', the parish minister would be assisted by neighbouring ministers, who would preach in turn to the crowds on communion Sunday, sometimes out of doors if attendance was too large for the parish church. Other ministers would serve the communion elements, in both kinds, to groups of twelve communicants at a time, seated around a table. Because of the 'fencing of the table', or the strict admonishment to people not to come forward for communion if unworthy, the number of actual communicants was often small. But many non-communicants were drawn to the events – some to hear sermons and join in prayer meetings, and some simply to drink ale, exchange news and gossip, or engage in flirtations with members of the opposite sex. As Robert Burns described a typical crowd in his poem, *The Holy Fair*:

On this hand sits a chosen swatch,
Wi' screw'd up, grace-proud faces;
On that, a set o' chaps, at watch,
Thrang winkin on the lasses.

The ministers of the Scottish establishment were supported mainly from the teind, the Scottish version of tithe. The teind was a form of heritable property, which granted the teind-holder the right to collect a notional 10 per cent of the produce of agricultural land and fisheries, including sea catches in coastal parishes. The teind-holder paid a proportion of the teind to the board of heritors (principal landowners in the parish), and from this amount the heritors paid the stipend of the minister and paid for the repair of the manse, or minister's house. In most rural parishes there was also the glebe, or land, usually about four acres, that was set aside for the support of the minister. In burgh parishes ministers were supported largely from rents charged for seats in the churches.

The minister and elders shared responsibility with the heritors for education in the parish. At the Reformation, the Church of Scotland had committed itself to the goal of universal literacy, to ensure that every person could read the Bible. By the Act for Settling of Schools in 1696, the heritors in each parish were responsible for financially supporting a school and schoolmaster. The parish schools were to provide primary education for both boys and girls, with most children attending school for about five years. The schools were also intended to identify boys with the potential for university study, and to prepare them for admission to one of Scotland's five universities. Schoolmasters were expected to have competence in Latin, and most apparently did; indeed, many were university-educated probationer ministers, who had failed to obtain church livings. They were selected by the heritors, examined and approved by the kirk-session, and required to subscribe to the Westminster Confession of Faith. In 1816 Scotland had 942 parish schools, or nearly one in every parish. Although in many districts, and especially towns, the parish schools were inadequate for the growing population, Scotland's literacy rate was one of the highest in Europe.

The minister and kirk-session supervised moral discipline and helped maintain order in the parish. In the Scottish church discipline was corporate in its character. The elders were expected to discover moral and religious infractions, including extramarital sex, drunkenness, lying, quarrelling, deceit and profanity. Suspected offenders would be summoned to appear before the kirk-session and examined on oath. If found guilty, they would be admonished and assigned a penance. The penance might take the form of a fine, with the money paid to the poor relief fund, or it might mean standing or sitting prominently before the congregation for a specified number of Sundays, sometimes barefooted and dressed in sackcloth. Those who refused to accept kirk-session discipline could be excommunicated. On the other hand, those who accepted admonishment and performed their penance were reconciled to the community in the eyes of the church. By the end of the century, most kirk-session discipline involved cases of extramarital sex. Elders placed pressure on unmarried pregnant women to reveal the names of fathers, who could then be legally required to pay for their children's support, thus sparing parish communities the expense of maintaining illegitimate children from the poor relief fund. The disciplinary proceedings could be humiliating, and the wealthy usually evaded discipline.

Charity was regarded as a religious duty, and the church played a major role in poor relief. According to the Scottish poor law of 1672 the minister and kirk-session shared responsibility for poor relief with the heritors in rural parishes and the magistrates in burgh parishes. The poor relief funds came primarily from voluntary church door collections for the poor. If these funds proved insufficient, the kirk-session and heritors were empowered to levy an assessment, or poor rate, on property in the parish, either short term, in response to a crop failure or other emergency, or long term. In rural parishes the minister and kirk-session distributed the poor relief. By law kirk-sessions were to restrict relief to legal residents of the parish, with residency determined either by birth in a parish or three years of self-supporting habitation. Furthermore, kirk-sessions were not permitted by law to grant relief to the able-bodied poor, that is, those who were judged able to work. In practice kirk-sessions frequently ignored this rule, especially during periods of poor harvests and high unemployment. In burghs the situation was more complex, with both kirk-sessions and magistrates distributing poor relief. In larger towns poor relief came to be distributed mainly through such institutions as the Glasgow Town Hospital (1733), the Aberdeen Poor's Hospital (1739) or the Edinburgh City Workhouse (1740).

Church–State Relations

The close cooperation of the religious and civil authorities at the local level helped to shape a distinctive Christian communal culture in Scotland. The parish resembled a miniature state, with kirk-sessions and heritors jointly administering poor relief, education and basic law and order. None the less, despite this local cooperation, Scottish Presbyterian political theory insisted that church and state were two separate and distinct societies – 'two kingdoms' – one under the sole headship of Christ and one under the worldly monarch. This view was rooted in the reformed political theory of such figures as Theodore Beza (1519–1605) of Geneva, and it implied a Christian right to resist an 'ungodly' monarch who declined to uphold the true Reformed faith. It had received one of its most eloquent expressions in 1596, when at Falkland Palace the clergyman, Andrew Melville, had plucked James VI's sleeve, called him 'God's sillie vassal', and instructed him that the church was the kingdom of Christ, 'whose subject King James the Sixth is, and of whose kingdom not a king, nor a lord, nor a head, but a member' (Burleigh 1960: 204–5). In respect of this separation of powers Church of Scotland ministers could not be elected to the House of Commons or vote in parliamentary elections, and the church had no official representation at the coronation ceremony or representatives in the House of Lords.

There was, moreover, no movement in eighteenth-century Scotland similar to that in England for the appointment of clerical magistrates. (A few were appointed, mainly in the Highlands, but only when there was a shortage of landed gentlemen able to serve.) Unlike England, Scotland had no Test Act, requiring candidates for civil office to take communion within the established church.

Such perfection was difficult to achieve and the relations of church and state were not without tensions. The greatest of these involved patronage or the right of laymen to present ministers to vacant church livings. Patronage was a form of heritable property, and could be bought and sold. It had its origins in the medieval church, and was supported by the crown and landed interest, which together possessed the patronage of most parish livings in Scotland. Strict Presbyterians, however, opposed patronage and sought its abolition. They believed that it gave patrons a privileged status within God's church, and that it offended against the principle, sacred to most Scots, that Christ's church must be no respecter of persons and that all people were equal before God. In 1690, when Presbyterianism had been re-established, the church had moved to end private patronage and instead to place the right of presenting ministers in the hands of the kirk-sessions and heritors in the parishes. In 1712, however, during a period of Tory ascendancy, parliament restored lay patronage in the Church of Scotland, despite the guarantees given at the Union of 1707 that parliament would not interfere in Scotland's religious settlement. In doing so, parliament had acted without consulting the Scottish church.

The Scottish church courts reacted strenuously with petitions and protests against the new Patronage Act, which was deeply unpopular. Initially, most lay patrons had declined to exercise their right of presentation. From about 1730, however, patrons began presenting candidates, viewing it as a means of increasing their local influence by placing right-thinking ministers in local churches, men who would emphasize in their sermons the importance of civil order and deference to the powers that be, and who might also be congenial companions for dinner and cards at the patron's house. The increased exercise of patronage resulted in bitter conflicts, with parishioners violently resisting the 'intrusions' of patron's candidates into parish churches, and presbyteries often refusing to ordain the candidates. Ordinations sometimes had to be conducted in the presence of armed troops, by special committees of the General Assembly; there were clashes between parishioners and troops, and loss of life. Individuals and whole congregations seceded from the established church rather than submit to patronage. But repeated church petitions to parliament to remove the law proved unavailing, and gradually the protests died down. By the end of the century, the majority in the Scottish church had grown, however reluctantly, to live with patronage.

Problems and Controversies

The Church of Scotland did not suffer to the same extent as the Church of England from the abuses of clerical pluralism and non-residence. There was only one type of pluralism permitted within the Church of Scotland – the uniting of a parish living with a university chair – and this was made necessary by the poor endowments of most professorships. Clerical non-residence was comparatively rare. Church law required residence from all parish clergy and presbyteries were usually strict in enforcing this law. The Scottish church did, however, suffer from serious financial problems, many of them stemming from the lay seizures of church property at the Reformation. Clerical stipends were often meagre. In 1750 no fewer than 273 parish livings, over 28 per cent of the total, provided less than £50 a year. From the later 1740s the General Assembly repeatedly petitioned parliament for an increase of the stipends. But its efforts were thwarted by the Scottish landowners, who had no wish to share a larger proportion of the teind with the clergy.

By the end of the century, moreover, the rapid growth of population in the central Lowland belt was resulting in a lack of adequate church accommodation. The parish boundaries had been largely defined in the later Middle Ages, with the result that new population centres had an insufficient number of parish churches. In the industrializing city of Glasgow there were by 1815 parishes with over 12,000 inhabitants, far beyond the capacity of a single pastor to provide spiritual supervision. The pew-rents in the urban churches, moreover, effectively excluded the poor from Sunday worship. In the Highlands and Islands, moreover, there was a shortage of parish churches and ministers. There the parishes were often of vast territorial extent, with sea, mountains, lochs and moors making travel difficult and dangerous. Many communities were far removed from any church or school. The Reformation had had only a localized impact in the Highlands, and much of the largely Gaelic-speaking population there was semi-pagan. Beginning in the early eighteenth century, the established church pursued a mission to the Highlands and Islands, sending out Gaelic-speaking missionaries and catechists – assisted after 1724 by a royal bounty of £1,000 a year. The Society in Scotland for Propagating of Christian Knowledge (1709) was also active in supporting missionaries and schools in the region. These efforts proved successful in bringing the Reformed faith to the region, often through the heroic struggles of such figures as Donald Ross Mitchell of Ross-shire or James MacDonald of Reay.

The early eighteenth century witnessed a movement away from an uncompromising, oppressive Calvinist order in the Scottish church towards a more open and tolerant faith. The change can be seen in two episodes. First, in 1697, Scotland witnessed its last execution for blasphemy when Thomas Aitkenhead, an eighteen-year-old Edinburgh University student, was hanged for having denied in private conversation the divinity of Christ. Although he had fully recanted his words, this had not satisfied the Edinburgh clergy and magistrates. Public opinion, however, recoiled against the savage sentence, and there were no more such executions. Second, in 1727 there occurred Scotland's last recorded execution for witchcraft. A confused and senile Janet Horne was burned in a pitch barrel in Dornoch, after trial and conviction for the crime of riding upon her daughter, whom the devil had temporarily transformed into a pony. But educated opinion had already turned against the belief in witchcraft, and in 1735 parliament repealed the Witchcraft Act of 1563, under which an estimated 1,500 persons had been put to death in Scotland. Theological controversy was being removed from the shadow of the gibbet and the stake. By the later 1740s the Edinburgh philosopher David Hume was openly questioning the miraculous events that formed the foundation of the Christian faith.

In the eighteenth-century Church of Scotland theological controversy was conducted between two main parties – the Moderate party and the Popular or Evangelical party. These were loose groupings: party or faction was generally regarded as an evil in Christ's church, and most church members would not have admitted to being an adherent of any party. None the less, the existence of the two parties was undeniable. The Moderates had emerged as an identifiable group in the early years of the eighteenth century, and maintained an ascendancy in the Scottish church from the 1760s until the early 1830s. Under the leadership of the versatile William Robertson (1721–93), celebrated historian, minister of an Edinburgh church and principal of Edinburgh University, Moderates worked to move the church away from the rough-hewn, militant religion of the seventeenth century towards a more cultivated, tolerant, world-affirming faith. Reflecting the ethos of the Scottish enlightenment, Moderates called on the church to promote a culture of improvement. The clergy were to be active in all aspects of intellectual life, and to seek a more cooperative relationship of church and state. While Moderates did not directly challenge the Calvinism of the Westminster Confession of Faith, they did tend to ignore the doctrine of predestination and emphasize practical morality, the harmonies of nature and the capacity of human reason. Many would have wished to revise the church's Confession, but held back to avoid division within the church. Moderate ecclesiastical policy was based on acceptance of patronage in the church. The established church, they insisted, was obligated to enforce patronage so long as it remained the law of the land. More than that, some Moderates came to believe that patrons, mainly educated landed gentlemen or crown agents, presented a superior quality of clergymen to Scottish churches – men of refinement, good manners and intellectual accomplishments, who would exercise a civilizing influence over their parishioners. Moderates opposed movements to increase the popular voice in politics. During the political unrest of the 1790s, the Moderate party aligned itself with the government party of William Pitt and Henry Dundas, denouncing popular reform movements and religious enthusiasm, while insisting on non-resistance to the powers that be. As a consequence, the Moderate clergy became stigmatized in the popular mind as the servile flatterers of men in power, who had no regard to the spiritual interests of their flock. None the less, they received most crown patronage and they retained control of the General Assembly.

The Evangelical movement in the Church of Scotland was part of the larger eighteenth-century Evangelical awakening in the North Atlantic world. It placed emphasis on the individual conversion experience, regular Bible reading, participation in prayer meetings and an emotional, heartfelt piety. Evangelicals disliked the moralistic preaching of the Moderates. Their own preaching focused on human depravity and salvation by grace alone. Their warm piety sometimes found expression in revivals, such as that at Cambuslang in 1742, which attracted thousands. Within the church courts, the Evangelical or Popular party led the opposition to patronage. For them, patronage was corrupting the church, subordinating the spiritual needs of parish communities to the will of individual patrons, and filling pulpits with worldly ministers. They believed that the kirk-sessions and heritors, or the male heads of family in the parish, should select the minister. By the 1790s, however, having failed to secure the abolition of patronage, the Popular party directed its attention to other matters, and especially the need to evangelize among the growing numbers of people who were growing up outside the church. A new generation of Evangelicals now came of age, people strongly influenced by both the thought of the Scottish enlightenment and the Evangelical movement in England, who viewed themselves as part of a larger North Atlantic Protestantism. Led by John Erskine and Sir Henry Moncrieff Wellwood (the only titled clergyman in the Scottish church), Scottish Evangelicals began embracing the anti-slavery and missionary commitments of trans-Atlantic Evangelicalism.

Religious Minorities

Not everyone in eighteenth-century Scotland was part of the established Presbyterian church. Some continued to hold to the old, pre-Reformation faith. Small groups of Roman Catholics, probably numbering several thousand in all, had survived the persecution that had followed the Reformation. Located mainly in the more remote areas of the Highlands and Islands, especially Banffshire, they were served by missionary priests, some trained at the small Catholic seminary at Scanlan. Threatened continually with persecution, especially after the failed Jacobite risings of 1715 and 1745, they kept a low profile and endured until granted a measure of toleration in 1793.

A growing number of Scottish Protestants also withdrew from the established church in the course of the eighteenth century. In obedience to their consciences, they removed themselves from the parish structures of the national church, with its historic associations and communal rituals. They became Dissenters from the established order in church and state. Among those withdrawing from the established church were the Episcopalians. With the Revolution of 1688–9 and the restoration of Presbyterianism in the established church, many devout Episcopalian clergymen could not conform. Some sixty Episcopalian clergy were 'rabbled' out of their churches and manses by Presbyterian mobs in 1689; others were later removed from their livings by legal action. The deprived clergymen often retained support in their local communities. Illegal Episcopalian congregations took shape and survived, mainly in the northeast and the Highlands and Islands, and often under the protection of aristocratic families. In 1712 the overwhelmingly Anglican British parliament passed a Toleration Act for Scottish Episcopalians, despite angry protests from the Church of Scotland. Most Episcopalians, however, continued to give their allegiance to the Stuarts: they viewed the overthrow of James II in 1688 as a sinful act of rebellion against Scotland's divinely ordained king, and they dreamed of the 'tall ships' that would bring a Stuart king back from exile in France. They suffered heavily for their support of the Jacobite risings in 1715 and 1745. Penal acts were imposed in 1719, 1746 and 1748 upon Scottish Episcopalians who did not 'qualify' by renouncing allegiance to the Stuarts and adopting the English Prayer Book. In suppressing the Jacobite rising in 1745–6, Hanoverian forces burned Episcopal meeting houses and scattered congregations. With the waning of the Jacobite threat after 1760, and the growth of enlightenment ideas of toleration, the persecution gradually eased. In 1792 parliament finally rescinded the penal laws. The Scottish Episcopal church emerged from the penal times as a remnant, with perhaps 15,000 adherents, or about 1 per cent of the population. But with toleration the Episcopal church began to revive, gaining influential converts among the landed and urban professional classes.

Other Dissenting bodies also emerged. There were Cameronians – severe Presbyterian Covenanters who took their name from Richard Cameron, killed in 1680 while resisting rule by the 'uncovenanted' Charles II. Alienated by the refusal of the British crown to adopt the Covenants, the Cameronians withdrew from the established church in 1690 and worshipped as Dissenters. There were Glassites – a gentle, charitable sect of followers of John Glas (1695–1773), who was deposed from the ministry of the Church of Scotland in 1730 after he embraced the view that the church must be entirely independent of the state. The Glassite churches had about 1,000 members in 1790. There were Baptist and Congregational churches, with perhaps 4,000 adherents in the 1790s. After 1733, these small groups of Dissenters were joined by larger bodies of Presbyterian seceders from the national church. Many devout Presbyterians had by now grown disenchanted with the established church, objecting to the rising influence of the Moderates and the church's failure to resist more forcibly parliament's reimposition of lay patronage in 1712. In 1733, following a dispute over patronage in the General Assembly, four ministers in the neighbourhood of Stirling, including the brothers Ralph and Ebenezer Erskine, withdrew from the Church of Scotland and formed themselves into the Associate Presbytery, commonly known as the Secession church. They gained a growing number of adherents, mainly tough-minded, independent Lowland farmers and artisans who hated patronage and believed in strict Calvinist discipline. The Secession church split in 1747 over a dispute concerning whether or not Christians, on becoming magistrates or town councillors, should take a required oath of loyalty to the state. Despite the split, both branches of the Secession churches continued to expand, establishing seminaries for the training of ministers and creating additional presbyteries. The year 1761 saw the formation of the Relief church, under the leadership of Thomas Gillespie, who had been deposed from the ministry of the Church of Scotland in 1752 for his outspoken opposition to patronage. The Relief church attracted Presbyterians who opposed patronage but were uncomfortable with the uncompromising Calvinism of the older Secession churches. Embracing a more liberal interpretation of Calvinist doctrine – Gillespie said he would share communion with all who recognized Christ – the Relief church expanded steadily, mainly in the rural Lowlands. By the end of the century, there were over 300 Secession or Relief congregations, with perhaps 150,000 adherents, representing nearly 10 per cent of Scotland's population.

Amid the social and political unrest of the 1790s, a new movement of Evangelical Dissent appeared in Scotland. The leading figures in this movement were the brothers James and Robert Haldane, the one a former captain of an East India Company ship, the other a wealthy landowner. Converted to Evangelical Christianity in the mid-1790s, the Haldanes organized a home mission directed to the growing numbers in Scotland who were outside organized Christianity, especially in the towns and more remote rural districts. In 1798 they created the Society for Propagating the Gospel at Home, which supported itinerant preachers who travelled on circuits through the country and established new churches on a congregational pattern.

The new Evangelical spirit also permeated the older Presbyterian Secession churches, bringing a more personal, less communal piety. In the later 1790s some members of the Secession churches began experiencing 'new light' regarding the teachings of the Westminster Confession on church and state. They came to view any established church as un-Christian and to embrace instead the belief that church membership must be purely voluntary, based on an individual decision for Christ. Between 1799 and 1804 the majority in both branches of the Secession church embraced these New Light teachings, breaking with their more traditionalist brethren. The New Light movement marked a major shift of attitude among Presbyterian Dissenters, from one of hope that the established church would eventually be purified, to a rejection of any connection of church and state. For New Light Dissenters, religion grew more individualistic. They ceased looking back to the seventeenth-century Covenants and were drawn to democratic and reformist ideas.

The years after 1790 witnessed an unprecedented growth of Dissent in Scotland. In 1790 probably only 10 per cent of the population were outside the established church. By the 1820s, however, perhaps 30 per cent of the Scottish population were Dissenters. Most of them had rejected belief in the connection of church and state. They stepped out of the traditional communal culture of the parish, with its kirk-session discipline, parish poor relief, parish education and communion seasons. In so doing, they were shaping a more individualist piety and a more pluralist Scotland.

FURTHER READING

Brown, C. G.: *Religion and Society in Scotland since 1707* (Edinburgh, 1997).

Burleigh, J. H. S.: *A Church History of Scotland* (Oxford, 1960).

Clark, I. D. L.: 'From protest to reaction: the moderate regime in the Church of Scotland, 1752–1805', in N. T. Phillipson and R. Mitchison (eds), *Scotland in the Age of Improvement* (Edinburgh, 1970).

Cunningham, J.: *The Church History of Scotland* (2 vols, Edinburgh, 1859).

Drummond, A. L. and Bulloch, J.: *The Scottish Church 1688–1843: The Age of the Moderates* (Edinburgh, 1973).

Grub, G.: *An Ecclesiastical History of Scotland* (4 vols, Edinburgh, 1861).

Henderson, G. D.: *The Scottish Ruling Elder* (London, 1935).

Macinnes, J.: *The Evangelical Movement in the Highlands of Scotland, 1688–1800* (Aberdeen, 1951).

McIntosh, John R.: *Church and Theology in Enlightenment Scotland: The Popular Party, 1740–1800* (East Linton, East Lothian, 1998).

McKerrow, J.: *History of the Secession Church* (Edinburgh, 1854).

Mitchison, Rosalind and Leneman, Leah: *Sexuality and Social Control: Scotland 1660–1780* (Oxford, 1989).

Schmidt, L. E.: *Holy Fairs: Scottish Communions and American Revivals in the Early Modern Period* (Princeton, NJ, 1989).

Sher, R. B.: *Church and University in the Scottish Enlightenment: The Moderate Literati of Edinburgh* (Princeton, NJ, 1985).

Struthers, G.: *The History of the Rise, Progress and Principles of the Relief Church* (Glasgow, 1843).

Vincent, Emma: 'The responses of Scottish Churchmen to the French Revolution, 1789–1802', *Scottish Historical Review*, 73 (1994), pp. 191–215.

Chapter Twenty-One

Religion in Ireland

Sean J. Connolly

Ireland entered the eighteenth century with a legacy of religious division and conflict. The civil war of 1641–53 had given the Protestant minority, mainly the descendants of Elizabethan or later settlers, control of some three-quarters of Irish land and a virtual monopoly of political power. During 1686–8 James II's viceroy, the Catholic earl of Tyrconnel, had sought to reverse this earlier defeat. Catholics displaced Protestants in the army, the magistracy and judiciary, and the civil administration. The Catholic clergy regained the right to operate openly and received funds diverted from the Protestant Church of Ireland. In 1689, following the overthrow of James II in England, a Catholic-dominated parliament in Dublin declared that all land was to be restored to its 1641 proprietors. Before and during the war of 1689–91, in which the forces of William III overran Ireland in a hard-fought campaign, Protestants were imprisoned, intimidated and plundered. These events were to be cited for decades to follow as proof that Irish Catholics were a ruthless and implacable enemy, bent on the destruction of their Protestant neighbours by all means possible.

Protestant Divisions

Yet Irish Protestantism itself also inherited a legacy of internal division. When Charles II was restored to the throne in 1660 the Church of Ireland was immediately restored to its former status as an Episcopal state church. But it had now to coexist with other Protestant denominations that had grown up during the upheavals of the previous two decades. In the reign of Charles II these Protestant Dissenters endured sporadic harassment and repression. During the war of 1689–91 Anglicans and Dissenters had temporarily come together to defend their religion and property. But their unity had lasted only as long as the common danger. Once the war ended Anglicans sought once again to restrict both the religious rights and the political power of their former allies.

There are no wholly reliable statistics on the size of the different religious denominations at any point in the eighteenth century. Figures based on returns made by collectors of the hearth tax in 1732–3, however, suggest that Catholics made up between three-quarters and four-fifths of the total population. The other 20–25 per cent were divided roughly equally between Anglicans and Presbyterians, with small groups of other Protestants: Baptists, Congregationalists, Quakers, Palatines and Huguenots. The geographical distribution of the three major denominations was highly uneven. The great majority of Presbyterians, perhaps 90 per cent, lived in Ulster. About half of all Anglicans likewise lived in Ulster; the remainder were distributed throughout the other three provinces, with particularly large concentrations in some of the towns. Dublin, in particular, remained a predominantly Protestant city up to the middle of the eighteenth century. In the countryside Catholics were a minority in the north-east, where English and Scots had settled in large numbers during the seventeenth century. Elsewhere they made up a large majority, in most places accounting for 80 per cent or more of the population.

The Church of Ireland thus combined privilege and prestige with numerical weakness. It was the established church: its bishops sat in the House of Lords; it was legally entitled to tithes collected from the entire population for the support of its clergy; its religious rivals were subjected to a variety of restrictions; its rituals were a central part of state occasions such as the opening of parliament or the commemoration of military victories. It was also the church of the political and social elite. All but a handful of landowners were members of the Church of Ireland, as were, outside Ulster, the majority of merchants and professional men. At the same time its adherents remained a minority, heavily outnumbered by the Catholics and equalled if not exceeded by Dissenters. This helps to explain the acute concern of the established church with the defence of what it saw as its rightful privileges. In the early eighteenth century, in particular, many churchmen, in Ireland as in England, believed that the real threat to the established order in both church and state came not from a defeated and politically neutralized Catholicism, but from the forces of atheism, Deism and Dissent. An Irish high church movement, closely linked to its English counterpart, campaigned vigorously for the reimposition of religious orthodoxy and social discipline. Its demands included not just the repression of Dissent, but a revival of the church courts, a restoration of censorship, and legislation against blasphemy and sabbath-breaking.

As in England the high church movement became closely entangled in party politics. Its leaders and propagandists openly opposed what they denounced as the dangerous attempts of the Whigs to justify the overthrow of James II in terms of 'Revolution principles', and they looked to the Tory party to implement their programme of moral and religious coercion. After 1714 the victorious Whigs took firm action to curb their ecclesiastical opponents. Trinity College, Dublin, the training ground for most Anglican clergy and a centre of high church sentiment, and at times of at least a rhetorical Jacobitism, was brought under strict political control. Henceforth, episcopal and other senior appointments went exclusively to clergymen unambiguously committed both to the Hanoverian succession and to a pragmatic acceptance of the subordination of the church to the state.

The condition of the Church of Ireland in the decades following the Revolution was generally agreed to be poor. The most common problems were absenteeism and pluralism, where the same clergyman held more than one benefice. To some extent these deficiencies arose from a lack of resources. Parochial revenues were often low, most commonly because the tithes from which they derived had been alienated to lay impropriators. This in turn made pluralism unavoidable, if the clergyman concerned was to receive even a minimum income. The glebe lands intended to supplement the incomes of parish clergy had also frequently been alienated, while many parishes did not have a house fit for a resident minister. Churches, too, were often ruinous or in poor repair. Such practical problems, however, were often compounded by lack of pastoral commitment, on the part both of the lower clergy and of their bishops, some of whom paid only occasional visits to the dioceses nominally under their care. Neglect, in turn, was partly a reflection of the incorporation of the Irish church into the spoils system of eighteenth-century politics. Appointments to bishoprics and other senior positions were prizes within an elaborate system of patronage, awarded primarily on the basis of past or future political services or of personal and family connections. For a period following the Revolution there were hopes that the new monarchy could be persuaded to undertake a thorough overall reform. A group of bishops including William King (1650–1729), bishop of Derry 1690–1703 and thereafter archbishop of Dublin, pressed for legislative action to restore church property and tighten internal discipline. Later they turned instead to Convocation, the representative body of the Irish clergy, which met between 1703 and 1714. But neither government nor Convocation was willing to undertake more than minor changes to the existing ecclesiastical system.

At the same time the venality and pastoral ineffectiveness of the Irish church should not be overstated. The vivid depictions of rampant careerism and a decaying physical fabric that have helped to shape historians' estimates come in many cases from senior clergymen such as King, whose comments must be read as the polemics of frustrated reformers rather than as a balanced assessment. Where more systematic statistical information is available, it suggests that problems like non-residence, though genuine, were not as widespread as has sometimes been suggested. If the church was poorly equipped to undertake its theoretical mission as a national church, it was better placed to fulfil its actual task of ministering to the Anglican minority. In the early eighteenth century it had one clergyman for every 310 or so members, and a functioning place of worship for every 300 to 350. How many of this lay population actually sought the services of their church with any regularity remains a mystery. But scattered evidence from middle- and upper-class households suggests that an orthodox piety, unobtrusive but genuine enough, was at least as common as indifference. If some of the senior clergy appointed through the all-pervasive system of political patronage were neglectful careerists, others, like Hugh Boulter, archbishop of Armagh (1724–42), combined their political role with a conscientious and effective discharge of their ecclesiastical duties. In the last decades of the century the first stirrings of an Evangelical movement introduced a new vigour into the religious lives of both clergy and laity.

Ulster Presbyterians were overwhelmingly the descendants of immigrants from Scotland who had moved into the region in large numbers from the early seventeenth century onwards. Their Scottish origins remained evident, throughout the eighteenth century and beyond, in their speech, a variety of Lowland Scots, and in aspects of popular custom and manners. Initially accommodated, somewhat uneasily, within the Church of Ireland, they had begun to develop a separate religious organization in 1642. The establishment in 1691 of the Synod of Ulster completed the creation of a Presbyterian structure. In the early eighteenth century there was growing tension between supporters of the traditional theology enshrined in the Westminster Confession of Faith, and a 'New Light' party unwilling to subscribe to any man-made statement of doctrine. In 1725 the New Light party were first grouped in a separate presbytery of Antrim, then excluded from the Synod of Ulster. When a dispute over lay patronage led to a secession from the Church of Scotland in 1733, a conservative minority within the Synod, dissatisfied with what they still saw as its theological laxity, took the opportunity, commencing in 1746, to form their own Seceding congregations. A second Scottish secession of the ultra-orthodox, by the Reformed Presbyterians or Covenanters in 1743, was likewise replicated in Ulster, where the first Covenanting congregation was established in 1757.

In contrast to the hierarchical organization of both the Church of Ireland and the Catholic church, where the clergy were appointed and directed by diocesan bishops, Presbyterian church government was decentralized. Ministers were appointed by a call from the congregation concerned. Senior members of each congregation ('elders') sat alongside the clergy in the Synod of Ulster. Yet despite this more broadly based system of management, internal discipline was strict. Members of Presbyterian congregations were subjected to constant close supervision by clergy and elders. Couples whose first child was born less than nine months after marriage, for example, were almost invariably made to perform public penance. Other moral offences, such as drunkenness, neglect of religious duties, slander, quarrelling, even unduly competitive economic behaviour, could likewise lead to public admonition or a requirement to perform public penance.

To the clergy of the Church of Ireland, and to many Anglican laymen, the Presbyterians of Ulster seemed to represent a formidable threat. Their tight internal discipline led critics to characterize them as a virtually autonomous community, whose ministers and elders usurped the functions of the civil magistrate. Their numerical strength and geographical concentration in the northeast aroused fears that they would at some stage seek to displace Episcopalian Anglicanism as the established church, as their co-religionists had already done in Scotland. Such fears were reinforced when economic crisis in Scotland led to a last great surge of immigration into Ulster in the 1690s and early 1700s. Against this background clergy and magistrates sought to prevent the erection of Presbyterian meeting houses in new areas. Ulster bishops also sought to force Presbyterians to resort to the established church for weddings and funerals, using the ecclesiastical courts to prosecute Presbyterian couples who had been married by their own ministers for fornication and refusing Dissenting clergymen access to graveyards. An act of parliament in 1704 was amended in London to impose the sacramental test, requiring all those holding offices of profit or trust under the crown to produce a certificate of having taken communion in the established church. The Whig triumph in 1714 put an end to direct interference with Presbyterian religious practice. The Irish Anglican gentry, however, even those who on other issues counted as Whigs, were not anxious to share power on equal terms with such a large body of Dissenters. A Toleration Act in 1719 secured the right of nonconforming Protestants to maintain their own religious organization and worship, but attempts to repeal the sacramental test, in 1719 and again in 1733, failed conclusively. In addition, Presbyterians continued to be required to pay tithes and other dues to the established church.

These tokens of continued subordination to an Episcopalian establishment were all the more galling because of the economic and social strength of the Presbyterian population. There were few Presbyterian landowners. On the other hand, Presbyterians dominated much of the commercial life of Ulster, including the rapidly expanding linen trade. This made their exclusion, by the sacramental test, from the government of the towns in which they did business a particular grievance. The Presbyterian rank and file, likewise, was largely composed of tenant farmers, self-employed weavers and other artisans, literate, relatively prosperous and economically independent. Taken together with resentment of Anglican hegemony, these characteristics help to explain why the Presbyterian northeast should have been a particularly fertile recruiting ground for radical political movements, from the first stirrings of an independent electorate in the 1760s to the United Irishmen of the 1790s.

Other Protestant denominations were, by comparison, numerically insignificant. In the mid-seventeenth century Dissent had briefly flourished in the southern counties: one estimate in 1672 suggested that as many as half of the non-Scottish Protestant population were Dissenters. But the main strength of all such groups had been among the soldiers and other servants of the Cromwellian regime. After 1660 many of these had returned to England. In the longer term the predominantly rural south, dominated by an Anglican squirearchy, was a less favourable base for Dissent than the more commercialized and socially variegated northeast. Already by 1695 the number of Independent or Congregationalist ministers had fallen to six, as compared with thirty during the 1650s. Around the same time the southern Presbyterians, English rather than Scottish by tradition and not always clearly distinguished from the Independents, had about 4,500 adherents. Irish Quakers, in the mid-eighteenth century, numbered no more than about 5,000, while in the 1720s there were perhaps 1,500–2,000 Irish Baptists. There were also small colonies of foreign Protestants: Huguenot refugees from France and Palatines from the Rhineland. In the 1740s and 1750s the Moravian evangelist John Cennick established a network of religious societies, mainly in Co. Antrim. Another new society, concentrated mainly in the Anglican areas of south and west Ulster, was the Methodists. John Wesley himself visited Ireland on twenty-one occasions between 1747 and his death in 1791, and Methodist numbers rose from just over 3,000 in 1770 to more than 15,000 by 1795.

The Catholic Position

Irish Catholics were unequivocally the losers in the prolonged religious conflict that had dominated much of the seventeenth century. In the civil war of 1689–91 they had supported James II against William III, in a last attempt to reverse earlier losses and establish Catholic hegemony. The Treaty of Limerick (3 October 1691) offered minimal guarantees: those still in arms when the treaty was signed were given immunity from prosecution or forfeiture, while Catholics in general were to enjoy the same religious freedom as in the reign of Charles II. Over the next few years, however, a series of statutes imposed severe legal disabilities. Catholics were excluded from voting, sitting in parliament or holding public office at any level. They could not possess weapons or practise law. Catholics were not permitted to acquire land by purchase, long lease, mortgage, or inheritance from a Protestant, while a Protestant heiress who married a Catholic forfeited her inheritance. Existing Catholic landed estates were to be equally divided among all the sons of a deceased proprietor; but an eldest son could secure his succession to the whole estate by conforming to the Church of Ireland. A single Catholic priest was allowed to minister in each Catholic parish, provided he registered with the authorities. But all bishops and members of religious orders were banished from the kingdom, and no priests were to be permitted to enter from abroad. Catholics were also forbidden to manage or teach in schools within Ireland, or to travel abroad for the purpose of education. The initiative for this body of legislation, introduced piecemeal between the 1690s and the 1720s, came from the Irish parliament, sometimes overriding the reservations of British ministers reluctant to accept measures that might jeopardize Britain's relations with European Catholic powers. Irish Protestant determination to secure themselves against any renewed political threat was reinforced not just by memories of events under James II, but by the continued attachment of the Catholic population to the cause of the exiled Stuarts and their supporters in Catholic Europe. Up to 1766 the pope appointed Irish Catholic bishops on the nomination of the Jacobite court. Meanwhile, large numbers of Catholic men went abroad to serve in the armies of France, Spain and Austria.

The range and severity of anti-Catholic legislation has led some historians to describe the eighteenth century as 'the penal era'. It is important, however, not to exaggerate the practical impact of the laws. Some of the prohibitions they embodied were of long standing. Catholic schools had repeatedly been suppressed during the seventeenth century. No Catholics had sat in the Irish House of Commons in the parliament of 1661–6. During the Popish Plot crisis the Irish government had ordered the seizure of all weapons held by Catholics. All that had really changed in such cases was that, in the new political culture created by the Revolution, what had previously been done informally or by royal proclamation was now being done by statute. The impact of the laws on the Catholic landed class was undeniably catastrophic. Excluded from participation in public life, prohibited from enlarging their estates by purchase or marriage, and faced with the prospect of seeing their property subdivided with the death of each proprietor, the majority of landowners conformed to the Church of Ireland. The major transfer of landed property, however, had taken place much earlier, during the Cromwellian confiscation of the 1650s. It was at this point that the Catholic share of landed property had fallen from 59 per cent in 1641 to 22 per cent after 1660. Forfeitures by Jacobite landowners unable to claim the benefit of the Treaty of Limerick, because they had been captured or killed in battle, or because they had accepted protection from the Williamite forces, brought the figure down to 14 per cent. A further fall in response to penal legislation, to an estimated 5 per cent by the late eighteenth century, was thus only the last stage in a much longer historical process. Unlike the Cromwellian confiscations, moreover, penal legislation did not lead to the actual loss of lands and the installation of a new class of Protestant proprietors. Instead it was existing landowners who changed their religion in order to retain their estates.

Beyond the small Catholic landed class, the real impact of penal legislation was much more limited. The laws did not significantly inhibit Catholic business activity. Catholics, mainly through lack of access to the capital provided by land, were underrepresented among manufacturers and merchants, holding perhaps one-third of total commercial wealth. On the other hand, this still substantial Catholic middle class shared in the benefits of the dramatic expansion of the Irish economy that began in the 1740s, and by the end of the century had emerged as a powerful pressure group. In the countryside the laws that had crippled the Catholic landowning class did not seriously inhibit the emergence, in the same climate of rapid economic expansion, of two other social groups. Catholic middlemen, many of them descendants of former landed families, maintained the lifestyle of minor gentry from the profits of reletting leasehold land. Lower down the social scale, what had been a largely undifferentiated peasantry broke up into two classes: a growing army of labourers, landless or land poor, and a smaller but still important class of reasonably prosperous and independent tenant farmers. In other ways, too, assertions that the laws served to impose a subordinate status on the population as a whole, often supported by comparisons with the former apartheid legislation of South Africa, are wildly unrealistic. The poverty of the majority of the population, and the concentration of political power in the hands of a small propertied elite, must be seen in the context of an *ancien régime* Europe in which such conditions were the norm. Since land was the key to political power, the virtual elimination of the Catholic landowning class was in itself sufficient to establish what came to be referred to as 'Protestant ascendancy'. Indeed, the dominance of Irish parliamentary politics by members of a small, wealthy class of landed Protestants was to continue up to the 1870s, long after formal religious discrimination had been abolished. Penal legislation permitted a great deal of petty harassment, and what was no doubt an irksome flaunting of their superior status by Protestants. But it did not radically alter the structure of Irish society.

Where Catholic religious practice is concerned, the picture is more mixed. There was initially a serious effort to enforce the laws against Catholic ecclesiastics. In the early months of 1698, 424 members of religious orders were transported from Ireland, while another 300 or so left voluntarily. By 1707 only two bishops remained in the country, one of whom was in prison. But the obstacles to consistent repression were always formidable. Much of the countryside remained underdeveloped, with poor roads and extensive tracts of bog and mountain in which law enforcement of any kind was a problem. In the absence of anything resembling a police force, the responsibility for proceeding against bishops, friars and unlicensed priests lay with what was in most areas a thinly spread Protestant propertied class, often disinclined to antagonize the surrounding Catholic population. There are also indications that many Protestants never really believed that it would be possible to suppress the religious institutions of such a large majority; instead they were content to see the laws against Catholic ecclesiastics as a threat to be kept in reserve, to enforce good behaviour and legalize prompt preventive action at times of crisis. For all of these reasons sustained attempts to suppress Catholic religious institutions had been abandoned by about 1720. Thereafter, bishops, priests and even regular clergy could generally operate without serious harassment, provided they observed a decent discretion. In 1744–5 the threat of a French invasion led to the temporary closure of Catholic churches. But this was the last occasion of its kind.

The slackening of persecution allowed the Catholic church to rebuild its ecclesiastical organization. By the end of the 1720s most dioceses once again had a resident bishop. Universities in the Austrian Netherlands, France, Spain and Portugal ensured an adequate supply of priests to serve in Irish parishes. In the 1730s there appears to have been one parish priest or curate for about every 1,600 Catholics. (By the end of the century, however, rapid population growth, concentrated among those social classes least able to contribute towards the support of their clergy, had increased this figure to around 2,700.) A semi-legal status, combined with limited material resources and the strong localism of a peripheral and economically underdeveloped society, meant that it was difficult to maintain a rigorous internal discipline. Bishops were sometimes censured for neglecting the dioceses committed to their care. One, Anthony Blake, archbishop of Armagh, was actually dismissed in 1787 for his persistent failure to reside. Parish priests in some cases defied bishops who attempted to regulate their conduct or make alternative appointments to parishes which they regarded as their personal property. Among sections of the laity, likewise, levels of religious instruction were not always high, and there is some evidence to suggest that attendance at Sunday mass and other services was often irregular. The religion of the Catholic poor, in fact, blended orthodox doctrine and ritual with a variety of folkloric elements. The 'patterns' (comparable to English wakes) celebrated at so-called holy wells, for example, combined prayers at the shrine of a Christian saint with rituals of healing or protection, and also provided the occasion for carnivalesque celebration. During the early and mid-nineteenth century a new generation of Catholic bishops found it necessary to engage in a major campaign of internal reform, both to raise standards of conduct and performance among the parish clergy and to encourage a more regular pattern of religious practice among the laity.

Religion and Politics

The period saw radical changes in the relationship between religion and political identity. In the early eighteenth century Protestants normally referred to themselves as 'English', using 'Irish' as a synonym for Catholic. Over time, however, these descendants of late sixteenth- and seventeenth-century settlers began to develop their own sense of Irish identity, expressed in an increasingly vigorous patriot politics. Many saw no contradiction in campaigning passionately against British encroachments on Irish constitutional rights, while simultaneously upholding the laws that excluded four-fifths of the population from any participation in public affairs. Others, such as Henry Grattan, however, came to believe that patriotism, to be either genuine or effective, had also to include the Catholic population. Meanwhile, other influences also strengthened the case for a relaxation of the penal laws. Enlightenment social and political thinking favoured religious toleration. Catholic politics themselves had changed. Jacobitism quickly ceased to be a credible cause after 1745; by 1766 even the pope had abandoned the Stuarts. Against this background the Catholic gentry, middle classes and clergy became willing to offer explicit declarations of allegiance to the Hanoverian state, while petitioning for a relaxation of their legal disabilities. For its part the British government, engaged in a century-long struggle against France for world supremacy, was anxious to draw on the large potential reserve of military manpower available if Irish Catholics could be incorporated into the

state. Ministers were also alienated by the increasing unruliness of the Protestant patriots both in and outside the Dublin parliament. Irish Catholics were thus able to appeal directly to the London government, over the heads of a still largely unsympathetic Irish parliament, in effect outbidding their Protestant opponents in terms of loyalty to the crown. Against this background Catholic Relief Acts in 1778 and 1782 removed the main restrictions on Catholic education and religious practice, and allowed Catholics to deal in land on broadly the same terms as Protestants. Later acts in 1792–3 admitted them to the practice of the law, the armed forces and to lesser offices, and restored the right to vote subject to the usual property qualifications.

By the 1780s many observers believed that Ireland was entering a new age of harmony, in which longstanding religious divisions would at last be left behind. Instead, however, the last years of the eighteenth century saw a widespread revival of sectarian antagonism. The origins of the violence lay partly in local circumstances in the south Ulster county of Armagh, where the growth of the linen industry had brought Catholics and Protestants into direct competition for land and employment. But plebeian Protestants were also reacting to the dismantling of the penal laws, and to the growing assertiveness of the Catholics, by attempting to reassert their traditional superiority. Revolution in France further contributed to political and sectarian polarization. Against this background, some Protestants carried the rhetoric of the patriot tradition to its logical conclusion. By the mid-1790s the Society of United Irishmen had moved beyond mere reform to a programme of democratic republicanism and complete religious equality, to be achieved by a French-backed insurrection. The Society also sought to mobilize the Catholic masses, through an alliance with the Defenders, a Catholic secret society that had arisen out of the sectarian conflict in Armagh but had also adopted a crude republican and egalitarian ideology of its own. For other Protestants, however, the threat of a resurgent Catholicism was a signal instead to rally to the defence of the existing constitution in church and state. The Orange Order, founded in 1795 following a sectarian skirmish in Co. Armagh, provided the vehicle for a new alliance between conservative gentry and plebeian Protestants. When the long-awaited radical insurrection came, in May 1798, both sides proved unable to control their plebeian allies. In Co. Wexford in particular the rising degenerated into brutal violence against Protestant non-combatants. The suppression of the rebellion, equally, brought an indiscriminate counter-revolutionary terror directed against the Catholic population as a whole by regular and part-time crown forces, many of whom openly identified with Orangeism. The eighteenth century thus ended as it had begun, with religious civil war.

FURTHER READING

Bartlett, Thomas: *The Fall and Rise of the Irish Nation: The Catholic Question 1690–1830* (Dublin, 1992).

Beckett, J. C.: *Protestant Dissent in Ireland 1687–1780* (London, 1948).

Connolly, Sean J.: *Religion, Law and Power: The Making of Protestant Ireland 1660–1760* (Oxford, 1992).

Corish, Patrick: *The Catholic Community in the Seventeenth and Eighteenth Centuries* (Dublin, 1981).

Ford, Alan, McGuire, J. and Milne, K. (eds): *As By Law Established: The Church of Ireland since the Reformation* (Dublin, 1995).

Greaves, R. L.: *God's Other Children: Protestant Nonconformists and the Emergence of Denominational Churches in Ireland 1660–1700* (Stanford, CA, 1997).
Herlihy, Kevin (ed.): *The Irish Dissenting Tradition 1650–1750* (Dublin, 1995).
Kilroy, Phil: *Protestant Dissent and Controversy in Ireland 1660–1714* (Cork, 1994).
Power, T. P. and Whelan, Kevin (eds): *Endurance and Emergence: Catholics in Ireland in the Eighteenth Century* (Dublin, 1990).

Part IV

Culture

Chapter Twenty-Two

Print Culture

Bob Harris

To explore print culture in eighteenth-century Britain is to examine a world of striking change. The period saw a proliferation of print, both in terms of the quantity of print produced and in respect of its diversifying forms. In the course of the century, novels, periodicals, newspapers and children's literature joined books, pamphlets, sermons and ballads as common forms of printed material. At the same time, the nature of reading for many altered, reflecting the increasing presence of print in the lives of the elite and the expanding middling ranks in particular. More and more people also began to see themselves and the society of which they were a part through the medium of print; no society had hitherto chronicled its activities and changing habits with the eagerness with which Britons of the eighteenth century did. Change was particularly marked in the early decades of the century, and again in the final third. Underlying this pattern was the influence of commercialization, broadening prosperity and the growing sophistication and scope of what increasingly was a national and international marketplace for print.

The Press before 1700

Discussions of eighteenth-century print culture tend to emphasize (as this chapter will do) the scale and historic importance of changes in this sphere. It is, nevertheless, important not to underestimate the role and availability of print before this period, or to neglect some important continuities. Under the impact of the Reformation, religious books – Bibles, prayer books and other devotional works – were widely printed and circulated from the later sixteenth century. Other types of print available in the sixteenth and even more so in the seventeenth century included school books, scholarly volumes and maps. Itinerant chapmen and ballad and almanac sellers were common figures in society in the two centuries before 1700. It is worth noting that it was in these forms – chapbooks, ballad and almanacs – that the printed word reached and influenced more individuals than conventional books, other perhaps than the Bible and several much reprinted devotional works. This was to be true in the eighteenth century, and it is a dimension to print culture about which we know frustratingly little. Several periods during the seventeenth century also saw explosions of controversial political material – including newsbooks and newspapers – notably during the mid-century civil wars and the Exclusion crisis (1679–81). The desire for news was evident from at least the 1620s, and, once stimulated by print, could not be extinguished. We are, nevertheless, still describing a world that was very different to the one that was to come into existence during the subsequent century. In 1662, the Licensing Act put on to a new statutory basis a system of pre-publication censorship which had been reimposed by the republican regime in the early 1650s. In England and Wales, printing was limited to London and the two university towns, Oxford and Cambridge. Book publication was a monopoly of the Stationers Company in London, and subject to pre-publication censorship. Most books published were either expensive scholarly volumes or devotional and religious works. Newspaper publication in the later seventeenth century was a government monopoly focused after 1665 on a single newspaper – the *London Gazette* – a monopoly broken only for a few years during the Exclusion crisis and the crisis of the Glorious Revolution. Otherwise, serial publication in London was limited to a few advertising or trade sheets. In so far as the dissemination of news was concerned, manuscript newsletters and private communication, written and spoken (including through the pulpit), were more important than print. Scottish seventeenth-century printers produced very few newspapers. Even during the disruption of the civil wars, most papers printed in Scotland – which were far fewer in number, in any case, than those produced south of the border – were either reprints of English newsbooks or, in the 1650s, newsbooks aimed at English troops and administrators. There were also relatively few books printed in Scotland, and Scots were largely reliant on volumes printed on the continent or in England. Printing outside of London, Edinburgh and Dublin was rare, and the number of provincial booksellers in England and Wales was small, certainly when compared to a century later.

A Free Press

The eighteenth-century British press was by contemporary European standards remarkably free. In retrospect, 1695 was a crucial date in this context; it was in this year that pre-publication censorship in England and Wales finally ended. Thereafter, government relied, ultimately, on the power of prosecution for libel under common law in order to police the press. The failure to renew the Licensing Act in 1695 was motivated primarily by dissatisfaction with the ways in which the system had operated in its final years, not by widespread conviction about the merits of a free press. In the years that followed, as particularly London was deluged in controversial print, demands for censorship to be reimposed were commonplace. The leading London booksellers – who feared the effects of an uncontrolled market – were the source of many of these, as were churchmen alarmed by a rapid growth in Deistical writings. Calls to reimpose regulation became much less frequent, however, from the 1720s, although they were heard sporadically thereafter.

Credit for ensuring that toleration was the outcome of these debates has been given to Robert Harley, Tory first minister in 1710–14. Harley, who was a very skilled exploiter of press propaganda and of journalists and writers such as Daniel Defoe and Jonathan Swift, was the architect of the Stamp Act of 1712. This imposed taxation on newspapers for the first time; a levy on advertising quickly followed. The stamp tax was periodically increased during the century (in 1757, 1776, 1780, 1789 and 1797), but only in the last case was this done with the express purpose of restraining the press. In 1712, in the same session in which the Stamp Act was passed, a bill to impose a new system of licensing was allowed to die with the end of the session.

Political support for a free press grew from the 1720s, amongst all stripes of political opinion. This acted as an important restraint on government efforts to police the press, although much depended on political circumstances and the degree of political and financial support that an author or newspaper had. Recent assessments have tended to stress the limitations on government powers in this area, although there may have been rather more self-censorship amongst printers and publishers than is often assumed. Ministries rarely sought new powers over the press, and those that they did seek were relatively minor in effect. In 1743 legislation was passed which allowed for heavy fines and imprisonment for those found guilty of selling unstamped newspapers, but this was politically uncontroversial and had the full support of the legitimate, stamped press. In 1789 an act was passed banning the hiring of newspapers from hawkers; in 1798 another piece of legislation made publication of names and addresses of printers and publishers on every paper mandatory; while in 1799 a register of printing presses was introduced. In Scotland and Ireland, pre-publication censorship did not end in 1695. In Scotland, it effectively seems to have lapsed in the 1700s, a trend expedited by the abolition of the Scottish privy council in 1708, although, during the 1715 Jacobite rebellion, there appears to have been an attempt to reimpose some control on newspapers and newsletters appearing in the coffee houses of the Scottish capital.

Political restrictions on the press were also weaker at the end of the century than at the beginning. The final extinction of Jacobitism as a practical political and military threat on the accession of George III (in 1760) made ministerial powers over the press more difficult to defend. In 1765 the legal authority of the general warrant – which allowed ministers to detain unnamed authors, printers and publishers of libels, and which had been frequently used before 1760 – was undermined by a series of judgements in the courts. In 1771 there was a successful challenge to the Commons privilege of prohibiting reporting of its proceedings in the press, a privilege MPs had jealously defended before the late 1760s. From the early 1770s press reporting of parliamentary debates became a crucial and very prominent feature of press reporting of politics. In the 1770s the Lords followed the Commons in giving up its defence of the prohibition on the reporting of its proceedings. In 1792 Charles James Fox successfully introduced into parliament a bill to confer on juries power to decide what constituted a libel; hitherto, in libel cases judges and ministers had argued that juries should confine their deliberations to the facts of publication.

Ministers did retain, nevertheless, important powers with which to police the press, most notably ex officio informations. These were filed by government officers in the Court of King's Bench and meant that a preliminary hearing of a case of seditious libel did not have to be heard before a grand jury. This device was a very useful means of harassing the print trade – at the very least it meant attendance at the court was necessary, which could be time-consuming and expensive – and was often employed without the case being prosecuted in court. In the 1790s ex officio informations, as well as prosecutions for seditious libel, were frequently used to harry radical newspaper printers and publishers in London and the provinces and with a great deal of success. When judging ministerial attitudes towards press control in this period – and judgements in recent years have tended to emphasize the relatively liberal nature of government policy and attitudes – we need to bear in mind the efficacy of existing powers, especially where repression was, as in the 1790s, supported by a substantial body of public opinion. In Scotland in the same period, a radical presence in the newspaper press was easily suppressed through the courts.

The Growth of the Press

From 1695 the number and influence of newspapers and other serial publications grew rapidly in Britain. The first daily paper in London, the *Daily Courant*, was established in 1702, while the first provincial paper was probably founded in 1700, in Bristol. The overall pattern was one of impressive expansion in the first three decades or so of the century, particularly as measured by the total number of papers printed. By 1723 there were twenty-four provincial papers in existence. They continued to expand in number until the mid-1740s, falling back to a total of thirty-five in 1760. Not all attempts at founding a newspaper succeeded, either in London or the provinces, and failure was commonplace. This could reflect lack of judgement and skill, but, in some cases and areas, it indicated a market that was either too small or already too saturated to sustain a profitable paper. Halifax's only paper in this period was the *Union Journal or Halifax Advertiser*, which made its brief appearance between 1759 and *c.*1763; a successor only appeared in the early nineteenth century. In the case of provincial papers, another important variable was speed of access to newspapers and printed newsletters from London, their main source of news and comment. In Liverpool an enduring newspaper was only founded after the establishment of a daily post to the city in 1755. In Scotland the much slower development of papers outside of Edinburgh and Glasgow reflected the relatively underdeveloped state of postal services beyond the two cities, as well as the less urbanized and commercialized nature of society. Before the 1780s, the only other place to see the establishment of a paper north of the border was Aberdeen, where from 1748 James Chalmers produced his *Aberdeen Journal*. The rising costs of newspapers, a result of successive increases in stamp duty, also imposed important restraints on growth, as the development of a cheap and unstamped press in the 1730s indicates, a press that collapsed in the early 1740s, partly as a consequence of legal action. By the middle of the century, nevertheless, the newspaper press had acquired a maturity of influence, in the political and other spheres, and of form, which was to provide the basis for further rapid expansion and growing influence in the second half of the century.

In the final third of the century, expansion in the newspaper trade accelerated again. In 1782 there were about fifty provincial papers; by 1808 this figure had risen to over 100. These papers were also beginning to carry a greater volume of local news than their counterparts earlier in the century, although their principal role continued to be that of a weekly digest of national and international news culled from the London and international press. In London there was growth, as well as a shift in the relative importance of different types of newspaper. In 1760 London had four dailies and five or six tri-weeklies; by 1790 there were thirteen morning and one evening dailies, seven tri-weeklies and two bi-weeklies. The year 1779 saw the publication of the first Sunday paper in London, the *British Gazette and Sunday Monitor*. London papers were also circulating in growing quantities throughout Britain and in Ireland. A Welsh newspaper had to wait until the first decade of the nineteenth century – although London and several provincial papers had a Welsh circulation in the eighteenth century. (The second half of the eighteenth century also saw the spread of professional printing to Wales, including Welsh-language printing.) In Scotland both the American and the French Revolutions and the Revolutionary War boosted newspaper production, while in Ireland it was a similar story, as ministerial concern about the influence of the press reflected in the first Irish stamp act (1774) and a press act (1784) indicates. By the final third of the century, newspapers, in London and the provinces, were also generating income and profits, from advertising as well as readers, which conferred on them a degree of independence from political manipulation which an earlier generation of newspaper historians tended to underestimate. To this extent, the potential of the press as a vehicle of independent opinion (or opinions) strengthened considerably during the century.

The development of periodicals was, if anything, even more striking than that of the newspaper. Periodicals tended to assume several common forms. First, there were papers in which the dominant feature was an essay on political, literary or moral affairs. The potential influence of such papers was demonstrated most spectacularly by Joseph Addison's and Richard Steele's *Spectator*. Between 1 March 1711 and 5 December 1712, this daily publication may have had a readership of around 40,000 per issue, and it was read widely throughout Britain and Ireland. (It was revived between June and December 1714 as a thrice-weekly publication. It was also produced in many collected editions during the rest of the century.) The formula adopted by the *Spectator*, of a club of correspondents writing on polite letters, philosophy and moral issues, provided the model for numerous subsequent imitators. Another feature of the eighteenth-century periodical was that authors and editors tended to seek out quite closely defined readerships; circulations were also generally significantly lower than for successful newspapers, of the order of several hundred. Several were aimed at women or at a certain profession, for example medicine. The first periodical to be specifically aimed at women readers was John Dunton's *The Ladies Mercury*, although it only ran to four issues in 1693; Dunton thought that women should be better educated than merely to 'distinguish between their Husband's Breeches and another man's'. Political essay papers achieved great influence in the early Hanoverian period, although this was partly because they were so widely extracted in other newspapers and the monthly magazines that began to appear from the early 1730s. The pioneer of the latter was Edward Cave, whose *Gentleman's Magazine; or Monthly Intelligencer*, which first appeared in 1731, was a compendium of everything that attracted the interest of educated, informed readers in the eighteenth century; it also helped to produce and define a cultural accommodation between the landed and urban elites in eighteenth-century Britain which was the source of both considerable social flexibility and a deeper-lying stability in society. The essence of Cave's achievement was to recognize earlier than anyone else the potential for a magazine of this type amongst provincial as well as London readers. (He had been the London correspondent of several provincial papers in the 1720s.) It too was a formula which many tried to repeat in subsequent years, but few had quite Cave's success. In Scotland the first monthly magazine, and the most successful during the century, was the *Scots Magazine*, published from 1739. The 1750s, meanwhile, saw the emergence of successful monthly journals – the *Monthly Review* and the *Critical Review* – devoted to reviewing books and pamphlets. By the end of the century, 250 periodicals had been launched in England; and there had also been a significant number published in the provinces and north of the border.

Newspapers and periodicals were just two parts, however, of a wider world of publishing that was also growing and developing rapidly. The relationship is underlined by the fact that booksellers were amongst the most common owners of London newspapers. Provincial newspaper printers were also often booksellers and, in some cases – for example, Benjamin Collins of Salisbury – bookseller-publishers themselves. London was utterly dominant in the eighteenth-century print trade, a fact that reflected and further enhanced the unifying cultural role which it played in this period. London was synonymous with fashion, and provincial society looked on the metropolis in this period with envy, astonishment as well as, on occasion, alarm. It was through print that many people encountered London and the values with which it was associated. The *Spectator* played a hugely influential role in this context, as a disseminator of metropolitan values and taste. Important books were nearly always published first in London. Major figures in the Scottish enlightenment, for example William Robertson, looked to London bookseller-publishers to publish the works which made them nationally and internationally famous. This was partly a matter of cultural prestige – Lawrence Sterne deliberately disguised the provincial provenance of the first edition of *Tristram Shandy* – but also of the strategic position of the capital in an increasing far-flung network of relationships that linked printers, booksellers and readers throughout the rest of Britain and, in some cases, North America and the continent. Print in the eighteenth century streamed across national boundaries, and the continental anglomania of the third quarter of the century, strongly present in both France and many German states, owed much to the vogue for British novels and other writing overseas.

Viewed in purely economic terms, bookselling and publishing represented a complex world of cooperation and competition, where risks and profits were frequently shared between bookseller-publishers. (A clear distinction between wholesale and retail bookselling and publishing was only beginning to emerge at the end of our period.) The development of the trade was partly shaped by legal factors – notably, shifting legal definitions of copyright – but also by the elaboration of different sets of relationships between the various components of the print trade. The complexity and variety of these relationships defy quick summary, but the main effect was to distribute risk, protect literary property and to create a trade which was increasingly national and international in scope. From the middle of the century, competitive pressures also exerted a strengthening influence on the world of publishing and book retailing, a factor promoting further change and innovation. A major element of the Scottish and Irish book trades was the production of cheaper reprints of works originally published in London. The import of Irish (and other foreign) reprints was illegal after 1739, but there was a considerable (if necessarily unquantifiable) smuggling trade into Scotland through several west coast ports. This appears to have been a trade which several leading Scottish bookseller-publishers had a part in, although they also had connections with the London businesses who were damaged by the subterfuges in which the Irish and Scots engaged. Provincial printing in the eighteenth century was largely limited, apart from newspapers and jobbing printing (handbills, forms, advertisements, tickets), to books of local interest (antiquarian or local histories) and sermons. Several provincial towns – notable among them Newcastle-upon-Tyne – did see, however, the establishment of firms that printed vast quantities of popular literature. (In Scotland popular publishing was concentrated in the capital, Glasgow, Stirling, Falkirk and Paisley.) The spread of printing outside of London was also heavily concentrated in the final decades of the century. In Scotland printing remained heavily focused on Edinburgh, with only Glasgow, Aberdeen and Perth seeing the publication of significant numbers of items (other than popular literature) during the century.

The eighteenth-century book trade underwent notable expansion, although it is easier to document in the later stages of the century than at the beginning, partly because of the spread of another type of publication in this period – the town directory. A subscription list to one publication issued in 1744 named 294 country booksellers. This number included twenty-two from Scotland and four from Wales. At the end of the century the *Universal British Directory* listed 988 booksellers in 316 towns in England and Wales. In Scotland specialist booksellers had spread to most Lowland towns of any size by 1775; even where a specialist bookseller was not present, it was likely that there would be an agent for a London or Edinburgh bookseller. In Cupar, a small market town in Fife, in the 1740s this individual was a glover. Later in the century, itinerant booksellers, such as George Miller of Dunbar, may have been operating in many parts of Lowland Scotland, selling books second-hand. In London, the average annual output of new and reprinted works in English in the period 1790–5 was 3,472; in the middle of the century (1750–9), the same figure had been 1,567. In Edinburgh, the corresponding figures are 216 and 375.

Several other important patterns underpinning the growth of print and the book trade in this period are worth picking out. First, under the impact of improving communications and spreading prosperity – at least amongst the top third of society – the print trade was expanding away from the market and county towns that had earlier dominated it at the provincial level – places such as York, Canterbury or Shrewsbury. By the final decades of the century it was tending to grow fastest in the burgeoning towns and cities of the north, the new centres of wealth and population. In Liverpool there were eleven firms in the book trade in 1766; fourteen in 1774; thirty-four were listed in the *Universal British Directory* (1794); and by 1800 there were ninety-eight. Second, the final decade of the century saw growth at unprecedented levels. This was especially evident in Scotland, although partly because it took place from a lower base. In the case of Glasgow, another buoyant centre of manufacturing, books and other items bearing local imprints – a good measure of local publishing activity – surged in the 1790s.

The Impact of the Press

Establishing the outlines of the growth of a new world of print in the eighteenth century is relatively simple. Figures for newspaper circulation, a fair number of pamphlet and book editions are fairly widely available, and they provide a basis for assessing the expansion of the print trade. They show, for example, that amongst London newspapers circulations did not grow significantly during the century; what changed was the number of titles. They also show that it was school books and almanacs that were commonly printed in the largest editions. What is much more difficult, however, is to assess who the new culture of print reached and how it affected them. Part of the problem is the sheer volume and growing diversity of print published across the century. There is also a general lack of data on who bought or read what, quite apart from the issue of how things were read and with what effect.

Some generalizations are, nevertheless, possible. Literacy was probably less of a constraint than cost. Problems surround the measurement and definition of literacy, but some reading ability seems to have been very widely diffused in urban communities by the middle of the eighteenth century and throughout much of Lowland Scottish society. Apart from popular literature, print was relatively expensive. There was a dynamic in some sections of the print trade towards searching out new and expanded readerships. In the 1730s part-books began to appear, so lowering their cost with each instalment and making them marketable on the lines of other popular literature. At the end of the century Matthew Brown, a printer-publisher from North Shields, produced a Bible, illustrated with engravings by the Newcastle engraver Thomas Bewick, in ninety-three parts at 5 d a part. Brown claimed that it was the cheapest family Bible that had ever been offered to the public. Yet the impression left by the sources is that the purchase and readership of newspapers, books and other forms of print, apart from popular literature, were heavily concentrated amongst the elites and the increasingly numerous and prosperous middling ranks. It is notable that when groups of different sorts wished to reach a popular audience through print, their publications typically were sold in large numbers at a heavy discount to be given away, recognition of the fact that cost would otherwise seriously limit the extent of their influence. Much of the loyalist literature during the Jacobite rebellions of 1715 and 1745–6, and again during the 1790s, was of this kind, as was literature produced by religious Evangelicals, including Methodists, and by societies for the reformation of manners in the 1690s and again in the 1780s. Provincial newspapers needed to circulate on a regional basis to survive and prosper, suggesting a relatively socially circumscribed market for them, especially outside of larger towns and cities. Christopher Etherington's *York Chronicle* had 2,230 subscribers in 1776. By this date, this was not a notably high figure, and Etherington's business collapsed in 1777. These subscribers were distributed throughout and around towns and cities in Yorkshire and neighbouring counties.

Access to books, periodicals, newspapers and pamphlets was facilitated by the emergence of circulating, subscription and proprietary libraries and book clubs from the later 1730s and – in the later eighteenth century – purpose-built newsrooms. Between the 1720s and the end of the century 112 book-rental establishments were founded in the capital, and around 270 in the provinces. In Scotland the first circulating library was established by Allan Ramsay in Edinburgh in 1725, but they were relatively slow to spread in the next few decades; the real expansion in libraries north of the border, of various sorts, was in the final decades of the century. Throughout Britain an unknown number of booksellers also rented out books. John Clay, who had bookshops in Daventry, Rugby and Lutterworth in the west midlands in the 1770s, lent out books at the cost of 3 d a volume, imposing no annual fee as was the practice of most libraries. Coffee houses and taverns supplied newspapers and pamphlets, and in some cases books, for their clientele. Yet again, we must be wary about exaggerating the extent to which these bodies opened up readership to groups much below the prosperous middling sort. Subscriptions to libraries and book clubs were relatively costly, although in the case of commercial libraries in larger towns and cities scales of tariffs could be fairly elaborate, including rates for borrowing individual items overnight or for a week. We know relatively little about coffee houses outside of a small number of relatively famous ones in London and one or two in the provinces. In 1715 a report from Aberdeen described neighbouring Jacobite gentry spreading rumours in the local coffee house, suggesting that at least part of their clientele was the local elite. Where information is available, membership of subscription libraries and book clubs appears to have been typically confined to a fairly representative cross-section of the local elite. This was especially true of book clubs, which often comprised no more than ten to twenty members. Some subscription libraries involved many more people. The Liverpool subscription library, founded in 1758, had over 400 members by 1799. Yet the bulk of their membership was still focused on the relatively prosperous classes, typically, clergymen, manufacturers, merchants and various professionals. The Perth subscription library, founded in 1786, had a membership largely comprised of the town elite – professionals and merchants – and neighbouring gentry and ministers of the church.

Several things appear to have been happening, therefore. First, books, periodicals and newspapers were by the later eighteenth century being read more extensively by the upper and middling ranks, both men and women. This simply reflected the much greater wealth of publications available, and also the book clubs and libraries of various kinds. They fed an appetite for fashionable literature, often of a serious kind, which was being produced in ever-increasing volumes by the final third of the century. As book prices rose in the later eighteenth century, and as the number of publications proliferated, few individuals could afford to purchase more than a small selection of them on their own. Many moralists complained about circulating libraries as sources of the moral corruption of women, who were borrowing cheap novels and filling their heads with unsuitable expectations and ideals. (The publication of novels grew rapidly in the 1740s, and then surged again in the 1770s, partly to feed the appetite of users of the commercial and subscription libraries.) The reality seems to have been slightly different – many libraries flourished also because of the great demand for books such as histories and travel literature, although there are very few extant borrowing records. Newsrooms, which emerged at the very end of the century, furnished the same service in respect of periodicals and newspapers, providing a range of these far beyond what an individual would consider purchasing. Books and newspapers also attracted a large readership amongst the commercial classes, for practical as well as cultural reasons. Up-to-date information about international affairs was crucial to traders and merchants, and newspapers offered unexampled breadth and continuity of coverage in this sphere.

Nevertheless, other readerships, some of which stretched further down the social scale, were also coming into clearer definition in the course of the eighteenth century. Weavers, colliers and shoemakers from the west and southwest of Lowland Scotland can be found subscribing to religious works in the middle and at the end of the eighteenth century. Many religious works were also published in serial form, and popular devotional works continued to be, as they had in the previous century, some of the most widely circulated and read. These and other religious works provided one of the staples of the country book trade; they also provided a staple of a growing Welsh-language print trade based in Carmarthen. Such facts warn us against assuming too readily that print was predominantly a secularizing force in this period, at least outside of 'polite' society. The market for children's and popular literature was a buoyant and extremely large one. Practical books and guides proliferated. It was the gaps between these different readerships that may have been widening during the eighteenth century, although in some cases they were overlapping. Working-class autobiographies of individuals who were children in the 1780s and 1790s tend to evoke a world in which books and newspapers were rare, although the fortunate had some access to popular literature. Relatively few new fictional works crossed the divide between high and low culture, one notable exception being Defoe's *Robinson Crusoe*, which was printed in cheap abridgements.

For those resident in towns and cities, however, print was colonizing increasing areas of society. Urban society was in various ways moving towards much greater print dependency, although this is a process which has yet to be systematically documented. A growing number of professions – such as attorneys and auctioneers – called on the services of printers, for advertisements and forms. The relationships between print and the medical world, amateur and professional, were close and developing ones. Local government in its various guises increasingly exploited the possibilities for communication created by print and newspapers. When a section of the populace rioted because of a shortage of meal in Leith in 1751, a handbill was quickly distributed explaining how the authorities were seeking to redress the grievances of the crowd. Already by 1760 an increasing number of individuals and groups in society (commercial bodies, ministers and politicians of all stripes, charitable organizations, religious groups, victims of crime, tradesmen and merchants, even well-organized sections of the labouring classes such as colliers and weavers) were recognizing that the newspaper represented an unrivalled vehicle for publicity and the dissemination of information. The world of print in the eighteenth century also encompassed a growing number of artisans and members of the skilled labouring classes, as well as the middling and upper ranks. By the later eighteenth century artisans lent one another books and went to debating clubs. They also had access to newspapers through less fashionable coffee houses and taverns in many parts of urban Britain. Newspapers could also be hired from hawkers in the streets; they were also purchased collectively and passed around. In the 1790s, under the impact of the French Revolution and French Revolutionary Wars, these practices appear to have expanded significantly amongst sections of the labouring classes, although it may also be simply that they became more politically threatening and therefore visible to the historian. In Cupar, Fife, weavers were clubbing together to buy copies of the *Scots Chronicle* in the later 1790s. Nor were artisans and shopkeepers who lived in rural villages necessarily cut off from the world of books and print, even before the 1790s. In very remote places, for example Cromarty on the edge of the Highlands, there was the possibility of borrowing books from local merchants. In the aftermath of the Jacobite rebellion of 1745–6, Catholic priests carried political pamphlets and tracts through the disaffected areas of the Highlands. Chapbooks, and indeed in some places other books, were carried by itinerant sellers on extended circuits through the country and to places such as fairs and markets; a flood of print seeped into the most obscure rural areas.

During the eighteenth century, therefore, the tentacles of the print trade extended across many parts of British society. In so doing, they helped to bring into being a culture of unprecedented diversity. It was also a culture in which for many amongst the elites and middling sort, what a person read became an increasingly important mark of taste and, consequently, social status. This should not disguise the fact, however, that many forms of print in the eighteenth century were not simply a facet of either elite or popular culture, but rather they formed an important bridge between them. As the editor of the *Sheffield Register* declared on 9 June 1797: 'All ranks of people from the Peer of the realm to the industrious mechanic find something to please them in a newspaper.'

FURTHER READING

Aspinall, Arthur: *Politics and the Press c.1780–1850* (London, 1949).

Barker, Hannah: *Newspapers, Politics and Public Opinion in Late Eighteenth-Century England* (Oxford, 1998).

Barker, Hannah: *Newspapers, Politics and English Society 1695–1855* (London, 2000).

Black, Jeremy: *The English Press in the Eighteenth Century* (London, 1987).

Carlson, C. Lennart: *The First Magazine: A History of the Gentleman's Magazine* (Providence, RI, 1938).

Cranfield, G. A.: *The Development of the Provincial Newspaper 1700–1760* (Oxford, 1962).

Feather, John: *The Provincial Book Trade in Eighteenth-Century England* (Cambridge, 1985).

Harris, Bob: *Politics and the Rise of the Press: Britain and France, 1620–1800* (London, 1996).

Harris, Michael: *London Newspapers in the Age of Walpole: A Study in the Origins of the Modern English Press* (London, 1987).

Munter, Robert: *The History of the Irish Newspaper 1685–1760* (Cambridge, 1967).

Myers, Robin and Harris, Michael (eds): *Development of the English Book Trade, 1700–1793* (Oxford, 1981).

O'Ciorsain, Niall: *Print and Popular Culture in Ireland, 1750–1800* (London, 1997).

Raven, James: *Judging New Wealth: Popular Publishing and Responses to Commerce in England 1750–1800* (Oxford, 1992).

Raymond, Joad (ed.): *News, Newspapers and Society in Early Modern Britain* (London, 1999).

Sullivan, Alvin (ed.): *British Literary Magazines: The Augustan Age and the Age of Johnson, 1698–1788* (London, 1983).

Wiles, R. M.: *Freshest Advices: Early Provincial Newspapers in England* (Columbus, OH, 1965).

Chapter Twenty-Three

Political Ideas from Locke to Paine

Pamela Edwards

The political thought of eighteenth-century Britain differed from the political thought of the previous century in three significant ways. First, to an even greater degree than in the time of Hobbes and Locke, political theory developed as an extension of the debate on human nature. The application of an empirical epistemology to questions of obligation, entitlement, volition, instinct, rationality, sensibility and (most importantly) sociability characterizes much of the effort of eighteenth-century political writers to consider the problem of constituted political authority. These questions – both moral and scientific – underpinned the more immediate and practical question of the relationship between appropriate forms of social organization and the best (and it was assumed most natural) forms of government. The debates on nature and artifice paralleled and intersected with the revival of classical and Renaissance narratives of virtue and corruption, as well as with Christian medieval doctrines of providence and design, to produce new explanations of power and legitimacy. Second, these new explanations of power and legitimacy increasingly depended on a civil juridical discourse of contract and by the mid-century admitted an expanded and broadening definition of 'the people'. Third, spurred by Union with Scotland (1707) and rapid expansion of empire, the eighteenth century marked the appearance of a nationalizing discourse of British, rather than narrowly English, political thought.

If these three developments suggest an innovative or modern tendency in the political thought of eighteenth-century Britain, three assumptions may be offered to explain the persistence of its nostalgic, and some would argue, elegiac qualities. Theorists drew their political inspiration and metaphor and lexicon not only from the ancient Greeks and Romans, but from the ancient Hebrews and from the seventeenth century. The inheritance of civil war and Restoration memory and polemic, therefore, as filtered through understandings of the Bible and the classics, constituted much of the early eighteenth-century debate on the 'Revolution Principles'. Commonwealth writers such as Algernon Sidney, Whig apologists such as John Locke, and Tory constitutionalists such as George Savile, marquess of Halifax, suggest three such inheritances. Published posthumously, after his execution for treason in 1685,

Algernon Sidney's *Discourses Concerning Government* suggested that the rights of a free people rested on a liberty secured by war. Rebellion, in Sidney's account, was a powerful and improving scourge. The citizen not only had an individual right of rebellion, to be claimed *in extremis*, he also had a positive obligation, as a citizen of the republic, to resist tyranny and to restore liberty.

Sidney's argument rested heavily on historical precedent. He pointed to the history of Rome for evidence of the cleansing merits of armed rebellion. Social wars and civil wars had been the engine of political and constitutional advancement throughout Rome's history. The history of Rome, like that of the free Germans and the Scots, was characterized as free and pure during its eras of agrarian militarism. The Roman republic's demise was occasioned by social and political corruptions consequent on the rise of luxury and the advent of commercial empire. Such rapid transformations of the political significance of property produced instabilities. Social instability, it was observed, often facilitated the concentration of power in a single tyrant. Sidney had refused to attend the trial of Charles I and had personally balked at the execution of the king. But, in his abstract account of government, he recognized regicide as a just component of the right of resistance, the right to banish tyranny. For Sidney, republicanism not only acknowledged sovereignty as originating in the people; it recognized consent as a power that remained resident in the people. Sidney's perspective may be viewed as radical in action, but it rested on arguments that fit well within the philosophical and juridical assumptions of the Renaissance. Arguably, his extensive use of historical example and his emphasis on the corrupting and destabilizing influence of new forms of wealth, in conjunction with his consistent aggrandizement of martial prowess as the foundation of political virtue, mark Sidney as a defender of tradition. While popular sovereignty arguments suggest a more innovative perspective, the question for Sidney, as for most late seventeenth- and early eighteenth-century political thinkers, was how that sovereignty might be mediated in a parliament. This question, of the limits of popular sovereignty within a government constituted in parliament, provided the central premise of the Revolution Settlement after 1688.

Sidney may have provided one ideal of the classical republicanism of the seventeenth-century Commonwealthman, but it was another of the Rye House conspirators who would most completely articulate the philosophy of the Revolution of 1688. The foundations of what would be described as 'Whig principles' by the late eighteenth century were most completely advanced in the writings of John Locke. Educated at Oxford University within the limits of scholastic philosophical tradition, Locke produced novel arguments in epistemology and political thought that escaped and transcended the traditional limits of medieval philosophical discourse. This in part accounts for the persistence of his influence on philosophers and political theorists. It is arguable that his immediate influence was limited and that his reputation, far greater at the end of the eighteenth century than at the end of the seventeenth, was enhanced by a political future he could not have anticipated.

Locke's philosophy suggested an alternative to tradition and mystical idealism in a world constructed and understood through principles of common sense and reason. Rejecting the philosophical assumptions of the scholastics, Locke was deeply influenced by the radical rationalist scepticism of Descartes and the new scientific and empirical approaches of Bacon, Hobbes and Bayle. The world was not to be known intuitively, as faint perceptions of some deeper hidden truth; it was to be tested empirically and scrutinized through the perception of those phenomena available to the senses. In his *Essay on Human Understanding* (1687–90), Locke produced arguments for cognition and reality that broke with ancient and medieval assumptions about man and nature. The world was materially and tangibly real, in a way it had not been for the Platonists, either of classical antiquity or those Renaissance neo-Platonic thinkers, who accorded some degree of a divine spark to human essence. Perception, and through perception cognizance, was dependent on the experience of the qualities, primary and secondary, which resided in material objects. There were, for Locke, no innate ideas. Man's nature, therefore, was a book to be written on an initially blank sheet of paper. These two assertions, that there was a world which was real and knowable in some physical material sense, and that human nature was the consequence of interaction with that world, had profound significance both theologically and politically.

Locke's political arguments are most closely advanced in his *Two Treatises of Government* (written in the 1680s but published in 1690). The first of these was a response to the arguments for the divine right of kings, which Sir Robert Filmer advanced in his *Patriarcha* (1680). Filmer argued that all kingly political authority derived from God as a power of fathers over children, directly inherited from Adam. Locke attacked this assertion on both historical and logical grounds as an absurd fallacy. While rejecting the coherence and demonstrability of Filmer's historical evidence, Locke did not reject a theological foundation for the legitimacy of government and law. Indeed, the presumption of divine law as the foundation of all natural law was the cornerstone of Locke's accounts of justice and morality. It was in the second *Treatise*, however, that Locke laid out the principles of the laws of nature and the foundations of civil society from which all government and all contract emerged. Describing metaphorically an original state of nature ordered by certain natural general laws, Locke conceived of man as born possessed of certain concomitant and inalienable natural rights. These are life, liberty and property.

Life was given, asserted Locke, by God and nature; liberty and property were its consequence. Liberty as a natural right was the capacity to consent; it was as such an innate faculty or power. While each man had a power in himself he also had a property in himself or a natural dominion over himself. Man, in Locke's account, was quite literally in possession of his faculties; his free capacity to choose, to act, to consent. Where the sphere of action was combined with the natural world, man also had dominion over such nature as he acted upon in the first instance. Simply put, the admixture of labour and nature produced property, and that property by extension of natural right became a just entitlement or possession. These entitlements or possessions would remain absolute if they were not challenged by competing claims of dominion. It was the need to arbitrate between competing entitlements, or competing claims of property, that necessitated the original contracts of government. As government was fashioned for the principle of protecting individual rights to property, it was best, Locke deemed, that government rest heavily on the principle of property that constituted the most stable and enduring interest: namely, land. Locke's second *Treatise on Government*, while advancing strong arguments for the natural moral and juridical equality of men, was none the less a powerful defence of a civilly constituted landed oligarchy in the sphere of contract and governance.

Whilst assuredly a republican of the kind who viewed the republic in any of its forms as the sovereignty of law, it is unlikely that Locke was a democratic thinker in the modern sense. He did not advocate the abolition of monarchy and he certainly did not envision the abolition of the Lords, who embodied the principle of property and constituted a senatorial continuity. He did acknowledge that sovereignty originated in the people, in their consent to be governed by the rule of law through a social and civil contract. If, however, the people's trust is violated and the contract broken by those who hold the sovereign power, then Locke acknowledged a right of limited resistance, *in extremis*. Trust, and the capacity to promise, are critically important in Locke's account of social and civil contract. Indeed, the foundation of all community rests on man's capacity to choose to recognize another's right by acknowledging his own duty. This reciprocity is only possible if trust exists. While this has been viewed as a cornerstone of all of Locke's political and moral writings, it is most evident in Locke's *Letter on Toleration*. In the *Letter* Locke argues that toleration for religious Dissenters should be extended to all varieties of heterodoxy excepting Roman Catholics and atheists, because neither could swear an oath of loyalty to the crown as constituted in church and state. Catholics could not swear the oath because of divided loyalty. The conflict of interest between pope and emperor would preclude Catholic subjects from swearing such an oath. Atheists could not swear any oath because they did not believe in God; they had no fidelity. In either case the problem which made political inclusion impossible was quite simply an absence of trust. Trust, for Locke, is the foundation of all contracts: moral, social and civil.

The years after the accession of the new sovereigns William and Mary, following the Glorious Revolution that swept them to power in 1688–9, were characterized by the need to consolidate and legitimate not only these new monarchs but arguably a newly constituted form of monarchy. The Whigs were both the bringers of the harvest and the beneficiaries of the feast of Williamite succession. But as so often happens at a long-awaited festivity, arguments quickly emerge as to seating order and portion size. Who would have the new king's ear? Which counsel would he pursue? Where would the balance of interest lie in the new government? What work would particular arguments do? It is therefore difficult to characterize a unified Whig ideology during this period, beyond those principles that justified the resistance to James while simultaneously asserting the legitimacy of William. Anti-monarchical arguments were bad, while anti-tyrannical arguments were good. Some, like Robert Molesworth and Walter Moyle, wanted a far more radical transformation of the constitution, one which more closely embodied the more republican spirit of Commonwealthmen such as Algernon Sidney. Others hoped that the constitutional settlement would strongly limit royal power and even enhance the powers of the House of Commons. Those Tories who had not fled into exile with James II were now confronted by the need first to survive, and then to conserve. While a chief preoccupation of these Williamite Tories was undoubtedly the privileges of the Church of England, they were also mindful of their own properties and offices. In the light of the particularly difficult position of these Tories, who must protect their church even if they had abandoned their king, a number of interesting critical positions may be detected. The most ingenious of these was that of Halifax's 'Trimmer'.

George Savile, marquess of Halifax (1633–95), was a politician of great pragmatism. He was before everything else a king's man, whether that king was Charles II or indeed William III. He was strongly associated with the Tory position during the last years of Charles's reign, but was one of the architects of the Whig transition under William III. It is important to distinguish Halifax's royalism from his Toryism. While Halifax had spoken out against the exclusion of James, duke of York, he had worked to find some accommodation that would reconcile Charles with his illegitimate son the duke of Monmouth in 1683. It was the effort to bring the king to some constructive resolution of the highly partisan succession controversy that prompted Halifax to write and distribute his pamphlet on *The Character of a Trimmer*. Although written in 1684, it was not published until 1688, after which it enjoyed numerous reprintings and transformations. Arguing that the best politicians served the national interest and the crown, through the spirit of compromise, Halifax may be viewed as an advocate of the politics of independence, or as the original expositor of 'governing from the centre'. Compromise, however, was not to be taken as unqualified accommodation. While Halifax's party loyalties tended to be tied to those interests which upheld his view of crown priorities as national priorities, he shrank from lending support to a monarch whose publicly and privately stated beliefs ran foul of the best interests of the nation as expressed in the constitution.

If Whiggism, throughout its long history, has been associated with the principles of parliamentary supremacy and the rule of law, Toryism has been (from its inception as a political creed) tied to party interests associated with the causes of church and king. But where these interests clashed rather than cohered, more flexible and subtle arguments were advanced. Halifax's view of constitutionalism identified the legitimacy of the crown with the constitution of an independent English state church. He believed that the power of parliament was supreme where it acted through the love and consent of the people as expressed through the monarch's will. For many defenders of this high constitutionalist line a choice would finally be required between a king who defined the church or a church which underscored and fortified the powers and purposes of monarchy.

While James chose to define himself through actions that regarded all institutions as subject to the personal faith and personal will of the king, he threatened the very foundations of the constitution which he was held, in Whig doctrine, to embody. In short, the English church could not be contained within the sovereign body of a Catholic prince. It is instructive, therefore, to notice the intentions and the uses of *The Character of a Trimmer* as they were transformed by the rapidly changing interests of the day. Said to be a Whig polemic, because it supported the interests of Monmouth against York, and because Halifax survived and flourished in the aftermath of the Revolution, it none the less placed a high importance on the role of a prince who governed with the people's love. The role of all servants of the crown, including the people, was to steady the ship of state as it sailed on a swiftly flowing river of political events and currents of opinion. Monarchs captained such ships, while ministers and members of parliament pulled to the centre, or 'trimmed', to right the load and steady the craft.

Pursuing this golden mean precluded both absolutist and republican extremes. While Halifax defined the purposes of princely power as the guardianship of the people's freedom, he also suggested that the necessity of that same freedom was as an instrument of the sovereign power; that the people should have as much liberty as was necessary to make them useful to the crown. The wise prince governed with love rather than fear. Such a prince, Halifax concluded, would be 'secure'. For his brand of monarchalism, his constitutionalism and his principled pragmatism, Halifax later became a great hero of moderate constitutionalists such as Edmund Burke.

While Halifax represented the constitutional Toryism of seventeenth-century thinkers like Edward Hyde, earl of Clarendon, he defended and indeed celebrated the virtues of trimming as among the best qualities of good politicians as loyal national servants. Later Tory polemic identified trimming with duplicity, political cynicism, and as definitively Whiggish. Trimmers, as characterized by later Tory polemicists, were political insiders who practised the politics of consensus as no more than a self-interested strategy for their own political survival. In partial response to this early eighteenth-century Whig ethos of pragmatism and conciliation, a Tory polemic of outsidership emerged. Characterized well by the satire of Swift, the rhetoric of the outsider, deployed especially by old veterans of the partisan fray, reached its apotheosis in the 'Country' polemic of Henry St John, Viscount Bolingbroke, by the 1730s.

Jonathan Swift (1667–1745) held questions of toleration and religious liberty in an interesting tension with views on political freedom. As a dean in the Church of Ireland, his loyalties and interests were complex. While his writings have been considered characteristically Tory, and indeed he wrote extensively for the Tory *Examiner* after 1710, he entered English political life in the service of Sir William Temple, who supported Whig interests in government. Swift's deep mistrust of Presbyterianism made him uneasy about the extension of religious toleration to Protestant Dissenters. At the same time his criticism of the corruptions and inefficiencies of English government policy, and his refusal to regard Ireland as a 'dependent kingdom', made him a strong advocate of political liberty through a popular sovereignty. A forceful defender of the doctrine of government by popular consent, usually viewed as the cornerstone of Whig ideology, Swift was an early critic of the Whig Junto's prudentialist arguments either as rationales for protecting the church or for social and charitable projects. *An Argument for Abolishing Christianity* (1708) was a satirical rebuke to those who would protect the church purely as a matter of expedience. *A Modest Proposal* (1729) extended the metaphor of the Irish poor as cattle or swine to a quite literal extreme. In both works, Swift rejected the cynical reduction of all conscience and all human tragedy to no more than the object of a prudential political calculus.

If Whiggism had grown cynical as well as 'sceptical' by the 1720s, Swift suggested Tory alternatives of conscience and principle, which stopped short of the Jacobite and absolutist ideals of divine right, passive obedience and non-resistance. While Swift had initially deployed these arguments in 1710–14 in the service of the Tory ministry's attack on the policies and personalities of the outgoing Whig administration, he carried much of Commonwealth and revolutionary or 'Real' Whig principles into the late days of Queen Anne's reign and beyond. But, he had reappropriated and refashioned these ideas as arguments that, while Tory, were generically oppositional rather than conventionally partisan in their rhetorical appeal. Swift's many years of service as a Tory polemicist hardly mark him out as a political independent. Yet, his celebration in the fourth part of *Gulliver's Travels* (1726) of the impartial and reasonable calm of the world of the Houyhnhnm, when combined with his own increasing distaste for the 'Yahoo' nature of all interested parties in social, and most especially political life, suggest his affinities for what eventually developed as an ideology of outsidership by 1724.

'Country party' polemic was not an exclusively Tory nor Whig ideology. It was a broadly oppositional omnibus response to fears of centralization and the encroaching corruptions of money in government. These worries were not entirely unreasonable and may be associated with two important changes in British political life after 1715. The first was a change that had been evolving as a social and political force since the end of the seventeenth century, but came into remarkable prominence after the Glorious Revolution. The commercial, then rapidly financial, revolution of the late seventeenth and early eighteenth centuries was increasingly given cognizance by the law, both through the creation of the Bank of England in 1694 and the growing efforts to regulate the stock market, particularly after the bursting of the South Sea Bubble in 1720. With new forms of wealth and the rising prosperity of the 'city interest', the balance of social and political power shifted; subtly at first, but with increasing significance to the gentry and the old landed elites before long. New alliances emerged. At times the coherence of interests appeared to be between the court and the city, at other moments, between the city and parliament. In either case the perception of those outside the coalescence of money and magnate oligarchy, whether they were 'Country Whigs' or 'Country Tories', was that a new monopoly of wealth and rank was threatening the traditional balance of the constitution. The second critical change, while a matter of administration rather than broad social and economic forces, provided further evidence of the deepening constitutional significance of the rising tide of money in politics. Some regarded the administration of Sir Robert Walpole (1721–42) as a direct consequence of the corrupting influences of money on government.

Competing languages of virtue and corruption suffused early eighteenth-century political rhetoric. Particularly during the reign of the first two Georges, British political thought was deeply influenced by the discourse of classical republicanism. The classical example had the rhetorical advantage of offering a secular pagan model as an alternative to the charged and often sectarian language of scripture. It would be wrong, however, to suggest that the classical and profane obliterated the medieval and sacred. It surfaced as a competitor to rather than a replacement for Christian polemic. In the early Country party uses of classical republicanism, this discourse celebrated the ideals of duty and virtuous citizenship in a republic. It drew heavily on ancient Greek city-state and Roman republican examples. The Greek example of virtuous oligarchy focused on Sparta, its martial independence and bucolic simplicity both preserved by the ideal of an aristocratic citizen militia. The Roman example tended to emphasize a broader construction of the gentry. It celebrated the values of Cato the Censor's republic, where again the secret to a free and virtuous polity was the model of an independent landed patriciate, but also the preservation of a citizenry that drew its strength through the duties and prerogatives of freeholding. Agrarian republicanism, in both the Spartan and the Roman republican forms, celebrated the virtues of the citizen soldier, the interests of whom were independently sustained by his status as a member of a freeholding gentry. Whether a writer emphasized the examples offered by Cato or Lycurgus depended on the critical issue at hand. The militia argument had always, from its first appearance in seventeenth-century Commonwealth writings, been an argument directed against newly professional 'standing armies'. Country party writers depicted the domestic billeting of a standing army in peacetime as an obvious tool of absolutism and therefore an instrument of tyranny. The recent history of the civil wars and the Glorious Revolution had, they argued, provided ample evidence of this.

For Country or Independent Whig writers, such as John Trenchard and Thomas Gordon, cautionary example could be drawn from the Tory despotism of James II and his billeting of a standing army outside London for the purpose of intimidating parliament. Similarly, for the Tory polemicist, tyranny could be personified through Oliver Cromwell and his imperial direction of the New Model Army during the Protectorate. Such examples and precedents could be subtly combined and fluidly rolled, one into the other, to provide an 'ideal type' of military despotism. Of more immediate concern to Tory critics, from Swift to Bolingbroke, was the caesarism of the duke of Marlborough. Standing armies were also the instruments of rapid fiscal expansion and an enhanced power for the Treasury. They were also implicated in the growing concerns over the corrupting influence of the monied interest on the principle of landed property itself.

Both John Trenchard and Thomas Gordon wrote of the need for an agrarian law to prevent the development of landed monopolies by a narrow elite. In *Cato's Letters* (1720–3) they wrote of the central connection between liberty and equality of property in a free and just republic. Strongly hostile to both Catholic and Church of England establishment viewpoints, in *The Independent Whig* Gordon, in particular, was vehemently anti-clerical. Both viewed religious freedom as a necessary corollary of political freedom, and tended to sympathize with Dissenting or freethinking opinion. On the subject of human nature, Gordon seems to have viewed men as possessing a natural equality, not only of moral worth but of talents. In this, he differed from Locke. Discrepancies of talent were of course more than evident in man as found within civil society, as it was presently constituted. But this was the fault of iniquitous government and inadequate education rather than a consequence of any natural lottery. The political and moral necessity of man's natural equality and inherent freedom of conscience was that free speech (preserved in spoken and written forms through concomitant liberties of assembly and press) was the birthright of the citizen of the virtuous republic.

While the Country arguments, both Whig and Tory, tended to defend the interests of the gentry, there were those among the great nobility who also wished to attack the growing powers of central government. Henry St John, Viscount Bolingbroke, had a career of great dexterity and, in the finest tradition of Halifax's 'Trimmer', great flexibility. Unlike Halifax's temperate and mediating pragmatist, however, Bolingbroke's grasp at statesmanship was always overreached by his naked personal ambition, impetuosity of judgement and an irredeemably poor sense of timing. Having failed to secure the highest preferment under Queen Anne in 1714, he fled to the continent and then rashly enlisted in support of the Jacobite Old Pretender's cause. Disappointed by the possibilities of the Jacobite court in exile by 1716, Bolingbroke managed eventually to accomplish his own partial rehabilitation back in Britain by the mid-1720s. Much of the rest of his career was devoted to the destruction of Walpole's ministry, and most of Bolingbroke's literary output followed his period of exile abroad and later marginalization at home. As is often observed of Machiavelli, Hobbes and Locke, the writing of political theory is often an introspective consequence of the failure of political action. Certainly, Bolingbroke's *Idea of a Patriot King* may be viewed as a bid for the patronage of George II's son

(Frederick, Prince of Wales), much as *The Prince* was Machiavelli's final application to Lorenzo de' Medici for his own return to political service.

Critics have tended to mark *The Idea of a Patriot King* (1738), following on *The Spirit of Patriotism* (1736), as constituting a watershed in Bolingbroke's career. He had throughout his life remained an implacable enemy of the Whigs: as a Tory (1701–15), a Jacobite (1715–16), a coalitionist (1716–35) and finally as a 'patriot' (1735–51). The ethos of patriotism, while having its roots deeply embedded in Commonwealth and Country ideology, was in no small degree Bolingbroke's own creation. The patriot, as Bolingbroke presented him, was the ultimate loyalist *because* he was the ultimate independent. Having no interest but that of his country, the patriot was free from the pull of clientage and faction. In a world of party, place and purchased loyalty, he alone could be trusted to exercise impartial and virtuous judgement and so serve the sovereign and the nation. In *The Spirit of Patriotism* and in *The Idea of a Patriot King*, Bolingbroke established the limits of obligation to the nation. The duties that men owe to the sovereign and the duties that the sovereign owes to the nation are both expressed in terms of love of country or patriotism.

Bolingbroke was especially careful to distinguish his conception of patriotic obligation, as limited by tradition, consent and natural law, from those Tory traditionalist polemics that preserved any remnant of divine right argument. Indeed, Bolingbroke, as did many of his Whig competitors, based his arguments for political obligation on the twin pillars of contract and natural law. He leaned heavily on the philosophy of Locke. But it was Locke's epistemology rather than a strictly Lockean view of contract and sovereignty which influenced him. Bolingbroke used strong empiricist arguments against the Tory idealist presumptions of sacred kingship and those intrinsically Platonic notions of human nature as fallen and corrupt that underpinned both Augustinian and Filmerian accounts of patriarchalism. In the area of natural law argument, Bolingbroke reached back beyond Locke to late medieval juridical arguments that may be traced from Marsilius to Grotius, on the continent, and then, through Hooker and Coke, into common law argument in England. This tradition antedated the seventeenth-century innovation of divine right rhetoric as a buttress of centralization. While Locke's debt to the 'judicious Hooker' has long been recognized, the Lockean solution to the problem of sovereignty based on divine right theory had been grounded in a highly individualistic account of contract. By contract, Locke meant a volitional exchange of political and economic interests which secured and recognized the mutual reciprocity of rights.

Bolingbroke's divergence from the Lockean account of contract turns on a number of differing assumptions as to human nature, the origins of civil society and the purpose of contract itself. While Locke viewed man before experience as initially a *tabula rasa*, Bolingbroke emphasized the role of instinct in the formation of human character. While Locke had proposed the event of an original social contract – a fiction some would argue – Bolingbroke contended there had always been civil society and that government was 'natural'. While Locke stressed the individual sphere of human rights as a platform for the individual scope of human actions, Bolingbroke emphasized the social qualities of human nature. While Locke advanced an argument for the innate moral equality of human beings, Bolingbroke rejected the assertion of any relevant a priori foundations for assessing human nature, contending instead that as there were evident natural inequalities among men, there were also natural social orders and in particular a natural aristocracy. While Locke regarded contract as a discrete set of promises for the securing of rights, Bolingbroke understood contract as a broader complex of agreements for the delineation of duties. As these arguments translated into practical formulations of political power, it is evident that Bolingbroke, while an anti-patriarchalist, was a staunch paternalist in governance. He preferred time-honoured, customary right to any metaphysical account of transcendental natural rights. He viewed civil society and social contract as a natural expression of human community. Consequently, he conceived of the separation of powers as the rightful, traditional and natural evolution of social organization in its constitutional form. The combination of powers, particularly the encroachment of the executive into the legislative branches, Bolingbroke considered to be the leading source of despotism in government. It was also, he argued, an unnatural innovation. As an artificial transformation of the constitution through the increasing influence of new wealth, it embodied the very essence of political corruption. Bolingbroke's argument, attacking the Hanoverian Whig government for its perversion of the 'ancient constitution', even as it rejected the foundations of a Jacobite Tory polemic based on the conceits of divine right and sacred kingship, was perhaps the highest articulation of 'Country' or 'patriot' rhetoric. Reaching its apotheosis in the last political moments of Jacobite possibility, it provided a shrewd alternative to the fatal inefficacy of an undiluted Tory loyalist polemic. In Bolingbroke, Commonwealth, Real Whig and classical republican ideology all cohered in a rhetoric of nationalist independence, which pronounced a plague on all the various houses of party, interest and faction.

Yet classical republican examples were not the exclusive preserve of the Country party writers. The rising influence of the new urban interest also had defenders who employed the great republican authors of Greek and Roman antiquity. But the defenders of virtuous commerce and the civilizing influences of cosmopolitan society celebrated the achievements of the Athenians over the Spartans and the merits of Cicero's (rather than Cato the Censor's) Rome. Cicero, after all, was a cosmopolite: a man of the world and fluent in Greek. He was not prejudiced by tradition or country, not a provincial, rather a man of the city and, as such, a man of contracts, a man of the law.

The Ciceronian model of classical republicanism has also been conceived of as civic humanism. It celebrated the civic pride of Athens, Rome and the great commercial republics of Renaissance Italy. Trade was a nexus for the exchange not only of goods, but also of language and ideas. A transactional society promoted a 'civilized' world of polite sociability and liberal urbanity. Its culture depended on a balance between the moderating and refining influence of manners in the social sphere and the extension of liberties through the commercial evolution of civil law in the political sphere. The celebration of the civic humanist conception of political virtue was embraced by those practitioners of sceptical Whiggism, Joseph Addison and Richard Steele, whose *Spectator* papers appeared in 1711–12. The argument that the city was not invariably a source of corruption, that commerce could actually be morally improving, was a reasonably novel one in the early eighteenth century. Earlier Christian and Stoic neoclassical defences of money had tended to regard it through the lens of prudence; as a necessary evil that must be tolerated for pragmatic reasons.

Bernard Mandeville, whose *Fable of the Bees* appeared in numerous editions from 1714 until 1732, was possibly the first political and social thinker in eighteenth-century Britain to envision a world where an enlightened commerce would translate the selfish into a social principle. While Mandeville stopped short of the aphorism 'greed is good', he contributed to the growing analysis of politics and human nature that assumed what might be described as a sociological view of interest, exchange and order. This new 'moral science' also had its continental practitioners – notably Montesquieu and Rousseau in France – but achieved a critical mass in British political thought through the works of the Scots literati. Francis Hutcheson, Dugald Stewart, Adam Ferguson, and particularly David Hume and Adam Smith, wrote extensively on the moral, social and political consequences of human sensibilities and interests.

The Scots moralists offered more nuanced investigations of a human psychology of the senses than Locke had done. They considered the interactions of interests, instincts and passions that attached to the formation of human nature and the development of the social bond as a consequence of time and place. The idea of an evolving social bond rather than a static social contract was a central element of these accounts. Scots moralism advanced a dynamic economic analysis of man in society. It was, therefore, profoundly historical in approach. This is particularly true in the case of thinkers like Adam Ferguson who, along with Vico, believed that political institutions were never created deliberately, but emerged as the consequence of actions rather than deliberate intentions. Even Hume, who strove to prove the inherent moral uniformity of mankind, used historical events as examples of recurrent pattern rather than as a means of mapping diversity or as a record of aberrant innovation. Answering Locke's *Essay on Human Understanding* with his own phenomenologically constructed arguments in the *Treatise on Human Nature* (1738–40), Hume posited a world of discrete events where pattern and causal necessity were the constructions of human association and perception rather than objectively and deductively valid. Two separate phenomena could therefore appear to coalesce and yet actually be causally distinct from each other. While Hume extended this epistemology into his theological writings – notably with regard to natural versus revealed religion and the possibility of miracles – he also drew conclusions based on these assumptions for political questions. In particular, Hume was concerned with the association of political liberty with religious Dissent.

Hume's *History of England* (1754–62) considered the tensions that existed between rationality, as the foundation of moral and political liberty on the one hand, and the cause of liberty as a mask for Puritan enthusiasm on the other. Hume disliked the vulgar populism of democratical opinion. But, he made it clear that the English had no reason to be in love with the picture of absolute monarchy. Hume cautioned against the unlimited authority of the prince and his unbounded prerogatives, recommending instead that noble liberty, that sweet equality, and that happy security by which the English were at present distinguished above all nations in the universe. His fears of an unrestrained religious bigotry, the vulgarity and license of the people and the irrational prejudices of an unbounded prerogative must be taken together when assessing Hume's Toryism. Certainly, his empirically grounded defences of reason, uniformity and predictability distinguish him as a conservative thinker.

Arguably, the Scots moral science culminated in the writings of Adam Smith. Smith investigated the social bonds of sympathy and dignity in his accounts of human character. In *The Theory of Moral Sentiments*, which he began in 1752 but first published in 1759, Smith distinguished between the purely selfish motive and an internal moral sense that originated in an appropriate regard for the self. Rousseau would delineate between the higher and baser forms of self-love in his *Social Contract*, which appeared three years later in 1762, but is likely a simultaneous composition. Smith described something more akin to self-respect than the childish selfishness of immediate gratification. It is this higher love of self, or self-esteem, Smith argued, rather than empathy or the fear of punishment, that is the key to all human morality. This better self, he contended, is not the love of our neighbour and is not the love of mankind. It is, rather, a stronger love, a more powerful affection, in short, it is the love of what is honourable and noble of the grandeur and dignity and superiority of our own characters. Smith translated his account of the moral qualities of self-esteem into political principle in his Epicurean association of virtue with prudence. Prudence, as wise and judicious conduct, is to be reckoned above benevolence as the leading principle of political justice. Prudence operating with the free expansion of an enlightened self-interest would bring about the greatest prosperity and the greatest general welfare.

Smith's claim must be distinguished from later 'prudentialist' arguments as advanced by English Utilitarians such as William Paley and Jeremy Bentham. Bentham's 'greatest happiness principle' was grounded on a narrower and more hedonistic account of gratification than the Epicurean assumptions in Smith's account. It was Smith's attack on mercantilism, *The Wealth of Nations* (1776), that fit more easily into the political and social agendas of philosophical radicals and political economists by 1800. In *The Wealth of Nations* Smith considered the development of society in terms of four stages, each of which suggested appropriate forms of social and political organization. The fourth and final stage was the commercial world; a world in which rapid and extensive trade rendered the government control of markets a moribund and inefficient form of regulation. Mercantilism was an obsolete system, Smith contended, and the new fourth-stage economies should be self-regulating, for in a free market everything would achieve its natural level. Only a divine intelligence could plan such a complex and rapid system of exchange. The market, argued Smith, if left to itself, would be regulated providentially by a hidden hand.

Smith's *Wealth of Nations*, while focusing specifically on the problems of mercantilism, was also a broad attack on the colonial system of governance as a whole. The critical timing of its 1776 publication fits well into the Whig rhetorical strategies of the American War. The political arguments which defined and articulated the war at home and in America were, like the crisis itself, the culmination of a series of interests and events that had been building since the conclusion of the Seven Years' War in 1763. The 'Old Corps' Whigs took their political rhetoric out of office with them in 1761 and old anti-Jacobite sentiment was retailored as a broad hostility to Scottish issues in general, and Scottish ministers in particular. John Wilkes's *The North Briton* was a thinly veiled attack on Bute.

The revival of high 'Tory' interests in the reign of George III transformed the possibilities of British political argument in two critical ways. First, while there were some exceptions, the political thought of the first half of the eighteenth century, whether Jacobite or Hanoverian, Whig or Tory, Court or Country, tended to define the 'people' in a rather narrow and elite sense. The poor, the marginal and, most importantly, the landless were of moral significance but of no political consequence. Towns, wider literacy, coffee houses and an expanding press altered that tendency by mid-century. In short, the rise of the middling sort to economic and social prominence necessitated a politics of greater inclusion by 1760. Second, after 1746 the old Jacobite threat seemed well and truly banished. At long last, celebrated jubilant Tories, a Hanoverian king could choose a Scottish noble as his principal minister, and with seeming impunity. But, the rehabilitation of the 'Tory' interest at court required certain polemical accommodations. The Tory abandonment of divine right rhetoric in favour of patriot arguments subtly but irrevocably altered the foundations of loyalty, and changed the idea of monarchy in the popular imagination. These two trends, the growing voice of the people and the desanctification of the monarchy, combined to produce more radical and democratical political ideas by the late 1760s. The cry of 'Wilkes and Liberty', therefore, suggested change in two ways. First, that it was politically tenable to call the king a liar, and second, that the credibility of that charge would be asserted by the *vox populi*.

The use of what would increasingly be understood as 'out-of-doors' influence transformed the political language of eighteenth-century Britain. Yet it would be going too far to characterize the organization and use of this force as plebeian. The new political clubs and gentlemen's associations, formed across the country as well as in the capital, still reflected the polite and propertied expectations of the gentry and the urban middling classes. County petitions, such as those organized by Christopher Wyvill and Major Cartwright, extended what had formerly been a 'top-down' national political culture, emanating from the capital, to a regional and localist base. The critical question for these new middling interests was the distribution of the franchise and the adjustment of county and borough representation rather than any radical extension of the franchise as universal manhood suffrage. New corruption was tarred with the rhetorical brush of 'old corruption' and concerns about the increase of pocket boroughs, rotten boroughs, pensioners and placemen were all associated with the corrupting influence of money. A critical change had taken place in the deployment of the anti-corruption polemic since the reign of George II.

During the years of Whig hegemony under Walpole and the first two Georges, Country Tories and Independents had assailed the ministry for its corrupt bargain with the monied interest. Now the opposition Whigs defended the gentry, railing against the Tory ministry's use of money to expand the king's prerogative through pension and place. Commonwealth and Country arguments were stood on their heads once again by the 1770s. Opposition Whig pamphleteers and politicians drew heavily on the strategies of the past. Many of these ideas had been conveniently drawn together into compilations. Histories like Hume's, legal treatises like William Blackstone's *Commentaries on the Laws of England* (1765–9), and source books of all work like James Burgh's *Political Disquisitions* (1774) provided the opposition Whigs with a rich rhetorical arsenal.

Edmund Burke, like Jonathan Swift, was a product of the Irish Ascendancy culture of the eighteenth century. While Burke chose a career in the law rather than the church, like Swift he sought his professional advancement in England in the service of the Whigs. The terms Whig and Tory must be used cautiously in the reign of George III. Certainly Burke, after his breach with the Foxites in 1791, offered his own *Appeal from the New to the Old Whigs*, defending what he characterized as the 'honest' principles of Walpole's day against the opportunistic and partisan politics of new and more radical Foxites of the age of reform. In turn, Burke's critics attacked him as a place-seeker. Burke's late defence of his own pension, *A Letter to A Noble Lord* (1796), certainly exposed him to this charge. Like Locke, and to a lesser degree Swift, Burke's talent as a man of letters brought him into the service of a great aristocratic patron. Yet he moved beyond the role of secretary and private philosopher, obtaining direct influence in parliament. Making his way from his 1765 election as MP to rising rhetorical star in the Rockingham party, Burke none the less regarded himself, from first to last, as a constitutionalist and a patriot.

While a Rockinghamite Whig in the 1770s Burke attacked the unconstitutional actions of the king in his choice of ministers and in his use of crown patronage. He also criticized Lord North's policies towards both the American colonists and the king's Catholic subjects in Quebec. He believed that such policies were a prelude to the erosion of the constitutional liberties of his majesty's subjects, first in the American colonies and then inevitably at home. In the long tradition of Whig constitutionalist writings, however, Burke's criticism of the king turned on his defence of the constitution in church and state. George III had extended a level of toleration to his erstwhile Tory enemies that he had persistently withheld from the English and adamantly denied to the Irish. He had also allowed the creation of a new colonial government in Quebec that excluded any assembly representation, resting almost exclusively on an executive base. Burke argued for the ancient constitutional liberties of all Britons, supporting American claims by comparing colonial bids for representation to those of the Welsh and the Scots. His arguments appealed to a growing understanding of Britishness, as common heritage and shared kinship. Even in his early writings, Burke emphasized the historical construction of a national consciousness through inherited tradition, racial memory and customary law.

In Burke's account of a British national state (as opposed to nation-state), the past was linked through the present to the future in a living and organic interdependency of land and kinship. The institutions that ordered and preserved these affinities were in keeping with Whig traditions of both the 'ancient' and the 'balanced' constitution. Through the checks and balances of mixed government, monarchy, nobility and episcopacy were preserved in a delicate and dynamic tension. The ancient constitution evolved and endured. Through the providence of the common law inheritance it culminated in the sovereignty of parliament and the Revolution Settlement of 1688–9. While the patriot and common-law assumptions of Burke's earlier writings would not look out of place amongst Bolingbroke's arguments, Burke quite consciously distanced himself from Bolingbroke's reputation as an irreligious Deist and an unprincipled rebel. Closer affinities may be suggested in Burke's association with Adam Smith. Indeed, Burke relied heavily on Smith in the composition of his *Letters on Scarcity*. The sociological approach of the Scot's moral and economic science allowed Burke to employ a more sophisticated understanding of history in his accounts of an evolving and organic society. While these arguments may be detected in Burke's defence of the patriot side during the American War, they achieved their most resonant formulations during Burke's rejection of radical revolutionary principles and mob rule in his *Reflections on the Revolution in France* (1790).

Burke's paternalism and his distrust of the vulgar opinion of the unenlightened and unenfranchised – the swinish multitude – drew a response from an erstwhile ally in the patriot fray. Thomas Paine, whose *Common Sense* (1776) had defended the colonists' bid for independence, answered Burke's extended letter on the French Revolution with a radical appeal for the civil and natural rights of ordinary men. While Paine may have believed himself once to have common cause with Burke on the issue of the American War, it is unlikely that Burke would have recognized much fellow-feeling in *Common Sense*. Burke had argued for conciliation, Paine championed independence. Burke censured the king for constitutional abuses, Paine challenged the constitution itself in his undiluted attack on monarchy, the hereditary principle and a complicated constitution of checks and balances.

Paine's *Rights of Man* (1791–2) parted company with earlier opposition Whig polemic in several interesting ways. It abandoned the gradualist and paternalist reform platforms of the moderates. These had argued for 'economical' reforms that would eliminate corruption and emolument, make the distribution of seats more representative of the balance of interests in the nation, and essentially restore the constitution to its pristine and, it was assumed, ideal form. A radical extension of the franchise through the elimination of any property qualification had not, however, been suggested by the opposition Whigs. Even many of those reformers who embraced the ideal of universal franchise as a just principle agreed that education and enlightenment must precede the revolution. Paine, on the other hand, argued that the natural rights of man demanded his civil inclusion; that reason, not birth, wealth or education, was the fundamental qualification for citizenship. In doing so, Paine also suggested that ancient institutions that preserved deference and subjugation were unjust. There was no natural hierarchical order of sovereign to subject, no political justice that did not reconcile natural rights to civil institutions. Monarchy was as unjust as it was unnatural, hereditary right was no more than custom and prejudice, and organized religion was an impediment to faith. Paine's anti-clerical views were both consistent with his anti-Test sympathies for the Dissenters and his own personal Deism.

Paine's arguments on politics and religion were, for some, the fulfilment of the Lockean prophecy of natural religion and natural right. Yet the Locke remembered by the popular and democratical republicans of 1791 was very different from the Locke who had defended the rights of magnate oligarchy in 1690. The rights of nature emerged as the civilly constructed rights of man in the writings of Thomas Paine. But Painite radicalism was not the last word in the debate on late eighteenth-century reform. Thomas Spence's various pamphlets and his penny periodical *Pig's Meat* (1793–5) argued for a far more radical agrarian reform than that considered by Paine in his own *Agrarian Justice* (1796). Mary Wollstonecraft suggested that Paine's *Rights of Man* failed to offer an adequate *Vindication of the Rights of Woman* (1792), while William Godwin contended that all governments, indeed all forms of contract, were oppressive, coercive, and should be abolished. Beyond that, Godwin argued that benevolence and duty and not contract and right were the keys to *Political Justice* (1793).

Dissenters, who made common cause with radicals for the repeal of the Test and Corporation Acts, differed profoundly on issues ranging from Christological opinion to ecclesio-political settlement based variously on toleration, comprehension and disestablishment. Richard Price and Joseph Priestley, variously described as Rational Dissenters or radical Unitarians, were judged for their political opinions more than their religious convictions. This was certainly true of Price, whose *Discourse on the Love of Our Country* (1790) had provoked Edmund Burke's response in the *Reflections* and had ignited the intense political controversy on the French Revolution. Still others, from a moderate opposition perspective, amalgamated patriot and constitutional rhetoric to suggest a more paternalistic approach to the social and political crisis of reform. Samuel Taylor Coleridge leaned heavily on James Burgh's *Political Disquisitions*, Edmund Burke's early speeches, as well as his own extraordinary scholarship as a classicist in his 1795 'Addresses to the People'. Published under the Latin title *Conciones ad Populum*, these public lectures on politics and revealed religion addressed a very different audience than that to which Paine's plain vernacular appealed.

Political thinkers of late eighteenth-century Britain continued to revisit the ideas and rhetorical strategies of the past. As the balance of interests changed, however, so too did the resonance of these earlier arguments. Rather than considering a choice between the divine right of kings and the sovereignty of parliament, political writers of the late eighteenth century sought to explain differing forms of constitutionalism. The language of contract and law, even when applied to its Gothic or feudal origins, had eclipsed the language of covenant and sacrament as the foundation of civil polity. Seventeenth-century natural philosophy had given way, first to moral science and then to political economy. Political thought from Locke to Paine expanded the idea of subject, to patriot and citizen, and transformed the idea of commonwealth into nation.

FURTHER READING

Ashcraft, Richard: *Revolution Politics and John Locke's 'Two Treatises on Government'* (Princeton, NJ, 1986).

Browning, Reed: *Political and Constitutional Ideas of the Court Whigs* (Baton Rouge, LA, 1982).

Burtt, Shelley: *Virtue Transformed: Political Argument in England, 1688–1740* (Cambridge, 1992).

Claeys, Gregory: *Thomas Paine: Social and Political Thought* (London, 1989).

Clark, J. C. D.: *English Society 1688–1832: Ideology, Social Structure and Political Practice during the Ancien Régime* (1985; rev. edn, Cambridge, 2000).

Colley, Linda: *Britons: Forging the Nation 1701–1837* (London, 1992).

Dickinson, H. T.: *Bolingbroke* (London, 1970).

Dickinson, H. T.: *Liberty and Property: Political Ideology in Eighteenth-Century Britain* (London, 1977).

Forbes, Duncan: *Hume's Philosophical Politics* (Cambridge, 1975).

Hont, Istvan and Ignatieff, Michael: *Wealth and Virtue: The Shaping of Political Economy in the Scottish Enlightenment* (Cambridge, 1983).

Kenyon, John P.: *Revolution Principles: The Politics of Party 1689–1720* (Cambridge, 1977).

O'Gorman, Frank: *Edmund Burke: His Political Philosophy* (London, 1973).
Pocock, J. G. A.: *Virtue, Commerce and History: Essays in Political Thought and History Chiefly in the Eighteenth Century* (Cambridge, 1985).
Robbins, Caroline: *The Eighteenth-Century Commonwealthman* (Cambridge, MA, 1959).
Winch, Donald: *Adam Smith's Politics: An Essay in Historiographical Revision* (Cambridge, 1978).

Chapter Twenty-Four

The Making of Elite Culture

Maura A. Henry

Through their cultural practices and values the elite of eighteenth-century Britain forged a shared identity, distinguished themselves from other social groups, and justified their dominance of British society, politics and economy. Culture served as one of the most prominent and powerful markers of Britain's landed ranks. Furthermore, elite culture helped to account for the triumph of the aristocracy and gentry during the long eighteenth century (1688–1815). In a society where the lines separating social groups had traditionally been indeterminate and elastic, cultural practices and values held considerable significance. Culture assumed greater importance during the eighteenth century when Britain's professional and merchant classes appeared to challenge the existing pre-eminence of the landed class by aspiring to increased political, economic and cultural power. In such a context, culture served as an even more vital distinguishing feature. Taken together, the shared habits, ideas and material objects marked the elite as a distinct and distinctly dominant social group atop British society.

This chapter explores the range of elite cultural pursuits, and analyses the means and meanings of elite cultural construction and expression. After defining the terms 'culture' and 'elite', we will discover the ways in which a wide range of social and economic activities distinguished the aristocracy and gentry. Central to our study are the most significant constituent practices of elite culture, namely: wealth management and consumption; education and training; the Grand Tour; sociability in the country and city; estate building and improving; art collecting; and domestic travel. Through these activities, the elite defined themselves, grew more homogeneous, and strengthened and maintained their position of superiority throughout the period.

Eighteenth-century British elite culture, like that of any other social group in the century, represented the spirit of its members. It comprised the actions, values, unspoken assumptions, representations, material objects and myths of the elite. Since its prevailing 'general idiom' at once grew out of and governed the activities, beliefs and values of its individual members, elite culture was constantly evolving. Elite culture was not a static set of rules for behaviour and interaction, a singular aesthetic, or a rigid structure designed simply to organize and perpetuate political and economic power. Rather, individual men and women lived their lives within a given context of possibilities of action and mental frameworks. They exercised considerable agency in their self-definition, and collectively, in their class definition. The elite were, like their middle-class and working-class counterparts, present at their own making.

Wealth, Expenditure and Consumption

The culture of Britain's elite was the creation of an exclusive, small and privileged ring of landowners. The elite were rooted in the land, which served as their primary source of wealth and status and symbolized their right to rule. Since landed society privileged men, this chapter focuses more on the cultural pursuits of elite men than on those of their female counterparts. Through the prevailing legal structures of primogeniture (whereby the eldest surviving male heir inherited estates and titles) and entail (which prevented estates from being alienated), men controlled the land and therefore occupied the centre of the elite society. Very few women, mostly single women (widows and spinsters), held property in their own name during the period, while most married women did not receive separate property rights until the passage of the Married Women's Separate Property Act in 1836. During the long eighteenth century a few women possessed titles in their own right, such as the fourth duchess of Beaufort, who inherited the barony of Botetourt in 1771 from her brother Norborne Berkeley, who died while serving as Governor of Virginia. These titled and propertied women were the exception, however, not the rule. As a consequence of women's limited formal power within the elite, their ability to shape the culture was confined to informal means. Britain's elite was overwhelmingly male in its membership and ethos.

Elite culture was forged by relatively few individuals. Although precise demographic numbers for the eighteenth century are hard to determine, a number of contemporary eighteenth-century accounts are highly suggestive of the elite's compact size. According to Gregory King, large landowners numbered a mere 1.2 per cent of the nation's population. In the early nineteenth century Patrick Colquhoun, although he employed criteria and methods different from those used by King, arrived at the same percentage: the landed elite comprised 1.1 per cent of the overall population. Thus, in a century when the British nation doubled in size from 5.5 million in 1700 to roughly 10 million by 1810, the elite remained a small percentage of the population and thus formed a tight-knit group.

Though limited in number, the landed elite contained a range of landholders that can be easily divided into three major subgroups: the aristocracy, baronetcy and gentry. Within each of these three major subgroups there were still more subdivisions and hierarchies. The aristocracy, numbering around 180 titleholders and their families across the century, stood at the apex of landed society. Within the peerage there was a clearly graded hierarchy of status, power and wealth. At the top stood the great noble families. While there was no direct correlation between noble rank and wealth, protocol and prestige dictated that dukes took precedence over marquesses who took precedence over earls who took precedence over viscounts who took precedence over barons who took precedence over commoners who comprised the rest of society. The second subgroup of landed elite consisted of a small number of baronets who were titled landowners of estates generally more modest than those held by the nobility. Although oftentimes mistakenly considered part of the aristocracy because they possessed titles, baronets were decidedly not part of the nobility. Rather, the baronetcy was clearly and unequivocally a step below. The third and largest subgroup of landowners comprised the gentry. The gentry, like the baronetcy, had no formal subdivisions but ranged across a spectrum of greater to lesser sorts based on the size of their landholdings and their wealth.

Elite culture grew out of and reflected the wealth of the propertied ranks. The social activities and interests of propertied men and women, from their dress to their art collecting, were made possible by their vast incomes. Over the course of the eighteenth century substantial landowners became wealthier (both relatively and absolutely) than their grandfathers before them. The money in elite coffers rose dramatically due to increases in both the size of many individual estates and the overall percentage of their total landholdings. Whereas peers owned 15–20 per cent of England's land in 1700, they controlled between 20 and 25 per cent by 1800. A half-dozen peers owned over 100,000 acres each. Not only did the elites own a greater percentage of the country, but they also benefited from rising rents. During the last half of the century alone, rental incomes increased between 70 and 90 per cent in England. In Wales, rent income rose an average of 60 per cent, and in some areas by 200 per cent. Rents in Ireland jumped by an extraordinary 90 per cent, and by a similarly staggering eightfold in Scotland between 1750 and 1815. Individual landowners, such as Thomas Coke of Holkham, doubled their estate rentals between 1776 and 1816. In addition to rents, landowners derived increased profits from mining operations of coal, lead and other natural resources on their properties. Urban landholdings also brought vast sums into elite families by way of rentals and urban development, as demonstrated by the two great aristocratic London land magnates, the Bedfords and Grosvenors. In 1700, the duke of Bedford collected £2,000 from his Bloomsbury properties; in 1771 he took in £8,000. Similarly, the Grosvenors' London properties yielded spectacular increases. In 1779 the family collected £7,000 from their Oxford Street properties; by 1812, they were raking in an astounding £12,000 per year. As a direct result of rising incomes, elites enjoyed increased prosperity and greater disposable income, which they spent on their cultural pursuits. Flush with money, the eighteenth-century aristocracy and gentry lived in very grand style, undertook expensive educational programmes, rebuilt their ancestral seats, purchased new estates, established and embellished urban homes, and filled their country and town residences with a vast array of luxury goods.

Like the gradations of social standing, wealth also reflected a hierarchy among Britain's propertied ranks. Although there was no direct correlation between elite rank and wealth, the two criteria were related. In general, aristocrats were the wealthiest at the start of the century, with the baronetcy and gentry less well off than the nobles but generally better off than the professional and middling ranks below them. Aristocratic incomes steamed ahead during the eighteenth century, leaving the baronetcy and gentry behind and creating a significant gap between the titled and untitled. In 1700 aristocratic wealth averaged £5,000 to £8,000 per year. Of course, these sums are only averages and do not reflect the incomes of those far above and below the middle range. Some nobles, such as the first duke of Newcastle, enjoyed extremely large annual incomes; in 1715 alone Newcastle grossed £32,000 from his estates scattered across thirteen counties. By 1790 the 400 great landowning families collected annual incomes that ranged from £5,000 to £50,000, according to contemporary estimates. Many of the great families, notably the Bedfords, Bridgewaters, Devonshires and Northumberlands, were raking in sums greater than £50,000 per annum.

At the start of the century a baronet's income likely hovered around £1,700 per annum. Gentry income reflected the wide range of estates and spanned the spectrum from tens of thousands of pounds per year to a few hundred pounds. The greater gentry, those 200 or so families who owned estates over 10,000 acres apiece, lived off incomes that rivalled and even surpassed those of some less well-to-do aristocrats. Meanwhile, the lesser gentry, the approximately 10,000 to 15,000 families who owned estates under 10,000 acres, averaged a few thousand to a few hundred per year. The ubiquitous country squire was generally the least well-off landowner, living on an annual income of approximately £300 at the beginning of the century. While not all landowners were created equal, owing to the varying sizes and values of holdings, all members of the landed elite derived wealth from their holdings which they regularly spent in the creation of a shared culture.

Expenditure was as vital as income in the world of Britain's landed families. Consumption, the purchase and use of goods and services, was inseparable from elite social activities. The key cultural practices of education, travel, art collecting and sociability necessitated expenditures before, during and after the events. As a result, elite men and women were consumers *par excellence*. With overstuffed accounts, many landed elites purchased a vast array of goods with gusto. It is reckoned that Sir Robert Walpole spent some £90,000 between 1714 and 1718 on his private expenditures. Years later, in 1733, Walpole's account records show that he and his elite guests spent more than £3,000 on White Lisbon wine and chocolate. The lord mayor of London and his guests quaffed some 626 cases of wine during the annual lord mayor's dinner at Mansion House in 1774. In addition to buying goods, elites incurred considerable costs for services, the most significant of which were provided by their large household staffs.

Because it was ubiquitous and integral to elite life, the buying habits of gentlemen and ladies attracted a great deal of attention. While some contemporaries, notably Henry Fielding and Bernard Mandeville, declared elite consumption to be both a social and economic good (provided of course that it did not ruin the family fortune), other social commentators fretted that the elites were feckless and wanton in their spending. Why did they engage in such an orgy of conspicuous consumption? Members of the landed elite spent their money and accumulated goods in order to meet their personal needs and desires as well as to impress themselves, their cohorts and their inferiors. Whatever the motivations, and amidst discrepancies in relative wealth and expenditure, members of the eighteenth-century landed class constructed a shared material culture built to a large degree by their money and their passion to consume.

While birth and money formed the foundation of elite society, cultural perceptions by individuals across the social hierarchy (from the landed to the poor) conferred elite status. Thus, a gentleman was a gentleman only if he was accepted as one by the rest of society based on an assessment of his manners, behaviour, education and upbringing. Women were similarly subject to social scrutiny of their behaviour, especially their sexuality. The duchess of Kingston, for example, was spurned by polite society because although she had married the duke of Kingston, she had once been his mistress. Whereas a man's sexual exploits (such as the duke of Kingston's) would not necessarily bar him from elite circles, a woman's past (notably his duchess's) could and often did keep her out of that rarefied orbit. Elite society (from the magnates down to the least of the country gentry) served as gatekeepers, allowing those adjudged elite to enter and barring those who failed the test. Thus, while Jonas Hanway complained in 1752 that 'the labourer and mechanic will ape the lord', it was a certainty that emulation alone would get them nowhere. Acknowledgement by all ranks of society that one possessed the appropriate habits, training, interests and appearance made one elite.

The product of many individuals, elite culture reflected the great variety of personalities who comprised the group. While idealized images of polite and genteel gentlemen were promulgated by the likes of the earl of Chesterfield, not every gentleman obtained, let alone aspired to, such noble ends. For every propertied gentleman who articulated learning and open-mindedness, there were those who often displayed bigotry and narrow-mindedness. Their manners could be polished as well as crude. As Lady Mary Wortley Montagu noted, many rough squires spent their mornings 'among the hounds and their nights with as beastly companions – with what liquor they can get'. While some property-holders were business-minded, such as Colonel Walpole (JP and MP in North Norfolk, and father of Sir Robert), others were hopeless spendthrifts, as symbolized by Hogarth's caricature, the earl of Squander, in *Marriage à la Mode.*

Whatever the relative merits or demerits of individual members of the elite, their collective cultural practices and values both shaped and reflected their enduring dominance. By 1815 a more coherent elite culture had developed out of the actions and beliefs of thousands of men and women. This increased homogeneity was not the result of conscious and deliberate planning. Rather, it emerged from the ebb and flow of elite life. As we shall now explore, landed culture was forged through the key practices of education and training; the Grand Tour; country sociability; estate building and improving; urban sociability; and domestic travel.

Education and Training

Education and training played a pivotal role in elite culture by breeding a distinct social group. Through both formal instruction and informal training, elite boys in particular not only acquired similar knowledge, attitudes, manners, dress, speech, behaviour and accomplishments, they also forged a close and exclusive network of friends, and equipped themselves for their leading roles in society and government. Their education continued to exert influence well beyond their childhood; the lessons learned and manners acquired both informed and were reflected in their adult leisure pursuits. Moreover, their education supported and validated the social and political dominance of landed gentlemen.

Formal education, both at home and at school, was the privilege of elite boys. Their sisters, in sharp contrast, received mostly informal instruction of uneven quality. A girl's education was a hit or miss proposition that depended almost exclusively on the attitudes of her parents. For instance, John Symes Berkeley (a Gloucestershire MP) and his wife Lady Hereford thought it worthwhile that their only daughter, Elizabeth (1719–99), be taught a range of intellectual subjects by an Oxford don who had been hired to tutor her brother. Elizabeth's experience was the exception, not the rule. Most daughters of the landed class were educated at home by governesses who were often notorious for providing an indifferent education to their charges. Governesses emphasized female accomplishments such as needlepoint, dancing and handwriting over scholarly subjects, which were thought to be irrelevant to a young lady's life. While a few boarding schools for girls existed at the start of the century, and many more were established throughout the period, most elite parents and social commentators worried about the appropriateness of sending elite daughters away from home to be schooled. Thus, girls' boarding schools catered to the daughters of the aspiring professional and middle ranks, rather than to those of the landed elite.

Public schools exercised profound influence on elite boys and by extension elite culture. Whereas, at the start of the century, most elite boys were tutored at home where they were thought to derive both intellectual and moral benefits, by mid-century public schools had become the predominant means of educating the sons of the landed ranks. Public schools constituted exclusive clubs where elite boys acquired shared cultural norms, ideas and tastes, and were socialized to assume their leadership roles in society. Within the rarefied world of public schools, the landed elite favoured a select number of public schools that became known as the 'Great Seven'. Counted among this august group were Eton, Harrow, Winchester, Westminster, Rugby, Charterhouse and Shrewsbury. Among these, there was still greater exclusivity and clustering of elite boys. By 1800, 70 per cent of English peers had been educated at only four public schools: Eton, Westminster, Winchester and Harrow. In this way, public schools, like many other aspects of elite culture, can be seen as self-perpetuating and self-selecting clubs. Simply put, elite boys were sent generation after generation to the same schools attended by their fathers and grandfathers before them. Collectively, public schools fostered and reinforced a pronounced aura of exclusivity, which in turn forged close and abiding ties among their chosen students.

No matter which particular school a boy attended, he studied a curriculum that had become standardized across all schools over the course of the long eighteenth century. Uniformly, the public school curriculum centred on the classics, which fostered a sense of superiority, a spirit of British patriotism and a distinct masculinity in pupils. Boys immersed themselves in Greek and Latin classics that celebrated the heroics and powers of a privileged elite like themselves. At Eton, boys spent twenty-one hours per week studying Greek and Latin, according to the notes left by one master. The study of Latin was a rite of passage into an exclusive men's club. Latin was a 'secret tongue' that displayed learning, social superiority and gender hierarchies that operated not only in the halls of power, but also in the drawing rooms of the landed elite and across the wider society.

By studying the classics, young boys acquired a strong sense of British patriotism. Ancient heroes, notably Homer, Cicero and Plutarch, revered for their courage, duty and service to the state, served as role models for young British boys. Boys also developed pride in both the nation and their place in it through the study of the history of Britain and other nations. Students entered essay-prize contests that focused on patriotic themes such as heroism, honour, country, duty and empire. They celebrated national victories and participated in national subscriptions that supported Britain through its many wars waged throughout the long eighteenth century.

Through their environment and activities, public schools bred in their charges a particular sense of masculinity rooted in both social graces and physical prowess. Boys studied art, music, poetry and language in order that they become polite, cultured and graceful. They practised public speaking, a skill deemed essential to their future careers in the House of Commons or Lords. The social manners and habits of British gentlemen were acquired through lessons in dancing, fencing, drawing and riding, which remained at the centre of their leisure activities throughout their lives. While fencing constituted a male accomplishment, it could when employed in a duel have deadly consequences. Such was the case in the early morning hours of 15 November 1712, when two of Britain's peers (the fifth Baron Mohun and the fourth duke of Hamilton) fatally stabbed each other as they battled for a contested estate and their personal honour. Although duelling had been banned in the seventeenth century, gentlemen continued to take up the sword or the pistol throughout the eighteenth century. In 1789 the duke of York duelled with Colonel Lennox, while in 1798 William Pitt, the prime minister, exchanged shots with George Tierney, a leading opposition politician.

Team sports also inculcated a virile masculinity in public school boys that stood in sharp contrast to the longstanding stereotype of elite boys as being effeminate and weak. Removed from the comforts of home and the supposed undue influence of their mothers, boys lived in an all-male world where physical ability, courage and resilience were valued. Students played a never-ending round of sports at school; chief among these was cricket. Competitive games were thought to toughen up boys so that they could assume their rightful place as Britain's leaders. Cricket, a sport once played on the village common, moved in the eighteenth century to the confines of the public school pitch where it became a gentleman's game. Cricket symbolized a new elite masculinity: polite and amateur, yet athletic and virile. Lord Chesterfield embraced the sport and encouraged his son to excel as a cricketer. Famously, Thomas Lord so loved the game that he founded the Marylebone Cricket Club (MCC) in 1787 on his property in London's Marylebone district.

The atmosphere that bred this toughness was seen by many as too easily crossing over to brutality. School heads and tutors physically (and often harshly) disciplined boys for a variety of infractions, both large and small. Aside from the few teachers on staff, public schools offered little in the way of adult supervision, thus leaving boys to their devices. Pupils established a hierarchy based on age and maintained it through power and fear. Senior boys regularly and sometimes cruelly disciplined junior boys, often to the point of terrorizing them. At times, the violence exploded out of control. For example, a pupil rebellion at Eton subsided only after the militia stormed the school to quell the rioters. In 1770, the Riot Act was read to students at Winchester following a particularly violent uprising. More limited acts of rebellion and mischief were routinely carried out by students against the school staff. Students at Rugby planted gunpowder in the study of their school headmaster. While many parents, graduates and proponents of public schools extolled the virtues of masculinity that the schools instilled, Henry Fielding, for one, condemned public schools as 'nurseries of all vice and immorality'. Boys were initiated into the wanton ways of some British gentlemen: they drank, gambled and fought.

Perhaps even more significant than the lessons learned at school were the bonds forged and the common understandings shared. Gibbon, who had attended

Westminster, sang the praises of public schools for they had produced many eminent characters and thus were best adapted to the genius and constitution of the English people. Public schools bred the nation's leaders, the ministers and patriots of the rising generation by supplying boys with a shared education, similar habits and an exclusive network of friends for life.

For the better part of the eighteenth century universities, unlike public schools, were not deemed necessary to the education and training of elite gentlemen. While gentlemen had nearly exclusive access to Oxford and Cambridge, most young men (as likely decided by their families) did not matriculate due to the universities' reputations for drinking, whoring and suspect political leanings. The universities were widely perceived to fail in their educational mission. Edward Gibbon, for one, disappointedly recalled his own days at Oxford in the 1750s when the dons were 'free from the toil of reading, or thinking, or writing'. Horace Walpole similarly declared Oxford to be 'a nursery of nonsense and bigotry'. Furthermore, Oxford's politics were suspect, as it was thought to lean towards the Jacobites, supporters of the exiled Stuarts. Cambridge fared little better, as Lord Chesterfield branded it 'an illiberal seminary'. Elite guardians, concerned for the welfare, intellect and scruples of their young sons, tried to persuade their charges to pursue other endeavours instead of attending university. Enrolment figures reflect the poor reputation of and low confidence in the universities. In 1700 only 35 per cent of English peers attended either Oxford or Cambridge (the percentages of Scottish, Welsh and Irish peers are significantly smaller). In 1733 Christ College, Cambridge admitted only three students in its first-year class. By mid-century Oxford's total enrolment of new students across all its colleges had dropped below 200. For those elites who did attend, however, Oxford and Cambridge (like the elite public schools) functioned as private clubs where the sons of the landed ranks acquired similar customs and ideas, cemented their exclusive social networks, and prepared to assume their leadership roles in society.

By 1800 a significant change had occurred in the universities, as well as in the elite perceptions of them. Families had developed renewed faith in Oxford and Cambridge, which, like the Inns of Court, were seen as essential components of a gentleman's education. By attending university and spending some time at one of the Inns, a gentleman would acquire a smattering of knowledge that would help him to run his estate, the country and the empire. By the end of the century, over 60 per cent of English peers spent some time at university. By 1815 60 per cent of all peers (English, Scottish, Welsh and Irish) had matriculated at Oxford or Cambridge.

Whether at university or outside of it, many landed gentlemen pursued knowledge and understanding by reading, participating in philosophical and cultural societies, conducting scientific experiments, and pursuing the natural sciences of botany, zoology and mineralogy, to name a few. Some, like Horace Walpole, contributed to eighteenth-century intellectual life by writing a variety of literary works, running a printing press and exchanging ideas with others through thousands of letters. Walpole's letters remain the most famous and richly revealing of eighteenth-century elite life. Many landed gentlemen stocked their private libraries with a great many texts covering a wide range of subjects, including history, art, architecture, music, poetry, language, philosophy, religion and travel. While estate inventories reveal the extent of the elite's acquisition of books, these documents often have little to say on whether or not the books were read, by whom, and with what effect. The answers to these questions about the habits of reading can only be found in marginalia written in the texts as well as in commonplace books, diaries, memoranda and letters.

The Grand Tour constituted the final component of a gentleman's education and served as one of the most distinctive and powerful rituals that defined a British gentleman. Essentially, the Grand Tour entailed an extended journey lasting two to three years and centred around a set of prescribed activities intended to finish and polish the mind, habits and qualities of a young man. The grand tourist engaged in scholarly, athletic and social pursuits under the supervision of one or two tutors. Academic study focused on history, languages and natural sciences. Additionally, tourists studied art and architecture in order to cultivate the proper aesthetic and thus make elite boys into connoisseurs who bought artworks and luxury goods while on the Tour. Boys were expected to hone their skills in the male accomplishments of riding, fencing, shooting and dancing. Socially, they were meant to mix with continental nobles and notables as well as other British travellers, thereby refining and displaying their manners. Together, these activities were thought to enhance the gentleman's learning and sophistication.

Every grand tourist followed a fairly standard itinerary. After setting sail from Dover, he landed at Calais from whence he travelled southeast towards Paris. Before reaching the metropolis, however, many British travellers stopped in a provincial town in order to improve their language skills. Paris was a premier destination where young British gentlemen would become acquainted with continental fashions, manners and society. Here, in the emporium of Europe, they purchased the finest goods, from rich cloth to handmade books to delicate china and glass. After Paris, the grand tourist made extended stops in France's southern provinces to concentrate on his study of history, art and architecture, while enjoying the pastoral setting and temperate climate along the Mediterranean. After a few months, the traveller would take to the road once more, this time crossing the Alps, sometimes via a trip to Geneva. Finally, an extensive tour was made of Italian cities, including Venice, Florence, Rome, Naples and Pompeii, in no particular order, to tour the relics of classical civilization and to purchase paintings, sculptures and *objets d'art* that attempted to recapture its grandeur.

The Grand Tour was one of the formative rituals that distinguished British landowners as a class. The Grand Tour spoke volumes about the elite's unparalleled learning, vast wealth and limitless leisure. The mere fact that the well-born had the means and opportunity to take an extended Tour set them apart from fellow Britons who could afford neither the time (the average Tour lasted two to three years) nor the expense (typically, tours cost upwards of £5,000). Of course, few men of any status could afford the ten-year Grand Tour taken by the duke of Kingston from 1726 to 1736 that cost well over £40,000. The Grand Tour, with its principal components of international socializing, education and art collecting, was thought to foster cosmopolitanism among the landed ranks, and thus further distinguished them as a class apart. Not only did the Grand Tour differentiate the gentleman from his more common countrymen, it also enabled the British elite to create and participate in an international elite culture. It fostered a homogeneity perhaps never achieved since by any class on such an international scale. Furthermore, although the completion of the Grand Tour marked the end of a gentleman's formal education, its after-effects lingered throughout his life. Upon his return from the continent, a British grand tourist displayed his acquired manners and accomplishments, his goods and riches; and it was these social and material attainments that helped legitimize his rule at home and ensure his cultural dominance.

Social and Cultural Pursuits

The landed orders of eighteenth-century Britain constituted the quintessential leisure class. Having acquired their social graces and habits of mind in their youth, the landed elite spent the overwhelming majority of their adult lives engaged in a dizzying array of continuous sociability: they dined, danced, promenaded, hunted, gambled, travelled and gossiped together. In a variety of settings and through myriad social activities, members of the landed elite forged intimate ties amongst themselves and created a powerful sense of group identity. Elite social activities were ordered by both time and place; the social calendar and the location of the social world moved in unison. Elite social life became amphibious in the eighteenth century. While the landed ranks maintained their strong roots in the country through a wide variety of leisure pursuits including hunting, shooting and visiting on their newly built and refashioned estates, they simultaneously forged a new urban ethos by flocking to London and other towns where they partook of the delights of the city, including attending the 'Season', assemblies and theatres. In this way, their new urban identity complemented rather than displaced their age-old country ethos. Eighteenth-century landed men and women were peripatetic creatures who travelled on an established circuit, from country house to country house, from countryside to London, from spa to spa, from race meetings to assemblies. They rediscovered and reclaimed towns, and uncovered Britain's natural wonders of the Lake District, the Peaks, Wales and even the Scottish Highlands. As a whole, the leisure activities of the landed ranks clearly defined them as a social group at the apex of the British nation.

Elite sociability was remarkably exclusive and tightly knit. The active and continuous social activities strengthened existing ties of blood, affinity and upbringing and enabled members of the elite to forge a shared identity that fostered cohesiveness among themselves while distinguishing them from those below. While the landed elite continued to hold and attend traditional feasts and national celebrations that brought them into contact with their less privileged neighbours, these occasions were few and far between. Such events tended to emphasize, rather than downplay, the elite's social distinctions and local authority. For example, many ceremonies celebrated the rites of passage of the great, such as the births, coming-of-age, weddings and funerals of the landed elite. These occasions demonstrated the hierarchical order of social relations and showcased the superior status of landlords, while pointedly reminding the local community of their inferior position and the deference they owed to the elite. The stark divide between elites and commoners was evident in the vast resources that the landlord spent to host a traditional feast. For example, the duke of Rutland's three-day coming-of-age party in 1799 cost over £60,000. Thus, despite the continuation of traditional intra-class mixing, the landed elite forged a culture separate and distinct from that of the people at large.

The foundations of elite social life were firmly laid in the country. Their wealth, status and power had long been derived from the land, and so too did their way of life.

The family seat, with its grand house and extensive grounds, was the setting for a variety of leisure pursuits, including the rebuilding and redesign of the estate, amassing art collections, and hosting family and friends for long stays during which they dined, danced, gambled and hunted. During the eighteenth century elite families started a craze for the fashioning and refashioning of their country estates. In this way, country house 'improvements' constituted a significant leisure activity in itself that also created the setting for hundreds of additional social activities. Across the century and across Britain, country homes were redesigned, rebuilt and refurbished in a range of architectural styles, including Palladianism, neo-classicism, Grecian, Italianate, Chinese and Gothic. Among the most famous and famously expensive were the earl of Leicester's £90,000 bill for Holkham Hall; the £100,000 of improvements to Audley End; and the sixteen-year (1747–63) rebuilding project of Woburn Abbey that cost the duke of Bedford £84,000. Famously, the cost of building Blenheim Palace, designed by Sir John Vanbrugh, was borne by a grateful nation for the military successes of the first duke of Marlborough. Inside, rooms were redesigned so that a variety of specific social practices, from card-playing to dancing to dining, could take place simultaneously. Libraries, saloons and drawing rooms inside as well as temples and menageries outside on the grounds of the estate became venues for elite sociability.

The interior spaces of the house underwent similar transformations. British grand tourists carried back to Britain a great variety of art objects and material goods that displayed their acquired knowledge, vast wealth and refined taste. Through the exercise of their cultivated aesthetic, members of the aristocracy and gentry fostered a shared sensibility that drew them more closely together while distancing them from Britain's professional and middling orders. Gentlemen connoisseurs established impressive art collections. Some, like Viscount Palmerston, snapped up considerable collections at bargain prices. Palmerston purchased some 300 old masters for a mere £8,000. Others paid dearly for a few well-chosen pieces, such as the second Earl Grosvenor, who paid £10,000 for four paintings by Rubens. In the aftermath of the French Revolution elite connoisseurs were able to snap up more continental works of art. In 1803, for example, the duke of Bridgewater and some of his noble friends bought the Orleans collection of old masters for £43,000.

While many gentlemen collected continental art across the century, other members of the elite filled their homes with works created by British artists. The eighteenth century witnessed a tremendous flowering of British art by the hands of some of the nation's most celebrated artists, including William Hogarth, Sir Joshua Reynolds, Thomas Gainsborough, Sir Thomas Lawrence, George Romney and John Constable. Elite patronage fuelled this extraordinary creative output. Some nobles, such as the third earl of Egremont, bought only British artists (in stark contrast to his father, who had collected European works exclusively). The third earl collected not only acknowledged British masters such as Gainsborough and Reynolds, but also works by new artists including Constable, William Blake, Sir David Wilkie and J. M. W. Turner, who captured elite life in a series of paintings he made while staying at Egremont's Petworth House. One direct consequence of this new-found interest in British art was an increase in prices for British works, which meant that only the elite could afford them. The interest in British paintings was mirrored by a craze for British furniture, with gentlemen filling their homes with the creations of Chippendale, Mayhew and Ince, and Linnell.

In addition to building, redesigning and redecorating their stately homes, the landed elite spent substantial sums remaking and enlarging their estate parks and gardens. Where possible, houses were reoriented to sit in the centre of the park through the practice of engrossing and enclosure. The park at Holkham Hall, for example, was redesigned and expanded throughout the period so that by 1800 it covered more than 3,000 acres. Similarly, the duke of Norfolk expanded his Cumberland estate to 5,000 acres. Parks, like that at Woburn Abbey, were filled with a variety of deer, thus symbolizing the owner's status and power. Within the park, the family seat (once nestled alongside its local neighbours) was resituated in a large, private park that literally insulated the house and its occupants from the unwelcome noise from the roads, markets and local villagers. If privacy could not be ensured by enclosure or engrossing, the local village was moved or, more dramatically, razed and rebuilt at a suitable distance. Landlords employed the artistic vision of William Kent, 'Capability' Brown and Humphrey Repton to redesign their parks in order to make them 'natural' by building serpentine lakes and moving earth into mounds. By 1780 the landscaped park had become the sine qua non of elite status; the countryside had been refashioned in a similar manner thanks to the efforts of Brown (who transformed 188 estates between 1750 and 1783) and his successor Repton (who redesigned over 220 parks from 1780 to 1818). The landed class also displayed a taste for the exotic by collecting foreign animals, notably monkeys, parrots and goldfish, as well as imported plants such as fuchsias, acacias, pineapples and citrus trees.

The family seat was the setting for hundreds of social activities. The elite entertained one another and a constant flow of friends who came and went as part of the practice of country house visiting. During visits, ladies and gentlemen shared meals, took tea, attended elaborate balls and parties, played all manner of card games from whist to faro, rambled across the countryside, gambled continuously, read aloud to one another, put on amateur theatricals, performed musical concerts, and gossiped throughout all these activities. Many of the elite distinguished themselves as patrons of music: the duke of Chandos kept his own private twenty-seven piece orchestra at Cannons; the duchess of Newcastle supported the composer Greene; and the royal family as well as the earl of Burlington supported Handel. Some members of the elite not only supported music, they also made it. Charles Jennens, a member of the Leicestershire gentry, composed the libretto of Handel's *Messiah*, *Saul* and *Belshazzar*. Many ladies and gentlemen, having studied music as part of their education, frequently showcased their accomplishments during small concerts at home.

The landed elite opened their homes and gardens to one another. By the 1770s some of the more popular landscape parks and estate houses had established open days and, in the 1780s, a few of these began to issue admission tickets. Many landlords capitalized on the developing commercialization of leisure by selling teas, prints, guidebooks and souvenirs to visitors. Others, such as the duke of Norfolk, built accommodations for visitors close to their estates, thus encouraging longer stays. The great noble landed estates, such as Chatsworth, Wilton and Warwick Castle, attracted thousands of visitors each year. Wilton, for example, welcomed more than 2,300 'strangers' in 1776. Although country houses and the practice of country house visiting were intended to impress the middling sorts rather than fellow elite, it remains the case that the middle class merely visited while the landed elites stayed. Elite visitors, who might be related to or acquainted with an estate owner, were generally more welcome than middle-class tourists. Elite guests were, however, still expected to pay the entrance fee. The earl and countess of Bath, along with their son, paid a half-crown for a tour led by servants of the earl of Leicester's estate at Holkham Hall. Fees and tips paid to servants acting as tour guides were related to the status of the visitor: the higher the social degree, the larger the fee expected. Servants could earn substantial sums from entrance fees. Mrs Home, who worked at Warwick Castle for more than seventy years, collected more than £30,000 by showing visitors around.

For the visitor, country houses offered spectacular viewing, inside and out. Rooms were sumptuously furnished with exquisite paintings, sculpture and *objets d'art*. The practice of country house visiting helped to extend the significance of the elite habit of art collecting well beyond the confines of any single country house. Indeed, elite collections exerted considerable influence in shaping the aesthetic sensibilities of the British nation. Aristocrats such as the duke of Bridgewater, the marquess of Stafford and Earl Grosvenor opened up their galleries and published guidebooks for the use of visitors. From this practice grew a belief that private art collections held in elite country homes constituted treasures that both belonged to and enhanced the British nation. The elite connoisseur played an important role in the establishment of Britain's national cultural institutions. The genesis of the National Gallery (which was not built until the late 1830s) lay in the British Institution for Promoting the Fine Arts, which was founded in 1805 by elite art collectors. Similarly, members of the landed ranks founded other British cultural institutions, including the Society of Dilettanti and Royal Academy.

Complementing their indoor sociability was their outdoor leisure. Out-of-doors, elite men pursued their love of sport: they rode and raced horses, hunted fox and went shooting. Horses and riding had been associated with the landed classes since the early Middle Ages when horsemanship was considered a vital part of knightly status. Riding instruction was a key component of a gentleman's education. Horseracing, which was a natural extension of riding, became a favourite elite pastime in the eighteenth century. Race meets became a regular feature of elite sociability, and significantly races bore the names of their elite sponsor's house or estate. Horseracing quickly became a British national institution. Many towns established their own race meets, thereby making racing a more public occasion. Horseracing however remained the sport of kings and landlords, since the most prestigious meets were those sponsored by the landed elite. Furthermore, the obsession with pedigrees and thoroughbreds meant only the well-to-do could afford to keep and train the horses. Earl Grosvenor, for one, spent some £7,000 annually on his stable in the later eighteenth century. Nobles and gentry proudly shared the sport with the people who served to enhance their own social prestige. Thus, while horseracing became revered as a national sport, it remained an elite pursuit.

The elite sport *par excellence* was foxhunting. Foxhunting was invented in the middle of the century when breeding practices created new types of horses (with greater speed and increased agility) and hounds (with a more acute sense of smell). Organized hunts were quickly established across the countryside; by the 1830s, there were more than ninety different hunts in Great Britain and still more in Ireland. The establishment of these numerous hunts, each with their own distinctive colours and dates, symbolically carved the nation up into different 'countries', while at the same time they united the elite in a new activity that powerfully symbolized the status and homogeneity of landowners. The hunt prompted landowners to reshape their land, and by extension, the landscape of the country. Ditches were filled, gates and bridges built and hedges torn down so that elite men might pursue the hapless and inedible fox and display their skills as riders. Foxhunting enabled gentlemen to flaunt both their leisure and their manliness while shedding their effete and idle image. Hunters, dressed in tight-fitting outfits that resembled military uniforms and engaged in a violent pursuit, looked like warrior men.

Shooting, like the hunt, was a pastime exclusive to the landed ranks. Gaming laws ensured that hunting remained the privileged activity of the landed. Only landowners had the rights to the game that populated their estates, and thus only landowners had the right to hunt that game. Hunting all manner of prey became wildly popular among the elite in the period. In the eighteenth century marksmanship became a highly valued ability in gentlemen as the landed ranks no longer shot low-flying, ground-dwelling game (such as partridges), but preferred to shoot at high-flying pheasant (whose tendency to be more densely packed than the partridge promised more birds to shoot). Shooting parties were eminently social occasions in which houseguests stayed on an estate for days. In this way, shooting, like the hunt, helped to foster strong ties among the landed ranks.

Eighteenth-century elites gambled away their days, and sometimes their fortunes, by wagering on nearly every conceivable game of chance. Gentlemen and ladies flocked to the gaming tables, where they bet on horseracing, card-playing, cock-fighting, political events, as well as births, deaths and daredevil feats. They bet on sports; Horace Mann once wagered £1,000 on a cricket match. Despite their good fortune of being to the manor born, gentlemen often lost huge sums. Charles James Fox, for example, had lost £140,000 by the age of twenty-five. The tides of fortune could quickly turn, as was the case for young Lord Stavordale, who, not yet twenty-one, lost £21,000 in one card game at the London gentlemen's club White's, only to recover it in a following hand. Gaming fever was not limited to men. Ladies, most (in)famously Georgiana, duchess of Devonshire, suffered equally staggering losses totalling more than £100,000.

No longer content to live exclusively in the country, the elite sought the society and sophistication found only in towns. Many elites believed that they must acquire the polish of the urban and urbane lest they be mistaken for a mean fellow, or a country bumpkin. Britain's eighteenth-century landed classes spent much more time on their country estates and less in towns than did their continental counterparts, although they spent more time in the city than their predecessors had. The increasingly urban life of the landed elite prompted concern among contemporary observers, who feared that the landed elite were abandoning the countryside entirely in favour of a love of the fashionable life in London and spa towns such as Bath. Their extensive social calendar and continuous movement across the nation was prompted by 'an urban renaissance' and was made possible by the eighteenth century's transportation revolution that brought turnpike roads, canals and improvements in carriage design and comfort. Elites flocked to once-moribund cities, like Bath and York, which sprang back to life during the period and offered a range of social activities to genteel visitors. Similarly, resorts were established to cater to the leisure pursuits of the landed.

The Season (complete with the definite pronoun and a capital S) called the landed elite from their country estates to London and helped to make the elite 'amphibious' by linking the country house (with its rural and sometimes parochial pursuits) to the arguably more cosmopolitan life of the townhouse. The Season, which was tied to parliamentary sessions, powerfully represented the political and cultural dominance of the landed ranks. The Season began in November with the presentation of the daughters of the landed elite to the monarch and to elite society as a whole. In this way, the London Season served as a marriage market for eligible young gentlemen and ladies. While many attendees (both male and female) hoped to exchange wedding vows, all engaged in seven months' worth of parties, balls, visits, gambling, eating and drinking. By the later half of the eighteenth century, the Season had been elongated on both ends and formed into two Seasons, the Spring Season (which ran from March to June) and the Winter Season (which started in September and closed in December).

The aristocracy and the greater gentry bought and established townhouses in London, thereby confirming the capital's status as the premier urban destination. Throughout the century, the elite migrated ever westward and northward in greater London in an attempt to create fashionable neighbourhoods and avoid the ever-encroaching middle and lower orders. This trend can clearly be seen when elite districts are plotted on a city map: Covent Garden, St Giles, Leicester Square, Grosvenor Square, Hyde Park. These fashionable districts were built on property owned by some of the great landowners, the duke of Bedford and marquess of Westminster among others, who either developed the lands themselves or leased them out to builders. Like their country estates, elite townhouses were filled with exquisite collections and luxury goods. Unlike their country houses, the townhouses were not open to visitors, but rather served as the private settings for exclusive sociability among the elite. Similarly, new venues, such as assembly halls, townhouses, clubs, salons, theatres and parks, were constructed to meet the needs of an elite clientele.

In London the landed elite pursued an elaborate daily round of amusements: visits, dinners, teas, suppers, balls, attending music, opera and drama, playing a variety of games of chance, especially cards, participating in private clubs, societies and institutions, and promenading in landscaped gardens. Elite men and women promenaded and socialized in London's famed parks, Hyde, Ranelagh and the Spring Gardens at Vauxhall. The gardens offered a variety of fashionable amusements where the elites could dine, dance, converse, gossip and promenade. London's gardens were open to all who could afford the price of an admission ticket. Ranelagh cost 2 s 6 d per person, while Vauxhall was less expensive and perhaps less discriminating, charging a mere one shilling a head up until 1792. Although the gardens were open to the public and therefore not the exclusive preserve of the elite, they were tellingly located in the west and southwest of the city, home of the elite. While the social ranks might encounter one another every now and again in London's pleasure gardens, they did not socialize together. While elite men and women mingled in the majority of elite social occasions, elite men congregated exclusively in their private clubs, such as White's and Almack's, or at all-male societies, such as the Dilettanti Society or the Royal Society.

While the upper stratum of landed society claimed the fashionable districts of London as its own, the lesser gentry staked their claims in select provincial urban centres such as Durham, Lincoln, Maidstone, Salisbury, Winchester and Bury St Edmunds. These towns experienced considerable growth in tourism and leisure industries during the long eighteenth century. In these towns the genteel pursued a social life similar to that found in London, albeit on a smaller scale. Regional centres boasted theatres, assemblies, shops and gardens. For those lesser gentry with estates close to a major town, gentlemen and women were able to enjoy the best of both worlds. They could reside on their landed estate while making day trips into a nearby town in order to take advantage of its many amusements.

The elites not only travelled the circuit from country to town, they also began to explore Britain in the eighteenth century. Domestic travel grew increasingly popular among the landed elite during the period as frequent warfare between Britain and France made travel to the continent more dangerous, and many times simply impossible. Indeed, in the 1760s and 1770s, gentlemen and ladies explored Britain more frequently than they did the continent. With the continent effectively out of bounds, the landed elite turned to Britain for vistas similar to those of the continent. For example, Sir George Beaumont, an Essex baronet, substituted the Lake District and Wales for his beloved Italy after it had been cut off from him. Similarly, Sir Watkin Williams Wynn, fourth baronet, explored north Wales in 1771 during a two-week tour of the region, taking the artist Paul Sandy to capture the landscape and nine servants to tend to his comforts. When it came to domestic travel, the farther afield the better, as destinations off the beaten track obtained special cachet. Travelling to places where others could not demonstrated elite leisure and wealth, and reflected the elite's exclusivity and superiority. Furthermore, travel enabled the elite to appropriate the land and thus declare their dominance over it. While on their travels, the elite displayed their ownership over the land by collecting flora, fauna and minerals, capturing views on canvas, and hunting the wild animal life. Like other Highland landlords, the duke of Gordon advertised 'hunting and fishing opportunities' on his estate in *The Times*. Angling for genteel clients, the duke charged £70 per rental for each hunting lodge on his estate.

Bath became *the* elite spa resort in the early eighteenth century. Drinking the waters at Bath was thought effective in treating glandular diseases. Although Bath and other spas boasted salubrious effects, the full spectrum of landed elite flocked to these resorts primarily for their social benefits. In Bath elite men and women pursued an elaborate and intensive social circuit throughout the day and night. Their lives revolved around the baths, balls, assemblies, theatres, concerts, promenades, excursions, gaming, gossip and intrigues. There were three distinct baths, each serving a different purpose and constituency. Only the King's Bath catered to the genuinely ill. The rest of elite society, those in good health and in mixed company, convened at the Cross Gate Bath for social bathing. Male and female bathers alike were clothed in canvas garments for propriety's sake. Although there was some criticism levelled against mixed bathing during the eighteenth century, the sexes were not segregated until the nineteenth century. The third bath, the Queen's Bath, was for ladies only. In addition to bathing in the mornings, genteel men and women congregated at the Pump Room to drink the alkaline waters. By late morning they had taken refreshments and listened to a musical concert at newly built theatres. In the afternoon they promenaded, played cards and took excursions around town and the surrounding countryside. Their evenings were filled with gaming, concerts, discussions, gossip and dancing at the assemblies. The next day, the cycle began again.

In the latter half of the eighteenth century Bath began to lose some of its appeal for the landed elite as more and more people from the aspiring professional and middle ranks gained a foothold in town. In response, the elite closed ranks. As the social range of visitors widened, more and more of the landed elite held private parties and 'at homes', a practice that earlier in the century would have been unthinkable as well as unwelcome. This trend toward reaffirming elite social space as exclusive even applied to the baths. The duke of Kingston built a private, fee-only bath in 1766. Admission was five shillings per visit, a sum that clearly excluded many. The wealthier pleasure-seekers happily paid the admission fee in exchange for some modicum of privacy and exclusivity.

Other spa towns, notably Tunbridge Wells and Scarborough, served as regional resorts that catered to local country gentry. Between 1660 and 1815 more than forty-eight spas were founded in Britain, more than half of which were established by elite landowners (who had discovered springs on their estates). These smaller, less famous towns offered similar social amenities to those found in Bath. Local grandees gathered at assemblies, attended the theatre and dined together according to the cycle of the social season. Seaside resorts, notably Brighton and Scarborough, were quickly established in the eighteenth century. By 1806 Britain had sixteen marine resorts that boasted elite residences built in exclusive elegant crescents and squares, theatres, assemblies, pleasure gardens, libraries, shops selling all manner of goods, and sometimes specialized card, dancing and music rooms which catered to an elite clientele.

Over the long eighteenth century the landed elite developed distinct patterns of social behaviour, and with these a more cohesive culture that enabled them to maintain their power and position in society. The elite became more cohesive as a result of an increasingly standardized upbringing. The sons of the landed elite pursued a uniform education at a few exclusive public schools and universities where they acquired similar habits of mind, ideas and values. Over the course of the century, the landed ranks became more exclusive, and more British. Furthermore, the landed elite became amphibious, equally at home in the country and in town. As the century progressed, elite culture turned its gaze away from the continent and looked inward for inspiration and identity. Elites were more closely drawn together through their education and upbringing, which grew increasingly more standardized in form, substance and ideas. The aristocracy and gentry remained in control of British society, due to a large extent to their cultural practices. On the whole, eighteenth-century Britain embraced and was governed by elite values and leadership rather than middle-class habits. Through their cultural activities, elite men and women consolidated their power and authority, and thus remained at the apex of British society throughout the long eighteenth century and beyond.

FURTHER READING

Bermingham, Ann and Brewer, John (eds): *The Consumption of Culture, 1600–1800: Image, Object, Text* (London, 1995).

Black, Jeremy: *The British Abroad: The Grand Tour in the Eighteenth Century* (Stroud, 1997).
Brewer, John: *The Pleasures of the Imagination: English Culture in the Eighteenth Century* (London, 1997).
Cannadine, David: *Lords and Landlords* (Leicester, 1980).
Cannon, John: *Aristocratic Century: The Peerage of Eighteenth-Century England* (Cambridge, 1984).
Christie, Christopher: *The British Country House in the Eighteenth Century* (Manchester, 2000).
Cohen, Michèle: *Fashioning Masculinity: National Identity and Language in the Eighteenth Century* (London, 1996).
Colley, Linda: *Britons: Forging the Nation 1701–1837* (London, 1992).
Davidoff, Leonore: *Best Circles: Society, Etiquette, and the Season* (London, 1973).
Ford, Boris: *The Cambridge Cultural History of Britain: Eighteenth-Century Britain* (Cambridge, 1992).
Jackson-Stops, Gervase (ed.): *The Treasure Houses of Britain: Five Hundred Years of Private Patronage and Art Collecting* (London, 1985).
Jenkins, Philip: *The Making of a Ruling Class: The Glamorgan Gentry, 1640–1790* (Cambridge, 1983).
Stone, Lawrence and Stone, Jeanne C. Fawtier: *An Open Elite? England 1540–1880* (Oxford, 1984).
Tillyard, Stella: *Aristocrats: Caroline, Emily, Louisa and Sarah Lennox, 1750–1832* (London, 1994).
Vickery, Amanda: *The Gentleman's Daughter: Women's Lives in Georgian England* (New Haven, CT, 1998).
Williamson, Tom: *Polite Landscapes: Gardens and Society in Eighteenth-Century England* (Stroud, 1995).

Chapter Twenty-Five

Literature and Drama

J. Alan Downie

Augustan Poetry

Inevitably, literary history is concerned with writers and with texts. Divisions into periods are arbitrary, and dates of publication are at best indicative, at worst misleading. This applies to divisions into centuries also. William Cowper died in 1800, exactly 100 years after the death of Dryden. The second edition of *Lyrical Ballads*, which included Wordsworth's famous *Preface*, was published in the same year. These events, then, offer vantage points from which to view the development of eighteenth-century verse. Two anthologies edited by Roger Lonsdale, *The New Oxford Book of Eighteenth-Century Verse* (1984) and *Eighteenth-Century Women Poets: An Oxford Anthology* (1989), have changed our perception of what was written during the period. By reprinting work which had languished out of print since its first publication, particularly poems by women writers, Lonsdale succeeded in demonstrating how eighteenth-century poetry was more diverse in style, form and subject matter than we had been led to believe by previous critics. Where Lonsdale first ventured, others were eager to follow, and competing anthologies of verse by women now vie for our attention.

Indeed there is a danger that this recent emphasis on the diversity of eighteenth-century verse forms and the 'discovery' of 'new' eighteenth-century poets might result in the importance of 'Dryden, Pope, and all their school', and the dominance of the heroic couplet, being understated. To point to the idiosyncrasies of Smart's *Jubilate Agno* (written *c.*1759–61, published 1939) or Macpherson's spurious *Fragments of Ancient Poetry* (1760), let alone Blake's *Marriage of Heaven and Hell* (*c.*1793), as examples of experimental verse is one thing. To dispute the hegemony of the heroic couplet is another matter entirely. True, lyric poets exploited other verse forms, and ballads, hymns and odes of several kinds were published throughout the period. True, not everyone wrote in pentameter couplets; the commonest variations were blank verse and octosyllabic couplets. Nevertheless, it is seriously misleading not to acknowledge that couplets dominated all poetry for more than 200 years. Dryden installed the heroic couplet in its position of hegemony almost single-handedly. More satire was published between 1660 and 1714 than any other type of verse, and Dryden's influence on the poetry of these years, particularly political poetry, would be difficult to overstate. Yet to limit our appreciation of Dryden's achievement to satire written in heroic couplets would be to ignore his mastery of other metres and moods. As his numerous odes attest, he was equally innovative as a lyric poet. Dryden's poetical versatility epitomizes the diversity of eighteenth-century verse itself, and Pope was Dryden's true poetic heir not only because of his mastery of the heroic couplet and his tremendous satiric gift, but on account of the astonishing variety of his output.

Dryden and Pope are called 'Augustan' satirists because they looked back to Roman writers who flourished during the reign of Augustus Caesar, to Virgil and Horace in particular. Although recent critics have questioned both its applicability and its usefulness as an adjective to describe the period, the term 'Augustan' was used by contemporaries to indicate a period of high literary achievement, measured by a self-conscious subscription to classical models. Thus, Goldsmith's *An Account of the Augustan Age of England* (1759) refers to the decades between the 1680s and the 1740s when 'taste was united to genius' and writers shone 'like stars lost in each other's brightness'. In this way, Goldsmith deliberately links Dryden with Pope, Swift and their contemporaries, as well as insinuating that this literary golden age died with Pope and Swift.

That Pope found Augustan literary models congenial cannot be denied, and his first essay in verse was an imitation of Virgil's *Eclogues.* The youthful Pope is a difficult poet to pigeonhole, however. He also wrote imitations of Chaucer, Spenser and various seventeenth-century English poets before making a statement of his own about the poet's art – in heroic couplets of course – with the *Essay on Criticism* (1711). He followed this with two versions of the brilliant heroi-comical *The Rape of the Lock* (1712, 1714), a mock-epic which pokes fun at society's inability to distinguish the serious from the trivial, as the repeated zeugmas – Pope's master trope – illustrate perfectly:

> Whether the nymph shall break Diana's law,
> Or some frail china jar receive a flaw,
> Or stain her honour, or her new brocade,
> Forget her prayers, or miss a masquerade,
> Or lose her heart, or necklace, at a ball . . .

Although *The Rape of the Lock* deals with serious subjects, as social satire it is fairly inoffensive. Pope's next major poem, *Windsor-Forest* (1713), is a poem of celebration rather than a satire, a paean to nascent British imperialism, while his *Elegy to the Memory of an Unfortunate Lady* (1717) is a contemplative poem which is included in the *Penguin Book of English Romantic Verse.*

If Pope had died before writing *The Dunciad* (1728), his poetical reputation would have been very different. His disturbing account of the way in which the 'Smithfield Muses' had been legitimized and brought 'to the ear of Kings' during the reign of George II, 'Th' Augustus born to bring Saturnian times', was part of a determined literary assault on the administration of Robert Walpole, and *The Dunciad* was published in the wake of Swift's *Gulliver's Travels* (1726) and Gay's *Beggar's Opera*

(1728). The figure of Pope-the-satirist known to posterity is based on *The Dunciad*, the *Moral Essays* and the *Imitations of Horace*, in which Pope uses classical models to accentuate not the similarities, but the differences between Augustan Rome and eighteenth-century Britain. In the *Epistle to Burlington*, the description of a day spent at Timon's villa interrogates the ideology underpinning the Augustan vision of peace and plenty in an ordered, paternalistic society, while the closing lines urge Burlington to 'make falling Arts your care . . . Till Kings call forth th' Idea's of your mind':

> These Honours, Peace to happy Britain brings,
> These are Imperial Works, and worthy Kings.

The sustained irony of the *Epistle to Augustus* takes the argument one stage further, intimating the utter inadequacy of any comparison between Augustus Caesar and George Augustus – the Hanoverian George II – pointedly addressed as the 'great Patron of Mankind' in the opening line.

What had changed? Why was Pope's satire increasingly vitriolic? What were the Augustans so angry about? The great age of English satire coincided with the conclusion of a period of acute political instability. The financial revolution required to secure the safety of the Protestant succession threatened the traditional position in society of the landed man, as power and wealth appeared to shift to those with property in stocks and shares rather than in real estate. Augustan satire is basically a response to this threat, and the most striking voices raised in opposition to political and social change are those of Swift, Pope and Gay – the Scriblerian satirists – and their imitators and disciples. Interestingly, Augustan Rome provided yet another model for the English Augustans in Virgil's *Georgics*, which was also written after a violent civil war. In *Windsor-Forest*, Pope follows Virgil in envisaging a period of 'Peace and Plenty' under Queen Anne just as Virgil anticipated the *pax Augusta*. The Scriblerians believed that a golden opportunity had been thrown away after the Hanoverian succession, which is why they attacked the abuse of trust by self-interested landlords and, by implication, politicians such as Walpole and monarchs such as George Augustus.

The alleged effects of these political and social changes were still being lamented by Oliver Goldsmith a generation later in *The Deserted Village* (1770):

> A time there was, ere England's griefs began,
> When every rood of ground maintained its man;
> For him light labour spread her wholesome store,
> Just gave what life required, but gave no more:
> His best companions, innocence and health;
> And his best riches, ignorance of wealth.
> But times are altered; trade's unfeeling train
> Usurp the land and dispossess the swain . . .

Goldsmith's eloquent construction of a bygone paternalistic society in which everyone recognized and accepted his place in the social hierarchy was deeply indebted to the *Georgics*, as well as to verse-epistles of Horace filtered through Pope's *Moral Essays*. In *The Village* (1783) – a sort of answer to *The Deserted Village* – George Crabbe was quick to point out how far Goldsmith's nostalgic vision of rural life was removed from reality. The appeal of the Augustan vision was a very powerful one, however. It provided the ideological underpinning for a society in which most of the wealth and power were concentrated in the hands of a few men. Satire is predominantly a conservative mode which operates by contrasting *what is* and *what should be*, according to the ideology of the satirist. Satire implies the condemnation of society by reference to an ideal, and challenges any deviation from this ideal. It often tends, therefore, to be backward-looking if not downright reactionary, and this is true of Augustan satire.

The satiric thrust was felt throughout the century and other distinctive voices were heard in verse. Gay's early output, culminating in his fine three-book poem, *Trivia: Or, the Art of Walking the Streets of London* (1716), is heavily indebted to the *Georgics.* The second volume of his *Fables* (1738), however, was advertised as 'mostly on subjects of a graver and more political turn', and the collection was pervaded by the darker tone more readily associated with Swift. Although he affected to be nothing more than a 'man of rhimes', Swift's own range as a writer of verse is remarkable. Preferring to imitate Horace in octosyllabics rather than heroic couplets, he could also be surprisingly effective (like Blake) in energetic anapaests. Humorous, witty and angry by turns, Swift, like Gay, reveals his Augustan face in the self-consciousness of his method of satiric attack, interrogating the values underpinning his literary models through parody. Poets such as Churchill and Goldsmith continued the Scriblerian line of wit in verse after the deaths of Swift, Pope and Gay, and traces can be detected even in Byron. Writers more readily associated with the literature of sensibility – such as Gray and Cowper – occasionally operated within the satiric mode, as did Crabbe and Burns. After the Scriblerians, the most distinctive satiric voice belongs to Samuel Johnson, however, who, with Juvenal rather than Horace as his satiric model, contributed two superb imitations of the third and the tenth satire, respectively, in *London* (1738) and *The Vanity of Human Wishes* (1749) – 'among the greatest verse Satires of the English or any other language', according to T. S. Eliot.

Women tended to write social rather than political satire. The uncompromisingly feminist stance of many female poets of the early eighteenth century is not always appreciated. In her *Poems on Several Occasions* (1703), Sarah Fyge Egerton acknowledged that love poems were traditionally the subject of 'a woman's pen' before lambasting masculine pretensions in 'The Liberty' and 'The Emulation'. The former opens with a rhetorical question:

> Shall I be one of those obsequious Fools,
> That square their lives by Custom[']s scanty Rules . . .

and, as if in response, the latter ends by answering

> And shall these finite Males reverse their Rules?
> No, we'll be Wits, and then Men must be Fools.

The argument of *The Ladies Defence* (1703) by Mary, Lady Chudleigh, runs along similar lines, while in *Miscellany Poems on Several Subjects* (1722), Elizabeth Thomas bids to outdo even Egerton in her scorn of male small-mindedness:

. . . if we enquire for a book,
Beyond a novel or a play,
Good lord! how soon th' alarm's took,
How soon your eyes your souls betray,
And with what spite ye look!

Although Anne Finch, countess of Winchilsea, is mostly remembered for the 'pre-Romantic' sensibility of poems like 'A Nocturnal Reverie' or 'To the Nightingale', she was not immune to the satiric impulse that permeated the age. Nor was Lady Mary Wortley Montagu, whose *Six Town Eclogues* (written 1716, published 1747) bear the hallmarks of her early friendship with Pope and Gay. That the intimacy did not last is made abundantly clear by *Verses Address'd to the Imitator of Horace*, her witty riposte to Pope's *Epistle to Arbuthnot.*

Poetry in the Age of Sensibility

The period from the 1740s to the 1790s has been dubbed the 'Age of Sensibility' in an attempt to distinguish it from the preceding 'Augustan' period, and to avoid the implications of using the term 'pre-Romantic'. Sensibility is linked to the cult of 'feeling' that emerged in drama with Steele's *Conscious Lovers* (1722), in the novel with Richardson's *Pamela* (1740–1) and *Clarissa* (1747–8), and finally, from the 1740s onwards, in the poetry of Gray, Collins and the Wartons. Whereas the Augustans are said to have shied away from intimacy, preferring to write 'public' poetry in a satiric mode, the verse of poets such as Gray and Cowper is thought to anticipate the Romantics in the way in which it focuses on the reflective, solitary poet, as exemplified in Gray's *Elegy Written in a Country Churchyard* (1751).

The vocabulary of sensibility can be readily discerned by comparing a couple of the opening stanzas of Gray's *Elegy* with a few lines from Thomas Warton the younger's *The Pleasures of Melancholy* (1747). The italics in each passage are mine.

Save that from *yonder ivy*-mantled *tow'r*
The mopeing *owl* does to the moon complain
Of such, as wand'ring near her secret *bow'r*,
Molest her ancient solitary reign

Beneath those rugged elms, that yew-tree's shade,
Where heaves the turf in many a *mould'ring* heap,
Each in his narrow cell for ever laid,
The rude forefathers of the hamlet sleep.

Beneath yon' ruin'd abbey's moss-grown piles
Oft let me sit, at twilight hour of eve,
Where thro' some western window the pale moon
Pours her long-levell'd rule of streaming light;
While sullen sacred silence reigns around,
Save the lone screech-*owl*'s note, who builds his *bow'r*
Amid the *mould'ring* caverns dark and damp,
Or the calm breeze, that rustles in the leaves
Of flaunting *ivy*, that with mantle green
Invests some wasted *tow'r*.

The poems clearly have a number of features in common in addition to their 'poetic' diction. Mood and setting are key elements of the reflective poetry associated with Gray and Collins in particular. Delineating literary periods is complex, however, and we only have to look back to poems like Finch's *A Nocturnal Reverie* (1713), Parnell's *A Night-Piece on Death* (1721) and, above all, Young's *Night Thoughts* (1742–5) in order to appreciate that certain features of the 'melancholy' verse which Gray made so popular had been anticipated.

The same is true of 'nature' poetry. James Thomson claimed to draw the inspiration for his philosophical poem in blank verse, *The Seasons* (1726–30), from 'the Works of Nature'. Yet Thomson's poetical models were Virgil's *Georgics* (again) and the blank verse of Milton. In *The Pleasures of the Imagination* (1744), Mark Akenside followed Thomson in adapting his diction from Miltonic blank verse, as well as focusing on 'whatever our imagination feels from the agreeable appearances of nature', as did Joseph Warton in *The Enthusiast, or The Lover of Nature* (1744). Crucially, however, Cowper's long autobiographical poem, *The Task* (1785), best illustrates the way in which, taking Thomson's lead, the forms and conventions of earlier Augustan verse could be invested with an intimacy more in tune with the sensibility of the age.

'The Progress of Poesy' and 'The Bard', published together as *Odes, by Mr. Gray* (1757), illustrate other elements of the continuing awareness of tradition. Whereas earlier exponents of the Pindaric ode, following Cowley, had chosen the form because of the freedom it appeared to offer to indulge their flights of fancy, Gray uses it as a vehicle to demonstrate how his desire for lyrical intensity is matched by his Augustan instinct for correctness of form. 'The Progress of Poesy' typically traces the development of poetry from ancient Greece to England via Rome. Allusions to Shakespeare ('Nature's darling') and Milton ('second he, that rode sublime') lead on to a reference to 'Dryden's less presumptuous car' borne, significantly, by 'Two Coursers of ethereal race, / With necks of thunder cloath'd, and long-resounding pace' – heroic couplets. Gray then acknowledges Dryden's lyric accomplishments before reflecting on the poetical ambition of his own 'daring spirit'.

'The Bard', on the other hand, nods in the direction of an alternative poetical tradition of the Celtic Bard in which non-classical mythologies are exploited for their emotional intensity. Other poets were attracted to native traditions. The contrived passionate spontaneity of Macpherson's spurious *Fragments of Ancient Poetry Collected in the Highlands of Scotland* (1760) is far removed from the controlled classical correctness of the Augustans. Chatterton made similar claims of authenticity for his extraordinary imitations of 'medieval' verse, while Percy's *Reliques of Ancient English Poetry* (1765) included poems by contemporary poets alongside genuine ballads and romances. Interest in other styles, forms and poetic languages continued unabated through the final decades of the century, as can be seen variously in Burns's *Poems, Chiefly in the Scottish Dialect* (1785), Blake's early writings, and of course in *Lyrical Ballads* itself.

Significantly, Wordsworth's and Coleridge's collection opens with 'The Rime of the Ancient Mariner' – not the most obvious example to choose as an 'experiment . . . to ascertain how far the language of conversation in the middle and lower classes of society is adapted to the purposes of poetic pleasure' – and the Preface is an apology for a type of 'prosaic' poetry which Wordsworth was concerned, rightly, might not appeal to contemporaries. Reviewers largely felt that the 'experiments' had failed, Coleridge's wife, Sara, noting that 'The Lyrical Ballads are laughed at and disliked by all with very few excepted'. Readers either still preferred 'the sweet and polished measures on lofty subjects, of Dryden, Pope, and Gray' or, like Marianne Dashwood in Jane Austen's *Sense and Sensibility* (1811), the newer poetry of sensibility as epitomized by Cowper. The same is true of Blake. According to A. C. Swinburne, *The Marriage of Heaven and Hell* is the greatest work produced by the eighteenth century, yet it was virtually unknown in its own day and only acquired its immense popularity after its rediscovery by subsequent generations.

Drama

It would be difficult to make a case for the eighteenth century as a golden age of new writing for the stage. The managers of the patent theatres were more interested in proven favourites than in new plays. Concern about the indecency and profanity of contemporary drama was an added complication. The unfortunate response of theatre managers, actors and playwrights was an attempt to 'chasten and moralize the stage'. The effects on new writing for the theatre were far-reaching. In the early years of the century, the theatre at Drury Lane, having secured the services of Farquhar and Vanbrugh, gradually gained a reputation for comedy, interspersing new plays with revivals of 'carefully revised' Restoration comedies. Although Vanbrugh had already produced his best plays, *The Relapse* (1696) and *The Provoked Wife* (1697), by the beginning of the century, Farquhar's *The Recruiting Officer* (1706) and *The Beaux' Stratagem* (1707) succeeded in introducing a new vein of comedy which was less bawdy yet unsentimental, more situational without becoming farcical, and which, while less witty than the work of his Restoration predecessors, still contrived to retain a semblance of verbal humour. Unfortunately, Farquhar died the month *The Beaux' Stratagem* was produced. There were box-office successes such as Susanna Centlivre's *The Busy Body* (1709) and *The Wonder! A Woman Keeps a Secret* (1714), as well as Steele's sententious *The Conscious Lovers* (1722), but, by the 1720s, very few new plays were being performed each season, and most of the revivals were of plays written prior to 1707.

If comedy fared indifferently in the early eighteenth century, tragedy fared even worse. Contemporaries were aware that 'the great Success of one very faulty Play', Addison's *Cato* (1713), could be imputed almost entirely to its studied political overtones. *Cato*'s political thrust had in any case been anticipated by the most accomplished of the century's comparatively few tragedians, Nicholas Rowe. In *Tamerlane* (1701), the eponymous hero is a strange choice to represent William III, although the tyrannical Bajazet is a more conventional counterpart for Louis XIV. More interestingly, Rowe wrote a series of three 'she-tragedies', *The Fair Penitent* (1703), *Jane Shore* (1714) and *Lady Jane Grey* (1715), which, while acknowledging a heavy debt to Shakespeare's style in general and his history plays in particular, ruthlessly exploited female distress on stage for pathetic effect and moral improvement. No other new tragedy of note was produced until George Lillo's domestic tragedy in prose, *The London Merchant*, began its successful run in 1730.

By then, the London theatre world had been turned upside down as a consequence of *The Beggar's Opera*'s record-breaking run at the theatre in Lincoln's

Inn Fields which began on 28 January 1728. The originality of Gay's 'Newgate Pastoral' ushered in a period of intense political interest in the theatre, leading not only to renewed competition between the companies, but to significant dramatic experiments. The political nuances of *The Beggar's Opera* were apparent from the opening bars of the very first song, sung by the thief-taker Peachum, which concludes:

> And the Statesman, because he's so great,
> Thinks his Trade as honest as mine.

References to 'great men' as well as to Walpole's many other sobriquets – 'Robin of Bagshot, alias Gorgon, alias Bluff Bob, alias Carbuncle, alias Bob Booty' – clinched the connection between politics and corruption. Gay subverted more than literary genre. Substituting old English airs for Italian arias, doing away with recitative in favour of the spoken word, and contrasting the machismo of Macheath with the eunuchs who starred in the Italian opera which dominated musical taste, *The Beggar's Opera* not only looked forward to Gilbert and Sullivan, it followed *Gulliver's Travels* in drawing attention to the threat which the Scriblerians and their allies perceived upstarts like Walpole to be posing to the old, paternalistic ways. Peachum and Lockit stood for those monied men who seemed to be undermining the authority of the traditional leaders of society.

Where Gay led, others followed, and a brief but brilliant period of political drama revitalized the theatre until Walpole put a stop to it with the theatrical Licensing Act of 1737. That the inventiveness and exuberance of this type of theatre did not appeal to mid-twentieth-century critics preoccupied with other agendas is scarcely surprising, for it does not conform to preconceptions about what makes good drama. Instead, in its refusal to adhere to traditional ideas of comedy, it appears astonishingly modern. Robert D. Hume has remarked that what the most important of these dramatists, Henry Fielding, was 'moving towards' in the 'plotlessness' of a play like *The Historical Register* (1736) – a biting satirical attack on Walpole's use of hush money – was nothing less than 'political cabaret' (Hume 1988: 259). Fielding, in other words, was writing for the fringe and, like the fringe, his best work resonates with political overtones.

After 1737, however, the conditions that had so circumscribed London theatre at the start of the century were largely reimposed. There were still only two patent theatres (Wren's Drury Lane theatre and the new Covent Garden theatre, built in 1732) – and John Rich, who managed the Covent Garden company, owned both patents. According to *The London Stage*, Rich staged three new plays per season on average from 1732 until his death in 1761. Even under Garrick's management from 1747 until it passed into the hands of Sheridan, Drury Lane managed to produce only twice that number. In addition, the effects of the Licensing Act were far-reaching. Fielding eventually turned his hand to prose fiction, and the experimental comedy of the early 1730s came to an end. Few writers followed the lead of Lillo's *The London Merchant*, and none with conspicuous success. 'Political' tragedies were banned, while Samuel Johnson's unstageable *Irene* (1749, written 1736) is notable only because it is by Johnson – that it lasted nine nights was due entirely to the good offices of David Garrick.

Garrick wrote comedies, too. Indeed, he was known as a playwright before becoming famous as an actor. There was, however, another twenty-year period from 1737 until the late 1750s when very little of interest that was new found its way onto the London stage. Then, during the Seven Years' War (1756–63), there was a further renewal of interest in comedy. Most of it, particularly the vogue for sentimental comedy, was pretty shallow stuff, although one or two of the plays of these years have been successfully revived – George Colman and Garrick's *The Clandestine Marriage* (1766), for instance, or Cumberland's *The West Indian* (1771). But it is really only in the 1770s with the plays of Goldsmith and Sheridan that eighteenth-century comedy briefly escaped from the doldrums. *She Stoops to Conquer* (1773), *The Rivals* (1775) and *The School for Scandal* (1777) have remained in the repertory ever since their first production. They were 'laughing' comedies which exploited their theatricality to contrive comic situations, with 'screen' devices and mistaken identities and other misunderstandings between the central characters very much in evidence. Disguise is a crucial component of each play. The potential for hypocrisy – a straightforward-enough satire on the vogue for sentimentality – is exploited ruthlessly by Sheridan in his satiric exposure of Joseph Surface (the name gives him away), who cynically manipulates those around him in *The School for Scandal* in a way familiar to readers from the behaviour of the utterly self-interested Blifil in Fielding's *Tom Jones*.

That Sheridan 'borrows' a number of his characters and plot devices (including Mrs Malaprop) from earlier writers need not concern us unduly. Although his comedy is largely situational, Sheridan also clearly looks back to the verbal humour of Restoration comedy and, while he might not be able to pull off the wit of Etherege, Wycherley and Congreve – his audiences almost certainly would not have let him – his successful deconstruction of the plot of sentimental comedy in *The Rivals*, his triumphant return to the formula of the 'rehearsal' play in *The Critic* (1779), which closed not only his own career but the resurgence of interest in innovative comedy, and above all the virtuosity of *The School for Scandal* guarantee his position as the century's most successful playwright.

Prose

If the eighteenth century has been undervalued as a period in which something has gone wrong as far as its poetry is concerned, if its drama largely fails to live up to the brilliance of earlier eras, then it is redeemed, with interest, by its innovations in prose. As contemporary booksellers' lists indicate, plays and poems comprised only a fraction of what was published in English, as a significant expansion in the book trade led to a growth in supply and demand.

The enduring contemporary popularity of history, biography and travels is borne out by the catalogues of circulating libraries. Two monumental achievements stand out: Gibbon's *Decline and Fall of the Roman Empire* (6 volumes, 1776–88) exemplifies the transformation from insular, personal memoir to philosophical, interpretative history, while Boswell's *Life of Johnson* (1791) changed expectations of what could be accomplished by the biographer. Similarly, cosy assumptions about human behaviour were challenged by Mandeville's *Fable of the Bees* (1723) and Hume's *Treatise on Human Nature* (1740), and these, in turn, paved the way for Adam Smith's pioneering economic analysis, *The Wealth of Nations* (1776). Mention should also be made of Tom Paine's radical treatise, *Rights of Man* (1791–2), an answer to Edmund Burke's *Reflections on the Revolution in France* (1790).

One of the preconditions for the expansion of the book trade was the end of pre-publication censorship in 1695. This coincided with a period of intense political activity and generated an unprecedented amount of political literature. The rise of the newspaper press was one manifestation of this new-found freedom. Accompanying this development was a significant increase in the number of political pamphlets published during the party conflict of Queen Anne's reign, and the appearance of periodicals such as Defoe's *Review* (1704–13). This, in turn, led to the periodical essays of Addison and Steele. Virtually all the major writers of the period were involved in political journalism of one kind or another. Defoe, Swift, Addison, Steele, Fielding and Johnson wrote political pamphlets as well as being involved with journals either as editor or contributor or both.

Although Swift first came to prominence as the author of *A Tale of a Tub* (1704), a risky exposure of abuses in religion and learning, his contemporary reputation was cemented by his political writings on behalf of the Oxford ministry, especially his *Examiner* essays (1710–11), *The Conduct of the Allies* (1711) and *The Publick Spirit of the Whigs* (1714). A series of pamphlets on Irish politics followed in the 1720s, culminating in the notorious *Modest Proposal* (1729) for eating beggars' babies as a solution to Ireland's economic problems. *Gulliver's Travels*, his most accessible and far-ranging satire, was published during the same period, as his experiences in his native Dublin drove him to anger. '[W]hat I do', he wrote to Pope in 1728, 'is owing to perfect rage and resentment, and the mortifying sight of slavery, folly, and baseness about me, among which I am forced to live'. It is this anger – what Swift himself described as 'savage indignation' – allied to his extraordinarily inventive imagination and ironic tone, which constitutes 'Swiftian' satire. Tone is crucial to Swift's achievement as a satirist. Here we see understatement (litotes) at work, but Swift also uses hyperbole ('I desire the reader will observe, that I calculate my remedy *for this one individual Kingdom of IRELAND, and for no other that ever was, is, or, I think, ever can be upon earth*') and moves between the two with consummate ease. Swift's awareness of the need to manipulate his target reader is at the heart of his ability both as satirist and political writer, and the principal reason for his enduring appeal. His satire transcends its period not only because of his subject matter – *Gulliver's Travels* and *A Modest Proposal* remain relevant in the twenty-first century – but because of Swift's method of attack.

As a figure of indeterminacy, irony is appealing in the postmodern world. All one can be sure about if one decides to interpret a statement ironically is that it does not mean what it appears to mean. Acutely aware of the reader's role, Swift ruthlessly exploits this uncertainty. His satiric works have certain features in common. Swift 'personates' styles and probes the weakness of existing forms in his most accomplished prose writings as well as in verse. A tactical shifting of ground in the middle of the work, entrapping and then dislocating the reader, is also typically 'Swiftian'. Swift realized that, as 'satire is a sort of glass, wherein beholders do generally discover everybody's face but their own', various strategies to defamiliarize his readers needed to be adopted so that they could begin to appreciate how they constructed 'reality'. It is for this reason that Swift, like Sterne, has been called a deconstructionist *avant la lettre*. Then, having manoeuvred his readers into the uncomfortable position of having to question their values and value-systems, Swift refuses to spell out his positive alternative. Thus, at the end of *Gulliver's Travels*, we appear to be faced with the choice of following either the example of the 'Glorious *Houyhnhnms*' or the Brobdingnagians, 'whose wise Maxims in Morality and Government, it would be our Happiness to observe'. Where does Swift stand in all of this? He will not say. 'I forbear descanting further', Gulliver concludes, 'and rather leave the judicious Reader to his own Remarks and Applications'.

In the first half of the eighteenth century, Swift, along with Pope, towered over the English literary scene. Their personalities have intruded into our appreciation of their achievements, and Swift's alleged madness, misanthropy, misogyny and undeniable scatology scandalized the Victorians. The massive presence of Samuel Johnson came to dominate the second half of the century in a similar way. Although scholars have their reservations about the authenticity of the figure that emerges from Boswell's *Life* (1791), the fame of 'Doctor Johnson' is assured. Boswell had his reasons for courting Johnson and for inflating his reputation because, as he explained, 'everything relative to so great a man is worth recording'. Johnson's contemporary reputation was founded on his periodical essays in *The Rambler* (1750–2) and *The Idler* (1758–60) – his was the first truly distinctive voice to emerge since Addison and Steele's *Spectator* essays (1711–12) – the *Dictionary* (1755), the importance of which cannot be overstated, and his moral tale, *Rasselas* (1759), a sort of prose version of *The Vanity of Human Wishes*. Johnson's varied output also includes political pamphlets, *A Journey to the Western Islands of Scotland* (1775), and a series of seminal works of criticism encompassing the Preface to the *English Dictionary*, the Preface to the edition of Shakespeare (1765), and the prefaces collected as the *Lives of the English Poets* (1779–81). While the Johnson known to posterity largely lives in quotations drawn from Boswell's *Life*, Johnson's own moral vision is intimately revealed in the characteristically measured cadences and the symmetry of his instantly recognizable prose style.

The Novel

I have left the most important literary legacy of the century until last. With the benefit of hindsight, we can confidently claim that the ascent to its current position of preeminence of that upstart genre, the novel, took place during this period. Although works calling themselves 'novels' had been appearing in English since the middle of the sixteenth century, the emergence of 'the novel' was an eighteenth-century phenomenon. In his classic account, *The Rise of the Novel* (1957), however, Ian Watt worked from the assumption that the novel was 'a new literary form . . . begun by Defoe, Richardson, and Fielding', and that what distinguishes it from other literary forms – and other prose fiction – is 'formal realism':

> the premise, or primary convention, that the novel is a full and authentic report of human experience, and is therefore under an obligation to satisfy its readers with such details of the story as the individuality of the actors concerned, the particulars of the times and places of their actions, details which are presented through a more largely referential use of language than is common in other literary forms. (Watt 1957: 32)

Largely neglecting Italian, Spanish and French precursors, Watt simply ignored contemporaries of Defoe, Richardson and Fielding. This not only appears odd as far as Swift's *Gulliver's Travels* is concerned, it excludes highly popular women writers such as Aphra Behn, Delarivier Manley, Eliza Haywood, Jane Barker, Elizabeth Rowe, Penelope Aubin and Mary Davys. At the beginning of the eighteenth century, the term 'novel' meant a short tale of romantic love, and 'novels' were mostly written by and for women.

Yet it is only very recently that the hugely influential 'triple rise' thesis has itself been seriously challenged. Initially persuasive and immensely attractive, Watt's argument runs as follows: the rise of the middle class leads to the rise of the reading public which, in turn, leads to the rise of the novel. Unfortunately, as scholarship since 1957 has convincingly demonstrated, there are serious difficulties with each plank of Watt's thesis. First, there are problems with the timing of certain social and economic developments as described by Watt. By attempting to have them coincide with the publication of key works by Defoe, Richardson and Fielding, he appears to have brought them forward by half a century or so. For Watt's thesis to work, it would seem reasonable to expect this 'middle class' to have been in existence prior to the period in which Defoe, Richardson and Fielding were writing. Similarly, although there was a marked growth in literacy between 1600 and 1800, the most significant growth did not occur during this period. Thus, a link between the 'rise of the novel' and the rise of the reading public has yet to be established. Finally, Watt's thesis about the growth in popularity of 'the novel' in the early eighteenth century is simply not borne out by recent research.

Indeed, it could be argued that, in asserting the factuality of his narratives, Defoe destabilized the terminology used by contemporaries to describe prose fiction. Although he had earlier models from which to work, Defoe's spurious autobiographies were sufficiently ambiguous to confuse readers' expectations. *Robinson Crusoe* presented itself as 'a just History of Fact, neither is there any appearance of Fiction in it', exploiting the contemporary interest in travel writing, marrying it with earlier fiction which had laid claim to authenticity, such as Aphra Behn's *Oroonoko* (1689), and adding a religious dimension. Defoe's *Colonel Jack* (1721), *Moll Flanders* (1722) and *Roxana* (1724), on the other hand, played off a tradition of popular 'rogue' literature going back to Spanish picaresque novels of the sixteenth century. Modern critics have found the apparent unreliability of Defoe's first-person narrators appealing, and the seeming conflict between the material and the spiritual guidance offered by their narratives as well as the narrators' reluctance to accept responsibility for their actions have been taken as indications that a sophisticated, ironic fiction writer is at work.

The publication in 1726 of a bogus traveller's tale that strained the credulity of even the most willing suspender of disbelief appears to have brought the vogue for spurious 'History and Travels' to an abrupt end. Like *Robinson Crusoe*, *Gulliver's Travels* purported to be an authentic account of strange, surprising adventures in distant lands. Whereas Defoe contented himself with having Crusoe travel to genuine geographical locations, however, Swift transported Gulliver to undiscovered lands inhabited by tiny pygmies and huge giants, grotesque ape-like creatures and talking horses. Gulliver is the unreliable narrator *par excellence*, and *Gulliver's Travels* complicates standard accounts of 'the rise of the novel' to such an extent that it is classified under 'satire and humour' rather than 'the novel' in the Dewey decimal system. Its effect on contemporary taste might be gauged by the fact that, after the brief upsurge in the amount of prose fiction published in the wake of *Robinson Crusoe*, very little was published during the 1730s.

This changed overnight with the publication of *Pamela* in 1740. Interestingly, instead of acknowledging that he was writing 'Probable Feign'd Stories', Richardson initially resorted to the claims of authenticity typical of Behn and Defoe. Posing as merely the editor of genuine letters, he exploited his readers' emotions for suspense and for pathetic effect by means of his most important technical innovation, 'writing to the moment'. This applies equally to Richardson's much more complex second novel, *Clarissa* (1747–8), in which multiple narrators offer multiple viewpoints on events. Epistolary fiction remained popular for the rest of the century. In his most accomplished novel, *Humphry Clinker* (1771), Tobias Smollett forsook the picaresque plots of his earlier fiction for a narrative made up of letters by various correspondents including the irascible hero, Matthew Bramble, while Burney's bestselling first novel, *Evelina* (1778), successfully married the epistolary formula with the grotesque characters and practical jokes with which Smollett had first found fame in *Roderick Random* (1748) and *Peregrine Pickle* (1751).

Paradoxically, although he chose to write in letters in order to give the illusion of direct access to his characters' thought processes, Richardson wished to control the reader's response to his novels. Although he was immensely interested in what goes on in his readers' minds, Fielding, on the other hand, refused to enter into those of his characters. Instead, in *Joseph Andrews* (1742), *Tom Jones* (1749) and, to a lesser extent, in *Amelia* (1751), Fielding remorselessly and self-consciously manipulates the reader for satiric effect through an intrusive, ironic narrator. Interestingly, Fielding insisted that although his were not factual fictions, they were really 'true histories' that described 'manners not men, not an individual but a species', and he claimed a literary model for his 'comic epics in prose' in Homer's lost *Margites.*

The creative dialogue between Richardson and Fielding in the 1740s was crucially important to the development of the novel. Not only did they pioneer strikingly different narrative styles, they inaugurated a critical debate on the means and ends of prose fiction. Each had his imitators, as the demand for new fiction steadily grew throughout the second half of the century. Gradually the terminology used to describe 'the novel' stabilized. The novel sought to present a picture of real life and manners, and of the times in which it is written. This remains true of the sentimental novel, despite its melodramatic tendencies. While Goldsmith's *The Vicar of Wakefield* (1766) and Smollett's *Humphry Clinker* exploited the sentimental for comic effect, Mackenzie's *The Man of Feeling* (1771), published when the cult of sensibility was at its height, best exemplifies the sentimental novel's formulaic character: 'I was somehow led to think of introducing a Man of Sensibility into different Scenes where his Feelings might be seen in their Effects'.

Although he acknowledged his satirical forbears, Laurence Sterne also worked within the new sentimental mode. *The Life and Opinions of Tristram Shandy, Gentleman* (1760–7) was an instant bestseller on the appearance of the first two volumes. Sterne's first-person narrator is never quite in control of his text, and it is this quasi-stream-of-consciousness technique that is so strikingly modern, if not post-modern. Johnson thought Sterne's fiction would not last, and F. R. Leavis relegated his 'nasty and irresponsible trifling' to a footnote in *The Great Tradition*. Yet of all the eighteenth-century writers of fiction (with the possible exception of Swift), it is Sterne's influence on modern novelists – from Joyce to Kundera – that is most openly acknowledged today and *Tristram Shandy* ranks alongside *A Tale of a Tub* and *Gulliver's Travels* as the greatest achievements of eighteenth-century fiction.

If the sentimental novel was the most popular form of fiction in the later eighteenth century, the other successful genre was the Gothic. Horace Walpole explained how, in *The Castle of Otranto* (1764), he wanted 'to blend the two kinds of romance, ancient and modern'. The Gothic novel's calculated flouting of the laws of probability and ruthless exploitation of its readership's craving for suspense took their cue from Walpole's insistence that 'the great resources of fancy have been dammed up, by a strict adherence to common life'. Numerous novelists followed Walpole's lead and reintroduced elements of the supernatural into fiction, while others, notably Ann Radcliffe in *The Mysteries of Udolpho* (1794), exploited the appeal of the supernatural before supplying a plausible explanation for the mysterious events in which her heroine had been involved.

While the sentimental novel and the Gothic novel are both remarkable for their lack of engagement with the pressing issues of their day, the effect of the French Revolution is apparent in the novels of the so-called 'English Jacobins', Thomas Holcroft, Mary Wollstonecraft and William Godwin. Influenced by the 'philosophical' novels of John Moore and Robert Bage, they turned from writing political treatises to propounding their ideas in fiction with notable success. Holcroft's *Anna St. Ives* (1792), Wollstonecraft's *The Wrongs of Woman: or, Maria* (published posthumously in 1798) and, above all, *Things As They Are; or, the Adventures of Caleb Williams* (1794), Godwin's fictional reworking of his *Enquiry Concerning Social Justice* (1793), suggested how the novel could become an effective vehicle for discourse on serious social and political issues.

By 1800, therefore, the novel had successfully established itself as an indispensable part of the life of the nation, along with those other novel manifestations of the cultural heritage of the eighteenth century, the newspaper, the periodical and the magazine. It is worth pausing to reflect that not only was there no daily newspaper in 1700, there were no journals of opinion of any kind. Similarly, as a cultural phenomenon, in 1700 'the novel' did not yet exist. One hundred years later it was very different. Publishers had realized that profits were to be made out of novels, and Barbauld's *British Novelists* was followed by Ballantyne's *Novelist's Library* (edited by Walter Scott in ten volumes, 1821–4), and Bentley's *Standard Novels* (1831 onwards). At the same time, readers learned not to apologize for reading novels because, as Jane Austen explained in her famous defence of the novelist's art in *Northanger Abbey* (finished 1803, published posthumously in 1818),

> there seems almost a general wish of decrying the capacity and undervaluing the labour of the novelist, and of slighting the performances which have only genius, wit, and taste to recommend them . . . 'And what are you reading, Miss?' – 'Oh! it is only a novel!' replies the young lady; while she lays down her book with affected indifference, or momentary shame. – 'It is only *Cecilia*, or *Camilla*, or *Belinda*;' or, in short, only

> some work in which the greatest powers of the mind are displayed, in which the most thorough knowledge of human nature, the happiest delineation of its varieties, the liveliest effusion of wit and humour are conveyed to the world in the best chosen language.

The novel, in other words, was here to stay.

FURTHER READING

Bevis, Richard W.: *English Drama: Restoration and Eighteenth Century, 1660–1789* (London, 1988).

Butler, Marilyn: *Romantics, Rebels and Reactionaries: English Literature and its Background 1760–1830* (Oxford, 1981).

Doody, Margaret Anne: *The Daring Muse: Augustan Poetry Reconsidered* (Cambridge, 1985).

Hume, Robert D.: *Henry Fielding and the London Theatre 1728–1737* (Oxford, 1988).

Kelly, Gary: *The English Jacobin Novel 1780–1805* (Oxford, 1976).

Lonsdale, Roger (ed.): *The New Oxford Book of Eighteenth-Century Verse* (Oxford, 1984).

Lonsdale, Roger (ed.): *Eighteenth-Century Women Poets: An Oxford Anthology* (Oxford, 1989).

Probyn, Clive T.: *English Fiction of the Eighteenth Century 1700–1789* (London, 1987).

Richetti, John J.: *Popular Fiction before Richardson: Narrative Patterns, 1700–1739* (2nd edn, Oxford, 1992).

Rogers, Pat: *The Augustan Vision* (London, 1974).

Rothstein, Eric: *Restoration and Eighteenth-Century Poetry 1660–1780* (London, 1981).

Spencer, Jane: *The Rise of the Woman Novelist: From Aphra Behn to Jane Austen* (Oxford, 1986).

Todd, Janet: *Sensibility: An Introduction* (London, 1986).

Watt, Ian: *The Rise of the Novel: Studies in Defoe, Richardson and Fielding* (London, 1957).

CHAPTER TWENTY-SIX

Popular Culture

BOB BUSHAWAY

Popular culture, as far as historians of Britain before the twentieth century are concerned, is a problematic term. Loose in meaning, non-specific in scope and general in application, the phrase is widely used to cover the non-material aspects of the lives and experiences of ordinary men and women and their families, comprising the vast majority of the British population from the seventeenth century onwards whose shared world has usually gone largely unrecorded, except when it collided with the worlds of elite and middle-class cultures, or intruded upon the stage of political and economic life.

'The Country', 'The People', 'the mob', 'the justices' and 'the better sort of people' were not interchangeable terms but were quite distinctive in meaning. At the beginning of the eighteenth century the preferred term for the ordinary people was 'the mob', to be differentiated from 'the better sort of people'. By mid-century the same bipolar terminology continued to be in widespread usage. In *Tom Jones*, published in 1749, Henry Fielding advised the historian interested in British society to consult with its different components for an accurate picture of its structure as a whole. That Fielding's two sections of society – highlife and lowlife – produced separate and distinctive cultures was also clear. Oliver Goldsmith wrote in 1762: 'to pursue trifles is the lot of humanity; . . . whether we bustle in a pantomime or strut at a coronation; whether we shout at a bonfire or harangue in a senate-house'.

The problem for historians has been the tendency to view the eighteenth century through the prism of the nineteenth and twentieth centuries and from the perspective of class. The terms descriptive of seventeenth-century British society are not entirely adequate for the eighteenth, particularly its latter decades, and general labels such as 'the labouring poor' or 'the lower orders' are usually employed. Some historians confront the issue by dividing their studies at the pivotal year of 1750, seeing closer links between the popular culture of the first half of the eighteenth century and the early modern world and linking the second half of the eighteenth century to the emergence of the working class in the nineteenth century. In his groundbreaking work, the late E. P. Thompson increasingly emphasized the importance of understanding eighteenth-century popular culture as the precursor to the emergence of a working class in Victorian Britain. Thompson wrote of 'the continuing popular traditions in the eighteenth century which influenced the crucial Jacobin agitation of the 1790s', and elsewhere, in a transcendent and justly celebrated passage, Thompson went on to identify the groups he sought to rescue from the 'enormous condescension of posterity', urging historians to realize that their 'aspirations were valid in terms of their own experience' (1963: 12–13). This goal is no less important for the historian of eighteenth-century popular culture as a whole. It was Thompson who first propounded the 'patrician–plebeian' dichotomy, a thesis that continues to hold the field, albeit revised by more recent postmodernist studies and yet not wholly replaced. Thompson's analysis, it should be stressed, accords with the views of eighteenth-century contemporaries such as Fielding and Goldsmith.

In the second half of the eighteenth century there was a European-wide interest in the culture of ordinary people. Philosophers and antiquaries began to search for examples of popular recreations, rituals and beliefs as evidence of the customary culture of the labouring poor in town and country. There was a process of discovery (or, perhaps, rediscovery) of popular culture during the enlightenment, closely linked to the rise of nationalism especially in Germany. Historians have noted that, towards the end of the eighteenth century, this popular culture was subjected to change through moral reform, the removal of elite support and commercialization. This reforming tendency was almost universal among the educated sections of society. Modern historians seek to restore the people to popular culture as actors in their own destinies rather than those who were merely acted upon: the largely urban popular culture that had emerged by the mid-century was to a considerable degree a culture created by the people themselves. The old culture of the labouring poor, dating from the early modern period, both transformed itself and was transformed by the melting pot of the social and economic changes at the end of the eighteenth century. But continuities were still to be discerned: people have always liked to sing, to get drunk in company, to enjoy competitive and violent games, to be entertained by storytellers or dramatists, to goggle at the unusual and to gamble.

The weakness of seeking to define popular culture in accordance with its lowest common denominators is that it minimizes the political dimension, the sense of cultural self-awareness and identity that people in eighteenth-century British society derived from those cultural practices. To view eighteenth-century popular culture as merely a surrender to animal passions is to take the stance of many contemporary critics, such as the radical reformer Francis Place, who emphasized those aspects whilst minimizing the richness and diversity of a culture which might connect the visionary world of William Blake and the literary aspirations of John Clare, as well as the complexity of alternative knowledge based upon the observation of the natural world or the opportunities for self-preservation and the ability to overcome the setbacks of fate which Place's own father demonstrated. Contemporary antiquaries, by contrast, understood the political context in which popular culture operated. After the American and French Revolutions, the British governing elite, collectors such as John Brand observed, would be wise to consider what motivated ordinary people.

In his tour of 1794 Colonel John Byng, later fifth Viscount Torrington, was acutely aware of the importance of popular culture as a vehicle of expression for labouring people. 'I took my evening ride alone', he wrote, 'thro St Neots where continue the relics of their fair as an elephant and the King of France guillotin'd (is not this a bad exhibition for the lower people?).' Byng had begun regular tours of different regions in 1781 and was an accurate observer of the effect on the labouring poor of the withdrawal of the rural elite from the countryside and from engagement with popular culture in general. He noted the ringing of a merry peal at the funeral of a bellringer at Westbury, Gloucestershire, in 1781 and, at Chepstow, 'the May-pole of this town, as of others I have passed through, is well hung round with garlands'. In 1785 he noted, with relish, an account of the revels at Yattendon in Berkshire which involved a cudgel match, wrestling, bowling, women's races and competitive grinning. His paternalist view did not obscure the nature of the customary culture he observed in the last decades of the eighteenth century, albeit that customary culture no longer engaged the upper sections of society who opposed or simply ignored its manifestations.

Contemporaries searched for the origins of popular customs, ceremonies, rituals and beliefs, as well as aspects of recreational activity in a remote past and attempted to explain their relationship to elite and middle-class culture in terms of the complicit engagement of the latter. The subtitle of John Brand's published collection of popular customs, *Antiquitates Vulgares*, expressed no doubt as to whose collective practices were represented. His examples of customary behaviour were those of the vulgar, that is, the common people. He introduced his subject using the following descriptive terms in an interchangeable manner: 'common life', 'vulgar rites and popular opinions', 'the common people', 'the humble labourer', 'the people', 'popular customs', 'the English antique'. Brand's sense was that such collective practices as those examples which he had collated originated in the history and practices of the unreformed church or the feudal past, but were maintained by the contemporary labouring poor, illustrative of their informal and unofficial popular beliefs, values and rituals in opposition to the prevailing forms of formal or official culture. In eighteenth-century Britain Brand's account might be considered as evidence for a customary culture that was of as much continuing relevance to the governed as to the governors who ignored them at their peril. Historians, too, have sought to understand this relationship in eighteenth-century Britain. Some write of an old or traditional, pre-existing culture in which the interests of high and low were united. Others draw on the work of anthropologists such as Robert Redfield, whose concept of the 'great tradition' of the literate few and the 'little tradition' of the illiterate majority seems to offer an alternative model for eighteenth-century society, albeit recently revised to account for more diversity and variety within the 'little tradition', particularly between its urban and rural forms, and in the complexity of the link between orality and literacy.

E. P. Thompson detected in much collective action in the eighteenth century an underlying meaning which he characterized as legitimation. He found this notion informed many forms of crowd action, including the perennial food riots which previous historians had simply viewed as the poor's spontaneous reaction to periods of economic hardship. Thompson argued that such crowd action reflected the popular conception of a moral economy within the strict framework of which poor people operated during food disturbances. He discovered, too, that the writers of anonymous letters often left their threats as an appeal to custom, and that popular behaviour such as charivari or 'rough music' contained explicit reference, often through ritual, to a shared sense of social and moral order. Others detected similar notions in the actions of Cornish wreckers, Sussex smugglers and midlands poachers who, although criminals according to eighteenth-century law, enjoyed popular support and saw their actions as defensible according to a community-based moral code. The concept of 'social crime', it was argued, underpinned similar activities by other eighteenth-century lawbreakers, such as illegal wood-gatherers and sheep-stealers. 'The plebs', Thompson urged, 'were aware that a ruling-class that rested its claim to legitimacy upon prescription and law had little authority to over-rule their own customs and rights' (1991: 74). For Thompson and others, the rites of plebeian culture in the eighteenth century defended and promoted the rights of that same plebeian culture against the imperatives of patrician society. With this view John Brand would probably have concurred.

Popular culture in Hanoverian Britain was increasingly isolated from elite and middle-class cultures and under assault by a consensus of possessive individualism, Evangelicalism, moral reform and radicalism. A straightforward account of oppositional cultures has been modified by recent studies such as those of Barry Reay and Tim Harris, where a multiplicity of cultures has been identified rather than a single undifferentiated popular culture. To date, most accounts have confined themselves to the study of a series of collective activities and forms of behaviour and belief as something which was shared by the common people. Harris argues for an approach that 'problematizes' popular culture. He discerns a plural and gendered popular culture reflecting regional variation, a metropolitan and a provincial popular culture, and even rural cultures differentiated by economic practice.

The most recent description of popular culture in eighteenth-century Britain continues to adopt a taxonomic approach. Popular culture is an elusive concept, though there is rough agreement that it encompasses the common people's world of work, attitudes to the natural world, education, literacy and knowledge, health practices, gender and generational roles, religious beliefs, recreational and leisure pursuits, and community customs. There is little with which to disagree in this classification, but it goes no further than contemporary antiquaries or modern folklorists who remained fascinated by collecting types of popular culture or belief rather than considering them in context as the products of a common or shared customary consciousness, pursued by individual and collective action. Francis Place described his father, Simon, as a resolute daring straightforward sort of a man, governed almost wholly by his passions and animal sensations, as careless of reputation except in some particulars in which he thought he excelled. His father liked to frequent London pleasure gardens (Bagnigge Wells) and was well acquainted with the principal boxers of his day. Place acknowledged a transformation in taste in his lifetime, accepting that his father's conduct was not then obnoxious to the censure of others, as such conduct would be in the 1820s. This partly reflects Place's insistence that working-class morals had improved since the days of his father and, partly, Place's own experience as a popular radical. Place, perhaps, exaggerated the extent of change by overdrawing the metropolitan world in which Simon Place moved in late eighteenth-century London.

John Clare, the Northamptonshire farm labourer and poet, whose father Parker Clare died in 1846 at the age of eighty-two, remembered the rich oral culture which he inhabited in rural Helpstone: 'My father, could read a little in a bible or testament, and was very fond of the superstitious tales that are hawked about a sheet for a penny, such as old Nixons Prophecies, Mother Bunches Fairy Tales and Mother

Shiptons legacy and he was likewise fond of Ballads and I have heard him make a boast of it over his horn of ale with his merry companions at the Blue Bell public house which was next door that he could sing or recite above a hundred' (Robinson 1983: 2). Both metropolitan and rural popular culture in the eighteenth century, essentially oral, drew upon chapbook literature and printed ballads as well as biblical texts, and shared a common interest in alternative knowledge and popular prophecy. But disembodied examples of street ballads, accounts of calendar customs, descriptions of rituals or collections of country wisdom from the eighteenth century tell us little about the process of popular culture; rather, it is the uses to which these were put, the reactions to them from others and the common consciousness which they reveal that should interest the historian. As E. P. Thompson concluded: 'We need to take this bundle apart, and examine the components with more care: rites, symbolic modes, the cultural attributes of hegemony, the inter-generational transmission of custom, and custom's evolution within historically specific forms of working and social relations' (1991: 13).

Popular culture should not, indeed cannot, be detached from its wider political context in eighteenth-century Britain. In his tour of the midlands in 1789 Byng recorded: 'The cottagers, every where, look wretchedly, like their cows; and slowly recovering from their wintry distress: Deserted by the gentry, they lack assistance, protection, and amusement; however, my landlord says that in May, there are mayers [alias Morris dancers] who go about with a fool, a man in woman's clothes [the maid Marion], and music'. The legitimation of custom motivated the mayers notwithstanding their economic circumstances, not as a spluttering example of residual deferential ritual in a rural society dominated by an increasingly distant elite, but through a common consciousness that such seasonal activities were part of a customary calendar and took place within a local frame of reference where the collection of largesse was legitimated. Byng went on to condemn an account of a public celebration at Stamford in 1789, sponsored for the poor, to mark the recovery of George III from his serious illness. 'Two sheep were roasted whole and the populace were regaled with barrels of ale . . . the parish also united and testified their loyalty by their bounty to the common people and liberality to the poor.' Byng called such festivities 'pompous treats' and condemned them as 'repugnant to jollity' as those 'poor wretches, who struggled for a piece of meat, or a draught of beer, have left at home a wife and children shivering with cold and perishing of hunger' (Andrews 1954: 140–2). Such crowd manipulation did not represent the conjunction of cultures but emphasized their very separation.

Nicholas Blundell of Crosby and Ditton near Liverpool participated wholeheartedly with popular culture in 1712, overseeing and joining in with the celebrations that accompanied the opening of his marling pit. He recorded in his journal:

> July 3rd. I made a sword dance against my marl pit is flowered.
>
> July 4th. Some of the young folks of the town (Crosby) met those of the Morehouses and Great Crosby to consider about the flowering of my Marl pit.
>
> July 7th. I was very busy most of the afternoon shaping Tinsall etc for the Garland of my new Marl pit, and after supper the women helped to paste some things on it. I began

> to teach the 8 sword dancers their dance which they are to dance at the flowering of my Marl pit. Dr Cawood played to them.
>
> July 8th. I was very busy making caps for my marlers and dancers, several of Great Crosby lasses helped me. The young women of this town, Moorehouses, and Great Crosby dressed the garlands in my barn. I taught my 8 sword dancers their dance, they had music and danced it in my barn.
>
> July 9th. I was very busy making some things to adorn marlers heads. My marl pit was flowered very much to the satisfaction of the spectators, all the 14 marlers had a particular dress upon their heads and carried each of them a musket or gun. The six garlands were carried by young women in procession, the 8 sword dancers went along with them to the Marl pit where they danced, . . .

Music and dancing then went on in Blundell's barn well into the night and the following day a bull was baited in the marl pit itself. When the marl was carried on 'the Finishing day' (23 July), a feast was held with more sword-dancing and a maypole. Blundell did not dominate or invent these rites of passage, he simply sanctioned, coordinated and participated as was his customary role.

Such elite sanction of popular culture was steadily withdrawn. The case of the long-standing local custom of bull-running at Tutbury in Staffordshire, where the inhabitants of the towns and villages around Needwood forest legitimated an annual calendar carnival, was increasingly at odds with polite society. The annual custom was suppressed in 1778 by the duke of Devonshire on receipt of a petition from the inhabitants of Tutbury. Custom was dismantled. Needwood forest was itself disafforested in 1801. The two events were not unconnected. The duke of Devonshire had previously provided the patronage to the medieval foundation of the Tutbury minstrels' court whose origins lay in the medieval period. Henry Coxon, the last 'king of the minstrels', petitioned the duke in 1772 to maintain the rights and dignities of the court. Six years later, the duke of Devonshire preferred to act upon the petition of what might be termed the polite and commercial people at Tutbury. Fifty years or so earlier, Nicholas Blundell, at his marl pit opening, represented only a commercial people.

The mid-eighteenth-century cleric and diarist James Woodforde accepted the imperatives of the local customary calendar in which he participated. He regularly entertained Christmas singers and mummers as well as offering commensality to a group of elderly parishioners at the Somerset parish of Castle Carey. In 1764, on Christmas Eve, he recorded that the new singers came very late in the evening and sang a Christmas carol and an anthem, and they were given cider 'as usual' and two shillings. The key phrase in this is 'as usual', which points clearly to the customary basis of the practice. When Woodforde moved to a different parish in Norfolk at Weston Longeville, he simply adapted to the prevailing but different local customary calendar, recording in 1777: 'to 36 children being Valentine's day and what is customary for them to go about in these parts this day gave [three shillings] being one penny apiece to each of them.' Valentine perambulatory practice had not existed in the customary calendar of Castle Carey, from whence he came. Again, the key phrase is: 'what is customary'.

Custom was the most powerful legitimating force for popular culture and the activities of the crowd in eighteenth-century Britain. Popular custom was not a separate and disconnected feature of social life; rather, it was an essential underpinning for a holistic structure of values, beliefs, mechanisms and forms. It is this mental world that is characterized as an ideology of custom. As the jurist Charles Calthrope pointed out, its true measure 'is when a custom or usage, or other things have been used, so long as a man's memory cannot remember the contrary. That is, when such matter is pleaded, that no man then in life, hath not heard anything, nor any proof to the contrary' (Calthrope 1917: 15).

In eighteenth-century Britain custom delineated the local calendar in which leisure pursuits and workplace usages were linked to seasonal events and community collective activities characteristic of the particular village or region of rural Britain or to the trade or district of the town. The reckoning of time was a customary one, which was highlighted when Britain adopted the Gregorian calendar in 1752 and the 'old' (that is Julian) fair and feast dates continued to be observed in some places. Custom described the community, the in-groups, the physical and social delineation of the parish, town, region, street, workshop or group connected by reference to the prevailing practices of the customary calendar or recreational pattern. Custom was dynamic and could be adapted flexibly to the circumstances of change in order to defend or promote the rights of the labouring poor, legitimating direct action or supporting customary consciousness. It legitimated dole collections on ritual occasions which would otherwise have been condemned as begging by providing opportunities for non-discretionary largesse. In the countryside custom legitimated seasonal doling rights from the mayers on May day, wassailing at Christmas, harvest workers at harvest and, in the town, Christmas box collection was widespread among trades, associations, apprentices, parish officials, shopkeepers and other retailers.

Thomas Turner, a shopkeeper from East Hoathly, near Uckfield in Sussex, combined both the public calendar of the local landed elite with the customary calendar prevailing in his district. On 5 August 1759 he went to the public day at Halland House, home of Thomas Pelham, duke of Newcastle, no doubt having enjoyed the occasion both as a public festival and as one of the retail suppliers. On 23 August 1764 he attended Lewes races, taking a knowledgeable and sociable interest in owners, runners and riders and using the occasion for legitimate conviviality which, in Turner's case, was usually taken to excess. The previous May, he noted in his diary, 'a main of cocks, at our public-house, between the gentlemen of East Grinstead and the gentlemen of East Hoathly, for half-a-guinea a battle and two guineas the old battle'. He recognized the true recreational nature of cock-fighting when he recorded on 10 June 1761 that 'was fought this day, at Jones's a main of cocks between the gentlemen of Hoathly and the gentlemen of Pevensey. Query is there a gentleman in either of the places that was concerned?' He played cricket on 28 June 1763 for half a crown's worth of punch and, not surprisingly, perhaps, recorded the next day that he was very stiff and disagreeable. He celebrated national military victories and peace treaties, royal births and visits, and criticized the duke of Newcastle for employing, apparently unpatriotically, 'so many Frenchmen, there being ten of his servants, cooks etc. . . . of that nation'. Yet, in 1756, he also supported the annual customary local hop-pickers' prerequisite and the perambulation of the pole-puller's nickcloth as a symbol to claim legitimate largesse. He was as fully a part of his local customary calendar as was Nicholas Blundell half a century earlier.

By the end of the eighteenth century there was a sharp divide between 'high culture', as examined by John Brewer, and 'popular culture', which studies by Malcolmson, Cunningham and others have indicated. The area of interaction in customary culture was greatly reduced. Elite society and others strove to reform customary culture and to tame its excesses. The rise of a consumer culture in eighteenth-century Britain, especially in the form of popular recreations, markets, commercial leisure pursuits, resorts and drinking establishments, where the role of the publican as sponsor accelerated the demise of independent customary culture, led to the transformation of popular culture in the wider society from an arena of shared or negotiated beliefs, events and venues to one of separate or contested beliefs, events and venues.

For most of the eighteenth century popular culture should be seen not simply as the accumulation of events, activities, forms of collective behaviour and systems of belief, beloved by antiquaries as survivals, but as the process by which these manifestations were produced and the customary consciousness that produced them. Popular culture was shaped not so much by external oppositional factors but from within by those who shared common experiences of work and leisure. Popular culture, however varied, was an expression of common perceptions of others and the external world, and operated within similar legal and moral frameworks, thereby nurturing similar ideas about identities, aspirations, objectives and motivations, and manifesting them in the context of a changing demographic, social and political order, against the transforming background of a burgeoning consumerism. The widespread custom in manufacturing trades of 'Saint Monday' – the holiday taken at their discretion at the start of the week by a variety of hand workers – illustrates this stubborn resistance to change. The eighteenth-century statute fair, where the world of carnival and role reversal rubbed shoulders with the new consumerism of the market, is a further example. Horn Fair, at Charlton in Kent, was notorious. 'The mob indeed', wrote Daniel Defoe, 'at that time take all kinds of liberties, and the women are especially impudent for that day; as if it was a day that justified themselves a loose to all manner of indecency and immodesty, without any reproach, or without suffering the censure which such behaviour would deserve at another time . . . I rather recommend it to public justice to be suppressed as a nuisance and offence to all sober people, than to spend any time to enquire into its origin' (Defoe 1971: 115). At the Easter Monday Fair in Greenwich park, parties of women demanded a kiss or a forfeit of male fairgoers. Cross-dressing was not uncommon at Horn Fair. In 1703 William Fuller attended, dressed in his landlady's best gown and other women's attire. At Weyhill Fair, near Andover, there was a custom of subjecting newcomers to a rite of passage known as 'homing the colt'. Having submitted to the ritual, initiates were referred to as having been 'made free' and the ceremonies used were closely paralleled by similar rituals for apprentices in the printing and coopers' trades. Weyhill, increasingly in the eighteenth century, took on a more dubious reputation for respectable provincial society as a haven for confidence tricksters, pranksters, sharps, gamblers, young bucks and ne'er-do-wells. In the poem *The Humours of Weyhill Fair* by the improbably named Maurice Mushroom, the twin functions of the fair in eighteenth-century Britain are well illustrated:

> When Michaelmas with welcome pace drawn near,
> The world of pleasure and of trade prepare,

To celebrate the feast at Weyhill fair.
These form within the fine perspective scene,
And interest is the great commanding queen:
Delight of profit is in every view,
And all are fraught with hopes of something new.

Of course, the fair had always been the resort of the credulous and sharpster, as writers had always recognized from Ben Jonson's *Bartholomew Fair* onwards. By the time of Mushroom's poem the scale of manufactured products available to fairgoers and the extent of market manipulation reflected the world of mass consumption. Mushroom comments:

Dealers in hops begin themselves t'exert;
But first at home they play the craft part:
The subtle sadlers say, they'll stay at home,
Until they know the buyers all are come:
Our hops shall lodge upon the road; for why,
The fewer there, the more they'll want to buy.

From mid-century onwards, as agriculture and industry were transformed by enclosure, capital investment, machinery and new techniques, it was increasingly the case that a hopmaster would understand better how to manipulate the hop price rather than worry about his hop-pickers, that a clothier would know more about his cloth prices than about his weavers, and that a farmer would be more concerned about his livestock improvements than his farm servants. To the elite and also to the more prosperous middling class of people, the worlds of the artisan, craftsman, field labourer and town worker were increasingly unfamiliar as they sought to distance themselves by defining their own aspirations and expectations in terms of the consumption of goods and the culture of new wealth.

The aspirations and expectations of the lowest ranks in society and of artisan culture remain equally hazy to historians of the eighteenth century, partly because of the nature of the sources that provide information on their forms. Records are either openly hostile or are official accounts of the prosecution of newly criminalized customary behaviour. More sympathetic collectors of examples of customary activities viewed them as quaint survivals or vulgar drolleries, spectacles and popular delusions – the crowd engaged in irrational, criminal or immoral behaviour. Under-reporting was also significant. For example, a Maypole at Cheriton in Hampshire in 1773 was mentioned in the *Hampshire Chronicle*, simply because of the fatal accident to the carpenter engaged in its erection. In 1785 a harvest home at Hursley in Hampshire was reported in the same provincial newspaper merely because a labouring man was found dead in a barn, allegedly as the result of excessive alcohol.

Some historians, wishing to stress cultural diversity in the eighteenth century, have moved towards models which classify popular culture into subcultures. Barry Reay writes of popular culture splintering into subcultures divided by locality, age, gender, religion and class. Others take a longer view and seek to identify activities within categories. Hugh Cunningham prefers to divide popular culture into groups. 'Boundaries', he writes, 'of class, of gender, of age and of geography are therefore likely to be represented in leisure; and leisure activities may themselves have reinforced or shifted those boundaries, and not merely passively reflected them' (in F. M. L. Thompson 1990, vol. 2: 290). The problem with a dichotomous view of eighteenth-century culture, whether between patrician and plebeian or between polite and popular, is that variety and diversity are not easily accommodated. A useful approach may be to analyse popular culture as a process which produced in eighteenth-century Britain a multiplicity of forms and expressions that were interlinked through the common element of customary consciousness. We need to differentiate by region, gender or age, bringing out the diversity of texture from one region to another and within the distinctive worlds of women's culture or youth culture. Such an analysis also helps to explain why, for example, eighteenth-century metropolitan printers could use a self-regulated system of work discipline, where those who infringed chapel practices were subjected to a punishment known as 'booting' or 'ten pound in the purse', a practice that was also to be found among rural harvest workers in the same period. The punishment, either in the harvest field or in the printer's chapel, was designed to humiliate rather than harm, a chastisement being ritually administered by the harvest lord or the chapel father on the miscreant in a way which scarcely could have been imposed by the farmer or master printer and which prevented disharmony among the working group itself.

A similar practice was also to be found in the army and the Royal Navy during the eighteenth century, carried into those institutions by recruits drawn, whether willingly or unwillingly, from the popular cultural world around them. 'Ten-pounding' existed in well-defined communities or associations of work where the quality of work was guaranteed by the workers themselves as part of collective self-interest and pride. The local customary calendar provides another example. 29 May was widely celebrated as Oak Apple Day – the date commemorated in the Book of Common Prayer to mark the anniversary of the restoration of Charles II in 1660. In the popular tongue this date was known variously in different parts of rural Britain as 'sick sack', 'shig shag', 'shick-shack' or 'zig-zag' day. Antiquaries attempted various explanations for this curious term. It is likely, however, that it derived from the widespread canting term of abuse for Protestant Dissenters – 'shit sack' – whose etymology was derived from the practice of hedgerow preaching. Oak Apple Day, formally associated with the established church, was seen as an occasion for the rebuke of Evangelicals and Dissenters, as a verse still chanted by the young in Somerset in 1910 indicates:

> Royal Oak
> The whigs to provoke,
> Plane tree leaves
> The church folk are thieves

A more direct rhyme was chorused by boys in the southwest in the mid-nineteenth century:

> Shit-sack, lousey-back,
> Go and tell the Lord of it

In the customary consciousness of the eighteenth century the popular celebrations of the season and of work were marked by parish bellringers, local workers, and rural and urban labourers alike, sometimes legitimated by reference to Anglican and loyalist rhetoric originally derived from the Stuart restoration. In the eighteenth century Oak Apple Day was sometimes appropriated by labouring people to register their protests against the Hanoverian succession in the form of popular Jacobitism. As late as 1750 in Walsall, some people were charged with having made an image of the king on 29 May and then shooting at it. The ringleader and some of those arrested were tried the following year at King's Bench and were sentenced to varying periods of imprisonment and pillorying.

If popular culture was linked by a customary consciousness, the separation from the culture of elite and gentry society whose own consciousness was derived from the market, progressive individualism and the dogma of 'improvement' was ever more marked towards the end of the century. E. P. Thompson's conclusions remain valid: 'While there was no novelty in the existence of a distinct plebeian culture', he argued, 'with its own rituals, festivals and superstitions, we have suggested that in the eighteenth century this culture was remarkably robust, greatly distanced from the polite culture, and that it no longer acknowledged, except in perfunctory ways, the hegemony of the church. As dialect and polite speech drifted apart, so the distance widened' (1991: 64). In politics the popular actions of the crowd, whether in support of the radical John Wilkes or against the radical Tom Paine, whether electing 'the mayor of Garrat' in a mock election at Wandsworth, in Surrey, or taking part in actual parliamentary elections, were a form of counter-theatre in which rituals and symbols of privation and protest could often be seen alongside those of popular patriotism or anti-Jacobinism. The occasion itself, rather than the temporary targets the crowd identified, was the most important common factor as the crowd sought to establish a temporary state of equilibrium in which customary consciousness could set up for a brief time a kind of counter-ideology of the governed in opposition to the prevailing one of the governors. There is a recognition of a generalized social bond that has ceased to be and has simultaneously yet to be fragmented into a multiplicity of structural ties. The same can be discerned in the popular culture of fairs and markets, during periods of seasonal carnival such as the playing of street football in various places at Shrovetide or in May day festivities, especially the urban frolics of the Jack-in-the-Green produced by chimney sweeps or the dances accompanying the showing of the milkmaid's garland. A similar motivation might also be seen in the actions of the crowd at public hangings where the counter-theatre expressed a sense of solidarity with the victim or, on other occasions, condemned his actions. Jonathan Swift's mythic bandit, Tom Clinch, hanged in 1726, was not intended to be seen as either primitive rebel or pro-revolutionary, but in the manner of his end is presented the ritual interplay with the crowd, characteristic of the highwayman. Decked out in finery, taking a drink on the way with the promise of payment on the return journey, Clinch decries the ballad sellers whose account of his last words are already being peddled to the crowd. Clinch dies bravely:

> The hangman for pardon fell down on his knee.
> Tom gave him a kick in the guts for his fee.
> This said, I must speak to the people a little,
> but I'll see you all damn'd before I will whittle.
> My conscience is clear, and my spirits are calm,

> and thus I go off without pray'r, book or Psalm.
> Then follow the practice of clever Tom Clinch,
> who hung like a hero, and never would flinch.

The term 'whittle', notwithstanding Swift's need for a rhyme, was actually the canting expression 'whiddle' as in Francis Grose's lexicographical example: 'He whiddles the whole scrap' meaning 'he discovers all he knows'. Clinch was no informer. Grose compiled his *Dictionary of the Vulgar Tongue* in 1785, before his death in Dublin in 1791. He gave the word 'Bever' for an afternoon lunch, a term which was also familiar to John Clare and which he used in his poem of rural labour, *The Shepherd's Calendar*, in 1827 in an entirely rural environment – the harvest.

> They seek an awthorn bush or willow tree
> or stouk or shock where coolest shadows be
> where bookets heaped and unbroached bottles lye
> which dogs in absence watched with wary eye
> To catch their breath awhile and share the boon
> While beavering time allows their toil at noon
> All gathering sit on stubbs and share the hour.

Popular culture in the eighteenth century was essentially oral even where printed texts were intermixed with the world of memory. Reay writes convincingly that the orality of print and language was widely shared, even within the varied context of dialect, accent, specialist words and regional variation.

In millenarian movements or other forms of popular religious or alternative belief in the eighteenth century, evidence of similar imperatives to those of the crowd can be discovered. The followers of Joanna Southcott, the prophetess, or members of the United Society of Believers in Christ's Second Appearing (Shakers) who followed Ann Lee to America, sought their own ritualized community emerging initially from the world of popular literacy, chapbooks, astrologies, prophetic pamphlets, foretellings, divinations and popular sermons. Some, such as Southcott herself, passed through more orthodox forms such as Methodism and were able to write and publish. Added to popular tales, manuals, ballads, companions and the vast range of other cheap printed matter available, popular literacy in the eighteenth century, at least measured by some ability to read, was widespread. The ability to be read to was even more common.

The expectations, objects and motives of the eighteenth-century crowd may have become steadily unfamiliar to patrician culture, but they were none the less legitimate to the *mentalité* of popular culture. The seasons of trades and manufacturers and the calendar of the workplace, including holidays and festivals specific to particular trades, can also be traced in eighteenth-century popular celebration. In 1785, on the festival of St Blaize, on 3 February, 'a great number of wool-combers, from Romsey, and other places met in a large body and paraded the streets . . . They were chiefly dressed in white shirts and were attended by the Bishop [Blaize] dressed in character, and mounted on a horse, attended by a band of music, and colours flying'. So reported the *Hampshire Chronicle* four days later. Woollen clothworkers, but especially woolcombers whose implements of work were reminiscent of the manner of St Blaize's legendary martyrdom, took the saint's festival as their labour holiday and the occasion on which the prestige and status of their trade were marked with public display, ritual and celebration. The same people, when gathered together for the defence of customary rights in the workplace, were regarded less indulgently. In 1791, at a clothworkers' riot in Bradford-upon-Avon, a crowd of some 500 gathered before a clothier's house and stoned his windows. In the ensuing struggle, the crowd was fired upon and three people were killed. The *Hampshire Chronicle* took a more censorious line on such behaviour. The events at Bradford-upon-Avon occurred in the same year as a sixty-four-year-old woolcomber was hanged at Salisbury for stealing a lamb. As Adrian Randall has shown, the coming of the machine economy resulted in community resistance citing customary practice as its justification: 'It was the structure and customs of the woollen industry which shaped community as a dynamic force for social cohesion and resistance to change' (1991: 7).

Calendar customs, recreational pursuits, national celebrations, regional or local festivals, trade and workplace customs, political events or occasions when the needs of the moral economy required, were occasions when the crowd in eighteenth-century Britain asserted itself in protest against apparent violations or in an attempt to balance perceived injustices or simply to enjoy itself. The form of these events might appear, at one extreme of the continuum, polite, respectful, complicit and even deferential, or, at the other, violent, hostile and even proto-revolutionary, but the crowd's underlying characteristic was the notion of legitimation by reference to the framework of customary consciousness unifying a vibrant popular culture.

FURTHER READING

Primary Material

Andrews, Fanny (ed.): *The Torrington Diaries: A Selection from the Tours of the Hon. John Byng between the Years 1781 and 1794* (abridged edn, London, 1954).

Beresford, John (ed.): *The Diary of a Country Parson 1758–1802: James Woodforde* (London, 1935).

Blencoe, R. W. and Lower, M. A. (eds): *Thomas Turner: The Diary of a Georgian Shopkeeper* (Oxford, 1979).

Blundell, Margaret (ed.): *Blundell's Diary and Letter Book 1702–1728* (Liverpool, 1952).

Brand, John: *Observations on Popular Antiquities*, ed. Henry Ellis (2 vols, London, 1813).

Calthrope, Charles: *The Relation between the Lord of the Manor and the Copyholder his Tenant* (London, 1917).

Defoe, Daniel: *A Tour through the Whole Island of Great Britain* (London, 1971).

Grose, Francis: *A Classical Dictionary of the Vulgar Tongue* (London, 1788).

Robinson, Eric (ed.): *John Clare's Autobiographical Writings* (Oxford, 1983).

Thale, Mary (ed.): *The Autobiography of Francis Place* (Cambridge, 1972).

Secondary Sources

Burke, Peter: *Popular Culture in Early Modern Europe* (London, 1978).

Bushaway, Bob: *By Rite: Custom, Ceremony and Community in England 1700–1880* (London, 1982).

Cunningham, Hugh: *Leisure in the Industrial Revolution 1780–1880* (London, 1980).

Golby, J. M. and Purdue, A. W.: *The Civilisation of the Crowd: Popular Culture in England 1750–1900* (London, 1984).

Harris, Tim (ed.): *Popular Culture in England, c.1500–1850* (Basingstoke, 1995).
Hay, Douglas, Linebaugh, Peter and Thompson, E. P.: *Albion's Fatal Tree: Crime and Society in Eighteenth-Century England* (London, 1975).
Malcolmson, Robert W.: *Popular Recreations in English Society, 1700–1850* (Cambridge, 1973).
Randall, Adrian J.: *Before the Luddites: Custom, Community and Machinery in the English Woollen Industry 1776–1809* (Cambridge, 1991).
Reay, Barry: *Popular Cultures in England 1550–1750* (London, 1998).
Rogers, Nicholas: *Crowds, Culture and Politics in Georgian Britain* (Oxford, 1998).
Thompson, E. P.: *The Making of the English Working Class* (1963; 2nd edn, London, 1968).
Thompson, E. P.: *Customs in Common* (London, 1991).
Thompson, F. M. L. (ed.): *The Cambridge Social History of Britain 1750–1950*, vol. 2: *People and their Environment* (Cambridge, 1990).

Chapter Twenty-Seven

Crime and Punishment

James A. Sharpe

The history of crime and punishment has, since the 1970s, established itself as an important sub-genre of eighteenth-century British history. This situation, itself one facet of the more general blossoming of scholarly social history for the early modern period, has, in academic circles at least, done much to overturn earlier portrayals of Hanoverian crime and punishment. Typically, these phenomena have been interpreted simply as evidence of the brutality and sordidness of the past, to be treated on a par with the excessive gin-drinking, bad sanitation and poor public health provision which were regularly adduced as central features of social life before the coming of the age of reform in the nineteenth century. Most thinking on the history of crime and punishment before the advent of new approaches in the 1970s fitted neatly into a Whig interpretation, where all was disorganization and sanguinary chaos before the arrival of professional police forces and the prison system. Modern research has demonstrated that the eighteenth-century criminal justice system was neither as brutal nor as chaotic as earlier generations of historians had claimed.

Most of the work so far completed on this subject has focused on England, partly because of a greater availability of sources for that country, partly because historians of England became aware of the potential of the subject earlier than their colleagues in other parts of the British Isles. Wales had been integrated into the English legal and administrative system since the 1530s, and patterns of crime and punishment there were very similar to those found in upland England. Writing the history of crime and punishment for Scotland is hampered, over the first half of the eighteenth century at least, by the complexity of the court system. The High Court of Justiciary at Edinburgh dealt with most forms of serious crimes, but petty offences were dealt with by a multiplicity of local courts: there were the church courts, above all the kirk-sessions, which as well as treating purely religious matters dealt with cases of sexual morality, unseemly behaviour such as swearing or drunkenness, and slander; there were the justices of the peace courts, which were more concerned with administrative matters and economic regulation than serious crime; there were the sheriff courts, which by the early eighteenth century were concerned mainly with debt cases; the burgh courts, which were again concerned mainly with debt, but which had some criminal business; and the barony and regality courts, franchise courts whose business was not unlike that of English manorial courts of an earlier period, and included the punishment of local nuisance offenders.[4] In 1747, however, the Abolition of Heritable Jurisdictions (Scotland) Act swept away many of the traditional courts, and power over criminal matters was increasingly concentrated in the High Court of Justiciary and the justices of the peace courts. Scotland now had a bureaucratic and more centrally directed system, and there are thus good prospects for writing the history of crime and punishment in Scotland in the second half of the eighteenth century.

Study of the history of crime and punishment in Ireland is inhibited by the loss of many of the relevant records when the Irish Public Record Office suffered a severe fire in 1922 during the Irish civil war. The outlines of the criminal justice system can, however, be reconstructed. The criminal law operating in Ireland in the eighteenth century was a mixture of English common law, English statute law in so far as it extended to Ireland, and statute law as enacted by the Irish parliament. This law can, of course, be characterized as a component of English colonization, but it should be remembered that this point of view is probably clearer to modern historians than it was to most inhabitants of eighteenth-century Ireland. The court structures were also essentially similar to those existing in England. There was a court of King's Bench, theoretically the most important court in the kingdom, at Dublin. There was also an assize system, with Ireland being divided into five circuits, the city of Dublin and County Dublin being independent of the assizes and possessing their own courts. There were also quarter sessions, dealing with administrative matters and less serious crimes. Petty sessions in the English sense do not seem to have existed before the early nineteenth century, but it is possible that in some areas manorial courts leet were dealing with minor offenders, while throughout the eighteenth century, as in England, justices of the peace in private meetings exercised summary justice over petty offenders. These justices were, of course, all Protestants, the oaths they had to swear on taking office effectively excluding Catholics. Yet Catholics figured prominently among the local officers of law enforcement, such as watchmen and constables, these latter officials, as in England, being frequently represented by substitutes.

It is, however, with work on crime and punishment in England that we shall be mainly concerned. The arrival of the new scholarship in this field was heralded by the publication of two books in 1975: the first of these, *Whigs and Hunters*, was written by Edward Thompson, the second, *Albion's Fatal Tree*, consisted of a collection of essays written by a team of young scholars, most of them Thompson's graduate students. Of these essays, Douglas Hay's on 'Property, Authority and the Criminal Law' has maintained a lasting impact, although all the contributions to this collection opened up new subject areas. The main interest of this group, which adopted a broadly Marxist or neo-Marxist stance, was with 'social crime', that is, not crimes like murder, rape, burglary or robbery, but rather poaching, rioting and wrecking: offences which, although illegal in the eyes of the authorities, were often regarded as legitimate by those committing them and the communities within which they lived, thus allowing historians to detect early signs of class consciousness among 'social' criminals. This approach has not found much favour among later historians of crime, but it served a useful purpose in opening up some of the definitional problems surrounding 'crime', and demonstrating that it was not a simple or unproblematic historical phenomenon. Perhaps the other major contribution from these two pioneering works was a section in *Whigs and Hunters* where Thompson stated his views on the importance of law as an ideological force in eighteenth-century society, and demonstrated how this issue could be subjected to a sophisticated Marxist interpretation that jettisoned any simplistic 'law as a tool of class oppression' model.

Despite some early publications, it was not until 1986 that a full-scale regional study of eighteenth-century crime appeared, with John Beattie's important *Crime and the Courts in England 1660–1800*. The starting date of this study, incidentally, reminds us that a large body of work has been completed on Elizabethan and Stuart crime and punishment, and that this demonstrated, perhaps surprisingly, that both levels of prosecuted crime and levels of capital punishment were, with the partial exception of the London area, running at much higher levels in the later sixteenth and early seventeenth centuries than they were in the eighteenth. Beattie essentially picked the story up in 1660, and demonstrated what happened in at least two English counties (Surrey and Sussex) over the next century and a half. Beattie, like most scholars dealing with serious crime in England, concentrated on the records of the assizes, the courts that tried most cases of felony – murder, manslaughter, burglary, grand larceny, highway robbery and arson, to take the most obvious examples. He discovered that homicide cases (murder and manslaughter) showed a steady drop away from a comparatively high level in the 1660s to a lower one in the late eighteenth century, with a rate of guilty verdicts in homicide cases falling from about 2.5 per 100,000 population in 1660–79 to 0.3 per 100,000 in 1780–1802. Property offences, mainly grand larceny and burglary or housebreaking, but also robbery and pickpocketing, were far more numerous than homicides, increasing steadily towards 1800 after something of a dip in the middle of the eighteenth century. As well as showing these long-term trends, however, property offences were also prone to marked short-term variations. This was normally the outcome of high grain prices, showing a connection between property offences and want, or of the end of a period of warfare. The coming of peace meant the demobilization of tens of thousands of soldiers and sailors, most of whom were simply dumped on the English shore with minimal means of support, and, as the eighteenth century progressed, it became axiomatic that the end of any large-scale war would be followed by a crime wave.

Beattie's findings for southeastern England offer some interesting points of comparison with the only other full-scale regional study of English crime and punishment in this period, by Morgan and Rushton, dealing with County Durham, Northumberland and Newcastle-upon-Tyne over the period 1718–1800. Here, as in the southeast, other offences were dwarfed by property crimes. Less than 10 per cent of indictments, involving some 250 accused (of whom only nineteen were hanged), involved homicide, while other felonies, such as rape, were tried very rarely. But the assizes and quarter sessions in this region over the period of study witnessed 4,396 property offences. There was a peak in such offences, with 584 indictments, in the 1750s, then, as in Surrey, indictments took off massively in the 1780s and 1790s, with a total of 1,593 indictments in these two decades. Here, too, bad harvests sent theft indictments up, notably in 1740–1, while the arrival of peace also witnessed a rise in criminal prosecutions. This study of the northeast, however, emphasizes two other points. The first of these was the high level of participation by women, relative to modern expectations, in property offences: in Durham and Northumberland nearly a third of those accused of theft at the assizes and quarter sessions were women, while in Newcastle the proportion rose to a half. Second, the northeastern experience emphasized that as the eighteenth century progressed, crime became an increasingly urban phenomenon, with both levels of prosecution and evidence of organized criminality becoming more marked not only in Newcastle, but also in smaller towns like Sunderland, and even Morpeth.

The most obvious connections between criminality and urbanization were, of course, to be found in London. With a population in excess of 500,000 by the mid-eighteenth century, London and its environs formed by far the biggest urban centre in the British Isles. Contemporaries were convinced that this metropolis offered unique opportunities to criminals, and by the mid-eighteenth century social commentators were in agreement that London presented a unique law and order problem. There were certainly ample opportunities for crime there, especially property crime, while prostitution flourished, and, as the career of Britain's first great criminal entrepreneur, Jonathan Wild, had demonstrated, London could support relatively sophisticated organized and professional crime. Unfortunately, there has so far been little scholarly research investigating whether the opinions of contemporary commentators were well founded, and what the realities of crime, organized crime and law enforcement in the capital were. There has also, unfortunately, been comparatively little research into crime in English provincial towns, which would deepen our understanding of crime as an urban phenomenon.

For most readers, however, perhaps the most potent image of London crime is provided by hangings at Tyburn. Capital punishment lay at the heart of the eighteenth-century criminal justice system, and it is knowledge of this which has encouraged that conventional wisdom which would portray that system as barbaric. Eighteenth-century England, indeed, experienced the construction of a 'bloody code' of capital statutes, which meant that, by 1800, perhaps 200 offences existed under English law, most of them crimes against property, for which the perpetrator could incur the death penalty. What is striking, however, once the sentences meted out by various courts are studied in detail, is how frequently capital punishment was avoided. Characteristically, larger numbers of people were sentenced to death than were hanged. Thus, in London and Middlesex between 1775 and 1784, some 185 persons were capitally convicted for burglary and 318 for highway robbery, but only 108 of the former and 124 of the latter were actually executed (Emsley 1996: 256). The law operated a principle of selectivity: in theory, anybody convicted of burglary could be executed, but in practice only about a half were. An offender convicted of almost any property crime, if he or she were young, of previous good reputation, came from a respectable family, committed the offence in a period when the authorities felt no great urge to make examples, and could find locally important people to intercede on his or her behalf, was likely to receive a conditional pardon and be subjected to a lesser punishment than hanging. Conversely, known offenders who committed especially atrocious crimes in periods when the authorities felt there was a severe law and order problem, and who could find nobody to intercede for them, were likely to be hanged. This selectivity and flexibility helped build a regular dimension of clemency into what was a draconian system, and thus helped preclude the revulsion against the system that might have occurred if really high levels of execution had obtained.

Nevertheless, the totals of those hanged seem striking enough to the modern observer, especially given that the majority of those executed died for property offences, most of them for simple grand larceny, burglary or pickpocketing. Over the period 1788–1802, of those executed in Surrey, 81 per cent were hanged for property offences, with robbery and burglary each forming about a third of this total, and a further 6.3 per cent for coining. Against these percentages, two men (2.5 per cent) were hanged for homicide, one woman (1.3 per cent) for infanticide, and one man (again 1.3 per cent) for rape (Beattie 1986: 536–7). During this period, the place of execution in London was moved from Tyburn to Newgate, and the old carnivalesque parade of convicted persons through the streets of London ended. But, at both Tyburn and Newgate, and elsewhere throughout the British Isles, persons undergoing the death penalty met their end in public, in a ritualized theatre of death. Again, however, recent research has suggested that the public execution was a complex cultural phenomenon which can be decoded to reveal a sometimes complex set of objectives on the part of the authorities and yet more complex responses on the part of the spectators.

The emphasis on capital punishment should not obscure the importance of secondary punishments. Many petty thieves were whipped, while the common practice of undervaluing stolen goods meant that many of those convicted of theft avoided the possibility of being hanged for grand larceny (that is, the theft of goods valued at a shilling or more). At the beginning of the century, many were saved by the 'pious perjury' of benefit of clergy, by which many convicted of theft or manslaughter escaped with being branded in the hand for a first offence rather than being hanged. There was a growing feeling, however, that more effective forms of secondary punishment were needed, and the first significant innovation in this area came in 1718, in the wake of a crime wave that accompanied the end of the War of the Spanish Succession in 1713. Legislation was passed which enacted that many of those convicted for capital offences might be pardoned on condition that they were transported to the American colonies. Between that date and the outbreak of the American War of Independence in 1775, some 30,000 convicted felons went to the colonies from England, 13,000 from Ireland, and a mere 700 (evidence of the independence of that country's penal system) from Scotland. Indeed, the refusal of the American colonists to take any more convicts left the English and Irish penal systems in some disarray: execution rates increased, while another penal experiment, that of incarcerating convicts in prison hulks on the Thames, was put into place (this measure, initially introduced as a stop-gap, was finally discontinued in 1857). A lasting solution was finally indicated in January 1788, when the first convict fleet sent to Australia arrived at Botany Bay.

Thus, over much of the eighteenth century transportation to the Americas, and subsequently to Australia, was of vital importance to the English and Irish penal systems. Less obviously, and without any statutory basis, imprisonment was also beginning to feature as a secondary punishment. It was not, of course, until the early nineteenth century that the penitentiary prison arrived as the most important practical and symbolic means of dealing with serious offenders. But from the early eighteenth century, on a piecemeal local basis, county and urban authorities began to send convicted criminals for short spells in the county gaol or the local house of correction; this practice sometimes being complemented by hard labour or corporal punishment. So, as the eighteenth century progressed, the criminal justice system, above all in England, found itself with a range of penalties to apply to convicted criminals, although it should be noted that here as elsewhere there could be considerable variations in local penal practices.

Encountering such variations leads us back to the role of discretion, and hence the presence of a considerable degree of flexibility, in the legal system. This theme has been most thoroughly explored by historians of crime in England, but there is no reason to reject its presence in other parts of the British Isles, and, one suspects, over most of continental Europe. The law was enforced, it must be remembered, for the most part not by professional law enforcers backed by a fully bureaucratized criminal justice system, but rather by unpaid amateur officials upon whose opinions, often operating in the context of face-to-face communities, the decision on whether to prosecute an offence, and how that offence might be categorized, might depend. In particular, it has been argued that the existence, progress and outcome of a criminal trial in England in the eighteenth century would depend upon a process of decision making that might involve a broad range of decision makers. As a result of the general absence of 'police' officers in the modern sense, the decision to prosecute (assuming that a suspect had been identified) normally lay with the person offended against, who had to decide whether his or her annoyance at being a victim of crime was sufficient to overcome the knowledge that prosecuting a criminal offence would involve time, trouble and expense. The prosecutor had then to convince local officials, typically parish constables and local justices of the peace, that there was a good possibility that the person suspected might have a criminal charge to answer; the evidence of witnesses and community opinion possibly being important at this stage. Assuming a suspected person was then held for trial, the charges against him or her, in England and Wales at least, would be screened by a grand jury of twelve or more men, usually substantial local figures, who would decide if a trial were justifiable. If that was the grand jury's decision, the accused would then stand trial before a petty or trial jury of a further twelve men, who would reach a verdict, usually with a heavy input, in the assizes, from the presiding judge. If a guilty verdict was reached, its consequences (most obviously, of course, whether it should lead to execution) were frequently the outcome of a number of interested parties attempting to influence the judges. The eventual conviction of a criminal was therefore the outcome of the input of a wide variety of individuals, and the whole of the eighteenth-century criminal justice system was shot through with discretion.

It is, of course, the trial and punishment of serious crime that has attracted the most attention. Yet in eighteenth-century Britain, as in the majority of societies, most crime was petty crime, and the methods of dealing with petty criminals were as distinctive as those invoked against their more serious counterparts. In earlier periods, other courts and agents than those which predominated in the eighteenth century had been involved in the prosecution of petty offenders. In late medieval England, manorial courts leet had been active in the prosecution and fining of local nuisance offenders, although the current conventional wisdom is that these courts were, for the most part, in terminal decline by the mid-seventeenth century. Ecclesiastical courts had also been concerned with certain categories of local nuisance offender, although the correction business of these courts was generally falling off in England by the late seventeenth century, and in Scotland by the late eighteenth. In an interesting regional variation, however, church courts in the Isle of Man seem to have been more active in the early eighteenth century than in earlier periods, largely as a result of the energies of the then bishop of Sodor and Man, Thomas Wilson.

But in England the eighteenth century witnessed a near monopoly of petty crime by the justices of the peace, perhaps most frequently in petty sessions, where two or three justices might sit to try petty crime in a subdivision of a county, or on summary conviction, when a justice of the peace might decide on a case of petty crime in the privacy of his own parlour. The one major study of the prosecution of petty crime so far completed for our period (by Shoemaker), dealing with London and Middlesex in the years 1660–1725, has traced the emergence of a flexible and seemingly effective system. This dealt with petty offenders through indictment, binding over to keep the peace or be of good behaviour, or (this last being frequently used against prostitutes) by sentencing to a short period of incarceration in a house of correction, these practices being supplemented by summary justice by the justices of the peace.

Although most of the evidence so far adduced relates to England, patterns of the prosecution and punishment of serious offences have also been reconstructed for at least parts of Ireland. As we have noted, most Irish criminal records have been lost, but an important study by Garnham has analysed one of the few sources that do exist, records of indictments in Co. Armagh between 1735 and 1797. To some extent, these offences reflect one of the peculiarities of Irish criminal law in this period: in Ireland, trespass was defined by statute, and was a matter for the criminal rather than the civil law. Trespass, for example, formed about a third of all property offences indicted at the Armagh assizes, with grand larceny, the largest category, forming 61 per cent of property offences, and burglary, housebreaking and robbery a mere 3 per cent. As in England, fluctuations in property offences were closely linked to the state of the harvest, although the connection between the end of warfare and peaks in the indictment of property offences was much less apparent. The Armagh assize indictments include many prosecutions of assault, with 1,192 individuals being prosecuted for that offence in 1771–5. Rape, conversely, was very rarely prosecuted (only nineteen indictments in 1771–5). Homicide was likewise a rarely indicted offence, with, for example, only forty-three cases being prosecuted at the Armagh assizes in 1772–81; a figure which does, however, suggest that the homicide rate in that Irish county was three or four times higher than that obtaining in southern England in the same period. Crime and punishment in Dublin demonstrated a pattern that would probably have been familiar in British cities. Between 1780 and 1795 somewhere between 199 and 242 felons were hanged in Dublin, the larger total including thirteen women and 229 men. Most of them were executed for property offences: burglary, robbery and thefts of various types. Over the period the Dublin courts recorded 390 fatalities of one sort or another, including 189 murders, thirty-four manslaughters, thirty-four infanticides and nine deaths resulting from duels, along with fifty-three rapes, 3,600 robberies and burglaries and 1,300 thefts.

It is thus hardly surprising that from the mid-eighteenth century there developed a debate over crime, a debate that was conducted in terms which would be recognizable to the modern reader. Crime had long been a matter of interest to the popular press. Pamphlets describing horrible murders and other especially newsworthy crimes had been published since the Elizabethan era, and continued to flourish over the eighteenth century. They were joined by more compendious works describing the lives of highwaymen, murderers and other notorious criminals, and, as the century progressed, by a wide range of literary treatments of crime and criminals. Something like more straightforward reportage arrived, notably, from the late seventeenth century onwards, with the regular printed accounts of the proceedings of each session of the Old Bailey. But from about 1750, in England at least, major works appeared that discussed crime, its causes and its possible remedies in a way which would, for example, have been unthinkable a century earlier. The work that symbolized the arrival of this new attitude to crime and punishment was Henry Fielding's *An Enquiry into the Causes of the late Increase of Robbers, and some Proposals for Remedying this growing Evil* of 1751. The debate on crime and punishment that developed over the second half of the century attracted a number of participants, among whom perhaps the most notable were Martin Madan and Patrick Colquhoun. Its overall effect was to alert public opinion to the fact that crime was a matter of urgent concern, and that there were a number of possible schemes on hand for curbing it.

These debates, however uncertainly, were moving law enforcement in Britain towards that emergence of 'modern' thought on the problem which the nineteenth-century reforms are commonly held to have heralded. What is becoming clear, however, is that the suddenness of the nineteenth-century break has often been overestimated, an assertion that is nowhere more true than of the history of the police and policing. The conventional 'Whig' history of the subject has portrayed the foundation of the Metropolitan Police by Robert Peel in 1829 as an important watershed, and has tended to gloss over the objections that existed to the new police, and the slowness with which professional policing was adopted in many parts of the country. It also made Peel's achievements look all the more impressive by creating a portrayal of earlier policing systems that is little more than a negative caricature. Obviously the old system of parish constables was ill-adapted to the needs of an industrializing and urbanizing society, yet it probably continued to work well enough (albeit supported by local societies for the prosecution of felony) in many rural areas. In the towns, as research is just beginning to reveal, there were many local initiatives, which included the improvement and rationalization of local policing as one facet of improved urban government. Other parts of the British Isles saw earlier experiments in 'modern policing'. In Dublin, for example, in the face of a perceived law and order crisis, a new uniformed police of forty mounted and 400 foot constables went into action in 1786, although the expense this force involved made it a political liability, and it was in effect ditched in 1795. In that year, coincidentally, the first private act for setting up a local police force in Scotland was passed, for Aberdeen, with Glasgow following in 1800 and Edinburgh in 1805. The history of policing in eighteenth-century Britain, like that of so many other aspects of crime and punishment, was therefore much more complex than the standard accounts would suggest.

This conclusion reminds us that it is impossible in a brief review such as this to do more than indicate the main lines of research into eighteenth-century crime and punishment that have so far been explored, and to make some suggestions about future developments. It is hoped, however, that this short introduction will have demonstrated the exciting and diverse nature of the subject, and shown how the research that has been completed offers a profound challenge to any 'Whig interpretation' of the history of crime and criminal justice.

FURTHER READING

Beattie, J. M.: *Crime and the Courts in England 1660–1800* (Oxford, 1986).

Beattie, J. M.: *Policing and Punishment in London: Urban Crime and the Limits of Terror* (Oxford, 2001).

Bell, Ian A.: *Literature and Crime in Augustan England* (London, 1991).

Davies, Stephen J.: 'The courts and the Scottish legal system 1600–1747: the case of Stirlingshire', in V. A. C. Gatrell, Bruce Lenman and Geoffrey Parker (eds), *Crime and the Law: The Social History of Crime in Western Europe since 1500* (London, 1980).

Ekirch, A. Roger: *Bound for America: The Transportation of British Convicts to the Colonies, 1718–1775* (Oxford, 1987).

Emsley, Clive: *Crime and Society in England 1750–1900* (2nd edn, London, 1996).

Garnham, Neal: *The Courts, Crime and the Criminal Law in Ireland, 1692–1760* (Blackrock, Co. Dublin, 1996).

Gatrell, V. A. C.: *The Hanging Tree: Execution and the English People 1770–1868* (Oxford, 1994).

Hay, Douglas, Linebaugh, Peter and Thompson, E. P.: *Albion's Fatal Tree: Crime and Society in Eighteenth-Century England* (London, 1975).

Hay, Douglas and Snyder, Francis (eds): *Policing and Prosecution in England 1750–1850* (Oxford, 1989).

Henry, Brian: *The Dublin Hanged: Crime, Law Enforcement and Punishment in Late Eighteenth-Century Dublin* (Blackrock, Co. Dublin, 1994).

King, Peter: *Crime, Justice and Discretion in England 1740–1820* (Oxford, 2000).

Linebaugh, Peter: *The London Hanged: Crime and Civil Society in the Eighteenth Century* (London, 1991).

Morgan, Gwenda and Rushton, Peter: *Rogues, Thieves and the Rule of Law: The Problem of Law Enforcement in North-East England, 1718–1800* (London, 1998).

Sharpe, J. A.: *Crime in Early Modern England 1550–1750* (2nd edn, London, 1996).

Shoemaker, Robert B.: *Prosecution and Punishment: Petty Crime and the Law in London and Rural Middlesex, c.1660–1725* (Cambridge, 1991).

Thompson, Edward: *Whigs and Hunters: The Origin of the Black Act* (London, 1975).

PART V

Union and Disunion in the British Isles

Chapter Twenty-Eight

Integration: Patriotism and Nationalism

Colin Kidd

Curiously, historians of eighteenth-century Britain had paid little attention to the processes of British integration until the appearance in 1992 of Linda Colley's pioneering survey, *Britons: Forging the Nation 1701–1837.* Yet, as Colley pointed out, Britain is an eighteenth-century creation, though one whose significance seemed dim for generations of – nominally – 'British' historians guided by a longstanding anglocentric agenda. Nor should Scottish historians escape censure. Although a number of figures working on Scottish topics had addressed the origins of the Anglo-Scottish Union of 1707 and the initial instability of the new state arising from the threat of Jacobitism, Scottish historians seemed to assume, just as much as their English counterparts, that, from 1746 onwards, Britain was a given of political life.

Yet from thc mid-1960s the message which historians working on the union sent out was that union had been a short-term solution to a high political crisis and that its long-term success had been far from inevitable. P. W. J. Riley argued that union had come about as a means of controlling a refractory Scottish parliament that had escaped the tight management of the estate of bishops and the Lords of the Articles (a steering committee whose composition reflected royal influence) after both were abolished in the Revolution of 1688–90. Working on parallel lines, William Ferguson saw a union which had emerged as an alternative method of winning an increasingly anglophobic Scotland over to the *fait accompli* of the Hanoverian succession, which was England's unilateral answer to the death in 1700 of Queen Anne's last surviving heir. Moreover, he detected bribery in the way in which it passed the Scottish parliament, estimating that the union was generally unpopular in Scotland and, as far as England was concerned, largely an anti-Jacobite device deployed for strategic reasons. In other words, the union was not the result of Anglo-Scottish convergence; if anything, English and Scottish interests were perceived to be diverging in the first decade of the eighteenth century, especially after the English had frustrated Scottish attempts in 1698–1700 to establish a colony at Darien in Central America. At best, the union was a shady deal, elements of which met the respective national interests of the contracting parties.

Nowhere was the hollowness at the heart of Britishness more apparent than in Ireland where the ruling Church of Ireland, though proud of the Irish parliamentary heritage, was much keener than the Scots political nation on the idea of an incorporating union with England, and aware too that, by comparison with Scotland's Presbyterian kirk and Roman jurisprudence, its own values and institutions displayed much closer affinities to those of England, which the 'English nation in Ireland' regarded as the motherland. By no means did Irish patriots, such as William Molyneux, the author of the influential and much reprinted treatise, *The Case of Ireland's being bound by Acts of Parliament in England, stated* (1698), want the Irish parliament to be treated – as it had been – like a powerless subordinate of Westminster; but full incorporating union within a British parliament was an acceptable alternative to the status quo. Indeed, the Irish House of Commons called for a union with England in 1703; and there would be further Irish petitions for union in 1707 and 1709. In his *Essay towards an union of Ireland with England* (1703), Henry Maxwell justified Anglo-Irish integration on the grounds of blood: the Protestants of Ireland were the biological offspring of the English nation. Thus, it came as a shock to the self-image of the English nation in Ireland, which discriminated both against Presbyterians and Roman Catholics, when England united with Presbyterian Scotland. In 1707 Jonathan Swift, a fierce critic of Scots Presbyterianism, wrote his *Story of the Injured Lady* (eventually published in 1746), which related how Ireland, symbolized by the noble lady of the title, had been jilted by her inconstant lover (England) for a rival mistress (a beggarly, disloyal Scotland). Although Irish patriots criticized English policy towards Ireland, it seems clear that during the early part of the eighteenth century the idea of union with England was more warmly espoused in Dublin than in Edinburgh.

The Britain of 1707, as cynical Irish observers recognized, was a freshly minted state which failed to inspire any emotional enthusiasm in its peoples and lacked any enduring *raison d'être*. Unsurprisingly, in 1713 there was a motion in the House of Lords to repeal the union, which failed by only four votes, and in 1715, after the Hanoverian succession had taken place, there were calls in Scotland for the union to be dissolved now that its principal objective had been achieved. Not only did Scots Jacobites oppose the union, in its early years there was also opposition from the Whiggish trading communities of Lowland Scotland where perceptions reigned that the union had done little to regenerate the Scottish economy. This low-intensity hostility to the union flared spectacularly in 1725 with the Shawfield Riots in Glasgow against the malt tax. If the union was seen, on both sides of the border, as an instrument of politics rather than an end in itself, how did Britain come to inspire such loyalty in its subjects, Scots as well as English, throughout the various wars of the eighteenth century?

Linda Colley believes that empire and the Franco-British warfare of the period provided a crucial part of the answer. Indeed, from the Reformation onwards a British imperial unionism had acted within Scottish political culture as a counter-current to the dominant discourse of assertive ethnocentric nationhood. More immediately, the failure of the Darien scheme indicated to Scots that their yearnings for overseas colonies were unlikely to be achieved in the absence of a partnership with a better-established power, a prospect realized in Article IV of the Union which granted Scots full access to England's overseas colonies and trade. Glasgow's merchants struck up a successful entrepôt trade in tobacco with the Chesapeake region, while also exporting Scottish-made goods, such as linen, to North America, and using the profits to diversify into other sectors of the Scottish economy. Ambitious Scots, such as Robert Hunter in New York, and Alexander Spotswood and Robert Dinwiddie in Virginia, also obtained governorships and lieutenant-governorships within the North American colonies. The loss of the thirteen colonies between 1776 and 1783 barely dented Scottish opportunities in the empire; for by then Scots had already infiltrated the East India Company, not least the officer corps of its army. The domination exercised by the Scots political manager Henry Dundas over the fledgling Board of Control for India (where he sat formally as president from 1793 to 1801) merely confirmed the Scots ascendancy in Indian affairs. The career of James Macpherson demonstrates most poignantly how the empire could neutralize and co-opt potentially nationalist sentiments. Macpherson, the patriotic mythmaker responsible for promoting his 'translations' of the supposedly ancient Gaelic epics of Ossian, was a proud Scoto-British imperialist who served as secretary to the governor of Pensacola, West Florida, and as London agent to the nawab of Arcot, while also figuring within an influential Highland 'mafia' that included Sir John Macpherson, the governor-general of India 1785–6, the son of the Reverend John Macpherson of Sleat, like James Macpherson another patriotic historian of Caledonian antiquity. Impecunious but educated, Scots were, perhaps, more willing than their English counterparts to risk death and disease in the far-flung corners of the empire. On balance, however, Scots manpower was not exploited in the cause of imperial expansion. The Scots, just as much as their English partners-in-empire, were oppressors of non-white ethnic groups. For example, a Scots connection from the Spey valley, Caithness and Glasgow – areas associated with the proprietors Grant, Oswald and Co. – dominated the management of the African slave entrepôt at Bance Island near the mouth of the Sierra Leone River. In addition, the empire offered Scots a number of creative outlets for self-expression. The Scottish enlightenment did not flourish only within Scotland's university towns, but its values were exported throughout the empire, as was the distinctive agrarian patriotism of the Scottish improvers.

Although, as Colley notes, a 'British' empire offered Scots parity of esteem, profits and the pecuniary rewards of office, it was warfare, above all, that superimposed a British national identity on the peoples of England and Scotland. Contemporaries – most notably, the Scottish moral philosopher and former chaplain to the Black Watch regiment, Adam Ferguson – recognized that conflict with some external 'Other' helped to consolidate the domestic bonds that held a community together. Certainly, warfare encouraged a more vivid sense of Britain as an 'imagined community': news of British actions abroad and on the high seas constituted the staple information of newspapers and magazines, and led to a heightening of local interest in Westminster politics. By the end of the Napoleonic Wars, the achievements of Wolfe earlier, and then of Nelson and Wellington, had generated an authentic matter of Britain – an heroic history shared collectively by the nations of Britain, unlike the traditional histories of England, Scotland and Wales.

At a practical level, moreover, the growth of the fiscal-military state from the 1690s paved the way to fuller British integration. Indeed, the army was the first major British institution to be colonized by ambitious Scots, a process that had begun even before the Union of 1707, with a number of Scots soldiers winning renown under

Marlborough. By 1752 Scots accounted for a quarter of the British officer corps. Certainly, the rise of Scots within the army – such as John Dalrymple, second earl of Stair, and John Campbell, fourth earl of Loudoun – provoked nothing like the degree of alarm associated with the ascent of Scots politicians and jurists to high civil office in London, most notably the storm over Lord Bute's short-lived premiership of 1762–3 and the controversy that dogged the career of William Murray, first earl of Mansfield and lord chief justice from 1756 to 1788. Both were accused of importing a quasi-Jacobite Scottish authoritarianism into the laws of England. On the contrary, loyal military service also proved a stepping stone to diplomatic preferment for Scots, including Stair and Sir Robert Murray Keith, ambassador to Vienna from 1772 to 1792.

A growing recognition of the shared Anglo-Scottish values of Protestantism, liberty and constitutional government also emerged out of conflict with an alien, despotic and Roman Catholic France. Catholic Spain was another bugbear. The oppositional and imperialist cult of Admiral Vernon, the victor over the Spaniards at Porto Bello (1739), was to be celebrated across Lowland Scotland as well as throughout England between 1740 and 1742, as Kathleen Wilson has shown. The continent as a whole, with the odd exception, seemed to be a scene of tyranny and superstition, of absolutist kingcraft and popish priestcraft. Scots and English, for all their differences, it seemed, had much more in common with one another than they did with an alien and hostile continent. Some of the advocates of Anglo-Scottish union – which took place, of course, during the War of the Spanish Succession – emphasized the need for the limited monarchies of England and Scotland to unite in the face of Bourbon expansionism. French backing for the Jacobite uprising of 1745, itself a theatre of the War of the Austrian Succession, reinforced this impression of an authoritarian France conspiring to impose alien political values on a predominantly Whiggish Britain. By the time of the Seven Years' War, this pan-British front against France was also fuelled by a popular imperialism. Scots played crucial roles in the Indian and North American theatres of the war. In India the officer corps of the East India Company already contained a high proportion of Scots, while in North America Highlanders played a heroic role in the conquest of Quebec.

The Seven Years' War also led to a reiteration of the old francophobic stereotypes, though with the added force of warnings – most famously in the Reverend John Brown's *Estimate of the Manners and Principles of the Times* (1757) – that the spread of luxury threatened to weaken Britons' moral fibre, turning sturdy liberty-loving John Bulls into effeminate Frenchmen. This argument later found elegant expression in *The Expedition of Humphry Clinker* (1771), an epistolary novel by the Scottish author Tobias Smollett which exploded conventional anti-Scottish prejudices and contrasted the manly virtues of North Britain – and rural Wales – with the corruption of the *beau monde* in Bath and London. Within the prevailing idiom of civic humanism, national characters were not conceived as immutable. Rather, there was a widespread perception that the manners of a nation could easily lapse into luxury and corruption – of the sort which English chauvinists decried in France.

Anxieties of this sort serve as a reminder not to exaggerate the nature and degree of the gulf contemporaries perceived between free-born Britons and the benighted subjects of Catholic and absolutist France. Have historians such as Colley and Gerald Newman exaggerated the otherness of the Other? Whatever the xenophobic views of the public at large, the elites of Britain did not regard the French with contempt. The patriotic champions of England's Anglo-Saxon origins and Gothic inheritance of parliament and common law were keenly aware that other peoples had emerged from what was known as the Gothic 'hive of nations', including the Frankish ancestors of the French. The English and French nations, despite their considerable differences by the eighteenth century, stemmed from the same Gothic family tree. In the beginning, ran the historiographical consensus among eighteenth-century British commentators (Scots and Irish included), there must have been a close degree of similarity in the manners and institutions of the kindred Anglo-Saxons and Franks. The sharp contrast between English liberty and French despotism which became such a cliché of eighteenth-century English popular culture, not least in political caricatures, had arisen only from the later Middle Ages with the rise of the French monarchy relative to the nobility and the kingdom's historic institutions. Whereas the French estates-general had last met in 1614 – and would not meet again until the French Revolution – in England, so the argument ran, the powers of parliament had grown during the Reformation era, as the dissolution of the monasteries led to a wider distribution of land among the gentry, while the security England enjoyed through its maritime detachment from continental Europe had inhibited the expansion of a standing army. The intellectual leaders of British society perceived that the gulf between England and France was a recent, historical contingency; yet, at a popular level, they did little to discourage a politically useful francophobia. Although eighteenth-century wars were not the result of deep-seated antagonisms between nation-states, propaganda nevertheless assumed strikingly ethnocentric forms. It seems unlikely that francophobia provides an explanation for the cultural integration of Britain's elites. The Scottish philosopher David Hume, a proponent of British integration and critic of the solipsism which fuelled patriotic boasting and national prejudices, informed Englishmen that a modern civilized monarchy such as France was far from the oppressive state depicted in English Whig mythology. The cosmopolitan attractions of the Grand Tour further qualified British demonization of a French otherness. Nevertheless, as Gerald Newman has noted, during the second half of the eighteenth century a growing Evangelical sincerity gradually displaced this cosmopolitan outlook, a trend exacerbated with the French Revolution and the rise of radical irreligion.

Nor should we exaggerate the extent to which confessional differences shaped anti-French sentiment. Within the ranks of the Anglican clergy, there was a marked degree of sympathy for Gallicanism, the desire of the Catholic church in France – expressed most forcefully in its Four Articles of 1682 – for a large measure of national autonomy from the temporal claims of the papacy. Indeed, William Wake, archbishop of Canterbury between 1716 and 1737 and a former chaplain to the embassy in Paris (1682–5), engaged in negotiations from 1717 to 1720 for a possible union of the Anglican and Gallican churches, though this plan did not come to fruition. Beyond the immediate sphere of Anglo-French relations, the eighteenth century witnessed – again at the elite level – a marked diminution of the anti-Catholicism that had been such a characteristic feature of British Protestant identities during the seventeenth century. The collapse of Jacobitism after the failure of 1745–6 happened to coincide with a time of obvious tensions within the Catholic world. Britons came to recognize that continental Catholicism – contrary to the image they once held of a doctrinaire Counter-Reformation militancy – encompassed considerable ecclesiastical diversity. In 1763 the Catholic theologian Febronius issued his treatise *De statu ecclesiae*, which advocated a more decentralized church. In practice, Febronianism was held to legitimize a Catholic Erastianism which reached its apogee in the secular utilitarian calculus adopted by Joseph II of Austria to review the church's role in his dominions. No group epitomized the old ways more than the Jesuits, whose star waned with the eclipse of ultramontane confessionalism. Portugal's enlightened minister Pombal expelled the Jesuits in 1759, France quickly followed suit in 1764, and in 1767 Charles III was persuaded of the wisdom of suppressing the order within Spain and throughout his colonial empire. Under considerable international pressure, Pope Clement XIV formally dissolved the Jesuit order in 1773. Papal foreign policy also began to assume a more benign aspect. In 1766 Clement XIII took the opportunity of the death of the Old Pretender to refuse diplomatic recognition to his successor Charles, the Young Pretender. The cold wars of religion were clearly thawing in the sun of the European enlightenment, whose effects were also felt upon British policy making.

Roman Catholic relief legislation for England and Scotland was introduced in 1778–9 (though the Scottish bill was dropped after popular pressure). The Quebec Act (1774) accorded formal recognition to the Roman Catholic religion in that province. Even in Ireland the Protestant ruling classes began to dismantle the anti-Catholic penal laws instituted between 1695 and 1727. As early as the 1720s Archbishop Synge had begun to wrestle with the problem of formulating a test of allegiance to the Hanoverian monarchy which would have facilitated a measure of toleration for Catholic clergy and laity in Ireland. The passivity of Irish Catholics in 1715 and 1745 began to dampen the anti-Catholic fears of the Protestant Irish elite. By the 1760s and 1770s the term 'papist' had fallen into disuse among enlightened Irish Protestants. The Irish Catholic community began to reflect the wider divisions of the church, with Archbishop Butler of Cashel emerging in the 1770s as the leader of its Gallican wing. Moreover, by now the moral imperatives of enlightenment had been reinforced by the need to draw upon Irish Catholic manpower to serve the growing military needs of the British empire. An act of 1771 eased restrictions on Catholic tenancies and the Oath Act of 1774 permitted Catholics to take a new non-papal oath of allegiance to the Hanoverian monarchy. Further Irish Catholic relief acts followed in 1778, 1782, 1792 and 1793 which, collectively, gave Catholics the same property rights as Protestants, removed many of the restrictions that had been imposed on Catholic worship, and allowed Catholics to practise law and to vote in elections (though not, of course, the right to sit themselves as MPs). By the end of the century full Catholic emancipation – including Catholic representation – seemed close at hand. Pitt the Younger attempted to make Catholic emancipation a cornerstone of the union with Ireland agreed in 1800, but was frustrated by George III, who judged it a betrayal of the Protestant constitution he had sworn to uphold in his coronation oath.

Anti-Catholicism remained a staple of popular Britishness. There were serious riots in Edinburgh against Roman Catholic relief, targeted against the residence of William Robertson, the principal of Edinburgh University and leader of the liberal Moderates in the kirk. In England a Protestant Association was formed in the spring of 1780, and that summer's Gordon Riots constituted the century's largest explosion of popular violence on mainland Britain. In North America too the Quebec Act seemed to confirm suspicions among British colonists that the motherland was in the grip of a crypto-Catholic absolutist conspiracy, in turn fuelling demands for separation. Moreover, in Ireland the century of enlightenment ended with a renewal of popular sectarianism, with the Catholic Whiteboy and Rightboy movements succeeded by the more intense hostilities of the late 1790s. This disjunction between the liberalism of enlightened elites and the prejudice of the populace has to be taken into account when generalizing about the identities of eighteenth-century Britons. By a similar token, the Jewish Naturalization Act of 1753 prompted an outpouring of anti-Judaic bigotry and was promptly repealed. Confessional prejudice, while perhaps not the uncomplicated given assumed by Colley, was none the less a major component of popular identities throughout the eighteenth-century British world.

The undoubted strength of these animosities, however, was not matched by an equally powerful positive identification with Britain's family of Protestant churches. If continental Catholicism was not quite the alien monolith that Colley imagines, then neither was British Protestantism as homogeneous or tension-free as the Colley thesis suggests. There was considerable conflict within the Protestant community. Although anti-Catholicism was enshrined at the heart of the Union of 1707 – in Article II, which confirmed the Protestant succession – the acts accompanying union which secured the privileges of the Church of England and the Presbyterian Church of Scotland were the product of genuine Presbyterian fears of Anglican imperialism. The legislative intrusion of the English Tory ministry of 1710–14 into the reserved area of Scottish church matters served only to exacerbate Presbyterian anxieties. Indeed, the non-Jacobite opposition to union of the 1720s and 1730s has been generally overlooked. Yet, from 1712 through to 1783 the General Assembly of the kirk issued an annual grievance to the British state against the intolerable grievance of lay patronage, and patronage provoked significant secessions from the established kirk in 1733 and 1761. The Seceders were unenthusiastic Britons, critical not only of the abomination of patronage, but also of a union which had at its rotten heart an Erastian multi-confessional arrangement: not only did Anglicans – notionally – recognize the inviolable privileges of the Scots Presbyterian kirk, but Scots reciprocally acknowledged an Episcopal Church of England. This was offensive enough to Presbyterians sensitive to any usurpations on the rights of Christ over his church, but doubly galling was the presence of the bishops in the British House of Lords which involved a breach of the Presbyterian principle of the two kingdoms – a parallel division of spheres between civil and spiritual interests. Indeed, at the extremes of the Scots Presbyterian community, the Cameronian heirs of the radical Covenanters of the seventeenth century openly rejected the Glorious Revolution and the Union of 1707, denouncing the Hanoverians – equally with the Stuarts – for their failure to take the Covenants.

Even in Ireland, where Protestants shared deep-seated fears of Catholic insurrection, the Episcopal Church of Ireland discriminated against Presbyterians in much the same way that it did against Catholics. High church Irish Anglicans – Swift is the most notorious example – despised Presbyterians almost as much as they did Roman Catholics. In 1704 an act – ostensibly directed against popery – included a requirement that officeholders under the crown take communion within the Church of Ireland. Given that Catholics were already effectively excluded from office, this sacramental test was an anti-Presbyterian measure whose main effect was to disqualify Presbyterian burgesses from local government in towns such as Belfast and Derry. The Tory ascendancy at the end of Queen Anne's reign saw a further worsening of the status of Irish Presbyterians. Presbyterians were harassed by the authorities and in 1714 the *regium donum*, a state subsidy to Presbyterian ministers, was suspended, though it was to be restored from 1715 with the accession of George I and the demise of the Tories. Despite the passage of a Toleration Act in 1719, Presbyterians continued to experience certain legal disabilities. An attempt to repeal the sacramental test in 1719 failed, as did a further vote on the measure in the Irish parliament in 1733. Presbyterian marriages were also outlawed. Only by an act of 1737 did marriages conducted by Presbyterian clergymen gain official validity – and only if both parties were themselves Presbyterian. The sacramental test was eventually repealed in 1780, but only after the anti-Catholic penal laws had already begun to be dismantled. The experience of Ireland's Presbyterians – with their strong Scottish connections – sits uneasily with Colley's thesis that Protestantism was a major force of British integration.

The vital missing ingredient from Colley's work is the phenomenon of anglicization, whether in the fields of culture, economics or politics. The *Spectator* of Addison and Steele was widely imitated throughout the provincial capitals of the British world. North Britain saw a craze for elocution and a mania for the eradication of unseemly scotticisms in speech and prose. The emergence of a consumer society encouraged provincials to ape the fashions and accoutrements of the sophisticated metropolitan lifestyle. It would be a mistake to underestimate the appeal of English liberties to the wider British world. Britain did not only unite against an external Other, but the emulation of Englishness acted – up to a point – as a glue of integration. Throughout the eighteenth-century British world there was a strong identification with the values and institutions of the English motherland. Colonial Americans and Protestant Irishmen believed themselves to be of English stock, and heirs to the precious English liberties of their Anglo-Saxon ancestors. North Britons, though clearly not of English stock, quickly lost their former patriotic shibboleths, coming to the conclusion that the Union of 1707 had entitled them to full incorporation within a more advanced and liberal England. After all, British provincials, such as Scots, Protestant Irishmen and Americans perceived the liberal essentials beneath the outer ethnic cladding of Englishness: civil, political and religious liberty, trial by jury, government by parliaments and the need for the collective assent of the people's representatives to taxation. English liberties embodied universal aspirations to freedom and self-government. To be under the protection of England, either as a North Briton fortuitously admitted in 1707, or an Englishman in a colonial setting, it seemed, was to enjoy the natural rights of mankind.

In Scotland, for example, a controversy begun during the 1690s over Scotland's economic failures eventually ushered in a wide-ranging critique of Scottish institutions, a process of self-examination which was to be one of the characteristic features of the Scottish enlightenment. A philosophy of progress emerged during the Scottish enlightenment, associated not only with celebrated figures such as Lord Kames, Adam Smith and John Millar, but also with the likes of Sir John Dalrymple, who contrasted the legal histories of England and Scotland in his *Essay towards a*

General History of Feudal Property in Great Britain (1757). The history of mankind was a story of progress from the primitive hunter-gatherer state through pastoral and agrarian stages to the refinement of modern commercial society. As a result, the propriety and utility of institutions and laws came to be assessed against a yardstick of commercial modernity, set by Scotland's liberal post-feudal southern neighbour. The movement for agricultural improvement which gathered steam from the establishment of the Honourable Society of Improvers in 1723 was directed not only towards encouraging the introduction of new techniques, but also towards the removal of political, legal and social obstacles that hindered the emergence of a more dynamic and commercialized agrarian economy. Within the discourse of the improvers, the goals of prosperity and modernization were closely linked to anglicization and the attainment of English-style civil liberties. Criticism of Scotland's economic mismanagement and illiberal, stagnant feudal law rapidly displaced sentimental nostalgia for the old Scots parliament lost in 1707. Indeed, commentators identified this unicameral magnate-dominated body as an obstacle to the development of pre-union Scotland. While Scots had thankfully been liberated from their oligarchic parliament, other problems remained to be tackled. During the first half of the century some Scots even campaigned to 'complete the union' – to extend to Scots, conscious of their comparative subordination to the still extensive powers and jurisdictions of a feudal baronage guaranteed by Articles XVIII and XX of the Union, the freedoms enjoyed by the English nation. This goal was realized in good part by the legal reforms that followed the Jacobite rebellion of 1745–6: the abolition of strict feudal vassalage and most heritable jurisdictions (private feudal courts held by Scots barons which appeared to taint the justice administered to their subjects). Thereafter, many Scots jurists and historians celebrated this legislation of 1747–8 as the eventual admission of formerly oppressed North Britons to their proper entitlement of English liberties. In succeeding decades, however, Scots anglicizers perceived other defects in Scots law that needed to be rectified, including a law of entails which hindered investment in agriculture and the lack of a civil jury in Scotland. During the 1760s several writers issued calls for the curtailment of Scots entails, achieving a partial success in the Montgomery Act of 1770, while in 1785 a campaign began for the introduction to Scotland of the civil juries enjoyed by Englishmen. Scots also remained aware that the electoral franchise north of the border was much narrower than in England, a defect of the union that would be addressed in 1832. The value attached to Englishness was strikingly demonstrated during the 1790s when Scots radicals agitated not for a Scottish Jacobin nationalism, but for the restoration of ancient Anglo-Saxon liberties. This anglophilic fantasy was but the culmination of eighteenth-century Scots' progressive loss of confidence in their own historical nationhood. In 1729 the Jacobite antiquary Father Thomas Innes had exploded the myth of Scotland's national origins, which had endured since the fourteenth century. Enlightenment historians went further, not only criticizing the backwardness of Scotland's institutional and economic progress relative to England's, but, in the case of Hume's *History of England* and John Millar's *Historical View of English Government*, reducing the history of Scotland to a mere aspect of the decisive and all-important history of England. Although enlightened Scots challenged some of the more vulgar errors of England's Whig mythology, such correctives did little to inhibit either the Scottish critique of Scottishness or a well-entrenched North British anglophilia.

The experiences of colonial America and Protestant Ireland, however, indicate that a narrow line separated this enthusiastic emulation of the liberal English core from a colonial irritation with the exclusiveness of the English motherland. Historians are agreed that colonial Americans described themselves as Englishmen and Britons. Indeed, John Murrin has shown that anglicization was the dominant trend in colonial society until the 1760s. Among the contingencies of that decade which suddenly eroded this strong identification with England were not only new fiscal strategies, but also the changed political environment at the seat of imperial government associated with the rise of the Scots politician Lord Bute, the favourite of the new monarch George III. Despite Bute's rapid downfall in 1763, his influence seemed to persist in court and government circles, a rhetorical ploy of his opponents which found a purchase far from home in the colonies. Scotophobia – whether directed against Bute, the grasping factors of Glasgow tobacco houses who controlled the credit lines of an indebted planter class, zealous imperial officials and, eventually, Scots loyalists – was to be a prominent characteristic of revolutionary American political culture. The perception that London was in the grip of an authoritarian quasi-Jacobite Scottish 'mafia' determined to undermine English liberties helped to ease the transition from colonial anglophilia to more assertive demands for colonial autonomy. Nevertheless, the colonial cult of Anglo-Saxon liberties that had helped to foster colonial radicalism and a revolutionary outlook survived the break with England. Thomas Jefferson, who penned the Saxonist pamphlet *Vindication of the Rights of British America* in 1774, remained obsessed with Anglo-Saxon jurisprudence, philology and religious institutions long after the winning of independence.

Eighteenth-century Ireland followed a pattern of anglicization midway between the Scottish and American experiences. During the first half of the century a defiant Protestant Irish patriotism which asserted the status and privileges of the Irish parliament was counterbalanced by an equally proud acknowledgement of English ancestry and values and a willingness to contemplate union with the motherland. Indeed, both sets of values were as likely as not to be articulated by the same politicians and pamphleteers. Swift contended that Englishmen in Ireland wanted only to be treated as such by their compatriots in England. At the turn of the century, Protestant Irishmen were provoked by English interference in, and restrictions upon, Irish trade. Although Ireland was formally excluded from the Navigation Acts until the winning of concessions in 1779, Ireland did participate in the Atlantic economy throughout the eighteenth century – as historians now recognize – exporting linen and salted beef to England and the West Indies.

Economic complaints were compounded by constitutional fears, as in the heightened patriotism of the 1720s. First, the legal case of 'Sherlock versus Annesley' provoked the Westminster parliament's Declaratory Act of 1720, which decreed that the British, not the Irish, House of Lords should be Ireland's ultimate court of appeal, and also made clear the right of the superior British parliament to pass legislation applicable to Ireland. Furthermore, the grant of a patent to mint copper coin for Ireland to William Wood, a Wolverhampton manufacturer, was attacked during the Wood's Halfpence controversy (1722–5) for its economic consequences, and by some, including Swift in the *Drapier's Letters*, as an example of how Ireland's political subordination to England led to poor governance. Swift's patriotism was also symptomatic of discontent within the Church of Ireland where there was resentment among native-born Protestants at the appointment of English-born bishops to Irish sees.

Nevertheless, Irish patriots remained conscious of their identity as the English nation in Ireland. During the 1750s the Dublin radical Charles Lucas still spoke the language of Anglo-Saxon constitutionalism. The climate was changing, however. In 1759 rumours of an impending union provoked a riot in Dublin. Moreover, from 1767 the government abandoned the system of managing the Irish parliament through the agency of native-born magnates, or 'undertakers'. Henceforth there was an escalation of Irish political grievances which culminated during the crisis of the American War of Independence when a weak British government was driven to concede greater autonomy to the Irish parliament. The Irish constitutional revolution of 1782 included the repeal of the Declaratory Act and the modification of Poynings' Law. Although a new edition of Molyneux's *Case of Ireland* was published in 1782 which, significantly, dropped the balanced pro-unionist sentiment of the original, there was still – as in Revolutionary America – an anglophilic dimension to the campaign for independence from the mother country. The Irish patriot leader Henry Grattan still spoke the language of English constitutionalism.

Parliamentary autonomy was short-lived. The French Revolutionary Wars created new fears about the security of the British Isles, paralleling the anxieties which had brought about the Union of 1707. Moreover, the danger posed to the English connection by the establishment of the radical non-sectarian Society of United Irishmen in 1791 – designed to unite Catholics, Presbyterians and establishment Protestants to liberate Ireland from English interference – was exacerbated from another direction by the renewal of sectarian violence, not least from Catholic Defenderism. Over the course of the decade, the initial dream of the United Irishmen collapsed, the organization was driven underground and into insurrectionist conspiracy with Revolutionary France. The traumatic Irish rebellion of 1798 – confirming twin fears of Jacobinism and political Catholicism – led mainland politicians to work for union as a political and strategic necessity. The Union of 1800 that united the British parliament with a reluctant – but pliable and anxious – Irish parliament was, like the Union of 1707, a contingency which ran against the patriotic grain of recent history. While the prime motive behind union in 1800 was strategic, the rhetorical justifications of union – most famously advanced by Dundas, the Scots-imperial politician – revolved around the opportunities of commerce and empire and the chance to emulate Scotland's successful integration with the English core.

The new United Kingdom of 1801 was not a nation-state. An allegiance to the British state and empire coexisted with the perpetuation – and, as often as not, reinvention – of the national traditions of Wales, Scotland and Ireland. The eighteenth-century Welsh cultural renaissance was not directed against Britishness: quite the reverse, the Welsh considered themselves to be the biological heirs of the first Britons and believed that the primitive Christianity of their ancient British ancestors which preceded the arrival of popery constituted the proto-Protestant foundations of the Church of England, a position recognized by Anglican commentators. Among the foremost Welsh organizations were the Society of Ancient Britons (founded in 1715) and the Honourable Society of Cymmrodorion (or aborigines), both London-based. The Welsh revival, whether in the form of linguistic patriotism or Druidism, was shaped more by theological than by political considerations. Throughout the Celtic peripheries, indeed, cultural patriotism tended, as often as not, to take religious forms. There was a pride in Welsh and Gaelic as the primeval languages of Adam and in the ancient Celtic roots of pre-Roman Christianity in the British Isles. The longstanding interest of Church of Ireland clergymen in ancient Celtic Christianity blossomed during the second half of the eighteenth century into a wider Protestant identification with Gaelic culture. Yet, such cross-cultural overtures did not pave the way to enduring confessional reconciliation. Irish Catholicism would remain the main obstacle to fuller British integration.

FURTHER READING

Bailyn, Bernard and Morgan, Philip D. (eds): *Strangers within the Realm: The Cultural Margins of the First British Empire* (Chapel Hill, NC, 1991).

Bartlett, Thomas: *The Fall and Rise of the Irish Nation: The Catholic Question 1690–1830* (Dublin, 1992).

Claydon, Tony and McBride, Ian (eds): *Protestantism and National Identity: Britain and Ireland c.1650–c.1850* (Cambridge, 1998).

Colley, Linda: *Britons: Forging the Nation 1701–1837* (London, 1992).

Connolly, Sean J.: *Religion, Law and Power: The Making of Protestant Ireland 1660–1760* (Oxford, 1992).

Ferguson, William: *Scotland's Relations with England: A Survey to 1707* (Edinburgh, 1977).

Greene, Jack P.: *Peripheries and Center: Constitutional Development in the Extended Polities of the British Empire and the United States 1607–1788* (Athens, GA, 1986).

Hancock, David: *Citizens of the World: London Merchants and the Integration of the British Atlantic Community, 1735–1785* (Cambridge, 1995).

Haydon, Colin: *Anti-Catholicism in Eighteenth-Century England c.1714–80: A Political and Social Study* (Manchester, 1994).

Kidd, Colin: *Subverting Scotland's Past: Scottish Whig Historians and the Creation of an Anglo-British Identity, 1689–c.1830* (Cambridge, 1993).

Kidd, Colin: *British Identities before Nationalism: Ethnicity and Nationhood in the Atlantic World, 1600–1800* (Cambridge, 1999).

Marshall, P. J. (ed.): *The Oxford History of the British Empire*, vol. 2: *The Eighteenth Century* (Oxford, 1998).

Morgan, Prys: *A New History of Wales: The Eighteenth-Century Renaissance* (Llandybïe, 1981).

Newman, Gerald: *The Rise of English Nationalism: A Cultural History 1740–1830* (London, 1987).

Riley, P. W. J.: *The Union of England and Scotland* (Manchester, 1978).

Robertson, John (ed.): *A Union for Empire: Political Thought and the Union of 1707* (Cambridge, 1995).

Wilson, Kathleen: *The Sense of the People: Politics, Culture and Imperialism in England, 1715–1785* (Cambridge, 1995).

Chapter Twenty-Nine

Scotland and the Union

Alexander Murdoch

Eighteenth-century Britain arguably came into existence with the acceptance by the parliaments of Scotland and England of a Treaty of Union creating the kingdom of Great Britain with its parliament in London at Westminster. Under the terms of the treaty a judicial system was retained in Scotland in which some autonomy was devolved to the supreme courts of the ancient kingdom of Scotland meeting in Edinburgh, the Court of Session for civil cases and in criminal cases the Court of Justiciary, whose judges were drawn from the senior members of the Court of Session. The union was a wartime measure pursued by an English ministry intent on military success against absolutist France through its wars in Flanders in alliance with the Dutch Republic and the German states of the Holy Roman Empire. It was achieved despite considerable opposition in Scotland and great indifference in England because it was favoured by the monarch of both countries, Queen Anne, who was accepted by both Jacobite adherents of the Stuart dynasty and those who had opposed the loyalty to the Roman Catholic religion and the absolutist ambitions of her father, James II of England (but seventh of that title in Scotland). Leading members of the nobility in Scotland also perceived the possibilities for advancement in increased access to English office that union represented to them, and the young and intensely ambitious second duke of Argyll in particular became crucial to the success of union negotiations. Having the effrontery to offend the queen by the scale of his demands, which included a commission as a field marshal in the English army that was deferred and an English dukedom that was not, Argyll and his retinue of Campbells arrived in Edinburgh in 1705, marshalled the unicameral Scots parliament as if it were on parade, and got it to delegate to the crown the appointment of commissioners to negotiate the terms of union on behalf of Scotland rather than assert its own authority to do so. His role in persuading his great rival and possible claimant to the Scottish throne, the duke of Hamilton, to agree to this is still shrouded in mystery. Having informed the anti-union party that there would be no business of substance on 1 September 1705, Hamilton proceeded to move to a chamber dominated by astonished pro-union members that the queen appoint the Scottish commissioners for the latest round of negotiations for a parliamentary union (another round had preceded it in 1702–3).

The second duke of Argyll was able to treat Scotland like a satrap because he had inherited the political legacy of his family in the seventeenth century, when his great-grandfather the marquess of Argyll had become a leading member and at times *the* leading member of the Scottish Covenanting movement which in effect precipitated the English civil wars and caused the fall of Charles I. After many vicissitudes, Argyll's father had returned from Holland with William and Mary in 1688 and played a key role in ensuring that the Scottish crown was offered to them both in 1689. William had raised the then earl of Argyll to a dukedom in 1701, and his young sons (twenty-four and twenty) inherited his influence on his death in 1703. The second duke of Argyll was an arrogant aristocrat who, because of his family history, inherited the mantle of representing the political interest of the continuing Presbyterian Covenanting religious movement in Scotland which was strongest in the western Lowlands of the country. Due to the sectarian legacy of the seventeenth century, most of the rest of the Scottish nobility were Episcopalian and indeed, although tutored by Presbyterian ministers as boys, both the second duke of Argyll and his brother had been sent to Eton to help them place the wider claims of Presbyterianism to divine authority in a broader context. Under William II (as William III was in Scotland), the Church of Scotland was restored to a Presbyterianism that was related to the Covenanting Presbyterianism of the seventeenth century, without inheriting its broader ambitions to eliminate episcopacy throughout the British Isles, and the Campbells of Argyll had played an important role in that development. For the Church of Scotland, parliamentary union with the kingdom of England and Wales threatened ecclesiastical union with the Episcopalian Church of England. Once Argyll refused to act as its champion – other than to help arrange that the Scots parliament would pass an act guaranteeing the Presbyterian basis of the Church of Scotland before voting itself out of existence – the Covenanting Presbyterian legacy of the seventeenth century was sidelined in eighteenth-century Scotland, and it was the Campbell/Argyll interest which carried this out.

One man, or even one overmighty aristocratic interest, did not create the British state in 1707, but arguably the second duke of Argyll played a key role in preserving it in 1715. In the years following the union Scotland essentially was left to the administration of those who formerly had acted for the monarch there, led by politicians such as the duke of Queensberry, the earl of Mar and the second duke of Argyll's younger brother the earl of Ilay, who pursued politics while his brother followed his personal quest for military glory on the continent. Pro-union 'country' opposition politicians like George Baillie of Jerviswood were able to persuade the first parliament of Great Britain to abolish the privy council of Scotland on the grounds that it was not necessary in a united kingdom, but this was a ploy to weaken the influence of the politicians who dominated Scottish court politics rather than a coherent move towards administrative integration. Without a privy council in Scotland, the leading English ministers, Earl Godolphin and Robert Harley, tried to work with Scottish politicians resident in London who assured them of their ability to represent government authority in Scotland, principally for the purpose of ensuring the return of MPs at elections who were favourable to the existing ministry.

One major issue in the government of Scotland after the union was the acceptance of the English taxation system by the Scots under its terms. This involved the introduction of a much more bureaucratic system of tax collection whose purpose was the levying of significantly higher taxes than had been the case in Scotland since the Cromwellian union of the 1650s. The ministry in London tried to carry this out by working through the leading Scottish politicians, such as the duke of Montrose in Glasgow as well as Queensberry, Hamilton and Argyll. Their response was to distribute customs and excise posts as patronage in support of their political interest and their pursuit of influence at court in London. This helped in the return of pro-government MPs, but it failed absolutely in terms of establishing an efficient tax administration in Scotland. The new Court of Exchequer established in Edinburgh to help enforce the new revenue system did not operate with any efficiency, although a young English bureaucrat, John Scrope, who was sent to be its secretary, used the experience of over twenty years as a witness to maladministration in Scotland as the basis of his success in administering the British Treasury under Robert Walpole. Scotland immediately after the union, however, paid little tax. Otherwise, during the war years immediately after the union, Scotland was ignored by the now 'British' ministry in London and by the queen, who viewed its union with England as a desirable end in itself.

This changed with the prospect of peace in 1713. The ministry in London led by Harley, now earl of Oxford, was Tory-dominated and its supporters in parliament could not distinguish between the union and the integration of Scotland as a subordinate province of England, which was after all the precedent set by the incorporation of Wales into an essentially English polity in the sixteenth century. The failure to generate significant levels of tax revenue in Scotland did not go unnoticed in the House of Commons and led to the ministry's attempt to extend the full level of malt tax to Scotland, from which Scotland had been excused under Article XIII of the Treaty of Union. Article XIV had guaranteed that the malt tax would not be levied in Scotland 'during this present war', but left 'consideration of any Exemptions beyond what are already agreed on' to the determination of the parliament of Great Britain. The Scottish political nation united in fury at what was perceived as English oppression. Landowners in Scotland, whether Jacobite or Whig, were convinced that the introduction of a tax regime that had evolved for use in a far wealthier country would reduce Scotland to the status of an oppressed province or colony, and that the malt tax was the thin end of a wedge which would bankrupt their impoverished country. The economic improvement that had motivated many of those who supported the union was little in evidence by 1713, and to those who had supported it, including the Campbells, the earl of Mar and others, the proffered partnership in 1707 had led to subjugation by 1713. This provoked the motion to dissolve the union introduced by the Scots in the House of Lords in 1713, a move which failed by four votes, only after proxies were taken into account.

Politically Scotland remained a different country after the union, with the Whig and Tory politics of the English meaningless in a Scottish context. English high church Toryism was very different from the Scottish Jacobite Episcopal tradition, although the latter were intent on using their shared episcopacy as a weapon in their battle to counter the influence of the Covenanting Presbyterian tradition in Scotland and the Church of Scotland. It was difficult for Anglicans, who believed that the

Catholicism of the son of James II limited his sympathy for the cause of the Church of England, to understand the depth of the commitment to the Stuart dynasty of the Episcopalians of Scotland. This was demonstrated clearly by the Greenshields case of 1712, in which an Episcopalian minister had been imprisoned by the town council of Edinburgh on the grounds that the only publicly recognized form of worship in Scotland was the Presbyterian liturgy of the Church of Scotland. The Court of Session upheld the town council, but Greenshields's supporters appealed to the House of Lords in 1712, and the upper house asserted its jurisdiction as a court of final appeal in all civil cases in Britain, including those from Scottish courts. It ruled that Greenshields was within his rights and, providing an Episcopalian minister followed the Prayer Book of the Church of England and was willing to take the oath of loyalty to the crown, no bar could be put on his ability to hold worship publicly in Scotland. The case also set a pattern for the rest of the eighteenth century whereby important Scottish civil cases always went on appeal to a House of Lords in which understanding of Scots law was a scarce commodity. Interference in the legal system was another of the grievances of those Scots who voted to end the union in the House of Lords in 1713.

This was the background to the Jacobite rebellion in Scotland of 1715 following the accession of George, elector of Hanover, as king of Great Britain in 1714. The rebellion was led by the earl of Mar, who had been pro-union in 1707 but had supported the attempt to end the union in 1713. He had played a role in Scottish government at various times following the union, most recently in the government led by Robert Harley (later earl of Oxford) from 1710 to 1713. George I, however, had been advised against him and literally turned his back on him when he appeared at court. Mar's response was to leave London and travel to northeast Scotland in order to raise the Stuart standard, bearing the legend 'No Union' in August 1715. The resulting encounter was a civil war in Scotland, resolved by belated intervention from England.

The second duke of Argyll acted as commander-in-chief of the government forces in Scotland and managed to concentrate the small number of government troops available in the country at Stirling to prevent the larger Jacobite army from breaking out into the Lowlands and beyond. When Mar attempted to outflank him by sending a detachment of Highlanders, under the command of John Macintosh, across the Forth estuary in order to capture Edinburgh from the east, Argyll managed to mount enough infantry to join his few dragoons in a race from Stirling to the capital which just managed to outface Macintosh, whose force ended up marching south to join the small Jacobite force in the north of England. At Sheriffmuir, outside Stirling, in November 1715 Argyll managed to force a draw with a Jacobite force three times as large, but was sacked by the government early in 1716 on suspicion of favouring amnesty for the rebels after General Cadogan had arrived in Scotland with Dutch troops (which were provided under the terms of the British alliance with the United Provinces of the Netherlands).

The aftermath of the rebellion of 1715 in Scotland did not witness large-scale reprisals against the Jacobites. A substantial number of the leadership in the Highlands and the Lowlands had their lands confiscated by the crown, but those Scots suspected of attempting to take advantage of the situation to further their careers as Hanoverian loyalists, such as Patrick Haldane of Gleneagles, quickly found themselves ostracized by the rest of the Highland elite. The York Building Company of London purchased forfeited Scottish estates as an investment, but found that it was impossible to manage the estates without recourse to local elites who favoured the preservation of the interests of the former owners. Nevertheless, by the time Sir Robert Walpole set about consolidating his power at the Treasury, he soon turned his attention to the problem of integrating Scotland fiscally if not socially. He was ably abetted by the former secretary of the Court of Exchequer in Scotland, John Scrope, now at the Treasury in London. Walpole's starting point of poor tax returns turned his attention to the growing Scottish involvement in the tobacco trade with the British colonies in America. This led to an attempted restructuring of the customs establishment that would bring more experienced English officers into Scottish posts. In the short term this ended the pervasive fraud that had categorized the service in Scotland. The Disarming Act of 1716 has often been associated with fear of Jacobitism, but Walpole and the Campbells used it to clear the way for the establishment in Scotland of what amounted to a garrison under the Irish Protestant, General Wade, that would help ensure that the government could make its writ run in most if not all of the country.

In 1725 Walpole was ready to move on the issue of the malt tax which had almost destroyed the union in 1713. Walpole's proposals were to levy the tax at a reduced level in Scotland, but to refuse to concede that a tax could be levied in England only. It was an issue which presaged later and larger conflicts elsewhere in what became the British empire during the eighteenth century. When the existing Scottish administrative and legal establishment refused to implement the policy, because of its unpopularity in Scotland, they were sacked and replaced with the followers of the duke of Argyll, whose younger brother the earl of Ilay came to Scotland personally to work with Wade and the new Scottish lord advocate, Duncan Forbes of Inverness, to consolidate government authority in the country. The office of secretary of state for Scotland was abolished, but Ilay received high office additional to those he already held, and his elder brother received the promise of still more military honours.

The relationship between the Argathelians, as the followers of the duke of Argyll were known in Scotland, and Walpole's ministry was not entirely a one-sided one, as the Campbells argued for investment in and development of Scotland coincident with greater integration, as well as demanding high office for themselves. Their role in Scottish politics was not unlike that of the Irish 'undertakers' who managed the parliament of Ireland during the Walpole years, but arguably they were more successful in promoting Scottish national interests within a British union than the Irish undertakers were in defending Irish interests outside it. This is not to argue that the Campbells were altruistic, although the combination of patriotism and self-interest is not unknown in British history. They had befriended the financial expert John Law when in Edinburgh to promote the union, encouraged him then, and continued to be in contact with him during his heady career in France, the lessons of which they attempted to apply in Scotland. Walpole cannily channelled them in that direction in order to limit their potential importance in a British context.

Walpole authorized the establishment in Scotland of a Board of Trustees for the Encouragement of Fisheries and Manufactures, dominated by Argathelian lawyers, who were to administer funds promised for economic development at the time of the union under Article XV, but not released by the Treasury until 1727. He also obtained legislation for the foundation under parliamentary charter of the Royal Bank of Scotland, which was capitalized by the so-called 'Equivalent debentures' issued by the Treasury after the union to those who had claims for compensation under its terms (shareholders in the former Company of Scotland Trading to Africa and the Indies, for example), but who were unable to obtain cash payment after 1707. It was the foundation of a modern Scottish system of banking whose purpose was to make maximum credit available for economic expansion in Scotland. While the Campbells sought to maximize their political influence through expanding their financial power, they also attracted a broad spectrum of support in all parts of Scotland drawn from landed gentry, professionals and merchants who sought to promote the economic development of the country within the union. It was also in many ways the beginning of the Scottish enlightenment.

Economic improvement was limited in Scotland after 1725 despite the initiatives made in government subsidies and the development of banking facilities. As the Walpole regime became more unpopular, so the opposition to the Argathelians in Scotland grew, both on the part of the Jacobites and the so-called Squadrone Whigs (strongest in the area around Edinburgh) who favoured even greater integration with England. In 1737 the duke of Argyll and his brother broke over the issue of government reprisals in Scotland following the so-called Porteous Riots in Edinburgh, which demonstrated the fragility of administrative and legal authority even in Scotland's capital. Argyll's accession to the opposition in parliament gave them a powerful addition of strength, and, despite his younger brother's efforts to maintain government influence, a majority of Scottish MPs returned in the general election of 1741 supported the opposition to Walpole and played a key role in forcing him from power. Shortly afterwards Argyll died, his ideas of a 'broad-bottom' coalition government unable to transcend the continuing influence of Jacobitism on politics. The uneasy alliance of former members of Walpole's government and opposition Whigs was unstable, although the Scottish opposition Whigs insisted on reviving the office of secretary of state for Scotland. The occupant, the marquess of Tweeddale, had no idea of how Scottish government beyond Edinburgh worked, and he increasingly lapsed into inactivity while the government became preoccupied with prosecuting the war with Spain and France that had contributed to Walpole's downfall.

Thus, the Jacobite rebellion of 1745 in Scotland occurred in a political vacuum. Remembering his elder brother's treatment during the 1715 rebellion, the third duke of Argyll, as the former earl of Ilay now was, left Scotland for the court in London. Tweeddale, as secretary of state in London, did nothing. Only Andrew Fletcher, nephew of the famous Scottish patriot (who sat in the Scottish law courts under the judicial title of Lord Milton), continued to represent civil authority in Scotland by gathering intelligence through the network of Argathelian political contacts that continued to exist throughout the country. The third duke of Argyll's former colleagues in the Walpole ministry, particularly the duke of Newcastle and the earl of Hardwicke, blamed him for the collapse of Hanoverian Scotland, as did the former Scottish Squadrone opposition Whigs, who argued that the success of the Jacobites was an indictment of the Campbells' long years of supremacy in Scottish politics. When the rebellion was suppressed finally, it was at the hands of an army of veteran regiments returned from the front in Europe under the leadership of George II's son, the duke of Cumberland. Victory at Culloden led to the government army acting as an army of occupation, with the Highlands bearing the brunt of the defeat, but with all Scots, including Whigs, sharing in the national stigma of rebellion.

The Walpole Whigs within the ministry, led by Henry Pelham, completed the expulsion of the former members of the opposition early in 1746. Pelham and his colleagues were convinced that Walpole had made a mistake in relying so completely on the Argathelian political interest in Scotland, and he returned to the earlier policy of attempting to work with both Argathelian and Squadrone Whigs. Lord Chancellor Hardwicke embarked on a major reform of the Scottish legal system (in violation of the Treaty of Union), convinced that its shortcomings had been responsible for the initial success of the Jacobite rebellion. The third duke of Argyll, now over seventy, acted as a representative of the old Scottish polity, defending the integrity of the Scottish legal system. The old Argyll interest was the only political interest which operated across all of Scotland, although equally in all of Scotland there were those who resented its pervasive influence, whether they were Jacobites or Squadrone Whigs. Argyll and Milton began to recruit younger lawyers, ministers of religion, politicians and merchants to the idea of countering the effects of the rebellion by attempting another effort at national economic improvement. By 1752 these efforts bore fruit in government legislation to establish a commission based in Edinburgh to administer the larger estates confiscated from Jacobites after the rebellion. Its purpose was to run the estates as models of agrarian commercial improvement in the hope that this would provide a lead for those landowners in Scotland who had not yet begun to try to reorganize their estates on a more commercial basis.

Although the achievements of the commission were limited, it set a lead, supported by the Scottish financial system, that did finally bring about significant gains for the Scottish economy, which was also stimulated by the Seven Years' War from 1756 to 1763. One neglected impact of the decision to annex the larger Jacobite estates was that the British Treasury took responsibility for their debts, and the large payments to the creditors of the Perth and Lovat estates in 1759 (£70,000 sterling) and 1770 (£72,000 sterling) put as much capital into the underdeveloped Scottish economy as the compensation paid by the British Treasury (£164,000 sterling) for the heritable jurisdictions abolished by the act of parliament introduced by Lord Chancellor Hardwicke in 1748. Of much greater economic value, however, was the decision of the French Farmers' General Tobacco monopoly to source almost all of its tobacco through Scottish merchants despite, or perhaps because of, the fact that France was at war with Britain in 1742–8 and 1756–63. They paid cash worth more than £100,000 sterling per annum through the Edinburgh merchant bank of William Alexander, backed by the Royal Bank of Scotland. These payments, even more than the money from the British Treasury after 1745, helped to provide the capital which began the economic development of Scotland that Scottish Unionists had hoped for fifty years previously.

By 1763 agrarian improvements had begun to make as much impact on the Scottish economy as the tobacco trade, although there was a postwar depression which led to high levels of emigration from the west of Scotland and the Highlands. The war had been ended by a ministry led by the third earl of Bute, a Scottish aristocrat who was the nephew of the second and third dukes of Argyll. They had acted as his guardians after his father's early death and had directed his education at Eton and Utrecht in the Netherlands. Bute had married Mary Wortley Montagu, heiress to one of the largest fortunes in Britain, and had become attached to the court of the Prince of Wales in the 1750s, thus becoming associated with the opposition to the ministries led first by Henry Pelham and then by Pelham's elder brother, the duke of Newcastle. Bute also became responsible for the education of the Prince of Wales's son George after the death of the prince in 1751. By late 1760 young George was king, and his former tutor was not only one of the wealthiest men in Britain but also at the centre of political power at court. In 1761 he became a secretary of state and in 1762 he succeeded the duke of Newcastle as first lord of the Treasury. By 1763, however, he had been hounded from office at almost the very hour of the conclusion of a peace that marked the end of a victorious war.

Bute had been educated by his uncles to perceive himself as a Briton, an apotheosis his uncle the second duke of Argyll achieved with his burial and memorial in Westminster Abbey. He had joined the opposition to Walpole as a young man in the 1730s and retreated to his estate in Scotland, only leaving with the outbreak of the Jacobite rebellion in 1745. He taught the future George III also to perceive of himself as a Briton, only to find that he himself was widely denounced as a Scot. As he became more powerful between 1761 and 1763, so resentment of his position as a political interloper grew, and this increasingly found expression in terms of national prejudice. Although resentment at Bute's rise to power within parliament was substantial, it was greater 'out-of-doors' in the expanding urban areas in England where many craftsmen and shopkeepers without the vote had acquired enough substance to aspire to a role in politics. This opposition came to perceive of Bute as a crypto-Jacobite interloper intent on undermining the liberties enshrined in the English constitution. It was no accident that John Wilkes's opposition periodical was called the *North Briton*, or that issue 45, attacking Bute's influence, acquired particular resonance in opposition politics. The fact that Bute's surname was Stuart also contributed to the anti-Scottish hysteria, which later extended to the duke of Newcastle's former protégé, Lord Mansfield, an English judge of Scottish birth from a family (Murray) with many Jacobite connections, even though Mansfield himself had little or no political connection with Bute.

Although national prejudice had something to do with the opposition Bute encountered, and although it can now be established that his ambitions were as modest as his ability, he was a royal favourite who had no connection with parliament other than through the king. (Under the terms of the Treaty of Union throughout the eighteenth century the Scottish nobility elected sixteen of their number to represent them in the House of Lords – Bute had served as one of these representatives in the parliament of 1727–34 and he returned to the House of Lords in 1761 after the accession of George III.) The anti-Scottish climate in the politics of the 1760s, however, had the effect of driving almost all Scots out of any significant role in British politics for two decades. The Scottish nobility who had long looked to an expanded field of ambition and endeavour in a new British state now returned to their estates in Scotland intent on maximizing their commercial potential. They sought to expand their own income and to develop the Scottish economy in an endeavour which justifies the term 'agrarian patriotism'.

It was this period that witnessed the great achievements of the Scottish enlightenment. The Scottish nobility returned to seek common cause with an urban professional and mercantile elite that had grown in wealth and confidence over the course of the century, and in particular in the decades following the Jacobite rebellion of 1745. The experience of what amounted to military occupation led to a determination to increase the country's wealth, its cultural standing and, ultimately, its role in the British state. Led by a 'Moderate' party in the Church of Scotland that sought to ally itself with the landowners of the country in modernizing not just the church but society itself, the Scottish universities and the intellectuals associated with them such as David Hume and Adam Smith confronted the problems of economic and social development from a cosmopolitan rather than a nationalist perspective. Their legacy in Scotland was a willingness to confront social change whatever the costs, which by the early nineteenth century would prove to be substantial, but in the eighteenth century they transformed the landscape and productivity of the countryside, while constructing idealized New Town urban environments across Lowland Scotland to house the beneficiaries of change.

Eventually, economic improvement and cultural enlightenment led to a revival of Scottish participation in a British state which, by the last two decades of the eighteenth century, had emphatically become imperial. The personification of this integration – a generation after it had been impossible for Lord Bute to achieve it – was Henry Dundas, a member of an Edinburgh legal family who had long been prominent in the opposition to the Argyll interest. Family influence had obtained high Scottish legal office for him at an early age (he was lord advocate of Scotland by the age of thirty), but it was his friendship with the wealthy Scottish peer the duke of Buccleuch, a pupil of Adam Smith, that gave him the backing to bring him to the attention of the Westminster government as a potential political manager or undertaker of Scotland. Buccleuch was the grandson of the second duke of Argyll, through his mother, and, like his mother's cousin the earl of Bute, he married into the wealthy English Montagu family. Unlike Bute, Buccleuch chose to make Scotland his principal country of residence for the rest of his life, remaining close to his tutor Adam Smith. Henry Dundas, from the first arrival of Buccleuch in Scotland at the age of twenty-one, became the duke's close collaborator and he eventually, in 1776, helped him to obtain high civil office for Adam Smith in the form of an appointment as one of the commissioners of customs in Scotland.

In London Dundas soon attracted the attention of William Pitt the Younger, or rather William Pitt attracted the attention of Dundas just as the North ministry was breaking up following the debacle of the American War of 1775–83. It was Dundas who early identified Pitt as a possible prime minister and it was Dundas, almost alone, who spoke in Pitt's defence in the House of Commons in 1783–4, during Pitt's beleaguered first ministry, when the rest of the cabinet sat in the House of Lords. The general election of 1784 was as much a triumph for Dundas in Scotland as it was for Pitt in Britain as a whole, with an emphatic return to the situation where Scotland returned a pronounced majority of pro-government MPs. Dundas rose through government ranks to a place in the cabinet as home secretary and later, first lord of the Admiralty, acquiring in addition a particular expertise in Indian affairs as president of the Board of Control for India. Indeed, at one point Dundas was a prime candidate for office as viceroy of India, but persuaded Lord Cornwallis to accept that place instead. By 1798 Dundas had emerged as the architect of the campaign for the British union with Ireland which created the United Kingdom in 1801. He was convinced that the union of England with Scotland had created a template that would allow Britain to use union with Ireland to solve the increasingly intractable problems of Irish affairs. Dundas was wrong, but at the time he appeared right, and his advocacy of Catholic emancipation not just in Ireland but for the whole of what became the United Kingdom established his genuine claim to statesmanship.

In the meantime, the growing movement for the reform of the British constitution had not been without influence in Scotland. What is not often grasped by outside observers is that reform was a British issue which, because of the particularities of the Treaty of Union, had a very specific Scottish context. At first, reform in Scotland took as its objective the reformation of the Scottish franchise, exceptionally narrow even by British standards, at least from the perspective of the end of the century. From 1784 an annual convention to promote the cause of reforming the feudal constitutions of the royal burghs of Scotland met in Edinburgh. By 1792, following events in France, the Association of the Friends of the People in Scotland was formed in Edinburgh, mirroring developments in England without exactly following them. By 1796 the United Scotsmen, patterned on the United Irishmen, were meeting in Scotland, establishing an alternative point of reference that would resonate in Scotland far beyond the eighteenth century in establishing a distinctive radical political tradition in Scotland.

Yet the reform movement in Scotland never really challenged the old regime, in part because of the latter's success in keeping control of the constitutional agenda from 1707 right to the end of the eighteenth century. Ownership of land and influence over the courts meeting in Edinburgh continued to be at the centre of the Scottish constitution. After 1792 in particular the urban professional and mercantile class were no longer satisfied with subordinate status, although they sought common cause with the landed class when the weight of the political demands of the 'people below' – the artisans and farm labourers – began to be felt in Scottish politics. The Scottish aristocracy who made the union were not finished, but their time was coming. By the end of the eighteenth century, along with the middle classes that had flourished in part because of their largesse, they sought to perpetuate the influence of an enlightenment in Scotland that had reached eventide. The cause of meaningful Scottish integration in a greater Britain would in future be pursued by the Scottish Whigs, who would spend a generation in opposition to the old regime in Scotland as represented by the Dundas family before finally achieving government office in 1832, bringing the reform ideology of the 1790s to bear on the vastly different circumstances of an emerging industrialized society in the 1830s, with political consequences that would create an entirely new series of issues in Scottish public life in the mid-nineteenth century.

FURTHER READING

Devine, T. M. and Young, J. R. (eds): *Eighteenth-Century Scotland: New Perspectives* (East Linton, East Lothian, 1999).

Fry, Michael: *The Dundas Despotism* (Edinburgh, 1992).

Kidd, Colin: *Subverting Scotland's Past: Scottish Whig Historians and the Creation of an Anglo-British Identity, 1689–c.1830* (Cambridge, 1993).

McFarland, E. W.: *Ireland and Scotland in the Age of Revolution* (Edinburgh, 1994).

McIntosh, John R.: *Church and Theology in Enlightenment Scotland: The Popular Party, 1740–1800* (East Linton, East Lothian, 1998).
Mackillop, Andrew: *'More Fruitful Than The Soil': Army, Empire and the Scottish Highlands, 1715–1815* (East Linton, East Lothian, 2000).
Murdoch, Alexander: *'The People Above': Politics and Administration in Mid-Eighteenth-Century Scotland* (Edinburgh, 1980).
Riley, P. W. J.: *The English Ministers and Scotland 1707–1727* (London, 1964).
Robertson, John: *The Scottish Enlightenment and the Militia Issue* (Edinburgh, 1985).
Robertson, John (ed.): *A Union for Empire: Political Thought and the Union of 1707* (Cambridge, 1995).
Shaw, John Stuart: *The Management of Scottish Society, 1707–1764* (Edinburgh, 1983).
Shaw, John Stuart: *The Political History of Eighteenth-Century Scotland* (Basingstoke, 1999).
Sher, Richard B.: *Church and University in the Scottish Enlightenment: The Moderate Literati of Edinburgh* (Princeton, NJ, 1985).
Sunter, Ronald M.: *Patronage and Politics in Scotland 1707–1832* (Edinburgh, 1986).
Whatley, Christopher A.: *Scottish Society 1707–1830* (Manchester, 2000).

Chapter Thirty

Wales in the Eighteenth Century

Geraint H. Jenkins

The beauty of eighteenth-century Wales lies in the eye of the beholder. Fifty years ago, most Welsh history was reckoned to be of marginal importance and Georgian Wales stirred hardly any passions. Echoing many of the xenophobic and negative stereotypes so assiduously cultivated by eighteenth-century celtophobes, historians depicted Wales in the most unflattering light. By general consensus, it was a quiescent backwater, comatized by economic inertia and dominated by a unified and unchanging landed caste. Since 98 per cent of the population were disenfranchised, there was no 'Welsh question' or any possibility of contesting English hegemony. The moribund established church, an unloved institution staffed by absentee prelates and their favourites, awaited the trumpet call of Methodism. The administrative and political integration of Wales into the English state in 1536–43, an initiative compounded by the abolition of the Council of Wales and the Marches in 1689 and the determination to undermine the Courts of Great Sessions, meant that even the most fervent cultural patriots were unable to create distinctive national institutions and, as a result, any worthwhile intellectual endeavour was confined to expatriates in London.

Mercifully, two generations of historical revisionism have opened up new fields of investigation and changed our perception and appreciation of this period. A remarkable upsurge of interest in social history has created a more generous and cheerful picture. Moreover, whereas in the past the Welsh experience was judged against the English model, recent constitutional changes and the new demands of the postcolonial era have led to a major re-examination of 'Britishness' as a cultural issue and a greater appreciation of the complex realities of multiple identities. In short, there are good reasons for telling the story from the point of view of the Celtic nations rather than through the distorting prism of anglocentric perspectives. Not least among these reasons is the opportunity to highlight internal differences, the distinctive features of Welsh society, and the 'otherness' of Wales.

It seems logical to begin with numbers. Owing to the lack of hard data in the pre-census period, little serious attention has been given to the historical demography of eighteenth-century Wales. Preliminary studies, however, suggest that John Rickman's calculations significantly underestimated the scale of population growth. Following fitful growth during the first half-century, a striking upturn occurred from the mid-1740s. Over the century as a whole, numbers increased from *c*.390,000 in 1700 to 601,000 in 1801. If the causes of population growth in Wales continue to puzzle historians and if the rate of growth was unimpressive in a European context, the appreciable upward trend after 1750 was nevertheless a significant turning-point in a pre-industrial economy which had formerly been so vulnerable to devastating mortality crises caused by harvest failures and killing diseases such as smallpox, typhus and diphtheria, which nourished the melancholy preoccupation with death in the literature of the age. Although epidemic diseases continued to prune local populations, as the economy grew stronger rising birth rates set the pace. Dense concentrations of populations emerged in the fertile low-lying valleys, on the coast, and in burgeoning industrial parishes in Glamorgan, Denbighshire and Flintshire. In some advanced parts of Wales the average mean household size increased from 4.4 in the 1680s to 5.5 by the 1790s. It is worth emphasizing here that one of the results of population growth was a marked increase in the number of Welsh speakers. By 1801, nine of every ten inhabitants were still monoglot Welsh to all intents and purposes, and both to insiders and outsiders the native tongue was the most tangible badge of difference. It is no accident that eighteenth-century tracts, squibs and caricatures depicted 'Poor Taffy' as a derisory figure whose devotion to the 'Gibberish of Taphydome' was as incomprehensible as his fondness for the ancient pedigrees, leeks and cheese of 'Goatlandshire'.

Even the traditionally robust landed gentry were vulnerable to demographic quirks and one of the most popular topics of conversation in drawing rooms and salons was the prevailing biological defect which rendered Welsh landowners barren of male heirs, the result of which was a proliferation in most Welsh counties of Welsh heiresses whose hands were swiftly taken in marriage by English and Scottish magnates. The gentry had never formed a rigid caste, but the general trend was for native landed families to slip down the social scale rather than climb upwards. Laid low by crippling mortgages, improvidence, heavy drinking, bad luck (as well as biological failures), they suffered the indignity of losing their foothold in the upper echelons of society. The principal beneficiaries were the substantial landlords who, by a variety of legal and illegal stratagems, assimilated other estates and employed non-Welsh-speaking stewards and agents to fortify their grip on the lives of increasingly beleaguered tenant farmers. Land gravitated into the hands of a small number of absentee 'Leviathans' or 'petty princes' whose annual incomes yielded anything between £2,000 and £5,000. Such behemoths were very different from the native-born *uchelwyr* whose local esteem since Tudor times had been based on a reputable ancestry, *noblesse oblige*, and a deep sense of responsibility for the social and cultural well-being of their communities. In the 1770s Thomas Pennant lamented the proliferation of deserted mansions swallowed by Welsh Leviathans, and by the end of the century large numbers of commentators mourned the passing of the old patriarchs and deplored the influence and behaviour of parasitic absentee landlords who entrusted the management of their estates to unscrupulous resident stewards and who privately and publicly derided the plebeian culture of the mountain Welsh. A yawning gulf had emerged between the new landed Titans bearing such un-Welsh names as Bute, Campbell, Douglas-Pennant, Plymouth, Stanley and Talbot and the smaller squires, and by the period of the Napoleonic Wars the firing of hayricks and game heaths, as well as corn and anti-enclosure riots, were indications of mounting discontent and anger among farmers and poor people. Insecurity of tenure, substantial rent increases and a general perception that the Welsh were a disinherited people fuelled this resentment.

New patterns of ownership, the advance of trade, the growth of urban communities and the commercialization of leisure led to the emergence of a diverse group of middling sorts who, although numerically small, exercised a growing influence on urban and cultural life. Shopkeepers, merchants, civil servants, surgeons, clergymen, attorneys, excisemen, schoolmasters and ship's captains were clearly in no position to challenge the socio-economic supremacy of the gentry, but, by hobnobbing diligently and wisely with the privileged elite and by investing their money carefully, they acquired modest property and filled their homes with such luxury items as books, clocks, china, looking-glasses and paintings. As the pace of the economy quickened and social life became more lively and diverse, there were new opportunities for industrious people with distinctive identities and ideologies. Their material aspirations were matched by their desire to effect cultural improvements and, although some of those who ventured to the metropolis to make their fortunes became anglicized lotus-eaters (or 'Dic Siôn Dafyddion' in Welsh parlance), most of them readily identified themselves with the native culture and were instrumental in advancing Welsh-language religious and educational causes and in promoting the printed word as the key to civility and cultural renewal. The dispiriting dearth of influential cultural institutions made the middling sorts all the more determined to don the mantle of the old gentry families as the true guardians of Welsh society.

Important though the middling sorts were, it is a commonplace that Wales was a land of small farmers and labourers and that the state of its agricultural base was of critical significance to the economy. Most Welsh people were dependent on the soil for their living and, although large tracts of open and waste land remained unenclosed, the general pattern was of tenant farmers with holdings of around fifty acres. The economic fortunes of these smallholders were determined by the accident of geography, terrain, climate and the disposition of their landlords. Sheep and cattle rearing provided the mainstay of the economy and drovers who shepherded thousands of beasts to be fattened on pastures in the midlands and sold in London were key middle men. In general, agricultural progress remained slow and piecemeal during the first half of the century, but improvements were swiftly stimulated by demographic and urban growth and by the accumulation of capital in trade and industry. In the progressive parts of Glamorgan and along the Welsh Marches the Norfolk crop rotation system prevailed, and a substantial increase occurred in the use of lime and the planting of turnips and potatoes. From 1755 onwards the county agricultural societies revised the profile of scientific methods of cultivation and spirited improvers such as Thomas Johnes of Hafod (Cards.) and Alexander Maddocks at Traeth Mawr (Caerns.) spent enormous sums of money in a bid to transform the rural environment. It is a mistake, however, to exaggerate the extent of agricultural progress. There were sharp contrasts between the rugged upland fastnesses, where wheeled traffic, if it existed at all, moved at a snail's pace, and the more fertile and affluent lowland plains. Small farmers lacked the necessary capital to effect improvements and since most of them were tenants rather than owner-occupiers there was little incentive to farm efficiently. There are good grounds for believing that in many counties the word improvement was a catch-all euphemism for the imposition of annual tenancies, rack-renting and the enclosure of hill and moorland terrain, all of which were detrimental to the interests of farmers, cottagers and squatters.

The lower orders, as might be expected, were perennially vulnerable to the effects of demographic growth, employment fluctuations, high food prices and the loss of customary rights. It used to be thought that the labouring and dependent poor were so deeply rooted in their own communities that they were reluctant to travel far from the narrow confines of their place of birth. But abundant evidence exists of considerable mobility on the part of craftsmen, artisans, labourers, garden girls and weeders, especially during years of harvest failure, dearth and high prices. The lot of those at the bottom of the heap was particularly hazardous and, as the old sense of paternalism and mutual dependence withered from the 1770s onwards, expenditure on poor relief rocketed dramatically. The total annual expenditure on the poor rose from £10,529 in 1748–50 to £154,802 in 1803. The upshot was that parishes rooted out beggars, strollers and vagabonds, and went to some pains to ensure that they were brutally escorted to their place of legal settlement. The propensity for violence among the lower orders was just as evident in the multitude of bawdy, boisterous and cruel recreations that were so roundly condemned by Methodist killjoys. Belief in the power of the occult continued to provide the most popular and convincing explanation for the daily misfortunes and brutalities which befell those who dwelt in 'habitations of wretchedness', and the 'sour spirit' of religious reformers proved no match for the ingenious army of cunning men, white witches and astrologers who served the needs of common people with great skill and panache. Over the century as a whole, there occurred a decline in the warmth of natural affection. As a result, there were few practical safety nets for working people and paupers at the base of society.

Although town and countryside were still clearly dependent on one another, more attention is now being paid to the manner in which Welsh towns shed their rural ambience as a result of demographic growth, improved communications and regional specialization. It is certainly true that in terms of population and wealth Wales was dwarfed by London, that even its largest towns never approached the size of the surrogate Welsh cities of Liverpool, Chester, Shrewsbury and Bristol, that even as late as 1801 less than 15 per cent of the total population lived in towns of over a thousand inhabitants, and that Aberystwyth was larger than Cardiff. But over the course of the century the urban profile of Wales changed markedly as towns began to sport prosperous gentry and middling sorts and to fulfil vital commercial, industrial and social functions. The most appreciable demographic developments occurred in industrial communities, all of which had their own specialisms (iron, copper, lead, coal, brass). In Glamorgan the sprawling parish of Merthyr Tydfil, the cradle of the iron industry, boasted a population of 7,700 by 1801, while Swansea, which combined a taste for fashion with industrial prowess (exemplified in the proximity of bathing machines on its well-appointed beaches to toxic fumes emanating from its remarkable copper-smelting works), became the first industrial urban community of consequence during the second half of the century. In northeast Wales the brass and copper works of Holywell were reckoned to be superior to any in Britain, while Wrexham, the most populous town in north Wales, was a busy, extensive and well-built town. Carmarthen acquired a reputation for turbulence on account of its flourishing printing press, radical academy, pockets of Jacobitism and fractious political disputes between the Blues and the Reds. Along the coastline maritime activity quickened as vessels extended their voyages to North America and the Caribbean as well as to western Europe, and the prospering slave trade, together with technological developments, enabled the woollen town of Newtown to become known as 'the Leeds of Wales'. The proliferation of tourist resorts and spa towns attracted visitors in growing numbers, and the building of elegant and innovative town halls, assembly rooms and villas designed by professional architects, the most gifted of whom was John Nash at Carmarthen, was testament to growing civic pride as well as economic expansion.

As the century unfolded, Wales's sluggish industrial economy also embarked on a process of improvement which culminated in the emergence of some of the most dynamic and innovative enterprises in the world. Indeed, a new Welsh identity was forged based on entrepreneurial capitalism and industrial prowess. The diffusion of new technology, the inflow of merchant capitalism, improvements in communications and the demands of successive continental wars accelerated the pace of industrial change. Even the most unfashionable counties experienced significant economic change. The discovery of rich veins of lead in rural Cardiganshire prompted the hard-nosed surveyor Lewis Morris to dub the county the 'Cambrian Peru', while in distant Anglesey Thomas Williams, a solicitor from Llanidan, became a millionaire following the extraordinary excavation and shipping of high-quality copper ore at Parys Mountain, near Amlwch, an open cast mine memorably depicted by the artist Julius Caesar Ibbetson. Even as early as the 1730s, partly as a result of Sir Humphrey Mackworth's remarkable entrepreneurship in iron, coal and copper in the Neath area, Swansea had become a major European metallurgical centre which, by 1800, supplied 90 per cent of Britain's copper requirements. Prolonged and costly wars, fuelled by the deeply rooted fear of Catholicism, led to remarkable developments at Bersham in northeast Wales and along the northern rim of the south Wales coalfield, where the manufacture of cannon and of cylinders for the steam engines of Boulton and Watt filled the personal coffers of modernizing families like the Bacons, Crawshays, Guests and Wilkinsons. In 1803 it was confidently claimed that the Cyfarthfa ironworks at Merthyr was the largest in the world. The 'flaming labyrinths' which constituted the four giant ironworks – Cyfarthfa, Dowlais, Plymouth and Penydarren – acquired an iconic significance in Welsh labour history. The sheer scale of some of these advanced capitalist enterprises was unmatched in the rest of Britain and helped Wales to acquire a deserved reputation for industrial modernity.

If their attention has only recently been engaged by the foregoing socio-economic changes, historians have long been familiar (perhaps even obsessed) with the role that religion played in eighteenth-century life. As Welsh bibliographies amply reveal, few subjects have commanded their attention as much as the rise of Methodism. Indeed, one of the most persistent historical myths is the notion that Wales experienced a 'Great Awakening' that transformed the spiritual life of the nation. This simplistic one-dimensional view, however, has been abandoned by most reputable writers for at least three reasons. First, to attribute the coming of Methodism to the intervention of Providence is to circumvent our responsibility to discover deep underlying causes. Second, the portrait of the pre-Methodist age as one of unrelieved spiritual torpor ignores or underplays the assiduous labour of previous generations of Anglicans, Puritans and Dissenters, all of whom were just as capable of stoking up the fires of revivalism. Third, it is abundantly clear that the growth of Methodism was so slow and piecemeal that it could not possibly have taken Wales by storm. The most sensible approach is to view Methodism, in so far as it represented a new form of personal commitment, as the ultimate fulfilment within the established church of the Welsh Protestant faith first introduced in the Elizabethan period. After all, Methodism was a church within a church and not until the 1790s did there emerge a desire to prise it from the stubborn grip of its deeply loyalist and hidebound leaders.

By the 1730s the reputation of the established church was deeply tarnished not simply by the abuses caused by the maldistribution of wealth, but also by the apparent desire of its leaders to de-Cymricize the institution even though the overwhelming majority of Anglican communicants were Welsh-speaking. While English-speaking Wesleyan Methodists from England were prone to refer to the benighted Welsh as if they were Cherokee Indians, one of the great assets of Welsh Calvinistic Methodism was that it was very much 'of the people'. Boldly led by young and attractive evangelists – Howell Harris, self-styled commander-in-chief, Daniel Rowland, pulpit preacher *par excellence*, and William Williams of Pantycelyn, the legendary 'Sweet Singer' whose hymns conveyed the intense enthusiasm which lay at the heart of Methodism – the movement prospered best in Welsh-speaking mid- and southwest Wales, where the Welsh circulating schools were most numerous. Its principal epicentre was Llangeitho (Cards.), where Rowland's emotional preaching precipitated remarkable Pentecostal scenes. A network of societies, which attracted modestly well-to-do, self-improving young farmers and craftsmen, helped to consolidate the faith of the twice-born and met the spiritual and psychological needs of those who yearned for effective pastoral care. Some interesting recent work on shifting gender identities in Wales has confirmed that pious young women discovered new niches of opportunity within these cells. Yet even though the leaders drove themselves to the point of exhaustion in their determination to bring Satan's kingdom tumbling down, they were given a dusty reception in north Wales. Riven by personal antagonisms and factionalism, the movement might easily have foundered after 1750, when the disgraced Harris (to some degree the victim of a smear campaign) retreated to his 'monastery' at Trefeca, had not Rowland established his authority, triggered off a major revival at Llangeitho in 1762, and most of all, won the heart of Thomas Charles, who turned Bala into a major fiefdom of Methodism and the Sunday school movement in north Wales. Ironically, though, in the long run Charles was primarily responsible for cutting the umbilical cord that had bound Methodism to the mother church. How the founding fathers must have shivered in their graves.

A precondition for the emergence and relative success of revivalist movements was the growth of literacy. It is a matter for regret that the extraordinary success of the Welsh-medium peripatetic schools established between 1731 and 1776 by Griffith Jones, Llanddowror, and his doting benefactress Madam Bridget Bevan of Laugharne have escaped the notice of scholars outside Wales. As rector of Llanddowror (Carms.), Jones initially committed himself to a programme of reform and renewal based on charity school teaching, itinerant preaching and at least tacit support for the early Methodists. But as he entered middle age he abandoned the discredited English-medium tuition based on the 'three Rs' in SPCK schools and established a remarkably flexible and effective Welsh-medium system of circulating schools for the benefit of the 'vulgar sorts', both young and old. Formidably hard-working, Griffith Jones succeeded in gaining the munificent support of those who had their hands on the strongest social levers and also of his fellow clergy. Contemporaries referred to him with unstinting admiration as he assembled an army of schoolteachers, plied them with Bibles and catechisms, and urged them to encourage the reading habit among a people who had hitherto been indifferent or hostile to schooling. Jones and his assistants worked wonders and the Welsh became one of the most literate peoples in Europe. By the end of the century more than half the population had learned to read. *The Welch Piety*, Jones's annual report, is peppered with examples of illiterate septuagenarians weeping with joy as they acquired rudimentary reading skills in their twilight years and of precocious five-year-old children who became fluent readers of Welsh within three months. Common people carried fuel and candles to draughty church vestries in order to extend their hours of tuition. Such enthusiasm betokened a powerful desire for education and self-improvement, all of which created a more widespread religious and cultural dynamic. The upsurge in educational provision revitalized the established church, helped Calvinistic Methodism to prosper, and injected new life into the native tongue. In an age when most religious reformers were less troubled by the future well-being of the Welsh language than by the salvation of souls and when so-called 'improvers' nursed a deeply rooted aversion to all the Celtic languages, the veneration which Griffith Jones publicly displayed for his native language was of the highest importance.

A second associated precondition of the success of religious revivals was the influence of the printed word. Hailed in 1735 by Lewis Morris as 'the Candle of the World', the Welsh printing press played a far-reaching role in the transformation of spiritual and cultural life. Only one printer – at Trerhedyn in the vale of Teifi – earned a living in Wales in 1718, but within a hundred years there were fifty printers sustaining a flourishing book trade throughout Wales. More than 2,600 Welsh books (excluding ephemera) were published over the course of the century and the proliferation of charity, circulating and Sunday schools, book clubs, subscription ventures, academies and literary societies clearly helped to nourish a new respect and affection for the printed word. Whereas early seventeenth-century Puritans had counted themselves fortunate if they managed to publish one Welsh book, eighteenth-century authors avidly seized growing opportunities to publicize their missions in print. William Williams of Pantycelyn, Welsh Methodism's principal literary icon, published ninety books and pamphlets (including a thousand hymns) during his lifetime, and we should not ignore also the enormous popularity of the cheap, rough and ready Welsh almanacs and ballads which were published in their thousands and sold by armies of agents, itinerant booksellers, carriers and hawkers. It would be hard to overestimate, too, the contribution of printed books to the efforts of cultural patriots to persuade the Welsh to shrug off the psychologically debilitating effects of being so cruelly caricaturized as illiterate country bumpkins.

The fact that the overwhelming bulk of printed material was in Welsh rendered Wales different from the English model. The native language was not only the most distinctive badge of national identity, but also a much more powerful dividing factor than religion or politics. Nine of every ten of the population spoke only Welsh and, although there was a widespread feeling in 'anglicizing' and 'civilizing' circles that Welsh could never truly be considered a learned tongue, it flourished not only as the medium of daily discourse but also as the linchpin of a remarkable renaissance of Welsh letters. In the absence of a robust cultural infrastructure and in the wake of the anglicizing of the gentry, the Welsh middling sorts were obliged to devise their own agents of cultural change, to exhume usable elements from the past, and to concoct new theories. The initial impetus was provided by the Celtic scholar Edward Lhuyd, whose groundbreaking volume *Archaeologia Britannica* (1707), published by a delicious irony in the year in which the British state was strengthened by the parliamentary union of England, Wales and Scotland, demonstrated the common Celtic origin of the Breton, Cornish and Welsh languages. Here was proof from an impeccable source that multiple identities, under a Celtic banner, existed within the union. Lhuyd's untimely death in 1709, however, meant that the new appreciation of the affinity of the Celtic languages and peoples was overtaken by a propensity for fantasy and myth-making. Celtomania and Druidomania flourished as never before, and were encouraged by scholars and savants who established London-based societies like the Cymmrodorion (1751) and the Gwyneddigion (1770) in order to restore what they believed to be the oldest living literary language in Europe to its former glory. Led by the redoubtable Morris brothers of Anglesey, the Welsh middling sorts began to punch their weight in cultural circles. Scholars who belonged to the Morris Circle developed a passion for transcribing and preserving dust-laden manuscripts locked away in gentry libraries, and the growing interest in romanticism and primitivism meant that in no part of Britain was the invention of the past more splendidly invoked than in Wales. One of the finest exemplars of this vogue was Evan Evans's *Some Specimens of the Poetry of the Antient Welsh Bards* (1764), the Welsh equivalent of James Macpherson's Ossianic writings in Scotland and Charlotte Brooke's effusions in Ireland, which celebrated the iconic status of the Celtic bard and the noble savage, an image memorably depicted in *The Bard* (1774) by the artist Thomas Jones, Pencerrig.

Tourists who ventured in increasing numbers into Wales during the latter decades of the eighteenth century were surprised and thrilled to discover that barren 'Goatlandshire' was in fact a land of extraordinary picturesque beauty, filled with druidic altars and temples and a variety of arresting legends, symbols and mythical creations. The fact that Wales was so lamentably deficient in cultural institutions prompted the most adventurous of romantics to indulge in myth-making on a grand scale. The key figure was Iolo Morganwg (Edward Williams or Edward of Glamorgan), a prodigiously gifted stonemason whose curious passion for both authentic and bogus material enabled him to provide the Welsh with a striking visual pageant focused on *Gorsedd Beirdd Ynys Prydain* (The Gorsedd of the Bards of the Isle of Britain), founded in 1792. Druids were viewed as a fount of wisdom, as guardians of the Welsh memory, and as transmitters of a uniquely fascinating lore. From 1789, too, the Gwyneddigion Society, with the enthusiastic support of Iolo Morganwg and others, rescued the traditional *eisteddfod* from beery rhymesters and transformed it into a formal and properly constituted event in which a Chair was the reward of the undisputed *prifardd* (chief poet). These central features of Welsh cultural life were lovingly nurtured and cherished in order to prove to the world at large that a five-foot nation, long despised by the English, was determined to clamber on to the historical stage and assert its rights as a distinct and distinctive people.

Somewhat grudgingly, historians are now beginning to abandon the study of the Eatanswill world of patronage, jobbery and corruption, and to recognize that a political imperative was at least implicit in the remit and activities of these new cultural institutions: after all, druidic bards had the potential to become political activists on behalf of the Freeborn Welsh. Ever since the Acts of Union (1536–43) the practice of politics had been dominated by powerful landed families (most of whom had annual incomes of £3,000–£5,000 by the eighteenth century), from among whom twenty-seven MPs were returned to Westminster by a tiny electorate which never exceeded 25,000. Contested elections were frowned upon because they entailed prohibitive costs and disturbed the peace of the county. Somnolent Montgomeryshire prided itself on its political 'virginity' in this respect, and party divisions, in the traditional sense of Whig versus Tory, counted for little. Jacobite activity was desultory and even in 1745–6 it caused few shock waves west of Offa's Dyke. Its leaders, past masters at noisy inertia, simply drank the health of the Pretender behind closed doors. Welsh MPs were conspicuous by their absence in the parliamentary bear-pit, but the electorate, notwithstanding those cowed into submission by threats of coercion by heavy-handed stewards and agents, remained loyal and deferential to their betters.

Belatedly, but not surprisingly, Welsh historians now tend to shun high politics of this kind and focus their attention on places where the winds of change were blowing more vigorously. It is becoming increasingly evident that considerable turbulence existed at local levels and that this manifested itself in public disorder, physical intimidation and lawlessness. A recent study based on the gaol files of the Courts of Great Sessions concluded that this was 'a violent, unsqueamish, brutal society' in which physical assault, theft of property and wilful damage were rife (Howell 2000: 177). There is little doubt that political inequalities, large-scale changes in landownership and the depredations of middle men like stewards and agents encouraged criminality and disorderly behaviour. Most decades witnessed violent food riots and bitter clashes over manorial rights and the enclosure of common land, and some borough constituencies were prone to erupt in stormy conflict whenever economic issues and religious differences led to conspiratorial activity.

A new kind of politics was also emerging from masonic lodges and academies where progressive thinkers were constructing alternative models to conservative politics and predestination theology. Whereas Methodism, despite its potential for turbulent enthusiasm, was a stabilizing force within society, there existed within Dissent, especially its Arminian wing, agencies of social and political reconstruction. Far from being the dry, fractious and ineffectual groups which Methodist apologists deemed them to be, Dissenters were in fact an active leaven in the lump. Dissent prospered best among pious small farmers, craftsmen and artisans who thrived on the lively sermons, warm fellowship and spirit of inquiry which made their meeting houses and chapels so hospitable and lively. The most historically minded of them, especially Congregationalists, Baptists and Unitarians, rejoiced in the fact that their ancestors had chopped off the head of the king of England and they also forged fruitful trans-Atlantic links with fellow Dissenters who had ventured to the New World. Relatively well-to-do Dissenters were the mainstays of the Welsh branch of the Wilkeite and Wyvill reform movements, and within masonic lodges revolutionary ideas emanating from America and France were widely canvassed. In the 1790s Wales boasted lively groups of politically active Jacobins who cherished the ideals of Tom Paine, loathed the deference of Methodist evangelists, and denounced the baneful influence of oligarchic power, tithes and rack-rents, insecurity of tenure and anglocentrism. Most

Dissenting radicals peddled their ideas through printed texts (including *Y Cylchgrawn Cyn-mraeg*, 1793, the first Welsh-language journal devoted to politics), *eisteddfodau* and the newly formed *Gorsedd* of the Bards, though Richard Price of Tyn-ton in the parish of Llangeinor, Glamorgan, one of the founding fathers of the American Republic and a major economist, statistician and philosopher, became a powerful agent of change on the international stage. More recognizable than Price in Welsh circles was Iolo Morganwg, who revelled in the name 'Bard of Liberty' and deployed the *Gorsedd* as a vehicle for propaganda. Even in the fastnesses of rural Cardiganshire, a Unitarian fiefdom known disparagingly in Methodist circles as *Y Smotyn Du* (The Black Spot) bred active ministers fired by enlightenment ideals, political theory and a fierce determination to secure full legal recognition of the right to freedom of worship and political liberty. The number of Welsh-language publications of a political nature decupled during the 1790s and other clandestine material which has survived in manuscript suggests that subversive correspondence, squibs, songs and graphic prints were much more prevalent than has previously been supposed. Had not the French Wars dragged on interminably, Welsh radicals might have become even more openly critical of the government. From such people would develop, in the fullness of time, a burning desire to bring down old corruption and take control of their own political destiny.

By the end of the century the shrewdest Welsh commentators were keenly aware that the old order was passing away swiftly and that the Wales of 1800 was profoundly different from that of 1700. Significant changes had occurred during the course of the century. A sluggish economy had embarked on a process of improvement catalysed by demographic upturn, striking industrial growth and urban development. A critical split had deepened between the cultures of powerful absentee non-Welsh-speaking landowners and industrious, Bible-reading cultural patriots who increasingly claimed to represent and articulate the aspirations of the Welsh people. Within a religiously pluralistic society Methodists were marching towards secession from the mother church, Dissent was poised to become part and parcel of the 'Welsh way of life', and the old 'merrie Wales' had been undermined by a reformation of manners sponsored by pious middling sorts. Religious revivals had coincided with an extraordinary upsurge in literacy rates which, in turn, had created both a book culture and an infectiously new cultural confidence. Welsh remembrancers celebrated the Celtic inheritance by establishing an unbroken cultural umbilical cord binding them to the remotest past and by reminding the wider world of the language and culture of one of the forgotten peoples of western Europe. The search for national roots was accompanied by a taste for the romantic fashions of the day and, increasingly by the 1790s, for myth-making, sans-culottisme and free thinking. Ironically, the external drive for homogenization, ideological control and the elimination of undesirable differences had created a new framework for cultural, political and social debate.

FURTHER READING

Evans, E. D.: *A History of Wales 1660–1815* (Cardiff, 1976).

Herbert, Trevor and Elwyn Jones, Gareth (eds): *The Remaking of Wales in the Eighteenth Century* (Cardiff, 1988).

Howell, David W.: *Patriarchs and Parasites: The Gentry of South-West Wales in the Eighteenth Century* (Cardiff, 1986).
Howell, David W.: *The Rural Poor in Eighteenth-Century Wales* (Cardiff, 2000).
Jenkins, Geraint H.: *Literature, Religion and Society in Wales, 1660–1730* (Cardiff, 1978).
Jenkins, Geraint H.: *The Foundations of Modern Wales: Wales 1642–1780* (Oxford, 1987).
Jenkins, Geraint H. (ed.): *The Welsh Language before the Industrial Revolution* (Cardiff, 1997).
Jenkins, Philip: *The Making of a Ruling Class: The Glamorgan Gentry 1640–1790* (Cambridge, 1983).
Jenkins, Philip: *A History of Modern Wales 1536–1990* (London, 1992).
Moore, Donald (ed.): *Wales in the Eighteenth Century* (Swansea, 1976).
Morgan, Derec Llwyd: *The Great Awakening in Wales* (London, 1988).
Morgan, Prys: *A New History of Wales: The Eighteenth-Century Renaissance* (Llandybïe, 1981).
Thomas, Peter D. G.: *Politics in Eighteenth-Century Wales* (Cardiff, 1998).
Williams, Gwyn A.: *The Search for Beulah Land* (London, 1980).

Chapter Thirty-One

Ireland: The Making of the 'Protestant Ascendancy', 1690–1760

Paddy McNally

It has been a longstanding tradition within British historiography to characterize the 'Glorious Revolution' of 1688–9 as 'bloodless'. In Ireland this was most certainly not the case. Whereas James II's flight to France in December 1688 rapidly led to the establishment of William and Mary as joint monarchs of England and Scotland, the issue was not to be so quickly nor so effectively settled across the Irish Sea. It would require a war lasting over two years, fought by two large, professional, multinational armies and costing the lives of over 20,000 men to achieve a stable political outcome in Ireland.

The Revolution Settlement in Ireland

William of Orange's invasion of England in November 1688 and the flight of James II to France the following month placed the Irish government under James's protégé, the Catholic earl of Tyrconnel, in an unenviable position. The reign of the Catholic James II had witnessed a resurgence in the influence of the 'Old English' Catholic elite. On the eve of the Glorious Revolution the Irish army was overwhelmingly Catholic, the judiciary was dominated by Catholics, and national and local government had undergone a purge of Protestants. The restoration of the Protestant monarchy in England, however, inevitably meant that the Protestant domination of Ireland would be restored. The Irish Catholic leadership was thus faced with the choice of making the best terms possible with the de facto monarchy in England or continuing to support the exiled James. Once Louis XIV of France decided to support an attempt by James to recover his crowns, Tyrconnel determined to risk all in an attempt to preserve the gains made in Ireland since 1685. The scene was thus set for a military resolution to the longstanding struggle for power between the Catholic and Protestant elites of Irish society.

While some Protestants attempted to cooperate with the Jacobite regime, the majority fled to England or sought refuge in the major areas of Protestant settlement. By the time James II arrived in Ireland in March 1689 the whole of Ireland, with the exception of isolated areas of Ulster (most significantly the besieged city of

Londonderry), was in Jacobite hands. Although the relief of Londonderry in July 1689 provided William with an invaluable base for launching the recovery of the island, his initial attempts to recover the kingdom proved inauspicious. A Williamite army of 14,000 men under the duke of Schomberg secured Ulster in the summer of 1689, but made little headway otherwise. Only when William took personal control of his army in Ireland in June 1690 did events come to a head. Anxious to end the Irish war as quickly as possible in order to concentrate on the European theatre of operations against Louis XIV, William wasted no time in leading his force of 37,000 men to confront James's army of 25,000 on the River Boyne a few miles west of Drogheda. Although William's victory at the Battle of the Boyne of 1 July 1690 did not finally decide the outcome of the war (the Battle of Aughrim in July the following year was more significant militarily), the Jacobite forces never recovered from a setback which gave William control of the eastern half of the country, including Dublin. The war, indeed, dragged on for over a year after the Boyne but the issue had effectively been settled. Certainly after Aughrim, the question for the Jacobites was not so much how to continue the war but how to achieve the best peace terms possible.

While the Battle of the Boyne was essentially fought over the issue of who should be king of England, Scotland and Ireland, the outcome of the battle had a particular significance for the future of Ireland. William's victory represented for the people of Ireland a triumph of Protestantism over Catholicism. Ever since the failure of the sixteenth-century Reformation to convert the majority of the Irish to Protestantism, a struggle for power had been waged between the Catholic and Protestant elites of Irish society. The status of the Catholic Irish had been steadily undermined by the 'New English' Protestants who acquired in the seventeenth century a greater proportion of landownership and public office. Although the restoration of Charles II had allowed some Catholics to regain a proportion of the land confiscated during the Cromwellian period, by the 1680s Protestants still owned over three-quarters of Irish landed property. The reign of James II, however, threatened to overturn Protestant control of Ireland and had James remained as king there is little doubt that the Restoration land settlement would have been significantly altered to the benefit of Catholics. William of Orange's victory, however, rendered the achievements of Tyrconnel's regime null and void and Protestant domination of Ireland after 1691 was to be even more complete than it had been in 1685.

The war in Ireland eventually ended in October 1691 with the surrender of the Jacobite forces besieged at Limerick. The Treaty of Limerick which ended the war has ever since been a subject of controversy. The military articles of the treaty were quickly agreed and proved to be relatively uncontroversial. It was agreed that those among the Jacobite army who chose to do so would be transferred to France and 12,000 Irish troops eventually went into foreign service to continue the struggle in Europe, beginning the tradition whereby thousands of Irish Catholics would serve in continental armies for most of the eighteenth century. Much more contentious were the civil articles of the treaty, specifically the question of the civil and political rights of Catholics in post-revolutionary Ireland. Whereas William and his commanders offered relatively generous terms in order to achieve a speedy peace, the leaders of the Irish Protestant community were determined to crush the Catholic threat once and for all. A community which had faced the prospect of a 'Catholic Ascendancy'

under James II was unlikely to display much generosity in triumph, particularly while the threat of a Jacobite restoration remained very much alive. It was not until 1697 that the Irish parliament agreed to ratify the Treaty of Limerick and even then it was in a modified form. A clause which appeared to guarantee Irish Catholics significant political, civil and religious liberties was deliberately omitted and, although it has been argued that this missing clause would have given Catholics little protection in practice, historians have generally regarded the failure to ratify the treaty in full as a breach of faith. The episode demonstrates above all what was to be the dominant feature of Irish history for the next hundred years: the determination of Irish Protestants to keep Catholic power in check.

The important constitutional changes brought about by the Glorious Revolution in England are well known. After 1688 there was a transformation in the respective roles of monarch and parliament with the power and influence of the latter significantly increasing. Similar developments were seen in Ireland and largely for the same reasons. While the formal constitutional changes brought about by the Revolution (notably the Bill of Rights) were slight, the implications of England's involvement in the continental wars of the next twenty-five years were momentous. As in England, the main impact in Ireland of the continental wars was to increase dramatically the Irish government's need for additional taxation. Whereas Irish government finances under Charles II and James II had been normally in surplus, the impact of the Irish war and the expansion of the Irish military establishment under William meant that the government had to recall the Irish parliament to seek additional supplies. A combination of governmental complacency and suspicion on the part of Irish Protestants meant that the first parliament to meet after the revolution in 1692 ended disastrously, being prorogued only four weeks after it had met. The 1695 parliament, however, saw the establishment of better relations between the court and local political managers or 'undertakers'. The latter 'undertook' to manage the Irish parliament on the government's behalf in return for a share of government patronage and some influence over legislation. Moreover, from 1695 the court agreed to allow the Irish House of Commons the dominant role in the drafting of financial legislation, the issue which had led to the breakdown in relations in 1692. From now on Irish MPs were to decide both the level and nature of Irish taxation. This parliament also passed the first of the 'popery laws' and for the next decade or so in particular the government's toleration of further anti-Catholic legislation was an important aspect of the successful management of parliament. The result of the deal done in 1695 was that the power of locally based politicians was significantly enhanced. The decision of the English parliament in 1697 to allow William to maintain a 12,000-strong Irish standing army, combined with the fact that Irish MPs would not grant taxes for more than two years at a time, effectively ensured that the Irish parliament would be recalled at least every other year. In return for additional taxation to support the military, the government had little option but to take on board the concerns of the representatives of the Protestant community in parliament.

The Connection between Britain and Ireland

The establishment of permanent parliamentary government in both Ireland and England brought to the fore the question of the constitutional relationship between the two kingdoms. Strictly speaking, Ireland was a possession of the English crown with the Westminster parliament having no say in the government of the country. The expansion in the power of the English parliament after 1688, however, led to a blurring of the situation. English parliamentarians were inclined to view Ireland as a colony rather than as a kingdom and certainly did not accept the notion that the parliament in Dublin had equal status with that at Westminster. This confusion regarding Ireland's constitutional status was a recurrent cause of conflict in the eighteenth century until the issue appeared to have been finally settled with the Act of Union of 1800.

An act passed by the Irish parliament in 1494 (Poynings' Law) prohibited the Dublin legislature from initiating any legislation whatsoever. In theory all Irish bills were drawn up by either the English or Irish privy councils and then presented to the Irish parliament for approval or rejection. During the 1660s, however, Irish parliamentarians began to circumvent Poynings' Law by drawing up 'heads of bills' or requests for legislation which, once approved by the Irish Lords or Commons (but not both), were forwarded to the Irish privy council to be drafted as bills proper. This procedure became the normal practice in the 1690s and, effectively, heads of bills came to assume the status of formal bills. Consequently, the overwhelming majority of eighteenth-century Irish legislation was initiated by either house of the Irish parliament, although bills still required the approval of and could be amended by the privy councils in Dublin and London.

The first major dispute between the English and Irish parliaments was over an act passed by the Westminster legislature to restrict the export of Irish woollen manufactures. Currency rates in the 1690s gave Irish exporters a temporary advantage over their English rivals and Westminster MPs legislated in 1699 to secure foreign markets from Irish competition. Quite apart from the economic consequences of the Woollen Act (which historians now tend to minimize), the fact that the English parliament was legislating to control an important aspect of the Irish economy raised important constitutional issues. The most important consequence of the dispute was the publication in 1698 of William Molyneux's *The Case of Ireland's being bound by Acts of Parliament in England, stated* (Dublin, 1698). Molyneux argued that, since Ireland was a separate kingdom and the Irish people had no representation at Westminster, the English parliament had no right to pass legislation binding Ireland. Molyneux's book, although regarded by some Protestants at the time as provocative, quickly assumed the status of one of the key texts of Irish patriotism and was often reprinted during the eighteenth century. Simultaneous with the dispute over the Woollen Act, a conflict had arisen as to the respective judicial powers of the English and Irish Houses of Lords. A disagreement between William King, the bishop of Derry, and the Irish Society over the rights to various lands and fisheries had been taken on appeal to the English Lords, who overturned a previous ruling of the Irish upper house. Eventually the decision of the English Lords was upheld, resulting in an acceptance that the Lords at Westminster had supremacy in Chancery cases. The broader issue of which body was the supreme judicial authority in Irish cases was left unresolved, however, and would be the cause of a much more serious dispute between 1717 and 1720.

Molyneux's *Case* had raised a fundamental issue, however, for Irish Protestant patriots regarded it as unacceptable to be bound by legislation passed by a parliament in which they had no representation. Logically speaking there were two possible solutions to this problem – a recognition on the part of the English legislature that it had no authority over internal Irish affairs or a legislative union between the two kingdoms. Given the attention devoted to the eighteenth-century Irish patriot tradition (which has often been portrayed as an important contributor to the development of Irish nationalism), it is important to note that in the decade or two after the Boyne most Irish Protestants appeared to prefer the latter solution. Notable patriots such as Molyneux and Jonathan Swift, for example, favoured a union and the Irish House of Commons petitioned Queen Anne for a union in 1703. Once it became clear, however, that there was little enthusiasm in England for such a step, Irish Protestants had little alternative but to protect their interests as best they could through their dominance of the Dublin legislature.

The Religious Question

While Irish parliamentarians were attempting to establish a *modus vivendi* with the English government, they were simultaneously addressing the question of internal relationships, specifically those between the Anglican elite and the Catholic and Protestant Dissenting communities. While Anglicans comprised around 10 per cent of the Irish population, their possession of approximately nine-tenths of Irish land gave them a virtual monopoly over central and local government. The proceedings of a succession of Irish parliaments in the 1690s illustrated that Irish Protestants were determined to give their de facto dominance of Ireland legislative teeth and from 1695 until 1728 a succession of 'popery laws' was passed by the Dublin parliament. The most important legislation was passed between 1695 and 1704 and had the effect of imposing severe restrictions on the civil and religious rights of Catholics. Officially Catholics could not bear arms, vote, sit in parliament, enter the professions, hold public office, buy land or lease it for longer than thirty-one years, establish schools or be educated abroad. Significant restrictions were also placed on the ability of the Catholic church to function. From 1697 Catholic bishops and members of monastic orders were banished from the country and from 1709 the remaining Catholic clergy were also liable to transportation if caught. If these measures had been systematically implemented, the Catholic church would have ceased to exist within little more than a generation. The motivation behind these 'penal laws', as they have become known, and their practical impact on the Catholic population have in recent years been the subject of much debate. Most historians (Catholic, Dissenter and Anglican) were extremely critical of the laws and their deleterious effects. W. E. H. Lecky argued that the legislation went far beyond the necessities of self-defence, was continued long after all serious danger had passed, and was primarily intended to make the Catholics poor and to keep them poor. Others, such as Maureen Wall, have compared the penal laws to the apartheid legislation of twentieth-century South Africa and likened the status of Irish Catholics to that of native populations or slaves in eighteenth-century colonial territories.

Recent historiography has offered a more complex analysis both of the motivation behind the legislation and of its practical effects. Sean Connolly has argued that the penal laws had no single purpose, that they did not represent a coherent and systematic code, but were introduced by different people at different times for a variety of purposes. Connolly is also prepared to give more credence than most to the desire to convert Catholics to Protestantism as a motivating factor behind the legislation. Perhaps most controversially, he argues that the penal laws had little practical impact on Catholics since many laws were not enforced in practice and that only wealthy Catholics were affected by those which were.

It is true that after an initial period of persecution lasting a decade or so, the laws affecting the Catholic church were largely ignored by the Protestant authorities, many of whom regarded this aspect of the penal laws with some embarrassment and distaste. Apart from during times of tension with Britain's foreign enemies, the Catholic clergy were generally left to their own devices. In fact, the decades following the accession of George I in 1714 witnessed a considerable recovery on the part of the Catholic church in Ireland, a phenomenon often commented on with concern by Protestant clergymen. This tendency in recent historiography to minimize the practical impact of penal legislation has been augmented by researches into the nature of the eighteenth-century Irish economy. Louis Cullen stresses the importance of 'nominal conversion' as a mechanism by which Catholics could protect their property and engage in 'forbidden' areas such as politics and the professions. Kevin Whelan has gone even further, arguing that conversion from Catholic to Protestant cannot be taken as an erosion of the Catholic position; rather, in many cases, it strengthened it. While such portrayals of a 'flourishing' Irish Catholic community in the first half of the eighteenth century may be regarded as an example of 'revisionism' going too far, it is undeniable that recent historiography has provided a more rounded and nuanced picture of the Catholic experience in the decades after the Boyne.

Penal legislation also impacted upon the Protestant Dissenting community of which the most important element by far was the Presbyterian presence concentrated in Ulster. The 1690s had seen another large wave of Scots Presbyterian immigration into Ulster and Dissent made major advances in that province over the next two decades. Emigration from Ulster to North America, however, was under way from the 1710s and continued throughout the remainder of the eighteenth century. The reasons for such emigration were a matter of dispute for contemporaries. Protestant landlords laid the blame squarely with the Episcopal Church of Ireland, pointing to the impact of the sacramental test, which, officially at least, debarred Protestant Dissenters from public office and local government, and resentment among Dissenters at being forced to pay tithes to support the established church. Churchmen, on the other hand, argued that material considerations were more important, particularly the renewal of leases on more unfavourable terms from the late 1710s onwards and Protestant landlords' alleged preference for Catholic tenants who were willing to pay higher rents. It is likely that a combination of such 'push' factors and the 'pull' of religious toleration and the prospect of economic advancement in the new world explains the phenomenon.

While Dissenters were not subjected to most of the penal laws that affected Catholics (they retained the right to vote and to sit in parliament, for example), it appears that the imposition of the sacramental test in 1704 did have a significant impact on the influence of Dissenters in local government, especially in Ulster. The response of Dissenters to penal legislation largely mirrored that of Catholics, with the wealthy tending to conform to the established church and the remainder of the population (who chose not to emigrate) being largely unaffected in practical, if not psychological, terms.

Managing the Irish Parliament

The parliamentary politics of the 1690s had been dominated by the attempts of the viceregal court in Dublin to come to a working arrangement with Irish parliamentarians. The emergence of 'undertakers' from within the ranks of leading Irish politicians certainly led to a more productive relationship. The outbreak, however, of a Whig–Tory party conflict in England – which was quickly transported to Ireland – seriously complicated the situation. It is perhaps a sign of the security of the Protestant community that they felt able to participate in such a divisive party-political squabble. Potentially at least, the issues dividing Whigs from Tories had serious implications for the position of the Irish Protestant community. The question of the succession to the throne was certainly a matter of contention between the English parties. While the Whigs were determined to uphold the Protestant succession at all costs, at least some Tories were willing to flirt with the Jacobite cause. Given the experience of Irish Protestants during the reign of James II, it is hardly surprising that Jacobite sympathy was virtually non-existent among that community. Irish Whigs, however, feared that by acting in concert with the English Tory party, Irish Tories were risking a Jacobite restoration which could have disastrous consequences in Ireland. A more serious cause of conflict between the parties in Ireland was the question of religion. As followers of the self-styled 'Church party', the Tories were determined to uphold the privileged position of the Church of Ireland. The Whigs on the other hand were more distrustful of the political influence of the established church, relatively more sympathetic to Protestant Dissent and more inclined than the Tories to legislate against the Catholic community. The party conflict, therefore, raised issues fundamental to the security and dominant position of the Anglican community within Ireland.

There is no doubt that the politics of party dominated the parliamentary scene in Dublin during the latter half of the reign of Queen Anne. Following the peaceful Hanoverian succession in 1714, however, the Irish Tory party went into rapid decline, virtually ceasing to exist by the time of George I's death in 1727. A rump Tory party continued to exist for about fifteen years after 1714, providing a group of MPs and peers who could cooperate with 'discontented Whigs' and 'patriots' over specific issues. The absence of significant Jacobite sympathies among Irish Tories, however, and the willingness of the Irish government to dispense patronage to at least some repentant Tories, removed two of the main factors that served to preserve the Tory party in Britain intact for a much longer period.

Parliamentary politics in the first decade and a half after the Hanoverian succession tended to be concentrated on three main areas – the battle for dominance between the two chief undertakers of the period, Speaker of the Commons William Conolly and the lord chancellor, Viscount Midleton; a conflict among the Anglican episcopate in the House of Lords between the so-called 'Irish' and 'English interests'; and various 'patriot' issues. Conolly and Midleton had been two of the most important leaders of the Whig party during the reign of Queen Anne, the latter being recognized as the senior figure within the party. Just as the British Whigs quickly began to squabble over the spoils of victory after 1714, however, their Irish counterparts did likewise. Successive British governments appeared unwilling to make a decisive choice between the two candidates for the position of chief undertaker, preferring to try to keep both men in government and, therefore, to some extent under their influence. Over the years Conolly proved to be more adept at keeping on good terms with the British ministry and Midleton's resignation towards the end of the Wood's Halfpence crisis of 1722–5 (see below) allowed the former to emerge as the court's chief parliamentary manager. The conflict between the Irish and English interests within the Anglican episcopate was initially over the distribution of church patronage, the Irish-born clergy increasingly resenting the appointment of Englishmen to senior positions within the Church of Ireland. The fact that most English appointees after 1714 were generally more sympathetic to Dissent and hostile to Catholicism further exacerbated the schism. It was a 'patriotic' issue, however, that served to turn this simmering resentment into an all-out political conflict.

The vexed question of whether the Irish or British House of Lords was the ultimate court of appeal in Irish legal cases re-emerged in 1717 when the upper house of the British parliament overturned a ruling of the Irish Lords regarding a land dispute between Maurice Annesley and Hester Sherlock. On this occasion the defenders of Irish parliamentary authority appeared determined to push the issue to a final resolution and, led by Archbishop William King of Dublin, the Irish interest vigorously defended the right of the Irish House of Lords to have the final say in Irish cases. Prominent among the very few members of the Irish upper house to support the supremacy of the British Lords were those English-born bishops appointed since 1714. Thus, the ecclesiastical conflict was quickly superseded by an overtly constitutional one. Eventually the British parliament responded to what they regarded as the provocative claims of the Irish Lords by passing the Declaratory Act in 1720. This act not only asserted the judicial supremacy of the British Lords but explicitly asserted the right of the Westminster parliament to legislate for Ireland. While the theoretical implication of the Declaratory Act was that the Irish parliament could be dispensed with, in practice its effects were minimal. There is little evidence that any British government ever seriously considered legislating at Westminster for Ireland and the government of Ireland after 1720 carried on exactly as before. Quite simply, to have attempted to use the powers theoretically available after 1720 by, for example, taxing Ireland from Westminster would have aroused more trouble than it was worth.

It is ironic that Irish patriots failed miserably over the overtly constitutional Sherlock–Annesley dispute, yet succeeded in the next patriotic conflict when, legally speaking, they were on much shakier ground. In 1722 a patent was sold through an approach to one of the king's mistresses to William Wood to coin £100,800 worth of copper halfpence for Ireland. No one in Ireland had been consulted about the desirability of minting 'brass money' in such quantities and when news of the patent reached Ireland opposition soon manifested itself. Constitutionally the king was perfectly within his rights in granting such a patent, so Irish opposition focused on the alleged damage that would be done to the economy of the country by introducing halfpence in such numbers. The opposition of leading politicians was quickly followed by a popular campaign against the patent that proved remarkably successful. Jonathan Swift's *Drapier's Letters* attacking the patent were particularly important in uniting the Protestant community in opposition to the patent. The most immediate political implication of the dispute was that parliament quickly became unmanageable, with no one daring to undertake a defence of the patent for fear of losing all political credibility in the country. Midleton actively opposed the patent and Conolly refused to defend it. When the discredited duke of Grafton was replaced as viceroy by Lord Carteret in 1724, the latter decided to try to govern without the aid of an undertaker by forming a sufficient parliamentary following based on the viceregal court. Carteret's bold attempt completely failed. Even after he secured the withdrawal of Wood's patent to appease public opinion he found it impossible to command a stable majority when parliament reconvened in September 1725. Only when Carteret turned again to Conolly to manage parliament on his behalf did the situation improve. This experiment in checking the power of the undertakers would not be attempted again until the Townshend administration of the late 1760s.

Conolly continued as the unrivalled undertaker until his death in 1729. His long-term successor as chief undertaker emerged in 1733 when Henry Boyle was elected with government support as Speaker of the Commons and Boyle dominated Irish parliamentary politics for the next twenty years. It appeared during this period that the British and Irish political establishments had finally come to terms with each other and that mutually acceptable conventions for the government of Ireland had emerged from the disputes of the period from 1692 to 1725. So long as the British government and parliament was prepared to manage the Dublin parliament through locally based undertakers and to recognize the right of Irish Protestants to have the predominant say over internal Irish affairs, the latter appeared content to accept the ultimate authority of Westminster over broader 'imperial' matters such as foreign policy and trade.

This mutually beneficial arrangement, however, began to come under pressure during the 1750s when a dispute over whether the king or Irish House of Commons controlled the disposal of surplus Irish revenues caused a serious crisis between 1753 and 1755. This 'patriotic' cause was exploited by Boyle in order to prove his indispensability as a parliamentary manager. His position as chief undertaker had for some time come under threat from a coalition of the English-born archbishop of Armagh, George Stone, and the chief rival to the Boyle interest in parliament based around the Ponsonby family, headed by the earl of Bessborough. While the Ponsonbys had traditionally had very close connections with Dublin Castle, Boyle from the outset of his career had always emphasized his independence from the court. The money bill crisis presented Boyle with the perfect opportunity to assert his authority by assuming the leadership of a popular 'patriot' cause.

The immediate cause of the dispute was the Irish House of Commons' rejection of a money bill which had been amended by the British privy council. As in 1692, Irish MPs were determined to uphold their control over finance legislation. Fully realizing Boyle's true motivation, the government responded with the dismissal from government posts of key members of the Boyle faction, including the removal of Boyle himself as Chancellor of the Exchequer. Such a firm stand, however, did not bring Boyle to heel and only the combination of the appointment of a new viceroy in 1755 and the threat of war with France brought about a resolution. In return for the government's agreement to diminish Primate Stone's authority, Boyle supported the election of John Ponsonby as Speaker of the Commons and was rewarded with an earldom and a pension of £2,000 a year. Although on the face of it the old arrangement of governing by undertaker had been re-established, the money bill crisis had a number of important implications. The British ministry was once more made aware of the danger of allowing any single Irish politician to accumulate too much power. Moreover, the strength and extent of public support for the patriot cause evidenced during the dispute was, for the government, an alarming development.

Just as it had been a lengthy military conflict that had provided Irish Protestants with the opportunity to establish significant control over the government of their country, the outbreak of the Seven Years' War in 1756 began the process by which the accepted forms of government in Ireland would be progressively undermined. Just as the requirement to govern and defend a much-increased empire would lead to important consequences for Britain's relations with the North American colonies, so the military needs of the British government and the implications of governing a Catholic community in Canada were eventually to have important consequences for the government of Ireland. The 1760s would witness the beginning of a process whereby the British ministry adopted a more direct form of rule in Ireland. The common factor in all of these developments would be the military needs of the British state. During the Seven Years' War, Irish Catholics began to be illicitly enlisted into the British army and the desire to expand the Irish standing army from 12,000 to 15,000 men produced another political crisis in the late 1760s which effectively ended the undertaker system as it previously operated. The granting of toleration to Canadian Catholics by the Quebec Act of 1774 and the government's wish for Irish Catholic support during the American War of Independence put the 'Catholic question' firmly onto the political agenda. Although Irish Protestants were able to exploit the weakness of the British government in 1782 to achieve parliamentary independence (that is, the repeal of the Declaratory Act and the amendment of Poynings' Law), such a victory for the patriot cause proved to be a pyrrhic one. For the decades after 1760 gradually saw a dismantling of the penal laws (virtually abolished on the eve of war in 1793) and a significant increase in the government's ability to control directly the Irish parliament. Ironically, the term 'Protestant Ascendancy' was coined only in the 1780s as part of a vain attempt to defend a regime which had by that time been fatally undermined.

FURTHER READING

Bartlett, Thomas: *The Fall and Rise of the Irish Nation: The Catholic Question 1690–1830* (Dublin, 1992).

Bartlett, Thomas and Hayton, David (eds): *Penal Era and Golden Age: Essays in Irish History, 1690–1800* (Belfast, 1979).

Connolly, Sean J.: *Religion, Law and Power: The Making of Protestant Ireland 1660–1760* (Oxford, 1992).

Cullen, Louis: *An Economic History of Ireland since 1660* (2nd edn, London, 1987).

Dickson, David: *New Foundations: Ireland 1660–1800* (Dublin, 1987).

Foster, R. F.: *Modern Ireland, 1600–1972* (London, 1988).

James, F. G.: *Ireland in the Empire, 1688–1770* (Cambridge, MA, 1973).

Johnston, E. M.: *Ireland in the Eighteenth Century* (Dublin, 1974).

Lecky, W. E. H.: *A History of Ireland in the Eighteenth Century* (abridged edn, Chicago, 1972).

Leighton, C. D. A.: *Catholicism in a Protestant Kingdom: A Study of the Irish 'Ancien Régime'* (Dublin, 1994).
McGrath, Charles Ivar: *The Making of the Eighteenth-Century Irish Constitution: Government, Parliament and the Revenue, 1692–1714* (Dublin, 2000).
McNally, Patrick: *Parties, Patriots and Undertakers: Parliamentary Politics in Early Hanoverian Ireland* (Dublin, 1997).
Moody, T. W. and Vaughan, W. E. (eds): *A New History of Ireland*, vol. 4: *Eighteenth-Century Ireland 1691–1800* (Oxford, 1986).
Wall, Maureen: *Catholic Ireland in the Eighteenth Century* (Dublin, 1989).
Whelan, Kevin: *The Tree of Liberty: Radicalism, Catholicism and the Construction of Irish Identity 1760–1830* (Cork, 1996).

Chapter Thirty-Two

Ireland: Radicalism, Rebellion and Union

Martyn J. Powell

For much of the second half of the eighteenth century Ireland felt the effects of imperial conflict, playing, as it did, a major role in the Seven Years' War, the American War of Independence and the French Revolutionary Wars. The development of the fiscal-military British state during this period had a profound impact upon Irish social and political life. Britain, having acquired extensive new territories all around the globe, was forced to rationalize its conquests, and Ireland was included in this reassessment, although for historians its colonial status remains a matter of debate. Ireland was therefore left in a peculiar position. On the one hand war forced the British government to think of Irish security, an efficient system of Irish government and the need to gain additional funds from the Irish parliament. But it was also clear that the British ministry did not really have the leisure to attend to Ireland and make policy with any great degree of consistency. From the perspective of patriotic Irish politicians, resentful of British commercial and constitutional restrictions, this was a period in which Britain's difficulties could be put to national advantage. Ultimately, however, the presence of the Catholic majority, and the issue of dependence on British security, meant that Irish patriotism had both internal and external limits. Moderate Irish Protestants were unwilling to push the issue too far as long as the Catholic question was left unsolved. This left a political vacuum that was filled by radicals, from a variety of religious backgrounds, who were prepared to envisage substantive, even revolutionary, political and social change. Equally, those with a vested interest in the secular and religious status quo sought to preserve the Protestant state, thus setting the stage for political and sectarian conflict. Faced with these circumstances the British government's patience was finite, and as instability increased, it was evident that action would have to be taken if the weak underbelly of the British empire was not to be exploited by foreign aggressors.

Free Trade and Legislative Independence

The beginning of the reign of George III found Irish politics acting as a mirror to its British counterpart. Political ideologies were a firm second best to party factionalism and the more mercenary interests of MPs. In Ireland the 'undertaker system' provided a means by which the British government was able to manage the Irish parliament. Patronage was distributed to the most powerful political operators in exchange for the votes of their followers. This system had its faults, however, and the independent mind-set of the undertakers, along with a keen rivalry that bordered on outright hostility, contributed to the frustration felt by British ministers. British misgivings were heightened by the development in the late 1750s of a patriotic reform programme focusing on constitutional restrictions. The primary grievances were Poynings' Law, allowing the British and Irish privy councils to interfere in the legislative process, and the Declaratory Act, which gave the Westminster parliament the right to legislate directly for Ireland, and reserved to the British House of Lords the right of final judicature. Other complaints included Ireland's lack of a habeas corpus act, and the uncertain security of tenure enjoyed by Irish judges, who served only during the king's pleasure. This constitutional programme provided a rallying point for an independent patriot opposition, which when joined by the large undertaker-led parties was capable of defeating the British government in Ireland. Patriotic politics was also bolstered by the arrival in parliament of a new generation of leaders, initially Henry Flood and the unscrupulous John Hely-Hutchinson, and then later Henry Grattan. These politicians were successful in fomenting Irish resentment against British constitutional and commercial restraints, and the impact of their rhetoric was felt inside and outside of parliament. Indeed, the tail end of the Bedford viceroyalty saw mutinous behaviour by the lords justices (leading Irish 'undertakers' who acted in the viceroy's frequent absences), an anti-union riot and popular protest against British cattle exports.

During the 1760s Britain found it increasingly difficult to control the Irish parliament. Consequently, the Bute and Grenville ministries, with half an eye on similar administrative problems in America, resolved to reform the Irish system of government. The mechanism chosen to tighten Britain's control over Ireland was a resident lord lieutenant, which would make redundant the commission of lords justices, and thus reduce the power of the undertakers. It was probably hoped that the undertakers themselves would also be removed from the equation, but a succession of viceroys found that it was impossible to manage parliament without the support of the local power brokers. Although it was the Grenville ministry, in a cabinet decision of 1765, which first resolved on imposing a resident viceroy, it was left to the Grafton administration to send a viceroy who was actually prepared to remain there. Thomas Bartlett has shown that Lord George Townshend, who was chosen as lord lieutenant, played a key role in ensuring that the British ministry put its plans into action.

The Townshend and Harcourt viceroyalties were formative periods in Irish political development because their attempts to form a solid bloc of voters in the Irish parliament that would support the Irish executive in Dublin Castle alienated some of the old-style undertakers and drove them into the arms of the patriot opposition. From this point John Ponsonby and the duke of Leinster were regular critics of government, and their connections with the Rockingham Whigs at Westminster fused a bond between British and Irish opposition groups. Moreover, Townshend's decision to prorogue the Irish parliament, following the rejection of a British-inspired money bill, rekindled popular opposition to government on a scale not seen since the money bill dispute of 1753. The growth of popular politics in Dublin illustrates the increasing importance of public opinion in late eighteenth-century Ireland. It was most evident in the actions of the crowd, which protested outside parliament, in the proliferation of anti-government pamphlets and newspapers, and in the strident patriotic voices provided by a phalanx of MPs and city radicals, many of whom were directly accused of attempting to excite the common people.

Although Lord Harcourt was able to tease Henry Flood away from the opposition ranks, a solid core, including Henry Grattan, Walter Hussey Burgh, Hercules Langrishe, Gervase Parker Bushe and Denis Daly, gave voice to patriot concerns within the Irish parliament. The outbreak of the American Revolution acted as a bonding agent for this group, as did broader social connections in patriot clubs such as the Monks of Screw, and even in amateur theatrical entertainments. Yet, despite the renewed vigour of the opposition, Harcourt, aided by the judicious distribution of patronage, and the not inconsiderable body within the Irish political community that sympathized with Britain's war aims, was able to ensure that the Castle's parliamentary majority remained secure. But his successor as lord lieutenant, the earl of Buckinghamshire, was less successful, losing control of parliament to the patriot opposition. The free trade dispute, which was the result of longstanding resentment against British restrictions on Irish commerce, and the imposition of a wartime embargo on the Irish provision trade, strengthened the popular dimension to Irish politics. In imitation of the American rebels, an anti-importation movement was set up, along with 'buy Irish' societies. The British government failed to have these pronounced illegal. But its concern was probably an overreaction, as the non-importation societies were not as effective as they might have been. Expectations of the detrimental effect which the societies would have upon its vibrant linen trade, buoyed by export bounties, persuaded Ulster to opt out. At the same time the non-importation associations were often short-lived and targeted only selected British ports.

These associations, however, were backed by the military force of the Volunteers: locally raised companies ostensibly for the protection of Ireland against a threatened French invasion. Though companies had been raised during Harcourt's viceroyalty, the first of a new breed of Irish Volunteers were formed in Belfast in March 1778; these men went out of their way to declare their independence of government and their determination not to receive either reward or wages from the Castle. When the privateer John Paul Jones, acting for the American colonies, entered the Irish Sea and attacked Whitehaven, the Volunteers spread from a Belfast-based organization into a national movement. The Dublin branches were more moderate than those in Ulster, and they were willing to put themselves under the control of government, describing themselves as 'armed societies' rather than, as in Belfast, 'Volunteer companies'. Although a militia bill was passed, the lack of adequate funds, and the prevarication of the North ministry, meant that it was ineffectual in stemming the proliferation of Volunteer companies. The Protestant community's insecurity, which emanated from the awareness of their minority position within Ireland, and was exacerbated by the threat of a foreign Catholic invasion, quickly prompted the adoption of this attractive alternative to the Irish standing army. Later attempts to subvert the Volunteer leadership by offering their officers commissions on behalf of the crown were doomed to failure. The British government was in the unenviable position of having to deal with an armed force which, paradoxically, it was both threatened by and reliant upon. The viceroy, the earl of Buckinghamshire, was almost certainly guilty of encouraging Volunteering. But it must be acknowledged that the depletion of the Irish standing army and the lack of money available to fund a militia left him with no other viable alternative. The Volunteers were allowed to recruit freely; and the government was left reliant on the end of the war to bring about the disbanding of this force.

The Volunteers quickly became politicized and entered into the campaign for Irish free trade with some vigour. Parliament added to this pressure by passing a short money bill. Irish MPs were high on a tide of patriotic fervour, and no doubt a riot outside parliament further encouraged them to vote with the popular cause. The North ministry, distracted by the American War, and broadly sympathetic to Irish grievances, agreed to a generous programme of concessions. This legislation effectively allowed Ireland to trade directly with Britain's colonies, provided the Irish levied the same duties as Britain on goods imported from the plantations. In other words North continued to espouse a mercantilist theory, in that the mother country had the exclusive right to trade with her colonies, but as a great favour Ireland was to be allowed to enjoy similar commercial benefits.

The concession of free trade came too late to quell popular patriotic feeling, and Irish attention turned to the constitutional restrictions on the operation of the Irish parliament. Britain's war with America provided the Irish patriots with both opportunity and justification for a challenge upon Poynings' Law. Backed by the Volunteers, many companies of which had installed prominent patriots as their commanders, the Irish parliament regularly voted in favour of constitutional concessions. On 19 April 1780 Henry Grattan introduced a motion in the Irish Commons designed to confirm Ireland's legislative independence. His speech was one of the most impressive of his career. He pointed out that Britain had been willing to allow the rebellious colonies control over their own taxation and powers of internal legislation, and that it was therefore hypocritical to deny the same concessions to the loyal Irish.

Until this point, Irish patriots had received support from both the Rockingham and Chathamite wings of the British opposition. But their fast-forming reservations were confirmed by the fall of North, which meant that, now that they were in power, they would have to deal with the Irish crisis. Lord Shelburne and Charles James Fox harboured hopes of a partial submission to Irish demands, and a 'final adjustment' to the Anglo-Irish connection. The weight of pressure from the Volunteers and a united parliament forced them, however, to concede the alteration of Poynings' Law and the mutiny bill, the repeal of the Declaratory Act of 1720, and the restoration of appellant judicature to the Irish House of Lords. The situation created on 17 May 1782 was imperfect and ambiguous. It was certainly not the revolution in Irish government portrayed by many historians. Indeed, it can be argued that a revolution was precisely what Grattan and his followers wanted to avoid, because, as a Protestant minority dependent on British power, they could not countenance any serious rupture with Britain. After 1782 Ireland continued to remain in a subordinate position to Britain. The amended version of Poynings' Law still required Irish bills to be signified under the great seal of Great Britain; the Irish administration, through its control of parliament, could use its influence to block bills; the lord lieutenant was still appointed, through the great seal, through the influence of the British government; and the British ministry continued to make foreign policy for the whole of the empire, including Ireland. Above all there was a strong suspicion in Ireland that Britain could just as easily renege on its agreement, and impose once again the statutes previously used to control Ireland, particularly as a final adjustment, and perhaps even a union, was still on the agenda of the British government.

This partly explains why, although the Rockingham ministry believed that it had drawn a line in the sand, the momentum of Irish reform continued, and the more radical patriots looked for a renunciation act, freeing Ireland from all de jure legislative subordination to Westminster. This additional British concession was forced by Henry Flood, who was determined to regain the political initiative from Henry Grattan. Public opinion was also of vital importance in forcing the Irish parliament and the British government into action, and the more radical Volunteers and Irish newspapers gave Flood's campaign critical impetus. Yet, due to some canny intriguing by a grouping within the government, the measure eventually passed was a bill of recognition, which in effect recognized the status quo at the point of the repeal of the Declaratory Act.

Grattan's Parliament

The conflict over renunciation illustrated the divisions that existed within Irish patriotism. Similar signs had appeared in 1782, at the first Dungannon convention of the Volunteers, when a split had emerged in the Volunteers between the leadership and the rank-and-file. Indeed, the failure to call for immediate action left an implicit threat of rebellion stirring among the more radical sections of the Ulster Volunteers. The second Dungannon convention in September 1783 saw the Volunteers call for parliamentary reform, which had been put on the political agenda by Sir Edward Newenham. Their demands included the redistribution of seats, a wider franchise, annual parliaments, a secret ballot and the exclusion of placemen from the Irish House of Commons. They also advocated the limited enfranchisement of Catholics. It was this issue, however, that contained the seeds of its own destruction. The already fragile coalition of Volunteers and their parliamentary supporters was shattered over the question of the extension of the franchise to Catholics, ensuring that the bill to achieve this end, introduced in the Commons by Henry Flood, was defeated.

Catholic relief had periodically been on the government's agenda since the formation of the Catholic Committee in 1760, during the sympathetic Bedford administration. Later viceroys, Townshend and Harcourt, had both made minor concessions, and in 1778 and 1782 major Catholic relief acts were passed, albeit prompted by the British government. The Irish parliament, buoyed with Protestant confidence during the struggle for free trade and legislative independence, was not ill-disposed towards the Irish Catholics. The Dungannon convention of 1782 had called for the relaxation of the penal code, and Henry Grattan was firmly committed to Catholic relief. Many loyal Castle supporters, however, most notably the Shannon squadron, and also some of the more radical patriots, including Sir Edward Newenham, George Ogle, Lord Charlemont and Henry Flood, were much less enthusiastic. Catholic relief was left to languish on the Irish political back-burner, until a violent change in circumstances forced it once again onto the agenda.

Defeat on parliamentary reform, however, did not dampen the reforming zeal of Irish patriots. James Napper Tandy and Archibald Hamilton Rowan looked to a more radical approach and the strength of popular politics as a means of gaining redress. In parliament, Flood and his followers turned their attention back to Irish commerce, expressing reservations at the incomplete nature of free trade when it was conceded. Legislative independence only intensified patriot disaffection towards the remaining restrictions on Irish commerce, and in particular about the state of the Irish sugar-refining industry. Following a campaign to boycott British goods, in which merchants who would not bow to pressure were tarred and feathered, the viceroy was pressurized by parliament into raising the issue with William Pitt, the prime minister. As a result, Pitt began to formulate a distinctive Irish policy – based on the reformation of Anglo-Irish commerce. The new scheme was designed as a final adjustment to Anglo-Irish relations. Pitt planned to equalize duties between the two countries, allowing free traffic of foreign goods between them, and proposing to issue no further duties or bounties on goods moving from Britain to Ireland or vice versa. In return Ireland was expected to make a contribution to the imperial coffers, for defence purposes; a sum that would increase along with its prosperity. Pitt also intended to introduce a mild version of parliamentary reform, though this was abandoned at an early stage, following the failure of the British reform bill.

The Irish Commons accepted the resolutions regulating trade between Britain and Ireland without rancour, as they appeared to benefit Ireland. But a clause that provided for the appropriation of future surpluses in the Irish hereditary revenue, for the financing of the empire's naval protection, created a storm of protest. Government supporters led by John Beresford, patriots led by Henry Grattan, and Protestant public opinion were vehemently opposed to the measure. The Irish government was forced to backtrack, and it encouraged the amendment of the bill. The British privy council added its own alterations, including a clause that forced Ireland to recognize the Navigation Acts, and any further British legislation on shipping and the colonial trade that affected Britain and Ireland. Although the commercial propositions passed safely through the British House of Commons, they finally came to grief in Ireland. It is clear that Dublin Castle could not hope to overcome the three main points of objection by Irish MPs who were angered by the watering down of the concessions; unwilling to contribute to imperial expenditure; and convinced that the proposals were an infringement on the Irish parliament's legislative independence. The abandonment of the commercial propositions was a landmark defeat for the Pitt ministry. But although the government was forced to jettison its plans for Anglo-Irish trade reform, ultimately Irish tariffs were adjusted and an Irish Navigation Act was passed. The intransigence of the Irish Commons, however, had frustrated Pitt's attempt to secure a greater financial contribution towards the cost of empire. Such action prevented the British ministry from regarding the constitution of 1782–3 as a permanent settlement and made it reluctant to abandon its plans for a union.

The realization that legislative independence as it stood represented a dangerous halfway house was given further weight when the Irish parliament took the initiative in the regency crisis in the late 1780s. It presented an address to the viceroy asking the Prince of Wales immediately to take on the regency of Ireland with full and unrestricted powers. Like its British counterpart the Irish parliament had debated feverishly the possible outcome of the king's illness. The question exercising Irish MPs was: did the Irish parliament have the independent right to elect a regent during the king's illness? Moreover, even if they possessed this right, was it politic to use it at this point in time? Henry Grattan saw in the crisis another opportunity for the Irish parliament to exercise its newly won independence, and the parliamentary opposition also believed that a regency would be more sympathetic to their cause and that of their Foxite allies. Although the viceroy refused to receive their address, a delegation was sent to London, only to be welcomed by a deluge of hostile caricatures and the news that the king had in fact recovered.

The United Irishmen

It was the outbreak of the French Revolution, and the formation of more radical and more assertive organizations demanding Catholic rights, that finally dashed the patriotic optimism of Grattan's parliament. The Belfast Society of United Irishmen was formed in October 1791, under the leadership of the Protestant Theobald Wolfe Tone. Other important members included Dr William Drennan, Samuel Neilson and Thomas Russell. In November James Napper Tandy formed the Dublin branch. It was more successful in attracting Catholic members, and its membership was probably split evenly between Catholics and Protestants, though most of the leading activists were Protestants. There was certainly a sprinkling of artisans and, in its later stages, Catholic agricultural workers, but recent research by Nancy Curtin confirms that the two societies were dominated by the middle classes, particularly by professional men and merchants. Influenced by the political ideas of John Locke and Thomas Paine, by civic humanism and natural rights ideology, the United Irishmen pressed for parliamentary reform – including an extension of the franchise, equal electoral districts and annual parliaments – but they were also eager to end religious discrimination against Presbyterians and Catholics in Irish society. Although the core of United Irish activity remained restricted to Dublin and Belfast, the movement gradually became national. But this expansion brought ideological contradictions, because the success in enlisting Catholics from the lower orders, with their radical social and even sectarian aims, sat uneasily with the enlightened though essentially bourgeois world-view of the United Irish leadership. The social conservatism of the United Irishmen has probably been exaggerated, but it is notable that they did not embrace universal manhood suffrage until 1794, when their programme was first published, and even then they rejected the secret ballot.

From an early stage Wolfe Tone was determined to embrace the Irish Catholic community within the united Irish movement, and his pamphlet of 1791, *An Argument on behalf of the Catholics of Ireland*, was designed to persuade Irish Dissenters of the benefits of Catholic relief. In the same year the Catholic Committee demanded the complete repeal of the penal laws. A shift in power was occurring in this body from aristocratic conservatives to middle-class radicals, although admittedly even the more assertive members were calling only for the entrance of Catholics into the Irish political nation on the basis of their property qualifications. It is clear that they had some sympathy amongst the wider Protestant political nation, as the Irish Whigs wrested the initiative from the British government on Catholic relief. Sir Hercules Langrishe introduced a relief bill in the Irish Commons, offering relatively minor concessions relating to restrictions on Catholic entry into the legal profession, into education and into mixed marriages. Moderate Irish Whigs led by Grattan and William Ponsonby also formed The Irish Friends of the Constitution, Liberty and

Peace, modelled on the Association of the Friends of the People society in England. Many members of the Irish Whig Club joined, preferring its more moderate reformist agenda to that of the United Irishmen. It was not a republican organization. They saw a role for the monarchy, aristocracy and commons in government, though they acknowledged that the Irish parliament required radical reform and that this could not be separated from the question of Catholic relief.

Initially the Irish parliament, with the support of the Castle government, attempted to counter the threat posed by the United Irishmen by introducing legislation designed to limit their popular appeal. Place and civil list acts were passed, the latter in response to calls for a reduction of the pension list. A Libel Act, based on a similar act introduced by Fox in Britain, was also approved. In February 1793 an Irish Catholic enfranchisement act was introduced, allowing Irish Catholics to vote, bear arms and be appointed to civil and military posts. They were, however, still prevented from becoming MPs and from holding military rank above colonel. They also remained unable to break into borough guilds and corporations. These concessions owed much to the continued pressure exerted on government by the Catholic Committee, who had begun to make overtures to the Defenders, a body of sectarian Catholic rural agitators. The refusal of the Catholic Committee to abandon its campaign alienated not only bulwarks of the Castle party such as Beresford and Fitzgibbon, but also those more amenable to Catholic relief, such as the Ponsonbys.

The failure of the parliamentary reform programme in the face of the intransigence of the Protestant elite and the vacillation of the British government pushed the United Irishmen towards a more militant strategy. According to Curtin, key factors included the failure of the Catholic convention at Dungannon, the patriot response to war with France, and the beginning of government repression. Lord Edward Fitzgerald and Arthur O'Connor became increasingly prominent in the leadership of the United Irishmen, and they favoured a more radical secret society committed by oath to both nationalism and republicanism. French military assistance was essential for the achievement of their aims, as was a mass-based movement, and at this stage – rather than as a response to the Fitzwilliam viceroyalty – a recruitment drive was initiated, with the aim of forging an alliance with the Catholic Defenders. The increasingly militant United Irishmen, imbued not only with the enlightened ideals of the early French revolutionaries, but also with an embryonic form of Irish nationalism, were regarded as a threat to both the security of Protestant dominance and rule by Dublin Castle. The British government intensified its repression, declaring the Dublin United Irishmen organization to be illegal. But this pushed the movement underground, and increased the likelihood of a common language and goals being shared with the Defenders.

Matters came to a head in 1795 when the Pitt ministry, having welcomed a political alliance at Westminster with the more conservative Whigs under Portland, appointed Earl Fitzwilliam as viceroy. The appointment of such an inexperienced administrator to this challenging post was something of a gamble. He certainly would not have been chosen by Pitt, but the Portland group insisted on a share of the offices of state, and were particularly keen on addressing Irish affairs. Fitzwilliam, like many of his Whig colleagues, was a supporter of Catholic relief, and he determined to put such a plan into operation on arrival in Ireland, despite not having cabinet approval. In Fitzwilliam's defence, it is clear that the terms of his appointment were unclear and that he believed he had been given responsibility for the management of Ireland. But when Pitt found that he was making overtures to the Irish opposition, he made Fitzwilliam's instructions more explicit and, at a cabinet meeting prior to Fitzwilliam's departure, it was confirmed that there would be no change in government policy. Fitzwilliam, however, still seemed to be convinced that his instructions were not orders but simply advice which he was free to ignore if he wished. On his arrival in Ireland he dismissed a number of officeholders, including John Beresford, the powerful revenue commissioner, on charges of corruption and maladministration, and he allowed Grattan leave to introduce a bill for full Catholic emancipation. Given Protestant anger, his actions left Pitt with little choice but to recall the hapless viceroy. Fitzwilliam argued in vain that the peace of Ireland depended upon Catholic emancipation and that this concession would enable the government to raise regiments of Catholic yeomanry for local defence purposes.

Fitzwilliam had clearly made a political misjudgement. But he shares the blame with the ministers in Westminster who were willing to appoint someone who had no conception of the mechanism of the Irish government; with Pitt personally, who dallied when confronted with the question of emancipation; and with Portland, who was rather slow in replying to Fitzwilliam's correspondence and had not warned his friend against making rash commitments. Feelings in Ireland were mixed on Fitzwilliam's departure. It was evident that many Catholics and Protestants had regarded him as their saviour. But Pitt's government remained unsure about emancipation; they were not convinced of the trustworthiness of Catholic yeomen regiments, and they feared for the survival of the established Church of Ireland in a legislature dominated by Catholics. It is also clear that the defensive measures that would probably have been taken by fearful and belligerent Protestants would have been an unwelcome distraction to a government embroiled in war with France. The king was also offended by Fitzwilliam's premature agitation of Catholic emancipation and became more determined in his opposition to the measure. In Ireland the Fitzwilliam affair intensified hostility between Catholics and Protestants which had been simmering since the collapse of the parliamentary reform movement and the shift in the stance of the Catholic Committee towards radicalism. At the same time his departure, and the defeat of Grattan's Catholic emancipation bill, appeared to mark the last gasp for moderate Irish Whiggism. Henceforth, moderate Irish patriots such as Grattan and the Ponsonbys were marginalized. Grattan eventually followed Fox's example at Westminster and seceded from the Irish parliament; he was rendered powerless as the transformation of the United Irishmen into an armed society picked up speed.

By the spring of 1795 the United Irishmen had established a firm alliance with the Catholic Defenders. Despite profound differences in class structure and ideology, the Defenders were valued for their numerical strength in Catholic areas. The United Irishmen had yet to make much of an impression outside Dublin and Belfast, and large numbers were required if an insurrection was going to be successful. Kevin Whelan, however, has argued that the heightening of tension in Ireland was due less to the proliferation of the United Irish movement through their alliance with the Defenders, and more to the deliberate sectarian policies of the Protestant ultras. In his view, conservative Protestant MPs, with the tacit approval of the British government, deliberately fomented sectarianism in Ulster in the hopes that moderate

Protestants and radical Dissenters would split from their Catholic allies. Despite Defenderism's socially diverse support base, links with liberal freemasonry and similarities in structure with the United Irishmen, it is clear that the United Irishmen found difficulty in incorporating the traditions of sectarian violence associated with the Defenders, and their demands for social reform, and that these features tainted the movement, at least in the eyes of Ulster Presbyterians. Certainly, the bond between Presbyterians and Catholics in the urban United Irishmen societies was not replicated in rural Armagh, where sectarianism had returned to prevent any political alliance between Catholics and Protestants. Protestant Peep O'Day Boys attempted to take their own action against government concessions to Catholics, and when they used intimidation to drive Catholic families from their homes, they clashed with the Defenders. This activity had much deeper roots than the response to the French Revolution, out of which the United Irishmen were born. The Peep O'Day Boys were probably formed sometime in the late 1770s, the Defenders following in 1784. Both fit into the tradition of agrarian secret societies in Ireland, characterized by violent reprisal, secret oaths, attacks on cattle and the intimidation of judges.

If sectarianism was deliberately encouraged by Protestant ultras and their sympathizers in the Castle, then the keystone of this policy came with the Irish government's countenancing of the Orange Order. The foundation of this movement occurred after the defeat of the pro-government candidate in the Armagh by-election of January 1795 and after a violent incident later in the year known as the Battle of the Diamond, when Peep O'Day Boys routed a body of Defenders. The movement quickly spread, using the established network of Volunteer corps. Although the Orange Order initially met with a cold reception in governmental circles, ministers eventually concluded that the only means of counteracting the United Irish radicals was by supporting an equivalent avowedly Protestant organization. Exclusive Protestant rights were preached against the enlightened inclusiveness of the United Irish mission. There is no doubt that government authorities turned a blind eye towards heavy-handed tactics by the Orange Order and the yeomanry. But it should be recognized that this latter body did at least have non-sectarian antecedents, based as it was on old Volunteer regiments. More important, it also contained a substantial proportion of Catholic troops. Nevertheless, Armagh Catholics had their homes looted and burned in brutal searches for weapons, and many were forced to leave the province.

When the government received information about United Irishmen preparations for insurrection, the restoration of civil authority became a matter of some urgency, especially as it had uncovered Wolfe Tone's connections with Revolutionary France. The Castle was initially able to reflect with satisfaction on the final undermining of any credibility that the United Irishmen may have had left with moderate Whigs, and when Tone offered to go into voluntary exile in America, the government accepted this promise, without asking for any kind of security. This, of course, allowed him to make his way to his French allies. Government leniency towards the United Irishmen, however, was short-lived, and its legal and military servants were given a freer hand by the introduction of an Insurrection Act, which made it a capital offence to administer an illegal oath and which gave magistrates powers of search and seizure. The government also passed a series of indemnity acts, sanctioning police operations that stepped outside legal restrictions, including the partial suspension of habeas corpus.

The evidence that the United Irishmen were opening up discussions with the French gave particular cause for alarm, as it was far from certain that the British navy would be able to protect the coast from a combined attack by the French, Spanish and Dutch navies. In December 1796 a French force of 15,000 troops in forty-three ships under the command of General Hoche was dispatched to Ireland to aid in an insurrection, even though it was rather late in the year to mount such an expedition. An attempt to land 6,000 men eventually foundered in storms off Bantry Bay. The publicity surrounding the failed invasion acted, however, as a spur to United Irish recruitment. The United Irishmen were also able to connect with like-minded groups in Britain, and Benjamin Binns travelled to Ireland on behalf of the London Corresponding Society in order to meet with the revolutionary wing of the United Irishmen.

The failed invasion marked a critical point in the intensification of Castle-sponsored repression. The government was persuaded to look to the Orangemen for military assistance. Then, faced with rising tension and the increase in reports of a possible insurrection, it took the decision to disarm Ulster, which was done with brutal efficiency by General Lake. This effectively neutralized the ideological home of the rebellion, although a hostile undercurrent continued to exist for some time against the government's actions. Lake's efforts were not the only factor that induced the majority of Ulster's citizens to remain loyal. Much of the province was riven by sectarianism, and the Orange Order quickly overtook the United Irishmen as Ulster's most popular extra-parliamentary organization. At the same time, the middle classes and commercial interests began to realize that continued political upheaval was deleterious to their livelihoods. Finally, the Presbyterians were disappointed by the policies adopted by Revolutionary France towards Switzerland and America.

Although initially somewhat erratic, the British government's network of spies managed a major coup in February 1798, when Arthur O'Connor, John Binns and the Reverend James O'Coigley were arrested for treason. It was alleged that they had attempted to coordinate an uprising involving British and Irish radicals. O'Coigley was arrested after documents were found that named him as a member of the 'Secret Committee of England', which had called on the French government to aid a British insurrection. He was convicted and executed, but his co-conspirator Arthur O'Connor was found not guilty, largely due to the efforts of his lawyer, Thomas Erskine, and a number of prominent character witnesses from the opposition Whigs, including Fox, Sheridan and Charles Grey. Despite their acquittals, O'Connor, Marcus Despard and Binns remained in jail, as the suspension of habeas corpus allowed the government to keep them confined indefinitely. In March 1798 the Leinster directory of the United Irishmen were arrested after the government received information from its most valuable informer, Thomas Reynolds. Lord Edward Fitzgerald evaded capture, however, and he was not apprehended until 19 May 1798, when he was mortally wounded, supposedly while trying to escape arrest.

The Rebellion of 1798

When the rebellion eventually began, in May 1798, it was a disastrous failure. There was no insurrection in Dublin thanks to the arrest of the main leaders. Militant Belfast had been violently disarmed by General Lake in 1797, so it failed to rise. Eastern

Ulster had been pacified using a combination of arson and torture, much of it levied by the Irish yeomanry. There was a limited uprising in Ulster in June 1798 led by Henry Joy McCracken and Henry Munro, but they could rely only on the more determined republicans and they were quickly defeated and the leaders executed. Minor revolts also occurred in the countryside around Dublin, in Wicklow and Kildare. The main focus of the rebellion was Co. Wexford, involving 30,000 insurgents. It was not noted to be a centre of United Irish activity and the Irish rebellion can no longer be regarded as simply a rural riot on an enormous scale. Formerly, the Wexford rebellion has been portrayed as a spontaneous, disorganized and savage outbreak of sectarianism led by priests. Recent research, however, has downplayed priestly involvement, showing that the hierarchy were staunch loyalists, and has pointed to the strains of enlightened republicanism that can be found in the Wexford branches of the United Irishmen. The United Irishmen in Wexford were much more numerous and widespread than was hitherto thought, and the revolt was part of a wider United Irish plan. The Wexford rebels were capable of acting as a disciplined military force in the field and only later resorted to guerrilla tactics.

The Wexford rebellion, after initial successes due to the fact that landlords in this area were woefully unprepared for trouble, was eventually defeated at the Battle of Vinegar Hill, near Enniscorthy. Casualties were heavy during the rebellion, with atrocities committed on both sides. But Whelan argues that the savagery of the insurgents at Scullabogue and Wexford Bridge was due to a collapse of discipline among the rebels, whereas serious offences by the military were part of a deliberate policy. This, however, is somewhat misleading; such actions on the part of the rebels were not wild aberrations and the uncompromising tactics adopted by the pro-government forces were not the deliberate policy of the new viceroy, Lord Cornwallis, who replaced Lord Camden in June, and also took over as commander-in-chief. He was genuinely sympathetic to the Catholic cause and was determined not to undertake a vendetta against the defeated rebels, despite pressure exerted by Protestant ultras such as John Beresford and Lord Fitzgibbon.

The United Irish rising was to be supported by a French invasion. But lamentable organization resulted in the small French expeditionary force led by General Humbert being landed at Killala in Connaught where there was little rebel activity, and where he received paltry aid from the Catholic peasantry. Humbert and his forces defeated a British army in an open engagement, but their success was short-lived and the French troops making their way towards Dublin were swiftly rounded up at Ballinamuck by British forces under Cornwallis. In October 1798 Wolfe Tone was apprehended in a ship, part of a small French fleet, in Lough Swilly, Co. Donegal, by a British squadron. He was court-martialled and sentenced to death, in spite of the fact that though he was a French military officer, he had never been part of the British army, and civil courts were sitting at the time. He eventually committed suicide, dying on 19 November, before he could be executed.

The Castle administration under Cornwallis was eager to restore calm to Ireland, and was well disposed towards leniency for all rebels, excepting the commanders. The Protestant ultras, however, were less inclined towards clemency, but generally Cornwallis managed to win this argument. Although retribution occurred on a local level, officially sanctioned reprisals were minimal. A number of prominent United Irish leaders, including Arthur O'Connor and Oliver Bond, were saved from the gallows on condition that they would provide written evidence of their treason and that of their comrades, though without implicating other individuals by name. But this deal came too late for the Sheares brothers, who were executed along with William Byrne and John McCann.

The Act of Union

Although Cornwallis had achieved some success in pacifying Ireland, the Pitt ministry, which had been considering the constitutional position of Ireland for some time, determined to take action, and a union was its preferred solution. The British government had spent much of the latter half of the eighteenth century in trying to implement a more efficient mechanism of ruling Ireland. After undertakers, constant residency by the viceroy and legislative independence, union remained the only viable option. The 1798 rebellion persuaded the government that the minority Protestant interest could no longer act as the legitimate Irish legislature. While war continued with France, the security of Ireland was of vital importance to the British government.

The union scheme enveloped another strand of Pitt's policy, in that after the rebellion, the prime minister, with the firm support of Grenville, was determined to reconcile Irish Catholics. He had no intention of further alienating this section of the Irish population by a policy of repression and reprisals. He hoped to replace the sacramental test with a more general oath of allegiance, which included a disavowal of Jacobinism – to be taken by all officeholders, teachers and clergymen. Provision would be made for Catholic clergy, and Catholics would be eligible to all public offices; though Pitt remained unsure whether they should be allowed to sit in the united parliament. There was, however, little chance of emancipation being accepted by Irish Protestants while they remained a minority. Union would solve this problem by placing Irish Catholics in a minority position within the newly constituted British nation. At the same time, Irish Protestants were more willing to consider union following the rebellion. It had all too plainly emphasized that their privileged position – even with legislative independence – was untenable without British military aid.

When union was placed on the table, however, Catholic, Protestant and Presbyterian communities were divided on the issue. The Catholic population was generally apathetic, though their religious leaders were reasonably positive following intimations that emancipation would follow union. They were also disaffected with the anticlerical excesses of the French Revolution. Presbyterians were cautiously in favour of the measure, and Belfast mercantile interests were assuaged by the benefits offered by improved access to imperial markets that it was indicated would accompany union. But, ultimately, the union only had to be ratified by the Protestant parliament. It was hoped that the rebellion and the prospect of an insecure future with a restless and bitter Catholic majority would persuade the Protestant elite to vote its parliament out of existence.

None the less, the security argument and hints that agrarian disturbances would lessen the rent roll of Protestant estates were not sufficient to win over the Irish Commons. Protestant landlords representing county seats and MPs with seats in Dublin proved most reluctant to vote for union. Henry Grattan was hostile to the measure, as was Speaker John Foster, and a majority of the Orange lodges. It was clear that the removal of the parliament from Dublin would have a disastrous effect on Dublin society and its economy. In Britain the Foxites stood against union, but it was eventually passed with few problems at Westminster. Despite the persuasion of Lord Cornwallis, and his chief secretary, Lord Castlereagh, the Irish parliament was a different matter. After an effective opposition campaign led by Sir John Parnell, George Ponsonby and Sir Lawrence Parsons, the union bill was rejected.

This victory, however, was short-lived as on 6 February 1800 the Irish Act of Union was finally passed by 158 votes to 115 in Dublin. Longstanding historical accounts of this process focus primarily on the application of patronage – peerages and pensions – in order to purchase votes, but very few individuals actually changed their minds as a consequence of the distribution of favours by government. The true picture is rather complicated, and it can be argued with some assurance that patronage did play an important role, even if it is classed as legitimate compensation. It is certainly fair to say that Pitt had to distribute a great deal of patronage before Irish MPs came round to his way of thinking. Irish landowners who returned a number of MPs were promised financial recompense at the rate of £15,000 per borough seat at the final dissolution of the Irish parliament, and this soothed the tempers of many of the most notorious borough-mongers. Castlereagh used government funds to purchase the allegiance of opponents and persuade hostile MPs to retire from active politics. By the second vote around sixty MPs had retired and were replaced by pro-union politicians. This was of undoubted importance as the government was only able to persuade twelve MPs who had voted against the measure to alter their stance and vote for union on the second bill. Forty creations and promotions in the peerage were offered to ensure compliance in the Lords; though in this case these were part of compensation packages rather than an attempt to bribe the recalcitrant.

The newly constituted British parliament removed many of the abuses that had tarnished the reputation of the Irish body. During the process of reorganizing Irish electoral representation many of the most rotten boroughs were removed from the political landscape, and the number of placeholders was cut dramatically. The real key to future stability, Catholic emancipation, was not part of the settlement, however, and there was no attempt to solve the controversial tithe question. Prompted by the machinations of Lord Loughborough, George III expressed his implacable opposition to Catholic emancipation, and the former Irish viceroys, Camden and Westmorland, added their support to this intransigent policy. The Anglo-Irish union therefore was fundamentally flawed from the outset, and it arguably created as many problems as it solved. But the divisions within Irish society, even without exacerbation, would surely have come to the fore even if emancipation had been granted. In any case, the French Revolution pushed both republicanism and nationalism onto the agenda, perhaps ending the prospect of a peaceful absorption of the Catholic nation into the Irish state, something which had looked seriously possible only in the early heady days of Grattan's parliament. It must be emphasized, however, that this phase of Protestant optimism was short-lived. Indeed, given the continued sectarian agitation in Ulster, it was always something of a mirage; a creation that ignored the reality of both Anglo-Irish relations and Protestant disunity. Ultimately, the Irish rebellion solved the question of Protestant divisions, and union was the solution to the British government's security concerns. But Irish Catholics had gained little from this period of crisis, other than a greater sense of national awareness, defined through a sense of their ill-treatment, which in turn did not bode well for the stability of the newly United Kingdom.

FURTHER READING

Bartlett, Thomas: *The Fall and Rise of the Irish Nation: The Catholic Question 1690–1830* (Dublin, 1992).

Bolton, G. C.: *The Passing of the Irish Act of Union* (Oxford, 1966).

Curtin, Nancy J.: *The United Irishmen: Popular Politics in Ulster and Dublin 1791–1798* (Oxford, 1994).

Dickson, David, Keogh, Dáire and Whelan, Kevin (eds): *The United Irishmen: Republicanism, Radicalism and Rebellion* (Dublin, 1993).

Elliott, Marianne: *Partners in Revolution: The United Irishmen and France* (New Haven, CT, 1982).

Elliott, Marianne: *Wolfe Tone: Prophet of Irish Independence* (New Haven, CT, 1990).

Gahan, D. J.: *The People's Rising, Wexford 1798* (Dublin, 1995).

Geoghegan, Patrick M.: *The Irish Act of Union* (Dublin, 1999).

Kelly, James: *Prelude to Union: Anglo-Irish Politics in the 1780s* (Dublin, 1992).

Keogh, Dáire: *The French Disease: The Catholic Church and Irish Radicalism, 1790–1800* (Dublin, 1993).

Keogh, Dáire and Furlong, Nicholas (eds): *The Mighty Wave: The 1798 Rebellion in Wexford* (Dublin, 1996).

McDowell, R. B.: *Ireland in the Age of Imperialism and Revolution, 1760–1801* (Oxford, 1979).

O'Brien, Gerard: *Anglo-Irish Politics in the Age of Grattan and Pitt* (Dublin, 1987).

Smyth, Jim: *The Men of No Property* (Basingstoke, 1992).

Whelan, Kevin: *The Tree of Liberty: Radicalism, Catholicism and the Construction of Irish Identity 1760–1830* (Cork, 1996).

Part VI

Britain and the Wider World

Chapter Thirty-Three

Britain's Emergence as a European Power, 1688–1815

H. M. Scott

Britain's Discovery of Europe

In November 1815 Britain signed the final act of the Congress of Vienna, restoring peace at the end of the wars of 1792–1815, as one of Europe's five great powers. Her naval and financial strength, and finally her army, had contributed significantly to the defeat of France, while her diplomacy and especially that of her foreign secretary, Viscount Castlereagh (1812–22), had shaped the final settlement. Britain's territorial, political and economic gains from the conflict eclipsed those of any other state with the single exception of Russia, with whom she now contested the position of dominant European power. Such an exalted role would have been inconceivable little more than a century before. In the 1680s England had been a state of the second rank, significant only in the rivalries of western Europe but no match for the Bourbon and Habsburg Leviathans who controlled the continent's political destiny.

The long eighteenth century saw a series of linked transformations that changed Britain quite fundamentally. The modern United Kingdom was created by the extension of England's control over Scotland, with whom an incorporating union was concluded (1707), and then with union with Ireland (1800). The Revolution of 1688–9 and the wars that followed secured parliament's place in government, establishing a constitutional monarchy which soon became the envy of progressive opinion throughout Europe. The long and successful warfare that ranged across the entire eighteenth century established a fiscal-military state and contributed to the acquisition of a worldwide empire. This in turn fuelled a notable commercial advance, reinforced by a striking expansion of manufacturing from the later eighteenth century as Britain became the first industrial nation. Underlying several of these changes was the creation of a less stratified, more commercial society. Yet, in some ways, the remarkable expansion of Britain's political role in Europe and her connections with the continent eclipsed all of these changes and was the most fundamental transformation of all, though this has not always been fully appreciated. The eighteenth century saw Britain reconnected to Europe, becoming once more part of the mainstream of western Christendom in a way England at least had not been since the Protestant Reformation of the sixteenth century.

This was far more than a revolution in political relations, crucial though that was. It was also a two-way process. During these decades Europe became much more aware of its island neighbour, admiring its distinctive constitution, scientific and intellectual achievements, political success and, eventually, its territorial and economic power. There was a parallel and, in the longer perspective, more important British discovery of Europe, which has to be placed alongside the emphasis currently given to the growth of English and even British national consciousness at this period. The British elite sent its own sons on the fashionable Grand Tour in increasing numbers, bought paintings and employed architects and landscape gardeners from the continent, in keeping with the dictates of an increasingly cosmopolitan age. Some – and far more than in earlier generations – even learned a European language, above all French, which was the *lingua franca* of monarchical and aristocratic society, though rather fewer spoke a continental tongue at all satisfactorily. The linguistic aptitude of the leading later eighteenth-century diplomat, Sir James Harris, first earl of Malmesbury, who spoke French and – even more remarkably – Dutch fluently, was as unusual as it was laudable. Above all Britain embraced European music. Georg Friedrich Handel made a career in England as a composer of truly European stature and was buried in Westminster Abbey. The 'English Bach', Johann Christian, settled here and Wolfgang Amadeus Mozart thought seriously of doing so, while Joseph Haydn's dozen 'London' symphonies rank among his greatest compositions. The astonishing spread of both oratorio and Italian opera during the eighteenth century symbolized the new importance of Europe to the British Isles.

These cultural links, in the widest sense, were strengthened and even created by political events. Between 1688 and 1815 Britain became a European power, with consequences that have endured to the present day. One symptom was the notable expansion of her involvement in the enlarged diplomatic network linking the continent's capitals which was completed during and immediately after the long reign of Louis XIV (1661–1715). The Revolution of 1688–9 was a turning-point, after which the British monarchy came to maintain permanent and reciprocal diplomatic relations with most European countries of any size, except when these were interrupted during hostilities. This brought about a notable expansion of Britain's diplomatic service during these decades. Yet, even at the end of this period, it remained far less professional than that of its rival, France. Indeed, to speak of a 'diplomatic service', even by the later eighteenth century, may give a misleading impression of the degree of professionalization and coherent organization possessed by the assembled ranks of British representatives in foreign capitals. Diplomatic vacancies were usually filled on a casual, ad hoc basis, and political influence was at least as important as previous experience or relevant expertise. Many posts were difficult to fill, particularly those outside western Europe, while major embassies – such as Paris or Madrid – long remained in practice reserved for aristocratic amateurs who lacked relevant experience and often took only one embassy. The second tier of posts contained more career diplomats, who added a valuable leavening of professionalism, but the diplomatic service was always likely to be an obstacle to the success of London's policy.

Formal responsibility for day-to-day control of diplomacy lay, until the establishment of the Foreign Office in 1782, with the Northern and Southern secretaries. For much of the eighteenth century these men divided the conduct of foreign policy between them on a geographical basis. The secretary of state for the Southern Department was the senior minister, responsible for relations with France, Spain, Portugal, the Italian states, Switzerland and the Ottoman empire. His colleague at the Northern Department dealt with the remaining continental countries: the Dutch Republic, Prussia, Austria, the smaller German states, Denmark, Sweden, Poland and Russia. Assisted only by two under-secretaries with a handful of clerks and decipherers, the two secretaries were responsible for conducting a regular correspondence with diplomats and consuls abroad. The establishment was decidedly small: in the mid-1780s Britain's newly created Foreign Office probably had fewer than twenty permanent officials when its French counterpart contained more than seventy. The responsibility of the two secretaries was also far wider than the conduct of diplomacy: as the principal executors of all government policy, they were responsible for implementing cabinet decisions and maintaining the routine correspondence in almost every area of domestic and colonial affairs. Such dual responsibility for diplomacy and for a wide area of internal and colonial policy was not unique to Britain: this was a period when purely functional departments of state were still emerging. What was without parallel at least in the major continental states was the geographical division of responsibility before the establishment of the Foreign Office. The potential for tension and even rival policies was clear, though for much of the period the two secretaries either cooperated reasonably well or one assumed a leading role, thereby providing integrated direction.

During the Hanoverian period foreign policy remained the preserve of the political elite. In strict constitutional theory its conduct remained the crown's exclusive prerogative. The king concluded treaties and signed alliances, made peace and declared war. The ruler himself also participated in policy making. The three Hanoverian monarchs all exerted considerable influence upon diplomatic strategy. The existence of a 'German Chancery' in London, supplying a steady stream of information from the electorate's protean diplomatic service, often made monarchs better informed than their ministers. Two other influences upon British policy can be noted. The cabinet discussed major issues, especially if the question of war or peace was involved, while individual ministers were always likely to intervene over particular diplomatic questions. During the generation after 1688 parliament and especially the House of Commons had come to assume a general supervisory role over foreign policy, and it had a specific right to inspect any treaty concluded while it was in session, or which involved a financial charge or a change in the law of Great Britain. Ministers also had to take some account of the views of the political nation at large, but such public opinion as existed at this time did not directly affect policy, beyond reinforcing hostility towards France and her allies.

The process by which Britain became a European power was not linear. Periods of close involvement in continental politics and participation in its wars – 1688–*c*.1718; 1744–63; 1788–1815 – were interspersed with phases of insularity and even isolationism. There were always those in public life and even in the ministry of the day prepared to argue that Britain's status as an island enabled her to stand above Europe's rivalries and so isolate herself from its wars. Except during the 1730s, however, the advocates of an active continental policy were usually more influential within government. The dynastic links, first with the Dutch Republic (1689–1702) and then the personal union with Hanover (1714–1837), were important motives for involvement. There was considerable truth in the earl of Chesterfield's observation in 1742 that the electorate robbed Britain of the benefit of being an island. It was also true that, since merchants from throughout the British Isles traded extensively with Europe, London could not be indifferent to developments there. Britain's political emergence, however, was brought about not by such considerations but by her participation in the wars against Louis XIV's France.

The Political Consequences of William III, 1688–1716

Britain's career as a European power was launched by the Revolution of 1688–9. The Dutch stadtholder (1672–1702), William III, had invaded England in order to secure English resources for the anti-French coalition which he was assembling: his life's work was the attempt to weaken and even destroy France's dominance in western Europe, which menaced the republic's independence. The collapse of James II's regime and his precipitate flight ensured that William became king (1689–1702) with his wife Mary – James II's daughter – as queen. The new monarch's first important action in foreign policy was a declaration of war against Louis XIV in May 1689, and this opened four generations of Anglo-French rivalry and periodic warfare which historians have styled the second 'Hundred Years' War', in recollection of the equally extended struggle during the later Middle Ages. The British state was to be at war with France and sometimes Spain too for over half the period from 1688 to 1815. The principal conflicts were the Nine Years' War (1689–97), the War of the Spanish Succession (1702–13), the Anglo-Spanish War/War of the Austrian Succession (1740–8), the Seven Years' War (1756–63), the War of American Independence (1775–83), and the wars against Revolutionary and Napoleonic France (1793–1815). There were also periods of considerable tension amounting to undeclared hostilities, for example in colonial North America before 1756, which reinforced James Stanhope's view that the two states were 'natural and necessary enemies'.

The intensity and continuity of this rivalry, from 1688 to 1815 and beyond, were to be striking. Its importance for British foreign policy lay in the way it dominated London's diplomatic horizon throughout these decades. There were other issues of concern to eighteenth-century British statesmen. The security of the Low Countries and, after the accession of the House of Hanover in 1714, of northwestern Germany were enduring British preoccupations. A longstanding alliance with Portugal, important principally because of the trading connection with Brazil which it protected, and the more recent dynastic and political links with the Dutch Republic were also supported in London. The growing importance of the Baltic, dominated by Russia after the early eighteenth century, as a source of the crucial naval stores on which Britain's seapower depended, was apparent to ministers who also sought to defend British commercial interests wherever they believed this necessary. But these concerns were all subordinated to the needs of the established rivalry with France and, usually, Spain. Foreign policy was here subordinated to military and naval strategy, as diplomacy was shaped by the legacies of the last – or the requirements of the current or next – war. A corollary was that large areas of northern, central and eastern Europe were really only interesting to British statesmen in so far as they were able to provide support against her major enemy. Self-interest dictated the foreign policy of all states, but

Britain's approach was more one-sided than that of most chanceries. Her search for allies during the eighteenth century was really a search for armies to confront France's military power.

This European role was initiated by William III, whose accession ensured that Britain was a leading member of the coalitions which waged the Nine Years' War and the War of the Spanish Succession. Her participation was arranged through her signature of the Grand Alliance of 1689 and its successor concluded at The Hague in 1701. In both wars Britain fought alongside the Dutch Republic and Austria, together with a changing cast of second- and third-rank states. During the 1690s her naval power had developed impressively and this fleet, rather than the previously dominant Dutch navy, had borne the brunt of the conflict at sea. It was increasingly waged not against France's royal navy but against a well-organized, effective privateering campaign supported by the French government. Britain simultaneously re-emerged as a continental military power, sending large armies to fight the French and subsidizing lesser states to put their troops into the field. In 1704–8 the duke of Marlborough, at the head of an allied army, won a remarkable series of victories over France's forces, hitherto dominant. This raised British military prestige on the continent to a level it had not enjoyed since the great English victory at Agincourt almost three centuries before.

The military and naval effort was made possible by a simultaneous financial revolution. The establishment of a national debt (1693) and the founding of the Bank of England (1694) created a modern financial system for the new European power. Backed by parliament, which guaranteed government borrowing, and invested in by the landed and commercial classes, who were also willing to pay high taxes in wartime, this financial system provided the British state with stable loans and sufficient fiscal income to fight and win its eighteenth-century wars with France. This was in sharp contrast to its French rival, whose escalating financial problems would be one principal cause of the Revolution of 1789.

William III's principal legacy to British foreign policy was to establish its anti-French direction, which would endure until the nineteenth century. In the short term his impact was sufficiently strong to survive his own death in April 1702, at the outset of the conflict over the Spanish succession. During the fighting that followed his policies were continued, at least until 1710, by his political executors: the Dutch Grand Pensionary Antonie Heinsius, the Englishmen Sidney Godolphin at the Treasury in London, and Marlborough in command of the army in the Low Countries. In the longer perspective, too, what came to be termed 'Williamite' ideas – by which was meant essentially opposition to France pursued through continental alliances – were to be central to Hanoverian foreign policy, though they only became so from the later 1740s. The age of the stadtholder-king also produced much of the language in which Britain's eighteenth-century diplomacy was clothed: the 'Grand Alliance', a 'Common Cause', the 'Liberties of Europe'. While William III's influence was considerable, however, he alone did not establish Britain's enduring suspicion of and rivalry with Bourbon France.

During the final four decades of the seventeenth century England's traditional international outlook, that of hostility towards and rivalry with Habsburg Spain, had come to be replaced by opposition to France. The Spanish Armada was integral to England's national consciousness. The Protestant English were deeply hostile towards

Spain, who dominated western Europe during the later sixteenth and first half of the seventeenth centuries. This fundamental antagonism had been reinforced by the development of serious rivalry in the colonial sphere and by Madrid's rule over the Southern Netherlands, which endured until the early eighteenth century. But during the final third of the seventeenth century Spain's political and economic decline, together with the parallel rise of the Bourbon monarchy in France, brought about a fundamental change in England's outlook. This had linked internal and international dimensions. Domestically the two rulers of Restoration England had looked across the Channel for inspiration and support. The danger that French-style absolutism would be introduced by Charles II and James II may not have been very great, but it aroused real fears among the Protestant political nation towards France herself. The contemporaneous rise of French military, naval and economic power during the 1660s and 1670s had posed a new threat to the security of the Low Countries and revealed Louis XIV's appetite for more annexations. Colbert's rebuilt navy made France more of a rival at sea than the Dutch now were, while his tariffs hit at England's economic growth. By the 1680s, if not actually earlier, all the elements – with the single exception of serious colonial rivalry – which made Anglo-French tension and hostility so continuous during the next century and more, were in existence. William III benefited from this latent hostility rather than creating it.

There was, however, one important difference after 1688. Political, imperial and economic rivalry was to be crucial during the century of the second 'Hundred Years' War'. But at this period this rivalry was dwarfed by a different issue: the survival of Britain's Protestant Revolution Settlement of 1688–9, to which the Dutch Republic long remained committed. The Nine Years' War was, at one level, a struggle over the English succession, as contemporaries appreciated. Down at least to the accession of the Hanoverian elector as George I of Britain (1714–27), dynastic stability and political security were crucial, and strategic and economic issues were relegated to a back seat. Despite her numerous pregnancies, Queen Anne (1702–14) had no surviving children, imperilling the Protestant succession to the British throne. This was secured by the Act of Settlement (1701), which provided for the succession of the Hanoverian electors in the British Isles.

The Political Consequences of Sir Robert Walpole, 1716–48

A wish to defend the Protestant succession and the new Hanoverian dynasty that protected it dominated British diplomacy after the Treaty of Utrecht (1713). The serious Jacobite rising of 1715 suggested that the threat to George I's throne could not be neglected, and French power still appeared menacing. Security was sought through new treaties with the Dutch Republic and Austria, the principal members of earlier Grand Alliances. The anti-French coalition of the Spanish succession struggle had been sundered by the peace terms and the way they had been negotiated. Its restoration was not speedily accomplished, but during the first half of 1716 new treaties were signed with The Hague and Vienna. They were accompanied by the completion of a system of military defence against France in the Low Countries, the so-called 'Barrier'. The Dutch had the right to garrison certain fortresses in the Southern Netherlands, which had passed to Vienna's rule in 1713–14. The

Republic always attached considerable importance to these arrangements, which were underwritten by Britain and Austria.

By the end of 1716 the restored Grand Alliance had been eclipsed by the conclusion of an Anglo-French alliance that would survive until 1730–1 and whose consequences would shape British foreign policy down to the formal outbreak of a new war with France in 1744. The Anglo-French entente of 1716–31 was the principal and also the most extended occasion during the second 'Hundred Years' War' when London's diplomacy was based upon cooperation with France rather than automatic opposition to her. It was to be the 1740s before British diplomacy was definitively and permanently restored to its earlier anti-French orientation.

Cooperation after 1716 was rooted in shared dynastic and financial concerns. The efforts of the new Hanoverian regime to consolidate its own authority within the British Isles had their parallel across the Channel, where Louis XIV's long reign had ended in September 1715 with the accession of the old king's great-grandson, the five-year-old Louis XV. The regency for the boy-king was headed by the duc d'Orléans, who sought diplomatic cooperation with Britain in order to strengthen his own position and to deal with France's internal problems after a generation of warfare. The costly and large-scale wars of 1689–1714 had saddled both countries with considerable debts, and their financial problems were increased in 1720 by the instability created by two speculative schemes and their failures: the South Sea Bubble in England and the Mississippi venture across the Channel. This contributed to the initial success of the entente, and to a period of notable diplomatic cooperation which only began to break down during the later 1720s.

Cooperation with France facilitated a period of British diplomatic leadership in Europe during the later 1710s and 1720s. This dominance was rooted in the enhanced power and prestige of the fledgling British state, which had risen impressively during the generation of fighting after 1689, and especially in its naval power, which now eclipsed both the Dutch and French fleets. But as an island monarchy, Britain could never dominate western Europe militarily in the way in which Habsburg and Bourbon had done in earlier generations. London's diplomatic ascendancy after Utrecht ultimately rested on France's support, or at least acquiescence.

For a decade and more this was usually forthcoming from successive French regimes. It enabled British governments of Whig persuasion to follow what was essentially a Tory foreign policy. This had emerged during the 1690s and 1700s, in contrast to the interventionist approach which had prevailed under William III and his political heirs, and emphasized building up naval power and strengthening Britain's European position through diplomacy and, if possible, peace with France: exactly as was done during the generation after 1716. The Tory approach had in origin offered an alternative strategy during the conflicts with Louis XIV: naval and colonial warfare, rather than alliances and military campaigning on the continent. It was to be most influential during the generation after Utrecht, particularly during the ascendancy of Sir Robert Walpole.

Though in power domestically from the early 1720s, Walpole only really secured control over British foreign policy in 1730. Throughout the next decade he adopted a non-interventionist approach, keeping Britain out of the War of the Polish Succession (1733–8), in opposition to the views of the king, George II, and several of his own ministerial colleagues. This made possible a sharp reduction in the land tax together with a notable growth of British trade and a striking economic advance. Britain's passivity during the 1730s was encouraged by the good relations with France and by the repeated assurances of friendship which Louis XV's leading minister, the wily Cardinal Fleury (1726–43), was careful to extend to London. Fleury, a veteran clerical politician, had become chief minister at the age of seventy-three, and died in office in his ninetieth year. His domestic objectives mirrored those of Walpole: political stability, financial and economic recovery. But the cardinal never neglected France's international position to the extent that his British counterpart did. Fleury was determined to restore France to that position of leadership in Europe which her population and economic resources, together with the potent traditions of Louis XIV's reign, appeared to justify. This he accomplished by fighting in the War of the Polish Succession while simultaneously doing nothing to challenge the insular outlook that prevailed in London.

Fleury's ministry was decisive in a second respect. One purpose of the War of the Spanish Succession for Britain had been to prevent the crowns and kingdoms of France and Spain ever being united under one king, thereby creating a preponderant power. It had been accomplished in the Utrecht settlement, which had also partitioned the Spanish monarchy in Europe, awarding important territories in the Southern Netherlands and the Italian Peninsula to Austria. Although a minor branch of the French royal family now ruled south of the Pyrenees in the person of Philip V (1700–46), at first the two Bourbon monarchies did not act as a single unit in international relations, as British contemporaries feared. In the tangled international politics of the later 1710s and 1720s France and Spain had often been rivals and even actual antagonists. It was primarily due to the territorial and political ambitions of Philip V's second wife, the formidable Elisabeth Farnese, born in the Italian Peninsula and anxious to secure territories there for her own children, who were apparently excluded from the Spanish throne by the offspring of the king's first marriage. These hopes, together with Madrid's established interests in Italy and its rivalry with Austria, had disrupted Franco-Spanish relations. In 1733, however, Fleury's skilful diplomacy concluded the first Family Compact, establishing a secure Bourbon axis. Two further Family Compacts were concluded, in 1743 and 1761, and the alliance was usually a fixed point in the international constellation from the 1730s until the French Revolution. It was in practice suspended during Ferdinand VI's reign (1746–59), and much weakened during the early 1770s, but was otherwise a potent threat to Britain, at least in the eyes of ministers in London.

This became apparent during the final years of Walpole's ministry. In 1739 Britain went to war with Spain, against a background of clashes over efforts by British merchants to break into the profitable trade monopoly of the Spanish American empire. Though a wider European conflict, the War of the Austrian Succession (1740–8), began in the following year, Britain at first remained aloof. Both beyond Europe and especially on the continent the fighting did not favour British interests. Fleury provided Spain with unofficial naval support, ensuring that Britain's initial successes did not produce the clear-cut victory that had been anticipated. The confused campaigning and diplomacy of the Austrian succession struggle, which London finally entered in 1744 by declaring war on France, appeared equally unfavourable to British interests.

The fighting witnessed a notable revival of French military expansion, which appeared a return to the great days of Louis XIV. In 1741 a court faction headed by the maréchal-duc de Belle-Isle had carried France into the continental war. Its purpose had been to destroy Habsburg power once and for all, and there were moments during the 1740s when Austria's territorial and political survival appeared in jeopardy, as she was attacked first by the new military state of Prussia and then by a wider coalition. This seriously threatened British interests, since Austria was traditionally London's principal military ally on the continent. The revival of French power caused even more concern. It reached its peak during the second half of the war when the maréchal de Saxe won a brilliant series of victories and all but destroyed the Barrier in the Southern Netherlands. Simultaneously, the negligible contribution of the Dutch Republic to the fighting, even after the restoration of the stadtholderate in 1747, finally revealed its political and financial weakness and near bankruptcy. Both principal foundations of the former Grand Alliance appeared to be crumbling, increasing British anxieties. These had also been strengthened by Hanover's evident vulnerability to French attack, which became clear in 1741 when France had sent an army against the electorate and immediately compelled George II to conclude a neutrality convention for his German lands. The War of the Austrian Succession had also seen a revival of French naval power, which had been destroyed during the wars of 1689–1714 but once again threatened to rival that of Britain. The Jacobite rebellion in 1745 provided the most direct threat. It provoked a panic in Britain and, for a time, appeared to endanger the Protestant, Hanoverian succession. The duke of Newcastle, now extremely influential in the ministry headed by his brother Henry Pelham, was especially alarmed in 1745–6, less by the Jacobite clans themselves than by the way their rebellion distracted British attention from the formidable danger now posed by France.

The duke's concerns were increased by a firm Franco-Spanish axis, with the second Family Compact in 1743, renewing that concluded a decade before. For Britain and her allies it appeared as if the War of the Spanish Succession had been fought in vain, since the 'united House of Bourbon' represented an acute and direct threat to London's interests. In the short term, the threat was contained. Britain's colonial gains and particularly the capture of Louisburg, together with some weak French diplomacy, ensured that the Anglo-French settlement which formed part of the peace of Aix-la-Chapelle (1748) was on the basis of the status quo. But the perceived danger to British interests from the revived power of France could not be ignored: the consequences of the contrasting policies of Fleury and Walpole were now clear. With hindsight the 1740s was the decade when hostility to the Bourbons permanently established itself as the driving force behind British foreign policy. In many ways opposition to France only became the invariable basis of London's foreign policy from the 1740s onwards.

The Political Consequences of the Duke of Newcastle, 1748–88

Britain's response was to be distinctive and enduring. It was shaped by Newcastle, one of the longest-serving secretaries of state in the eighteenth century, if not one of the most distinguished. Though closely involved in foreign policy for two decades, it was only with the formation of the 'broad-bottom' ministry towards the end of

1744 that the duke was able to gain control over British diplomacy. By the later 1740s he believed in the absolute necessity of opposing France in Europe through alliances. That, he had concluded, was the principal lesson of the War of the Austrian Succession. After its conclusion British foreign policy was reconfigured. Henceforth, it assumed the necessity of opposition to France and diplomatic and military involvement on the continent to counter the Bourbon threat. Here, as throughout his career, Newcastle's ideas were derivative: his was not an original mind, and particular individuals were to have considerable influence on his policies, now styled the 'Old System'. By this the duke meant an anti-French alliance founded upon treaties with Austria and the Dutch Republic, and containing any other state which could be conscripted into military support against France.

Its wider context lay in Whig ideas about foreign policy, in contrast to the Tory policy of avoiding alliances and even accommodating France which had prevailed during the previous generation. The Old System arose naturally out of the assumptions of eighteenth-century Britons about their political world and the central importance of 1688–9 in its creation. Mid-eighteenth-century British ministers had been born and brought up during the decisive generation after 1688, and this shaped their thinking and actions. Their frame of reference and their political language remained that of the age of the stadtholder-king. George II sought to emulate William III, living in his palaces and marrying his eldest daughter to the prince of Orange, echoing the earlier dynastic marriage between Princess Mary and the stadtholder-king. Newcastle's own links with that age were both personal and political. Born into the Whig tradition, he had married Marlborough's granddaughter. Like many of his contemporaries, he saw the glorious quarter-century after 1688 as a storehouse of precedents to guide later generations. His views on how the War of the Austrian Succession should be fought and won had been directly inspired by Marlborough's strategy during the earlier conflict: an army was to be sent to Flanders, France was to be defeated in the field and forced to accept a negotiated settlement. The duke believed that Britain's difficulties during the 1740s demonstrated the enduring validity of Williamite ideas, and this conviction shaped his foreign policy after the peace of Aix-la-Chapelle.

A more immediate influence was the prominent Dutch statesman, Willem Bentinck, who was a leading figure in Orangist circles. Bentinck was himself a monument to the Anglo-Dutch partnership. Born in England in 1702 and educated there, he was the son by a second marriage of William III's most important adviser, an earlier Willem Bentinck, first earl of Portland, but he had pursued a career in the Republic. The younger Bentinck's outlook was always that of firm opposition to France, equally firm support for alliances with Britain and Austria, and devotion to the house of Orange. He wanted a revived Anglo-Dutch alliance to shore up the fragile domestic position of the restored stadtholderate. Bentinck's ideas, in this as in other respects, mirrored those of Newcastle. The two met on several occasions, particularly during the former's visit to London in 1747, and corresponded freely and extensively on the political questions of the day. It was following one of their meetings, in the Dutch Republic in 1748 when Newcastle was accompanying the king to Hanover, that the duke fully embraced the label 'Old System', which Bentinck and his Dutch friends may have furnished. This is exactly the point at which

Newcastle ceases to talk of the Grand Alliance and refers instead to the 'Old' or 'Antient' System. His advocacy of this was strengthened by G. A. von Münchhausen, the leading Hanoverian minister with whom the duke also conferred on this journey, and probably by George II.

By the end of 1748 Newcastle's plans for future British foreign policy had assumed their mature form. The components of the Old System had been familiar for decades, but they had been mobilized and given new coherence and direction at the aftermath of the War of Austrian Succession. The duke's aim between 1748 and 1756, against a background of continuing Anglo-French tension and before long an undeclared war in North America, was the full restoration of the Old System and its expansion to include Russia and even Prussia. A renewed Austrian alliance was sought in vain, while triangular negotiations were held in an unsuccessful attempt to restore and redefine the Barrier in the Southern Netherlands. A treaty with Prussia proved elusive, while a convention with Russia signed in autumn 1755 was never ratified. These initiatives were undermined by the rapidly changing diplomatic alignments of the mid-eighteenth century and related adjustments in the relative standing of European states.

The ideas for which the Old System was shorthand were becoming the basis of Britain's foreign policy at exactly the point at which its constituent elements were weakening and even dissolving. By the 1740s and 1750s the Anglo-Austrian alliance, always a marriage of political convenience, was breaking up. The principal solvent was Prussia's rise as a formidable military and political competitor for the Habsburgs in Germany, eclipsing Vienna's traditional rivalry with France. It provoked a fundamental realignment of Austrian foreign policy which sought a rapprochement with Versailles, secured in 1756 as the centrepiece of the celebrated diplomatic revolution of that year. The feebleness of the Dutch Republic, together with the breakdown of the link with Vienna, undermined Newcastle's foreign policy and in the longer perspective weakened British efforts to construct an anti-French alliance-system.

The Seven Years' War weakened the foundations of British foreign policy in two related ways. London's search for allies had been based on the threat, though at times exaggerated, of France's overweening power: testimony to the enduring influence of William III. The spectre of French hegemony had become frayed during the generation after Utrecht, and it was destroyed by the fighting after 1756. France's defeats in the continental war, in which she fought against Prussia as Austria's ally, and the even more serious reverses overseas against Britain, completely undermined her position as the leading European power, which was only to be recovered during the 1790s. Though her population and economic resources made her potentially the strongest state, military decline and mounting financial problems saw French power eclipsed for a generation. Simultaneously two new military powers emerged during the Seven Years' War, Prussia and Russia. This transformed continental diplomacy, and also weakened British foreign policy.

Since the later seventeenth century international relations had been dominated by fear of French hegemony. This coincided exactly with Britain's view, and it had enabled London to build alliance-systems against France by exploiting Dutch and Austrian hostility, particularly during the age of William III. By 1763 there were five 'great powers', as they were now beginning to be called: Britain, France, Austria,

Prussia and Russia. Their rivalries were more complex, as were the potential diplomatic permutations. The very simple alignments on which British foreign policy had been based after 1688 and which had hardened into a system in the late 1740s, principally Austro-Dutch rivalry with France, had disappeared. Britain's own victories in the Seven Years' War further weakened her international position. The decline of Louis XV's monarchy combined with Britain's own colonial and commercial power destroyed the strategy of building alliances on the basis of the danger of French hegemony, though her ministers were slow to appreciate this. If any state threatened to dominate Europe, or at least its western half, after 1763, it was Britain and not France.

Yet the Seven Years' War simultaneously appeared to have vindicated the strategy of fighting France in Europe while defeating her decisively in the colonial sphere, where British resources had been concentrated. The effectiveness of this strategy had been due to France's involvement in the continental war (albeit much reduced from 1759 onwards) and to Britain's support of Prussia through a subsidy and much higher expenditure on an 'Army of Observation' in western Germany protecting Prussia's western flank, which together prolonged the European struggle. It was why Britain's postwar foreign policy, against a background of continuing and even intensifying Anglo-Bourbon rivalry in the colonial and naval spheres – another Franco-Spanish alliance, the third Family Compact, had been signed in August 1761 – was concerned to secure alliances, in keeping with Newcastle's ideas, which had hardened into a doctrine. The search for allies during the decade after 1763 was unsuccessful: exactly as it was to be when it was resumed during and immediately after the War of American Independence (1775–83), in which France and Spain intervened openly in 1778–9. Britain retained her traditional commitments to Portugal and the Dutch Republic (though this was far weaker than hitherto and would dissolve in the later 1770s), but was unable to secure the major continental ally or allies during the War of American Independence which ministers believed were essential to combat the threat of France.

The lack of success owed something to the British approach to potential partners, who were sought in terms of a supposed threat of French hegemony which could now be clearly seen to be a phantom. This was strengthened by the resentment of other states at Britain's naval and commercial supremacy and the way this supremacy was exploited. It was accompanied by an overriding assumption – rooted in the hubris that took hold after the great victories during the Seven Years' War – that an alliance with Britain was a not-to-be-missed opportunity, which in turn encouraged ministers to react to failure by adopting a pose of studied insularity. The potentially commanding European position secured by 1763 was not exploited and was soon undermined. This failure, however, owed much more to changes within the international system, with the emergence of the eastern powers, the notable rise of Russia, and the decline of France. The result was that London was no longer able to manipulate continental diplomacy in its own interest. Britain, not its Bourbon rival, now appeared the preponderant power, while Austria, Prussia and Russia had other priorities than defending the 'liberties of Europe' or defeating the united house of Bourbon. Newcastle's fatal legacy for British foreign policy had been to establish the idea that alliances were essential against France and, usually, Spain when changes in the international system were making the conclusion of such treaties difficult and even impossible.

The Political Consequences of the French Revolution and Napoleon, 1788–1815

Britain's post-Seven Years' War insularity and, at times, outright isolationism lasted until the later 1780s and helped lose her the American colonies. London's concern to check the growth of French influence in the Dutch Republic and so defend the Low Countries led her to support actively the stadtholderate, when its authority was attacked by the so-called Patriot movement which advocated the establishment of a less oligarchical political system. British money and diplomatic backing, together with a Prussian army which invaded the republic in 1787, revived Orangist power. In 1788 the Dutch, Prussians and British signed a Triple Alliance, which ended Britain's quarter-century of exclusion from Europe. During the next few years London was to pursue a more interventionist and wide-ranging diplomacy, which extended for the first time to the Balkans. It sought to restrain Russia and to determine the outcome of her war with the Ottoman empire. Britain's full political re-emergence, however, was a consequence of the French Revolutionary and Napoleonic Wars, which finally established Britain as a leading European power.

The official British response to the outbreak of the French Revolution in summer 1789, and to the subsequent constitutional and administrative changes, was indifference. France's rapid international collapse had been welcomed, since the weakening of French power had been London's aim since 1689. It contributed to the breakdown of the Family Compact and to Britain's triumph over an isolated Spain in a colonial confrontation over Nootka Sound (on Vancouver Island) in 1790. The British attitude was transformed by the Revolution's increasing radicalism from mid-1792 onwards, culminating in the execution of Louis XVI. The prime minister, William Pitt the Younger, was less influenced by such ideological motives and more by a very traditional concern with the Low Countries, menaced by a French invasion. Together these considerations carried Britain into war with France in early 1793, to join the conservative German powers already fighting the Revolution. The warfare would continue until the final defeat of Napoleon in 1815, with only one short break in 1802–3.

This struggle transformed Britain's European role. Yet her approach was for long a very traditional one. For a decade and a half London's military commitments were limited to occasional – and invariably unsuccessful – expeditions, against targets in northwestern Europe, a region of traditional concern. In addition, naval and financial power and diplomacy were ranged against Revolutionary and Napoleonic France, very much in the Williamite tradition. Britain's role in organizing the First Coalition, though she was unable to turn a loose grouping of states into an effective alliance, set the precedent for the next two decades of warfare. It achieved less than London had anticipated, but it accustomed continental states to a greater degree of British political involvement and even direction. This was to reach its peak during the final stage of the military struggle. In other respects Britain's actions were familiar. The alliances which she sought to create and direct against the Revolution were for long analogous to the cooperation that had been secured against France in earlier generations. The foreign secretary Lord Grenville explicitly set out to create a new 'Grand Alliance' in 1798–9, hoping to persuade major continental states to field armies against France, and this remained Pitt's approach in assembling the Third Coalition after 1803. Subsidies were paid to allies: at first to minor states and then, as the scale of French military expansion became clear, to major powers who were also encouraged to seek loans from London's financial market.

The wars of 1792–1815 were distinctive in one respect. The unique scale of France's victories and her massive territorial annexations quickly eclipsed anything achieved under Louis XIV. The unprecedented size of the Revolutionary armies, based as these were on near-universal male conscription, together with their new *élan* and aggressive tactics, brought a remarkable series of military successes. Napoleon Bonaparte, after he seized power in 1799, harnessed this massive potential, added organization, leadership and direction, and in 1805–7 won an even more complete series of victories over the Third Coalition.

It was not only the scale of French victories which transformed European politics and revolutionized Britain's policy; it was also the extent of the resulting territorial and political changes that was so decisive. International rivalry before the French Revolution had been relatively limited in nature, in keeping with a style of warfare which yielded marginal gains to one side or the other. With the exception of Prussia's seizure of Silesia from Austria during the 1740s and France's losses to Britain in the colonial sphere, great powers did not make their territorial annexations from one another but from declining states: Sweden during the early decades of the eighteenth century, Poland and the Ottoman empire during its second half. This changed during the 1790s and 1800s, as victorious French regimes extorted considerable territorial cessions from the defeated states. They could do so because of the completeness of their military victories and the threat to continue these if the defeated country did not surrender what was demanded. In a second respect, moreover, the victorious power behaved in a way which was quite unknown before 1789. Revolutionary and Napoleonic France remodelled the domestic governments of the conquered territories, creating a series of satellite republics during the 1790s and satellite kingdoms during the 1800s. These transformed the political geography of continental Europe and highlighted the gulf which now divided the new regime in Paris from its enemies, the established monarchies.

Britain's seapower ensured that her own rivalry with France became a stalemate. Her naval mastery conferred a degree of political independence not possessed by any continental state and throughout the fighting she made an important series of colonial conquests from France and her Spanish and Dutch dependants. Yet the successive remodelling of states and regimes was creating a Europe less and less to London's taste, and more and more under French sway. By 1807, after his overwhelming defeat of the Third Coalition, the Emperor Napoleon (as he had now become) dominated the continent to an extent which had not been seen since the Roman empire. Britain, for her part, had been effectively shut out of Europe by his latest victories. The traditional strategy of finding continental armies to fight France was bankrupt. A recognition that this was so brought about a decisive change in London's policy, which was now controlled by more forceful and imaginative figures who were less influenced by eighteenth-century doctrines. George Canning, foreign secretary 1807–9, and his political rival Castlereagh, secretary for war and subsequently foreign secretary after 1812, gave a new direction to Britain's strategy. London announced that in effect it would underwrite any continental revolt against Napoleonic hegemony. British statesmen had been convinced by the emperor's great victories in

1805–7 that the previous and essentially traditional approach, of attacking France's commerce and colonies while subsidizing European allies, would not bring victory. London would have to increase her commitment and her troops would have to fight on the continent itself, where they were sent in increasing numbers.

Canning also supervised a fundamental change in British aid. Hitherto, London had concluded what were essentially troop-hiring agreements in which payment was carefully supervised and weighed against the number of soldiers actually provided. These treaties had aroused resentment, with repeated accusations of penny-pinching from hard-pressed allies. The foreign secretary now sought to aid them to Britain's full ability and to provide more generous subsidies. Such support also ceased to be a matter of simple cash payments. The duration and cost of the wars against France and, more recently, Napoleon's attempt to wage economic warfare through the 'Continental System' had left Britain short of bullion. Canning therefore reduced the amount of money and instead sent arms and equipment, particularly clothing, which industrial Britain could provide and which her continental allies needed almost as much as cash.

The expeditionary force sent to the Iberian Peninsula in August 1808, to aid the Spanish revolt against Napoleon, was the beginning of this enlarged commitment, which was to continue until the final defeat of France in 1814–15. It was accompanied by a sharply expanded diplomatic role, which finally established Britain as one of the two leading European powers by the Congress of Vienna. British diplomacy did not merely assemble the Fourth Coalition; the foreign secretary Castlereagh personally directed it during the crucial months in 1814–15 when he stayed on the continent. London's enlarged commitment in money and troops to the final defeat of Napoleon conferred a political initiative and enabled its diplomacy to shape the peace settlement at Vienna.

This reflected British ideas and strategic interests, some of which were long established. A series of strong buffer states – much more powerful than the arrangements set up at Utrecht a century before – was established around France's borders, to guard against any future aggression. Castlereagh also ensured that the Low Countries should be in friendly and strengthened hands, those of the restored Orangist rulers of the new kingdom of the Netherlands, comprising Holland and Belgium. The 1815 settlement in western Europe was dominated by the idea of containment and, as such, exactly matched traditional British interests. Further east, London embraced a second purpose of the settlement, that of seeking to contain Russia. To influence the continental settlement, Castlereagh handed back most of Britain's colonial conquests during the war, though sufficient were retained to protect her trade and imperial communications. The Vienna settlement enhanced her maritime, colonial and economic supremacy, the foundation of her position as a leading power. The Revolutionary and Napoleonic Wars had weakened her rivals overseas, especially France, and her domination in the colonial sphere was considerable. It was reinforced by the industrial revolution which, from the later eighteenth century, was simultaneously adding a formidable new dimension to British power, which had always depended heavily on her economic strength.

Britain's emergence as a European power had been truly spectacular since the later seventeenth century, but it had not been accompanied by a permanent commitment to continental diplomacy. Despite the personal union with Hanover, her island situation periodically enabled her – in contrast to other leading states – to abstain from European alliances and politics. It was a source both of strength and of suspicion. Britain had periodically played the role of a great land power, when France's territorial and military strength had appeared menacing and when the Low Countries or Hanover were in danger. She sent troops to the continent when absolutely necessary, but simultaneously pursued her own maritime and colonial interests overseas. The British involvement in Europe had at times been considerable, and cumulatively decisive, but it had been interspersed with long periods of insularity and even isolationism, and there was no reason in 1815 to believe that this ambivalent membership of the European states-system was in any way altered. Continental states could not ignore Britain, but British statesmen could relegate continental issues to a subordinate position. It was part of the explanation for Britain's greatness as a European power, which had been established during the long eighteenth century.

FURTHER READING

Black, Jeremy: *A System of Ambition? British Foreign Policy 1660–1793* (London, 1991).
Black, Jeremy: *British Foreign Policy in an Age of Revolutions 1783–1793* (Cambridge, 1994).
Browning, Reed: *The Duke of Newcastle* (New Haven, CT, 1975).
Ehrman, John: *The Younger Pitt* (3 vols, London, 1969–96).
Gibbs, G. C.: 'Parliament and foreign policy in the age of Stanhope and Walpole', *English Historical Review*, 77 (1962), pp. 18–37.
Gibbs, G. C.: 'The revolution in foreign policy', in Geoffrey Holmes (ed.), *Britain after the Glorious Revolution 1689–1714* (London, 1969), pp. 59–79.
Hatton, Ragnhild M.: *The Anglo-Hanoverian Connection 1714–1760* (London, 1982).
Hatton, Ragnhild M. and Bromley, J. S. (eds): *William III and Louis XIV: Essays 1680–1720 by and for Mark A. Thomson* (Liverpool, 1968).
Horn, D. B.: *The British Diplomatic Service, 1689–1789* (Oxford, 1961).
Horn, D. B.: *Great Britain and Europe in the Eighteenth Century* (Oxford, 1967).
McKay, Derek and Scott, H. M.: *The Rise of the Great Powers 1648–1815* (London, 1983).
Pares, Richard: 'American versus Continental warfare 1739–63', *English Historical Review*, 51 (1936), pp. 429–65.
Roberts, Michael: *Splendid Isolation 1763–1780* (Reading, 1970).
Scott, H. M.: '"The True Principles of the Revolution": the duke of Newcastle and the idea of the old system', in Jeremy Black (ed.), *Knights Errant and True Englishmen: British Foreign Policy, 1660–1800* (Edinburgh, 1989), pp. 55–91.
Scott, H. M.: *British Foreign Policy in the Age of the American Revolution* (Oxford, 1990).

Chapter Thirty-Four

Britain and the Atlantic World

W. A. Speck

The relationship of Great Britain to her American colonies in the century before the Declaration of Independence is too often treated in the shadow of that document. Thus a Whiggish view of their interaction tends to dominate studies of it. Many accounts, for instance, focus on the thirteen mainland colonies that declared their independence of Great Britain and became the United States. Treating the period 1689 to 1776 as the first chapter in the history of the USA, however, distorts its significance. For one thing it overlooks the fact that the thirteenth British colony to be acquired on the eastern seaboard of North America was not Georgia but Nova Scotia, which the French ceded to Britain at the Treaty of Utrecht in 1713, twenty years before the southern settlement. More seriously, it ignores the West Indies. By the beginning of the eighteenth century the English had acquired eleven islands in the Caribbean, of which the most significant were Antigua, Barbados, Jamaica, Montserrat, Nevis and St Kitts. These were regarded in many ways as more important than the continental colonies. Certainly Barbados was seen as the jewel in the crown, its sugar being more profitable to the royal revenues than the tobacco of the Chesapeake Bay or the rice of South Carolina. The sugar islands also contributed significantly to the value of British imports, their produce rising from 13 per cent of goods imported into Britain in 1700 to around 25 per cent by the 1770s. Britain retained possession of these colonies when the USA successfully seceded from the British empire.

The owners of plantations in the sugar islands carried more clout in the corridors of power for much of the eighteenth century than did the colonists on the mainland. This was partly due to the fact that most of them were absentee landlords, resident in Britain. They employed stewards to tend their West Indian estates and used slaves to cultivate the sugar, and lobbied MPs to safeguard their interests. Thus, the Sugar Act of 1733, which protected their exports from competition from the French islands of Guadeloupe and Martinique, was regarded by the seaboard colonies as being contrary to their interests. In 1731 the gentlemen of the northern colonies, representing all the seaboard settlements from Nova Scotia to South Carolina, in vain petitioned parliament to protest against the proposed duties on sugar from sources other than the British West Indies (*Pennsylvania Gazette*, 15 July 1731).

Colonies and Metropolis

The importance of the political world of Whitehall and Westminster to the politics of the American colonies was vital. That is why increasingly colonial assemblies employed agents to represent their interests in London, even though in the ultimate imperial crisis they were to prove 'ropes of sand'. Contacts in the imperial capital were crucial to any colony, whether its governor was appointed by the crown, or by a proprietor, as in Maryland, or even elected its own governor, as did Connecticut and Rhode Island. This can be illustrated from the case of colonial Pennsylvania. Pennsylvania was a proprietary colony, having been granted to William Penn in 1681. Penn and his sons, who succeeded him as proprietors, spent most of their time in England. They recognized that London, not Philadelphia, was the seat of their power. Although this was a constant factor in colonial politics, there were occasional crises which brought it home to politicians on both sides of the Atlantic.

The internal dynamics of politics in colonial Pennsylvania have been well established by several scholars, notably Gary Nash. Thus, the central tension between the so-called Quaker party and the proprietary interest of the Penn family has been substantiated, above all by Alan Tully. The Quaker party's hegemony in the assembly lasted for most of the proprietary period, being only temporarily disturbed by the voluntary secession of the strict pacifists in 1756. By contrast, the proprietary interest was so weak that it scarcely deserved the name of 'party'. Its weakness made it a failure in the internal political context of the colony. And yet the Penns survived a number of assaults upon their proprietorship, starting with the challenge to William Penn himself launched by Philip Ford, and ending with Benjamin Franklin's abortive bid to get the crown to take over the colony. The main cause of their ability to fend off their opponents was the strength of their interest not in Pennsylvania but in England.

After mending fences with William III following his ill-fated liaison with James II, William Penn cultivated contacts at court to consolidate his hold on Pennsylvania and the three lower counties of New Castle, Kent and Sussex, which subsequently became Delaware. His range of political acquaintances was wide. Although Quakers reputedly associated with Whigs, Penn did not confine his political alliances to that party. His allies spanned the political spectrum. Amongst the Whigs they included Sir William Cowper and his son, the lord chancellor. On the Tory side was Lord Poulett, who became an executor of Penn's will. But his most important political contacts were not so much Tory or Whig partisans as courtiers, men like Robert Spencer, earl of Sunderland, Robert Harley, earl of Oxford, who also became an executor, and John Churchill, duke of Marlborough. It was Penn's interest with such powerful political brokers which enabled him to regain his colony in 1694, after it had been taken from him because of his association with James II. It also enabled him to retain it when the Board of Trade, established in 1696, embarked on a policy of subordinating all colonies to the crown, and succeeded in the case of New Jersey, formerly a proprietary colony, in 1702.

Problems in Pennsylvania spilled over into the politics of Delaware and Maryland. Before Penn died the earl of Sutherland challenged his title to the three lower counties. The last governor of Pennsylvania to be appointed by Penn, Sir William Keith, exploited the situation created by the proprietor's death for his own advantage. Keith at first impressed Penn's friends in Pennsylvania, giving them a very favourable opinion of his good sense, sweetness of disposition and moderation. They were very glad when he arrived in the colony in June 1717, but they came to regret Keith's appointment soon after when he surprised his friends who had recommended him with his fondness for absolute power. One of the ways in which he displayed this penchant was by distinguishing between his appointment to the governorship of Pennsylvania and that of the lower counties. The first was without limitation, but the second was during the king's pleasure. Keith interpreted this to indicate that Delaware was now regarded as a crown colony, and proceeded to act as if he were the king's rather than the proprietor's deputy. Thus, he called himself Excellency, and issued a charter to New Castle with no reference to the proprietor. When Penn died, Keith even began to assert his own authority in Pennsylvania, being neither under the immediate cognizance of the crown nor under any proprietor. In 1726, however, the Penns thwarted his ambitions when he was dismissed as governor and replaced by Patrick Gordon.

Keith then sought to exploit his own interest at Whitehall, and therefore left Pennsylvania and sailed to England. He thereby showed that he too was aware that power lay ultimately not in Philadelphia but in London. There he tried to persuade the king to grant him the governorship of the three lower counties, but the Penn family showed that it had still too strong an interest at court for a successful challenge to be mounted against them there. Keith hoped that his own interest with the dukes of Argyll and Montrose would outweigh the influence of the Penns. In the event, though, the Penns outsmarted him when both sides of the family agreed to replace him with Patrick Gordon, detached Argyll to their side, and got their choice of a new governor endorsed by him, the dukes of Chandos and Newcastle, and the earls of Orkney, Oxford and Stair. How much clout the Penns had at court was revealed in 1733 when some of their opponents in Pennsylvania were denying the authority of their new governor, Colonel Gordon, on the grounds that he had not received the approbation of King George II. On application to the duke of Newcastle and the president of the Board of Trade, the royal approval of Gordon was obtained in fifteen days flat.

The long-lasting saga of the border dispute between Maryland and Pennsylvania was another colonial issue that was fought out more in the corridors of power in London than in North America. Thus, the moves and counter-moves of the Calverts and Penns were often reactions to developments at court rather than in the colonies. In 1733, for instance, the proprietor of Maryland put pressure on the British government to recognize his claim to the lower counties. John Penn responded by exploiting Quaker fears that the Calverts would not respect the religious toleration granted to the three lower counties by his father. He wrote from London on 17 July to his brother Thomas, who was then in Philadelphia:

> What I think would be of the greatest service is a letter of remonstrance from all the Quakers in the lower counties and if you could of the Province itself to the meeting of sufferings here setting forth their having gone over on the consideration of the grant of [Delaware] to my father under whose government they have injoyed the full liberty

> of their religion, and that if they should now fall under any other government it would be very much to their prejudice, especially as to the payment of tithes. If this could be managed as to get the meeting here to espouse their cause as a general concern . . . it would be the greatest interest we could make. For by endeavouring to get the Excise Act passed the last session the people are so prepossessed against the Court that the Quakers' interests will never be so considerable as before the chusing the next parliament, when they will stand in need of their assistance and consequently do anything to oblige them. (*Penn Letterbook*, vol. 1: 83–4)

Thomas Penn did succeed in acting on this suggestion, and an address was duly presented to the London Meeting for Sufferings from Quakers in Pennsylvania protesting against Baltimore's designs on Delaware. The eventual resolution of the boundary problem by the running of the Mason-Dixon line in the 1760s was a victory for the Penns over the Calverts, for the survey established the southern border of Pennsylvania significantly below the fortieth parallel, which the proprietors of Maryland claimed to be the northern boundary of their colony according to the charter granted to their family by Charles I. Although they spent considerable time and money in the law courts at Westminster fighting to make good their claim, in the end it was the superior influence of the Penns with successive ministries which prevailed.

The influence of the Penn family with the ministers was put to its severest test when Benjamin Franklin was sent by the Pennsylvania Assembly to England to protest against alleged abuse of the proprietary powers in 1757 and 1764. On the first occasion Franklin attempted to curtail the proprietors' prerogatives. On the second he tried to persuade the crown to take over the colony from the Penns. In both cases the interest of the Penns at the courts of George II and George III was too entrenched for Franklin to prevail. In 1757 Franklin appealed to the Board of Trade and subsequently to the privy council against the proprietary view that a bill passed by both the assembly and the governor could not be repealed unless it were contrary to natural justice or the laws of England. On both occasions the attorney-general and the solicitor-general appeared for the Penn family and persuaded the board and the council to find in favour of the proprietary view and against the assembly.

As long as George II lived the servants of the crown were associated with the old corps Whigs who had looked after the interests of the Penn family since the death of William Penn, the founder of Pennsylvania. The strength of their connections at court under the first two Georges had survived every attempt to shake it. Backed by the dukes of Cumberland and Newcastle, the interest of the Penns at court was unrivalled, as their opponents learned to their cost. In 1760, however, George II died and his grandson on succeeding him as George III declared his intention to remove the ministers who had served his grandfather for most of his reign. The so-called 'reversionary interest' then came into power. Among those who benefited from this change was Benjamin Franklin, whose son William obtained the governorship of New Jersey from the new favourite, the earl of Bute.

When the assembly next challenged the proprietors, therefore, the Penns could not automatically count on court support. On the contrary, the change of monarchs persuaded the anti-proprietary party that they could appeal to George III to take the colony out of the hands of the proprietors altogether and place it under the direct control of the crown. Franklin was sent over to England again, this time to present a petition from the assembly to the king requesting that Pennsylvania became a crown colony. In the event it was to be a trial of strength between the rival interests at court. Franklin was accused by the Penns of lacking any clout there, but he responded that his majesty had very lately honoured him with a nomination to a small employment, which indicated a favourable opinion of him among the ministers. He had indeed been recommended by the Board of Trade in July 1764 to be a commissioner for settling the boundary dispute between New Jersey and New York. Moreover, Richard Jackson, the assembly's agent in England, had been appointed as secretary to the leading minister, George Grenville. As long as the ministry was dominated by the likes of Bute and Grenville, therefore, Franklin could realistically hope to outmanoeuvre the Penns at court. Unfortunately for him and the anti-proprietary party, when he arrived there Grenville's days were numbered. In July 1765 Grenville was replaced by the duke of Cumberland and the marquess of Rockingham. The interest of the Penns thereby revived sufficiently to ensure that the move to wrest the province out of their hands would be thwarted. On 22 November 1765 the king in council rejected the assembly's petition. The movement for royal government was officially over.

The Imperial Crisis

Unfortunately, Franklin continued to hope for a successful outcome to his mission until 1768. By then, however, the internal politics of Pennsylvania had been overtaken by the imperial confrontation arising out of the Stamp Act and Townshend duties. This was to transform the context in which provincial politicians operated. The imperial connection became not so much an asset as a liability, as Franklin discovered almost too late, having to do some fancy footwork to extricate himself from being identified with the British court. Before then, however, influence there had been a key factor in the rivalry between the proprietary and anti-proprietary parties in Pennsylvania.

By the time Franklin went to Britain to argue the case against the Penns, colonial policy had changed significantly. Until the end of Sir Robert Walpole's ministry in 1742 the British government's imperial policy stressed commercial rather than territorial concerns. It was not primarily interested in the settlement of colonists in extensive plantations. Except by way of conquest the government did not take the initiative in colonizing ventures. All the American colonies established in peacetime, from Virginia in 1607 to Georgia in 1733, were the result of private rather than public enterprise. After Walpole's fall, however, the policy underwent significant adjustment. The 'War of Jenkins's Ear', which he tried to prevent in 1739, certainly began as a commercial conflict with Spain, but it ended as a struggle with France for mastery of North America. Although the British gave Cape Breton back to the French at the peace treaty in 1748, they accepted that the cessation of hostilities was but a breathing space before the next round began. Moreover, it began in North America before it broke out in Europe. The defeat of George Washington's Virginians, and the subsequent expedition and rout of General Braddock in 1755, sparked off a titanic conflict which ended with the expulsion of the French from most of North America. At the Treaty of Paris in 1763 the British decided to keep Canada rather than exchange it for Guadeloupe and Martinique. Nothing could more signify the transition from a commercial to a territorial concept of empire.

The growing imperial ambitions of Britain testified to its emergence as a major power after the Glorious Revolution and the subsequent development of the 'fiscal-military state'. Again traditional accounts of the relationship between the mother country and the American colonies failed to take into account the dynamism of the British state. They tended to juxtapose a largely static, unchanging Britain with a dynamic colonial trajectory. Britain in fact changed very significantly between the Glorious and American Revolutions. The population of England and Wales rose gradually in the first half-century after 1688, from about 4.8 million to about 5.4 million, then began to increase rapidly to top 6 million in the 1760s. Much of this growth was concentrated in towns. London alone accounted for over 10 per cent of the total number of inhabitants of England and Wales. Provincial towns, although dwarfed by the metropolis, shared in this process. Whereas in 1700 only seven contained more than 10,000 inhabitants, by mid-century a further seven had been added, Birmingham, Coventry, Leeds, Liverpool, Manchester, Nottingham and Sheffield – the principal manufacturing centres which were to experience the industrial revolution. Already they were producing manufactured goods that helped to transform the pattern of exports from one based largely on textiles to one where other manufactures featured. Although textiles remained the principal exports, their share did not increase as remarkably in the first half of the eighteenth century as did that of other products, many of them destined for the American colonies.

Even more significant for the imperial context were the constitutional and political changes in Britain consequent upon the Glorious Revolution. Constitutionally the seventeenth century had witnessed a struggle for sovereignty between the crown and the king-in-parliament. Under the early Stuarts the royal prerogative had challenged parliamentary claims that the polity of England was that of a limited monarchy. Proclamations enforceable in prerogative courts had rivalled statutes upheld in common law courts. The independent powers of the crown had been significantly shorn by the time the civil wars broke out. Subsequent republican governments had removed them completely. Meanwhile, with the rise of radical groups such as the Levellers the idea of the sovereignty of the people had also risen. At the Restoration, however, popular sovereignty received a setback, while many royal prerogatives were restored along with Charles II. Both he and his brother James II relied upon the surviving prerogatives in their disputes with parliament. For almost the whole of the 1680s there was no parliament in being to challenge the king's claims to rule without it. The Revolution Settlement decided the struggle for sovereignty. Although there were still claims made by 'real' or 'true' Whigs that it resided in the people, the outcome was to lodge it in the king-in-parliament. Contrary to a widely held view, this did not mean the supremacy of parliament. The House of Lords and the House of Commons were not made superior partners in the constitution but given equal authority with the crown. Some prerogatives even survived 1689 – the right to declare war and make peace, to summon and dissolve parliament at pleasure and to appoint ministers of the monarch's own choosing. But these were eroded in the 1690s and 1700s not because of the Revolution but by the wars with France. These, not the Bill of Rights, required the crown to summon parliament every year in order to get the resources voted for the war effort. Annual sessions date from 1689 thanks to the financial revolution rather than the Glorious Revolution.

The financial revolution put public credit on an institutional rather than a personal basis. Thus, the debt became that of the nation rather than of the reigning monarch. By 1713 the national debt stood at £36,000,000. It reached £76,000,000 in 1748 at the end of the War of the Austrian Succession and £132,000,000 in 1763 at the end of the Seven Years' War. Much of this was raised from taxes. At the outset of the century the main tax fell on land, or rather on income from landed property. The land tax, as it was called, accounted for some £2,000,000 per year at the wartime rate of four shillings in the pound. By the middle of the eighteenth century indirect taxation assumed more significance, particularly excises, the yields from which increased from £849,000 in 1700 to £1,600,000 by 1760. The government borrowed from the money market in anticipation of taxation and ultimately on the credit of the state. Such institutions as the Bank of England, founded in 1694, the East India Company, launched long before 1688 but relaunched with a new charter in 1709, and the South Sea Company, established in 1711, received privileges from the government in return for lending money to it. This created a financial nexus between the Treasury and the three great corporations which underpinned the fiscal side of the military-fiscal state. The military side was the growth of a standing army to fight the French. The army increased from some 8,000–17,000 men in peacetime to between 35,000 and 74,000 in wartime. This was a major commitment requiring arms, clothes, victuals and other resources. The navy fluctuated between 16,000 men in peacetime and 25,000 in wartime. Manning some 160 capital ships, that is, those with over fifty guns, they inhabited 'a wooden world' that was the greatest concentration of manpower employed in one activity anywhere during the century. To build, equip and keep seaworthy the fleet required dockyards and other facilities, which made it the state's main contribution to colonial activity before the mid-century wars with France.

The colonies were undergoing significant change, too, during the century. The growth of the white population from 223,000 in 1700 to 2,000,000 by 1776 is one impressive measure of this. Contemporaries were aware that the population was doubling every generation. This was due more to reproduction than emigration. Increasing numbers did not produce an overall decline in living standards, however much they resulted in a widening gap between rich and poor. On the contrary, the average standard of living for whites rose throughout the century as their per capita income increased in real terms by at least 0.5 per cent per year. That of the slaves, on whom the economies of the southern colonies became increasingly dependent, could not of course be measured in wage levels, though even they were probably better clothed, housed and fed on the eve of the Revolution than they had been a century before. By then certainly the white colonists were enjoying better material conditions than most of their counterparts in Britain. White adult males also enjoyed greater political rights than did those in the mother country. The franchise for voting in the provincial assemblies was much wider than it was for parliamentary elections. Where there has been much debate about its extent, the estimates range from 50 to 80 per cent in the colonies. Even accepting the most conservative estimate, it is twice the most generous reached of the proportion of adult males who made up the electorate of eighteenth-century Britain. The colonial assemblies were not only more representative than the British parliament, they also acted as a more effective check upon the executive. They eroded gubernatorial powers by gaining control of a whole range of executive activities. Perhaps the most crucial were their successful bids to appoint the colonial treasurers, which transferred from the governors to the assemblies considerable financial leverage. As the governor of South Carolina pointed out to the Board of Trade in 1748: 'the political balance in which consists the strength and beauty of the British Constitution being here entirely over turned . . . all the weights that should trim and poise it [are] by different laws thrown into the scale of the people . . . Almost all the places of either profit or trust are disposed by the General Assembly' (Greene 1974: 359). Much the same could be said of most colonial assemblies by the middle of the eighteenth century. Their rise at the expense of the governors was a crucial development which enabled them to function independently of the executive when the breach with Britain came.

Long before then the British government had been aware that the slender threads of patronage which governors could employ to influence the behaviour of assemblymen were snapping. In particular the promotion of Lord Halifax to the presidency of the Board of Trade is now generally seen as marking a turning-point in the attitude of the British government to its American colonies. Before that it had been characterized, in Edmund Burke's famous phrase, by 'salutary neglect'. Some American historians have criticized it as being more akin to culpable negligence. Thus, the duke of Newcastle, principal secretary of state for most of the period, and thereby primarily responsible for relations with the American colonies, has been accused of treating them as appendages to his English political interests. This perpetuates an image of Newcastle as an incompetent minister which British historians tend to reject. Certainly, in his concern for imperial defence after 1740, the duke was not guilty of neglect but initiated the strategic intervention in American affairs which Halifax was to continue.

Halifax implemented a series of measures that to some extent anticipated the functions of the secretaryship for the colonies which were to be established in 1768. He issued instructions to governors commanding them to curb the pretensions of the colonial assemblies. Both Halifax and Newcastle realized that the Treaty of Aix-la-Chapelle of 1748 marked a truce rather than a peace in North America. As P. J. Marshall observes, 'the end of the war in 1748 brought no real reduction in British military involvement overseas. Louisburg was returned to France at the peace, but a garrison of 4,000 men costing an average of about £95,000 a year, a figure of proportion with all previous spending, was established in Nova Scotia; and Halifax was built up as a base and made a home of the royal naval squadron maintained in North America after 1745' (1979: 200). The commitment to defence in North America can be gauged from the fact that where annual expenditure during the war between 1740 and 1748 had averaged £148,000, between 1748 and 1756 it actually rose to £268,000.

During the Seven Years' War, of course, it soared way beyond these figures to average £998,000 a year. The total amount expended in North America by the British government between 1756 and 1763 came to £7,984,000. It was to be its attempts to recoup some of that sum that brought on the dispute between Britain and the American colonists. The dispute sparked off a debate about the constitutional relationship between the mother country and the American colonies which still reverberates among historians. Put at its crudest, it polarizes those who insist that the Americans had no legal justification for their slogan 'no taxation without representation' from those who maintain that they did.

The classic response to the complaint that the Americans were being taxed despite not being represented in the parliament of Great Britain was George Grenville's claim that they were 'virtually' represented. Theories of representation in the eighteenth century did not apply to individuals. Few on either side of the Atlantic were proponents of democracy. At most one in four of adult males voted for MPs in England, and a much smaller proportion in Scotland. While the colonial assemblies had a wider franchise, the right to vote in elections to them was confined to white adult males who satisfied a property qualification. Consequently, many colonists could have complained that they too were taxed without being represented had the franchise been based on the rights of individuals. Instead, it was based on the concept of interest – the landed interest, the monied interest, and so on. The fact that complaints were being raised that industrializing centres such as Birmingham and Sheffield did not send members to the House of Commons stemmed not from any concern for the political rights of their inhabitants, but from an awareness that a new and growing interest, that of manufacturing, was not directly represented in parliament. Grenville's point was that it was virtually represented since there were MPs who acted as spokesmen for it. Where his theory of virtual representation was taken to mean that American interests were similarly represented, it was pointed out that MPs involved in colonial commerce were not partners but rivals of American entrepreneurs, and therefore could not be said to represent their interests.

The debate, however, moved on rapidly from arguments about representation to disagreements over the concept of sovereignty. As we have seen, the prevailing British view was that it lay with the king-in-parliament. The counter-claim of the crown had been eliminated in the Glorious Revolution. Although theories of popular sovereignty survived 1688, and were even to be revived in the reign of George III, they did not command enough support to challenge the dominant view. This was that the king-in-parliament was the sovereign power which could not be lawfully resisted. It had supreme authority over all British subjects, whether they were resident in Britain or in her American colonies.

Colonists opposed to taxation without representation objected to this assertion. They claimed that the colonies owed their origin to the authority of the crown in the seventeenth century and were still subject to it and not to parliament. The Stuarts had granted colonial charters, giving colonists the right to have representative assemblies and to pass laws which were not contrary to English law. This proviso indicated that the laws of England did not automatically apply to the colonies. While the independent power of the king might have been merged with that of parliament in the Revolution Settlement as far as England, and after 1707 Scotland, was concerned, this transfer had not comprehended the colonies too, which continued to be under the crown.

In recent years this argument has been revived by a number of historians. John Phillip Reid argues that there were in fact two constitutions within the dominions of the British monarchs. One applied to the United Kingdom of Great Britain, and embodied the sovereignty of the king-in-parliament. The other pertained to the remaining dependencies and concerned the crown alone. A major exception to this appears to have been Ireland. For although there was a separate Irish parliament, a British statute of 1720, the Declaratory Act, asserted the right of the parliament of Great Britain to legislate for Ireland 'in all cases whatsoever'. This was a precedent for the Declaratory Act of 1766, which declared parliamentary authority to legislate for the American colonies. Yet, as defenders of Irish and colonial independence of British legislation pointed out, this claim of theoretical sovereignty over Ireland was never used in practice to raise revenues there. The attempt to do so in America was a violation of what Jack P. Greene has dubbed 'the imperial constitution'.

Ian Steele has challenged this view that the resulting conflict with America was a 'war of the two constitutions'. As he points out, 'there were at least 95 British statutes passed between 1660 and 1753 concerning imperial trade. These acts . . . should be a central part of the constitutional history of the English Atlantic empire before 1760' (1995: 37–8). In his view the Revolution of 1688 had established the sovereignty of the king-in-parliament in all parts of the empire. The Navigation Acts demonstrated that sovereignty, however, was challenged by colonists at the time. They accepted that parliament could legislate to control colonial commerce, but not to raise revenues. That there was at least residual royal prerogative concerning the colonies operating independently of parliament was shown in the proclamation of 1763. This is remembered chiefly for its restriction of westward expansion beyond the crest of the Appalachian mountains, but it also created four new British colonies: Quebec in Canada, Grenada in the West Indies, and two in Florida. The Americans had a point when they appealed to George III against the claims of parliament. British politicians were apprehensive of this approach since the doctrine of parliamentary sovereignty had been developed to counter the claims of the crown. They were afraid that the influence of the crown was still a threat to the liberties of parliament. Were the king to succumb to American overtures they feared that it would result in a significant increase in his influence. Fortunately for them, George III sided with parliament and declared that he was fighting for its claims over the colonies. The Americans then blamed him for their troubles, and declared their independence by indicting the king for alleged acts of tyranny. It is a similar format to the English Bill of Rights of 1689, which levied a list of charges against James II, accusing him of subverting the constitution. One indeed, that he had maintained a standing army in peacetime without the consent of their legislatures, was a direct echo of the bill. Another, that he had appointed judges at pleasure, was an issue raised in 1689, though it was deferred because to legislate to make them appointable only on good behaviour was deemed to be new law. Since the bill was allegedly only declaring what was the existing law this could not be dealt with in it. It was, however, enacted in the Act of Settlement in 1701. These legal points were never extended to the colonies. In this respect the Glorious Revolution was not for export to America.

In many ways what the Americans were seeking in their dispute with Great Britain in George III's reign were the guarantees against abuse of the prerogative that the English sought from the Stuarts. As several historians have pointed out, the language of the dispute was more that of the seventeenth than of the eighteenth century, with parliament replacing the king as the alleged tyrant. Thus, the Americans insisted that they were defending the liberties of Englishmen. The British, by contrast, were maintaining those liberties of Britons as established by the Glorious Revolution and the legislative union of 1707. As John Phillip Reid observes, the Americans 'were constitutionalists of the English constitution, in the spirit of Sir Edward Coke, John Seldon and Algernon Sidney, sharing an English faith that government could be balanced and power could be restrained. They were not constitutionalists of the British constitution like Sir William Blackstone, Lord North and Lord Chief Justice Mansfield, who had been taught by the Glorious Revolution that power alone, subject to constitutional restraints, did not endanger liberty' (vol. 4: 60).

American views were shared by English writers who also believed that the balanced constitution established by the Revolution Settlement had lost its equilibrium. In theory the mixed monarchy of 1689 was self-sustaining. Attempts by the crown to exceed its powers would be offset by the Lords and the Commons. In practice, however, the influence of the crown over both houses had undermined the independence of the legislature. The classic argument that corruption was employed to eradicate resistance to the executive had been developed by John Trenchard and Thomas Gordon in *Cato's Letters*, published in the early 1720s and reprinted many times thereafter, not least in the colonies. There was a conspiracy thesis on both sides of the Atlantic which accused George III and his ministers of seeking to undo the Glorious Revolution and to increase the power of the crown. English historians have long held that this alleged threat was the invention of opposition propagandists, and that the charges against George III in the American Declaration of Independence were absurd. Yet they were clearly believed. There was a perception on the part of American and English radicals that the influence of the crown had increased, was increasing and ought to be diminished. The arguments of George Grenville in favour of virtual representation were as counter-productive in England as they were in America. Where he used the fact that many Englishmen were taxed without being represented to justify his raising revenues from the colonies, men such as John Wilkes used it to argue that representation should be extended. The Wilkesites and the Sons of Liberty sang much the same tune.

In the end, however, the Americans leaped out of history and justified their independence by appealing not to the historic liberties of Englishmen but to natural rights. Few English radicals were prepared to go that far. They still appealed to the past, as the Society of Supporters of the Bill of Rights implied by its very title. One who was to employ natural rights arguments, Thomas Paine, significantly first did so in the context of the War of American Independence, in his influential pamphlet *Common Sense*.

How far there was support for the American cause in Britain has been much debated. At one time it was assumed that the government of Lord North had the support of the majority of the king's British subjects for his coercive measures. He dissolved parliament in 1774 a year before a dissolution was statutorily due in order to get the approval of the electorate for the 'Intolerable Acts'. Dr Johnson registered the disapproval of his fellow subjects in his tract, *Taxation no Tyranny*, in which he denounced sympathizers with the rebels, claiming that their 'antipatriotic prejudices are the abortions of Folly impregnated with Faction'. A majority was duly returned at the polls for the ministry.

Yet the degree to which the electoral results reflected public opinion is open to grave doubt. Very few constituencies were contested and in most the electorates were too small to be representative of widespread views. More concrete evidence for the attitudes of Britons towards the colonists is to be found in the addresses and petitions for and against coercion which were drawn up in reaction to the repressive measures undertaken by the government. These document divisions in the British public. While many expressed support for Lord North, others, especially from large urban centres where dissent was strong, urged conciliation. When resistance turned to rebellion such indications of sympathy became muted, since it was disloyal to show support for the king's enemies. Nevertheless, enough evidence is available to suggest that there was significant sympathy for the American cause throughout the war. After the defeat of Cornwallis at Yorktown this became irresistible, playing a large part in the fall of North's administration and the formation of Rockingham's. Then it became safe to express solidarity with the Americans. None did so more flamboyantly than Sir Thomas Gascoigne, who erected a huge triumphal arch at the entrance of his Yorkshire estate displaying the legend 'Liberty Triumphant in N[orth] America, 1783'.

FURTHER READING

Brewer, John: *The Sinews of Power: War, Money and the English State 1688–1783* (London, 1989).

Conway, Stephen: *The British Isles and the War of American Independence* (Oxford, 2000).

Dickinson, H. T. (ed.): *Britain and the American Revolution* (London, 1998).

Dickinson, H. T.: '"The Friends of America': British sympathy with the American Revolution', in Michael T. Davis (ed.), *Radicalism and Revolution in Britain, 1775–1848* (Basingstoke, 2000), pp. 1–29.

Geiter, Mary K.: *William Penn* (London, 2000).

Gould, Eliga: *The Persistence of Empire: British Political Culture in the Age of the American Revolution* (Chapel Hill, NC, 2000).

Greene, Jack P.: *The Quest for Power: The Lower Houses of Assembly in the Southern Royal Colonies, 1689–1776* (Chapel Hill, NC, 1963).

Greene, Jack P.: *Settlement to Society 1607–1763: A Documentary History of Colonial America* (New York, 1974).

Greene, Jack P.: *Peripheries and Center: Constitutional Development in the Extended Polities of the British Empire and the United States 1607–1788* (Athens, GA, 1986).

Gwyn, Julian: 'British government spending and the North American colonies 1740–1775', in P. J. Marshall and Glyn Williams (eds), *The British Atlantic Empire before the American Revolution* (London, 1980), pp. 74–84.

Henretta, James: *'Salutary Neglect': Colonial Administration under the Duke of Newcastle* (Princeton, NJ, 1972).

Kammen, Michael G.: *A Rope of Sand: The Colonial Agents, British Politics and the American Revolution* (Ithaca, NY, 1968).

Katz, Stanley N.: *Newcastle's New York: Anglo-American Politics 1732–1753* (Cambridge, MA, 1968).

Marshall, P. J.: 'The British Empire in the age of the American Revolution: problems of interpretation', in William M. Fowler and Wallace Coyle (eds), *The American Revolution: Changing Perspectives* (Boston, 1979).

Middleton, Richard: *Colonial America: A History 1585–1776* (Oxford, 1996).

Nash, Gary: *Quakers and Politics: Pennsylvania 1681–1726* (Princeton, NJ, 1968).

Olson, Alison G.: *Making the Empire Work: London and American Interest Groups 1640–1790* (Cambridge, MA, 1992).

Penn Letterbook (manuscript): Historical Society of Pennsylvania, Philadelphia.
Reid, John Phillip: *Constitutional History of the American Revolution* (4 vols, Madison, WI, 1986–93).
Steele, Ian K.: 'The British parliament and the Atlantic colonies to 1760: new approaches to enduring questions', *Parliamentary History*, 14 (1995), pp. 29–46.
Tully, Alan: *William Penn's Legacy: Politics and Social Structure in Provincial Pennsylvania 1726–1755* (Baltimore, 1977).

Chapter Thirty-Five

Britain and India

Bruce P. Lenman

In 1700 both 'Britain' and 'India' were geographical terms. Europeans had only a very vague concept of the Indian subcontinent as a unit, and rightly so. The first significant English map of the region, drawn by William Baffin and engraved by Renold Elstrack in 1619, but based on information supplied by Sir Thomas Roe, was a map of 'The Empire of the Great Mogoll'. That tradition of concentrating on the domains of the great Muslim empire of the Moguls whose political pretensions extended over much of the subcontinent, as well as over much else, was continued by Dutch cartographers such as Jan Jansson, whose 1650 map of 'Magni Mogolis Imperium' stretched from Persia to China, excluding non-Mogul south India. Before 1849 the political entity called 'India', over which the government of the United Kingdom surrendered its claims to jurisdiction to two new states in August 1947, did not exist.

The Rise of the East India Company

The single most pervasive and influential unifying factor in the subcontinent *c.*1700 was Hinduism, though that culture is an intricate non-monolith. In practice relations between the kingdoms of Scotland, Ireland and England and the subcontinent *c.*1700 were shaped by two main players: the Mogul empire and the English East India Companies (there were two). Direct trade between England and all points east of the Cape of Good Hope had been, since the granting of its charter by Queen Elizabeth I on the last day of 1600, the legal monopoly of 'The Company of Merchants of London trading into the East Indies'. As its charter was virtually copied by the one granted to its rival the 'New' East India Company (chartered in 1698), the 'Old' East India Company established long-lasting parameters for the conduct of Anglo-Asian trade. It had a monopoly of English direct trade only. Private trade between Asian ports by approved 'free' merchants was always legal, as was a theoretically strictly limited amount of private trade by East India Company (EIC) servants. It was a corollary of the monopoly that Englishmen of any kind could usually reach Asia only on EIC ships, if the EIC would take them.

Before the Anglo-Scottish Act of Union of 1707, Scots were in no way bound by the monopolistic claims of the English EIC. The Company of Scotland Trading to Africa and the Indies, established in 1695, was referred to by some Englishmen as 'The Scotch East India Company'. Originally, half its capital and directorate were to be English and its headquarters were to be in London. Both the EIC and the English parliament reacted violently to make English participation impossible. The Company of Scotland did sponsor some preliminary voyaging in Asian waters, but by 1700 it had committed suicide by sinking irreplaceable assets in a disastrous plan sponsored by the London Scot, William Paterson, for a Scots colony at Darien on the Isthmus of Panama. The Act of Union compensated the company's shareholders and ensured there would be just one British EIC. By the 1720s the prime minister, Sir Robert Walpole, was using EIC patronage placed at the government's disposal by obliging members of the EIC directorate to help consolidate government influence in Scottish constituencies. A very large number of Scotsmen and Irishmen entered EIC service in the eighteenth century, especially its military service, where commissions were relatively cheap for the younger sons of non-affluent Scots lairds or Irish squireens. Irish and Scottish figures later rose very high on the civil side of EIC service, however, and in its central governance in London. Laurence Sulivan, an Irishman of obscure origins who has been described as 'one of the greatest of the Company's rulers', was Clive's arch-enemy in the appalling EIC civil wars of the 1760s, and still a director in the 1780s. By the late eighteenth and early nineteenth centuries by far the most influential voice on the directorate was that of the Evangelical Charles Grant, one of the poverty-stricken Grants of Shewglie from Glen Urquhart beside Loch Ness.

The 'Old' EIC had benefited from the very rapid rise in the import and re-export of tropical and subtropical products that was characteristic of the English economy in the Restoration era after 1660, but it had fared badly after 1688. Its dominant figure, Sir Josiah Child, had tied it too closely to the court of James VII and II. With King James, Child had embarked on an armed confrontation with the Mogul Emperor Aurangzeb, a war which between 1688 and 1690 the EIC lost, miserably. Unpopular with the new regime of William III and Mary II, the EIC suffered heavy shipping losses in William's war with France, which was concluded in 1697, but from 1698 there was a rival EIC. In practice the 'Old' EIC recovered rapidly after 1697, did not suffer so much from the renewed Anglo-French war of 1702–13, and retained the capacity by its competition to bankrupt the 'New' Company, whose directors soon became desperate for a merger. The 'Old' Company's volume of trade was far greater than that of its rival and its stock rose from a low point of 33.25 in 1698 to 60 by the end of 1699, touching 142 by 24 April 1700. By July 1702 the two EICs had agreed to trade as one under a joint committee for the next seven years, whilst an amalgamation was negotiated. Problems over compensation, valuation and debts made a ruling by a third-party arbitrator, the lord treasurer Earl Godolphin, necessary in 1708, but by 1709 a new United Company was formed. Theoretically, the 'Old' EIC was dissolved. In practice it had survived and absorbed its upstart competitor, and was flourishing. Between 1709 and 1711 it paid an annual dividend of 9 per cent.

The Crisis of the Mogul Empire

By 1707 it had become clear that the Mogul empire was facing a series of crises which it could not surmount and that the effective authority of its emperor over his nominal dominions was contracting dramatically. This was the case long before the death of the last great emperor, Aurangzeb, who reigned from 1658 to 1707. Inheriting an empire founded after 1525 by Babur, a central Asian Turk, Aurangzeb had emerged from a war of succession committed to giving his stalled Turkic conquest empire new and profitable frontiers of conquest. Only to the south could he make progress, so in a determined thirty-year thrust into the Deccan he pushed the empire by 1707 to its furthest physical limits, overrunning the erstwhile Muslim sultanates of Golconda and Bijapur and almost reaching the southern end of the peninsula. During his long absences from the northern heartland of the empire, cracks and fissures in the Mogul regime there became chasms. The sturdy Hindu peasantry of the Jat community rose in repeated rebellion around the Delhi–Agra area. In the Punjab the Sikh community, once a collection of pacifistic, mystical religious reformers, became militant rebels and totally intransigent after Aurangzeb executed their ninth guru, Tegh Bahadur, in 1675 for his refusal to embrace Islam. Afghan raids from the northwest frontier were matched by restlessness and spasms of violent rebellion from Rajput rajas who, historically, had been the most important Hindu allies of the empire.

That there was a 'crisis of empire' in eighteenth-century India is beyond question. Its underlying causes were obviously multiple, and there is no consensus among historians as to exactly what the decisive developments were. That there were structural flaws in the Mogul imperial system is a fact. The empire had always had an oblique relationship with local communities mediated through a nobility which consisted of *jagiradars* or imperial revenue assignees, who organized troop levies in accordance with a numerical rank assigned to them, but who were not allowed in theory to accumulate and pass on an hereditary estate. They in turn dealt with the local elites usually known as *zamindars*, who were not so much owners of land as possessors of extensive heritable rights over land, and they in turn dealt with the vast mass of the village-dwelling peasantry. The idea that the empire drove the peasantry into poverty and rebellion by the relentless racking up of fiscal demands by a nobility with no incentive to take long-term views that might lead to productive investment may be applicable in some regions, but not in all. In provinces such as the Punjab the development of irrigation and the ever-deeper commercialization of the economy benefited peasant society, to the point where previously nomadic pastoral peoples began to settle down and join it. Besides, from the beginning of the eighteenth century the military nobility began to resist regular transfers to other areas. In practice it was hereditary, and began to acquire local roots.

All Turkic conquest states tended to overexpand, to reach frontiers of diminishing returns for effort invested, and either to collapse or to undergo restructuring into more flexible regional units. The Mogul empire was no exception, nor was it very different from, say, Napoleon's empire, except in longevity. The Deccan was the Moguls' Russia. The high military nobility in the end – in both cases – reckoned they would survive better without the emperor. The Deccan wars left the Mogul empire financially crippled, because the destruction of the existing sultanates and the heavy-handed policies of Aurangzeb cleared the way for a sustained Mogul confrontation with the rising revivalist Hindu power of the Marathas of the northwest Deccan and western Ghats. The Moguls failed to co-opt the Maratha leadership. After the death of the great Maratha warrior-king Sivaji in 1680, pounding by Mogul armies did ensure that by 1714 the unitary monarchy of Sivaji was breaking up into an expanding military confederacy recognizing the general leadership of the peshwa, the hereditary first minister of the descendants of Sivaji, whose seat was at Poona in the west. After the Battle of Panipat in 1761 the peshwa's authority, though real, was limited when dealing with Maratha princely houses like the Sindias, Holkars, Gaikwars and Bhonslas, who ran autonomous regional conquest empires.

By 1760 the authority of the Mogul emperors was confined to a small area around Delhi. Their imperium had been replaced by regional successor-state empires, often in the hands of former Mogul court families. None of these families wished to abolish the theoretical primacy of the emperor, who remained the fount of honour. There were economic advantages in loose association. The Moguls had evolved a powerful, flexible uniform currency and monetary order based on a trimetallic imperial mint system which coined gold, silver and copper with no legally fixed ratio between them. The EIC before 1700 was minting silver rupees bearing imperial Mogul inscriptions in its mints at Bombay and Madras, as well as using Mogul mints in north India to coin the silver bullion that was its main export to Asia. Its trading activities leaned heavily on a grant of trade concessions and exemptions from customs duties obtained at the cost of £30,000 in presents to the evanescent Emperor Farrukhsiyar, who succeeded a murdered emperor in 1713 and was himself murdered in 1719. The EIC no more wanted to abolish a vague Mogul framework than did the dynasty of nawab-viziers who left the Delhi court to set up an autonomous regime in Awadh (Oudh); or the Mogul viceroy or nizam of the Deccan, who set up for himself in Hyderabad; or Alwardi Khan, who established a dynasty in Bengal and Bihar and fought the Marathas for Orissa. By the early 1790s a Maratha prince, Mahadaji Sindia, was protector and deputy regent of the Mogul empire.

The EIC's Intervention in Indian Affairs

The EIC was adamant that it was not any kind of competitor for a regional ascendancy. It was a trading body with agents and factories (walled compounds housing a mixture of warehouse facilities and accommodation for employees) all over Asia from Mokha on the Red Sea (an important source for coffee beans), to Bencoolen in Sumatra, where the pepper trade was the main business, to China. After unsuccessful attempts to push the China trade from Taiwan, Amoy, Chusan and even Pulo Condore (a small island off southern Vietnam), all trade with China was, after 1703, confined to the mouth of the Pearl River. Portuguese Macao, belonging to an ally with whom the EIC had had intimate relations since the signing of the Convention of Goa in 1635, provided a holding point while contracts were negotiated with Canton merchants, after which the EIC vessels went up the river to Canton's port of Whampoa. Final payment, in bar silver, would be made in Macao.

The huge jump in the China trade after 1720 was based on one commodity: tea. China also exported a great deal of lacquerware and ceramics. Europeans could not manufacture porcelain before the discoveries of the alchemist Johann Friedrich Böttger enabled the elector of Saxony to set up the Meissen factory in 1710. There had been a luxury trade in green tea in the late seventeenth century, but the London price was sixteen shillings a pound. Cheaper bohea or 'black' tea fuelled a leap in imports from 200,000 pounds in 1720 to over a million pounds by 1730. There was a simultaneous jump in imports of West Indian sugar, used to sweeten tea. By 1770 an average of fifteen EIC ships a year were importing 9 million pounds of tea, and the price of bohea had fallen to three shillings a pound. Porcelain teaware often formed the ballast on the six-month return voyage from Canton–Whampoa. The EIC was essentially an example of import-led growth in the eighteenth-century British economy and the China trade was an extreme example of its – much criticized – pattern of exporting silver bullion, ultimately obtained from the mines of Latin America, often through the agency of merchants from the persecuted Portuguese Jewish community who had settled in Amsterdam and London, where they dominated the diamond, coral and bullion trades.

Commercially, India was important to the EIC as a source both of commodities imported into Britain and re-exported to continental Europe, and as a source of commodities which could be traded further east in Asia, for primary profit, or as a means of obtaining more profitable goods such as spices or tea. Cheap, washable, light, dyed or less frequently plain cotton textiles (calicoes) ranked high in both categories of trade. The volume of calico imports into the United Kingdom of Great Britain raised fears of unemployment in the textile industry, stimulating heavy protectionist duties designed to curtail their consumption, but smuggling and evasion were rampant, as the government admitted when it introduced its second round of protectionist measures in 1719. Daniel Defoe had claimed that the original 1700 legislation was totally effective, but this was in a manipulative pamphlet on economics which bore no relationship to reality. British governments in wartime were always warmly welcoming of another EIC import – saltpetre (potassium nitrate), an essential constituent of gunpowder. In 1743 saltpetre imports were a record 53,162 cwt (a cwt = 112 pounds). Briefly, they fell off but by the mid-1750s European wars and competition between the British, Dutch and French for the once-cheap Bihari saltpetre meant prices were rising inexorably on the main saltpetre market at Patna in Bengal, where Bengali merchants like Omichund (who was to be a key figure in the Plassey revolution in 1757) showed skill in manipulating the market to the disadvantage of the Europeans. Patna was the main market for opium – a drug widely used in Europe as a medicinal product, and notoriously acceptable to a growing population of addicts in China, to the distress of the government of that empire. Bengal also produced raw silk to compete in European markets with Persian and Italian supplies.

The EIC had four major, as well as many minor, centres for its Indian trade. Surat was the oldest site. It was the great emporium of the west coast and the transit trade to the heart of Hindustan, the vast plains of north India. Despite the fact that in Surat they were under the direct rule of Mogul officers, the EIC always maintained a presence there. Their factory had to be to some extent fortified, with Mogul approval, as protection against recurring Maratha raids. Only in the 1740s did the EIC begin to complain about the econocidal impact of violent faction in the sub-Mogul administration of Surat, and only in 1759 did they, with backing from the local Indian banking community, take control of the city, with the Mogul fort which dominated the port and river. By then Surat was in decline, being finally overshadowed by Bombay, a crown colony, originally part of the dowry of Charles II's Portuguese queen transferred to the EIC for a peppercorn rent. Both the company and the increasingly numerous British 'free traders' cooperated there, to the point of occasional intermarriage, with the remarkable Parsi community (of pre-Islamic Persian origin) of merchants, shipowners, shipwrights and bankers. Bombay became one of the three EIC presidencies, though one constricted by proximity to Maratha power.

Calcutta was the seat of the youngest EIC presidency. It was a River Hooghly port which had grown from a village with a well-known shrine of the goddess Kali. From the 1690s it was the refuge of EIC servants, led by Job Charnock, after their defeat by Aurangzeb's able subadar or governor of Bengal, Shayista Khan. By 1750 Calcutta is thought to have had 120,000 inhabitants. It had a fort, built with Mogul approval, Fort William. People poured in from the *mofusil* or back country to take advantage of job opportunities provided by rapidly growing foreign trade. After 1757 it overshadowed the late Mogul urban centres of Bengal and Bihar: Murshidabad, Patna and Dacca. By 1800 it was a sprawling metropolis of 200,000 or so inhabitants. Foreigners flocked to the Hooghly. The Dutch were at Chinsura, the French at Chandernagore. Bengal was the third and last major economic frontier, after Surat and the Coromandel coast in the southeast of the Deccan, where fortunes could be made out of a huge regional export surplus of textile piece goods with an unbeatable price advantage on world markets. The Dutch East India Company (the VOC) was by the early 1700s drawing from Bengal 40 per cent by value of the Asian goods it sent to Holland and over half of all Asian textiles despatched. Since the exports were paid for by bullion mainly, the export economy did not lead to displacement of local consumption items. Sheer cheapness and abundance of labour discouraged technical innovation. British private traders complained then that there were signs of price inflation in the early 1750s. Maratha raids and the terrible 1770 famine created labour shortages which accelerated cost rises.

It was, however, the Madras presidency, where business opportunities were less spectacular, which first precipitated the EIC into serious power politics. Madras had a fort, Fort St George, started in the 1640s in the naive belief that the local raja who had approved it would pay for it. Despite the lack of a good harbour, Madras grew rapidly, attracting Indian merchants including key financial groups such as Jains, Armenians and Portuguese Jews. It faced the EIC's three main problems. One was controlling its own servants, which from 1600 it never quite managed. A second was avoiding being sucked into the endless Anglo-French wars after 1697. This they achieved before 1745 by a very sensible agreement with the French Compagnie des Indes that there would be a permanent state of truce between them east of the Cape of Good Hope. The third problem the EIC faced was Westminster politicians. Its original charter of 1600, renewed in 1609 by King James, was a royal grant viewed in common law as a species of property. It could be renegotiated by consent or indeed forfeited, but only by due legal process in the Court of the King's Bench on grounds of failure to fulfil or violation of the charter's terms. By the eighteenth century the king-in-parliament could by legislation alter the EIC charter. There were implicit guarantees for moderation in the shape first of the monarch, still the most important of the trinity of King, Lords and Commons. He could be relied upon to try to dampen any wild abuse of parliamentary sovereignty by faction leaders in the Commons, where most MPs respected property, while the Lords were there as a long stop.

In practice, during the long political ascendancy of Sir Robert Walpole between 1721 and 1742, the EIC, which needed periodic renewals of what was now a time-limited charter, ensured its own security from political harassment. Many of its directors sat in the House of Commons among the leaders of a powerful City of London interest. The EIC, however, was also a major lender to the government. Its entire notional capital was so loaned. Business was carried on by raising bearer bonds in London, and very significantly by raising large sums for short periods from cooperative Indian bankers. By cooperating in Walpole's drive to lower interest rates on the British national debt, the EIC could extract a reasonable degree of understanding from Westminster. Walpole's détente with France and his aversion to European war also suited the EIC. The collapse of the détente in the later 1730s, the ability of a factious opposition to drive Walpole into a disastrous war with Spain in 1739, the fall of Walpole, and the eventual outbreak of war with France, the other Bourbon power, in 1744, was a lethal sequence of events for the EIC. The usual neutrality in Asian waters was vetoed by a British government which regarded this as an arrangement too favourable to the weaker naval power – France.

The arrival of a Royal Navy squadron under Commodore Barnett in waters east of Cape Cormorin in 1745 spelled disaster for French shipping. Barnett captured three Compagnie des Indes ships returning from China, the French Manila ship, and others returning from Surat, Basra and Mokha. The servants of the Compagnie, in Pondicherry, like those of the EIC in nearby Madras, were mainly rogues more interested in building private fortunes than in the profitability of their company. In Pondicherry the leading figure, Joseph François Dupleix, appointed in 1742 governor-general of all French Indian establishments, lost a fortune in his private trade due to Barnett. When the Madras council of the EIC regretted it could neither call off the Royal Navy nor offer compensation, Dupleix called up naval reinforcements from the distant but excellent French naval base in the Ile de France (Mauritius), and struck. The defences of Madras were pathetic. The EIC directorate wanted 'Trade not Grandeur', and though it had reluctantly accepted the need for some fortification under the unstable circumstances of sub-Mogul India, it had been reluctant to pay for it. Madras fell and was plundered in September 1746. A British expedition under Admiral Boscawen failed to capture Pondicherry in 1748, but Madras was part of the mutual restoration of conquests agreed by the Treaty of Aix la Chapelle of that year. The British were lucky to secure *uti possidetis* terms, having lost to the French on the battlefield as comprehensively as they had lost to the Spanish.

In India the war never really ended. Conflict in his dominions had inevitably involved the nawab of the Carnatic, the half-formed Muslim conquest state which was the territory behind both Madras and Pondicherry. Technically, it was subordinate to the nizam of Hyderabad, still the notional Mogul viceroy of the Deccan. Since the seventeenth century European observers had guessed that a disciplined European infantry force would probably be able to rout a Mogul cavalry army, but the logistics of despatching and supplying a significant European army in India were quite beyond any European sovereign, even if one had wanted to try. Under Dupleix the French developed the technique of training local men in the same way as European regulars armed with the relatively fast-firing flintlock musket, with an offset ring-bayonet for repelling cavalry capable of braving the fire-storm. They proved as good as Europeans, but cost only a quarter to a fifth of the Europeans' wages. Having seen off the nawab's Mogul horse, the French embarked on an intricate game of intervention in succession struggles in the Carnatic and in Hyderabad. Since a French-controlled Carnatic would have choked off British access to the handloom weavers producing piece goods, the EIC had to fight back, which meant it too had to train Indian infantrymen or sepoys, like the French. By 1752 the EIC's new sepoy army, commanded by veterans such as Stringer Lawrence and the rising young company soldier Robert Clive, had gained control of the Carnatic for the British-backed candidate Nawab Mohammed Ali, although the French under de Bussy retained control in Hyderabad.

As France and Britain drifted towards war again in 1755, Clive was returning from a trip to England. He reached Bombay with 300–400 regular foot and three companies of Royal Artillery. Embarking on Admiral Charles Watson's squadron, Clive witnessed the decisive impact of heavy naval bombardment of seaboard defences when he and Watson stormed Gheria, the lair of the quasi-piratical Maratha admiral of the west coast, Tulaji Angria. Because there was no need for their services at Madras, Clive and Watson found themselves, reinforced with Madras sepoys, despatched to rescue the EIC's Calcutta base.

It was a crisis generated by the reaction of an inexperienced and insecure young nawab of Bengal to unintentional provocation. Fort William and Calcutta were rapidly retaken. The serious fighting on the campaign was a protracted, bloody artillery duel between Watson's ships and the French fortifications at Chandernagore. The battle of Plassey, where Clive routed Nawab Siraj-ud-daula, was a political intrigue complicated by a brisk skirmish. Clive exploited the deep divisions within the Muslim ruling elite to neutralize a large part of the nawabi force and to replace the murdered Siraj-ud-daula as nawab by one of his own generals, Mir Jafar. Clive had also been in touch with the important Hindu bankers of the house of Seth, Marwaris who had branches all over north India. They had helped fund Nawab Alwardi Khan, but were on bad terms with Siraj-ud-daula, who had threatened them with the circumcision preparatory to forcible Islamicization. Now the Seths preferred to cooperate with an EIC they knew and with which they had long done business.

After wisely crushing a Dutch attempt to intervene by attacking and routing their expeditionary force before it could move inland, Clive settled down behind a nawabi administration to enrich himself and his cronies of the 'Madras gang', appropriate territorial revenues and use them to create a huge sepoy army. The battle which confirmed the EIC grip on Bengal and Bihar against a massive counter-attack by three leading Muslim princes of north India was fought in Bihar at Buxar in October 1764. The nawab-vizier of Awadh proved a skilful, brave commander, giving the sepoys of the new Bengal army under the Scot, Hector Munro of Foulis, a severe contest before finally being defeated by their fire discipline. No regular troops of the British crown played any part in this action. The year 1765 saw Clive accept for the EIC the *Diwani* or financial administration of Bengal, Bihar and Orissa (the latter under Maratha occupation). The grant came from the Mogul emperor, to whom the EIC promised an annual tribute. As the nawabi government in Bengal sank to the status of an abused puppet, it became clear that the EIC was now a major 'country' power. Crucially, one of its three presidencies now controlled the two richest and most populous provinces in India.

By the end of the Seven Years' War in 1763 French military power in India had been fatally weakened. Pondicherry had fallen to the British in 1761. It was returned but after its defences had been slighted. It could not challenge Madras for control of the nawabiship of Arcot. French engineers and other soldiers helped, however, to provide expertise for a new regional empire in south India, that of Mysore, where an able, though illiterate, Muslim soldier, Hyder Ali, usurped the throne from a Hindu dynasty, and by the 1760s had supremacy over 80,000 square miles of territory, with an army of 150,000 and annual revenues equivalent to over £2 million. The Carnatic was enfeebled by the use of its revenues to service outrageous debts owing to individual members of the EIC Madras presidency council. Nawab Mohammed Ali (known as 'the nawab of Arcot') realized his creditors could never foreclose, so he shrewdly relaxed and enjoyed the rape of his incoherent state whilst propagating an image as Britain's noble and dignified ally, especially in fine portraits by European painters which found their way into the exhibitions of the Royal Academy in London. Hardly surprisingly, the first Anglo-Mysorean war of 1767–9, triggered by Madras aggression, proved that the Mysore ruler could fight the Madras presidency to a standstill. He repeated the performance in 1780–3 in the second Mysore war, destroying an entire EIC army at the battle of Pollilur. He had the assistance of his able son Tipu, but Hyder's death in 1783 helped secure for a defeated Madras the relatively generous peace of Mangalore in 1784.

The British Government and the EIC

After Plassey, Clive had deliberately given the elder William Pitt the impression that Bengal would yield a huge revenue surplus. The reality was that the EIC military expenditure in Bengal went up from £375,000 in 1756 to £885,000 in 1766. Yet by 1767, when the elder Pitt was at the head of the government and facing the massive burden of debt charges on war debt which he himself had recklessly piled up in the Seven Years' War, he tried to escape the problem by 'stealing' £1 million a year from the EIC (which could not faintly afford it) by act of parliament. George Grenville persuaded the House of Commons that the bill threatened all property rights by a cynical abuse of the dubious doctrine of parliamentary sovereignty, and the EIC bought off the government with a 'voluntary' gift of £400,000 a year (which it could not afford). A huge jobbing scandal involving EIC stock, and many members of the Commons and Lords, in 1768–9 left many speculators ruined. Lauchlin Maclean MP, parliamentary agent for the nawab of Arcot, may have emerged with debts in excess of £90,000. Hostility to wealthy returned EIC servants, known as 'nabobs' (a corruption of nawab), had long been mounting in Britain. Public paranoia exaggerated their numbers and financial weight until they were believed to threaten to corrupt the entire political system. A man like Clive, who bought his way into the Commons and then bought a small group of MPs to support him, threatened basic concepts of civic virtue and independence which underpinned respect for the House of Commons. By 1772 the EIC was both bankrupt and vulnerable. In exchange for a government loan of £1.45 million to keep it going, it had to submit to the first successful legislative assault on its autonomy.

Lord North's Regulating Act of 1773 embodied a series of compromises, negotiated in his usual conciliatory style. It limited dividends until debt was cleared, tried to strengthen the directorate against the rumbustious general court of the EIC, where it tried to limit the manipulation of stock to manufacture extra votes for rival factions, and in India it strove to curb what were seen as the corrupt and warmongering servants of the company by subjecting them to the authority of a governor-general who with four others was to constitute a supreme council, seated in Calcutta but with some power over the other presidencies. The members of the council were named. The governor-general was to be an experienced EIC servant, Warren Hastings. His period in office between 1774 and 1785 was to prove turbulent and contentious, not least because for much of the time he faced a hostile majority on the supreme council, a majority he lacked the power to overrule.

Like most company servants Hastings probably had no formal 'imperialist' ideology. Survival and enrichment, if they survived, were the main obsessions of men who usually died in India, many shortly after arriving, due to disease. 'Two monsoons' was the proverbial lifespan of the new European arrival. Hastings was less obsessed with self-enrichment than many, and faced horrendous military problems. Apart from the villains who ran the Madras presidency, he had to grapple with the logistical problems involved in saving the incompetents of the Bombay presidency. Interfering in Maratha politics in 1778, they sent an army against the peshwa's capital of Poona, only to meet with total, humiliating defeat in January 1779. Hastings had to march a sepoy army across north India to stabilize the front, a feat rendered possible only by the cooperation of a network of Indian bankers. Four years of indeterminate war ended in a standstill peace, despite reinforcements and a lot of money from Bengal. Similar support enabled Madras not to lose its war with Tipu too badly.

Hastings was anxious to shore up buffer states like Awadh, which stood between Bihar and the unstable central pivot of Hindustan, the region around Delhi. That imperial city had been sacked by a massive raid led by Nadir Shah, greatest of Persian soldiers, in 1739, and then twice by the Afghan ruler Ahmad Shah: first in 1757, then again after he defeated its Maratha protectors in 1761 at Panipat. Hastings earned criticism by renting troops to the nawab-vizier of Awadh to crush Afghan Rohilla chiefs on his northern marches. To his critics the Rohillas were the last free people in Asia. This was nonsense. They were Muslim military adventurers who had quite recently established authority over a Hindu peasantry. Hastings was ruthless in squeezing revenues out of Bengal and Bihar, but latterly he faced in south India a French bid, not for a French empire but to destabilize EIC territories by alliance with Indian enemies of the British. The French admiral, the Bailli de Suffren, was only narrowly prevented from destroying British naval power on the crucial Coromandel coast in 1782–3. By 1785 the EIC presidencies were safe.

During the latter stages of the Anglo-French war triggered by French intervention in the War of American Independence, the Fox–North coalition tried by legislation (owing much to the mind of Edmund Burke) to take over the EIC lock, stock and barrel, subjecting it to an effectively irremovable clique of Fox–North appointees. Their India bill passed the Commons but was defeated by the king and the Lords. Rightly seen by the political nation as an attempt to destroy the balanced constitution by reducing the crown to a fig-leaf for a prime minister controlling a Commons party majority cemented by patronage (much of it the EIC's), the reaction to it led to the massacre of Foxite candidates at the general election of 1784. After that, the premier, Pitt the Younger (who had been appointed by the king in December 1783), passed an India Act in 1784 which set a framework only finally abolished with the EIC in 1858. The power of the EIC general court was further curbed. The company directorate was subjected to a Board of Control headed by Pitt's India expert, the 'Satrap of Scotland' Henry Dundas, later first Viscount Melville. In India the governor-general was given ultimately dictatorial power over his own council and the three presidencies. The EIC had supported Pitt and accepted his India Act, though it had much of Fox's bill in it.

For a short period after Hastings's departure in 1785, a company man, Sir John Macpherson, acted as governor-general, following a perfectly sensible policy of retrenchment and non-intervention. It was typical of his successor, Lord Cornwallis, the first political appointee, to denounce him for 'the dirtiest Jobbing'. Cornwallis had shown in the American war tactical flair and disastrous lack of strategic sense. He was luckier in India, where he decisively defeated Tipu Sultan in the third Mysore war of 1790–2. Tipu, whose symbol was the tiger, had sent diplomatic missions to Louis XVI and the Ottoman Sultan, and hoped eventually to build a European-style navy on the Coromandel coast. He was the most radically progressive of all creators of a sub-Mogul imperium in India. His was an army disciplined and armed in European style. His cavalry were much superior to that of an EIC dependent on Indian allies to supply horses. He also understood that his multi-cultural state needed a comprehensive rather than exclusive elite, and economic development to generate real power. The Marathas had recovered after 1761, so it was still conceivable that the northern Deccan and Hindustan (north India south of the River Sutlej) would form a great, developed empire under the yellow royal banner of the Maratha confederacy, even after the tiger standards of Mysore had been daunted.

After a holding operation under governor-general Sir John Shore, however, the power represented by the British possessions in India fell into the hands of an ambitious, rising Westminster politician, Richard Wellesley, Lord Mornington, an Irishman and a self-conscious Indian Caesar. With some assistance from his soldier brother, Arthur Wellesley, the future duke of Wellington, he finally between 1795 and 1802 raised an imperial British Indian state. Tipu Sultan, under the influence of a shipwrecked French impostor, was given delusions about possible French military assistance and, quite improbably, allowed a Jacobin 'Tree of Liberty' to be raised in his capital, Seringapatam, in 1798. By February 1799 the British had declared war. On 10 May Tipu died most gallantly, fighting in a breach as Seringapatam was stormed. Wellesley formally took over governance in the Carnatic, showed contempt for the shadow emperor in Delhi, reduced Awadh to a puppet state, and began a process of political and military intervention in Maratha affairs which was to culminate in the early nineteenth century in their total defeat and in British hegemony. Wellesley does not seem to have believed his publicly trumpeted theme that he acted only to avert 'The Threat' of Napoleonic intervention in India.

The EIC was increasingly reduced to the role of victim. Already grossly abused by its own servants, it was bankrupted by Wellesley's wars, which is why the chairman of the company, Charles Grant, so bitterly opposed them. As early as 1778 John Robinson, secretary to the Treasury, had argued that Westminster should keep the EIC as a front, and as a scapegoat in case anything went wrong. For a period the EIC was able to use territorial revenues from Bengal to find 'the investment' needed to purchase tea at Canton–Whampoa. Previously bought with silver,

China tea was the core of the EIC's business by the 1780s, which is why Pitt the Younger balanced his India Act with a Commutation Act of 1784 reducing crippling levels of import duty on tea, which encouraged smuggling, to 12.5 per cent *ad valorem*.

British Views of India

Intercourse between the British and Indian peoples was minimal. Consumerism was the core of the connection, though, until Wellesley sucked all surplus revenue into war-debt servicing, India mainly facilitated the import of Chinese ceramics, lacquerwares and tea into Britain. Indian calicoes, latterly smuggled, did affect textile design patterns, but the patterns of Indian chintzes were themselves a version of European patterns sent out by purchasers. Shawls from Kashmir were popular in Britain by the 1770s. They were being imitated by English manufacturers of cashmere shawls in Norwich by the 1780s, whence the manufacture spread to Scotland, to Edinburgh and then famously to Paisley, whence cashmere shawls were by the 1820s being exported to Turkey and Persia.

The visual image of late eighteenth-century India, where the EIC still controlled directly only a small part of the subcontinent and indigenous cultures flourished, was conveyed to a British public mainly through the superb aquatints of Thomas Daniell and his young nephew William. These were published between 1795 and 1810, after the Daniells' Indian journeys of 1786–94. There have been few finer tributes to Indian topography and architecture, but the impact of Indian architectural styles in the British Isles was nugatory compared with even the 'Chinese' style peddled by architects such as Sir William Chambers. In the last quarter of the eighteenth century there was a brief 'Indian Revival' patronized by a small group of connoisseurs. This phenomenon does not appear elsewhere in Europe, and it could be reasonably true to its sources, as its two great monuments, Sezincote House in Gloucestershire (where the architect Samuel Cockerell cooperated with Thomas Daniell) and the Prince Regent's stables and pavilion at Brighton, show. After 1750 talented artists (disproportionately Scots and Irish) who had not quite succeeded in London, or had problems there, moved to exploit the lucrative market for portraits in India. Their art often rose under the stimulus of Indian light and indigenous society to heights of sympathetic brilliance, but their overall achievement was only recognized much later.

By the 1790s, under the patronage of Cornwallis and Wellesley, Robert Home was producing in India an appropriately triumphalist imperial art, competent rather than inspired, and underlining the increasing racial gap between the political appointees who ruled British India and the ruled. Europeans had hitherto recognized Indian as well as Chinese civilization as ancient and worthy of respect. They tended to regard Islam as a derivative religion, dangerous but in retreat. Buddhism baffled them. Hinduism they found confusing but they could approach it, with the aid of great scholars such as Sir William Jones (who recognized Sanskrit's affinity with Latin and Greek), with generosity and goodwill. British males in India, especially the military, normally lived with one or more Indian women and begat Eurasian children on a large scale. By the 1790s, however, Eurasians were being excluded from the EIC's elite covenanted civil service, and from military commissions except in irregular forces. They were becoming 'inferior' just as Indian societies began to be deemed 'corrupt' or 'effete'.

The still polycentric Indian subcontinent of 1800 was different from the late Victorian unified subcontinental British Raj, with its arrogant, racist elite bureaucracy. The Indian textile industry had only begun to feel the impact of mechanized competition, which was bound to doom it to a long, traumatic reconfiguration. The British in 1800, with no steamships or electric telegraphs, let alone a Suez Canal, had not yet brought out their own financial structures, nor kicked away many of the Indian ladders up which they had climbed. Without massive aid from within India and luck, they could not have won. Warren Hastings is a better guide to the process than Victorian ideologues, from Marx to Lord Curzon. Hastings said in effect that the rise of the EIC Raj was an odd outcome, explicable but not inevitable, and in the long run unsustainable.

FURTHER READING

Alavi, Seema: *The Sepoys and the Company: Tradition and Transition in Northern India 1770–1830* (Delhi, 1998).

Bayly, C. A.: *The New Cambridge History of India*, vol. 2 (1): *Indian Society and the Making of the British Empire* (Cambridge, 1988).

Bowen, H. V.: *Revenue and Reform: The Indian Problem in British Politics* (Cambridge, 1991).

Chaudhuri, K. N.: *The Trading World of Asia and the English East India Company 1660–1760* (Cambridge, 1978).

Embree, Ainslie: *Charles Grant and British Rule in India* (London, 1962).

Hoh-cheung Mui and Mui, Lorna H.: *The Management of Monopoly: A Study of the East India Company's Conduct of its Tea Trade 1784–1833* (Vancouver, 1984).

Keay, John: *The Honourable Company: A History of the English East India Company* (London, 1991).

Lawford, James P.: *Britain's Army in India from its Origins to the Conquest of Bengal* (London, 1978).

Marshall, P. J. (ed.): *Problems of Empire: Britain and India 1757–1813* (London, 1968).

Marshall, P. J.: *The British Discovery of Hinduism in the Eighteenth Century* (Cambridge, 1970).

Marshall, P. J.: *East India Fortunes: The British in Bengal in the Eighteenth Century* (Oxford, 1976).

Marshall, P. J.: *The New Cambridge History of India*, vol. 2 (2): *Bengal: The British Bridgehead: Eastern India 1740–1828* (Cambridge, 1987).

Mukherjee, S. N.: *Sir William Jones: A Study in Eighteenth-Century British Attitudes to India* (Cambridge, 1968).

Sutherland, Lucy S.: *The East India Company in Eighteenth-Century Politics* (Oxford, 1952).

Chapter Thirty-Six

The British Army

Stanley D. M. Carpenter

Despite its seminal importance to the expansion and maintenance of the British empire in the eighteenth century, the army chronically suffered from popular dislike and government neglect. The public viewed the common soldier as drunken, unreliable, prone to crime (particularly petty theft), a threat to individual liberty, property and women, and the tool of overweening monarchs. Essentially, a small, professional force composed of long-service volunteer enlistees, the army proved surprisingly effective despite the chronic lack of funds, low pay and social standing of the soldiers and the amateurishness of their officers. Despite its limitations, the eighteenth-century British army performed as well as or better than its adversaries. Typically, it suffered at the outbreak of hostilities from peacetime neglect and low funding, but with few exceptions (the prime example being the American War of Independence), it generally emerged victorious. A German observer commented (in 1748) that British soldiers possessed 'an unquenchable spirit, great stubbornness in defence, [and] bravery amounting to recklessness in the attack [but were] difficult to discipline, quarrelsome in quarters, [and] haughty in their attitude to other troops'.

Army Organization

Following the Restoration of 1660, the standing forces in England lacked constitutional legitimacy, and simply existed as a department of the royal household. With the first Mutiny Act (1689), passed by parliament to take control of the forces during the political and constitutional chaos that followed the invasion of William of Orange (William III) and the flight of James II, a standing constitutional army took shape. This statute acknowledged the legal existence of a standing peacetime force and also provided the authority for courts-martial to punish infractions of the 1663 Articles of War. In effect, the annually renewed Mutiny Act (it lapsed in 1698, but was soon reinstituted in 1701) along with the Statute of Rights (1694) sanctioned a permanent national army under parliamentary control, but with immense consequences for increased taxation and a concomitant growth of administrative bureaucracy, governmental borrowing and debt service throughout the eighteenth century. Although both Scotland and Ireland had maintained separate military establishments in the seventeenth century, these forces merged into an integrated British army during the Nine Years' War (1689–97).

The Mutiny Acts placed the military command structure under the king, but parliament controlled finance, administration and supply. The secretary for war served as the army's chief administrative officer. A captain-general, later the commander-in-chief of the army, represented the monarch and directed the home and theatre commanders. An adjutant general oversaw discipline, arms, clothing, regulations and orders; the quarter-master general directed troop movements, operations and quartering. The Board of Ordnance, under the master-general of the ordnance (a political appointee), regulated the artillery and engineers, neither of which became part of the army establishment until late in the eighteenth century. The creation of a Corps of Engineers (1788) and the Horse Artillery (1793) finally brought these branches under the regular army command structure.

Organized into battalions of 500 men each, the infantry regiment formed the basic tactical and administrative unit. After 1756, many regiments employed paired battalions, with one staying on home service to serve as a training, recruitment and replacement depot while the other deployed for overseas campaigns or imperial defence. Further subdivided into ten fifty-man companies (the principal administrative unit) and platoons (the primary tactical sub-unit), the regimental system proved highly successful as an organizational scheme. By mid-century, most regiments converted two companies to 'flank' companies. The grenadiers, generally the tallest, most athletic men, formed a heavy shock force posted on the right flank of the regimental line. On the left stood the light company, composed of the best marksmen and quick, agile and generally small soldiers, who performed scouting, ambush and force security roles, particularly along a line of march. After 1770, these 'flank' companies often brigaded together into unified 'grenadier' or 'light infantry' battalions. Moreover, the Guards infantry (three regiments of the monarch's household bodyguard), technically not part of the army establishment until the mid-nineteenth century, typically formed into one large unit while on campaign and was referred to as the 'Brigade of Guards'.

Cavalry regiments would be designated as either 'horse' or 'dragoon'. Horse regiments, composed of large men mounted on heavy horses, acted as mobile shock troops. Dragoons (originally organized in 1759 as light cavalry and later styled 'dragoon guards') rode into combat, dismounted and fought as mobile infantry. Dragoons gradually replaced the horse cavalry. Several cavalry regiments adopted the showy Hungarian 'Hussar' uniform (after 1806), characterized by a highly ornate outer shell jacket with one sleeve worn off the shoulder and the busby-style bonnet. Other regiments adopted the lance as the primary weapon, thus becoming the 'lancers' popular in the nineteenth century. Cavalry regiments gradually increased from six troops of thirty-six men each (1783) to ten troops of ninety men (1803).

Artillery, initially organized into 'brigades of guns' with twelve field pieces each, were transformed on operations from a single cohesive unit to individual batteries dispersed through the infantry battalions (two guns per battalion) to provide fire support; but administration remained with the brigade commander and staff. As artillery units gradually integrated into the army establishment, a Driver's Corps replaced the hitherto civilian contract caisson and wagon drivers.

Normal peacetime army strength generally ranged from 12,000 to 20,000 troops, never adequate for both home defence and colonial garrison duties. Wartime strength often exceeded 200,000 regulars and local militia (officered by local aristocrats, commanded by the lord lieutenant of the county and intended for homeland defence and constabulary duties only), which paled in the face of the French *levée en masse* conscription armies. However, given the army's limited scope of continental operations, the bulk of British manpower and financial resources could be better applied to British seapower. This relatively small force therefore served perfectly well in view of the nature of the British war effort against France. Local interests initially opposed government attempts to draw regular regiment replacements from the militia ranks by ballot in each parish; but the militia did gradually evolve into a regular regiment permanent reserve (typically organized into second battalions of line regiments by 1804). Militia volunteers accounted for 40 per cent of regular army recruits by 1815. Fencible regiments provided home defence during the French Revolutionary and Napoleonic Wars. Although regular, full-time troops, fencible units served only in the British Isles (particularly Ireland) and only for the war's duration.

Manpower, Recruitment and Army Life

Army officers came from the ranks of the gentry and titled nobility, a practice held over from the feudal levy and the later Tudor militia (established in 1573), a status that led to the public perception of the army as essentially private retainers led by officers with independent attitudes, resentful of higher authority, given to long absences from their units and often indifferent to their men's individual welfare. As the eighteenth century advanced, however, more officers of merchant and professional origins obtained commissions, particularly during the long period of French Revolutionary and Napoleonic warfare. In many respects, a regiment was indeed the private property of the colonel who was granted a royal warrant to raise a unit. The government supplied limited funds for horses, uniforms, recruiting expenses and basic equipment such as arms (issued from the royal armouries, notably the Tower of London), but the colonel generally supplemented the official allowance. Proceeds from the sale of commissions, viewed as private property and not eliminated until the Cardwell Army reforms of the 1870s, offset some of the additional cost of training and equipping a newly raised regiment. Each colonel selected the subordinate officers, often relatives, neighbours or sons of local aristocrats. Upon retirement, the colonel sold the royal warrant, thus recouping his investment. Regimental agents, representing the secretary for war, disbursed pay and funds to ensure some government control over essentially private military contractors.

Up through the rank of lieutenant-colonel, officers purchased commissions, initially from the colonel. Upon retirement or the purchase of a higher rank in a different regiment, the commission could be resold, thus preserving the socio-economic exclusiveness of the officer corps. The landed aristocracy supported the purchase system, which gave them a vested interest in the forces as well as a hedge against any royal abuse of power through crown-appointed officers; monarchs generally disliked the practice. An ensigncy in a line infantry regiment typically cost £400, while a lieutenant-colonelcy (and battalion command) could run to upwards of £5,000. Blatant abuses, such as commissions for infants, ultimately led to minimum age regulations (set at sixteen in 1809) and time in rank requirements for promotions. Promotion for merit, while existent, occurred infrequently; promotions by strict seniority filled vacancies caused by death or disability while on campaign.

Ancient patterns of aristocratic paternalism and deference to authority conditioned relations between officers and other ranks. Troops resented cowardice and cruelty among their officers more than incompetence (a condition particularly rife with the commission-purchase system). Ensuring the feeding, clothing, housing and addressal of grievances of his troops constituted the fundamental duties of a junior officer. Tactical skill and operational competence, expected at the field grade (major and above) level, remained less important for junior officers.

The army, always voluntary, continually struggled against adverse public perceptions at a time before nationalistic patriotism and the ethos of national service emerged as recruitment factors. Soldiers frequently enlisted for life; although shorter terms (seven, ten or twelve years) resulted from the need to raise ever more men in an age of chronic warfare and imperial expansion. Recruiters plied country fairs, races and urban public houses. For the rural poor, typically agricultural labourers and craftsmen, enlistment often appealed as a solution to poverty, debt or legal troubles. The army rarely employed impressments except for incarcerated debtors and felons, the unemployed (regarded as vagrants) and the 'chronically idle'. Scotland and Ireland, where grinding poverty and a traditional military ethic made army service attractive and honourable, supplied a high percentage of recruits. For example, between 1759 and 1793, twenty infantry regiments drew their recruits from the Scottish Highlands. Out of a total population of 300,000, a phenomenal 74,000 Highlanders fought in the wars against France in those years, while expatriate Scots in North America served in units such as the 84th Royal Highland Emigrants and North Carolina Highlanders, regiments raised for crown service in the American War of Independence. In wartime, the calibre of enlistees rose, particularly during the invasion scares of 1759 and 1803, perhaps indicating a nascent spirit of nationalism and patriotism.

Unlike the officer corps, promotion within the ranks depended on merit, literacy and leadership acumen. Most regiments provided basic reading, writing and arithmetic instruction to those privates identified as potential non-commissioned officers (corporals and sergeants). The highest enlisted rank of sergeant-major (created in 1797), to which every rank-and-file soldier of talent and leadership could aspire, earned extraordinary respect from soldiers and officers alike.

Logistical difficulties typically limited a soldier's diet while on campaign. The daily ration consisted of a pound of meat, a pound of bread, flour or biscuits and a pint of wine or one-third of a pint of spirits. Vegetables and fruits supplemented the diet as available, with peas and onions the most frequently available. Each mess (generally squad level) carried a camp kettle with the lid used for frying and the pot for boiling and stewing. On the march, each man carried three days' worth of rations. British forces preferred to subsist from established magazines and protected supply routes, a logistical apparatus honed by the duke of Marlborough in the War of the Spanish Succession. The system proved more reliable than the traditional European habit of foraging and living off the land. Of a private's eight pence per day pay, two pence, withheld as 'off reckonings', paid for clothing, uniforms and living expenses.

The balance, called 'subsistence pay', usually went towards food, drink and necessities. Very little disposable income remained.

The Petition of Right (1628) and Disbanding Act (1679) forbade the billeting of troops in private households without the owner's consent. None the less, the impoverished status of troops, after pay stoppages for food, quarters, uniforms, arms and other 'off reckonings', typically resulted in non-payment for quarters and exacerbated public dislike of the army. Soldiers typically took outside civilian work and volunteered for extra hazardous duty to supplement pay. By 1697, projects to build permanent barracks throughout England and Wales emerged to help resolve the housing dilemma, but these were not implemented and it was not until the 1790s that William Pitt's government began to build barracks on a significant scale.

The Mutiny Acts regulated virtually all activities connected with military discipline, including mutiny, desertion, sedition, unauthorized leave of absence, civil offences, damage by neglect, inebriation and 'misbehaviour before the enemy'. The legislation also established the office of judge advocate general to oversee enforcement and provide legal advice to military commanders. A 1717 act authorized the crown to draw up new Articles of War, while this and other acts (1757 and 1803) extended the range of courts-martial to include militia and imperial forces. Between 1689 and the mid-eighteenth century, the army suffered from rampant corruption, officer insubordination, high desertion rates, fraudulent enlistments and poor relations between officers and other ranks. Throughout the century conditions improved, particularly as royal military administrators increased their authority and suppressed the more egregious abuses.

For the troops, many senior officers believed that only severe corporal punishment (or death) maintained order and discipline. Regimental courts-martial imposed flogging by the lash, imprisonment or death as punishment for serious disciplinary infractions or Articles of War violations. Lesser infractions resulted in bread-and-water diets, extra duty, public reprimands or humiliation by having to wear the regimental coat inside-out. Convictions for mutiny, sedition or 'misbehaviour before the enemy' carried the death penalty for all ranks. For lesser offences, officers suffered cashierment and non-commissioned officers reduced in rank.

Military Education and Training

In eighteenth-century warfare, the ability to manoeuvre troop formations quickly and efficiently required arduous and constant close-order drill. Officers, relying on guides such as *The Exercise of the Horse, Dragoon, and Foot Forces* (1728), learned to direct complicated troop movements; soldiers learned to execute orders rapidly and almost by instinct.

The multi-step priming, loading and discharge of firelocks (military muskets) in volleys required precision, speed and efficiency. Unfortunately, the army allotted only thirty musket balls and sixty blank cartridges per year per man for live-fire training. Units conducted surprisingly little bayonet training despite the British propensity for bayonet charges.

Formal, inflexible, Prussian-style procedures dominated the reigns of the first two Georges, but after 1760, the experience of wilderness warfare in North America altered tactics and drill doctrine. Colonel Henry Bouquet (60th Royal Americans), who developed a training system designed to produce troops capable of effective wilderness combat, laid the foundation of the light infantry system adopted throughout the army in the 1770s. In 1792, Colonel David Dundas published the *Rules and Regulations for the Formations, Field Exercises, and Movements of His Majesty's Forces*, the first official manual to establish a standard drill throughout the army and applicable to the open terrain typical of European battlefields.

Cavalry training emphasized horsemanship, often polished at a riding school. Surprisingly, prior to the French wars at the end of the eighteenth century, the horse regiments conducted minimal sword training, a situation corrected by the general adoption of Colonel Le Marchant's *Rules and Regulations for the Attainment and Practice of the Sword Exercise* (1797).

Until 1800, officers received nearly all their training either at drill or on the battlefield. When at war, ensigns, the two most junior officers in each infantry battalion, carried the regimental colours, thus learning the art of command without actually directing formations in the field. Frederick, duke of York, commander-in-chief from 1798 to 1809, established the Royal Military College (1799), the first formal centre of military education for infantry and cavalry officers. For artillery officers, the Royal Military Academy at Woolwich had provided formal education since 1741. Education in the art of leadership and the science of warfare thus set in motion the nineteenth-century phenomenon of an increasingly professional, educated officer corps, in contrast to the gentleman amateur of previous centuries.

Tactics, Operational Art, Weapons and Doctrine

Military music relied on the drum and fife. Drums maintained the cadence on the march, signalled commands and provided music for ceremonies such as trooping the colours, military reviews, formal parades and funeral processions. In combat, a drummer stood beside the officer in command of a specific unit. Each tactical movement or firing command had a unique drum beating, which extended the effective arc of control far beyond the officer's voice range. In camp, musicians signalled specific evolutions such as officer call, assembly, beat to arms, reveille, retreat and so forth. Though popular in the seventeenth century, the fife had fallen out of favour until the mid-eighteenth century when it again became popular. Although it did not signal specific command orders, the fife provided music for ceremonies and on the march accompanying the drummers. In Scottish Highland units, the bagpipe, proscribed except in the army after the 1745–6 Jacobite rebellion, substituted for the fife.

The smooth-bore, muzzle-loading flintlock musket, affectionately known as the 'Brown Bess' because of the colour of the rust proofing, remained, in several variations, the standard infantry arm for a century and a half. With a forty-six-inch barrel length and twelve pounds weight, the musket proved awkward and cumbersome. After 1750, successive models reduced the length and weight, thus making it easier to handle. Rifled and breech-loading weapons, notably the Ferguson Rifle (1776) and Baker Rifle of the 1790s, while featuring tremendous improvements in firing speed, accuracy and effectiveness, never caught on in the army. Except for special duty units such as the 95th Regiment (Rifle Brigade), and other light infantry formations, the army did not adopt standardized rifled arms until the 1840s. Round, solid lead musket balls, typically weighing an ounce with a calibre of .77 or .80 and propelled by black powder charges, did not evolve into the conical bullet until the mid-nineteenth century. As such, the aerodynamics of the round ball limited both range and accuracy.

British troops could deliver three to four volleys a minute, far faster than any opposing period force. This skill gave British commanders a tremendous tactical advantage in the close quarters (100 yards and less) of the typical eighteenth-century engagement. Period tactical doctrine called for massed volleys delivered in the general direction of the enemy line rather than individual firing at a specific target. The woeful inaccuracy and limited effective range (100 yards at best) of smooth-bore weapons dictated that massed volley fire remained the principal tactical doctrine until the late nineteenth century.

Forces moved slowly and deliberately using linear formations to maintain unit integrity, ensure a maximum effect from massed volley fire, and maintain command and control. The British line, arranged three ranks deep, fired volleys by tactical unit (companies or platoons), by battalions or by roll fire (each rank fired in succession as the other two primed and loaded). During the American War of Independence, local commanders reduced the line to two ranks, giving greater weight of shot effect to a single rank volley, but increasing the priming and loading time between volleys. Movement over roads and across fields required a narrow front column, but once on the battlefield, formations rapidly deployed into an extended line.

The bayonet, consisting of a long blade on a socket handle attached below the musket muzzle so as not to interfere with firing, dated from 1690. The socket bayonet rapidly replaced the pike as a primary infantry weapon. The bayonet gave soldiers the ability to defend the line at close quarters while maintaining volley fire, or to deliver a devastating charge against an enemy line. As with volley rate of fire, the small, highly trained and professional British army excelled all adversaries in the bayonet charge. A typical battle tactic called for delivering three volleys at close range followed by a bayonet charge directly at the enemy line. Frequently, this tactic resulted in the complete disintegration of the opponent's formation, which gave British commanders a significant battlefield advantage against less disciplined troops.

The primary horse cavalry tactic called for a headlong charge at full gallop against an enemy line. While a disciplined infantry formation armed with bayonets employed in a hedgehog defensive position had little to fear from such a pell-mell assault, undefended artillery batteries and infantry whose linear formation had broken down suffered tremendous casualties. While on the march, cavalry functioned as scouts, pickets and foragers in support of the slow-marching infantry. While dragoons retained the capability to deliver a charge, their primary tactical doctrine called for riding into position, dismounting and fighting as infantry. Accordingly, in addition to the swords and pistols used by the horse cavalry, dragoons carried short-barrelled muskets (usually the fuzee).

By the time of the War of the Spanish Succession, cannon had evolved from the heavy, highly immobile moulded iron siege pieces to lighter, bored brass-barrelled field artillery. Guns could be dispersed for infantry support or arrayed in batteries for massed fire effect against infantry or cavalry. By 1750, the science of calculating flight trajectory resulted in lighter, more accurate gunnery. The *Treatise of Artillery* by John Muller (1768), based on technological and scientific advancements and experiments, provided a standard set of procedures adopted throughout the army as well as specifications for the manufacture of lighter but more powerful field guns (including shortened barrels, tapered castings, and thinner but stronger barrel walls). The mortar and howitzer, designed as short-barrelled ballistic trajectory weapons, could throw a heavy ball into or within defensive walls; but their great weight and the movement away from sieges against walled defensive sites towards open, pitched battles by the end of the eighteenth century reduced the requirement for these weapons.

FURTHER READING

Barnett, Corelli: *Britain and Her Army, 1509–1970: A Military, Political and Social Survey* (London, 1970).

Chandler, David and Beckett, Ian (eds): *The Oxford Illustrated History of the British Army* (Oxford, 1994).

Childs, John: *The British Army of William III, 1689–1702* (Manchester, 1987).

Dietz, Peter: *The Last of the Regiments: Their Rise and Fall* (London, 1990).

Fortescue, John W.: *A History of the British Army* (vols 2–10, 2nd edn, London, 1910–30).

Guy, Alan James: *Oeconomy and Discipline: Officership and Administration in the British Army, 1714–63* (Manchester, 1985).

Guy, Alan James: *The Road to Waterloo: The British Army and the Struggle against Revolutionary and Napoleonic France* (Stroud, 1990).

Hogg, O. F. G.: *Artillery: Its Origin, Heyday and Decline* (London, 1970).

Messenger, Charles: *For Love of Regiment: A History of the British Infantry*, vol. 1: *1660–1914* (London, 1994).

Pollard, Hugh B. C.: *A History of Firearms* (London, 1926).

Rogers, H. C. B.: *The British Army of the Eighteenth Century* (London, 1977).

Savory, Reginald Arthur: *His Britannic Majesty's Army in Germany during the Seven Years' War* (Oxford, 1966).

Strachan, Hew: *The Politics of the British Army* (Oxford, 1997).

CHAPTER THIRTY-SEVEN

The Royal Navy

RICHARD HARDING

By the end of the seventeenth century the English (from 1707 British) Royal Navy was the largest and probably the most capable naval force in the world. In the preceding fifty years it had built on solid administrative, technical and professional developments to outbuild and outfight its rivals. Within another twenty years, after the War of the Spanish Succession (1702–13), its greatest rival, the French royal navy, had withered to a shadow of its former self, and its ally in the wars against France since 1689, the Dutch fleet, had become very much the junior partner. This dominance lasted throughout the eighteenth century and by 1815 the Royal Navy was without a near equal in the world. An important factor in British naval domination was the numerical superiority of the Royal Navy in all classes of vessels. The numbers of ships in the Royal Navy suggest a correlation between the size of the navy and the rhythm of British naval fortunes. In 1760, towards the end of the Seven Years' War, which was the most successful conflict of the century, British superiority over the French battleships and cruisers peaked. When Spain entered the war in 1761, the numerical balance was slightly redressed, but, by then, the exhaustion of French maritime resources and the financial bankruptcy of her navy more than outweighed the value of additional Spanish ships. A similar outstripping of French naval resources is apparent during the Revolutionary War (1793–1802) and Napoleonic War (1803–15). The relative strength of the Royal Navy in small ships shows a similar pattern.

The periods of danger are also apparent from the figures. At the end of the Seven Years' War, Britain's vast naval superiority was slowly eroded. The results of the slow mobilization of the Royal Navy during the American War of Independence are evident in the figures for the 1775–80 period. With a broad numerical advantage and the Royal Navy stretched across the globe, the combined fleets of France and Spain threatened an invasion of the British Isles in 1779. When the Dutch joined the alliance against Britain in December 1780, Britain's worldwide position looked gloomy. By 1782 British victories at sea and a superior building rate had restored her numerical advantage, which made a relatively good peace possible. In the building boom that followed the war, Britain was unable to maintain a clear superiority over her rivals. After some initial successes against France in 1793–4, there were difficult years facing the combined fleets of France, Spain and the Netherlands, before victories and building again established a superiority that was to remain well into the nineteenth century.

The Navy's Role

Numbers do not tell the whole story. The course and consequences of naval power were by no means as clear-cut as the crude numbers suggest. Seapower is not a simple equation in which net numerical superiority can correspond to a particular naval advantage. Reach and robustness are critical factors. Over the course of the century the ability of the Royal Navy to operate across the globe steadily increased. Its impact upon other states and societies likewise developed. Its ability to recover from setbacks, such as in 1779 and 1796–7, was also highly significant. The great strength of the Royal Navy lay in its integration with British political expectations and the expanding maritime economy. With political support, sufficient legal and economic resources of the country were devoted to ensuring the navy's development. This is not to suggest that the period was a golden age of 'navalism'. The political and military struggles the navy faced were real and there was no inevitable trajectory in the eighteenth century that propelled Britain towards a maritime and imperial future. Instead, there were a variety of circumstances that worked in favour of the Royal Navy over a long period and so enabled it to consolidate its position as the world's paramount naval force.

The position of the Royal Navy as a central feature of British political ideology had been developing for over a hundred years by 1700. The experience of military government under the Protectorate and the rhetoric of continental versus maritime war that accompanied William III's war against Louis XIV (1689–97) progressively entrenched the navy as the bulwark of British liberties and prosperity. By 1713 this rhetoric had been further enhanced. Unlike the Treaty of Nijmegen, which ended the previous war, the peace of Utrecht (March/April 1713), which ended the War of the Spanish Succession, provided Britain with solid colonial and commercial gains. The duke of Marlborough remained a national hero, but the role of the allied armies in Flanders and Spain in securing these prizes was never clearly articulated in the political debates. In 1714 a new Hanoverian monarch, George I, ensured that British foreign policy would remain focused upon Europe. The collapse of the French navy and an alliance with France, which provided a first-rate army, enabled British ministers to think of the navy as the first line of military power to support diplomacy until the early 1730s. Naval intervention in the Baltic, the Mediterranean and the Caribbean had mixed success, but it was enough success, particularly against Spain, to ensure that the belief in the potency of naval power was preserved.

A critical point occurred between 1739 and 1748. The political pressure for war with Spain over navigational and commercial freedoms (the War of Jenkins's Ear) was based on the belief that British naval power would rapidly bring Spain to a favourable peace. This did not happen. Furthermore, when this war merged with the War of the Austrian Succession (1740–8) and France allied to Spain (1744), the Royal Navy signally failed to achieve the results expected of it. For a critical period between 1744 and 1747 public faith in the Royal Navy was in doubt. Threatened by invasion and rebellion, the public were scandalized by the performance of some naval officers. It was the two great victories off Cape Finisterre in May and October 1747, led by Admirals Anson and Hawke respectively, that restored public faith in the navy before the peace in 1748. At the same time the dismal results of the campaigns in Germany and Flanders eclipsed any hope that Britain would achieve great success against the Bourbons in Europe.

From this point on the political case for the Royal Navy as the defensive and offensive core of British military power strengthened. The tremendous successes of the Seven Years' War across the globe and the death of George II in 1760 further diminished the continental argument. This was followed by more diplomatic successes, backed by naval force in the 1760s, culminating in the humiliation of Spain, and to a lesser degree France, over the Falkland Islands in 1770–1. The need to concentrate finances upon the army to suppress the American rebellion from 1775, together with the multiple tasks required from the navy, left it stretched from the beginning of the war. French and Spanish building eliminated the navy's advantage and between 1779 and 1781 the Royal Navy faced a series of crises. While defeat at sea off the Chesapeake on 5 September 1781 sealed the fate of the war in America, it was once again victories at sea that enabled Britain to make peace. Vice-Admiral George Darby's solid defence of the Channel during 1781, Rodney's great victory at The Saintes in April 1782, Sir Edward Hughes's campaign in the East Indies (1779–83) and Lord Richard Howe's relief of Gibraltar in October 1782 contained the Bourbon threat and limited the losses suffered at the peace.

The recognition that the Royal Navy performed this vital function preserved it from the worst of the postwar economy measures. Despite the desire for 'economical reform' and the drive against corruption, the naval budgets were largely protected. Repair and maintenance continued and the government was able to mobilize significant forces in 1790 in response to crises with Russia and Spain. The new war with Revolutionary France in February 1793 initially posed no significant naval problems. The demoralization of the officer corps and the political upheavals within the French royal navy destroyed the fragile recovery that the navy had shown since 1783. The blockade of French commercial ports and the victory of the 'Glorious First of June' 1794 confirmed the supremacy of the Royal Navy. A real threat, however, emerged from the collapse of Britain's allies. First Spain and then the Netherlands succumbed to France in 1795–6. With their defection to the side of France, the material balance swung substantially against Britain. The Royal Navy abandoned the Mediterranean in order to concentrate on the defence of Britain and to maintain the offensive in the Caribbean. Gradually, by 1800, British victories at sea, such as Cape St Vincent in February 1797, Camperdown in October 1797 and the Nile in August 1798, eliminated the numerical superiority of the enemy. While invasion always remained a technical possibility and a significant public fear, the practical threat slowly diminished. The victory at Trafalgar in October 1805 did not prevent an invasion, for Napoleon was already on the march against Austria and the French and Spanish fleets were preparing for moves against Italy. Nevertheless, the popular perception was that Nelson had finally lifted the threat. While it is true that Napoleon possessed significant and growing naval forces until 1814, they were never large enough nor concentrated to pose a threat to the dominance of the Royal Navy. The navy continued to support the military campaigns against Napoleon, encouraged the breach of his trade embargo against Britain within the empire and provided security for British trade worldwide. The 'Nelson Legend' and the record of these successes, allied to the development of the second British empire, provided the political rationale for continued naval hegemony until after 1918.

Naval Administration and Strategy

While political support provided the vital financial resources for the large navy, it would not have been forthcoming if that navy had failed to meet the political expectations of victory and diplomatic success. This required a force that could do the job – defeating its enemies and converting those victories into solid material advantages for the nation.

The conversion of money into ships, designed, equipped and manned for the job, was the function of a large naval administration. While a great deal of work has been done on this in recent years, a great deal more needs to be done, particularly in relation to foreign naval administrations, which would enable us to understand better contemporary views of efficiency and effectiveness. Two impressions emerge regarding naval administration from our current state of knowledge. First, there was an exceptionally long period of steady state investment in the naval infrastructure from the sixteenth century onwards. There was the development of not just central state bodies, such as the Navy Board (which originated in 1546), the Admiralty (taking its eighteenth-century form from around 1654) and the Victualling Board (permanently established in 1683). The dockyards required effective local management and it was a major achievement of the seventeenth century that this developed in a similar, steady manner to the central administration. Second, and of equal importance, was the ability of the central administration to develop control of that local administration. This capability seems to have developed earlier and more fully than in France and Spain. While this might be an impression created by the lack of current research in the area, it is an important consideration in understanding the performance of the Royal Navy.

Naval strategy was formally the preserve of the monarch and the ministry. The Admiralty was responsible for ensuring that strategy was carried out. Under the Admiralty, the Navy Board was responsible for the material quality of the fleet. The design of British warships has not, traditionally, been seen as a strength of the Royal Navy in this period. Contemporaries drew unfavourable comparisons between British ships and those of France and Spain. The sailing warship did not change fundamentally between 1650 and 1815, but there is no doubt that during the eighteenth century there were significant developments in sail plan, building practice, hull design and armaments that improved the durability, manoeuvrability and robustness of most types of warship. It was a European phenomenon and most countries borrowed from their neighbours and developed designs with local shipbuilding experience. The British were no different. In the mid-century an understanding of French-designed frigates and battleships enabled the joint Surveyors of the Navy, Thomas Slade and William Bentley, to develop new two-deck seventy-four-gun battleships which became the backbone of the British line of battle until the end of the period. Slade also designed new powerful three-deck warships, including the '100'-gun *Victory*, which were instrumental in bringing the largest battleship type back into favour among European navies. Slade's *Southampton* and *Alarm* classes of thirty-two-gun frigates matched the larger and more heavily armed French vessels. The development of these types also held their own until met by the larger American 'forty-fours'.

From design to finished ship was the responsibility of the dockyards. As building and maintenance pressures grew in times of crisis, some building of warships was contracted to private yards. The majority always lay with the royal dockyards. These were the largest and most complex industrial organizations of the period. They were, for the most part, highly effective in building and maintaining the ships. More needs to be understood about how they operated and why they appear to have been relatively more effective than their French and Spanish counterparts. They had to cope with serious problems. Timber supplies, particularly, proved a constant problem, but, on the whole, the mercantile and contracting networks maintained supplies at adequate levels. Likewise, the Victualling Board seems to have managed the task of supplying the fleet with victuals across the world. Britain's growing maritime economy was both a boon and a burden. Merchants competed for the best materials, but the contracting networks established by the naval administrators, to supply items ranging from primary materials such as timber, iron, flax and hemp, through to wet and dry victuals, and on to the hire or building of complete vessels, were the foundation of British naval resources. They seem to have worked well enough throughout the century to keep pace with the expansion of the navy. Sea officers have, traditionally, held a poor view of administrators, and with the exception of Samuel Pepys (1633–1703), the Royal Navy's administrators have not yet received the attention they deserve. More is now known about some of the senior administrators, such as Josiah Burchett, Thomas Corbett, Richard Clevland and Philip Stephens, all successive secretaries to the Admiralty Board, whose individual long tenures of office helped to create an effective routine of administration. Far more needs to be known about the more junior officials who managed the contracts with merchants and the relations with workmen, local communities and sea officers. As British security at home and victories abroad increased, so the naval dockyards expanded overseas to support her extended commitments: Gibraltar (after 1704), Port Mahon (after 1708), English Harbour, Antigua (1728), Port Antonio (1729) and Port Royal (1735) on Jamaica, Halifax (after 1755), Bombay (1750), Malta (1806) and Bermuda (1809). It was an unrivalled network.

The manning of the fleet was another area in which competition with the mercantile marine created problems. Recent research has demonstrated that service in the Royal Navy was not as horrific as earlier stories of the press gang have suggested. None the less, it was not as popular as service on merchant vessels or on privateers. Certainly, the navy's demands for seamen far outstripped the available supply in wartime. It was the responsibility of each captain to man his ship. Many captains could rely upon a personal following among seamen, but in wartime, all had to rely upon the press to a degree. Popular legend has it that the press gangs indiscriminately swept through towns causing havoc and terror. Press warrants were not entirely arbitrary, however. Protections were offered to many seafarers occupied in essential duties such as fishing or on government contracts. The most effective pressing occurred at sea, where homeward bound merchantmen were intercepted off the coast and a quota of men taken from them. It was an acknowledged anomaly that seamen should be the only group of Britons subject to compulsory labour. Both on land and at sea the press sometimes met with violent resistance. In America, particularly, the press gang was resented and legally challenged. Serious rioting broke out in Boston in November 1747 as a result of naval pressing and seamen played a significant part in the disturbances that preceded the outbreak of the Revolution. Attempts to find different methods of manning the fleet were periodically raised in parliament, but all foundered on grounds of cost or practicability. This is a good example of how the political nation recognized that, despite the injustice, the law had to continue to support the press rather than the liberty of the subject. Once on board, life was hard, as it was for all seafarers. The petty irritations that made life miserable were possibly a little different from those on a merchant vessel or privateer, and hence more acute to the newcomer. They were not so outrageous as to render the service only possible by rum and the lash. To landsmen the seafaring community of the eighteenth century was heterogeneous and volatile, but these seamen had to work together to sail and fight their ship. Self-preservation was a powerful stimulus. Work discipline was maintained by different rewards and threats in the merchant marine and the Royal Navy, but in neither service did it systematically transgress the accepted norms of society. In all organizations where compulsion, violence and discipline are fundamental to the system, individual cases of injustice will occur. Mutiny and savage reprisal were sometimes the result. The most famous case of the mutinies at Spithead and the Nore in 1797 are good examples of this reaction. They were sparked by local irritations and feelings of injustice, particularly regarding pay. They were met with some concessions and ultimately reprisal for the ringleaders. Severe and worrying as they were, they did not significantly destabilize or alter the traditional work patterns and discipline.

In the final resort, beating the enemy did not just require large numbers of well-built, maintained and manned warships. It required tactical and strategic insights together with ships and fleets that were effectively fought in action. This was the contribution of the officers of the navy. From 1660 naval officers were increasingly subject to formal proofs of professional competence and commitment. In 1677 an oral examination of each candidate for a lieutenant's commission before a board of officers was introduced. Journals had to be kept and certificates obtained from commanding officers to prove good conduct. Half-pay, introduced in a limited but systematic way in 1668 and extended at different times until 1700, became part of the process of strengthening the officer's obligation of service. The obligation of the officer was to fight his ship and the tradition of aggressive engagement of the enemy was well established long before it became the hallmark of Nelsonian leadership. Rooke at Malaga in August 1704 tried, unsuccessfully, to batter the French fleet to destruction. A tactical draw, the battle was, nevertheless, a strategic victory as it forced the French to withdraw to Toulon. Failure to engage wholeheartedly was a most serious crime. Two captains who failed to support Admiral Benbow in 1702 were shot at Portsmouth. In the 1740s the battle off Toulon in February 1744 and other actions provoked considerable disquiet about the performance of the officer corps, leading eventually to the amendment of the Articles of War in 1748, which in turn paved the way to the conviction and execution of Vice-Admiral John Byng in March 1757 for failing to do his utmost to destroy the French fleet off Minorca in 1756. By the 1740s decisive victory at close quarters was difficult to achieve over numerically inferior French and Spanish fleets that, wisely, did not intend to engage in pitched battles. The pursuit was critical and it was officers like Anson and Hawke who trained their squadrons to expect this kind of action. Hawke's pursuit of the French into Quiberon Bay on a stormy day in November 1759 has become a symbol of mid-century British naval dominance.

Controlling a large fleet in bad weather required methods of command and control that developed in the second half of the century. Central to this was the signalling system. The discipline required from captains to obey the signals was well established. Indeed, much has been made of the rigidity of the line of battle and the discouragement it gave to officers with initiative. While this was undoubtedly an important factor operating on the minds of officers, and some work has been conducted on its impact, much more work is needed to be confident that we understand the relationship between signals and performance in battle. What is known is that gradual amendments to the established system and, from the 1770s, experiments by officers such as Richard Kempenfelt and Richard, Lord Howe, with different systems led by 1790 to an effective communication process. Howe's numerical system was amalgamated into the official Admiralty signal book in 1799. The problem was always the same: how to inflict decisive defeat upon the enemy. With a relatively small force of the enemy in flight, as was often the case in the mid-century, it was largely a question of cutting off the stragglers and bringing sections of the enemy force to battle. Ensuring an effective chase action dominated thinking in this period. During the war of 1778–83 the problem was rather different. The French numerical inferiority was not so marked and their fleets could stand their ground in line of battle. The problem then became how to break the line and defeat the enemy in detail by concentrating fire on the enemy from both sides. There were plenty of aggressive officers in the mould of Samuel Hood and George Rodney who would do this, but achieving it was not easy. At the battle of The Saintes in April 1782, Rodney achieved it and sparked an interesting dispute over who inspired it. The same imperative dominated the Revolutionary and Napoleonic Wars. Howe at the 'Glorious First of June' 1794 broke the French line after days of manoeuvre. Nelson, under Sir John Jervis's command, broke through an ill-formed Spanish line off Cape St Vincent in February 1797. Nelson's fleet doubled the anchored French line at the battle of the Nile in August 1798 and, most famously, his fleet pierced the Franco-Spanish line in two places to win the crushing victory off Cape Trafalgar in October 1805.

While tactical and operational methods were developed in the hands of an aggressive officer corps, which had been conditioned to victory, the strategic operation of naval power went far beyond the battlefleet. The dispositions of the battlefleet for offensive and defensive purposes were essential, but the conduct of war in the eighteenth century was much more complex than this. The importance of frigates cruising as the eyes of the fleet and government had been recognized throughout the century. Few admirals ever thought that they had enough frigates. Convoy escort was a tedious business, but it was also vital to Britain's worldwide trade. Throughout the century, cruising and convoys played an important role against enemy privateers. The defeat of these privateers was one side of the coin. The success of the British attack on enemy trade was the other. Along with naval vessels, British privateers played an important part. The law courts and government were also extremely significant. The attack on enemy trade inevitably created serious diplomatic tensions with neutrals and it was the proceedings of prize courts and the willingness of government to buy contraband that made effective blockade diplomatically practicable.

By the end of the eighteenth century, British seapower was a well-balanced and powerful tool. Its capability had developed slowly over the century, but by then it had an effective global reach, which was unparalleled. This reach does not automatically imply an equivalent diplomatic impact. Contemporaries overestimated this impact in the early part of the century, most notably in 1739. By 1763, however, that impact was evidently growing. By blockade and vigorous action, British fleets precluded the assembling of rival battlefleets that might cover an invasion force. They forced her enemies to despatch naval and merchant shipping in small numbers to avoid discovery. The same fleets covered British military expeditions across the globe – by far the most spectacular example of the impact of seapower upon the diplomatic balance. Military occupations, made possible by seapower, had a significant impact on European diplomacy from the middle of the century. Unlike trade disruptions, real changes were wrought in territorial possessions that could not be corrected by years of peace. Nevertheless, cruising forces did significant damage, disrupted enemy trade, and hindered their privateers and cruisers. The Royal Navy was the institution central to this power. Its battlefleets and cruisers carried out the operations. This in turn was made possible by an effective administration drawing upon an expanding maritime economy. Ultimately, the political nation was willing to pay the price of these expensive weapons and their infrastructure. Founded partly on the supposed ideological relationship between navies, commerce and political liberty, and partly upon the perceived effectiveness of that navy in battle and, as the century progressed, at the peace conferences, the Royal Navy became one of the central institutions of the eighteenth-century British state and helped define the emerging nature of 'Britishness'.

FURTHER READING

Baugh, Daniel: *British Naval Administration in the Age of Walpole* (Princeton, NJ, 1965).

Black, Jeremy and Woodfine, Philip (eds): *The British Navy and the Use of Naval Power in the Eighteenth Century* (Leicester, 1988).

Coad, J.: *The Royal Dockyards, 1690–1815: Architecture and Engineering Works of the Sailing Navy* (Aldershot, 1989).

Duffy, Michael: *Soldiers, Sugar and Seapower: The British Expeditions to the West Indies and the War against Revolutionary France* (Oxford, 1987).

Harding, Richard: *The Evolution of the Sailing Navy, 1509–1815* (Basingstoke, 1995).

Harding, Richard: *Seapower and Naval Warfare 1650–1830* (London, 1999).

Lavery, Brian: *Nelson's Navy: The Ships, Men and Organisation, 1793–1815* (London, 1989).

Lavery, Brian: *The Line of Battle: The Sailing Warship, 1650–1840* (London, 1992).

Le Fevre, Peter and Harding, Richard (eds): *Precursors of Nelson: British Admirals of the Eighteenth Century* (Rochester, 2000).

Morriss, Roger: *The Royal Dockyards during the Revolutionary and Napoleonic Wars* (Leicester, 1983).

Rodger, N. A. M.: *The Wooden World: An Anatomy of the Georgian Navy* (London, 1986).

Syrett, David: *The Royal Navy in American Waters, 1775–1783* (Aldershot, 1989).

Syrett, David: *The Royal Navy in European Waters during the American Revolutionary War* (Columbia, SC, 1998).

Chapter Thirty-Eight

Britain and the Slave Trade

John Oldfield

During the course of the eighteenth century the British perfected the Atlantic slave trade. At its height, British ships carried more slaves than any other nation, their slave colonies produced vast quantities of tropical goods, and the country as a whole grew rich on the profits of African slavery. The slave trade clearly brought the British prestige, as well as enormous material well-being. Yet, paradoxically, it was also the British who led the struggle to bring the traffic to an end. In fact, abolition was to emerge as one of the most popular reform movements of the eighteenth century. That it did so reflected not only broad economic, social and political changes, but also changes in the way the British perceived themselves and their nation.

The Slave Trade

The British entered the slave trade relatively late. Estimates vary, but it is unlikely that the number of slaves shipped by the British before 1660 was much in excess of 10,000. Starting in the 1660s, however, the British began to dominate the slave trade. Slave exports rose from 59,900 in 1662–70 to 125,600 in 1700–9 and 273,300 in 1750–9. The second half of the eighteenth century witnessed further expansion. During the 1780s and 1790s, for instance, decades that marked the emergence of the early abolitionist movement, the British exported a total of 656,000 slaves. Overall, between 1662 and 1807 British empire ships carried approximately 3.4 million slaves from Africa to America. This was about 50 per cent of all slave exports during this period.

The British probably tried some slave trading to the Spanish colonies in the West Indies as early as the 1560s. But without major tropical colonies of their own there was little incentive to enter the trade, at least not in a concerted or organized fashion. All of this was to change in the early seventeenth century, however, as the British claimed Bermuda and later, in 1625, Barbados. After initial experiments with tobacco and cotton, Barbados rapidly emerged as a major sugar colony with a rural labour force that was enslaved and African. Barbados, moreover, set the pattern for further expansion in both the West Indies and mainland America. The acquisition of Jamaica in 1655, and the spectacular expansion of tobacco production in Virginia and Maryland, secured the rise of a plantation complex that dominated the Atlantic economy of the seventeenth and eighteenth centuries.

Spurred on by the success of Barbados, British merchants began to take a much more active interest in the Atlantic slave trade. By the 1630s the British had their first fort in Africa, on the Gold Coast, and two decades later had staked out the Sierra Leone or Upper Guinea Coast. But the real expansion came after mid-century when the state became involved in the slave trade. In 1660 Charles II granted a 1,000-year monopoly of British trade to Africa to the Company of Royal Adventurers Trading into Africa. Reconstituted in 1663, the company had its rights transferred to the Royal African Company (RAC) in 1672. Like its predecessor, the RAC was a joint-stock company and enjoyed monopoly control over the British slave trade, as well as Britain's trade with Africa in commodity goods.

Between 1672 and 1713, when the last remnant of crown control over Britain's trade to Africa came to an end, the Royal African Company transported over 350,000 slaves to the British colonies in the West Indies. As such, it helped to establish Britain's position as the leading European carrier of slaves. But like all monopoly companies, the RAC eventually failed. Its monopoly was ended by parliament in 1698 and from 1713 onwards the slave trade was effectively privatized, although the RAC and its successor, the Company of Merchants Trading to Africa (established in 1750), did continue to maintain forts and factories along the west coast of Africa. Part of the reason for this change in the organization of the British Atlantic slave trade was undoubtedly the high fixed costs involved in maintaining the RAC's monopoly. But no less important was the damage caused by interlopers. According to one estimate, between 1674 and 1686 perhaps one in four of the slaves reaching British America arrived illegally.

After 1713 the Atlantic slave trade was carried on largely by private trading partnerships or, occasionally, joint-stock companies. Typically, these partnerships were made up of between two and five merchants, although the same men might have interests in a number of different slaving expeditions. Naturally, the firm or partnership bore the cost of preparing ships for their voyages. While hardly exorbitant, at least in comparison to the India trade, outfitting costs for slavers rose considerably during the course of the eighteenth century, and for most outport merchants represented a sizeable investment. Slaving, moreover, was fraught with exceptional risks. It could take anything up to eighteen months to complete a successful slave voyage and longer still (perhaps three or more years) to settle one's accounts. There was also the danger of shipwreck or, more likely, disease and death.

Given these risks and the high costs of slaving expeditions, it is not surprising that London merchants dominated the slave trade, at least in its early expansionary phases. The most recent estimates suggest that London merchants financed about 63 per cent of all British slave voyages between 1698 and 1725. By the 1730s, however, London was being challenged by Bristol. Between 1720 and 1749 a total of 975 slave ships sailed from Bristol, marginally more than London during the same period, and by the 1750s Bristol merchants were sinking £150,000 a year into the slave trade. But just as London was eclipsed by Bristol, so was Bristol eclipsed by Liverpool. During the 1750s 521 slave ships cleared the port of Liverpool, more than Bristol and London combined. In the following decades, Liverpool went on to dominate the British Atlantic slave trade. Indeed, between 1780 and 1807, when the traffic was abolished, Liverpool merchants financed 75 per cent of all slave voyages.

The growing dominance of Liverpool in the slave trade can be attributed to its strategic position (the Thames and the English Channel were much more vulnerable to enemy privateering), low wage rates, and the city's ties to Europe's valuable East India trade. But important as Liverpool's ascendancy was, it did not displace London entirely. In fact, London merchants continued to be involved in the slave trade, both as financiers and suppliers of trade goods on credit. Some historians have even gone so far as to suggest a division of labour within slave trafficking from the 1730s, with Bristol and Liverpool merchants acting as shippers of slaves and London merchants providing manufactured goods and financial services. Indeed, there seems little doubt that London contributed greatly to Liverpool's success.

The first leg of a slave expedition, from Europe to Africa, took anywhere from three to four months. Most slave ships made straight for the Atlantic coast of Africa; unlike the French, British slavers rarely ventured beyond the Cape of Good Hope. Statistically, the British took the largest number of slaves (1,172,800) from the Bight of Biafra, that is, the region between the mouth of the Niger River and Cape Lopez in present-day Gabon. But significant numbers were also taken from West-Central Africa (634,000), the Gold Coast (509,200), Sierra Leone (483,100), the Bight of Benin (359,600) and Senegambia (246,800). In fact, it is clear that different regions were important to the British at different times, depending on supply and competition with foreign traders. So, for instance, slave exports from West-Central Africa fell sharply after 1740 in the face of French competition, and recovered only when the French largely abandoned the slave trade in 1793. Correspondingly, British exports from Sierra Leone peaked between 1760 and 1780.

Insatiable as the demand for slaves was, supply was firmly in the hands of African traders and middlemen. The market, moreover, was volatile. African tastes changed, often with remarkable speed. Indian cottons, for instance, were in great demand in the seventeenth century, but gave way to German-produced linens in the early 1700s and, later, East Indian textiles. To be successful, therefore, and to beat off their competitors, British merchants and slave captains needed to monitor African market demands and to be able to respond accordingly. This was why outfitting slave ships was so expensive. Throughout the period of the slave trade Europeans poured into Africa the whole range of European manufactured goods and hardware, some of which became high-demand items while others aroused little or no interest.

Like their European counterparts, British slave ships regularly spent several months on the coast of Africa. Because there were no arrangements for holding slaves on the coast, slave captains were dependent on local African traders. As a result, most slave purchases were made in relatively small lots; it was simply impossible to buy large numbers of slaves from any one African trader. More often than not, slave captains were forced to deal directly with a number of different traders, sometimes visiting the same trading place several times over a period of four to six months. In most cases, the slaves were held ashore for as long as possible to prevent the outbreak of disease (smallpox was a particular menace), but even so the death rates for this coasting period were relatively high. And this was before the slave ships had even set sail for America.

What followed, the middle passage, was undoubtedly the most testing and, for many, the most horrific part of the Atlantic slave trade. Yet talk of 'tight packing' and dangerously high mortality rates can be misleading. What evidence we have suggests that losses of slaves on British ships roughly halved in the century after the 1680s. That they did so was owing to better provisioning and, in particular, the use of common African foods (rice, yams, beans); and to a shift from very-low-tonnage vessels carrying high ratios of slaves to middle-range-tonnage vessels carrying fewer slaves. Many of these same ships also had special design features, open ventilation ports, for instance, that were intended to improve conditions below deck. Nevertheless, it is unlikely that the mortality rate ever fell much below 10 per cent, a figure that for a healthy and economically active population would be considered truly astronomic.

While death, disease and violence were all significant factors in the middle passage, the overwhelming majority of slaves did reach America. Here they were sold directly to planters or their agents as quickly as possible, and on the most advantageous terms. This usually involved a number of sales or 'scrambles' that submitted slaves to further humiliation. Slavers then set out on the return leg to Europe. If a cargo was available, it would be taken, but more often than not slavers returned in ballast, carrying just sand and water. Most West Indian goods, in fact, were shipped to Europe in specially designed merchant vessels that were larger than the typical slaver. In other words, while we can properly talk of a triangular trade between Europe, Africa and America, it was not necessarily the case that the same ship was involved in each leg of the triangle. Indeed, slavers only really made a significant impact on two legs of the trip.

The Atlantic slave trade was a vast commercial enterprise that stretched across three continents and involved complex capital and credit arrangements. Yet for those who could afford the price of entry the benefits were obvious. Slave prices increased steadily during the second half of the eighteenth century, but so too did the gap between American and African prices. Put crudely, a slave bought on the Gold Coast during the 1790s for £25 sold for roughly twice that amount in the West Indies. Against this, of course, investors had to offset outfitting costs and incidental costs on the west coast of Africa. It is also true that American planters were extended lengthy credit terms of between eighteen and twenty-four months, and often paid off their slave debts in colonial goods and not cash. Nevertheless, historians are agreed that during the last half-century of British slave trading profits from slave voyages averaged about 8–10 per cent, not an excessively high return by the standards of the time but still considered very good.

That British merchants made money out of the slave trade is indisputable. But there is very little evidence to suggest that gains from the slave trade were directly invested in industry or that they were responsible for Britain's first industrial revolution; in fact, it has been estimated that slave-trade profits by the late eighteenth century formed only 1 per cent of total British domestic investment. Yet in a broader sense the slave trade did have an immense impact on the British economy and on British commerce. The traffic in slaves was the backbone of an Atlantic economy that not only stimulated British manufactures but also created a seemingly insatiable demand for tropical staples. This voluminous trade in goods back and forth across the Atlantic helped to transform Britain into a major mercantile and naval power. All the more remarkable, then, that during the late eighteenth century many Britons began to question the humanity of the slave trade and to call for its abolition.

The Abolition Campaign

Properly speaking the early abolitionist movement dates from the 1780s. But, of course, there were attacks on slavery and the slave trade before this date. Aphra Behn and the Quaker George Fox both expressed their disapproval of the Atlantic slave system, as did Rousseau and Montesquieu. For the most part, these early critics focused on the inhumanity, cruelty and immorality of the slave trade (themes that would be picked up by abolitionists in the 1780s). But the case against colonial slavery was greatly strengthened by political economists such as Adam Smith, who argued that slave labour was also costly and inefficient. Others went further, condemning slavery on the grounds that it was inimical to personal industry, profitable economy and family life. Slavery, in other words, was increasingly viewed as part of a mercantilist system that appeared outmoded and in urgent need of repair.

What gave added impetus to these attacks on slavery and the slave trade, particularly after 1750, was a more fundamental change in human affairs. During the second half of the eighteenth century Britain underwent rapid industrialization and as it did so evolved its own distinctive capitalist mode of production. None of this is to suggest that the spread of abolitionist ideas *had* to rest on industrialization and the growth of free wage labour. But that there was a link of some sort seems indisputable. Industrialization, moreover, was inextricably linked to urbanization and the emergence of an increasingly leisured middle class. The population of Britain's four largest manufacturing towns almost quadrupled between 1750 and 1800, a rate of increase that overturned the traditional urban hierarchy. Under-represented in parliament, eighteenth-century towns became the focus of enlightenment culture, of modernity, civility, sociability and political radicalism.

These different trends made organized anti-slavery possible. But of far greater moment, at least in the short term, was the American Revolution. At an ideological level the Revolution unleashed a heated debate about political representation that was quite often framed in terms of slavery (disenfranchisement) and freedom (the vote). The Revolution, in other words, gave slavery political meaning. But it also had a more far-reaching effect. Defeat in the American War (1775–83) brought with it a searching and sometimes painful re-evaluation of Britain's standing as a once-victorious Protestant nation. As is well known, one of the results of the loss of the American colonies was a move to tighten the reins of empire elsewhere, notably in Canada and Ireland. Another, however, was a rise in enthusiasm for parliamentary reform, religious liberalization and reform of gaols and lunatic asylums; for virtually anything, in fact, that might prevent a similar national humiliation in the future.

Significantly, the ending of the American War coincided with an upsurge in abolitionist activity. The Quakers, for instance, petitioned parliament against the slave trade in 1783. That same year the London Meeting for Sufferings also appointed a special committee to distribute abolitionist books and pamphlets. And in a quite unrelated move (or so it would seem), the inhabitants of Bridgwater in Somerset petitioned parliament in 1785. But by and large these were uncoordinated efforts, involving a relatively small number of people. It was the Society for the Abolition of the Slave Trade (SAST), or, to be more precise, the Society's guiding London Committee, which set the movement on its modern course, evolving a structure and organization that made it possible to mobilize public opinion against the slave trade.

Historians have been strangely divided over the role and importance of the London Committee. The Wilberforces, for instance, attached far greater significance to the opinion-building activities of their father, William Wilberforce. Then in the 1970s and 1980s the Committee fell foul of a broader attempt to arrive at a better understanding of the general social and cultural context of abolition and, in particular, the linkage between economic change, protest and reform. One of the effects of this search for the 'ecology' of British anti-slavery was to shift attention from London and the influence of an abolitionist elite to the provinces (notably Manchester and the northwest) and the dynamics of popular abolitionism. Recent studies, however, suggest that the Committee gave the early abolitionist movement coherence, impetus and, above all, political direction.

The London Committee was formally organized on 22 May 1787. The precise details are unclear, but the stimulus undoubtedly came from William Wilberforce, who by this date had already declared his intention to introduce the subject of the slave trade in the House of Commons. The nucleus of the group was provided by Samuel Hoare, George Harrison, William Dillwyn, John Lloyd and Joseph Woods, who had all been connected with the Quaker committee established in 1783. In all, nine of the twelve founding members of the original London Committee were Quakers, the exceptions being Philip Sansom, Granville Sharp (who served as chairman) and Thomas Clarkson. The other significant feature of the Committee was its middle-class origins in trade and business. Two members were bankers, four were merchants or had some experience of trade, while two, John Barton and James Phillips, were manufacturers. By and large these were practical men and, as it turned out, ideally suited to the task of mobilizing public opinion against the slave trade.

The London Committee was the prototype of the nineteenth-century reform organization. Its self-appointed task was to create a constituency for abolition through the distribution of books and pamphlets. Some idea of the size and scale of this activity emerges from the Committee's accounts. Between May 1787 and July 1788, for instance, the London Committee printed and distributed nearly 85,000 pamphlets, reports, circular letters and subscription lists at a total cost of £1,196. The members of the Committee also revealed a keen awareness of the influence of the press and how it could be used to mould public opinion. Moreover, in Josiah Wedgwood, who joined the Committee in August 1787, they possessed an intuitive genius who understood perfectly the demands and rigours of eighteenth-century business. Wedgwood's influence is discernible, above all, in the SAST's seal, adopted in October 1787, which depicted a kneeling slave together with the motto 'Am I not a Man and a Brother'. Produced at Wedgwood's factory at Etruria as a black and white jasper medallion, and distributed in large quantities to well-wishers on both sides of the Atlantic, this simple but effective image became an instantly recognizable feature of abolitionist activity between 1787 and 1807.

In these different ways the London Committee took abolition out into the country. A key figure here was Thomas Clarkson, who at this date was the movement's only full-time, professional reformer. An indefatigable and obsessive man, Clarkson not only popularized abolition through his various letters and pamphlets, but as the Committee's 'travelling agent' he provided a vital link between London and the provinces. In 1787 he visited the major slave ports. This was followed in 1788 by a tour of the south coast of England; in 1790 by a tour of Scotland and the northern parts of England; and in 1791 by a tour of Shropshire, the north and north-east of England. Clarkson, as a result, became the public face of abolition. He was the 'ostensible person' who, as the London Committee's representative, could be depended upon for advice, support and encouragement. It was a demanding role (indeed, it finally broke Clarkson), but one that was crucial to the SAST's success in mobilizing public opinion against the slave trade.

Working closely with William Wilberforce, the London Committee aimed to create enough momentum to launch a petition campaign. At last, soon after Christmas 1787, Wilberforce gave notice that early in the next session he would ask leave to bring in a bill for the abolition of the slave trade. Taking this as their cue, the members of the London Committee moved quickly to rouse local correspondents into action. At the same time, they worked hard to ensure that the petition campaign was as broadly based as possible. On 1 January 1788, for instance, a delegation was appointed to wait on the city aldermen 'to confer with them on the proper measures to obtain a petition from the Corporation of London'. Three weeks later two new members, Robert Hunter and Joseph Smith, were delegated to do all they could to procure a petition from Glasgow. The same meeting also directed a small subcommittee to send a circular letter to the mayor of every corporate town that had not yet petitioned.

The petition campaign of 1788 fully rewarded the efforts of the London Committee. Between 1 February and 9 May over 100 petitions dealing with the slave trade were presented to the House of Commons, more than half the total number of petitions received in the session. It was against the background of this campaign that on 11 February a committee of the privy council was appointed to look into the state of the slave trade. Encouraged by the privy council's interest, abolitionists stepped up their pressure on parliament, the intention being to lobby MPs before Wilberforce's motion came on in the House of Commons on 11 May. But far from being willing to discuss Wilberforce's proposals for an early abolition of the trade, the Commons resolved to hear evidence at its own bar, a compromise measure which left abolitionists playing a dangerous waiting game. Wilberforce and his supporters did win one concession, however. Late in the same session both houses passed Sir William Dolben's Slave Limitation (or Middle Passage) Bill, which reduced the number of slaves that British ships could carry by defining slaves-per-ton ratios.

In the event, the Commons' hearings dragged on for nearly two years, until February 1791. Undaunted, the London Committee went on collecting evidence, distributing tracts and, as the debate came on, lobbying MPs. Despite these efforts, Wilberforce's motion was again defeated, this time by 163 votes to 88. The size of this defeat prompted Wilberforce, who by this date was himself a member of the Committee, to propose launching another petition campaign. Everything indicated that public support for abolition was still strong. Help also came from an unexpected quarter in the shape of William Fox's *Address to the People of Great Britain, on the*

Propriety of Abstaining from West India Sugar and Rum (1791). Fox's pamphlet, which went through fourteen or fifteen editions, inspired a nationwide boycott of West Indian sugar that at its peak involved some 300,000 families. Even the king and Queen Charlotte were said to have joined the boycott, a scene visualized by James Gillray in his graphic satire *Anti-Saccharrites – Or – John Bull and his Family leaving off the Use of Sugar*.

By 1791–2, however, mass petitioning carried with it political risks. The rising tide of revolutionary violence in France caused widespread panic among the propertied classes, so much so that the London Committee had to proceed with great caution. In some quarters the petition campaign was looked upon as nothing more than a ploy, a pretence to disguise the deep designs of men dismissively referred to as the Jacobins of England. The slave rebellion in Santo Domingo of 1791 gave resonance and meaning to the association between abolition and revolution. Understandably, the London Committee was eager to refute the charge that abolition of the slave trade, or even abolitionist activity, might endanger West Indian property. Yet for many Britons the rebellion in Santo Domingo would remain synonymous with abolition, a potent symbol of violence, instability and unrest.

It is a measure of the strength of abolitionist support that the London Committee and its agents were able to overcome these obstacles. In all, 519 petitions were presented to the Commons, the largest number ever submitted to the house on a single subject or in a single session. The numbers involved are, indeed, startling. In Edinburgh 3,865 people signed the local petition 'on the spot at different tables all with the most admirable decorum'. The final figure was 10,885, exceeded only by the 15,000 to 20,000 reported to have signed the Manchester petition. But just as important as the size of the campaign was its range and diversity. In Northumberland, for instance, even market towns like Belford (400 signatures), Wooler (400 signatures) and Alnwick (600 signatures) organized petitions, adding their voices to the gentlemen and shipowners of North and South Shields.

The petition campaign of 1792 was an unqualified success. More to the point, the strategy worked, or so it seemed. In the ensuing debate the Commons resolved by 230 votes to 85 that the trade ought to be *gradually* abolished. Though clearly disappointed – Wilberforce and the Committee had wanted immediate and utter abolition – abolitionists had registered their first major victory. After lengthy discussion, 1 January 1796 was fixed as the date for the abolition of the slave trade. The Lords, however, rejected the Commons' resolution and on 5 June 1792 voted to postpone the business until the following session, when they would proceed by calling evidence to their own bar. Abolitionists suffered further humiliation in 1793 when the Commons refused to revive the subject of the slave trade, thus effectively reversing the resolution of the previous year. The abolitionist moment had passed. As the hearings in the Lords spluttered to a halt, even the gathering of fresh evidence lost its significance.

In retrospect it is easy to see that the French Revolution killed abolition in parliament, sapping the energies of its supporters and forcing the movement out of the political spotlight. Outside Westminster, too, the Revolution took its toll. In 1793 the London Committee met on no fewer than thirty-three occasions; in 1794 the figure fell to nine. That same year Thomas Clarkson withdrew from the fight, his health broken by a punishing round of tours and meetings. Thereafter, the Committee went into steep decline, finally ceasing operations in 1796. Many local committees also collapsed after 1793. Clarkson noticed the change in the public mood, admitting to Josiah Wedgwood in 1794 that his notions of liberty were unpopular and that many people now considered him a political apostate.

Ironically, however, the French Revolutionary Wars (1793–1802) helped to prepare the way for final victory. The acquisition of new territories in the West Indies, notably Trinidad, Berbice and Demerara, led many of the old planter elite, who were increasingly fearful of competition, to desert the anti-abolitionist ranks. Capitalizing on this change of heart, and the entry into parliament of a batch of new liberal Irish MPs, the abolitionists renewed their campaign. In 1804 the London Committee suddenly sprang back into life, presumably at the instigation of Wilberforce, who was about to revive the question of the slave trade in the House of Commons. At first he met with little success. But then in 1806 the Ministry of All Talents brought in a bill for the 'Guinea Order', prohibiting the slave trade to conquered Dutch Guinea. Seizing this opportunity, Wilberforce began quietly to attach the provisions of his own Foreign Slave Bill to the proposed legislation. The tactic worked. The Foreign Slave Bill passed into law in 1806, paving the way for the Abolition Act of 1807, which outlawed the British Atlantic slave trade *tout court*.

As this suggests, the final struggle took place in parliament. If anything, Wilberforce deliberately avoided the sort of tactics employed by abolitionists between 1778 and 1792, using the London Committee, for instance, as a vehicle only for information gathering. Yet there is little doubt that public opinion was behind abolition. The campaigns of 1787 and 1792 succeeded in sensitizing the British public to abolition. Through books, pamphlets, prints and cameos, the London Committee and its supporters set Britain on a course that would lead, ultimately, to the abolition of colonial slavery in 1833. Abolitionism, moreover, helped to redefine the shape of British politics, shifting attention away from the confines of parliament to the wider world outside Westminster. Other popular campaigns were to follow (the Corresponding Societies, Chartism, Free Trade), but all of them owed something to the methods and example of the early abolitionist movement.

FURTHER READING

Anstey, Roger T.: *The Atlantic Slave Trade and British Abolition, 1760–1810* (London, 1975).
Blackburn, Robin: *The Overthrow of Colonial Slavery, 1776–1848* (London, 1988).
Curtin, Philip D.: *The Atlantic Slave Trade: A Census* (Madison, WI, 1969).
Davis, David Brion: *The Problem of Slavery in the Age of Revolution, 1770–1823* (Ithaca, NY, 1975).
Drescher, Seymour: *Capitalism and Antislavery: British Mobilization in Comparative Perspective* (London, 1988).
Eltis, David: *Economic Growth and the Ending of the Transatlantic Slave Trade* (Oxford, 1987).
Jennings, Judith: *The Business of Abolishing the British Slave Trade, 1783–1807* (London, 1997).
Klein, Herbert S.: *The Atlantic Slave Trade* (Cambridge, 1999).
Oldfield, J. R.: *Popular Politics and British Anti-Slavery: The Mobilization of Public Opinion against the Slave Trade, 1787–1807* (Manchester, 1995).

Pollock, John: *Wilberforce* (London, 1977).
Temperley, Howard: *British Anti-Slavery 1833–1870* (London, 1972).
Walvin, James: *Making the Black Atlantic: Britain and the African Diaspora* (London, 2000).
Williams, Eric: *Capitalism and Slavery* (2nd edn, London, 1964).
Wilson, Ellen Gibson: *Thomas Clarkson: A Biography* (London, 1990).

Bibliography

Alavi, Seema: *The Sepoys and the Company: Tradition and Transition in Northern India 1770–1830* (Delhi, 1998).

Allan, David: *Scotland in the Eighteenth Century* (London, 2002).

Andrews, Fanny (ed.): *The Torrington Diaries: A Selection from the Tours of the Hon. John Byng between the Years 1781 and 1794* (abridged edn, London, 1954).

Anstey, Roger T.: *The Atlantic Slave Trade and British Abolition 1760–1810* (London, 1975).

Armstrong, Alan: *Farmworkers: A Social and Economic History, 1770–1980* (London, 1988).

Ashcraft, Richard: *Revolution Politics and John Locke's 'Two Treatises on Government'* (Princeton, NJ, 1986).

Aspinall, Arthur: *Politics and the Press c.1780–1850* (London, 1949).

Bailyn, Bernard and Morgan, Philip D. (eds): *Strangers within the Realm: The Cultural Margins of the First British Empire* (Chapel Hill, NC, 1991).

Barker, Hannah: *Newspapers, Politics and Public Opinion in Late Eighteenth-Century England* (Oxford, 1998).

Barker, Hannah: *Newspapers, Politics and English Society 1695–1855* (London, 2000).

Barnett, Corelli: *Britain and Her Army, 1509–1970: A Military, Political and Social Survey* (London, 1970).

Barry, Jonathan and Brooks, Christopher (eds): *The Middling Sort of People: Culture, Society and Politics in England, 1550–1800* (Basingstoke, 1994).

Bartlett, Thomas: *The Fall and Rise of the Irish Nation: The Catholic Question 1690–1830* (Dublin, 1992).

Bartlett, Thomas and Hayton, David (eds): *Penal Era and Golden Age: Essays in Irish History, 1690–1800* (Belfast, 1979).

Bateman, John: *The Great Landowners of Great Britain and Ireland* (London, 1883; reprinted Leicester, 1971).

Baugh, Daniel: *British Naval Administration in the Age of Walpole* (Princeton, NJ, 1965).

Bayly, C. A.: *The New Cambridge History of India*, vol. 2 (1): *Indian Society and the Making of the British Empire* (Cambridge, 1988).

Baynes, John: *The Jacobite Rising of 1715* (London, 1970).

Beattie, J. M.: *Crime and the Courts in England 1660–1800* (Oxford, 1986).

Beattie, J. M.: *Policing and Punishment in London: Urban Crime and the Limits of Terror* (Oxford, 2001).

Bebbington, D. W.: *Evangelicalism in Modern Britain: A History from the 1730s to the 1980s* (London, 1989).
Beckett, J. C.: *Protestant Dissent in Ireland 1687–1780* (London, 1948).
Beckett, J. V.: *The Aristocracy in England 1660–1914* (Oxford, 1986).
Bell, Ian A.: *Literature and Crime in Augustan England* (London, 1991).
Bennett, G. V.: 'Conflict in the church', in G. S. Holmes (ed.), *Britain after the Glorious Revolution, 1689–1714* (London, 1969).
Bennett, G. V.: *The Tory Crisis in Church and State, 1688–1730: The Career of Francis Atterbury, Bishop of Rochester* (Oxford, 1975).
Beresford, John (ed.): *The Diary of a Country Parson 1758–1802: James Woodforde* (London, 1935).
Berg, Maxine: *The Age of Manufactures, 1700–1820: Industry, Innovation and Work in Britain* (2nd edn, London, 1994).
Bermingham, Ann and Brewer, John (eds): *The Consumption of Culture, 1600–1800: Image, Object, Text* (London, 1995).
Bevis, Richard W.: *English Drama: Restoration and Eighteenth Century, 1660–1789* (London, 1988).
Black, Jeremy (ed.): *Britain in the Age of Walpole* (Basingstoke, 1984).
Black, Jeremy: *The English Press in the Eighteenth Century* (London, 1987).
Black, Jeremy (ed.): *British Politics and Society from Walpole to Pitt 1742–1789* (Basingstoke, 1990).
Black, Jeremy: *Robert Walpole and the Nature of Politics in Early Eighteenth-Century Britain* (London, 1990).
Black, Jeremy: *A System of Ambition? British Foreign Policy 1660–1793* (London, 1991).
Black, Jeremy: *British Foreign Policy in an Age of Revolutions 1783–1793* (Cambridge, 1994).
Black, Jeremy: *The British Abroad: The Grand Tour in the Eighteenth Century* (Stroud, 1997).
Black, Jeremy: *Britain as a Military Power, 1688–1815* (London, 1999).
Black, Jeremy and Woodfine, Philip (eds): *The British Navy and the Use of Naval Power in the Eighteenth Century* (Leicester, 1988).
Blackburn, Robin: *The Overthrow of Colonial Slavery, 1776–1848* (London, 1988).
Blencoe, R. W. and Lower, M. A. (eds): *Thomas Turner: The Diary of a Georgian Shopkeeper* (Oxford, 1979).
Blundell, Margaret (ed.): *Blundell's Diary and Letter Book 1702–1728* (Liverpool, 1952).
Bolton, G. C.: *The Passing of the Irish Act of Union* (Oxford, 1966).
Bonney, Richard (ed.): *Economic Systems and State Finance* (Oxford, 1995).
Bonwick, Colin: *English Radicals and the American Revolution* (Chapel Hill, NC, 1977).
Borsay, Peter: *The English Urban Renaissance: Culture and Society in the Provincial Town 1660–1770* (Oxford, 1989).
Borsay, Peter (ed.): *The Eighteenth-Century Town: A Reader in English Urban History 1688–1820* (London, 1990).
Bossy, John: *The English Catholic Community, 1570–1850* (London, 1975).
Bowen, H. V.: *Revenue and Reform: The Indian Problem in British Politics* (Cambridge, 1991).
Braddick, M. J.: *The Nerves of State: Taxation and the Financing of the English State, 1558–1714* (Manchester, 1996).
Bradley, James E.: *Religion, Revolution and English Radicalism: Nonconformity in Eighteenth-Century Politics and Society* (Cambridge, 1990).
Brand, John: *Observations on Popular Antiquities*, ed. Henry Ellis (2 vols, London, 1813).
Brewer, John: *Party Ideology and Popular Politics at the Accession of George III* (Cambridge, 1976).
Brewer, John: *The Sinews of Power: War, Money and the English State 1688–1783* (London, 1989).

Brewer, John: *The Pleasures of the Imagination: English Culture in the Eighteenth Century* (London, 1997).
Brewer, John and Hellmuth, Eckhart (eds): *Rethinking Leviathan: The Eighteenth-Century State in Britain and Germany* (Oxford, 1999).
Brooke, John: *King George III* (London, 1972).
Brown, C. G.: *Religion and Society in Scotland since 1707* (Edinburgh, 1997).
Browning, Reed: *The Duke of Newcastle* (New Haven, CT, 1975).
Browning, Reed: *Political and Constitutional Ideas of the Court Whigs* (Baton Rouge, LA, 1982).
Burke, Peter: *Popular Culture in Early Modern Europe* (London, 1978).
Burleigh, J. H. S.: *A Church History of Scotland* (Oxford, 1960).
Burtt, Shelley: *Virtue Transformed: Political Argument in England, 1688–1740* (Cambridge, 1992).
Bushaway, Bob: *By Rite: Custom, Ceremony and Community in England 1700–1880* (London, 1982).
Butler, Marilyn: *Romantics, Rebels and Reactionaries: English Literature and its Background 1760–1830* (Oxford, 1981).
Calthrope, Charles: *The Relation between the Lord of the Manor and the Copyholder his Tenant* (London, 1917).
Cannadine, David: *Lords and Landlords* (Leicester, 1980).
Cannon, John (ed.): *The Whig Ascendancy: Colloquies on Hanoverian England* (London, 1981).
Cannon, John: *Aristocratic Century: The Peerage of Eighteenth-Century England* (Cambridge, 1984).
Carlson, C. Lennart: *The First Magazine: A History of the Gentleman's Magazine* (Providence, RI, 1938).
Chamberlain, Jeffrey S.: *Accommodating High Churchmen: The Clergy of Sussex, 1700–1724* (Urbana, IL, 1997).
Chambers, J. D. and Mingay, G. E.: *The Agricultural Revolution 1750–1880* (London, 1966).
Champion, J. A. I.: *The Pillars of Priestcraft Shaken: The Church of England and its Enemies 1660–1730* (Cambridge, 1992).
Chandaman, C. D.: *The English Public Revenue 1660–1688* (Oxford, 1975).
Chandler, David and Beckett, Ian (eds): *The Oxford Illustrated History of the British Army* (Oxford, 1994).
Chaudhuri, K. N.: *The Trading World of Asia and the English East India Company 1660–1760* (Cambridge, 1978).
Childs, John: *The British Army of William III, 1689–1702* (Manchester, 1987).
Christie, Christopher: *The British Country House in the Eighteenth Century* (Manchester, 2000).
Christie, Ian R.: *Wilkes, Wyvill and Reform: The Parliamentary Reform Movement in British Politics, 1760–1785* (London, 1962).
Christie, Ian R.: *Stress and Stability in Late Eighteenth-Century Britain: The British Avoidance of Evolution* (Oxford, 1984).
Christie, Ian R.: *British 'Non-Élite' MPs 1715–1820* (Oxford, 1995).
Claeys, Gregory: *Thomas Paine: Social and Political Thought* (London, 1989).
Clark, Anna: *Women's Silence, Men's Violence: Sexual Assault in England, 1770–1845* (London, 1987).
Clark, Anna: *The Struggle for the Breeches: Gender and the Making of the British Working Class* (London, 1995).
Clark, I. D. L.: 'From protest to reaction: the moderate regime in the Church of Scotland,

1752–1805', in N. T. Phillipson and R. Mitchison (eds), *Scotland in the Age of Improvement* (Edinburgh, 1970).
Clark, J. C. D.: 'A general theory of party, opposition and government, 1688–1832', *Historical Journal*, 23 (1980), pp. 295–325.
Clark, J. C. D.: *The Dynamics of Change: The Crisis of the 1750s and the English Party Systems* (Cambridge, 1982).
Clark, J. C. D.: *The Language of Liberty 1660–1832: Political Discourse in the Anglo-American World* (Cambridge, 1994).
Clark, J. C. D.: *English Society 1688–1832: Ideology, Social Structure and Political Practice during the Ancien Régime* (1985;, rev. edn, Cambridge, 2000).
Clark, Peter (ed.): *The Transformation of English Provincial Towns* (London, 1984).
Clark, Peter: *British Clubs and Societies 1580–1800: The Origins of an Associational World* (Oxford, 2000).
Clark, Peter (ed.): *The Cambridge Urban History of Britain*, vol. 2: *1540–1840* (Cambridge, 2000).
Clarkson, L. A.: *Proto-industrialization: The First Phase of Industrialization?* (London, 1985).
Claydon, Tony and McBride, Ian (eds): *Protestantism and National Identity: Britain and Ireland c.1650–c.1850* (Cambridge, 1998).
Coad, J.: *The Royal Dockyards, 1690–1815: Architecture and Engineering Works of the Sailing Navy* (Aldershot, 1989).
Cohen, Michèle: *Fashioning Masculinity: National Identity and Language in the Eighteenth Century* (London, 1996).
Colley, Linda: *In Defiance of Oligarchy: The Tory Party 1714–1760* (Cambridge, 1982).
Colley, Linda: *Britons: Forging the Nation 1701–1837* (London, 1992).
Connolly, Sean J.: *Religion, Law and Power: The Making of Protestant Ireland 1660–1760* (Oxford, 1992).
Connolly, S. J. (ed.): *Political Ideas in Eighteenth-Century Ireland* (Dublin, 2000).
Conway, Stephen: *The British Isles and the War of American Independence* (Oxford, 2000).
Cookson, J. E.: *The Friends of Peace: Anti-War Liberalism in England, 1793–1815* (Cambridge, 1982).
Cookson, J. E.: *The British Armed Nation 1793–1815* (Oxford, 1997).
Corfield, Penelope J.: *The Impact of English Towns 1700–1800* (Oxford, 1982).
Corfield, P. J.: 'Class by name and number in eighteenth-century Britain', *History*, 72 (1987), pp. 38–61.
Corish, Patrick: *The Catholic Community in the Seventeenth and Eighteenth Centuries* (Dublin, 1981).
Court, W. C. B.: *The Rise of the Midland Industries, 1600–1838* (Oxford, 1953).
Crafts, N. F. R.: *British Economic Growth during the Industrial Revolution* (Oxford, 1985).
Cranfield, G. A.: *The Development of the Provincial Newspaper 1700–1760* (Oxford, 1962).
Cruickshank, Dan and Burton, Neil: *Life in the Georgian City* (London, 1990).
Cruickshanks, Eveline (ed.): *Ideology and Conspiracy: Aspects of Jacobitism, 1689–1759* (Edinburgh, 1982).
Cruickshanks, Eveline and Black, Jeremy (eds): *The Jacobite Challenge* (Edinburgh, 1988).
Cullen, Louis: *An Economic History of Ireland since 1660* (2nd edn, London, 1987).
Cunningham, Hugh: *Leisure in the Industrial Revolution 1780–1880* (London, 1980).
Cunningham, J.: *The Church History of Scotland* (2 vols, Edinburgh, 1859).
Curtin, Nancy J.: *The United Irishmen: Popular Politics in Ulster and Dublin 1791–1798* (Oxford, 1994).
Curtin, Philip D.: *The Atlantic Slave Trade: A Census* (Madison, WI, 1969).
Daunton, Martin: *Progress and Poverty: An Economic and Social History of Britain 1700–1850* (Oxford, 1995).

Davidoff, Leonore: *Best Circles: Society, Etiquette, and the Season* (London, 1973).
Davidoff, Leonore and Hall, Catherine: *Family Fortunes: Men and Women of the Middle Class* (London, 1987).
Davidson, Caroline: *A Woman's Work is Never Done: A History of Housework in the British Isles, 1650–1950* (London, 1982).
Davies, Stephen J.: 'The courts and the Scottish legal system 1600–1747: the case of Stirlingshire', in V. A. C. Gatrell, Bruce Lenman and Geoffrey Parker (eds), *Crime and the Law: The Social History of Crime in Western Europe since 1500* (London, 1980).
Davis, David Brion: *The Problem of Slavery in the Age of Revolution, 1770–1823* (Ithaca, NY, 1975).
Davis, Ralph: *The Industrial Revolution and British Overseas Trade* (Leicester, 1979).
Deane, Phyllis and Cole, W. A.: *British Economic Growth, 1688–1955* (Cambridge, 1962).
Defoe, Daniel: *A Tour through the Whole Island of Great Britain* (London, 1971).
Devine, T. M. and Jackson, Gordon (eds): *Glasgow*, vol. 1: *Beginnings to 1830* (Manchester, 1995).
Devine, T. M. and Young, J. R. (eds): *Eighteenth-Century Scotland: New Perspectives* (East Linton, East Lothian, 1999).
Dickinson, H. T.: *Bolingbroke* (London, 1970).
Dickinson, H. T.: *Walpole and the Whig Supremacy* (London, 1973).
Dickinson, H. T.: 'The eighteenth-century debate on the sovereignty of parliament', *Transactions of the Royal Historical Society*, 5th series, 26 (1976), pp. 198–210.
Dickinson, H. T.: *Liberty and Property: Political Ideology in Eighteenth-Century Britain* (London, 1977).
Dickinson, H. T.: *British Radicalism and the French Revolution 1789–1815* (Oxford, 1985).
Dickinson, H. T. (ed.): *Britain and the French Revolution 1789–1815* (Basingstoke, 1989).
Dickinson, H. T.: *The Politics of the People in Eighteenth-Century Britain* (Basingstoke, 1995).
Dickinson, H. T. (ed.): *Britain and the American Revolution* (London, 1998).
Dickinson, H. T.: '"The Friends of America": British sympathy with the American Revolution', in Michael T. Davis (ed.), *Radicalism and Revolution in Britain, 1775–1848* (Basingstoke, 2000), pp. 1–29.
Dickson, David: *New Foundations: Ireland 1660–1800* (Dublin, 1987).
Dickson, David (ed.): *The Gorgeous Mask: Dublin 1700–1850* (Dublin, 1987).
Dickson, David, Keogh, Dáire and Whelan, Kevin (eds): *The United Irishmen: Republicanism, Radicalism and Rebellion* (Dublin, 1993).
Dickson, P. M. G.: *The Financial Revolution in England: A Study in the Development of Public Credit 1688–1756* (London, 1967).
Dietz, Frederick C.: *English Public Finance 1558–1641* (London, 1932).
Dietz, Peter: *The Last of the Regiments: Their Rise and Fall* (London, 1990).
Ditchfield, G. M.: *The Evangelical Revival* (London, 1998).
Doody, Margaret Anne: *The Daring Muse: Augustan Poetry Reconsidered* (Cambridge, 1985).
Downing, Brian: *The Military Revolution and Political Change: Origins of Democracy and Autocracy in Early Modern Europe* (Princeton, NJ, 1992).
Drescher, Seymour: *Capitalism and Antislavery: British Mobilization in Comparative Perspective* (London, 1988).
Drummond, A. L. and Bulloch, J.: *The Scottish Church 1688–1843: The Age of the Moderates* (Edinburgh, 1973).
Duffy, Eamon (ed.): *Challoner and his Church: A Catholic Bishop in Georgian England* (London, 1981).
Duffy, Michael: *Soldiers, Sugar and Seapower: The British Expeditions to the West Indies and the War against Revolutionary France* (Oxford, 1987).

Earle, Peter: *The Making of the English Middle Class: Business, Society and Family Life in London, 1660–1730* (London, 1989).

Eastwood, David: *Government and Community in the English Provinces 1700–1800* (Basingstoke, 1997).

Ehrman, John: *The Younger Pitt* (3 vols, London, 1969–96).

Ekirch, A. Roger: *Bound for America: The Transportation of British Convicts to the Colonies, 1718–1775* (Oxford, 1987).

Elliott, Marianne: *Partners in Revolution: The United Irishmen and France* (New Haven, CT, 1982).

Elliott, Marianne: *Wolfe Tone: Prophet of Irish Independence* (New Haven, CT, 1990).

Eltis, David: *Economic Growth and the Ending of the Transatlantic Slave Trade* (Oxford, 1987).

Embree, Ainslie: *Charles Grant and British Rule in India* (London, 1962).

Emsley, Clive: *British Society and the French Wars 1793–1815* (Basingstoke, 1979).

Emsley, Clive: *Crime and Society in England 1750–1900* (2nd edn, London, 1996).

English, Barbara: *The Great Landowners of East Yorkshire 1530–1910* (Hemel Hempstead, 1990).

Ertman, Thomas: *The Birth of the Leviathan: Building States and Regimes in Medieval and Early Modern Europe* (Cambridge, 1997).

Estabrook, Carl B.: *Urbane and Rustic England: Cultural Ties and Social Spheres in the Provinces, 1660–1780* (Manchester, 1998).

Evans, E. D.: *A History of Wales 1660–1815* (Cardiff, 1976).

Feather, John: *The Provincial Book Trade in Eighteenth-Century England* (Cambridge, 1985).

Ferguson, William: *Scotland's Relations with England: A Survey to 1707* (Edinburgh, 1977).

Field, C. D.: 'The social composition of English Methodism to 1830: a membership analysis', *Bulletin of the John Rylands University Library of Manchester*, 76 (1994), pp. 153–69.

Fildes, Valerie (ed.): *Women as Mothers in Pre-industrial England* (London, 1990).

Fletcher, Anthony: *Gender, Sex, and Subordination in England, 1500–1800* (New Haven, CT, 1995).

Flinn, M. W.: *The History of the British Coal Industry*, vol. 2: *1700–1830: The Industrial Revolution* (Oxford, 1984).

Foord, A. S.: *His Majesty's Opposition 1714–1830* (Oxford, 1964).

Forbes, Duncan: *Hume's Philosophical Politics* (Cambridge, 1975).

Ford, Alan, McGuire, J. and Milne, K. (eds): *As By Law Established: The Church of Ireland since the Reformation* (Dublin, 1995).

Ford, Boris: *The Cambridge Cultural History of Britain: Eighteenth-Century Britain* (Cambridge, 1992).

Fortescue, John W.: *A History of the British Army* (vols 2–10, 2nd edn, London, 1910–30).

Foster, R. F.: *Modern Ireland, 1600–1972* (London, 1988).

Fritz, Paul S.: *The English Ministers and Jacobitism Between the Rebellions of 1715 and 1745* (Toronto, 1975).

Fry, Michael: *The Dundas Despotism* (Edinburgh, 1992).

Gahan, D. J.: *The People's Rising, Wexford 1798* (Dublin, 1995).

Garnham, Neal: *The Courts, Crime and the Criminal Law in Ireland, 1692–1760* (Blackrock, Co. Dublin, 1996).

Gascoigne, John: *Cambridge in the Age of the Enlightenment: Science, Religion and Politics from the Restoration to the French Revolution* (Cambridge, 1989).

Gatrell, V. A. C.: *The Hanging Tree: Execution and the English People 1770–1868* (Oxford, 1994).

Geiter, Mary K.: *William Penn* (London, 2000).

Geoghegan, Patrick M.: *The Irish Act of Union* (Dublin, 1999).

Gibbs, G. C.: 'Parliament and foreign policy in the age of Stanhope and Walpole', *English Historical Review*, 77 (1962), pp. 18–37.
Gibbs, G. C.: 'The revolution in foreign policy', in Geoffrey Holmes (ed.), *Britain after the Glorious Revolution 1689–1714* (London, 1969), pp. 59–79.
Gibson, William: *The Achievement of the Anglican Church 1689–1800: The Confessional State in Eighteenth-Century England* (Lewiston, 1995).
Gibson, William: *Religion and Society in England and Wales 1689–1800* (London, 1998).
Gibson, William: *The Church of England 1688–1832: Unity and Accord* (London, 2001).
Girouard, Mark: *Life in the English Country House* (London, 1978).
Golby, J. M. and Purdue, A. W.: *The Civilisation of the Crowd: Popular Culture in England 1750–1900* (London, 1984).
Goldsworthy, Jeffrey: *The Sovereignty of Parliament: History and Philosophy* (Oxford, 1999).
Goodwin, Albert: *The Friends of Liberty: The English Democratic Movement in the Age of the French Revolution* (London, 1979).
Gould, Eliga: *The Persistence of Empire: British Political Culture in the Age of the American Revolution* (Chapel Hill, NC, 2000).
Graham, Brian J. and Proudfoot, Lindsay J.: *Urban Improvement in Provincial Ireland 1700–1840* (Group for the Study of Irish Historic Settlement, np, 1994).
Greaves, R. L.: *God's Other Children: Protestant Nonconformists and the Emergence of Denominational Churches in Ireland 1660–1700* (Stanford, CA, 1997).
Greene, Jack P.: *The Quest for Power: The Lower Houses of Assembly in the Southern Royal Colonies, 1689–1776* (Chapel Hill, NC, 1963).
Greene, Jack P.: *Settlement to Society 1607–1763: A Documentary History of Colonial America* (New York, 1974).
Greene, Jack P.: *Peripheries and Center: Constitutional Development in the Extended Polities of the British Empire and the United States 1607–1788* (Athens, GA, 1986).
Gregg, Edward: *Queen Anne* (London, 1980).
Gregory, Jeremy: *Restoration, Reformation and Reform, 1660–1828: Archbishops of Canterbury and their Diocese* (Oxford, 2000).
Grenby, M. O.: *The Anti-Jacobin Novel: British Conservatism and the French Revolution* (Cambridge, 2001).
Grose, Francis: *A Classical Dictionary of the Vulgar Tongue* (London, 1788).
Grub, G.: *An Ecclesiastical History of Scotland* (4 vols, Edinburgh, 1861).
Gunn, J. A. W.: *Beyond Liberty and Property: The Process of Self-Recognition in Eighteenth-Century Political Thought* (Kingston and Montreal, 1987).
Guy, Alan James: *Economy and Discipline: Officership and Administration in the British Army, 1714–63* (Manchester, 1985).
Guy, Alan James: *The Road to Waterloo: The British Army and the Struggle against Revolutionary and Napoleonic France* (Stroud, 1990).
Gwyn, Julian: 'British government spending and the North American colonies 1740–1775', in P. J. Marshall and Glyn Williams (eds), *The British Atlantic Empire before the American Revolution* (London, 1980), pp. 74–84.
Habbakuk, John: *Marriage, Debt and the Estates System: English Landownership 1650–1950* (Oxford, 1994).
Hall, Catherine and Davidoff, Leonore: *Family Fortunes: Men and Women of the English Middle Class, 1780–1850* (Chicago, 1987).
Hammond, J. L. and Hammond, B.: *The Village Labourer* (new edn, London, 1978).
Hancock, David: *Citizens of the World: London Merchants and the Integration of the British Atlantic Community, 1735–1785* (Cambridge, 1995).
Harding, Richard: *The Evolution of the Sailing Navy, 1509–1815* (Basingstoke, 1995).
Harding, Richard: *Seapower and Naval Warfare 1650–1830* (London, 1999).

Harling, Philip: *The Waning of 'Old Corruption': The Politics of Economical Reform in Britain, 1779–1846* (Oxford, 1996).

Harling, Philip: *The Modern British State: An Historical Introduction* (Oxford, 2001).

Harling, Philip and Mandler, Peter: 'From "fiscal-military" state to laissez-faire state, 1760–1850', *Journal of British Studies*, 32 (1993), pp. 44–70.

Harris, Bob: *A Patriot Press: National Politics and the London Press in the 1740s* (Oxford, 1993).

Harris, Bob: *Politics and the Rise of the Press: Britain and France, 1620–1800* (London, 1996).

Harris, J. R.: *The British Iron Industry, 1700–1850* (London, 1988).

Harris, Michael: *London Newspapers in the Age of Walpole: A Study in the Origins of the Modern English Press* (London, 1987).

Harris, Tim (ed.): *Popular Culture in England, c.1500–1850* (Basingstoke, 1995).

Hatton, Ragnhild: *George I: Elector and King* (London, 1978).

Hatton, Ragnhild M.: *The Anglo-Hanoverian Connection 1714–1760* (London, 1982).

Hatton, Ragnhild M. and Bromley, J. S. (eds): *William III and Louis XIV: Essays 1680–1720 by and for Mark A. Thomson* (Liverpool, 1968).

Hay, Douglas and Rogers, Nicholas: *Eighteenth-Century English Society* (Oxford, 1997).

Hay, Douglas and Snyder, Francis (eds): *Policing and Prosecution in England 1750–1850* (Oxford, 1989).

Hay, Douglas, Linebaugh, Peter and Thompson, E. P.: *Albion's Fatal Tree: Crime and Society in Eighteenth-Century England* (London, 1975).

Haydon, Colin: *Anti-Catholicism in Eighteenth-Century England c.1714–80: A Political and Social Study* (Manchester, 1994).

Hellmuth, Eckhart: *The Transformation of Political Culture: England and Germany in the Late Eighteenth Century* (Oxford, 1990).

Hempton, David: *Methodism and Politics in British Society 1750–1850* (London, 1984).

Hempton, David: 'Religion in British society, 1740–90', in Jeremy Black (ed.), *British Politics and Society from Walpole to Pitt* (Basingstoke, 1990).

Henderson, G. D.: *The Scottish Ruling Elder* (London, 1935).

Henretta, James: *'Salutary Neglect': Colonial Administration under the Duke of Newcastle* (Princeton, NJ, 1972).

Henry, Brian: *The Dublin Hanged: Crime, Law Enforcement and Punishment in Late Eighteenth-Century Dublin* (Blackrock, Co. Dublin, 1994).

Herbert, Trevor and Elwyn Jones, Gareth (eds): *The Remaking of Wales in the Eighteenth Century* (Cardiff, 1988).

Herlihy, Kevin (ed.): *The Irish Dissenting Tradition 1650–1750* (Dublin, 1995).

Hey, David (ed.): *The History of Myddle: Richard Gough* (Harmondsworth, 1981).

Hill, B. W.: *The Growth of Parliamentary Parties, 1689–1742* (London, 1976).

Hill, Brian W.: *British Parliamentary Parties, 1742–1832* (London, 1985).

Hill, Bridget: *Women, Work and Sexual Politics in Eighteenth-Century England* (Oxford, 1989).

Hilton, Boyd: *The Age of Atonement: The Influence of Evangelicalism on Social and Economic Thought 1785–1865* (Oxford, 1991).

Hintze, Otto: 'Staatsverfassung und Heeresverfassung' and 'Machtpolitik und Regierungsverfassung', in Hintze, *Staat und Verfassung* (Göttingen, 3rd edn, 1970), pp. 52–83 and pp. 424–56.

Hobsbawm, E. J.: *Industry and Empire: The Economic History of Britain since 1750* (London, 1968).

Hoffman, Philip T. and Norberg, Kathryn (eds): *Fiscal Crises, Liberty and Representative Government* (Stanford, CA, 1994).

Hogg, O. F. G.: *Artillery: Its Origin, Heyday and Decline* (London, 1970).

Hoh-cheung Mui and Mui, Lorna H.: *The Management of Monopoly: A Study of the East India Company's Conduct of its Tea Trade 1784–1833* (Vancouver, 1984).

Hole, Robert: *Pulpits, Politics and Public Order in England 1760–1832* (Cambridge, 1989).
Holmes, G. S. (ed.): *Britain after the Glorious Revolution 1689–1714* (London, 1967).
Holmes, Geoffrey: *British Politics in the Age of Anne* (London, 1967).
Holmes, Geoffrey: *Augustan England: Professions, State and Society 1680–1730* (London, 1982).
Hont, Istvan and Ignatieff, Michael: *Wealth and Virtue: The Shaping of Political Economy in the Scottish Enlightenment* (Cambridge, 1983).
Hoon, Elizabeth E.: *The Organization of the English Customs System 1696–1786* (New York, 1938).
Hopkins, Paul: *Glencoe and the End of the Highland War* (rev. edn, Edinburgh, 1998).
Hoppit, Julian: *Risk and Failure in English Business 1700–1800* (Cambridge, 1987).
Horn, D. B.: *The British Diplomatic Service, 1689–1789* (Oxford, 1961).
Horn, D. B.: *Great Britain and Europe in the Eighteenth Century* (Oxford, 1967).
Houston, R. A.: *Social Change in the Age of Enlightenment: Edinburgh 1660–1760* (Oxford, 1994).
Howell, David W.: *Patriarchs and Parasites: The Gentry of South-West Wales in the Eighteenth Century* (Cardiff, 1986).
Howell, David W.: *The Rural Poor in Eighteenth-Century Wales* (Cardiff, 2000).
Hudson, Pat: *The Industrial Revolution* (London, 1992).
Hume, Robert D.: *Henry Fielding and the London Theatre 1728–1737* (Oxford, 1988).
Hunt, Margaret: *The Middling Sort: Commerce, Gender, and the Family in England 1680–1780* (Berkeley, CA, 1996).
Ignatieff, Michael: *A Just Measure of Pain: The Penitentiary in the Industrial Revolution 1750–1850* (London, 1978).
Innes, Joanna: 'Parliament and the shaping of eighteenth-century social policy', *Transactions of the Royal Historical Society*, 5th series, 40 (1990), pp. 63–92.
Innes, Joanna: 'The "mixed economy of welfare" in early modern England: assessments of the options from Hale to Malthus (*c.*1683–1803)', in Martin Daunton (ed.), *Charity, Self-Interest and Welfare in the English Past* (London, 1996).
Israel, Jonathan I.: *European Jewry in the Age of Mercantilism, 1550–1750* (Oxford, 1985).
Jackson-Stops, Gervase (ed.): *The Treasure Houses of Britain: Five Hundred Years of Private Patronage and Art Collecting* (London, 1985).
Jacob, W. M.: *Lay Piety and Religion in the Early Eighteenth Century* (Cambridge, 1996).
James, F. G.: *Ireland in the Empire, 1688–1770* (Cambridge, MA, 1973).
Jenkins, Geraint H.: *Literature, Religion and Society in Wales, 1660–1730* (Cardiff, 1978).
Jenkins, Geraint H.: *The Foundations of Modern Wales: Wales 1642–1780* (Oxford, 1987).
Jenkins, Geraint H. (ed.): *The Welsh Language before the Industrial Revolution* (Cardiff, 1997).
Jenkins, Philip: *The Making of a Ruling Class: The Glamorgan Gentry 1640–1790* (Cambridge, 1983).
Jenkins, Philip: *A History of Modern Wales 1536–1990* (London, 1992).
Jennings, Judith: *The Business of Abolishing the British Slave Trade, 1783–1807* (London, 1997).
Johnston, E. M.: *Ireland in the Eighteenth Century* (Dublin, 1974).
Jones, Clyve (ed.): *Britain in the First Age of Party 1680–1750* (London, 1987).
Jupp, Peter: *Lord Grenville 1759–1834* (Oxford, 1985).
Kammen, Michael G.: *A Rope of Sand: The Colonial Agents, British Politics and the American Revolution* (Ithaca, NY, 1968).
Katz, Stanley N.: *Newcastle's New York: Anglo-American Politics 1732–1753* (Cambridge, MA, 1968).
Keay, John: *The Honourable Company: A History of the English East India Company* (London, 1991).

Kelch, Ray A.: *Newcastle, A Duke without Money: Thomas Pelham-Holles, 1693–1768* (London, 1974).
Kelly, Gary: *The English Jacobin Novel 1780–1805* (Oxford, 1976).
Kelly, James: *Prelude to Union: Anglo-Irish Politics in the 1780s* (Dublin, 1992).
Kenyon, John P.: *Revolution Principles: The Politics of Party 1689–1720* (Cambridge, 1977).
Keogh, Dáire: *The French Disease: The Catholic Church and Irish Radicalism, 1790–1800* (Dublin, 1993).
Keogh, Dáire and Furlong, Nicholas (eds): *The Mighty Wave: The 1798 Rebellion in Wexford* (Dublin, 1996).
Keogh, Dáire and Whelan, Kevin (eds): *Acts of Union: The Causes, Contexts and Consequences of the Act of Union* (Dublin, 2001).
Kidd, Colin: *Subverting Scotland's Past: Scottish Whig Historians and the Creation of an Anglo-British Identity, 1689–c.1830* (Cambridge, 1993).
Kidd, Colin: *British Identities before Nationalism: Ethnicity and Nationhood in the Atlantic World, 1600–1800* (Cambridge, 1999).
Kilroy, Phil: *Protestant Dissent and Controversy in Ireland 1660–1714* (Cork, 1994).
King, Peter: *Crime, Justice and Discretion in England 1740–1820* (Oxford, 2000).
Klein, Herbert S.: *The Atlantic Slave Trade* (Cambridge, 1999).
Langford, Paul: *A Polite and Commercial People: England 1727–1783* (Oxford, 1989).
Langford, Paul: *Public Life and the Propertied Englishman 1689–1798* (Oxford, 1991).
Large, David: 'The decline of "the Party of the Crown" and the rise of parties in the House of Lords, 1783–1837', *English Historical Review*, 78 (1963), pp. 669–95.
Lavery, Brian: *Nelson's Navy: The Ships, Men and Organisation, 1793–1815* (London, 1989).
Lavery, Brian: *The Line of Battle: The Sailing Warship, 1650–1840* (London, 1992).
Lawford, James P.: *Britain's Army in India from its Origins to the Conquest of Bengal* (London, 1978).
Le Fevre, Peter and Harding, Richard (eds): *Precursors of Nelson: British Admirals of the Eighteenth Century* (Rochester, 2000).
Lecky, W. E. H.: *A History of Ireland in the Eighteenth Century* (abridged edn, Chicago, 1972).
Lees, Lynn Hollen: *The Solidarities of Strangers: The English Poor Law and the People, 1700–1948* (Cambridge, 1998).
Leighton, C. D. A.: *Catholicism in a Protestant Kingdom: A Study of the Irish 'Ancien Régime'* (Dublin, 1994).
Lenman, Bruce: *The Jacobite Risings in Britain 1689–1746* (London, 1980).
Lenman, Bruce: *Britain's Colonial Wars 1688–1783* (London, 2001).
Lewis, Judith: *In the Family Way: Childbearing in the British Aristocracy, 1760–1860* (New Brunswick, NJ, 1986).
Linebaugh, Peter: *The London Hanged: Crime and Civil Society in the Eighteenth Century* (London, 1991).
Lonsdale, Roger (ed.): *The New Oxford Book of Eighteenth-Century Verse* (Oxford, 1984).
Lonsdale, Roger (ed.): *Eighteenth-Century Women Poets: An Oxford Anthology* (Oxford, 1989).
McBride, I. R.: *Scripture Politics: Ulster Presbyterianism and Irish Radicalism in the Late Eighteenth Century* (Oxford, 1998).
McDowell, R. B.: *Ireland in the Age of Imperialism and Revolution, 1760–1801* (Oxford, 1979).
McFarland, E. W.: *Ireland and Scotland in the Age of Revolution* (Edinburgh, 1994).
McGrath, Charles Ivar: *The Making of the Eighteenth-Century Irish Constitution: Government, Parliament and the Revenue, 1692–1714* (Dublin, 2000).
Macinnes, J.: *The Evangelical Movement in the Highlands of Scotland, 1688–1800* (Aberdeen, 1951).

McIntosh, John R.: *Church and Theology in Enlightenment Scotland: The Popular Party, 1740–1800* (East Linton, East Lothian, 1998).
McKay, Derek and Scott, H. M.: *The Rise of the Great Powers 1648–1815* (London, 1983).
McKendrick, Neil, Brewer, John and Plumb, J. H.: *The Birth of a Consumer Society: The Commercialization of Eighteenth-Century England* (London, 1982).
McKerrow, J.: *History of the Secession Church* (Edinburgh, 1854).
Mackesy, Piers: *The War for America 1775–1783* (London, 1964).
Mackillop, Andrew: *'More Fruitful Than The Soil': Army, Empire and the Scottish Highlands, 1715–1815* (East Linton, East Lothian, 2000).
Macleod, Emma Vincent: *A War of Ideas? British Attitudes to the Wars against Revolutionary France, 1792–1802* (Aldershot, 1998).
McLynn, Frank J.: *France and the Jacobite Rising of 1745* (Edinburgh, 1981).
McLynn, Frank J.: *Charles Edward Stuart: A Tragedy in Many Acts* (London, 1988).
McNally, Patrick: *Parties, Patriots and Undertakers: Parliamentary Politics in Early Hanoverian Ireland* (Dublin, 1997).
Malcolmson, Robert W.: *Popular Recreations in English Society, 1700–1850* (Cambridge, 1973).
Malcolmson, R. W.: *Life and Labour in England, 1700–1780* (London, 1981).
Marshall, Dorothy: *The English Poor in the Eighteenth Century: A Study in Social and Administrative History* (London, 1969).
Marshall, P. J. (ed.): *Problems of Empire: Britain and India 1757–1813* (London, 1968).
Marshall, P. J.: *The British Discovery of Hinduism in the Eighteenth Century* (Cambridge, 1970).
Marshall, P. J.: *East India Fortunes: The British in Bengal in the Eighteenth Century* (Oxford, 1976).
Marshall, P. J.: 'The British Empire in the age of the American Revolution: problems of interpretation', in William M. Fowler and Wallace Coyle (eds), *The American Revolution: Changing Perspectives* (Boston, 1979).
Marshall, P. J.: *The New Cambridge History of India*, vol. 2 (2): *Bengal: The British Bridgehead: Eastern India 1740–1828* (Cambridge, 1987).
Marshall, P. J. (ed.): *The Oxford History of the British Empire*, vol. 2: *The Eighteenth Century* (Oxford, 1998).
Martins, Susanna Wade and Williamson, Tom: *Farming and the Landscape in East Anglia, c.1700–1870* (Exeter, 1999).
Mather, F. C.: *High Church Prophet: Bishop Samuel Horsley (1733–1806) and the Caroline Tradition in the Later Georgian Church* (Oxford, 1992).
Mathias, Peter and O'Brien, Patrick: 'Taxation in Britain and France, 1715–1810', *Journal of European Economic History*, 5 (1976), pp. 601–50.
Meikle, H. W.: *Scotland and the French Revolution* (Glasgow, 1912).
Mendleson, Sarah and Crawford, Patricia: *Women in Early Modern England, 1550–1750* (Oxford, 1998).
Messenger, Charles: *For Love of Regiment: A History of the British Infantry*, vol. 1: *1660–1914* (London, 1994).
Middleton, Richard: *Colonial America: A History 1585–1776* (Oxford, 1996).
Miller, John: *James II: A Study in Kingship* (Hove, 1978).
Mingay, G. E.: *English Landed Society in the Eighteenth Century* (London, 1963).
Mingay, G. E.: *The Gentry* (London, 1976).
Mingay, G. E. (ed.): *The Agrarian History of England and Wales*, vol. 6: *1750–1850* (Cambridge, 1989).
Mingay, G. E.: *Parliamentary Enclosure in England: An Introduction to its Causes, Incidence and Improvements 1750–1850* (London, 1997).
Mitchell, L. G.: *Charles James Fox* (Oxford, 1992).

Mitchison, Rosalind: 'The making of the old Scottish Poor Law', *Past and Present*, 63 (1974), pp. 58–93.

Mitchison, Rosalind and Leneman, Leah: *Sexuality and Social Control: Scotland 1660–1780* (Oxford, 1989).

Money, John: *Experience and Identity: Birmingham and the West Midlands 1760–1800* (Montreal, 1977).

Monod, Paul K.: *Jacobitism and the English People 1688–1788* (Cambridge, 1989).

Moody, T. W. and Vaughan, W. E. (eds): *A New History of Ireland*, vol. 4: *Eighteenth-Century Ireland 1691–1800* (Oxford, 1986).

Moore, Donald (ed.): *Wales in the Eighteenth Century* (Swansea, 1976).

Morgan, Derec Llwyd: *The Great Awakening in Wales* (London, 1988).

Morgan, Gwenda and Rushton, Peter: *Rogues, Thieves and the Rule of Law: The Problem of Law Enforcement in North-East England, 1718–1800* (London, 1998).

Morgan, Prys: *A New History of Wales: The Eighteenth-Century Renaissance* (Llandybïe, 1981).

Morris, Marilyn: *The British Monarchy and the French Revolution* (New Haven, CT, 1998).

Morriss, Roger: *The Royal Dockyards during the Revolutionary and Napoleonic Wars* (Leicester, 1983).

Mukherjee, S. N.: *Sir William Jones: A Study in Eighteenth-Century British Attitudes to India* (Cambridge, 1968).

Mullett, Michael A.: *Catholicism in Britain and Ireland, 1558–1829* (Basingstoke, 1998).

Munter, Robert: *The History of the Irish Newspaper 1685–1760* (Cambridge, 1967).

Murdoch, Alexander: *'The People Above': Politics and Administration in Mid-Eighteenth-Century Scotland* (Edinburgh, 1980).

Myers, Robin and Harris, Michael (eds): *Development of the English Book Trade, 1700–1793* (Oxford, 1981).

Namier, Lewis: *The Structure of Politics at the Accession of George III* (1929; 2nd edn, London, 1957).

Namier, Lewis B.: *England in the Age of the American Revolution* (London, 1930; 2nd edn, 1961).

Namier, Lewis and Brooke, John (eds): *The House of Commons 1754–1790* (3 vols, London, 1964).

Nash, Gary: *Quakers and Politics: Pennsylvania 1681–1726* (Princeton, NJ, 1968).

Neuman, Mark: *The Speenhamland County: Poverty and the Poor Laws in Berkshire 1782–1834* (London, 1982).

Newman, Gerald: *The Rise of English Nationalism: A Cultural History 1740–1830* (London, 1987).

O'Brien, Gerard: *Anglo-Irish Politics in the Age of Grattan and Pitt* (Dublin, 1987).

O'Brien, P. K.: 'The political economy of British taxation, 1660–1815', *Economic History Review*, 41 (1988), pp. 1–32.

O'Brien, P. K.: 'Public finance in the wars with France 1793–1815', in H. T. Dickinson (ed.), *Britain and the French Revolution 1789–1815* (London, 1989), pp. 165–87.

O'Brien, Patrick: *Power with Profit: The State and the Economy 1688–1815* (London, 1991).

O'Brien, P. K.: 'Central government and the economy 1688–1815', in Roderick Floud and Donald McCloskey (eds), *The Economic History of Britain since 1700* (3 vols, Cambridge, 1994), vol. 1, pp. 205–41.

O'Brien, Patrick and Hunt, Philip A.: 'The rise of a fiscal state in England, 1485–1815', *Historical Research*, 66 (1993), pp. 129–76.

O'Brien, P. K. and Hunt, P. A.: 'England 1485–1815', in R. Bonney (ed.), *The Rise of the Fiscal State in Europe 1200–1815* (Oxford, 1999), pp. 53–101.

O'Brien, P. K. and Hunt, P. A.: 'Excises and the rise of a fiscal state in England, 1586–1688',

in Mark Ormrod et al. (eds), *Crises, Revolutions and Self-Sustained Growth: Essays in European Fiscal History* (Stanford, CA, 1999).
O'Ciorsain, Niall: *Print and Popular Culture in Ireland, 1750–1800* (London, 1997).
O'Connell, Maurice R.: *Irish Politics and Social Conflict in the Age of the American Revolution* (Philadelphia, PA, 1965).
O'Gorman, Frank: *The Whig Party and the French Revolution* (Basingstoke, 1967).
O'Gorman, Frank: *Edmund Burke: His Political Philosophy* (London, 1973).
O'Gorman, Frank: *The Rise of Party in England: The Rockingham Whigs 1760–82* (London, 1975).
O'Gorman, Frank: *The Emergence of the British Two-Party System 1760–1832* (London, 1982).
O'Gorman, Frank: *Voters, Patrons, and Parties: The Unreformed Electoral System of Hanoverian England 1734–1832* (Oxford, 1989).
Oldfield, J. R.: *Popular Politics and British Anti-Slavery: The Mobilization of Public Opinion against the Slave Trade, 1787–1807* (Manchester, 1995).
Olson, Alison G.: *Making the Empire Work: London and American Interest Groups 1640–1790* (Cambridge, MA, 1992).
Overton, Mark: *Agricultural Revolution in England: The Transformation of the Agrarian Economy 1500–1850* (Cambridge, 1996).
Owen, John B.: *The Rise of the Pelhams* (London, 1957).
Packenham, Thomas: *The Year of Liberty: The Story of the Great Irish Rebellion of 1798* (London, 1969).
Pares, Richard: 'American versus Continental warfare 1739–63', *English Historical Review*, 51 (1936), pp. 429–65.
Pares, Richard: *King George III and the Politicians* (Oxford, 1953).
Parker, R. A. C.: *Coke of Norfolk: A Financial and Agricultural Study, 1707–1842* (Oxford, 1975).
Perry, Thomas W.: *Public Opinion, Propaganda and Politics in Eighteenth-Century England: A Study of the Jew Bill of 1753* (Cambridge, MA, 1962).
Peters, Marie: *The Elder Pitt* (London, 1998).
Phillips, John A.: *Electoral Behaviour in Unreformed England: Plumpers, Splitters and Straights* (Princeton, NJ, 1982).
Philp, Mark: *The French Revolution and British Popular Politics* (Cambridge, 1991).
Pittock, Murray G. H.: *The Myth of the Jacobite Clans* (Edinburgh, 1997).
Plumb, J. H.: *The Growth of Political Stability in England, 1675–1725* (London, 1967).
Pocock, J. G. A.: *Virtue, Commerce and History: Essays in Political Thought and History Chiefly in the Eighteenth Century* (Cambridge, 1985).
Podmore, Colin: *The Moravian Church in England, 1728–1760* (Oxford, 1998).
Pollard, Hugh B. C.: *A History of Firearms* (London, 1926).
Pollock, John: *Wilberforce* (London, 1977).
Porter, Roy: *English Society in the Eighteenth Century* (Harmondsworth, 1990).
Power, T. P. and Whelan, Kevin (eds): *Endurance and Emergence: Catholics in Ireland in the Eighteenth Century* (Dublin, 1990).
Prest, Wilfrid R. (ed.): *The Professions in Early Modern England* (London, 1987).
Price, Richard: *British Society 1680–1880: Dynamism, Containment and Change* (Cambridge, 1999).
Probyn, Clive T.: *English Fiction of the Eighteenth Century 1700–1789* (London, 1987).
Rack, Henry D.: *Reasonable Enthusiast: John Wesley and the Rise of Methodism* (London, 1989).
Randall, Adrian J.: *Before the Luddites: Custom, Community and Machinery in the English Woollen Industry 1776–1809* (Cambridge, 1991).
Raven, James: *Judging New Wealth: Popular Publishing and Responses to Commerce in England 1750–1800* (Oxford, 1992).

Raymond, Joad (ed.): *News, Newspapers and Society in Early Modern Britain* (London, 1999).
Reay, Barry: *Popular Cultures in England 1550–1750* (London, 1998).
Redwood, John: *Reason, Ridicule and Religion: The Age of Enlightenment in England, 1660–1750* (London, 1976).
Reid, John Phillip: *Constitutional History of the American Revolution* (4 vols, Madison, WI, 1986–93).
Rendall, Jane: *Women in an Industrializing Society: England, 1750–1880* (Oxford, 1990).
Richetti, John J.: *Popular Fiction before Richardson: Narrative Patterns, 1700–1739* (2nd edn, Oxford, 1992).
Riley, P. W. J.: *The English Ministers and Scotland 1707–1727* (London, 1964).
Riley, P. W. J.: *The Union of England and Scotland* (Manchester, 1978).
Ritcheson, Charles R.: *British Politics and the American Revolution* (Norman, OK, 1954).
Robbins, Caroline: *The Eighteenth-Century Commonwealthman* (Cambridge, MA, 1959).
Roberts, Michael: *Splendid Isolation 1763–1780* (Reading, 1970).
Robertson, John: *The Scottish Enlightenment and the Militia Issue* (Edinburgh, 1985).
Robertson, John (ed.): *A Union for Empire: Political Thought and the Union of 1707* (Cambridge, 1995).
Robinson, Eric (ed.): *John Clare's Autobiographical Writings* (Oxford, 1983).
Rodger, N. A. M.: *The Wooden World: An Anatomy of the Georgian Navy* (London, 1986).
Roebuck, Peter: *Yorkshire Baronets, 1640–1760: Families, Estates and Fortunes* (Oxford, 1980).
Rogers, H. C. B.: *The British Army of the Eighteenth Century* (London, 1977).
Rogers, Nicholas: *Whigs and Cities: Popular Politics in the Age of Walpole and Pitt* (Oxford, 1989).
Rogers, Nicholas: *Crowds, Culture and Politics in Georgian Britain* (Oxford, 1998).
Rogers, Pat: *The Augustan Vision* (London, 1974).
Roseveare, Henry: *The Treasury: The Evolution of a British Institution* (London, 1969).
Roseveare, Henry: *The Financial Revolution, 1660–1760* (London, 1991).
Rothstein, Eric: *Restoration and Eighteenth-Century Poetry 1660–1780* (London, 1981).
Rowlands, Marie B. (ed.): *English Catholics of Parish and Town, 1558–1778* (Totton, 1999).
Rubenstein, W. D.: *Elites and the Wealthy in Modern British Industry: Essays in Social and Economic History* (Brighton, 1987).
Rule, John: *The Experience of Labour in Eighteenth-Century Industry* (London, 1981).
Rule, John: *Albion's People: English Society 1714–1815* (London, 1992).
Rule, John: *The Vital Century: England's Developing Economy, 1714–1815* (London, 1992).
Sack, James J.: 'The memory of Burke and the memory of Pitt: English conservatism confronts its past, 1806–1829', *Historical Journal*, 30 (1987), pp. 623–40.
Sack, J. J.: *From Jacobite to Conservative: Reaction and Orthodoxy in Britain, c.1760–1832* (Cambridge, 1993).
Sanderson, Elizabeth C.: *Women and Work in Eighteenth-Century Edinburgh* (Basingstoke, 1996).
Savory, Reginald Arthur: *His Britannic Majesty's Army in Germany during the Seven Years' War* (Oxford, 1966).
Schmidt, L. E.: *Holy Fairs: Scottish Communions and American Revivals in the Early Modern Period* (Princeton, NJ, 1989).
Schwarz, L. D.: *London in the Age of Industrialisation: Entrepreneurs, Labour Force and Living Conditions, 1700–1850* (Cambridge, 1992).
Scott, H. M.: '"The True Principles of the Revolution": the duke of Newcastle and the idea of the old system', in Jeremy Black (ed.), *Knights Errant and True Englishmen: British Foreign Policy, 1660–1800* (Edinburgh, 1989), pp. 55–91.
Scott, H. M.: *British Foreign Policy in the Age of the American Revolution* (Oxford, 1990).

Sedgwick, Romney (ed.): *The History of Parliament: The House of Commons, 1715–1754* (2 vols, London, 1970).
Sharpe, J. A.: *Crime in Early Modern England 1550–1750* (2nd edn, London, 1996).
Sharpe, Pamela: *Adapting to Capitalism: Working Women in the English Economy, 1700–1850* (Basingstoke, 1996).
Sharpe, Pamela (ed.): *Women's Work: The English Experience 1650–1914* (London, 1998).
Shaw, John Stuart: *The Management of Scottish Society, 1707–1764* (Edinburgh, 1983).
Shaw, John Stuart: *The Political History of Eighteenth-Century Scotland* (Basingstoke, 1999).
Sher, Richard B.: *Church and University in the Scottish Enlightenment: The Moderate Literati of Edinburgh* (Princeton, NJ, 1985).
Shoemaker, Robert B.: *Prosecution and Punishment: Petty Crime and the Law in London and Rural Middlesex, c.1660–1725* (Cambridge, 1991).
Shoemaker, Robert B.: *Gender in English Society 1650–1850: The Emergence of Separate Spheres?* (London, 1998).
Smail, John: *The Origins of Middle-Class Culture: Halifax, Yorkshire, 1660–1780* (London, 1994).
Smith, Mark: *Religion in Industrial Society: Oldham and Saddleworth, 1740–1865* (Oxford, 1994).
Smout, T. C.: *A History of the Scottish People 1560–1830* (London, 1969).
Smyth, Jim: *The Men of No Property* (Basingstoke, 1992).
Smyth, Jim: *The Making of the United Kingdom 1660–1800* (London, 2001).
Snell, K. D. M.: *Annals of the Labouring Poor: Social Change and Agrarian England, 1600–1900* (Cambridge, 1985).
Speck, W. A.: *Tory and Whig: The Struggle in the Constituencies 1701–1715* (London, 1970).
Spence, Peter: *The Birth of Romantic Radicalism: War, Popular Politics and English Radical Reformism 1800–1815* (Aldershot, 1996).
Spencer, Jane: *The Rise of the Woman Novelist: From Aphra Behn to Jane Austen* (Oxford, 1986).
Spring, Eileen: *Law, Land and Family: Aristocratic Inheritance in England, 1300–1800* (Chapel Hill, NC, 1993).
Spufford, Margaret (ed.): *The World of Rural Dissenters, 1520–1725* (Cambridge, 1995).
Steele, Ian K.: 'The British parliament and the Atlantic colonies to 1760: new approaches to enduring questions', *Parliamentary History*, 14 (1995), pp. 29–46.
Stevenson, John: *Popular Disturbances in England 1700–1870* (London, 1979).
Stone, Lawrence: *The Family, Sex and Marriage in England, 1500–1800* (London, 1977).
Stone, Lawrence (ed.): *An Imperial State at War: Britain from 1689 to 1815* (London, 1994).
Stone, Lawrence and Stone, Jeanne C. Fawtier: *An Open Elite? England 1540–1880* (Oxford, 1984).
Strachan, Hew: *The Politics of the British Army* (Oxford, 1997).
Struthers, G.: *The History of the Rise, Progress and Principles of the Relief Church* (Glasgow, 1843).
Sullivan, Alvin (ed.): *British Literary Magazines: The Augustan Age and the Age of Johnson, 1698–1788* (London, 1983).
Sunter, Ronald M.: *Patronage and Politics in Scotland 1707–1832* (Edinburgh, 1986).
Sutherland, Lucy S.: *The East India Company in Eighteenth-Century Politics* (Oxford, 1952).
Sweet, Rosemary: *The English Town 1680–1840: Government, Society and Culture* (London, 1999).
Sykes, Norman: *Church and State in England in the Eighteenth Century* (Cambridge, 1934).
Syrett, David: *The Royal Navy in American Waters, 1775–1783* (Aldershot, 1989).
Syrett, David: *The Royal Navy in European Waters during the American Revolutionary War* (Columbia, SC, 1998).

Szechi, Daniel: *Jacobitism and Tory Politics, 1710–14* (Edinburgh, 1984).

Szechi, Daniel: *The Jacobites: Britain and Europe 1688–1788* (Manchester, 1994).

Tawney, R. H.: *Religion and the Rise of Capitalism: A Historical Study* (London, 1926).

Temperley, Howard: *British Anti-Slavery 1833–1870* (London, 1972).

Thale, Mary (ed.): *The Autobiography of Francis Place* (Cambridge, 1972).

Thirsk, Joan (ed.): *The Agrarian History of England and Wales*, vol. 5: *1640–1750* (Cambridge, 1985).

Thomas, P. D. G.: *The House of Commons in the Eighteenth Century* (Oxford, 1971).

Thomas, P. D. G.: *British Politics and the Stamp Act Crisis* (Oxford, 1975).

Thomas, Peter D. G.: *The Townshend Duties Crisis* (Oxford, 1987).

Thomas, Peter D. G.: *Tea Party to Independence* (Oxford, 1991).

Thomas, Peter D. G.: *John Wilkes: A Friend to Liberty* (Oxford, 1996).

Thomas, Peter D. G.: *Politics in Eighteenth-Century Wales* (Cardiff, 1998).

Thompson, E. P.: 'The moral economy of the English crowd in the eighteenth century', *Past and Present*, 50 (1971), pp. 76–136.

Thompson, E. P.: *Customs in Common* (London, 1991).

Thompson, E. P.: *The Making of the English Working Class* (1963; 2nd edn, London, 1968).

Thompson, Edward: *Whigs and Hunters: The Origin of the Black Act* (London, 1975).

Thompson, F. M. L. (ed.): *The Cambridge Social History of Britain 1750–1950*, vol. 2: *People and their Environment* (Cambridge, 1990).

Thompson, F. M. L.: *Gentrification and the Enterprise Culture: Britain 1780–1980* (Oxford, 2001).

Thorne, R. G. (ed.): *The House of Commons 1790–1820* (5 vols, London, 1986).

Tilly, Charles: 'War making and state making as organized crime', in Peter Evans, Dietrich Rueschemeyer and Theda Skocpol (eds), *Bringing the State Back In* (Cambridge, 1985), pp. 169–91.

Tillyard, Stella: *Aristocrats: Caroline, Emily, Louisa and Sarah Lennox, 1750–1832* (London, 1994).

Todd, Janet: *Sensibility: An Introduction* (London, 1986).

Todd, Janet: *Mary Wollstonecraft: A Revolutionary Life* (London, 2000).

Trumbach, Randolph: *The Rise of the Egalitarian Family: Aristocratic Kinship and Domestic Relations in Eighteenth-Century England* (New York, 1978).

Tucker, Robert W. and Hendrickson, David C.: *The Fall of the First British Empire: Origins of the War of American Independence* (Baltimore, MD, 1982).

Tudor, G.: *Howell Harris: From Conversion to Separation 1735–1750* (Cardiff, 2000).

Tully, Alan: *William Penn's Legacy: Politics and Social Structure in Provincial Pennsylvania 1726–1755* (Baltimore, 1977).

Turner, Michael: *English Parliamentary Enclosure: Its Historical Geography and Economic History* (Folkestone, 1980).

Valenze, Deborah: *The First Industrial Woman* (Oxford, 1995).

Vickery, Amanda: *The Gentleman's Daughter: Women's Lives in Georgian England* (New Haven, CT, 1998).

Vincent, Emma: 'The responses of Scottish Churchmen to the French Revolution, 1789–1802', *Scottish Historical Review*, 73 (1994), pp. 191–215.

Virgin, Peter: *The Church in an Age of Negligence* (Cambridge, 1989).

Wahrman, Dror: *Imagining the Middle Class: The Political Representation of Class in Britain, c.1780–1840* (Cambridge, 1995).

Wall, Maureen: *Catholic Ireland in the Eighteenth Century* (Dublin, 1989).

Walsh, J. D.: 'Origins of the Evangelical revival', in G. V. Bennett and J. D. Walsh (eds), *Essays in Modern English Church History: In Memory of Norman Sykes* (London, 1966).

Walsh, J. D.: *John Wesley, 1703–1791: A Bicentennial Tribute* (London, 1994).

Walsh, John, Haydon, Colin and Taylor, Stephen (eds): *The Church of England, c.1689–c.1833: From Toleration to Tractarianism* (Cambridge, 1993).
Walvin, James: *Making the Black Atlantic: Britain and the African Diaspora* (London, 2000).
Ward, W. R.: *The Protestant Evangelical Awakening* (Cambridge, 1992).
Ward, W. R. (ed.): *Parson and Parish in Eighteenth-Century Surrey: Replies to Bishops' Visitations* (Surrey Record Society, 34, 1994).
Watt, Ian: *The Rise of the Novel: Studies in Defoe, Richardson and Fielding* (London, 1957).
Watts, Michael R.: *The Dissenters*, vol. 1: *From the Reformation to the French Revolution* (Oxford, 1978).
Webb, Sidney and Webb, Beatrice: *History of English Local Government* (9 vols, London, 1906–29).
Wells, Roger: *Insurrection: The British Experience 1795–1803* (Gloucester, 1983).
Wells, R. A. E.: *Wretched Faces: Famine in Wartime England, 1793–1803* (Gloucester, 1988).
Whatley, Christopher A.: *Scottish Society 1707–1830* (Manchester, 2000).
Whelan, Kevin: *The Tree of Liberty: Radicalism, Catholicism and the Construction of Irish Identity 1760–1830* (Cork, 1996).
Whetstone, Ann E.: *Scottish County Government in the Eighteenth and Nineteenth Centuries* (Edinburgh, 1981).
Wiles, R. M.: *Freshest Advices: Early Provincial Newspapers in England* (Columbus, OH, 1965).
Williams, Eric: *Capitalism and Slavery* (2nd edn, London, 1964).
Williams, Gwyn A.: *The Search for Beulah Land* (London, 1980).
Williamson, Tom: *Polite Landscapes: Gardens and Society in Eighteenth-Century England* (Stroud, 1995).
Wilson, Ellen Gibson: *Thomas Clarkson: A Biography* (London, 1990).
Wilson, Kathleen: *The Sense of the People: Politics, Culture and Imperialism in England, 1715–1785* (Cambridge, 1995).
Wilson, Richard and Mackley, Alan: *Creating Paradise: The Building of the English Country House, 1660–1880* (London, 2000).
Winch, Donald: *Adam Smith's Politics: An Essay in Historiographical Revision* (Cambridge, 1978).
Wrigley, E. A.: *Continuity, Chance and Change: The Character of the Industrial Revolution in England* (Cambridge, 1988).
York, Neil Longley: *Neither Kingdom Nor Nation: The Irish Quest for Constitutional Rights 1698–1800* (Washington, DC, 1994).

Index